HISTORY
OF THE
CUMBERLAND PRESBYTERIAN CHURCH

BY BENJAMIN WILBURN MCDONNOLD, D.D., LL.D

There shall be a handful of corn in the earth upon the top of the mountains, the fruit thereof shall shake the Lebanon—**Psalm** 72:16

*Let us watch awhile the sowers,
Let us mark the tiny grain.
Scattered oft in doubt and trembling,
Sown in weakness or in pain.*

from ***The Sowers*** by Frances Ridley Havergal

BICENTENNIAL EDITION

MEMPHIS, TENNESSEE
CUMBERLAND PRESBYTERIAN CHURCH
2010

History of the Cumberland Presbyterian Church by Benjamin Wilburn McDonnold. Electronic processing for this edition by Matthew H. Gore for Cumberland Presbytery and the Historical Foundation of the Cumberland Presbyterian Church and the Cumberland Presbyterian Church in America. Entire contents ©2010 by the Cumberland Presbyterian Denomination.

World rights reserved. No part of this book may be reproduced or transmitted in any form or by any means, electronic or mechanical, including photocopying, recording, or by any information storage or retrieval system, without permission in writing from the publisher. A reviewer may quote brief passages in a review. Short passages may be reproduced for academic purposes.

Originally published by the Board of Publication of the Cumberland Presbyterian Church in 1888.

Fifth (Bicentennial) Edition, April 2010
Second Printing, March 2016

ISBN-13: 978-0692668924
ISBN-10: 0692668926

Cumberland Presbyterian Church, 8207 Traditional Place, Cordova (Memphis), Tennessee 38016-7414

Preface to the Bicentennial Edition

B. W. McDonnold's *History of the Cumberland Presbyterian Church*, originally published in 1888, has long been one of the most cherished and sought after books about the Cumberland Presbyterian Church. There were four editions of the book including the original but an unknown number of printings. As far as has yet been determined all of the original editions are textually identical for all practical purposes. These printings kept the title in print from 1888 until about 1942 at which time original supplies ran out and the book was not reprinted. It is likely that the final copies sold were part of the 1899 fourth edition but from a printing made after 1910.

With no more "new" copies available for sale, existing copies of "McDonnold," as it had become relevantly known, became heirlooms, handed down in families from generation to generation. On the rare occasion that sound copies entered the used and collectible book market it was not uncommon for them to command prices of $100 or more.

For many years we have wanted to make a relatively inexpensive edition available. The occasion of the 200th anniversary of the Cumberland Presbyterian Church seemed ideal for this dream to be fulfilled. The book you hold in your hands was reproduced from the fourth edition as it originally appeared in 1899. The decision to reproduce the book from an extant copy was not arrived at lightly. We hoped the entire text could be reset and properly indexed this turned out to be a labor intensive process that would have pushed publication past the 180th meeting of General Assembly in Dickson, Tennessee. We hope that this version will satisfy demand.

23 April 2010, Memphis, Tennessee.

PREFACE.

At the suggestion of Dr. D. M. Harris, the Board of Publication of the Cumberland Presbyterian church contracted with the writer for the preparation of this history. The size of the book was limited by the board before a line of it was written. It was also understood between us that only the *minimum* of time consistent with thoroughness was to be allowed. Casting the horoscope of the book under these limitations, there were found just three things to choose between. The first was to end the volume where my own life became a humble factor in our history, and where interested feelings might prevent clear-sightedness. The second was to condense our whole history, giving each event and actor a place. The third was to make such selections from the whole field as would furnish a volume of good reading for our people, and illustrate our life and progress. The first method was not acceptable to my counselors, either in the board or out of it. The second method would have produced a book which nobody would read. The third method involved the inevitable complaints of all those who might be omitted, besides opening other doors of complaints not found in the first method.

After many consultations the third method, with all its inevitable complaints and inevitable omissions of good men who deserve mention, was deliberately adopted, and the work of gathering material from the whole field, and studying every particle of this material so as to be able to make the best selections, was undertaken. I had gone but a little way in this work before I discovered the utter impossibility of accomplishing it without more time than was at first proposed. More was granted, but with the pressing demand that it be made as brief as thoroughness permitted. My only fears on that point are that it will be found by experts that I made that time far too brief.

Under the same limitations the plan was formed about the different States. It was to give the origin of the church in each State, with as much fullness of detail as could well be secured, extending the record only to the organization of the first presbytery, closing that chapter with a rapid summary view of the present condition of our church in that part of the field. There were certain subjects belonging to all periods to which special chapters were reserved, to be placed at the last of the book; and if they brought out any thing further from the work of our people in any particular State, at any later period, all well; and if not, there would be no further notice taken of that portion of the church.

The question of brief biographical sketches was also carefully weighed, and finally decided in the negative. To this decision an exception was made in the case of those generally called the fathers of the church. If a biography formed part of the very thread of the history which I was writing, just so far was it also made a part of this volume. There were placed in my hands some very interesting biographies which contained no single item that could be used according to my established programme of operations.

It was not so much to show how our church originated as to show what it has done since it originated that this book was undertaken. In showing this, my best strength has been put forth to the utmost. In that part of the work I was fortunate in gathering materials. I reaped, also, the fruit of past labors. The materials mostly relied on for this part of the history were manuscripts. Of these my collection was extensive. Among them were manuscripts from James McGready, Finis Ewing, Samuel McAdow Robert Bell, Robert Donnell, and Thomas Calhoun.

In 1845, while boarding at Calhoun's house, and often meeting there various actors in the events out of which our church originated, I commenced taking down from the lips of these old men a full history of the origin and work of our church. The statements from Calhoun, McSpeddin, Lowry, and Aston covered all the main points of our history up to 1845. In spite of war and fire these memoranda have been preserved, and were used in the preparation of this book. The habit of collecting such memoranda, begun in my boyhood, has been kept up ever since, and the accumulation of reliable materials in that way is now considerable.

At two different periods in my life I have been called upon to travel over the church. In the last period of travels I spent twelve years, visiting more than four fifths of the entire denomination; and though neither of these extensive tours had any reference to collecting materials for a history, yet that old habit of keeping memoranda was all the time unintentionally furnishing matter for such a work. So, too, did that old habit furnish me the only existing records which I can now find of the proceedings of the conventions held by our people in Chattanooga, Tennessee, in 1863, and in Selma, Alabama, in 1864.

There were placed in my hands for use in the preparation of this little volume sixty manuscript autobiographies, some brief, and some extending to five hundred pages of foolscap. Two of these were the lives of men who were arraigned before the commission of Kentucky Synod. The original record books of all our first judicatures have also been examined, and the archives of old Cumberland College and of Cumberland University were consulted, as well as many other official records.

The literary remains in full of Richard Beard, Milton Bird, David Lowry, and President Anderson, all very extensive, were all explored. Parts of the literary remains of various others were placed in my hands. Of this latter class I mention James Smith, W. A. Scott, John W. Ogden, Finis Ewing, F. R. Cossitt, Robert Donnell, H. A. Hunter, Isaac Shook, and Herschel S. Porter. Dr. Beard's old letters date back to 1830, and are from all the chief actors in our church from the beginning. There are perhaps eight thousand of these letters, and they discuss every important subject that has ever been before our denomination. They will all be filed in the library of Cumberland University.

The private diary of Dr. Beard has been of great service to me. Indeed, diaries are the most trustworthy of all manuscript authorities. There was a considerable number of these placed in my hands. Most of them are to be returned to their authors' families. Others, together with many manuscripts, are to be filed in the library of Cumberland University.

It required more than fifteen months' constant labor to explore all these authorities. Files of from one to five weekly papers (and various monthlies) for a period of fifty-seven years had to be examined. "The ninth ripening year" was not allowed me for all this work, but past studies rendered some little compensation for this lack of time. Dr. Lindsley's labors in collecting material also saved me much delay. The fruit of his noble toil has been freely used in preparing this volume.

The generous assistance of many brethren was extended to me in collecting material. The list of the names of those brethren would be too long to give here, but God keeps all the roll. He knows how generously some of them struggled to help me; and he will not forget their labor of love.

The board secured the services of a very learned committee to revise the manuscript before it went to press, and they had unlimited power not only to correct errors, but also to strike out from the manuscript whatever they saw fit. They corrected several minor errors, and there may be others which neither I nor the committee detected. Those who have read "The Biography of a Lie" know how even an accumulation of authorities may sometimes mislead a writer. I have detected mistakes in authorities where mistakes seemed to be impossible. It is by no means likely that I have detected all in the authorities relied on for this volume.

It is proper here to state that, with my full consent, the book editor made great changes, especially in certain parts of the last two periods of the history. In this he had the assistance of the able committee already mentioned. My history of the sixth period was prepared in such haste that great changes were no doubt needed.

And now to Him for whom every line of this book was written, and to whom all its future destiny is committed, I leave this volume to be used as His infinite wisdom may determine.

EDITOR'S PREFACE

Before the work of editing this volume was begun, the Board of Publication appointed a committee consisting of the Rev. J. C. Provine, D.D., the Rev. M. B. De Witt, D.D., the Rev. W. E. Ward, D.D., and the Rev. D. M. Harris, D.D., to assist the book editor in this task. Several meetings were held, and some of the chapters were read and discussed by the whole committee. But this method required so much time, and such difficulty was experienced in securing a full and regular attendance at the meetings, that it was arranged for the members of the committee separately to read the manuscript, indicating their suggestions, and leaving the work of making changes to the book editor.

As the work progressed, and especially when the record of the closing period of the history was reached, it seemed to the committee and to the editor necessary to give a somewhat fuller account of certain events and certain departments of the church's work than that found in the manuscript. Accordingly the editor greatly extended the history of the relation of Cumberland Presbyterians to the Presbyterian Alliance, the history of city and home missions since the war, and of the Trinidad, the Japan, and the Mexican missions; of Waynesburg College, of the first efforts of the church to establish schools in Pennsylvania and Ohio and in the West, of the revision of the Confession of Faith, and of several minor matters. As stated in the body of the work, Dr. Harris made large additions to the sketch of Lincoln University, and John M. Gaut, Esq., prepared the history of the Board of Publication found in the forty-seventh chapter. The sketch of Cane Hill College in the forty-sixth chapter was furnished by the Rev. F. R. Earle, D.D., president of that institution. The index at the close of the volume was prepared by the Rev. J. P. Sprowls, D.D. All these changes and additions were made with the cordial consent and approval of Dr. McDonnold.

The editor desires to acknowledge the valuable assistance he has received from his colleague and co-laborer, Dr. Harris, and the no less helpful suggestions of Dr. Provine and Dr. DeWitt. By reason of the illness and death of Dr. Ward, the committee was, except in the earlier stages of the work, deprived of the counsel and suggestions which his literary attainments and wide knowledge of our denominational history so well fitted him to give.

In reading and re-reading this volume, first in manuscript and afterward in the proof sheets, the editor has been more and more impressed with its value as a most important contribution to our denominational literature. By the simple naturalness and beauty of his style, by apt illustrations and well-selected incidents, Dr. McDonnold has imparted to these pages a living interest and a charm which it is believed will make their perusal a delight. This book is sent forth to the church and to the world with the confident hope that it will awaken, not only among our own people but wherever it shall be read, new interest in the history and doctrines and future work of the Cumberland Presbyterian church.

J. M. HOWARD, *Book Editor.*

NASHVILLE, January, 1888.

CONTENTS.

FIRST PERIOD.

FROM THE BEGINNING OF THE GREAT REVIVAL TO THE ORGANIZATION OF THE COUNCIL, 1796 TO 1806.

CHAPTER I.

STATE OF THE COUNTRY.

The country called Cumberland. Indian warfare. Anecdote of Daviess and Donnelson. Pioneer women. Colonel Joe Brown. Privations and hardships. Boating to New Orleans. Mail facilities, ... 1-4

CHAPTER II.

LITERATURE AND RELIGION.

Education without books. The first school in Cumberland. Tennessee's first "meeting-house." Charles Cummings. Kentucky. Rice and Craighead. Formal worship. Unconverted church members and ministers. Richard King. Lifeless preaching. Conversion of James McGready. His removal to Kentucky, ... 5-9

CHAPTER III.

THE GREAT REVIVAL.

Fasting and prayer. McGready's covenant. Gasper River. General awakening. Muddy River. Sinners falling prostrate.

Origin of camp-meetings. Spread of the revival. Its origin in McGready's churches. The "Cumberlands" not "New Lights." Shouting. Tokens. "The Union,"........10–19

CHAPTER IV.

THE REVIVAL A GENUINE WORK OF GOD'S SPIRIT.

Testimony of David Rice, and of the Presbyterian General Assembly. George Baxter's testimony. David Nelson in the "Western Sketch Book." James Gallagher. Methodist testimony. Dr. Speer's history. Infidelity and the revival of 1800. Modern missionary progress and the revival,.....20–26.

CHAPTER V.

A PENTECOSTAL BAPTISM.

The gift of the Holy Ghost the distinctive privilege of the new dispensation. Finis Ewing's testimony. Anecdote of Ewing. Mr. Moody and "the power." Anecdotes of Donnell and Calhoun. Dr. Samuel Miller and H. F. Delany. An ordination incident. James B. Porter in a Presbyterian camp-meeting. The sublime faith of our first preachers. Calhoun dealing with disturbers. Solemn covenants. Remarkable answers to prayer. Testimony of our first preachers,..........27–38.

CHAPTER VI.

OPPOSITION TO THE REVIVAL.

Opposition to McGready's work in North Carolina. Balch in McGready's Kentucky churches. Violence. Hyper-Calvinism logically anti-revival. "Old Side" objections to revival "measures." Camp-meetings and the "mourners' bench." Arguments. An "orderly" meeting. Misrepresentation. The "Stoneites." An editor's mistake. "The jerks,"....39–47

CHAPTER VII.

THE SECOND DIFFICULTY—MINISTERIAL EDUCATION.

Pressing need for more preachers. David Rice's advice. Anderson, Ewing, and King before the Transylvania Presbytery. Anderson received as a "candidate." The General Assembly's advice. The revival party's statement. Statement of James Hutchinson, Esq. King as a lay exhorter. Anderson. McLean. Porter. Chapman. Division of Transylvania Presbytery, and formation of Cumberland Presbytery. Ordination of Anderson, Ewing, and King. The educational question not the cause of division. Proofs. Efforts to secure education for young men. Presbyterian testimony then and now. How shall we evangelize the masses? 48–65

CHAPTER VIII.

THIRD DIFFICULTY—DOCTRINES—RESERVATIONS IN ADOPTING THE BOOK.

Reservations in adopting the Confession. Meanings of "fatality." Dr. Davidson's testimony. Two charges. Unsoundness of doctrine the chief difficulty. Platform of union with Southern Presbyterians proposed in 1867. "Elect infants," and the Westminster Assembly. Dr. MacCrae, of Scotland. The Westminster creed an incumbrance to revival preaching. Testimony of Dr. Chalmers and Dr. Schaff. Creeds and theodicies. Significant incidents in the Belfast Council. The mission of Cumberland Presbyterians, ... 66–76

CHAPTER IX.

FOURTH DIFFICULTY—TRAMPLING ON A PRESBYTERY'S CONSTITUTIONAL RIGHTS BY A SYNODICAL COMMISSION.

The two parties in Cumberland Presbytery. The Commission. Statement of charges. The young men appealed to. Forbidden to preach. This action pronounced unconstitutional by the Presbyterian General Assembly. Bitterness of the people against the Commission. Mr. Lyle, ... 77–81

SECOND PERIOD.

FROM THE FORMATION OF THE COUNCIL TO THE ORGANIZATION OF THE GENERAL ASSEMBLY, 1806 TO 1829.

CHAPTER X.

THE NEW CHURCH.

The Council. Why the revival party did not appeal from the Commission's decision. Cumberland Presbytery dissolved. The Council's efforts for reconciliation. Lyle's tears. The Assembly's final decision. The Council's last effort for reconciliation. Gloomy outlook. Cumberland Presbytery re-organized. "The Cumberland schism" not a schism. Measures adopted by the new Presbytery. Rigid rules and discipline. Strict Sabbath observance. Lack of regular pastorates. Methods of education and study. List of the ministers belonging to the new presbytery, ... 82–92

CHAPTER XI.

FIRST AIMS—NECESSITY FOR A SYNOD—ITS ORGANIZATION—SKETCHES OF ITS MEMBERS.

A separate denomination not at first aimed at. Formation of a Synod. Presbyterial boundaries. Pen-and-ink sketch of the members of the synod. McSpeddin. Harris. Philip McDonnold. William McGee's anxiety about the new creed, . 93–97

CHAPTER XII.

THE CONFESSION OF FAITH—SYNOPSIS OF DOCTRINES—FULLER CONFESSION—A MEDIUM SYSTEM—DIAGRAM.

Exceptions about fatality. Outline statement of doctrine. Fuller creed adopted. Exhibit of changes in the Westminster Confessions. Additions. "The medium system." Diagram of creeds. Conditions of communion, ... 98–108

CHAPTER XIII.

THE THREE PRESBYTERIES—OLD CUSTOMS NOW DROPPED.

Three Presbyteries. Tokens. Col. Joe Brown's case. Fencing the table. Elders in presbytery. Extended fields. Fast days. A three-fold plan. Plans for securing and supporting itinerants. Final failure of this system. Origin of the name, Cumberland Presbyterian. Presbyterial libraries. Preaching on a call to the ministry. Demand for preachers in new fields. Catechising. Necessity for a school discussed. Prejudice against statistics. Camp-meetings in neglected neighborhoods. The doctrines preached, ... 109–119

CHAPTER XIV.

HISTORIC CHURCHES—PLANTING CHURCHES IN TENNESSEE AND KENTUCKY.

Red River church, Kentucky. Gasper River. Beech church, Tennessee. Big Spring. Thomas Calhoun's pastorate. Smyrna. New Hope. Mt. Moriah. Goshen. Origin of the Nashville church, ... 120–127

CHAPTER XV.

EARLY MISSIONS TO THE INDIANS.

Proximity of the Indians. Quickening of the missionary spirit. Indians at camp-meetings. Mission work by the presbyteries. Mission of Samuel King and Robert Bell. Bell's Mission and school, 1820. Indian customs. Traditions of the Tombigbee. The first Board of Missions for the whole church. The Russellville church, Kentucky. Details of Bell's missionary work. Letter from an Indian chief. Mrs. Bell's diary. Removal of the Indians. End of Bell's mission, ... 128–141

CHAPTER XVI.

PLANTING CHURCHES IN THE NEW TERRITORIES OF EAST AND WEST TENNESSEE AND THE KENTUCKY PURCHASE.

New fields. East Tennessee. McGready's letter to East Tennessee Presbyterians. An ecclesiastical barrier. Calhoun and Robert Donnell in East Tennessee (1815). Calhoun's tour the next year. David Foster. The Rev. J. S. Guthrie. Other laborers. The Rev. George Donnell. Organization of Knoxville Presbytery. Hardships. West Tennessee. John L. Dillard and the Rev. James McDonnold first in this field (1820). Richard Beard (1821). Difficulties. Camp-meetings. Organization of Hopewell Presbytery. Jackson's Purchase, Kentucky. B. H. Pearson's labors. Missionary work of Logan Presbytery. M. H. Bone. Incidents. Church growth in Kentucky, ... 142–154

CHAPTER XVII.

PLANTING CHURCHES IN ALABAMA.

A glance at the history of Alabama. Robert Bell sent to Hunt's Spring. Calhoun. Robert Donnell. Other laborers. Circuits. South Alabama. Efforts to form a presbytery. Labors of William Moore, Samuel King, R. D. King and Daniel Patton. Tombigbee Presbytery organized. Anecdote of R. D. King. A sermon by William Moore. Alabama Presbytery. Reminiscences. Hindrances, ... 155–163

CHAPTER XVIII.

PLANTING CHURCHES IN INDIANA AND ILLINOIS.

Indiana. William Harris' visit. Missionaries sent to Wabash and Indiana. Hardships. Organization of Mt. Zion church. Other congregations. Incidents. Illinois. First Cumberland Presbyterian sermon in this territory. John Crawford. Incidents. Green P. Rice. First Illinois camp-meeting. D. W.

McLin. Second camp-meeting. Chapman's missionary tour. Sparse settlements. Hardships. Illinois Presbytery organized. Comparison of church growth in Indiana and Illinois, ... 164–174

CHAPTER XIX.

PLANTING THE CHURCH IN MISSOURI AND ARKANSAS, 1811–1829.

First Cumberland Presbyterian sermon in Missouri. Daniel Buie. R. D. Morrow sent to Missouri. J. T. A. Henderson's boyhood home. Morrow's second trip to Missouri. McGee Presbytery organized. Finis Ewing in Missouri. "School of the Prophets." Labors of R. D. King and Reuben Burrow. A home supply of preachers. Pioneer missionaries: Robert Sloan, Archibald McCorkle, H. R. Smith, Frank M. Braly. Anecdote of Braly. A. A. Young. Daniel Patton. Adventure of William Blackwell. Arkansas. Emigration thither of the Pyatts and Carnahans. John Carnahan's circuit. Ordination of Carnahan. The first sacramental meeting in Arkansas. Incidents. An "intermediate" session of McGee Presbytery. Labors of R. D. King and Reuben Burrow. Camp-meetings. Sickness. Return of Burrow and King to Missouri. Arkansas Presbytery. Settlement of Cane Hill. The Buchanans. Cane Hill College. Bands of robbers. Guilford Pylant, ... 175–200

CHAPTER XX.

THE COLLEGE—THE GENERAL ASSEMBLY—SUMMARY OF WHAT HAD BEEN DONE.

Need of a college recognized. Plan adopted. Details. Dr. Cossitt. Expediency of organizing a General Assembly discussed, 1823. Reasons for delay. Last meeting of the General Synod. List of the presbyteries and original members. Four synods formed. The synodical period, ... 201–206

THIRD PERIOD.

FROM THE ORGANIZATION OF THE GENERAL ASSEMBLY TO THE REMOVAL OF CUMBERLAND COLLEGE, 1829 TO 1842.

CHAPTER XXI.

GENERAL SURVEY.

The transition period. State of the church. Changed times. Progress. Mistakes. The college. Home missionary progress. Statistics. Revivals. Camp-meetings. Appeal cases. Samuel King's tour among the churches. Temperance. Fraternal intercourse with other churches. A theological school demanded. Church growth. Change from missionary evangelists to pastorates. New presbyteries and synods. Financial troubles, ... 207–213

CHAPTER XXII.

THE FIRST CUMBERLAND PRESBYTERIAN COLLEGE.

Outward and internal history. A manual labor institution. The college located at Princeton, Ky. Buildings. Debts. Lease of Barnett and Shelby. Cholera. Barnett's lease surrendered. A stock company formed. Threats. Reviving hope, followed by failure. The Assembly decides to select a new location. Lebanon, Tenn., chosen. Report of the Commissioners. Protest of the friends of Princeton. Resolution against the control of pecuniary matters by the Assembly. Cumberland College after "the removal." Internal history. A homespun costume prescribed. Refectory and dormitories. Presidents. Professors. Dr. Beard's administration. Dr. Azel Freeman. Alumni, ... 214–228

CHAPTER XXIII.

THE CHURCH PAPER.

Origin of the *Religious and Literary Intelligencer*. David Lowry. The paper moved to Nashville. Sold to James Smith.

Smith's multiplied labors. The paper becomes the *Cumberland Presbyterian*. Hopeless indebtedness. T. C. Anderson, assistant editor. Efforts to increase the circulation. Smith's agreement with the Assembly. Editorial denunciations. No General Assembly, 1839. Convention at Nashville. Its action. Smith's *Cumberland Presbyterian* at Springfield, Tenn. He denounces the convention. Strife and division. Smith's college at Springfield. The *Banner of Peace*. Action of the Assembly, 1840. Smith's subsequent course. Preachers who have joined the Presbyterians, ... 229–241

CHAPTER XXIV.

THE TRANSITION FROM MISSIONARY EVANGELISTS TO PAID PASTORS.

Self-denying missionaries. Opposition to settled pastors. Proposed abolition of pastorates, 1830. Action of West Tennessee Synod. Misconceptions. Pastors and evangelists. Calhoun's testimony. False ideas of "supporting the gospel." Two anecdotes of Dr. A. J. Baird. Wrong training. Robbing pastors. Meager pay of circuit riders. The credit system. The scriptural method, ... 242–252

CHAPTER XXV.

THE CHURCH IN MISSISSIPPI AND LOUISIANA.

Bell's Mission. Bad character of settlers in the Indian country. Anecdote of a slave trader. An Indian comment on the Bankrupt Law. Removal of the Indians from Mississippi. Rush of settlers. "Seizing the golden opportunity." Temptations. Religious apostasy. Isaac Shook's testimony. Formation of Mississippi Presbytery. Shook's meetings at Columbus. Denominational progress in Mississippi. Mississippi Synod organized. Presbyteries. Mississippi preachers. Anecdote of R. L. Ross. Louisiana. First congregation organized. Louisiana Presbytery, ... 253–262

CHAPTER XXVI.

PLANTING THE CHURCH IN TEXAS.

American colonist in Texas. Sumner Bacon. Bacon in Texas. Attacked by ruffians. First Texas camp-meeting. Bacon's work. The Rev. Mr. Chase. Bacon's ordination. A. J. McGown. San Jacinto. Texas Presbytery formed. Robert Tate. Samuel W. Frazier. James McDonnold. Work of R. O. Watkins. Other helpers. Darkness followed by revival. Table of dates, ...263–272

CHAPTER XXVII.

ORIGIN OF THE CHURCH IN PENNSYLVANIA.

The Rev. Jacob Lindley. Visit of M. H. Bone and John W. Ogden. Request of Presbyterians in Washington County, Pa. Action of the Assembly. Arrival of the missionaries. Morgan's account. Morgan's first sermon in Pennsylvania. First meetings, and their results. Formation of the first Cumberland Presbyterian church in this State. The first camp-meeting. An incident. Anecdote of Burrow and Donnell. Bryan at Pittsburg. Formation of a presbytery. LeRoy Woods' work. Jacob Lindley's testimony. The Carmichaels church. Uniontown. Hopewell. J. T. A. Henderson. Brownsville. Bryan at Meadville. Pittsburg. Anecdote of Bryan. Death of Morgan. The *Union and Evangelist*. Pennsylvania Synod formed, ...273–291

CHAPTER XXVIII.

ORIGIN OF THE CHURCH IN OHIO.

Visit of Bone and Ogden. Morgan's visit to Athens. His return. Result of his labors. Morgan's Ohio Camp-meeting. Incidents. Our first church in Ohio. Beverly. Mr. Lindley's labors there. Senecaville. A circus incident. Cumberland, Ohio. Lebanon. The Rev. F. G. Black's work. The Covington church. Our church in Ohio, ... 292–300

CHAPTER XXIX.

MISCELLANEOUS SKETCHES AND INCIDENTS.

Revival at Bowling Green, Kentucky. A Kentucky camp-meeting. A sample church under the supply system. Anecdote of Hugh B. Hill. "Stars falling." Beginnings of Cane Hill College, Arkansas. Anecdotes of John Buchanan and T. C. Anderson. Duelling condemned by the Missouri Synod. Andrew Jackson and J. M. Berry. Conversion of an infidel woman. Anecdote of R. D. King, ... 301–309

FOURTH PERIOD.

FROM THE "REMOVAL" OF THE COLLEGE TO THE ST. LOUIS ASSEMBLY, 1842 TO 1861.

CHAPTER XXX.

A GENERAL SURVEY.

Progress. Records of the General Synod and Assembly. Opening sermon of the Assembly of 1843, by Milton Bird. No Assembly in 1844. The Assembly of 1845. Organization of the Board of Missions. Work of this board. A Committee on Publication. A new Publishing Committee, 1847. Its work at Louisville. Transferred to Nashville 1858. Our Hymnbook history. The Board of Church Extension. Fraternal correspondence. Relations with the New School church. With the Old School. Efforts to secure a history of the church. Fast days. A last message from Robert Donnell. Colleges. New synods and presbyteries, ... 310–321

CHAPTER XXXI.

MISSIONS—1843–1860.

Missions in the new Territories. City missions. David Lowry's mission to the Winnebagoes. Cumberland Presbyterian missionaries under the American Board. David Lowry's visit to the Choctaw country, 1854. His report. R. W. Baker's work. Armstrong Academy. Burney Academy. Faithfulness of R. S. Bell and Mrs. Bell. Letters from Israel and George Folsom. The Foreign work. Edmond Weir in Liberia. His visit to America, 1857. Discouragements. Other foreign fields discussed. Candidates. J. C. Armstrong appointed missionary to Turkey, ... 322–335

CHAPTER XXXII.

PLANTING THE CHURCH IN THE NORTH-WEST—IOWA AND OTHER FIELDS.

David Lowry's work. Church organized in Joseph Howard's house. J. G. White in Iowa. The first Iowa camp-meeting. Iowa Presbytery formed. Neil Johnson's labor. Ruffianism. David Lowry's missionary plan for the North-west. J. C. Armstrong's work in Iowa. A camp-meeting. A horse-racer converted. Waukon. P. H. Crider. A letter from Armstrong. Organization of Colesburg Presbytery. Hardships and dangers. Our meager strength in Iowa. Other North-western States, ... 336–341

CHAPTER XXXIII.

OREGON AND CALIFORNIA, 1844–1860.

Gold and God's providence. Oregon. Difficulties in the way of its colonization. Fur traders. The first settlers. First Cumberland Presbyterian colony in Oregon. J. E. Braly. Crossing the plains. Whitman's Station massacre. Neil Johnson's journey. Cholera on the plains. Other dangers. Our first Oregon congregation. Oregon Presbytery. Efforts to establish a college. Jacob Gillespie. Self-sacrificing missionaries. Presbyteries. Acquisition of California. Gold. Transient settlements. Mixed population. An unfaithful missionary. Others who were faithful. John E. Braly. Letter from T. A. Ish. Cornelius Yager. Linville Dooley. Anecdote of E. C. Latta. Organization of California Presbytery. Mushroom churches. Mountain View church. J. M. Small at Napa City. Pacific Presbytery. Cumberland College at Sonoma. T. M. Johnson and the *Pacific Observer*. D. E. Bushnell's testimony. Johnson, a peace-maker. Fascinating opportunities. Difficulties and advantages. Our California presbyteries. Idaho, ... 342–356

CHAPTER XXXIV.

SUNDRY SMALL BEGINNINGS—NORTH CAROLINA, WEST VIRGINIA, GEORGIA, KANSAS.

Visit of Reuben Burrow and Robert Donnell to North Carolina. Feeble beginnings abandoned. West Virginia. Our work in Georgia. A. Templeton and Z. M. McGhee. A war anecdote. Georgia Presbytery. The political struggle in Kansas. Letter from an emigrant. Round Prairie church. Kansas Presbytery. Leavenworth Presbytery. Missionaries. Presbyteries, . . 357–361

CHAPTER XXXV.

MISCELLANEOUS.

Concentration. Mushroom colleges. Theological school. Disagreement. Theological School of Bethel College. Action of the Assembly. Dr. Burrow's teachings. A living question. Missions. Fear of centralization. Proposed consolidation of newspapers. Arguments *pro and con*. Books. Crisman's Origin and Doctrines. Dillard's Reply to Lewis A. Lowry. Cossitt's Life and Times of Ewing. Anderson's Life of Donnell. Beard's Theology. Dr. Beard as a theologian. Controversies. Dr. Burrow's departures from the traditional faith. Decay of camp-meetings. Church trials. Profitless controversies, ... 362–372

CHAPTER XXXVI.

SKETCHES AND INCIDENTS.

The Memphis church. Anecdote of Matthew H. Bone and Hugh B. Hill. Story of Benjamin Watson. Facts from P. G. Rea's

History of New Lebanon Presbytery. Compensation of preachers. Anecdote of James Johnson. An Indian's conversion. A mother's Sunday-school. A discouraged teacher. Anecdote of M. H. Bone and F. G. Black. Story of a stammering preacher, ... 373-379

FIFTH PERIOD.

FROM THE BEGINNING OF THE CIVIL WAR TO THE WARRENSBURG ASSEMBLY, 1861 TO 1870.

CHAPTER XXXVII.

TEN ASSEMBLIES, 1861-1870.

Presbyteries, North and South. Location of church boards. Representatives in the Assembly of 1861. Reports of boards. Assembly of 1862. Southern presbyteries unrepresented. Temporary Committees on Missions and Publication. Re-organization of these committees in 1863. Removal of publishing interests to Pittsburg. Assemblies of 1864 and 1865. State of things in the South. The Chattanooga Convention. Missionary committee. Convention at Selma, Ala. Letter from Milton Bird. The *Southern Observer*. Memphis Convention. Assembly of 1866. A general fast day. Missionary boards. Re-organization of the Board of Publication at Nashville. Proposed Organic Union with Southern Presbyterians. Conference of committees. Result. Proposed revision of form of government. Consolidation of missionary boards. Controversy about the plans of the Board of Missions. Action of the Assembly of 1870. Abolition of the synod discussed. Church periodicals. New presbyteries, 380-390

CHAPTER XXXVIII.

THE WAR RECORD.

Assemblies and Conventions. Milton Bird's opening sermon, 1861. Resolutions. Resolutions adopted in 1862 and in 1863. Deliverance of 1864. Protest. Action in 1865. Position of Southern Cumberland Presbyterians. The Chattanooga Convention. Deliverance of the Assembly of 1866. Action of Pennsylvania Synod. Of the Assembly at Memphis, 1867. At Lincoln, 1868. Relations of Cumberland Presbyterians to slavery. Finis Ewing's views. McAdow. Ephraim McLean. Robert Donnell's prayer. Testimony of Dr. Beard's diary. A typical case. The *Revivalist* on slavery. Testimony of the *Cumberland Presbyterian*, 1835. Changes wrought by political agitation. Action of the Assemblies of 1848 and 1851. Present attitude of the church. Its Southern membership, . . 391–419

CHAPTER XXXIX.

PREACHING TO SOLDIERS.

Chaplains. Army missionaries. Methods of work by chaplains. Their trying duties. Denominations forgotten. Work in the Union armies. Labors of A. W. White and G. N. Mattox. A. G. Osborne. H. H. Ashmore. Hiram A. Hunter. J. W. Woods. S. Richards. The Southern army. Resolutions adopted by Southern chaplains. Revival in Bragg's army. Death of George L. Winchester. Cumberland Presbyterian Committee on army missions. J. L. Cooper. Nightly services during Johnston's retreat. A picket incident. Other incidents. Hardships of Southern chaplains. M. B. DeWitt. A. G. Burrow. Revival in the Southern armies, ... 420–431

CHAPTER XL.

COLORED CUMBERLAND PRESBYTERIANS.

Order of things before the war. An illustrative case. Colored people at camp-meetings. Colored preachers before the war. The change wrought by the war. Conventions of colored Cumberland Presbyterians at Henderson, Kentucky, and Huntsville, Alabama. Action at Murfreesboro, May 1869. A separate organization. A colored commissioner at the Assembly of 1870. Progress of colored Cumberland Presbyterians. Their General Assembly. School at Bowling Green, Kentucky. Our duty to the colored people. Letter of J. F. Humphrey, ... 432–439

CHAPTER XLI.

MISSIONS—1860-1870.

Missions in towns and cities. Itinerant missionaries. New Territories entered. R. S. Bell's work among the Indians. Liberia and Turkey. Gloomy letters from Edmond Weir. His second visit to America. Abandonment of the Liberia mission. J. C. Armstrong's mission to Turkey. His voyage to England. Arrival at Constantinople. Greek Christians from Brusa. Troubles. Providential relief. Work done by Armstrong. His illness and return to America, ... 440-447

SIXTH PERIOD.

FROM THE ASSEMBLY AT WARRENSBURG, MISSOURI, TO THE ASSEMBLY AT COVINGTON, OHIO, 1870 TO 1887.

CHAPTER XLII.

SEVERAL GENERAL ASSEMBLIES.

Growing spirit of unity. Quarterly collections. Day of prayer for colleges. Need of ministers. Death of Milton Bird. John Frizzell elected stated clerk. Discussion of the revised Form of Government. Proposition for organic union with Northern Presbyterians. Proposed terms of union. Response of the Presbyterian committee. Result. False ideas. Visit of James Morrison and Fergus Ferguson. Anecdote of Ferguson. Corresponding delegates. Address of J. S. Hays of the Northern Presbyterian church. Old School Presbyterian delegates. Assembly at Jefferson, Texas. Other Assemblies. General Superintendent of Sunday-schools. M. B. DeWitt succeeded by J. H. Warren. Address of Dr. E. D. Morris, 1879. Semi-centennial meeting. The Woman's Board. Its work. A Woman's Board in 1818. Negotiations concerning organic union with Evangelical Lutherans. Important measures adopted in 1881. Revised Confession of Faith approved, 1882. Vote of the presbyteries. T. C. Blake elected stated clerk. John Frizzell the first elder moderator. The Assembly at Bentonville, Arkansas. Dancing condemned. Consolidation of papers. Board of Ministerial Relief. New books. History of the Presbyterian Alliance and the relations of Cumberland Presbyterians with it. Death of Dr. A. J. Baird. New synods and presbyteries. Statistics. Freedom from proselyting, ... 448–468

CHAPTER XLIII.

MISSIONS.

Progress. City missions. Our work in St. Louis. Mission at Little Rock, Ark. Kansas City, and Sedalia, Mo. Logansport, Ind. Chattanooga, Tenn. Other missions. Successful administration of the board's affairs. Importance of Home Missions. Indian missions. Bethel Presbytery. Work among the Cherokees. Foreign Missions. Action of the Assembly 1870–1873. Dr. S. T. Anderson sent to the Island of Trinidad. History of his work. His return. J. B. and A. D. Hail accepted as candidates. The Japan mission. M. L. Gordon. The Hail brothers. J. B. Hail in Osaka, Japan, 1877. Beginning work. A. D. Hail joins his brother, October, 1878. The first sermon. Interest in the work. Difficulties. A Sunday-school organized. First baptism and communion service. Fruits at home. The Woman's Board. Extending work. Denominational literature. Arrival of Misses Orr and Leavitt. "Denarii boxes." "A woman's meeting." The Osaka church. Missionary conference, 1883. A great revival. Scattered membership. Elders. Principles governing the work. Arrival of Mrs. A. M. Drennan. The Wilmina School. Other labors of Mrs. Drennan. Corea. Growing fruits. Organization of congregations. Churches built. A native council or presbytery. Work of Miss Orr. Arrival of Miss Duffield. Wakayama. Miss Leavitt's work. Shingu. Schools. Japanese young men in America. Arrival of G. E. Hudson and wife and Miss Rena Rezner, December, 1886. Members of the mission. Benefits of denominational work. Co-operation with other churches. The Mexican mission. Appointment of the Rev. A. H. Whatley. His preparatory visit to Mexico. Aguas Calientes. Needs of the work. Plans of the board. Consecration of F. P. Lawyer. Dr. Bell's lectures. The *Missionary Record*. General remarks, ... 469–508

CHAPTER XLIV.

CUMBERLAND UNIVERSITY—1842-1887.

"Removal" of the college. R. L. Caruthers. Trustees. The first faculty. A University charter. The buildings. Obligations to teachers. T. C. Anderson made president, 1845. Free tuition to candidates for the ministry. Free boarding. Endowment. J. M. McMurray's work. The law department. Other departments. High grade of scholarship. Extension of buildings. President Anderson's administration. The theological department. Dr. Beard. The University closed by the war. Buildings burned. "*Resurgam.*" Reopening of the school. Purchase of the Caruthers property. Prejudice and ill-feeling. Dr. McDonnold's presidency. How the work was sustained. Gifts to the University. "Camp Blake." Preparatory schools. The life insurance plan. The disaster it brought. Nathan Green made chancellor. Progress. Buildings. Relation of the theological school to the University. Education of young women. List of members of the faculty. The law school. Endowment. Duty of men of wealth, ... 509–526

CHAPTER XLV.

WAYNESBURG COLLEGE—LINCOLN UNIVERSITY— TRINITY UNIVERSITY.

Three educational centers. Efforts to establish denominational schools in Pennsylvania and Ohio. Action of Pennsylvania Synod, 1838. Greene Academy. Madison College. Anecdote of John Morgan. J. P. Weethee's work in Madison College. Beverly College. Mr. Weethee president. Expected results not realized. Beginnings of Waynesburg College. The building. First graduates. Charter. Professors. Joshua Loughran the first president. J. P. Weethee becomes president. Difficulties. Mr. Weethee's resignation. President *pro tem.* and faculty. A. B. Miller made president. Dr. Miller's labors. Mrs. Miller. Graduates. Teachers trained at Waynesburg. A new building. Endowment. Religious influence. Value of Waynesburg College. Lincoln University. Early efforts to found schools. Influence of public schools. Effect of the civil war. Action of Indiana Synod. Commissioners appointed. The school located at Lincoln. The charter. Endowment. The building. The first faculty. Dr. Freeman's presidency. Dr. Bowdon his successor. Death of Dr. Bowdon. Dr. McGlumphy made president. Law and theological departments. Losses and difficulties. Resignation of Dr. McGlumphy. Graduates. Standard of scholarship. Professors. Trustees. Endowing agents. Work of the University. A new faculty. List of teachers and professors. Value of property. Trinity University. Educational spirit. Pioneer schools in Texas. Chapel Hill College. Larissa College. Ewing College. Origin of Trinity University. Tehuacana selected as the location. Plans for endowment. Faculty elected. Description of Tehuacana. University buildings. Prudent financial management. The charter. Presidents of Board of Trustees. List of presidents and members of the faculty. Presidents Beeson and McLeskey. Agents. Benefactors, ... 527-562

CHAPTER XLVI.

OTHER SCHOOLS AND COLLEGES.

The spirit of education among Cumberland Presbyterians. Our pioneer schools. Reports and resolutions adopted by the General Assembly. A graded system recommended. Warnings against the multiplication of schools. Number of schools in 1849. In 1856. List of colleges in 1860. Effect of the war. McGee College. Greeneville Seminary for Young Ladies. Greenwood Seminary. Union Female College. Cumberland Female College. Bethel College. Cane Hill College. Ward's Seminary. Spring Hill Institute. Loudon High School. Educational work in Missouri. Reflections on the evils of cheap scholarships, ... 563-584

CHAPTER XLVII.

PUBLICATION, NEWSPAPERS, REVISION, AND TEMPERANCE.

Publication. Use of the printing press. The first edition of the Confession. Plan of Cumberland College. Ewing's lectures.

Hymn-book committee. Publishing Association. The Louisville Board. Dr. Bird president, agent, and editor. Succeeded by Le Roy Woods. Jesse Anderson, Woods' successor. Work done at Louisville. Committee of Publication at Nashville. W. S. Langdon, general agent. The board chartered. Loans and donations. Work transferred to Pittsburg. S. T. Stewart, agent. Re-organization of the board at Nashville. J. C. Provine, book editor and publishing agent. W. E. Dunaway, agent. T. C. Blake, financial agent. M. B. DeWitt, financial agent and book editor. Purchase of the *Sunday-School Gem* and *Theological Medium*. Consolidation of church papers. Sunday-school publications. T. C. Blake, business manager, 1874-'78. J. M. Gaut, 1878-'80. T. M. Hurst, 1880-'86. Jno. D. Wilson, 1886. Financial struggles. Efforts to secure a church history. A digest. Hymn and tune book. Dr. W. E. Ward. List of members of the board. Newspapers. *Banner of Peace*. Church papers in Pennsylvania. *Cumberland Presbyterian Pulpit. The Ark. The Texas Presbyterian. Texas Cumberland Presbyterian. Texas Observer. The Watchman and Evangelist.* Papers in Missouri and Illinois. *The Ladies' Pearl. The Pacific Observer. The Theological Medium.* Revision of the Confession of Faith, 1853-1883. Faults of our first Confession. Action in 1852. Committee on Revision, 1853. Its report discussed and rejected, 1854. Unsuccessful efforts to revise the Form of Government, 1867-'74. History of the new Confession of Faith. Improvements and defects. John L. Dillard's testimony. Temperance. Action of Elk Presbytery, 1816. Position of church papers. Le Roy Woods in the Indiana legislature, 1855. Temperance deliverances by the General Assembly. David Lowry's testimony. Anecdote of J. M. Berry, ... 585-617

CHAPTER XLVIII.

NEW FIELDS—EVANGELISTS—PROGRESS—REFLECTIONS.

Inadequate Home Mission funds. Organization of Rocky Mountain Presbytery. Colorado. Colorado Springs. Pueblo. Visit of J. Cal Littrell to New Mexico. Nebraska. Indian difficulties. Overland Express Companies. R. S. Reed's account of the work in Nebraska City and elsewhere. Another account. Formation of Nebraska Presbytery Nebraska statistics. Washington Territory. H. W. Eagan at Walla Walla. A. W. Sweeny's record of the work. Statistics. Evangelists. R. G. Pearson and Dixon C. Williams. Anecdote of R. J. Sims. Our first evangelist. Lay evangelists. Evangelistic work among the Choctaws. A. P. Stewart. An old preacher's estimate of Dixon C. Williams. Our denominational progress. Increase in numbers. Lack of candidates for the ministry. "Heresy of the pocket." Regular pastors. Theological school. Comparison with Presbyterians. John L. Dillard's view. Decline in spirituality. General reflections. The author's unrecorded impressions. Cumberland Presbyterian doctrine in the Presbyterian church. The mission of our church. Our debt to the Presbyterian church, ... 618–634

CHAPTER XLIX.

ANECDOTES.

Sources from which these anecdotes are derived. Anecdote of Mrs. Samuel King. A timely arrival. A quarrel settled by a song. Conquered by kindness. Through head and heart. Tardiness cured. "The root of the matter." Anecdote of R. D. Morrow. Ruling passion strong in death. Comfort through faithfulness. Anecdote of F. M. Fincher. A Missouri camp-meeting. A barn meeting. A trial and a triumph. Another dancing incident. A war incident. A case of fasting and prayer. A gainsayer converted. A band of rowdies conquered. The key-stone of the arch. A Presbyterian elder convinced. A Christmas party. Two cases contrasted. A defeat changed to victory. A mother's prayers. A Jew converted. L. C. Ransom's discipline. Presentiment of death, 635–652

LIST OF ENGRAVINGS.

                     PAGE.

PORTRAIT OF B. W. MCDONNOLD, D.D., ... *Frontispiece.*

MAP, ... *Facing* 1

PORTRAIT OF REV. FINIS EWING, ... " 48

PORTRAITS OF REV. THOMAS CALHOUN, REV. ROBERT DONNELL, AND REV. R. D. MORROW, D.D., ... " 96

PORTRAITS OF REV. F. R. COSSITT, D.D., REV. A. M. BRYAN, D.D., AND REV. MILTON BIRD, D.D., . . . " 241

PORTRAITS OF REV. R. O. WATKINS, REV. REUBEN BURROW, D.D., AND REV. J. B. LOGAN, D.D., . . . " 368

PORTRAITS OF REV. RICHARD BEARD, D.D., REV. A. J. BAIRD, D.D., AND REV. S. G. BURNEY, D.D., . . . " 464

PORTRAIT OF REV. JOHN MORGAN IN SILHOUETTE . . . " 529

(xxxii)

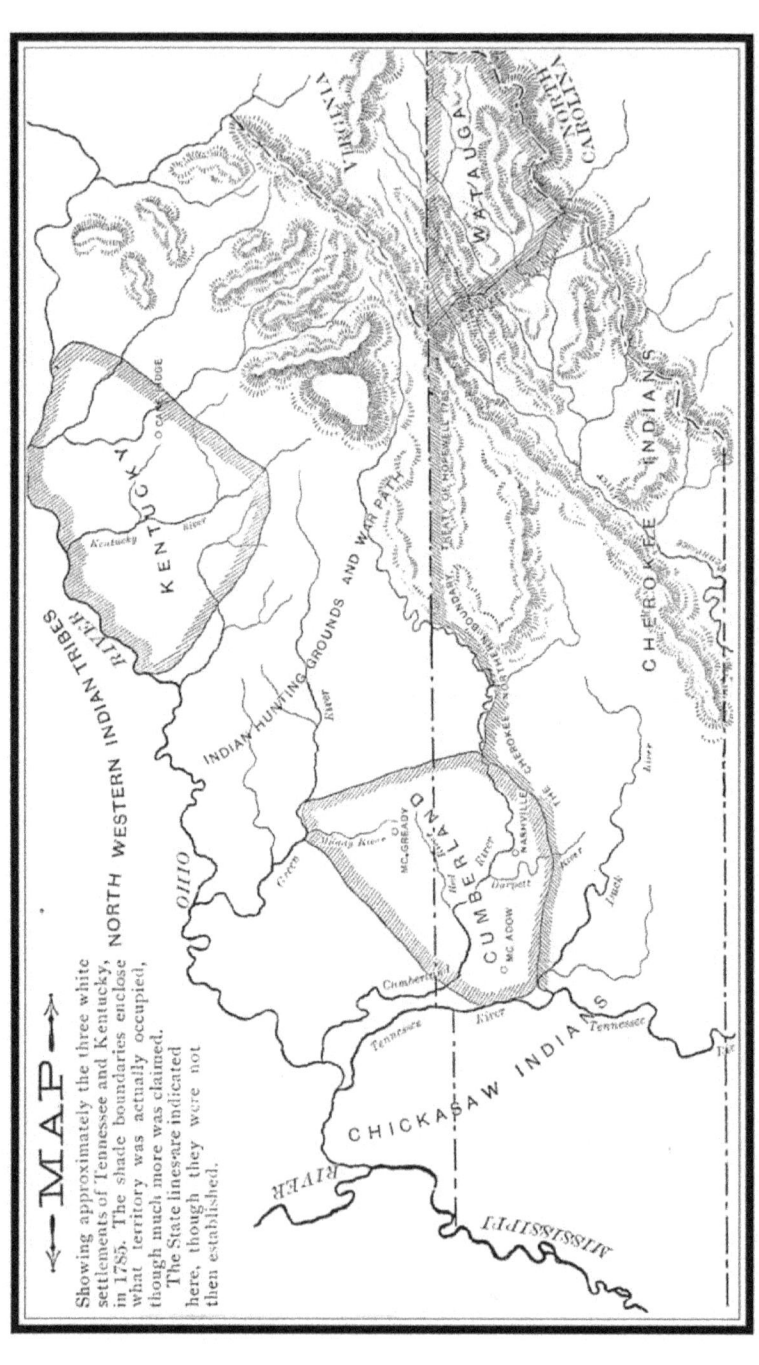

FIRST PERIOD.

CHAPTER I.

STATE OF THE COUNTRY.

*In the woodlands rang their axes,
Smoked their towns in all the valleys.*
—*Hiawatha.*

THE country called Cumberland on the accompanying map lay partly in Tennessee and partly in Kentucky. Its southern boundary was the dividing ridge between Cumberland and Duck rivers, in Tennessee; its northern boundary was the Green River, in Kentucky. When the Presbyterian church divided one of its large presbyteries, assigning one portion thereof to Cumberland, it gave the name of the country to the new presbytery. When this presbytery was engaged in exciting controversies with Kentucky Synod about the revival of 1800, the people called the revival party "Cumberland Presbyterians." When a new church grew out of the revival party, the name which the people had already given was neither repudiated nor formally adopted, but it clung to the new organization. The map belongs to a period a little earlier than the great revival of 1800. The shade lines include the white settlements, while all the rest of Tennessee and Kentucky was claimed by Indians.

There was constant warfare with these savages. No treaty could bind them. To this day, Indians claim that a treaty with their chiefs does not bind any one except the individuals who sign the treaty. Lands bought from them were still claimed by those who did not sign the deed—claimed and fought for, too. Hence, all these white settlers were soldiers. Men carried guns with them to church. When two men met and stopped to talk, they stood back to back, to watch both directions for the lurking Indian.

Men still wore hunting-shirts and moccasins. They still wore a belt in which were carried a large knife and a hatchet.

Their skill with the rifle was unsurpassed, but they reserved their display of it for living heads. At a later day, when powder and ball were not so precious, it is said they would throw up two apples and put a hole through both of them, with one bullet, when they crossed each other's path in the air.

There were men and women, too, in all the settlements, who had been scalped by the Indians and left for dead, but had afterward got well, and lived to pay back the debt of blood.

Two such, who afterward were actors in the great revival, were described to me by an aged, member of their family long ago. Their father was named Daviess, uncle of the Joe Daviess for whom Daviess County (Kentucky) was named. He had built his house a little distance from the fort which then stood at Gilmore's Lick, in Kentucky. The Indians surprised him at night, and took his two little children, son and daughter, prisoners. He escaped in his night-clothes, and with his utmost speed ran to the fort.

Colonel Donnelson, of Cumberland, was then visiting the fort. When he saw Daviess coming in his night clothing, he knew too well what that meant. He sprang instantly to his rifle, calling on the men in the fort to join him. Before Daviess had time to tell the whole story, they were all in hot pursuit, Daviess still in his *robe de nuit*. Donnelson knew that if the Indians discovered their pursuers they would instantly kill the prisoners, so he and his comrades tried to slip up on them. The barking of a dog gave the savages warning, and instantly they killed, as they supposed, and scalped the two children. The baby girl was taken by the heels and dashed against a sapling, her scalp was torn off, and the Indians fled. Colonel Donnelson took off his own shirt, and bound up the wounds of these children; and, though they suffered long, they ultimately recovered. There were, at that day, many such people among the sons of Cumberland and Kentucky.

All the women knew how to shoot, and not only knew how, but most of them had put their knowledge to practical use in self-defense. The memoir of Mrs. Margaret Hess, one of the early Cumberland Presbyterians, who lived to great age, tells how her mother and other ladies used their rifles in three different bloody struggles against the Indians. Wounded women were no uncommon thing in these settlements.

All the first generation of our preachers had been in the Indian wars. People who had been prisoners among the Indians, and afterward either escaped or were ransomed, entered into the general mass of material out of which the Cumberland Presbyterian church grew. Colonel Joe Brown, who was a Cumberland Presbyterian preacher, had for a whole year been a prisoner in the hands of the Indians. Nor was the schooling of these pioneers confined to fighting Indians. Privations and hardships helped to sharpen their wits. The first generation of children were brought up without "store goods." There were no shoes. All the people, men and women, wore moccasins made of untanned hides. Dresses were made of thread spun from buffalo wool for the filling, and the lint of the wild nettle for the chain.[1] There were no steamboats, or railroads, or steam factories, then, in the world. As to these settlements on the border, there were no stores, no mails, no good wagon roads, only blazed pathways. All the books or other luxuries they owned had been carried on pack-horses over the mountains, through the wilderness. Salt was worth sixteen dollars per bushel. Iron was equally dear. The country was nearly without trade or money. There was no South then, to buy mules and hogs. That South belonged, in part, to the Indians, and, in part, to the Spanish. There were no white settlements in what is now West Tennessee. The buffalo grazed quietly where Memphis now stands.

The only possibility for any trade at all was either by pack-horses to Philadelphia, or by flatboats to New Orleans. The latter avenue was not always open, whimsical Spaniards closing it sometimes, and always, when it was open, charging an enormous toll on every flatboat. These flatboats could not be brought back. The traders sold them for fuel, and walked back *through the Indian country*. Forty years ago these old boatmen abounded both in Tennessee and Kentucky, and the stories of their adventures held

---

[1] Life of Mrs. Hess.

many a group of children listening around the happy hearth-stones in these then peaceful and prosperous homes.

One incident, given in a manuscript history of the Presbyterian church in East Tennessee,[1] illustrates the mail facilities. Union Presbytery was about issuing a circular letter to its churches, when it received, for the first time, a copy of a circular letter issued by the General Assembly on the same subject more than two years before.

---

[1] This MS. was written by R. B. McMullen, D.D., and was loaned me by J. H. Bryson, D.D., of Huntsville, Ala. It is a very valuable MS. What a pity we have not a history of the Presbyterian church in the rest of the State!

CHAPTER II.

LITERATURE AND RELIGION.

"By heaven, and not a master, taught."—*Pope.*

"His passage lies across the brink
Of many a threatening wave,
And hell expects to see him sink,
But Jesus lives to save."

THERE have been highly educated men who could not read. In times and countries where education in the schools was impossible, strong native intellects learned from men, from events, from nature. Daniel Boone wrote, "Cilled a bar," and perhaps never in his life knew any better orthography; but if a profound knowledge of military strategy, if lightning-like grasp of resources for military emergencies, if a far-seeing anticipation of the enemy's movements, whether that enemy were Indian, French, or English, if an intellect that never made a mistake in any of the myriad military emergencies in which it was called to act, entitle a man to rank high among thinkers, then very few of the sons of West Point have ever been his equals.

This education without books, so common among a people who had no possible chance of schooling in the regular way, is never found at all in a country where schools are accessible to everybody. The thriftless laziness which will not avail itself of all the resources in reach, neither in old countries nor new ones, ever rises to the rank of a thinker. All the first settlements in Kentucky and Tennessee were for a while without schools. Circumstances made schools impossible. There were very few books. Among the treasures packed on horseback through the wilderness was the family Bible. It made the reading book. There were no novels. A few families had a tear-blotted copy of the Sacred League and Covenant, handed down for generations.

The first school in Cumberland was opened in Craighead's church, six miles from Nashville. It was called Spring Hill Academy, and was taught by a Presbyterian minister.[1] Among its early pupils were Finis Ewing, Samuel King, Samuel McSpeddin, and Robert Bell, all of them Cumberland Presbyterian ministers at a later day.

There is, it is said, a stone situated in the three States of Virginia, North Carolina, and Tennessee. A man seated on that stone on Sabbath morning, June, 1773, might have seen below him in the valley the first meeting-house ever erected on the soil of Tennessee.[2] That church was erected by that hardy and glorious race, the Scotch-Irish Presbyterians. The church was of logs, 40 by 80 feet. It was covered with clapboards. These Scotch-Irish settlers had profound respect for the Sabbath. Peep into their cabins. Every child is in its seat, reciting the catechism. This is that race of whom the Irishman said, that when the potato crop failed "they lived on the Shorter Catechism and the Sabbath." Peep into their cabins later in the morning. The male members, and in some cases the female members also, are taking down their rifles, preparatory to starting to church.

One hundred and thirty-eight heads of families had united in calling the Rev. Charles Cummings to come and settle among them as their pastor.[3] He ministered to these same people thirty-nine years. This man Cummings was the first man who ever preached in what is now Tennessee. His first years in this wild frontier were tracked with the blood of Indian battles. He fought often, and had many narrow escapes.

Farther north, in Kentucky, the first preacher was also a Presbyterian. The father of "Tippecanoe Joe Daviess" went back to his old home in Virginia after a preacher, and brought back with him the Rev. David Rice. He gave Mr. Rice the hire of a negro woman for two years, and helped build him a cabin.[4] But it appears from Dr. Davidson's history that Rice received very poor compensation for his services in after years.

---

[1] This minister was the Rev. Dr. Brooks. For reasons unknown to the writer his name never appeared on the roll of the Kentucky Synod, in whose bounds he lived.

[2] MS. History of Presbyterian church in East Tennessee, by Dr. McMullen.

[3] Dr. McMullen's MS., p. 6.

[4] Memoir of Mrs. Hess.

The Rev. Thomas B. Craighead was the first pastor who settled in Cumberland; though his first steps were not cold before the Rev. Benjamin Ogden, of the Methodist church, was proclaiming free salvation on the banks of the Cumberland River.

In this sketch of preachers and congregations my inquiries run in Presbyterian channels, since our church was of Presbyterian parentage. It would be *obiter dictum*, if I discussed other churches.

Orthodoxy, the catechism, a deathless attachment to principles and to ecclesiastical rights, a holy horror of any innovations on the traditional methods of work, singing Rouse's Psalms, and hearing sermons three hours long on election, made up the religion of many among the best citizens.

There seems to have been no great amount of dishonesty. The Nashville jail was a log cabin, fourteen feet square. But after the revolution, mainly through the influence of the French soldiers who had aided us in that struggle, infidelity swept over all this western frontier, and threatened for a while to carry all the population. All the historians are agreed in their testimony to this vast prevalence of infidelity. Some say nine tenths of the people were infidels. The general lack of regular preaching, and the bad character of many who did preach, helped to sweep faith away from the country. According to the testimony of the Rev. David Rice, the first Presbyterian minister who settled in Kentucky,[1] and of the Rev. Dr. Davidson, the historian of the Presbyterian church in that State, most of the ministers of that church, in Rice's day, were bad men. Drunkenness, wrangling, licentiousness, and heresy brought the most of them to grief sooner or later.[2]

The lives of unconverted preachers, elders, and members make a woful chapter in the history of this period. Of the church members in this country who, after being in the church for years, finally discovered their ruined condition, and made a profession of religion, there are several names whose prominence in our history justifies their introduction here. They are Richard King, Elder Hutchinson, Robert Guthrie, Samuel McSpeddin, Finis Ewing, together with their wives, and very many others.

The case of Richard King is interesting. He had been edu-

---

[1] Memoir of Mrs. Hess. [2] Davidson's Hist., pp. 103, 129, 130.

cated for the ministry. His father, Robert King, was an elder in the Presbyterian church, and one of those who opposed the revival. His brother, Samuel King, was he who made one of the three to organize our first presbytery. Although "Rich" had been educated for the ministry, he would not preach; but poor Sam, who had no education, when he felt that he was called of God to preach the gospel, would pray, "O Lord, send Rich!"

Men picked out and educated for the ministry, and thrust into the holy office without any conscious internal call to the work, made one of the troubles between Old Side and New Side in 1741. Dr. Charles Hodge's defense of Old Side views on this subject is a chapter which his reputation could easily spare from his writings.

The Rev. Samuel McSpeddin's testimony about the kind of preaching in the Presbyterian pulpits of that day is given at length in Dr. Cossitt's Life of Ewing. The substance of it is that they never said any thing to rouse the conscience; that they never discussed the new birth, or any conscious experience in grace; that people who by any means became uneasy about their religious state, and went to their pastors for help, were told that if they had been baptized, and believed that Jesus Christ was the Son of God, they need not trouble themselves about any conscious experience.

McSpeddin and Ewing both are specially severe on Craighead's preaching. Nor are these strictures by Cumberland Presbyterians any more severe than some occasionally found in Davidson's history of his own church. One of Craighead's sayings, handed down by tradition, was, "I would not give this old handkerchief for all the experimental religion in the world."

A curious statement is made by the Rev. James McGready, who was a Presbyterian minister in what is now Logan County, Kentucky, about one of the preachers of his own presbytery. It is that this preacher (the Rev. James Balch) in his sermons ridiculed the doctrines of faith, of repentance, and of regeneration. And although this preacher was finally brought to trial[1] for his heresies, it was not till he spent years traveling among the churches

---

[1] He had been tried and suspended before he came to Kentucky, and was restored to the ministry by a different presbytery without the consent of his own presbytery. He was a disturber of the peace wherever he went.—Dr. McMullen's MS.

of Cumberland, where the great revival prevailed, and doing his utmost to oppose the revival and check its progress. Nor were his efforts without success in some places.

The Rev. James McGready had entered the ministry without any religion. God led him to see his ruined condition, and he sought and found conscious salvation. He was then in Pennsylvania, but soon went to North Carolina. His preaching there was as much changed as he was himself. It aroused the conscience; it awakened unconverted church members; it was used of God to promote precious revivals of religion. These revivals in North Carolina were bitterly opposed by church members, and McGready was fiercely persecuted, even to the extent of endangering his life. There was also there, as there was at a later day in Cumberland, a strong revival party which sympathized with him, and worked heartily in his meetings.

A large number of McGready's North Carolina neighbors moved to Cumberland. Through their solicitations, in 1796, he changed his field of labor, and took charge of these scattered sheep in the wilderness. There were three small congregations to which he ministered, whose only preaching before his arrival had been from such men as Craighead and Balch. These churches were called Red River, Gasper River, and Muddy River, located in what is now Logan County, Kentucky. It was a strange contrast, these dead preachers and McGready. The result of his introduction into this mass of dead formalism belongs to the next chapter. His churches were located in the country then called Cumberland, but called at a later day the Cumberland and Green River Settlements. "Cumberland" was partly in Kentucky, but when this history opens the dividing line between the two States had not been run. Tennessee's first capital was east of the mountains.

CHAPTER III.

THE GREAT REVIVAL.[1]

Why should we crave a hallowed spot?
An altar is in each man's cot.
—Wordsworth.

WHAT share other churches had in the beginning and progress of that work of grace known as the revival of 1800, is not here discussed. Our origin was in the revival *in the Presbyterian church.* That revival had some very striking antecedents. It began in 1797. The year preceding its beginning was marked beyond all others for official calls to fasting and prayer by presbyteries, synods, and General Assembly—fasting and prayer for the outpouring of the Holy Spirit. Ohio Presbytery held a monthly fast-day all through the year 1796, to pray for a revival. The Synod of the Carolinas had appointed a synodical fast-day, in which all its congregations were to pray for the outpouring of the Holy Spirit. A large number of the congregations in western Pennsylvania had drawn up written covenants to pray for a revival. Accounts of these covenants and their precious fruits were afterward published in the *Western Missionary Magazine.* It is an item of interest to Cumberland Presbyterians that the very congregations which afterward called for our preaching were among those who joined in these solemn covenants to pray for a revival. The General Assembly also appointed a fast-day to be observed in all its churches—repentance, humiliation, and prayer for the outpouring of the Holy Spirit being specially mentioned. McGready drew up a very solemn covenant for his congregations. Every Saturday evening, every Sunday morning, and one whole Sabbath of each month, for a year, were to be observed as a season of special prayer

---

[1] McGready, Hodge, Ewing, Calhoun, Smith, Speer, Foote, and others, are my authorities for this chapter.

for the outpouring of the Holy Spirit in Logan County, Kentucky, and throughout the world. To this covenant he obtained the signatures of his church members.

It was not to sensational evangelists, but to God's Holy Spirit that our spiritual ancestors in the Presbyterian church looked for deliverance from the triumphant infidelity of the times. Nor did they look in vain. In Gasper River congregation, at McGready's regular sacramental meeting, in May, 1797, the grand work began. All through the preceding year McGready's church members had been coming to him about their spiritual condition. His preaching had opened their eyes to the fact that they were resting on a false hope. Finally, one of these — a lady — found the sure Rock, and was so filled with God's Spirit that she could no longer sit silent at home while so many of her friends were in the prison from which she had just escaped. She immediately visited her neighbors from house to house, and awakened among them a deep interest about their souls.

The next year a more general awakening occurred. After a solemn sacramental service in July, the profound claims of immortality followed the people to their homes. Secular business was forgotten, and men under deep conviction spent the days alone in the woods, weeping and praying. Groups that met in the houses talked of eternity, and wept together over their ruined condition. Thus for weeks, while there was no public preaching, God's Spirit was at work in the private houses. Godless church members talked together about the startling discoveries which they had made of their unconverted state.

In September, 1798, McGready held his sacramental meeting at Muddy River. God's power was there also. All over the field to which McGready ministered the home work became general. Surpassing any thing of the sort in all history was this revival without preaching, without public meetings, without any high pressure methods. The houses and the deep forests of Logan County rang with the prayers of souls in distress. While so many awakened souls were in solemn prayer, it is remarkable that deliverance was to most of them delayed. One who lived among them at that time has left his testimony, that in going from house to house all through

McGready's congregations he heard only one theme talked of. If he came upon a group of old people, they were weeping and talking about their souls. If he encountered the young people, either singly or in groups, they were in tears, and spoke only about their souls' salvation.

The next year (1799) the interest was still deeper, especially in Gasper congregation, but this year more of the burdened souls found salvation. The sacramental meeting was a time of victory to some. At this meeting began what was considered so strange then, though it had often occurred in the revivals of former generations. Men under overwhelming convictions fell to the floor, and though they were entirely conscious, as they afterward testified, yet they remained prostrate and motionless for hours. When they rose, it was with the shouts of victory on their tongues. This strange exercise drew vast crowds to McGready's meetings. A family who had recently moved to Kentucky from North Carolina heard of these strange things, and heard, also, that a sacramental meeting was soon to occur. Not having friends near the place of meeting, they resolved to go in their wagons and camp beside them, as they had done in their journey from North Carolina. This they did. At the next sacramental meeting their example was followed by several families, and most of the converts of that meeting were the campers. This meeting was at Red River, in Kentucky.

It is rather strange that mere *conjectural* accounts of the origin of camp-meetings should be extensively published, when we have the most reliable accounts from eye-witnesses. One of these accounts was written at the time by Captain Wallace Estill, who then lived in Kentucky, and was present at all these meetings. While he gives the date of the meeting at Gasper, soon to be described, he does not give the date of this Red River meeting, though he speaks of it. There is some conflict of authorities about the date of this meeting. The Rev. John McGee, of the Methodist church, who was present, places it in 1799, and there is traditional confirmation of this date. Smith, Estill, and others place it in 1800, with circumstantial confirmation.[1]

---

[1] John McGee's statements were written from memory, twenty years after the events, and contain internal proofs of inaccuracy in other matters.

This by some people, John McGee among them, is called the first camp-meeting in Christendom. It was at least the forerunner of the first camp-meeting, for the good results which McGready saw follow this *spontaneous* camp-meeting caused him to publish far and near that his sacramental meeting at Gasper, in July, 1800, would be a camp-meeting. The public responded fully, and campers with their wagons encircled all the place when the meeting began. This meeting at Gasper was the first meeting in Christendom that was *appointed* and *intended* for a camp-meeting. Estill calls this the first camp-meeting in Christendom. The grand revival flame kindled Saturday, while some pious women were talking about religion. It soon spread through all the gathered hosts. Among those attending this meeting at Gasper were several members of Shiloh church, Sumner County, Tennessee. The Rev. William Hodge, their pastor, who was a fast friend of the revival, was also present. At this meeting five of the regular members of Shiloh congregation became convinced that they were in an unconverted state, and, after a bitter struggle, made a profession of religion.

The elder brother of the Rev. Samuel King was one of these five members. The story of his conversion as told by the widow of the Rev. J. M. McMurray, Mrs. Elizabeth McMurray, of Lebanon, Tennessee, whose family were akin to the Kings, is here given. The father of this Richard King (Robert King) was an elder in the Shiloh congregation, and a Presbyterian after the straightest pattern. Before this Gasper River meeting, some members of the Shiloh church, while visiting one of McGready's sacramental meetings, had been converted, and had returned home shouting the praises of God. Robert King said it was all "fox-fire." "I'll send Rich; they can't fool Rich." It will be remembered that "Rich" was not only a member of the church, but had been educated for the ministry. It was to this grand meeting at Gasper, in 1800, that Rich was sent. It was there that he discovered the necessity of a change to which he had hitherto been a stranger. It was there, too, that his soul was set at liberty.

When he and the other Shiloh people returned from Gasper and met their friends, they rushed into their arms, shouting and telling what wonderful things God had done for their souls. Fire in dry stubble were these returned converts among their neighbors. The private houses rang with the cries of poor sinners who were now awakened to their ruined condition. Nor were their soul struggles protracted to the extent that others had been the previous year in McGready's field. Shouts of new converts were soon heard in these pioneer cabins. A nephew of Richard King, a little boy, was among those who were stricken down under deep conviction when all these rejoicing converts returned from the Gasper meeting. His friends sent for his grandfather, Robert King. Here was a situation for the old elder. His neighbors carried away with "fox-fire;" "Rich," whom he had relied on to ferret out the delusion, now carried away with it like the rest; and worse still, he himself sent for to play revivalist, and instruct a prostrate victim of the delusion. He, the anti-revivalist, Robert King! He took his lancet and his camphor, and went to the boy's relief, but a better Physician had preceded him. On his arrival he found the boy shouting the praises of God.

There were twenty conversions in the Shiloh neighborhood after the return of "Rich" King before there was a single sermon preached. Then they had a camp-meeting, and there were one hundred conversions: this, too, in that sparsely settled region.

The first camp-meetings were without tents or other shelter except the wagons. Later, people built double log-cabins, which were still called tents, for their families and visitors. So far as possible people cooked the provisions before they left home, and they moved to camps expecting to remain during the meeting. All who attended the camp-meeting were fed freely. Campers would go out into the crowd and make a public invitation for all to come and eat. The camps were supplied with straw, both on the ground and on the bed scaffolds. One tent was used by the ladies, and another by the gentlemen. A field of grain with a stream of water in it was secured, and the horses of the visitors were turned into it. A vast shelter covered with boards was built and seated for a preaching place. This, too, had an ample supply of clean straw for a floor. In the intervals between public services it was their universal custom to go alone, or in small groups, to secret prayer in the adjacent forest. The north and south line divided the grounds for retirement and prayer, and gentlemen were not allowed to go upon the ladies' grounds.

In all the early days, before railroads came along, these meetings were not only as orderly as any other kind of meetings, but they were generally seasons of unparalleled solemnity and unequaled moral grandeur. A Scotch traveler, who has seen most of the countries of the world, has left his written testimony that he had nowhere seen any thing to equal the moral grandeur of the great camp-meeting. No correct idea of these early camp-meetings can be formed from the so-called camp-meetings of modern times. They belong to a different economy. I have seen both, and I recognize in the modern one scarcely one single feature of those early gatherings of a pioneer people to worship God.

Although Craighead opposed the revival, his elders did not; and they determined to have a camp-meeting, and have some of the revival preachers attend it. They did so, and a precious meeting it proved to be; but the pastor gave it the cold shoulder.[1] This meeting was at the church near Nashville, in which Dr. Brooks, mentioned heretofore, was teaching a school.

Camp-meetings now became the order of the day. The Methodists especially took them up, and had grand victories in many of their meetings. Tennessee and Kentucky were transformed.

The dear old Beech church, in Sumner County, Tennessee, had that staunch friend of the revival, the Rev. William McGee, for its pastor. Its camp-meetings furnished surpassing displays of the Holy Spirit's power.

God's Spirit used the distant visitors to these camp-meetings to spread the revival, not only throughout Tennessee and Kentucky, but many other States. Foote's History of North Carolina[2] and his History of Virginia give us thrilling accounts of revivals started in these two States by people just returned from McGready's meetings.

Dr. Speer[3] tells us of revivals similarly started in western Pennsylvania. The Rev. James Gallagher, of the Presbyterian church, gives a most impressive account of its spread into East Tennessee.

---

[1] Several of his hard sayings on that occasion are preserved in the Kirkpatrick MSS., and in others.

[2] Foote's North Carolina, pp. 64–73.   [3] Speer, Rev., 1800, pp. 24, 43, 48, 84.

He says its awful solemnity made people think the day of judgment was at hand.[1]

An old claim, thoroughly refuted when first published,[2] has been recently revived. It is that the revival *in McGready's churches* was due to the preaching of John McGee, a Methodist. The sole foundation for this claim is that John McGee visited McGready's churches in 1799, and preached in them. McGee himself says his *first* visit to McGready's churches was in 1799.[3]

But the revival in McGready's churches began in 1797, before McGee moved away from North Carolina, and, at the meeting which McGee first visited, it was in full power before he ever took any part.

No one denies that both Methodists and Baptists had grand revivals about this period; but the claim that the particular revival out of which our church sprang originated with the Methodists has not the shadow of a foundation. The evidence on which the history usually given by our church rests is all that could be desired. The testimony of the pastor and various other actors in these events, all published right at the time, and in the midst of the people where these events occurred, remained unchallenged for twenty years. To this must be added the testimony of the several church judicatures in which these events became the theme of angry discussions. Official records of presbytery, synod, and Assembly speak of the revival which originated under McGready's preaching. Several official circulars[4] sent out by the actors in these events give the same history.

When the Rev. James Smith published his history, our General Assembly appointed a committee of eleven persons, most of whom had been eye-witnesses of these great events, to examine into its accuracy. Their report indorses the accuracy of this portion of the history in every particular.[5]

---

[1] Western Sketch Book. [2] Revivalist, Feb. 13, 1833.
[3] There is good reason to believe that he was wrong in the date. He describes events which seem to belong to the next year. He wrote from memory long after the events.
[4] See appendix to Life and Times of Ewing, Dr. Frizzell's semi-centennial pamphlet, and *Revivalist*, 1832, for these circulars.
[5] Assembly Minutes, Vol. I., p. 117, *et seq.*

Besides all this, John McGee set up no such claim. He knew better. Even his letter to Douglass, out of which men tried, after he was dead, to establish such a claim, itself disproves this claim. There were precious revivals among Presbyterians before the Methodist church was born.

There is in my possession a manuscript autobiography of the Rev. Robert Bell. He was present at all McGready's sacramental meetings from 1797 to 1800. Among the things which occupy a prominent place in this autobiography is the trouble he had over the doctrine of reprobation. He was under deep conviction in 1799 and 1800, but feared he was not one of the elect. The doctrine of a general atonement had never been preached in his hearing prior to his conversion, September, 1800. So far is it from being true that the doctrines preached in McGready's churches before the revival were Methodist doctrines, that many of McGready's people who regularly attended all his services, had never heard a general atonement preached in their lives. Robert Bell read and indorsed the Rev. James Smith's history of the great revival. We have a brief account of this great revival written by the Rev. Samuel McSpeddin.[1] He was an eye-witness. He says the revival began in Kentucky under McGready's preaching in 1797; that it extended in 1800 to Tennessee, and was heartily welcomed by the Methodists, who afterward became the chief agents for spreading it over all of Tennessee. He says the first Methodist preachers to aid in this revival work were John McGee, James Gwinn, and Bishop Asbury. Afterward McKendree came to this field, and, of course, entered heartily into the revival.

McSpeddin calls attention to the fact that there was a Cane Ridge church in Tennessee, which had been confounded with the Cane Ridge in Bourbon County, Kentucky, where the New Lights originated; and this fact, perhaps, helped to create that long-lived error which represents "New Lights" and "Cumberlands" as the same. McSpeddin points out several other minor errors in the published histories. He says, as do all the historians, that McGready had revivals in North Carolina before he came to Kentucky; that

---

[1] See McSpeddin's papers, filed in Cumberland University Library; also *Banner of Peace*, September 8, and October 26, 1853.

soon after his arrival in Kentucky (1796), revivals began under his preaching there. He also says: "McGready was the great instrument, under God, of the commencement of the great revival, called the revival of 1800."

McSpeddin says that Shiloh and DeSha's, so often mentioned in our early history as churches in Sumner County, Tennessee, were one and the same, and that Dry Fork church, in the same county, was composed of the revival party of both Hopewell and Shiloh. [See *Banner of Peace*, No. 15, Vol. xii.]

There was a controversy between "Uncle" Joe Brown and McSpeddin about the dates in McSpeddin's history, but the accuracy of these dates was thoroughly and triumphantly established by McSpeddin and acknowledged by Brown. His dates make it almost certain that John McGee's first visit to McGready's meetings was in 1800. One feature, however, of McGready's meetings at a later day was clearly due to McGee, who ran through the church shouting and telling the people to shout, until he succeeded in producing quite a tumult. The Presbyterians generally condemned shouting, and this feature of McGready's meetings, after McGee's visits, was one of the grounds of their bitter complaints. So it is probable that the "shouting," once so common, now so rare, among Cumberland Presbyterians was of Methodist parentage.

It is amusing to read the Rev. Dr. Fergus Ferguson's account of the shouting by one of our good sisters at our General Assembly in 1874, when he and Dr. Morrison were on their visit to America.[1] It really seems, from his account, that he had never heard any such thing before, and did not know what it was. I wonder if the Methodists of Scotland never shout.

It was, perhaps, through the brothers, John and William McGee—one a Methodist and the other a Presbyterian—that what was called "the union" was accomplished. Before that "union" it was not at all customary for different denominations to commune together at the Lord's table or work together in meetings—least of all for Methodists and Presbyterians to commune together.

---

[1] From Glasgow to Springfield, by Fergus Ferguson, D.D.

The history of "tokens"[1] is a strange one. Dr. Blackburn, liberal and progressive as he was, refused to admit Joe Brown to the communion table because Brown had communed with the Cumberland Presbyterians. It was this which drove Brown out of the Presbyterian church. "Fencing the table" was a more rigid thing than any of our Baptist brethren now practice in their "close communion."

"The union" formed in the time of the McGees was nothing more than a written contract to commune together and hold meetings together—union meetings.

---

[1] An explanation of what "tokens" were and what "fencing the table" was will be found in another chapter.

CHAPTER IV.

THE REVIVAL A GENUINE WORK OF GOD'S SPIRIT.

"He shall baptize you with the Holy Ghost and with fire."

NOT all so-called revivals are genuine. Was this one a genuine work of God? The testimonies here introduced are from that class of witnesses entitled to the greatest respect. They are conclusive, if human testimony can be conclusive in such a matter.

The Rev. David Rice, who visited McGready's churches during the revival, preached a sermon before his synod in reference to this wonderful work. This sermon was preached in 1803.[1] He says:

This revival has made its appearance in various places without any extraordinary means to produce it. . . . .

The revival appears to be granted in answer to prayer, and in confirmation of that gracious truth that God has "not said to the house of Jacob, Seek ye me in vain," when he says he will be inquired of by the house of Israel to do it for them.

As far as I can see, there appears to be in the subjects of this work a deep, heart humbling sense of the great unreasonableness, abominable nature, pernicious effects, and deadly consequences of sin; and the absolute unworthiness in the sinful creature of the smallest crumb of mercy from the hand of a holy God. . . . . Jesus Christ, and him crucified, appears to be the ALL IN ALL to the subjects of this revival and the creature nothing, and less than nothing.

They seem to have a very deep and affecting sense of the worth of precious immortal souls, ardent love to them, and an agonizing concern for their conviction, conversion, and complete salvation. . . . . Neighborhoods, noted for their vicious and profligate manners, are now as much noted for their piety and good order.

Drunkards, profane swearers, liars, quarrelsome persons, etc., are remarkably reformed. . . . . A number of families who had lived apparently without the fear of God, in folly and in vice, without any

---

[1] Quoted from Dr. Speer.

religious instruction or any proper government, are now reduced to order, and are daily joining in the worship of God, reading his word, singing his praises, and offering up their supplications to a Throne of Grace.

Parents who seemed formerly to have little or no regard for the souls of their children, are now anxiously concerned for their salvation, are pleading for them, and endeavoring to lead them to Christ and train them up in the way of piety and virtue. . . . .

The subjects of this work appear to be very sensible of the necessity of *sanctification* as well as justification, and that without holiness no man can see the Lord; to be greatly desirous that they and all that name the name of Christ should depart from iniquity. . . . .

Now, I have given you my reasons for concluding *the morning is come*, and that we are blessed with a real revival of the benign and heaven-born religion of Jesus Christ, which demands our grateful acknowledgements to God the Father, Son, and Holy Ghost.

Five years later, when the revival preachers had been placed under the interdict of a commission of synod, this same David Rice again testifies: "That we had *a revival of the spirit and power of Christianity*[1] among us, I did, do, and ever shall, believe . . . but we sadly mismanaged it; we have dashed it down and broken it to pieces."

How far the Presbyterian church suffered from its treatment of the revival preachers, he and others of his comrades had begun keenly to feel, and have left us clear testimony. Dr. Davidson tries to lay the blame for this injury to the Presbyterian church, in Kentucky and Tennessee, on the revival. Mr. Rice knew where to lay it. He says, "We have not acted as wise master-builders who have no need to be ashamed."[2]

From the beginning of this work, in 1797, for a series of years the General Assembly of the Presbyterian church gave its testimony to the precious fruits of this revival. In 1803, it adds to its former testimony many precious words about the revival in other parts of the field and then notices our field as follows:

In many southern and western presbyteries revivals more extensive and of a more extraordinary nature have taken place. It would be easy for the Assembly to select some very remarkable instances of the

---

[1] Italics his. [2] Bishop's Memoir of Rice, p. 367.

triumphs of divine grace which were exhibited before them in the course of the very interesting narratives presented in the free conversation—instances of the most malignant opposers of vital piety being convinced and reconciled; of some learned, active, and conspicuous infidels becoming signal monuments of that grace which they once despised; and various circumstances which display the holy efficacy of the gospel. . . . . In the course of the last year, there is reason to believe that several thousands within the bounds of the Presbyterian church have been brought to embrace the gospel of Christ. . . . . The Assembly consider it worthy of particular attention, that most of the accounts of revivals communicated to them stated that the institution of praying societies, or special seasons of special prayer to God for the outpouring of the Spirit, preceded the remarkable displays of divine grace with which our land has been blessed. In most cases, preparatory to signal effusions of the Holy Spirit, the pious have been stirred up to cry fervently and importunately that God would appear to vindicate his own cause. The Assembly see in this a confirmation of the word of God, and an ample encouragement of the prayers and hopes of the pious for future and more extensive manifestations of the divine power. And they trust that the churches under their care, while they see cause of abundant thankfulness for this dispensation, will also perceive that it presents new motives to zeal and fervor in application to that throne of grace from which *every good and perfect gift cometh*. The Assembly also observe with great pleasure that the desire for spreading the gospel among the blacks and among the savage tribes on our borders has been rapidly increasing during the last year. The Assembly take notice of this circumstance with the more satisfaction, as it not only affords a pleasing presage of the spread of the gospel, but also furnishes agreeable evidence of the genuineness and the benign tendency of that spirit, which God has been pleased to pour out upon his people. On the whole, the assembly can not but declare with joy and with most cordial congratulations to the churches under their care, that the state and prospects of vital religion in our country are more favorable and encouraging than at any period within the last forty years.

There was a long letter written by the Rev. George Baxter to Dr. A. Alexander, which I desire to introduce here. Dr. Baxter was for many years President of Washington College, in Virginia. At the time of his death he was Professor of Theology in the Union Theological Seminary, Virginia. He wrote from Kentucky, January 1, 1802. His statements, when published, were attacked by the anti-revival party. He defended them. Dr. Davidson says if he had lived long enough he would have corrected some of his statements. Well, it is not likely that he would have contradicted his testimony to facts. He says:

I will just observe that the last summer is the fourth since the revival commenced in those places, and that it has been more remarkable than any of the preceding, not only for lively and fervent devotion among Christians, but also for awakenings and conversions among the careless; and it is worthy of notice that very few instances of apostasy have hitherto appeared. As I was not myself in the Cumberland country, all I can say about it is from the testimony of others; but I was uniformly told by those who had been there, that their religious assemblies were more solemn and the appearance of the work much greater than what had been in Kentucky. Any enthusiastic symptoms which might at first have attended the revival had greatly subsided, while the serious concern and engagedness of the people were visibly increased.

Dr. Baxter then gives us many strong statements about the precious fruits of the revival in Kentucky, where he was then visiting. He says: "In October I attended three sacraments; at each there were supposed to be between four and five thousand people, and every thing was conducted with strict propriety." Dr. Baxter takes up the charge of enthusiasm made against the revival and denies it. He says:

Never have I seen more genuine marks of that humility which disclaims the merits of its own duties, and looks to the Lord Jesus Christ as the only way of acceptance with God. I was indeed highly pleased to find that Christ was all in all in their religion as well as in the religion of the gospel. Christians in their highest attainments seemed more sensible of their entire dependence upon divine grace, and it was truly affecting to hear with what agonizing anxiety awakened sinners inquired for Christ as the only physician who could give them any help. Those who call these things enthusiasm ought to tell us what they understand by the spirit of Christianity. In fact, sir, this revival operates as our Savior promised the Holy Spirit should when sent into the world—it convinces of sin, of righteousness, and of judgment, a strong confirmation, to my mind, both that the promise is divine and that this is a remarkable fulfillment of it.

Again he says in the same letter:

I think the revival in Kentucky among the most extraordinary that have ever visited the church of Christ, and, all things considered, peculiarly adapted to the circumstances of that country. Infidelity was triumphant and religion on the point of expiring. Something of an extraordinary nature seemed necessary to arrest the attention of giddy people, who were ready to conclude that Christianity was a fable and futurity a dream. The revival has done it. It has confounded infidelity and vice into silence, and brought numbers beyond calculation under serious impressions.

Dr. Baxter, in a letter quoted in Davidson, p. 186, tells of the wonderful reformation in morals and manners and the general religious solemnity which the revival produced over all Kentucky. He says, "I found Kentucky *the most moral place I had ever seen.*" And this was in that same frontier where he tells us that only four years before infidelity had been triumphant.

I am for the present excluding inside testimony. McGready and Hodge were actors in the revival, but the Rev. Gideon Blackburn ought to be accepted as good outside testimony. In 1804 he wrote a long letter to a friend in Philadelphia, in which he describes what he had seen of the revival, and defends it from the charges made against it. He says:

I am constrained to say that I have discovered far less extravagance, disorder, and irregularity than could be expected in so extraordinary an awakening, especially when part of it took place among persons settled in the back parts, and entirely destitute of the means of grace. If crowded audiences, earnest praying, practical preaching, and animated singing may be considered irregularity, if crying out for mercy, if shouting glory to God for salvation are disorderly, then there is some disorder, but I presume not more than there was on the day of Pentecost.[1]

The Rev. David Nelson's testimony is given in the Western Sketch Book. In speaking of the charge that the Kentucky revival ran into Shakerism, he says:

When God has been pleased graciously to visit a people with the quickening power of his Spirit, and many have been turned from sin to holiness, and from Satan to God, is it not marvelous that good men can be so deluded by the wiles of the great adversary as to become evidently eager to impute all the wrong things that may appear in that

---

[1] From the Western Sketch Book, published in East Tennessee by the Rev. James Gallagher, of the Presbyterian church.

community for ten or twenty years afterward to the influence of the revival? With as much propriety you might charge the apostasy of Judas to the ministry of Jesus Christ.

It is true that one of the preachers who co-operated with McGready afterward joined the Shakers. It is true, too, that one of the apostles who traveled along with Jesus afterward sold his Master. While one of the revival party did go at last to the Shakers, it is true, also, that the wealthiest and most influential acquisition which the Shakers of that day made in that community was an *anti-revival* Presbyterian. It is true, also, that no Cumberland Presbyterian joined them. But what does all that amount to? The Shakers neither originated there, nor prospered in that field to the extent they did in fields where the Presbyterian church had no revival. Nor did any men stand firmer against these heresies than the preachers who afterward composed the first presbytery of the Cumberland Presbyterian church. The Rev. James Gallagher says of these same heresies:

Certain it is that no men more regretted any departure from sound doctrines than did these good men whose labors were so abundantly blessed in that dispensation of the Holy Spirit by which the West, in its infancy, was consecrated to the service of God. Nor do I believe that now, after fifty years, there is in any part of the several evangelical denominations more of that religion which God approves than in the region visited by the revival of 1800.

He also speaks of the Cumberland Presbyterians thus:

This body of Christian people began their organized existence during that great divine visitation.[1] There are among them many strong men: workmen that need not be ashamed. And their blessed Master has been with them in every part of that wide field where they have labored, and has made his gospel the power of God unto salvation to many thousand believing souls. From my inmost soul I honor these men, and will speak of it in the presence of the church of my God. . . . I have no hesitation in declaring my belief that during the last forty years no body of ministers in America or in the world have preached so much good efficient preaching, and received such small compensation. That church now stands before heaven and earth a monument of God's great work in the revival of 1800.

---

[1] The revival of 1800.

Testimonies from Methodists about the revival could, of course, be produced; but these here quoted are all of them from that church in which the revival had such bitter opposition. It never had any opposition from the Methodists. Bishop Asbury and Bishop McKendree both visited the Presbyterian churches where it first prevailed, and both gave it their hearty indorsement.

The history of this revival, by Dr. Speer, is published and indorsed by the Presbyterian publishing board at Philadelphia, and on the cover the board say, among other things of like import, that their object in publishing the book is to "inspire the church to efforts for *another great revival* from on high." The whole book is one of unqualified indorsement of the revival: and except one paragraph, is, I believe, a correct history. That the revival of 1800 quickened into new life all the enterprises of the Christian churches is abundantly proved by this little book.

That revival in Tennessee and Kentucky, under God, rescued those two States, and, through them, the West and South, from French infidelity. Going out into a broader field, and studying the fruits of the revival in its whole broad extent over America and Europe, Dr. Speer shows that this work in the West was only a part of a grand forward movement of the kingdom of our Savior throughout the world.

Out of this grand movement sprang the Bible societies, the missionary boards, the tract societies, which have so wonderfully blessed the world. In a remarkable little book, by Dr. Rochester, on Christian progress, he gives us a diagram of progress. In missions, the line which shows that progress runs nearly parallel with the horizon till it reaches 1800, then it ascends at an angle of about sixty degrees.

For such a time as this are we come into the kingdom.

CHAPTER V.

A PENTECOSTAL BAPTISM.

"Have ye received the Holy Ghost since ye believed?"

> Awake, O spirit, that of old
> Did'st fire the watchmen of the church's youth,
> Who faced the foe, unshrinking, bold;
> Who witnessed, day and night, the eternal truth;
> Whose voices through the world are ringing still,
> And bringing hosts to know and do thy will.
> —*Bogatzky.*

’Ενδύσησθε δύναμιν ἐξ ὕψους.—*Luke xxiv. 49.*

IT is a truth too often forgotten that the gift of the Holy Ghost on the day of Pentecost was the beginning of what was henceforth to be the distinctive privilege of the new dispensation. The Holy Spirit had always been in the world, and every genuine conversion had been his work; but the Paraclete was that Spirit in a new office, and with new and abiding power on the believer. The Old Testament saints had the Spirit in occasional manifestations. Some who live earnestly, and are true Christians, have only these occasional or Old Testament gifts; but the Paraclete is an *abiding* power. "He shall give you another Comforter, that he may abide with you forever." It is a precious gift to be specially sought, as it was by the apostles after the ascension of Christ.

The object of this chapter is to show that the chief actors in the revival of 1800 had this New Testament baptism of the Holy Ghost. The first proof of this fact is found in the abiding nature of their spirituality. They all advocated daily communion with God as an attainable experience. In Finis Ewing's lecture on sanctification he uses many strong expressions on this subject, and adduces, as evidence of a low state of grace in some Christians, the fact that "they are not expecting daily communion with God, daily access to the throne, a daily or abiding witness that they are born of God."

Besides advocating the theory, their works show plainly that they had this abiding presence and power of the Holy Spirit with them, and knew the fact, and were made fearless by it. The Rev. H. A. Hunter, who knew them all, gave it as his opinion that the chief difference between them and modern preachers lay in their consciousness of God's abiding presence.

An anecdote of Ewing illustrates the truth that these men had abiding spiritual power.[1] A gentleman went with some wicked associates to hear Ewing preach. As he had never heard Ewing, his comrades offered to bet him twenty dollars that he could not go into the church and sit through the sermon without going to the mourner's bench when Ewing made the inevitable call for mourners. He took the bet, sat through the sermon, resisted the call for mourners, going, instead, out to his comrades, saying, "Gentlemen, I have won the bet, but I want none of your money. From this hour on, as long as I live, I shall not rest till I find salvation." It was not long until he was among the happy converts, and he long ornamented the church in which he cast his lot.

There is no part of Cumberland Presbyterian history of greater practical importance than the subject of this chapter. The danger in modern times is that men will forget to seek this new anointing from the Holy Spirit. Moody's testimony on this subject has been extensively published. "You lack *the power*," the ladies said to him. He sought the power. God gave it to him, and it abides with him. He said:

Eight years ago I was anxious for ministers and workers to see this truth and seek for this power. I remember that dear man, Rev. James Robertson, of Newington, telling me that when the work began in Edinburgh he could only preach once a week. He was suffering from heart disease. He prayed and the Spirit of God came upon him; he seemed to be anointed for his burial. "And now," said he, "I have preached eight times a week for a month, and enjoy better health than for years gone."

I can myself go back almost twelve years, and remember two holy women who used to come to my meetings. It was delightful to see them there. When I began to preach I could tell by the expression of their faces that they were praying for me. At the close of the Sab-

---

[1] Conversations with Old Kentuckians.

bath meeting they would say to me, "We have been praying for you." I said, "Why don't you pray for the people?" They answered, "You need the power." "I need the power!" I said to myself; "why I thought I had power." I had a large Sabbath-school and the largest congregation in Chicago. There were some conversions at the time. I was, in a sense, satisfied. But right along these two godly women kept praying for me, and their earnest talk about "anointing for special service" set me to thinking. I asked them to come and talk with me, and we got down on our knees. They poured out their hearts that I might receive an anointing from the Holy Spirit, and there came a great hunger into my soul. I did not know what it was. I began to cry as I never did before. The hunger increased. I really felt that I did not want to live any longer if I could not have this power for service. Then came the Chicago fire. I was burnt out of house and home at two o'clock in the morning. This did not so much affect me; my heart was full of the yearning for divine power. I was to go on a special mission to raise funds for the homeless, but my heart was not in the work of begging. I could not appeal. I was crying all the time that God would fill me with his Spirit. Well, one day in the city of New York—O what a day! I can not describe it; I seldom refer to it; it is almost too sacred an experience to name. Paul had an experience of which he never spoke for fourteen years. I can only say, God then revealed himself to me, and I had such an experience of his love that I had to ask him to stay his hand. I went to preaching again. I did not present any new truths. The sermons were not different, and yet hundreds were converted. I would not now be placed back where I was before that blessed experience if you would give me all Glasgow—it would be as the small dust of the balance. I tell you it is a sad day when a convert goes into the church, and that's the last you hear of him. If, however, you want this power for some selfish end— as, for example, to gratify your own ambition—you will not get it. "No flesh," says God, "shall glory in my presence." May he empty us of self and fill us with his Spirit.

Brought in to be a live factor in the grand progress of Christ's kingdom, the Cumberland Presbyterian church stands in wonderful relations to God. Her first ministers were flaming fires. Wherever they went there were revivals. When they stopped all night at a private house or at wayside hotels, there were professions of religion. They left homes and families and every earthly interest to go and preach Jesus to perishing souls. My father gave me an incident of Robert Donnell which illustrates the ever-abiding presence of God's Holy Spirit with these men. Father was traveling in the South and stopped at a wayside inn. Soon after another traveler put up at the same house. When the innkeeper proposed to take his guests to bed one of them said, "If you have no objections, I should like to have prayers with your family before I go to bed." The family were gathered. After the prayer the hotel keeper and his wife were seen to be weeping. The traveler labored with them that night till they both professed religion. The traveler was the Rev. Robert Donnell.

Another incident is here given to illustrate the same abiding presence of God's Holy Spirit with the preachers of that great revival. Many years ago I was traveling in the mountains of Tennessee. Passing by a large framed meeting-house, a gentleman who lived in the neighborhood, and had fallen in with me on the route, said to me: "That church has a strange history. Late one Saturday a stranger stopped at my father's to stay all night. After supper he told my father that he never traveled on Sunday, and would like to have religious services at his house on the Sabbath, if there were no objections. Next morning the neighbors were gathered in and the stranger preached. The very heavens came down to earth. Men fell to the floor crying for mercy. Before that stranger left the neighborhood the new converts were organized into a Cumberland Presbyterian church. That stranger was the Rev. Thomas Calhoun. That church grew until it was able to build the house of worship which we have just passed."

The next proof of this New Testament gift upon our fathers is found in the extraordinary power of their preaching. It was not learning or talents, but spiritual power. I have tried in vain to obtain a copy of a letter published by the Rev. Dr. Samuel Miller, of Princeton, New Jersey, in regard to this power in the preaching of H. F. Delany. The letter was often spoken of in my boyhood, and my recollections of the case are indorsed by several persons with whom I have compared notes, and the son of Delany[1] among them.

Dr. Miller had written some very bitter things against the Cum-

---

[1] Judge W. S. Delany, Columbus, Texas.

berland Presbyterians, being, as he afterward acknowledged,[1] wholly misinformed about them. He was traveling west and stopped over Sabbath. There was a Cumberland Presbyterian camp-meeting in the neighborhood, and Dr. Miller went. The Rev. H. F. Delany preached. Dr. Miller found his prejudices melting away, until he was all overcome at last with the simplicity and power of the gospel as Delany preached it. Dr. Miller wrote and published a glowing account of the sermon, declaring his conviction that the mighty power of God's Holy Spirit was on that preacher.

An old brother who had known Robert Donnell well attended the Chautauqua Assembly. I asked him what he thought of Chautauqua. His reply was: "If Robert Donnell could come back to earth and preach at Chautauqua just one such sermon as I have heard him preach at the camp-meetings it would set the whole vast thing on fire, until only the cries of lost sinners and the shouts of new converts could be heard."

At Cave Spring camp-ground, Overton County, Tennessee, the Chapman presbytery was in session. Some ordinations were appointed for the Sabbath. The camp-meeting was unusually large. Not only the shelter, but the whole lot was filled with people. When the presbytery gathered around the candidates for the imposition of hands, the congregation rose to their feet to see the ceremony. The prayer was offered by the Rev. Thomas Calhoun. His pleading with God for the Holy Spirit's power to be given to those young men impressed my boyish heart, as I listened, with new and grand ideas of the divine mission of the gospel ministry. Then the prayer shed a startling flash of light on a holy partnership and union between a truly spiritual preacher and God. Then came another flash sweeping out over the dark masses of fallen men to whom God was sending the gospel. O the gospel! how that prayer revealed and transformed it to my young eyes. The prayer went on, and people standing near the preacher sank down sobbing to the earth. The prayer went on, and others who stood next sank in like manner to the ground. Burning sentences,

---

[1] See *Revivalist*, 1833.

thrilling with the power of God's Spirit, went up from the preacher's heart to God, and the next circle of by-standers sank to the ground, sobbing and groaning. Finally, all under the shelter were alike bowed to the earth. Still the thrilling prayer seemed to gather more power. When at last it closed, not only under the shelter, but out to the fence and all around, and back even in the camps, men lay upon the ground weeping and praying.

Nobody rose when the amen was uttered. The remaining ceremonies were performed in choking, sobbing whispers. Then there was a pause. O that pause! Then the old man, the grand survivor of the revival preachers of 1800, uttered one little sentence: "Ye called of God, to your work!" and, leading the way, he and the other preachers went among the prostrate crowd, telling the lost what to do to be saved.

Our venerable and beloved brother, the Rev. W. H. Baldridge, who was a pupil first and afterward a fellow-laborer of the Rev. James B. Porter, gives me many precious facts about Porter's wonderful spiritual power. Although Brother Baldridge heard all our first preachers, being now eighty years old, he does not hesitate to pronounce Porter the most powerful one among them. One of the facts which he so kindly furnished me is as follows: The Rev. James Bowman, of the Presbyterian church, resolved to hold a camp-meeting in his congregation; but his brethren, in his presbytery, were nearly all Old Side, and would have nothing to do with camp-meetings. The few favorable to the revival had other engagements. Bowman could get no help. The ecclesiastical authorities of the mother church had forbidden its people either to recognize as ministers the preachers of the Cumberland Presbyterian church, or to commune with its members.[1] Notwithstanding this, Mr. Bowman invited James B. Porter to assist him in his camp-meeting. This was a new departure. Porter agreed to assist on two conditions. First, that he should be allowed to preach his own doctrines. Second, that there should be no tokens used at the communion service, but all Christians be allowed to participate. His conditions were accepted. While Porter preached

---

[1] This prohibition was revoked in 1825.

(text, "Turn, ye prisoners of hope"), the mighty power of God swept over the vast assembly. Sinners fell like men slain in battle. Going home was postponed one day after another. There were one hundred and twenty-five professions. Fifteen of the converts became ministers of the gospel.

Another proof that these spiritual heroes had this higher baptism is found in their lofty faith. What a difference Pentecost made in the faith of the apostles! The men of 1800 often announced results beforehand, because God had given them *assurance* in answer to their prayers. In Bird's life of Alexander Chapman, p. 178, is an incident illustrating this point. At Mount Moriah, in Logan County, Kentucky, after hours spent in the woods in solemn prayer, Chapman began his sermon with the words, "You shall all feel before I am done." The results vindicated his assurance. Not only feeling, but many conversions there were there that day.

There is an incident from Calhoun's ministry illustrating this point. He was at a camp-meeting at Rock Spring camp-ground, in Overton County, Tennessee. On Sabbath morning at breakfast some one told him that two desperate young men had bound themselves by a solemn oath to break up the meeting that day. Calhoun replied, "We'll see." Immediately after breakfast he went to his usual retreat, the woods, and there remained in prayer till time to commence the eleven o'clock sermon. Then he entered the rustic pulpit and announced his text. Then he stated what had been told him at breakfast, adding: "I am a preacher called and sent from God. You shall this day see, and know, and acknowledge that God is with me, and is able to give me the victory over all the opposition of men and devils." At that moment the two desperate young men before spoken of rose to their feet, and, with loud oaths, began cursing the preacher and the meeting, and moving through the crowd with noisy efforts at disturbance. Calhoun went on with his sermon. No human voice could keep his from being heard. The piercing power of his sentences made people forget all disturbances. That eagle eye of his held the eyes of the congregation. People were weeping. Hearts were lifted to God in prayer. The poor, silly young men who were trying to disturb the worship could not help hearing those wonderful sentences. No one could hear them without feeling the burning fire of God's Spirit which was in them. Presently one, then the other, of these two would-be disturbers of God's worship fell, like Saul of Tarsus, prostrate to the earth. They both were converted that day, and one of them became a minister of the gospel, and died proclaiming salvation to the lost. My parents were present at this meeting and gave me the incident. I knew the men.

Another proof that the men of 1800 had this Paraclete baptism is seen in their real, practical consecration to Christ, much like the consecration after Pentecost. Solemn covenants of consecration were written by some of them after their conversion, and were carried out in such a manner as to show that they were in earnest. From a long written covenant of consecration which was entered into by Robert Donnell, I make a brief extract: "And now, O Lord, I consecrate myself, ... my talents—whether one or five—my time, influence, all to thee."

A few years afterward when his little daughter died, he was absent in Alabama holding a camp-meeting. Writing to his wife, on receiving this sad intelligence, he says: "But for my appointments to preach, I would set out immediately to see my dear, afflicted wife. I have, however, given myself to the Lord to serve in his vineyard, and am not at liberty, like men of the world, to leave my Master's work."[1] Ah! consecration was no empty sound in such a life as that. [See Ezek. xxiv. 16, *et seq.*]

Take one more case. When Samuel King was in his sixtieth year the General Assembly asked him to make an evangelistic tour among the feeble churches of the frontier. Without hesitation he mounted his horse and made a grand tour through Tennessee, Kentucky, Arkansas, Alabama, Mississippi, Louisiana, and Missouri. He was absent from his family, on this tour, nearly two years. Do you say he did not love his family? I answer that you who say that do not know what real practical consecration to Christ, the King, means.

I find that written covenants of consecration were the rule, their

---

[1] Lowry's Life of Donnell, pp. 43, 45.

absence the exception. But this covenant is often made in words, while the after life shows there was no real consecration in deeds. The lives of all these heroes of 1800 show consecration in deeds.

When this higher baptism was given on the day of Pentecost, there followed grander answers to prayer than the apostles had ever known before. The men of 1800 had answers to prayer of such a nature as to provoke incredulous smiles when described in modern times.

About the year 1814, the Rev. William Harris was very sick with winter fever. It was thought he would die. The family stood round him weeping. He turned his face to the wall and prayed. At length he told his wife to cease weeping because the Lord had given him the clear assurance that he should recover from that sickness. He lived thirty years after that. The life-long friend of Harris, the Rev. Alexander Chapman, having heard of this dangerous illness of his fellow-laborer, called together the Little Muddy congregation, of which he was pastor, and notified them that the special object for which he had assembled them was that they might join him in praying for the recovery of Harris. It was at the same hour in which they were engaged in this prayer that Harris announced to his wife that he was going to get well.[1]

Thirty years ago all this country abounded with similar traditions of wonderful answers to prayer.

The wife of the Rev. W. W. Hendricks, D.D., witnessed the following incident and furnished me a written account thereof. The Rev. Thomas Calhoun was preaching the funeral sermon of the Rev. Robert Donnell. Vast crowds of people were present. A heavy rain was seen to be approaching. People began to be restless. Calhoun raised his hands to heaven and prayed God not to allow the rain to disturb the solemn worship. Then, turning to the congregation, he assured them that God would not allow the rain to come upon their saddles. The cloud parted, and it rained all around, hard and long, but none fell either on the camp-ground or on the multitude of horses which stood with saddles on them in the adjacent grove.

---

[1] Beard's Memoirs of the Rev. William Harris, p. 138.

Many years ago, some ladies, in Kentucky, who witnessed the following incident, gave me, substantially, this history thereof. There was a severe drouth. Chapman called his congregation together to pray for rain. He lead the first prayer. At first the prayer was very earnest pleading, then the prayer turned into thanksgiving for the rain which God had assured him was coming. It began raining abundantly that same day. O well, people laugh at such things now, and they who laugh go without any such answers to their prayers. *Every one* of our first preachers *has left us proof* that he believed that God healed the sick in answer to the prayer of faith. I am prepared to substantiate this assertion, if need be. Dr. Beard, in noticing this faith of our fathers, indorses and defends it. See biographical sketch of Harris. He gives his testimony, too, to the facts which I have been laboring to prove about this Paraclete power on the men of 1800. Hear him:

The first generation of Cumberland Presbyterians were the most intensely spiritual people that I have ever known. It is charged, I know, that old men look back and magnify the past, while young men look forward; but I can not be mistaken on this subject. Those people lived nearer heaven than ordinary Christians do now."[1]

The earnest advocacy of this Paraclete baptism, as a distinct blessing, after conversion, is found in many of the writings of our fathers. The McAdow MSS. before me contain two sermons devoted specially to this subject. One of them argues the general question; the other discusses the absolute necessity of this divine baptism in order to ministerial success. Some points in Mr. McAdow's arguments will be here condensed. He says: The gift of the Holy Ghost, in conviction and conversion, is not all its gifts. This is shown by the Holy Spirit giving messages and prophecies to unconverted men, like Balaam. It is shown by the gift of the Spirit to King Saul, not for his own sake at all, but for the sake of God's people over whom Saul was ruler. It is shown by the gifts of mechanical skill to Bezaleel, that he might construct cunningly the vessels of the sanctuary. It is shown by the gift of wisdom to Solomon that he might govern God's people wisely. It

---

[1] Dr. Frizzell's semi-centennial pamphlet, pp. 57, 58.

is shown by all the special "ascension gifts" mentioned in the New Testament—gifts suited to each special sphere of duty, in which men had their special callings; gifts conferred after conversion, fitting each recipient for some special service.

The other sermon takes the ground boldly, and argues it, that after a truly converted man is called of God to preach the gospel, and has received all the education which the schools can give, he may still be destitute of this New Testament baptism, and he is utterly unfit for his work in the gospel ministry until he does receive this superadded gift of power from the Paraclete, specially fitting him for the work of preaching the gospel. In this sermon Mr. McAdow argues the perpetuity of the order to tarry at Jerusalem till endued with the power from above. He insists that no one should go out to the preacher's work until this baptism of power has been conferred upon his soul. He shows that no amount of learning or professional training can give this power. Even the three years which the apostles spent traveling with Jesus failed to furnish it. He says: "I have no doubt but that there are men in our day who have received a genuine call to preach the gospel, ... but have never yet received that unction of the Holy Ghost." Again he says: "O that all our dear brethren who are looking forward to the ministry would heed the admonition of Christ to his disciples, and tarry at Jerusalem till they obtain this seal of their commission!"

The Rev. James Gallagher, a precious minister of the Presbyterian church, who witnessed some of the scenes of the great revival, discusses this very subject in "The Western Sketch Book," which he edited. He gives wonderful descriptions of the special gifts of prayer bestowed on some people. He insists that these were special enduements of power from God's Spirit. He says, while discussing the "bodily exercises:" "Of the professors of religion who were in this country when this revival began, perhaps one half became the subjects of this bodily exercise. These were invariably baptized with that spirit of prayer. The bodily exercises did not continue long, but that marvelous power of prayer was lasting as life." He goes on to describe the wonderful transformations of dull and formal and stupid church members by this baptism. He says many, personally known to him through a period of thirty years, whose prayers had always been cold and lifeless, when they received that divine enduement of power, "would at once rise above and beyond themselves—yea, above all I ever heard. This extraordinary power in prayer continued with them through their life." Again he says of this new power in prayer: "The man who has been acquainted with that strain or manner of prayer will know it in a moment whenever or wherever he may have the opportunity to hear it again."

Dr. Bird, in his life of Chapman, page 350, says he "valued the anointing of the Holy Spirit above every thing else. . . . Grace, the anointing of the Holy Spirit, was every thing to him."

Every one of these men whom I heard preach in my boyhood —Donnell, McSpeddin, Barnett, Calhoun, Harris, George Donnell, and many others of the next generation—laid special emphasis on this baptism of power from the Holy Spirit. This they did in all their preaching and their prayers.

Men try to apologize for the lack of this spiritual power now by pleading that the preachers of 1800 had uneducated, primitive, excitable people to preach to. Some of them cite the impulsiveness and inflammability of the colored race as a proof that the grand results of 1800 were due to similar conditions, instead of a superior spirituality. I ask, Was the Rev. Dr. Samuel Miller ignorant and excitable? Was the Rev. James Gallagher, of the Presbyterian church, or the Rev. Dr. Bird, or the Rev. Dr. Beard, or the Rev. Dr. H. A. Hunter, of our own church, ignorant and excitable? No, no! Let us turn to the stronghold and seek the divine gift for our own souls.

CHAPTER VI.

OPPOSITION TO THE REVIVAL.

> To see the blow, to feel the pain,
> But render only love again!
> This spirit, not to earth is given;
> *One* had it, but HE came from heaven.
> —*Hemans.*

IT is hard to be impartially just in writing this chapter. There is no doubt but that the manner in which the revival was managed gave some just grounds for complaint; neither is there any ground to doubt that most of the complaints made were undeserved. All genuine revivals are committed to human management, and stir up both just and unjust complaints.

Before McGready came to Kentucky his revivals stirred up opposition, even to the extent of threatening the preacher's life. A letter written in blood was sent to him warning him to leave the country.[1]

When, in his Kentucky field, the revival made its appearance, the Rev. Mr. Balch, of McGready's own presbytery, visited McGready's churches for the special purpose of preaching against the revival, and ridiculing what McGready had taught about faith, repentance, and regeneration.[2] Balch's preaching caused a vast amount of mischief. Nor did he stop with pulpit ministrations, but also visited the converts from house to house ridiculing their experience.[3] Nor was this preacher the only one who opposed the revival. In the same field were four others who opposed it. They were Craighead, Bowman, Templin, and Donnell. Balch made the fifth; just half the Presbyterian preachers in that field. Those who favored the revival and worked for it were McGready,

---

[1] Smith's History, p. 563; Foote, p. 50.
[2] Smith, p. 567, *et seq.*; McGready's Posthumous Papers
[3] See Mrs. Williamson's letters in Bird's Chapman.

Hodge, McGee, McAdow, and Rankin. The opposition was not confined to the ministry. King, with his lancet and camphor, going to minister to a soul seeking salvation, was only a sample of what many a church member was.

Before any other question arose between the two parties this one had split the churches asunder. The Muddy River church, in Kentucky, divided, and the revival party formed a new church called Liberty.

In 1801[1] the difficulty on this account in the Shiloh congregation, Sumner County, Tennessee, was brought before the presbytery. It had, of course, occurred before that date. The same year the revival part of Spring Creek church,[2] in Wilson County, Tennessee, having for a considerable time been locked out of the meeting-house, withdrew and built them another house, which they called Bethesda. This church still exists.

The Gasper church,[3] in Logan County, Kentucky, was closed against the revival party, and for years they held their meetings in the grove near the church. At a later day they built at Pilot Knob, in Simpson County. Their meeting place was in the adjacent grove when the Commission met at the church. This explains what Dr. Davidson says about Mr. Rankin's addressing the people in the grove while the Commission were at Gasper.

The Red River church,[4] in Logan County, Kentucky, was locked against the revival party, and McGready stood on the door steps and preached. One day while he or some other revival preacher stood there gesticulating violently, a backward stroke broke the lock, and the house was never locked against the revival party afterward.

There were several cases in which this opposition to the revival amounted to personal violence. The Calhoun MSS. give an account of one man who used a stick to enforce his views. The McAdow papers make several allusions to this personal violence. So do the Kirkpatrick MSS. In this opposition infidels and church members made common cause. A very wicked man saw

---

[1] Minutes of Transylvania Presbytery, 1801; *Revivalist*, April 16, 1834.
[2] Lowry's Life of Donnell, p. 26. [3] Bird's Chapman, p. 70.
[4] Conversations with Old People at Red River.

his wife go to the mourner's bench. In a rage he rushed to the place and dragged her away, cursing the revival as he went. While he was on his way to her horse a tree fell on him and killed him. The corpse was brought back to the shelter, and then and there McGready preached the poor sinner's funeral sermon. This was at Shiloh.[1]

Opposition to revivals *per se* is an exotic plant in Presbyterian gardens. Its importation began in the Established Church of Scotland, when state authority thrust unconverted men into the pastorates. We have already seen that unconverted preachers were common in McGready's day, according to the judgment of their contemporaries. Such men are generally opposed to revivals *per se*. But a far better class of Presbyterians have always opposed "revival measures." All honest hyper-Calvinists are logically opposed to such things. A recent writer in *The Southern Presbyterian Quarterly*, in arguing against our modern revivals, puts ultra-Calvinism in its legitimate expression when he says: "In the conversion and sanctification of the elect, the Almighty appoints a bound, and there is no margin for improvement. . . . . A faithful proclamation of the glad tidings is all the machinery that is needed in the salvation of those who are ordained to eternal life."[2] The same writer declares his conviction that all the modern revivals have been a disadvantage to the churches.

There were in 1800 many rigid notions among the churches which seem strange to us now. Singing hymns instead of psalms was one of McGready's offenses. The day for opposition to fireplaces or stoves in church was gone, but other things as unreasonable still held sway among the descendants of the Covenanters. Night meetings were considered scandalous. In the catalogue of "new measures" which the "Old Side" party objected to, were protracted meetings, night meetings, calling in other ministers to aid in meetings, inquiry meetings, propositions calling for action of any kind, weeping in the pulpit, great fervor in exhortation, itinerant preachers, evangelists both lay and clerical, singing hymns, all noise — shouting, groaning, or crying out for mercy; to all of

---

[1] John McGee locates this incident incorrectly.
[2] *Southern Quarterly*, 1868, p. 155.

which was added another long list after camp-meetings and the mourner's bench came into use. The Presbyterian church was at first divided about half and half on these questions, but the Old Side party to-day is everywhere in the minority. It counted the heaviest pens of the church from 1740 to 1800. Some of Dr. Samuel Miller's complaints against the revivals in which these new measures were used are very severe,[1] but scarcely less so than Dr. Charles Hodge's.[2]

There were in 1800 many ministers who believed the revival genuine, but objected to many of the measures used, and objected to such an extent that they were often classed with the anti-revival party. David Rice was one of this class. It was new measures which many good men conscientiously opposed. The revival preachers of the Presbyterian church, all the better class of them, admitted the necessity of caution in times of great popular excitement, and acknowledged the worthlessness of man-made revivals; but they said as God uses human beings in all genuine revivals, so will there always be human imperfections accompanying them. They illustrated the constants and the variables of Christianity by the art of printing. The truth was a constant, printing a variable, and not mentioned in Scripture; yet by its use the unchangeable truth could be carried to many who could never see a copy of the Bible by the old method. There is but one way of salvation, but the agencies by which that way may be taught and impressed are multiplying and improving every year.

The mourner's bench is one of the variables. The advocates of new measures presented strong arguments in its favor, such as these: It commits the sinner publicly to seeking salvation; it touches the hearts of his comrades; it enlists the prayers of Christians for him; it mortifies his stubborn pride. But the mourner's bench has been abused. Perhaps other methods are to take its place.

As for itinerant preaching it is willful blindness to call it a new measure. Christ and his apostles used it, and the commission was "go," not "stay."

The New Side showed that the revival on the day of Pentecost

---

[1] See his ninth letter to Presbyterians.
[2] See his History of the Presbyterian Church in America.

was one of excitement and noise, so much so that men said the apostles were drunk; and yet that great revival neither destroyed nor hindered the ordinary services, but souls were "daily added" to the church after the meeting. There was new life in those ordinary regular services. There was a consecration of men and money to Jesus far beyond what the ordinary services produced.

Then they turned the tables on the objectors. They showed what a routine of stagnation and death the ordinary services had reached before every one of the great revival periods. Men were taken into the church without conversion; unconverted men were taken into the ministry; infidelity, too, crept in under this cloak of lifeless forms; and vast multitudes were sweeping away to hell under a godless ministry.

If Dr. Miller's ninth letter is appalling, the answers to it are still more so. One of the writers (himself a Presbyterian)[1] asks: "Are any of these able men who are writing against the way we conduct our revivals themselves experts in revivals? Did any single one of them ever have a revival, either genuine or spurious, under his ministry?"

We are successful watch-makers. We have sent out thousands of good time-pieces, none of them faultless, but all serviceable. Up yonder in the college observatory is an able astronomer, and he sets himself to writing against our watches, and denouncing them for lack of that ideal perfection which, from his mathematical training, he sees in them. We ask him, Sir, did you ever make a watch?

There is a history by Dr. Robert Henderson, quoted in the McMullin MS., which seems in place here. Dr. Blackburn was holding a revival meeting on the New Side programme. Dr. Henderson, who was Old Side, and had no patience with Dr. Blackburn's meeting, was present. So he gathered a part of Dr. Blackburn's congregation into another house, and held an *orderly* meeting for them. Although some of Dr. Blackburn's most excitable followers were present, yet there was no noise or confusion of any sort at Dr. Henderson's meeting. It also comes out, incidentally, that there were no conversions there.

---

[1] See New York *Evangelist*, 1833.

In 1852 an earnest Methodist was holding a revival meeting in the church just opposite a great Catholic church in Philadelphia. Day and night for a hundred days the meeting swept on like a tempest. Finally the priest called on the Methodist preacher and inquired if there was no way "to have a stop put to that nuisance." The answer was, "Nothing easier, sir; you just come and preach in my pulpit and all the noise will stop." No doubt Dr. Henderson could produce order out of Dr. Blackburn's excitable materials, but Dr. Blackburn had thousands of seals to his ministry.

The reader will please look at the map. Kentucky Synod took in both the Cumberland settlement and the upper Kentucky settlement. A wilderness lay between them. None of "the Cumberland party" lived or preached in "upper Kentucky." Four Presbyterian ministers in upper Kentucky preached some wild doctrines, and used many strange methods at their meetings, all of which the Cumberland party earnestly condemned. Years before the "Cumberland schism" originated there was a schism in upper Kentucky, and those engaged therein were called Stoneites, after the name of their leader, the Rev. Barton W. Stone. The wildest and most wonderful of their meetings were at Cane Ridge, where miracles, prophesies, and other such wonderful things were said to take place. Afterward, when the Cumberland party sprang up in "Cumberland," some of the Stoneite preachers came to that field, but in every case "the revival party" of Cumberland Presbytery refused to allow these Stoneites to preach in their meetings. Ewing and others preached against the heresies of the Stoneites. Yet for years, and even now, "the anti-revival party" of the mother church holds up the Cane Ridge meetings and Stoneite theology as samples of what the meetings and doctrines of Cumberland Presbyterians are. Several writers who confounded McGready's meetings and the Cumberland meetings of a later day with these wild meetings in upper Kentucky, afterward discovered and corrected their mistake. Others have promised to correct theirs also. It is far more important to them than it is to us that they should do so. "An outrage," says Cervantes, "injures him who gives it, not him that receives it."

An illustration of these misrepresentations is seen in the published letters of Dr. Samuel Miller. He had so often heard and read the charge that the Stoneites, Shakers, and Cumberland Presbyterians were all branches of one tree, and all alike in their revival meetings, that he repeated the charge in his publications. He afterward published the following recantation; "I am now convinced that in representing the 'New Lights' or 'Stoneites,' the 'Shakers,' and the Cumberland Presbyterians as exfoliations from the same disorderly body, and of about the same time, I wrote under a misapprehension of the facts."[1] Again, in the same letter, he says: "Neither the Stoneites nor the Shakers ever made constituent parts of that body. The Stoneites and Shakers, I am now aware, were separated from the church several years anterior to the departure of the Cumberland Presbyterians."

Another sample is taken from the *Presbyterian*, 1847. After making some grave charges against us, the editor proceeds to prove them, thus, quoting from the Assembly's digest:

But we will give a brief extract in their own words, as these Minutes are accessible but to a few. "When we withdrew," they say, 'we considered ourselves freed from all creeds but the Bible; and since that time, by constant application to it, we are led further from the idea of adopting creeds and confessions as standards, than we were at first. We feel ourselves citizens of the world; God our common Father; all men our brethren by nature, and all Christians our brethren in Christ. This principle of universal love to Christians gains ground in our hearts in proportion as we get clear of particular attachments to party. We therefore can not put ourselves in a situation which would check the growth of so benign a temper, and make us fight under a party standard." Although these men had just denied the faith, rent the church, and set up a party standard, yet, with this high sounding language, they attempted to beguile the public, and said to the assembly, "Let us pray for more of the uniting, cementing spirit, and treat differences in lesser matters with Christian charity." They were ready for a reunion, but only on the terms that the whole church should give up its creed and descend to their level. Thus it was upwards of forty years ago in our own church; let the church now, as then, stand up for the maintenance and defense of its precious distinctive doctrines.

---

[1] *Revivalist*, June 18, 1834.

To which Milton Bird made the following reply, addressing himself to the *Presbyterian:*

By referring to Davidson's late history of Presbyterianism in Kentucky (pp. 197, 198, 200,), in connection with the Minutes from which you quote, you will find that you have mistaken the "New Lights" for the Cumberland Presbyterians. The two have no more fellowship with each other than night and day. The "Separatists," or "New Lights," to which these Minutes refer, soon disbanded without adopting any creed. Three of them joined the Shakers, two united again with the Presbyterian church, and the sixth, Barton Stone, joined the Campbellites.

Then the *Presbyterian* made the following statement:

A CORRECTION.—We incidentally referred in some remarks on distinctive Presbyterianism, to the schism of the Cumberland Presbyterians as illustrative of the views we were expressing, and quoted a document found in the Minutes of the General Assembly, which we attributed to the members of this presbytery. In this we erred. The sentiments we quoted were chargeable to the "New Light Schism" in Kentucky, and not to the Cumberland Presbyterians, who did not come on the stage until several years afterward.

How carelessly that editor read the Minutes of his own Assembly! There are still those who reiterate the old slander, perhaps really believing it. Thus Dr. Speer (1872), in his little book entitled "The Great Revival of 1800," represents "Cumberlandism" as originating out of the Cane Ridge furor, while he holds up in contrast the more orderly meetings in McGready's field in Logan County.[1] Dr. Speer wrote me that he would make some corrections when he published his next edition. It is not the purpose of this history to expose and refute the unfounded and bitter charges which the anti-revival party of that day made against the revival, and afterward against the church which took its rise from that revival. In most cases these bitter charges were never indorsed by the bulk of the Presbyterian church. Their refutation was given at the time. Let that suffice.

One of the *foci* of fury where opposition to the revival rallied was "the jerks." Of these strange matters a few words must be written. In many countries, both in the Old World and the New,

---

[1] See pp. 38-40.

and in many meetings, and especially Presbyterian meetings, not only in 1800, but in previous revivals, these bodily exercises made their appearance. Their first appearance in the revival of 1800 was not in McGready's churches, but in Gideon Blackburn's, in East Tennessee. The first person to have them in this western field was the Rev. Dr. Doak, a graduate of Princeton, New Jersey, and a thorough Presbyterian. These exercises have been investigated scientifically and often. All parties agree that they were involuntary. A curious story was current in my boyhood about a Presbyterian minister who came into Tennessee and was preaching against these bodily exercises, when he was himself seized with them in the pulpit and violently jerked about.

Dr. Blackburn, Dr. Baxter, McGready, and Hodge, and a host of others, all Presbyterians, and eye-witnesses, were fully persuaded that these strange manifestations were the direct work of God's Holy Spirit, sent to silence and convince the gainsayers of that day. Others thought them only the result of nervous excitement. Dr. Blackburn quoted Scripture to show that they were the legitimate work of the Holy Spirit. James Smith ("Scotch Smith," as our people called him) took the nervous view of the matter. So did Dr. Charles Hodge and Dr. Davidson. It is absolutely certain that these strange exercises made a deep and solemn impression on those who witnessed them. Proofs are in existence of the conversion of many an infidel through the agency, under God, of these strange manifestations. Advocates of the nervous theory were put to practical confusion at Gasper River at the first appearance of these wonders there. They plied medical remedies to those who fell prostrate and lay like dead men. The lancet was used to such an extent that the place was covered with bleeding bodies like a battle-field,[1] but no good ever came from this medical treatment; and no harm to life, limb, or reason ever came from the mysterious exercises. Dr. Charles Hodge's effort to connect these bodily exercises with nervous epidemics, whose origin had no connection with religion, is, it seems to me, a total failure.

---

[1] Hugh Kirkpatrick's MSS.

CHAPTER VII.

THE SECOND DIFFICULTY—MINISTERIAL EDUCATION.

"Shall we to men benighted,
The lamp of life deny?"

THERE was a vast field almost destitute of the means of grace. Most of the settlers had been accustomed to church privileges in their former homes, and were clamorous for them in their frontier cabins. Those who attended the camp-meetings returned to spread the religious interest in their neighborhoods. A sufficient supply of preachers could not be secured. The case was one of extreme urgency. The Rev. David Rice visited McGready's field, "and being informed of the destitute state of most of the churches, and the pressing demands for the means of grace, earnestly recommended that they should choose from among the laity some men who appeared to possess talents and a disposition to exercise their gifts publicly to preach the gospel, although they might not have acquired that degree of education required by the Book of Discipline. This proposition was cordially approved by both preachers and people. . . . . What still more clearly convinced them of the propriety of this measure was that in almost every congregation that had been blessed with the outpouring of the Holy Spirit, there were one or more intelligent and spiritual men whose gifts in exhortation had already been honored by the Head of the church in awakening and converting precious souls. Accordingly three zealous, intelligent, and influential members of the church—viz., Alexander Anderson, Finis Ewing, and Samuel King—were encouraged by the revival preachers to prepare written discourses and to present themselves before the Transylvania Presbytery at its session in 1801. All these persons had previously been under serious impressions that it was their duty to devote themselves to the ministry, but as they had not enjoyed the advantages of a

collegiate education, and were men of families and somewhat advanced in life, they had been laboring under difficulties. At the meeting of Transylvania Presbytery, in October, 1801, the case of these brethren was brought before that body, from some of whom they met with warm opposition. However, after a protracted discussion, it was agreed by the majority that they might be permitted to read their discourses privately to Mr. Rice."[1] They did so, and Rice reported favorably. They were then sent out as exhorters to the vacant congregations, and instructed to prepare written discourses for the next meeting of the presbytery.

In the spring of 1802 Anderson was received by a majority of one vote as a regular candidate for the ministry, and the others by a majority of one vote were retained in the category of catechists. In the fall of 1802 they were all licensed to preach.

Here was the second ground of complaint. The question was not then, nor is it now, about the great importance of a classical education, but it was, and still is, whether after we have done our utmost in educating men for the ministry, we may supplement the supply by licensing judicious men of piety and promise to work among the perishing, even when these men have not a collegiate education. Inasmuch as there was opposition, Mr. Rice, by direction of the presbytery, addressed a letter to the General Assembly on the subject. Here is the answer:[2]

A liberal education, though not absolutely essential, has been shown to be highly important and useful, from reason and experience and the prosperity of the Presbyterian and New England churches. But, whatever might be the Assembly's opinion, the standards are explicit on the subject. As to the apprehension of schism in consequence of rigid views, the reply must be that the path of duty is the path of safety, and events are to be committed to God. Parties formed under such circumstances would be neither important nor permanent. Notwithstanding, when the field is too extensive, catechists, like those of primitive times, may be found useful assistants. But great caution should be used in selecting *prudent and sound* men lest they run into extravagance and pride. Their duties should be carefully defined and subject to frequent inspection. They should not be considered stand-

---

[1] Quoted from Smith's History.
[2] Quoted from Cossitt's Life of Ewing, p. 346.

ing officers in the church, but, if possessed of uncommon talents, diligent in study, and promising usefulness, *they might in time purchase to themselves a good degree, and be admitted in regular course to the holy ministry.* [Italics mine.]

This advice of the General Assembly accords in every possible particular with the views then taken by the revival party. On those views they acted, and against them the other party planted themselves. Every Cumberland Presbyterian would consent to have all the licensures by Cumberland Presbytery tried by this rule. So, too, may the licensures of Ewing, King, and Anderson by the Transylvania Presbytery be tried. Though not fully up to the requirements in the classics, these three men were all men of respectable attainments in scholarship. Ewing had considerable classical knowledge. There were catechists sent out at a later day who never expected to become regular ministers. As a considerable number of these catechists were employed, it is not a matter of surprise that a few of them disappointed the expectations of the presbytery.

But, of all those whom the revival party licensed to preach, there is not one single name which is not held in the profoundest veneration to-day in all the field where they labored. Not one of them left a reputation tarnished by heresy, apostasy, or defection from the church and services of the Lord Jesus. They all died with their armor on after a noble warfare. Such things can not be said of those who constituted the other party of the Cumberland Presbytery.

At a later day the revival party sent a history of their action at this time to the General Assembly. An extract from that history is here given. The history is too long to quote in full[1] but it is all interesting, and is in perfect accord with the history of the revival given in this book, especially as to when, where, and how the revival originated.

After describing the origin of the revival and its wonderful spread over the whole country, they say:

Now, truly, the harvest was great and the laborers few. Unable to

---

[1] See *Revivalist*, May 14, 1834. See also appendix A, in Life and Times of Ewing.

resist the pressing solicitations from every quarter for preaching, with unutterable pleasure we went out, laboring day and night, until our bodies were worn down, and after all we could not supply one third of the places calling upon us for preaching. While thus engaged, and while the gracious work was still going on, we observed what was very remarkable, that in almost every neighborhood there was some one who appeared to have uncommon gifts for exhortation and prayer, and was zealously engaged in the exercises thereof, while the Lord wrought by him to the conversion of many. Viewing the infant state of the church in our country, the anxious desire for religious instruction, the gifts, diligence, and success of those we have mentioned, and the scriptural authority for exhortation, we were induced with almost every member in the presbytery, to open a door for the licensure of exhorters, well knowing it was a liberty that was, and would be taken; and concluding if taken by presbyterial authority it might prevent disorder and weakness. It was now agreed that any of those who might be licensed, and who manifested extraordinary talents and piety, should be considered as candidates for the ministry; also, that for their improvement they should have subjects appointed, on which they were to be heard at our stated sessions of presbytery; that if, by their improvement, piety, and usefulness, they purchased to themselves a good degree, they might be set apart to the holy ministry. Accordingly, several made application, who were examined on experimental religion, and the motives inducing them to public exhortation. Those we judged qualified were then licensed. The first were all men of families, and somewhat advanced in years. Out they went, leaving wives and children, houses and lands, for Christ's sake and the gospel; suffering hunger, cold, and weariness, for weeks in succession, but the Lord was with them and made them happy instruments in helping on his work in the conversion of many. After a long trial of those men in different parts of our country, there came forward to our presbytery several petitions for their licensure to the ministry, signed by hundreds of the most moral and religious characters where they had labored.

From our personal knowledge of those men's good talents, piety, and usefulness; from the numerous warm petitions of the people at large; from the example of many presbyteries; from the silence of Scripture on literary accomplishments; from your own declaration in answer to Mr. Rice's letter, viz.: "That human learning is not essential to the ministry;" from the exception made in the Book of Discipline, in extraordinary cases; we humbly conceived, that it would not be a transgression either of the laws of God or the rules of the church, to license men of such a description. We therefore did license them, and a few others at different times afterward; some of them with, and some with out, literary acquisitions; but all men of gifts, piety, and influence, having spent years previous in exhortation, before they were admitted to the ministry. Several were licensed to exhort, whose names are on our Minutes, whom we never had a design of admitting to the ministry. Now the work of the Lord went on. Numbers of young and promising congregations were formed. . . . . So that in a few years the wilds of our country echoed with the praises of the Lord. Savage ignorance was changed into a knowledge of God and his dear Son; and savage ferocity into the lamb-like spirit of Jesus."

James Hutchinson, Esq., of Montgomery County, Tennessee, gave to Dr. Cossitt a statement which will illustrate the circumstances under which these men were first sent out. He says:[1]

We emigrated from Virginia in 1796, and settled where we now live, in 1797. Both my Sarah and I had been religiously raised and accustomed to read our Bible. Away from all our friends and in this then solitary place, we felt that we needed an Almighty Protector. We sought the one thing needful as for goodly pearls. In 1800 we trust we both embraced that holy religion which has been our guide and comfort up to the present hour. The country was filling up rapidly, but there was no one to break to us the bread of life. O how we did long to hear the blessed gospel preached! We joined with David Beaty and Henry Anderson in a petition praying Transylvania Presbytery to send us a preacher. We were rejoicing in hope, but hungering for the word of God. We were Presbyterians, so far as we understood ourselves, and wanted to cast our lot with that people among whom God was carrying on his glorious work. The field was wide, the harvest plenteous, and the laborers few. A preacher could not come to us. We wept, we mourned, we prayed; we could take no denial. We petitioned again without success. Still we believed God would hear and help us. We could not be discouraged, seeing that God could, in answer to our prayers, incline the presbyters to favor us, if only a little. No mortal man can conceive our anxieties unless he has been placed in a like situation.

We could hear of other places within ten, twenty, thirty miles where the people, like us, were petitioning for a preacher. Some of them had attended the great meetings in Kentucky or higher up in Tennessee, and had returned glorifying God. We asked, Would not a God of love take care of his own cause and feed his own flock? . . . . We called to mind his precious promises and said, Surely he will.

There are two periods in my life which I never can forget while I

---

[1] Life and Times of Ewing, pp. 70-77.

remember any thing. One is when I found the Lord precious; the other is when, in answer to all our prayers, he sent his faithful servant to minister to our spiritual necessities. I often call to mind, as if it were but yesterday, the evening when a traveler, an entire stranger, as I supposed, rode up to my log-cabin. This house, built of stone, was not here then. His eyes were red with weeping, and the tears were scarcely dried on his cheeks. He inquired for James Hutchinson. On being informed that I was the man he seemed overjoyed. He said, "I have so long traveled this Indian path without seeing a house that I seriously feared it would be my lot to lie out this night and take my chances with the wolves. I have cried and prayed the Lord, my helper, ... and he has brought me to this hospitable home." I was filled with surprise and joy. I saw he was a man of genteel appearance, and, better still, his language savored of grace and piety. I had seen but few religious persons since I professed, and I greatly rejoiced that a pious traveler had done me the favor to call and spend a night with me at my cabin in the wilderness. . . . . He soon took occasion to let me know his business in these parts, and that his name was Finis Ewing. . . . . "Sarah, Sarah," I called. She was out preparing supper. Stepping to the door I said, "The preacher has come!" Sarah came in shouting, while I was crying for joy. God had answered our prayers and sent us a preacher!

When we had become a little composed, Mr. Ewing modestly observed, "Do not mistake me, my friends; I am not a preacher, but have been sent in the place of one. I am authorized publicly to exhort, expound the Scriptures, and, according to my ability, give all needful instructions, without the formalities of a sermon." Being mere babes in Christ, we cared but little for the formalities of a sermon. . . . .

We had long felt that we were in the midst of a people who were living without hope and without God in the world, actually perishing for lack of knowledge. Without the gospel, without schools, and almost without a Sabbath, we shuddered at the thought of raising our children in such a state of society.

Mr. Hutchinson gathered in his neighbors and Ewing preached and left another appointment. Hutchinson then accompanied him to other destitute neighborhoods. He speaks in strong terms about the great power of Ewing's sermons at all these places.

As for the other lay exhorters, each in separate fields, the one claiming attention next to Ewing is Samuel King. Like Ewing, he had been taken into the church while still unconverted; and, like Ewing, he had been truly converted afterward. Then he immediately began to exhort sinners. It is the general testimony that his exhortations were greatly blessed. While he had a circuit regularly appointed around which he traveled, he seems often to have wandered beyond its bounds. From the very first his heart yearned over the most destitute. Nor did he stop with the white settlements. An incident of his work among the Indians will be given here. It was furnished originally by his son, Judge R. M. King. King was addressing, through an interpreter, a large crowd of Choctaw Indians. The interpreter became so powerfully convicted that he could proceed no further, but like the sinners at McGready's meetings, he fell to the earth and began to cry for mercy. The preacher knew not what to do. He could speak none of their language, yet they were weeping all around him. He knew, though, that God could understand him. He fell to his knees and began to pray. While King prayed the interpreter was converted. Then the preacher had a new tongue. His sermon was blessed to the salvation of many souls before he left the place. To the visits of King to the Choctaws can be traced the conversion of our first native preachers among that people.[1]

But, returning to King's circuit, the indications are that it reached the wildest and sparsest portions of the field. He swam rivers; he slept often in the forest with his saddle-bags for a pillow; he preached under the trees, where there was no house of worship. Thomas Calhoun testified that King was the first man in all the West to take his stand against whisky.

All these men rode vast circuits on which they preached every day, besides riding from twenty to fifty miles on horseback. Riding, too, when there were no bridges, ferry-boats, or even good wagon roads. It took them four months to make one round on these circuits. To many of the new settlers visited by them these circuit appointments, once in four months, were their only dependence for the gospel. Even the daring pioneers of Methodism had not then reached some of these regions.

Alexander Anderson had gifts, in some particulars, superior to all the others. One who knew him well gave a long written statement to Dr. Beard[2] testifying to his spiritual power. Speak-

---

[1] Beard's King.   [2] Beard's Anderson.

ing of his selection by the presbytery he says: "They knew their man. They knew what he could do in prayer, exhortation, and other religious exercises. Nor were they disappointed." He says there were still living a few who remembered Anderson's sermons and could repeat whole paragraphs of them, and still wept at the mention of his name, after he had been in heaven fifty years. It is reported of him that he foresaw the schism which was threatened in his church, and prayed God that he might be taken home before it came. His prayer was answered.

Colonel Joe Brown gives this incident, as related to him by the father of the Rev. James B. Porter: "The Rev. Dr. Thomas Hall, while on his way to Natchez, where he had been sent as a missionary, stopped to rest a while in Sumner County, Tennessee. There he heard about these lay exhorters. He expressed himself in strong terms against the measure, and said he would see to it that the Presbyterian church should not be disgraced by lay preaching. That same night he attended a prayer-meeting at which Alexander Anderson exhorted. Dr. Hall was amazed. He said that man must preach. The Lord had some great work for him to do." [See *Banner of Peace*, March 16, 1856.]

As for Ephraim McLean, he is not in the same category as the others. While he was received as a candidate in 1802, he was not willing to be placed on the list of exceptions to the educational requirements. What little he lacked of coming up to those requirements he believed he could make up by private study while on the circuit. It is this that explains the omission of his name in the passage quoted from Smith's history. But in all the list there was no truer hero for Jesus than McLean. When he professed religion he had a wife and four children, and was living in a floorless cabin built of round poles. When he felt himself called to preach the gospel, his heroic wife urged him on, both in his preparation for the work of the ministry and in the discharge of its sacred duties afterward. He went out on his circuits, year after year, preaching to people where no other minister came. He received no pay. His wife raised the wool, spun the thread, wove the cloth, and made the clothing which he wore on his circuits. The anti-revival party sneered at his rough garments, but they will not sneer in the day of judgment, when they see him wearing a crown studded with many stars. His was not a long career. He fell just after the new church was organized, but his work lives on. He had two sons who were in the national Congress afterward, one a Senator. He has a grandson now in the ministry in our church, the Rev. E. G. McLean, of California.

Some idea of the way in which the revival spread, and how God pointed out to the presbytery what men to select as evangelists, may be received from the following incidents:

James B. Porter had educated himself for a physician. At Shiloh camp-meeting, in Sumner County, Tennessee, 1801, he found the Savior. Soon after the meeting his mother took him with her on a trip to South Carolina. At every house where they stopped on their journey, Porter told about the wonderful grace of God to his soul, and commended his Savior to the people. There were conversions all along the journey. On the return trip Lorenzo Dow had a public meeting in which he made Porter exhort, and God greatly blessed the exhortation.

The case of Alexander Chapman is similar. Soon after his conversion he went on a visit to his uncle in Virginia. On his arrival he found the family about starting to their weekly prayer-meeting. He accompanied them. After two or three prayers the way was opened for any one to read, or pray, or make remarks. Chapman, who had been brought up in the neighborhood, and whose profession of religion was unknown there, rose and gave an exhortation. A revival began at once, and spread over the community until more than one hundred persons professed faith in Christ. Among these were several of his cousins, who lived many years to adorn the profession which they had made. The Rev. Mr. Robinson, the pastor in that community, gave his hearty indorsement to the young man's zeal and usefulness.[1]

Owing to the great distance between the two settlements which belonged to Transylvania Presbytery, the synod divided it, and created the Cumberland Presbytery. This presbytery embraced all the Green River and Cumberland settlements, and all that portion of the synod in which those grave differences of opinion had

---

[1] Bird's Life of Chapman, p. 35.

arisen, out of which, at last, "the Cumberland schism" sprang. As the Transylvania Presbytery had received into membership a Methodist by the name of Hawe, and as he resided in the bounds assigned to Cumberland Presbytery, the revival party, by his aid, had a majority of one. The new presbytery ordained Anderson, Ewing, and King. That gave the revival party a decided majority.

Against all these measures in which men were employed as exhorters or preachers without a classical education, the anti-revival party took a decided stand. Their protests in several instances were entered on the Minutes of the presbytery; but the revival party were in the majority, and had things their own way for a season. The synod, however, came at last to the relief of the minority.

This question about the Westminster standard of ministerial education being made a *sine qua non* for the pulpit, is a live question yet. So, too, is the question about how to conduct revival meetings. Three out of the four questions of that day are still debated; though with a growing majority in all three in favor of the views then taken by the revival party. On the fourth question (the ecclesiastical one), all parties concede now that the founders of our church were right.

While we believe the course pursued by the revival party was wise and scriptural, we believe also that it has been abused by many of our presbyteries since. Three errors have prevailed. One, in overlooking "aptness to teach" and spirituality, which neither education nor the lack of it can ever supply. Another is in attributing the wonderful spiritual power of Calhoun and his associates to their lack of education. If lack of collegiate education gives this wonderful spiritual power, why is it that all the army of uneducated ministers in our church, and in other churches, to-day do not have it? The third error is in calling Ewing and Donnell and their comrades uneducated men, and holding up their example as an excuse for laziness and stupidity, as, alas! so many of our presbyteries have done. True, these men were not graduates of any college, and what scholarship they had was not obtained according to regulation methods, but for all that they were educated men and profound thinkers. Their education came as Daniel Boone's did. They availed themselves of all the facilities in their reach. They carried text-books in their saddle-bags and studied at night. They studied men, and profoundly studied their English Bibles. Most that colleges do for men is to teach them how to think; these men had that lesson, no matter how they obtained it. Between these men and the lazy boy of to-day who has it in his power to secure a college education and will not do it, there is no similarity at all, and their example is a rebuke rather than an apology to all such.

Akin to this error of some of our own people is a slander from some who do not understand us. "They went out of the Presbyterian church because they were opposed to education," is a threadbare slander still circulated. Many times utterly refuted, this slander is still peddled out as the most effective way of injuring our church. The real issue is not about the inestimable value of education, but about the propriety of allowing exceptions to the requirement of a *classical* education in cases of great pressure, like those of Ewing and King, when clearly demonstrated usefulness on the part of the aspirant combines with a very great demand for his special services on the part of the destitute. Whether it was better to allow whole vast areas of destitute settlements to remain without the gospel entirely, or to send them sound teachers who loved souls and knew the way of salvation, though they did not know either Latin or Greek—that was the question.

Neither the fathers of our church nor their sons failed to appreciate an educated ministry. It requires considerable grace patiently to argue such a proposition at this late day, but I think God will give me grace to do it.

Proof 1. Ephraim McLean was one of the fathers of our church. When he was ordered to prepare for ordination along with Ewing and King, he said: "Give me a little more time and I shall be able to come fully up to the standard. I am fully up now in every thing but Greek, and am working hard at that."[1] They granted his request, but with the understanding that he should pursue his studies on the circuit. This he diligently did. They cared for souls, but they cared for scholarship too. McLean then had a wife and six children, and was preaching without any compensa-

---

[1] Incidents furnished by his son, Finis E. McLean.

tion whatever. His wife and boys made their support on their Kentucky farm, and his wife with her own hands spun the thread and wove the cloth for his clothing. Our fathers thought it was worth while to endure trials that the perishing multitudes might have the gospel. Nor is this all in McLean's case. When his boys were old enough to go off to school he discussed the case with his noble wife, and fell upon a plan for their education. His wife took charge of the farm herself, and by heroic struggles and sacrifices supported the family and kept her boys at school and her husband on the circuit. Was that husband opposed to education?

Proof 2. All the men who took part in the organization of the Cumberland Presbyterian church left the strongest possible testimony that they held a thorough education in the highest esteem.

Finis Ewing left his testimony in several forms. He spent large sums of money in establishing a classical school near his home in Kentucky, and that before the organization of our first synod; and when this school was established he would have none but thorough classical teachers in it. This was the first classical school in all that portion of Kentucky.[1] Afterward he sent his own son, who was then looking to the ministry, to college and gave him a thorough education. When he moved to Missouri he set to work to establish a school for the *classical and theological* education of the ministry in Missouri, and he filled his large house full of young preachers going to school, to whom he gave gratuitous boarding.

Still further, when our first college was proposed, and the practicability of establishing both a classical and theological college, with ample endowment, was under discussion, Finis Ewing made a speech in favor of the enterprise which Dr. Cossitt, a graduate of a New England college, who heard it, pronounced the ablest of all the pleas for an educated ministry that he had ever listened to. To his dying day Dr. Cossitt maintained, and published, and reiterated his declaration that he had heard no plea for an educated ministry equal to Ewing's great speech. Ewing wrote for the college some of the ablest pleas I ever read. When I was president of Cumberland University, and struggling hard to lift the institu-

---

[1] Incidents reported by Hon. F. E. McLean.

tion up from the wreck where the civil war had left it, the most telling appeal I made to our people in behalf of our college was made by republishing some of Finis Ewing's pleas for old Cumberland College.

Samuel King traveled as agent for the endowment of our first college. Thomas Calhoun had a son who entered the ministry. He sent that son to college and afterward to a theological school. He nearly all his life was aiding some young preacher to obtain a college education.

Samuel McAdow was himself a graduate, but his infirm health prevented his taking any very active share in any kind of work after the organization of the new church.

Robert Donnell traveled as agent for our first college, at his own expense, and published many earnest pleas for it. He delivered a course of lectures to the theological class at Lebanon, Tennessee. He declared a thoroughly endowed theological school to be a necessity of the church. He himself gave large sums to that endowment. In discussing the necessity of a thoroughly endowed college he says, in a letter published in the *Banner of Peace*, "*Without it we can not prosper as a body.*"

All the first numbers of our church papers teem with earnest articles from those men who planted the church, urging the importance of thorough education.

Proof 3. Early ecclesiastical action. The council formed by the revival preachers before the organization of our first presbytery addressed a letter to the General Assembly, in which they say: "We never have embraced the idea of an unlearned ministry. The peculiar state of our country and the extent of the revival reduced us to the necessity of introducing more of that description than we otherwise would. We sincerely esteem a learned and pious ministry, and hope the church will never be destitute of such an ornament."[1]

The first presbytery of our church thought proper to place itself on record also. The very first year of that presbytery's existence it addressed a circular letter to the churches under its care, in which it told those churches, and all the others concerned in the

---
[1] Smith's History, p. 624.

case, to have no fears of any laxness in educational requirements; declaring its purpose to require a classical education in all cases where that was practicable, and when, in exceptional cases and emergencies *that* was dispensed with, in *no* case to dispense with a thorough English education.[1]

Our first presbytery, the first year of its existence, commenced raising money to educate its young preachers. It instructed those who came as candidates, while still young enough to secure an education, to go to school first. Philip McDonnold was a poor boy, who had shown his eagerness for an education before he applied to presbytery to be received as a candidate. Presbytery determined to receive him and defray the expenses of his thorough education, and it carried out this determination. This was the first year of that presbytery's life and its first official act about education. The official records of our first three presbyteries abound in strong declarations of the great importance of an educated ministry, and declare it to be "absolutely necessary for us to have a college of our own."

A convention of delegates from the presbyteries met in 1822 to consider the question of a college for the church. See Minutes of Elk Presbytery, and other minutes. Three years before we had a General Assembly, those founders of our church, who traveled in homespun clothing made by their wives, and carried text-books in their saddle-bags while they went seeking the lost among the pioneer settlements, established, through the General Synod, a college for the education of young preachers. Our later work need not now be mentioned.

A curious fact of history deserves now to be noticed. It is this: During the first twenty years of our existence, what was called "the anti-revival party" of the mother church strenuously denied that lack of classical education was one of the charges against us.[2] Heresy and disorderly conduct in revival meetings were then asserted to be the offenses. Our church had, at first, no theological literature, and it was an easy matter to make people who knew us not

---

[1] Dr. Frizzell's Semi-centennial Pamphlet, p. 14.
[2] See "The anonymous pamphlet of Kentucky Synod;" J. L. Wilson's letters in *The Standard*, 1832; *Religious and Literary Intelligencer*, April 5, 1832, etc.

believe that we held horrible heresies. Not only were we charged privately and publicly with the grossest heresies, but also with the most abominable practices in our meetings. Good and true men who lived where we were unknown believed these reports which appeared in pamphlets and newspapers, and repeated them in dignified volumes. The Rev. J. L. Wilson, D.D., who was one of the commission, and who never ceased to pursue and persecute "the Cumberlands" till he was called to his final account, wrote a long article for his church paper in 1832, taking the same ground, and declaring the statement in Buck's Theological Dictionary about the educational issue to be a falsehood. David Lowry, then editing our church paper, replied to Dr. Wilson, and argued that education was one of the issues. [See *Religious and Literary Intelligencer*, April 5, 1832.]

How the winds do change! Now the cry is that the question of ministerial education was the real cause of the schism, and the doctrinal difference is ignored or denied altogether. Once we were charged with denying the atonement, denying original sin, denying imputation,[1] and with various similar heresies. Now it is asserted even by the New York *Observer* that practically, and in our pulpits, "there is no difference." It would not be hard to point out the reason for this shifting of the winds, but it would not be edifying. No harm comes to us from these charges. The taunts about education have done us good. Let us go on our way trying to please God, and pay no attention to any misrepresentations which men may make of us or our doctrines.

The main question stands to-day about where it did in 1800. Many millions are perishing for lack of the gospel. It is a modern thought, revived from New Testament examples, after a long sleep, that the gospel is to be carried with the utmost zeal and speed to every perishing human being. To shut it up in a select circle, and deliver it officially from stately pulpits with learned illustrations and elegant diction before cultivated audiences, may suit the tastes of ambitious ecclesiastics; but there is a far more stirring view of its solemn mission which is beginning to break in upon the vision

---

[1] See Dr. Wilson's charges quoted in *Religious and Literary Intelligencer*, February and April, 1832. See also Pittsburgh *Herald*, 1835, *passim*.

of modern churches. The appalling spectacle of a city on fire presents no such stirring appeals for sympathy and assistance as do the millions of our fellow-men who are now perishing in their sins. There is no time to lose. Our generation will be beyond the reach of the gospel when we pass away.

God is dealing with the churches of this day. While lay evangelism has been abused, it is manifest that God is in it. Educate? Yes, to the utmost. Let all secure the best training possible. When good men have spirituality and aptness to teach, and feel it to be their duty to proclaim salvation to lost men, but have no opportunity to secure a classical education—hold them back? No, never.

Who would blot out the record of Moody's work? Ah! even Dr. McCosh, at staid old Princeton, gives Moody a hearty welcome to those classic seats; and God uses Moody even there. Yes, and uses him at the grand old colleges of England, too.

The Southern Presbyterian church, which has been so wonderfully conservative, is seriously considering the propriety of changing its standard on this subject. A standing committee has been appointed to investigate the question. A long circular has been sent out by one of that committee, ably advocating the change. This circular shows that the ratio of increase in a hundred years between the Presbyterian and Methodist churches is as 47 to 1051. It shows that "aptness to teach," which *is* a Bible qualification, is not proved by the possession of a college diploma, which *is not*. Indeed, there is no essential connection between the two. It shows that the evangelization of the masses was not in the plans of the Westminster Assembly.

The one great question which the awakened Christianity of to-day has to settle is how best to evangelize the masses. This one great work will require the diligent use of all the church's forces. We have not a man or a woman to spare. In some sphere or other all are to help. Men, women, and little children are all to share in this activity for Jesus. God will lead each trusting soul, and indicate to each one who is pliant in his hands just what work to do. Consecrated workers in still greater numbers, we trust, are coming up to give heart and life, tongue and pen, to the service of the

King. Ecclesiastical courts may advise and help, they may pray for and defend them; they may and they will soon be forced to provide a place in their ecclesiastical machinery for this uncanonical army, which cares a thousand times more for souls than it does for church canons and rubrics. The churches which refuse to do so will go into the same category with the Jewish church after it rejected its own Messiah.

One measure which is both scriptural and canonical needs to be revived by all the presbyteries: that is the policy of licensing catechists or exhorters. If that had been diligently followed, many of the embarrassing questions of the present day would have been forestalled.

Another step will have to be taken. God in his providence has sent us back to learn over again the teachings of his word about woman's sphere in helping on the gospel.

When Mrs. Ranyard, unaided by any ecclesiastical recognition, by the simple prayer of faith secures the necessary means and employs two hundred Bible-women to labor all the time for Jesus among the outcast portions of London; and when God blesses these labors to thousands of perishing souls, what church court would dare come in with its ecclesiastical gag to stop these women's mouths?

When Elizabeth Clay, leaving her aristocratic home among the high-churchmen of England, goes to heathen India, and year after year makes a regular circuit of a thousand miles preaching Jesus to the women of heathendom, and God uses her in leading many to salvation who never heard the gospel from other lips, shall any mitered churchman dare interpose his ecclesiastical gag, and say to this devoted woman, Stop! this is not canonical?

One of the bitter complaints against the revival methods of 1800 was that women would "get happy," and even dare to exhort sinners in church and in public. It was to one such exhortation that the church and the country owes, under God, the conversion of that holy servant of Jesus, the Rev. James B. Porter. Would that we had more such women now.

What, in my estimation, is needed in ecclesiastical courts is to provide for and lead this lay activity, and not sit still and be led and superseded by it. For lack of fatherly direction (not suppression), it has run into many hurtful errors, and may yet become extensively mischievous; while with proper direction it may yet be the church's right arm of power. In saying this it is not intended to reflect upon or set aside the regular ministry, but rather to stir up their pure minds by way of remembrance.

5

CHAPTER VIII.

THE THIRD DIFFICULTY—DOCTRINES—RESERVATIONS IN ADOPTING THE BOOK.

The wages of sin is death; the gift of God is eternal life.

Nell' mezzo del cammin.[1]—*Dante.*

THE young men, when licensed by the Cumberland Presbytery, made reservations in adopting the Confession of Faith. They thought that a particular and limited atonement and unconditional election amounted to fatality. They were willing to take the book "for substance," after precedents which could be cited in great numbers, but they are of no value to us now. If the traditional system of Calvinism, without any modern liberalizing, is to be maintained at all, then no reservation in the adoption of the book should be tolerated for one moment. Reservation is a leak in the dykes of Holland. The whole vast sea of modern thought presses on the barriers. "If the book were not in existence, there is no modern church which would ever produce it."[2] The one lingering hope is to hold the anchorage to "the time-honored standards." How long that anchorage will hold time will reveal.

There are meanings to the word fatality which all know do not attach to the Westminster Confession. There are others which many people still think apply to that book. Webster defines fate to mean, among other things, "A decree or word pronounced by God;" "A fixed sentence by which the order of things is prescribed;" "*inevitable necessity.*" These are the popular and common ideas of what fatality means: the doctrine of inevitable necessity. It carried the chief thinkers of the world once. Its reign took in the purest and best men of another age; but "*Ilium fuit.*"

I quote here an illustration of the doctrine which our fathers

---

[1] In the middle of the track.
[2] Dr. James H. Brooks said this in substance, if not *ipsissimis verbis.*

called fatality. The quotation is from grand old John Bunyan. "Is there ever a time in the life of a sinner, who is not one of the elect, when it is possible for him to repent and be saved? To this I answer emphatically, No."[1] This is the doctrine from which modern thought shrinks shivering away. If this doctrine be not in the Westminster Confession, then there are some very unfortunate paragraphs in the book which greatly need to be changed.

Our fathers believed that no man is sent to hell without having a chance to be saved. They preached the doctrine of a general atonement, and the operation of the Holy Spirit on all men.

And now I come to a vital part of this history. The one supreme difficulty which *could not be reconciled*, and which still stands an insuperable obstacle to a reunion, is this doctrinal difficulty.

Dr. Davidson, in his history of "the Cumberland schism,"[2] says: "It was not the want of classical learning, but *unsoundness in doctrine*, the adoption of the Confession with *reservations* (charge second, as already alluded to), that created the grand difficulty; and the removal of this would have wonderfully facilitated the accommodation of the other."

Samuel Hodge was one of "the young men." His literary qualifications were much lower than Ewing's or Anderson's, but when he agreed to adopt the Confession without reservation, he was taken back, and allowed to continue his ministry. All the young men who were involved in this difficulty, after some delay, made an offer to the Transylvania Presbytery that they would yield on all other points, and come back in a body,[3] if they might still be allowed to make this reservation about fatality; and their offer was rejected.

Two charges were brought officially against these preachers by the commission of Kentucky Synod: (1) That they were illiterate; (2) That they held erroneous doctrine.[4] In the apology for their proceedings, made by the members of Kentucky Synod to the Gen-

---

[1] This quotation is given from memory.
[2] Davidson's History Presbyterian church in Kentucky, p. 255.   [3] Ibid., p. 256.
[4] Davidson's History Presbyterian church in Kentucky, p. 239, where the Minutes of the Commission are quoted. "Not only illiterate, but erroneous in sentiment," is the wording.

eral Assembly, they stated explicitly that unsoundness in doctrine constituted the chief difficulty; and they deny that the lack of classical education was the greatest difficulty.[1]

The General Assembly, in 1814, gave a deliverance about the Cumberland Presbyterians, in which the following words were used: "'The grounds of their separation were that we would not relax our discipline *and surrender important doctrines*.[2] [Italics mine.]

The members of the council, after the Assembly gave its final decision against them in 1809, sent two commissioners to negotiate with the synod for a reconciliation. The terms laid down by the members of the synod, on which they were willing to be reconciled, included an unconditional adoption of the Confession of Faith.[3]

In 1811 there were three other ecclesiastical deliverances about this doctrinal difficulty. The West Tennessee Presbytery and the Muhlenberg Presbytery (Presbyterian) undertook to secure a reconciliation. First, they addressed, through an unofficial letter, some inquiries to the General Assembly about what terms could be accepted. The answer was, among other things, an unconditional adoption of the book.[4]

This doctrinal difficulty stands to-day the main barrier between the Cumberland Presbyterians and the mother church. Proof of this assertion can be found in the negotiations for organic union in 1866 and 1867 with the Southern church, and 1873 and 1874 with the Northern church. In both of these negotiations (neither of which originated *officially* with the Cumberland Presbyterians[5]), the Cumberland Presbyterian committees offered to surrender every existing difference except the doctrinal one. I have all the documents before me, but need not make extracts now. In the platform of union submitted by the Cumberland Presbyterian committee to the Southern church was a new creed, which contains about as much Calvinism as we ever hear in Presbyterian pulpits in modern times, but that platform was not accepted. It went as far as it is possible for us to go. That platform proposed to take the West-

---

[1] Davidson's History Presbyterian church in Kentucky, p. 255.
[2] Digest, p. 157.   [3] Smith, pp. 635, 681.
[4] Baird's Digest, pp. 157, 645.
[5] Presbyterian General Assembly Minutes (South), 1866, p. 30. Presbyterian General Assembly Minutes (North), 1873, p. 485.

minster Confession entire, except the third, fifth, and eighth chapters, for which it offered the following substitutes:

Chapter III.—Of God's eternal decrees.

Section 1. God did from all eternity adopt the whole plan of his creation and providence with a full knowledge of all the events which would transpire therein, including the sins of men and angels. These events he determined either to bring to pass by his own direct and absolute agency, or to permit them to come to pass in view of the results which his bounding and overruling providence would bring out of the whole plan.

Section 2. According to the determinate counsel and foreknowledge of God, he did from all eternity elect to salvation all true believers in Jesus Christ. This election was perfectly definite as to the persons elected, and also as to their number: and God did in like manner from eternity reprobate to eternal perdition all that finally reject Jesus Christ, and this reprobation was also definite as to person and number.

Section 3. Those of mankind that are predestinated unto life, God, before the foundation of the world was laid, according to his eternal and immutable purpose and the secret counsel and good pleasure of his will, hath chosen in Christ unto everlasting glory, out of mere free grace and love, all to the praise of his glorious grace.

Section 4. As God hath appointed the elect unto glory, so hath he by the eternal and most free purpose of his will, foreordained all the means thereunto. Wherefore they who are elected, being fallen in Adam, are redeemed by Christ, are effectually called unto faith in Christ by his Spirit working in due season, are justified, adopted, sanctified, and kept by his power through faith unto salvation.

Section 5. The doctrine of this high mystery of predestination is to be handled with special prudence and care, that men attending the will of God revealed in his word and yielding obedience thereunto, may from a certainty of their vocation be assured of their eternal election; so shall this doctrine afford matter of praise, reverence, and admiration of God, and of humility, diligence, and abundant consolation to all that sincerely obey the gospel.

We make the same references which are made in the Presbyterian Confession of Faith, with the addition of 1 Peter i. 2, and Romans viii. 29.

Chapter V. We offer the following modification for section fourth:

Section 4. The almighty power, unsearchable wisdom, and infinite goodness of God, so far manifest themselves in his providence, that it extendeth itself not only to those acts which God absolutely decrees, but also to those which he permits, joining with it a most wise and powerful bounding, and otherwise ordering and governing them in a manifold dispensation to his own holy ends.

Chapter VIII. We offer the following as a substitute for section eight:

Section 8. Although Jesus Christ tasted death for every man, according to the Scriptures, yet the benefits of this death are savingly applied to those only who are chosen unto life through sanctification of the Spirit and belief of the truth; but to all those thus chosen these benefits are so applied as to insure their eternal salvation.

We offer the tenth chapter in the Cumberland Presbyterian Confession of Faith, instead of the tenth chapter in the Presbyterian Confession of Faith.

In chapter seventeen we offer this change in section second: substitute for the phrase "not upon their own free will," the phrase "not upon their own ability or merit."

Finally, we propose to modify certain expressions in the Catechisms, so as to make them correspond with the changes indicated in reference to the Confession of Faith.

As far as possible the wording of the old book was retained, even when it required some explanation to fit that wording into the general scheme. The tenth chapter, on effectual calling, in our book differs from the old in the meaning put on the word "calling." Whether the hard places in the Westminster Confession be justly called fatality or not, they are too hard for us. We believe the doctrine of grace, but we think it needs to be restated.

One fact most clearly pointing to this necessity is that there are no Calvinists now of the type which composed the majority of the Westminster Assembly. Leaving Supralapsarian and Infralapsarian questions all out of the discussion, it is plain to all who study the writings of the Westminster divines that many of them believed, as Calvin before them did, that there are infants in hell. No modern Presbyterians believe any such a thing. No man dare preach any such a doctrine now.

In the first draft of Westminster doctrines, the majority stated their creed, "elect of infants." The liberal party objected. To compromise matters, the statement was so modified that both parties might claim it, but with a very decided advantage given to the interpretation which the majority wished to put on the deliverance: "Elect infants" are saved. So of other places. The creed is a compromise, but always with an immense advantage given to the views of that hyper-Calvinistic majority.

In modern times it is the hardest surviving type of rigid Calvinists who insist on an unconditional adoption of the creed. The liberal party insist on the phrase, "for substance." Robert Shaw had easy sailing in interpreting the book according to the hard old traditional Calvinism. Dr. Morris and Dr. Schaff have a hard time of it trying to fit the liberal system to the book. True, it can be done; but the process by which it is done is itself objectionable.

A genuine Calvinist of the liberal school gave utterance to this same view of the case while advocating before his presbytery a change in some of the hard places in the book. This Calvinist was the Rev. Dr. MacCrae, of the United Presbyterian church of Scotland. His speech was made in 1876, and reported by the press. He says:[1] "I am aware that every doctrine in the book can be defended or explained away. But some of the casuistry employed for this purpose is as discreditable as the doctrine it is used to defend. For instance, the Confession says 'elect infants' are saved. The other side of the doctrine obviously is that non-elect infants are cast into hell. This was not only, in former days, admitted and preached, but within the memory of fathers and brethren in this presbytery, one of the most eminent ministers of our church was like to have been brought before the church courts for denying it."

When the Synod of Diospolis arraigned Pelagius for heresy, one of the charges brought against him was that he taught that unbaptized infants dying in infancy are saved. It is vain to deny that the world, including the Calvinists, has been drifting slowly away from this and other hard doctrines since Pelagius.

Another proof that some of the hard expressions of the old book need to be changed, is found in the outburst of protest against it coming from real Calvinists whenever the spirit of evangelism comes upon them. To quote all these protests would fill many a volume. As Dr. Phelps (speaking of these stern doctrines) says: "A preacher . . . . finds them to be incumbrances upon the working power of the pulpit." Whenever his heart grows warm

---

[1] Quoted from the *Evangelical Repository*, March, 1877.

with the gospel he begins to feel that something is wrong in the creed. Thus Dr. Chalmers breaks forth:

The commission put into our hands is to go and preach the gospel to every creature under heaven, and the announcement sounding forth to all the world from heaven's vault was, Peace on earth, good-will to men. There is no freezing limitation here, but a largeness and munificence of mercy, boundless as space, free and open as the expanse of the firmament! We hope, therefore, that the gospel, the real gospel, is as unlike the views of some of its interpreters as creation in all its boundless extent is unlike the paltry schemes of some wretched scholastic of the middle ages. The middle age of science and civilization is now terminated; but Christianity also had its middle age, and this, perhaps, is not yet fully terminated. There is still a remainder of the old spell, even the spell of human authority, and by which a certain cramp or confinement is laid upon the genius of Christianity. We can not doubt that the time of its complete emancipation is coming, ... but meanwhile there is, as it were, a stricture upon it, ... and by virtue of which the largeness and liberality of Heaven's own purposes have been made to descend in partial and scanty droppings through the strainers of an artificial theology, instead of falling, as it ought, in a universal shower upon the world.[1]

That stanch leader among modern Calvinists, Dr. Philip Schaff, of Union Theological Seminary, says of the Westminster Confession: "Predestination to death and damnation . . . . ought never to be put in the creed or Confession of the church, but should be left to the theology of the school."[2] Again, he says of the seventh section of the third chapter: "This seventh section is one dark spot on the Confession, and mars its beauty and usefulness."[3] He has many other expressions showing that he holds the doctrine of grace in much the same sense that Cumberland Presbyterians do. Many conscientious men who hold about the same views which are preached by men like Dr. Schaff are, nevertheless, too conscientious to adopt the Westminster Confession. One of our men was talking with a modern Calvinist, when the latter said to him, "Why, you preach as much Calvinism as I do. You would have no difficulty in our church." The answer was, "O the ministry in your church is like a bottle: there is room enough when you get in, but there

---

[1] Inst., Vol. II., ch. vi.   [2] Creeds of Christendom, Vol. I., p. 791.
[3] Creeds of Christendom, Vol. I., p. 792. Note.

is such a narrow neck to pass through before you get in." Yes, that is the trouble.

Cumberland Presbyterians believe pretty much the same doctrines that the liberal modern Calvinists preach, but they can not get through the neck. They believe in total depravity. They believe that man is utterly unable to come to Christ till he is drawn by God's Spirit. They believe that all the initiative steps toward salvation are from God. They believe that even infants need regeneration. They believe the theory of justification by faith alone. They believe in the imputed righteousness of Christ. They believe that the Christian's legal standing is in Jesus and not in works. They believe that God's overruling providence extends to every thing, but is not the author of every thing. They believe in the perseverance of the saints, but they can not take that third chapter of the Westminster Confession. They would have no difficulty in accepting the doctrinal declaration[1] of the United Presbyterian Church of Scotland, if it were not for the book to which it is appended.

One trouble with all of us is that we want our creeds to be theodicies. When man knows all that God knows then he may write a theodicy, and not till then. As Dr. Schaff says, the Westminster Confession attempts to give deliverances on matters that ought never to go into a church creed. As Dr. Phelps says, that book contains doctrines which we can not use in our work for Jesus. While the Cumberland Presbyterians aimed at making a working creed, it is a pity that they still exhibited some of the old penchant for making a theodicy. In the main, though, theirs is a creed for the pulpit and the mission.

A typical fact exceedingly significant, is found in the debates of the Belfast council of Presbyterians about the admission of our delegates. A precious Presbyterian missionary to the heathen was the mover and the advocate of our admission. A Presbyterian preacher who, it is said, has charge of no congregation—a scholastic Calvinist—was the chief opponent to our admission. Both he and Dr. Worden, of Philadelphia, in their remarks, betrayed

---

[1] Declaration of 1879. I have a copy in the handwriting of its author, sent me by Dr. Ferguson, of Glasgow.

the profoundest ignorance of the transactions of their own General Assemblies, and provoked Dr. Morris, of Lane Seminary, to give them a whack over the shoulders which was heard clear across the Atlantic.

Workers, wherever we find them, who have their hearts set on the salvation of lost men, extend to Cumberland Presbyterians the most hearty co-operation. Even at a time when the ecclesiastical bitterness which "the Cumberland schism" produced was still a burning fire in Kentucky, the Presbyterian missionaries then in Mississippi Territory passed resolutions inviting the Cumberland Presbyterian church to send more preachers among them, and indorsing those already there.[1] Yes, this is our place, our field, our mission, beside those live workers who are struggling for souls. God never called us to scholasticism. Writing theodicies is not in our commission. Working for souls with all our forces is.

Side by side with every man that loves Christ more than all other things, to struggle for the evangelization of the world, is the high calling which God has given to the Cumberland Presbyterian church. With all our forces used, whether more or less learned; with all our creed, practical and available for the pulpit, to take our places in the solemn, thrilling struggle for those now perishing, is the mission to which God calls us. If aught in our policy or in our creed fits not into this mission, let it be abandoned. With sweet confidence to go wherever there are lost men, and without any "freezing limitations," to preach Christ, not theories about him, not works, not doctrines, but a personal divine Deliverer who will save all that accept and trust him—this is our first mission.

Our second mission is also Christ—to preach him to the Christian; Christ dwelling in us; realized by faith, as the way of victory over all evil habits, as the way of sanctification. To preach, not works, not self, not some imparted power, not some second conversion, not theories about sanctification, not growth, but that "same Jesus" who dwells in us, trusted for victory over sin's power, just as he was trusted for victory over sin's penalty, and

---

[1] *Revivalist*, April 17, 1833.

this also without any "freezing limitation"—this is our second mission.

Our third mission is also Christ—to preach the indwelling God, not some imparted thing, but Christ in us, realized by faith as the way of all power for service, with no "freezing limitation." Not human attainments, but Christ accepted and installed as King within, and his presence realized by faith, and his promise, "I will never leave thee nor forsake thee," clung to and believed in, in spite of all failures, not on account of the dead covenant of works, but on account of the everlasting covenant of grace—ah, this made our first preachers a race of invincible heroes! In this work, and with a faith like this, we can never make a failure.

In all three of these missions both the extremes between which we steer our way present "freezing limitations." If works are to be relied on in either of the three, then the limitation comes from the rottenness, and imperfections, and uncertainties of all human works. If the "unalterable necessity" of "unconditional" theology be the iron fence that bounds our hopes, then the "freezing limitation" in all three of these missions comes from that iron fence.

Our theology is belief in the boundless divinity of the Redeemer, able, ready, and willing, in each of the three missions, on the simple condition of trust and nothing else to give us the victory. No preparation is necessary, no human scaffolding up to salvation or other blessings, but Christ trusted just as we are. Our starting point is not God's eternal and unrevealed decrees, nor man's will nor man's powers, but Christ and his divine power, and his dying love, and his unfailing promises, and his gracious invitations. This is the tried corner-stone of our system.

Christ is the *truth* as well as the way. A theological school may cover a student all over with theories about Christ, and hide a personal Savior from his eyes so as to send him out at last a mere proclaimer of theories. Or it may be an institution conducted by men who are themselves filled with all the fullness of God; who not only know the power of the indwelling Savior, but have experience and success in leading others to that knowledge; and they may lead their pupils on and up in the blessed experience of the divine life till those pupils, when they go out into their life-work, will be an army filled with divine power. The latter is the only type of a theological school which will ever fit into the Cumberland Presbyterian system, or be in harmony with Cumberland Presbyterian antecedents. From all others may the good Lord deliver us.

CHAPTER IX.

FOURTH DIFFICULTY—TRAMPLING ON A PRESBYTERY'S CONSTITUTIONAL RIGHTS BY A SYNODICAL COMMISSION.

> In vain they smite me; men but do
> What God permits with different view;
> To outward sight they wield the rod,
> But faith proclaims it all of God.
> —*Madame Guyon.*

THE two parties in Cumberland Presbytery got further and further apart. The "anti-revival" party was in a hopeless minority in the presbytery, but it had a large majority in the Kentucky Synod. In 1805 that synod appointed a commission of ten ministers and six elders to meet at Gasper River meeting-house and investigate the proceedings of Cumberland Presbytery and take such action as the case required. This commission was composed of all the men in the "anti-revival" party of the synod who had rendered themselves most obnoxious to the other party. Whether justly or not, the revival party believed that the work aimed at by the commission was not the correction of abuses, but the suppression of the revival. All the preachers and probationers for the ministry belonging to the revival party of Cumberland Presbytery received a regular citation to appear before this commission. Most of them obeyed. The commission met December 3, 1805.

I have before me a full copy of the proceedings of the commission, taken from the record book by Lowry and Smith, while they were editing the church paper. The words of the charges are these:

They did license a number of young men to preach the gospel, and some of them they ordained to preach the gospel and administer ordinances in the church, contrary to the rules and regulations of the Presbyterian church in such cases made and provided; and, whereas, these men have been required by said presbytery to adopt the said Confession of Faith and Discipline of said church no further than they believe it to be agreeable to the word of God, etc.

These charges are repeated, in substance, three times in the records of the commission, and are, in substance, just what Dr. Davidson makes them. The General Assembly paraphrased the charges thus: "Licensing and ordaining a number of persons, not possessing the qualifications required by our Book of Discipline and without explicit adoption of our Confession of Faith."

No prosecutor was named. No specifications were made, but on these general charges the commission required the Cumberland Presbytery to submit all its probationers for the ministry, and also four of its ordained ministers, to the commission for re-examination. To this requirement the majority of the presbytery refused to submit, claiming that the constitution of the church made the presbytery the sole judge of the qualifications of its own probationers, and that no other church court had a right to arraign and try one of that presbytery's ordained ministers.[1] It was not a case of appeal or of reference. No charges had ever been brought against these four ordained ministers in their own presbytery. Neither the synod nor its commission had any right to originate process of trial in these cases.

The commission then appealed to "the young men," as the accused were called, to come forward and submit to the examination. The young men asked leave to retire and pray for divine direction. Their request was ridiculed, but a telling speech by a layman in favor of granting the request turned the current, and they were allowed to retire. Each went alone to the woods for silent prayer. Each returned alone. Each one separately declined to submit. Then the commission forbade all of them to preach by virtue of any authority received by them from Cumberland Presbytery. Ewing and King, however, did not receive their licensure from Cumberland Presbytery. Of course that fact was forgotten by the commission. The other young men placed under the interdict were numerous, including several mere catechists who never aspired to the work of the ministry; but those whose names

---

[1] Discipline, ch. v. sec. 2.

are of special interest to our people were Robert Guthrie, James B. Porter, David Foster, Hugh Kirkpatrick, Thomas Calhoun, Robert Bell, Ephraim McLean, Alexander Chapman, and William Moore.

But the commission had no right to *originate* process against a minister, nor to suspend or depose a minister. Its action was illegal, unconstitutional, null, and void. Precedents away back in the state church of Scotland are quoted, but there is not one of these precedents that does not reek with the odors of state tyranny, overriding and subduing the lawful church courts. Riding committees, high courts of commission, and popery all go together.

There was a written constitution in the Presbyterian church in America. No matter what was done in Scotland. No matter if the Westminster Assembly itself did ordain men to preach. In the constitution of the American Presbyterian church the sole and exclusive right to ordain was placed, where the Bible places it, in the hands of the presbytery.[1] Nor is there one single word in all the book giving that right to any other court.

As to trial of a preacher, the constitution fixes that beyond all dispute. "Process against a gospel minister shall always be entered before the presbytery of which he is a member." (Discipline, ch. v. 2.)

What then is the synod's redress when a whole presbytery goes wrong in its ordinations? It can dissolve that presbytery, and attach its members to some other.[2]

That intensely partisan history of the Presbyterian church in Kentucky, written by Dr. Davidson, has this remarkable concession about this commission: "Thus terminated one of the most interesting and important convocations ever known in the American church; *without precedent, and, thus far, without imitation.*" [Italics mine.] It seems to be the accepted policy of the Presbyterian church now to obey the constitution, and restrict the right to originate process against a minister to his own presbytery. [See McPherson's Hand Book, pp. 141, 144, 146.]

One significant fact is brought to light by Dr. Crisman's valuable little book, "Origin and Doctrines," pp. 77, 78, and that is that

---

[1] Form of Government, ch. x. sec. 8. [2] Ibid., ch. xi. sec. 4.

the very year in which the first presbytery of our church was organized, the General Assembly of the mother church pronounced the assumptions of a synod to try a minister when there was no appeal —that is, to originate process of trial against a minister—unconstitutional. When asked the next year to reconsider the deliverance of the preceding year on this subject, the Assembly declined to do so, and adhered firmly to its former decision. [See Baird's Digest, pp. 447, 448, 468.]

The General Assembly of 1807 disapproved this assumption of authority by the commission of Kentucky Synod, and if it had not been for the doctrinal trouble, an appeal to that Assembly would have settled all the difficulty.

But no matter what the Assembly did or would have done, the revival party stood on their constitutional rights when they refused to submit to the commission's demands. In doing so they gave a check to popish usurpations in the Presbyterian church so decided, that there has been no effort since to repeat them in that particular way.

Along with the traditions and written testimonies about this meeting of the commission at Gasper River church, come up two conflicting multitudes of angry voices, both, however, agreeing in two things: First, that "the young men" who were arraigned were prayerful, dignified, and firm. Second, that the chief manifestations of bitterness against the commission were made by the people, and not by the revival preachers. To this Mr. Rankin, who never joined the Cumberland Presbyterians, was the only exception.

For the popular feeling it would be easy to find an apology. The object of the commission was looked upon as one more effort to put a stop to the great revival. It was put in the same category with the visits to McGready's churches and McGready's members in 1798 by Mr. Balch, who went from house to house and from church to church, ridiculing the revival, and trying to embarrass the young converts.

The place of meeting was unfortunate. The revival party had been shut out of that meeting-house, and had established their place of worship in the adjacent grove. Among the members of the commission were men who had been the fiercest partisans against the revival. Mr. Lyle, who had succeeded in winning pre-eminence as an unscrupulous enemy of the revival, and who had traveled among the revival churches, as they thought, "in the capacity of a spy," preached the opening sermon—if a harangue three hours long against the measures of Cumberland Presbytery may be called a sermon. Mr. Rankin, the most excitable of the revival party, harangued the people on the other side of the question, going for that purpose to the grove where the revival party had established their place of worship.

The popular feeling of the neighborhood had been roused against "Mr. Lyle and his commission" to such an extent, that none of the people near the church out of which the revival party had been locked, would open their houses to the commissioners. Mr. Cameron, who had also won the title of "the spy," was present with these commissioners. Joshua L. Wilson, who to the day of his death pursued "the Cumberlands" with a malignity which would have disgraced a Romish priest in the days of Martin Luther, was also one of the commissioners. But Rice and other conservative men of the synod were not on the commission.

The revival party complained much of the haughty and dictatorial language used by the commission in all its demands upon them. It often reminded them that they were no longer where they were in a majority, and could have things their own way, but were standing at the bar of their masters, arraigned for trial.

Ah! well; we have had enough of that. God rules. The actors in that scene have all long ago gone before a tribunal which never makes any mistakes. One thing we do know. God still used the revival party in leading poor sinners to their Savior.

6

SECOND PERIOD.

CHAPTER X.

THE NEW CHURCH.

> Small, but a work divine,
> Frail, but of force to withstand,
> Year upon year, the shock
> Of cataract seas that snap
> The three-decker's oaken spine.
> —*Maud.*

AFTER the commission had delivered its verdict, the revival party organized themselves into a council. They agreed on several things. First, that they would not cease preaching on account of any interdict of the commission; second, that they would refrain from official presbyterial action; third, that they would try to keep the revival churches alive and foster the revival; and finally, that they would labor for a reconciliation with the synod and the Presbyterian church.

The revival party failed to appeal from the decision of the commission, because they utterly repudiated its right of jurisdiction in trying and silencing ordained ministers. The next meeting of the synod put all chances of appeal in the prescribed form out of their power, by dissolving the Cumberland Presbytery and remanding all the parties and their complaints to Transylvania Presbytery. It is plain that no appeal could have relieved the doctrinal difficulty, though all the other difficulties might have been settled.

The council spent four years in a vain struggle for reconciliation. It was not God's will that any reconciliation should be effected. The council sent a letter of remonstrance to the General Assembly in 1807. The case was warmly debated. The Assembly sent two letters, one to the synod approving some of its actions, but disapproving its assumption of right to originate trial against a minister, and advising the synod to revise its action. The other letter was to the members of the council, condemning their course in rejecting the doctrine of fatality, but expressing sympathy in other things.

The synod did revise its action, but it re-affirmed its decisions; explaining, however, that its interdict against the ordained preachers was not meant for suspension in the technical sense.[1]

Owing to the failure of the synod to send up its Minutes, the case did not reach the Assembly again till 1809—not in the regular way, at least. The council, however, had a letter before the Assembly of 1808. To this letter an unofficial answer was sent. It was written by Dr. J. P. Wilson. It pronounced the commission unconstitutional, and advised an appeal in the regular way.

In 1809 the Minutes of synod were sent up, accompanied by a letter from the synod, and John Lyle, the bitter enemy of the revival measures, was their bearer and defender. Lyle had, in a high degree, the *donum lachrymarum*—the gift of tears—and in his speech before the Assembly his weeping and his oratory carried the whole house. Dr. Davidson's account of Lyle's speech represents it as having completely turned the tide, so that the Assembly voted unanimously for sustaining all the actions of the synod, in this case, and added a vote of thanks to the synod for its fidelity.[2] Dr. Davidson uses these words about Lyle's speech: "Bursting into tears, he made a most impassioned appeal, and the Assembly were so affected that their final judgment was very different from that to which they had at first inclined." [History of church in Kentucky, p. 119.] The case was now finally and hopelessly decided against the revival party.

In August of the same year, 1809, the council decided to make one final effort at reconciliation with the synod, and if that failed, then to organize an independent presbytery. The council submitted to the synod its ultimatum, the chief point of which was that those who chose to do so should be allowed to make the reservation

---

[1] Davidson, p. 248. Minutes of the Synod, Vol. I., pp. 140, 142.
[2] Davidson's History, p. 250.

about fatality. To this the synod would not agree. The council met in October, 1809, and heard the synod's decision. McGready and Hodge being genuine Calvinists, withdrew and made terms for themselves with the synod. This left the council with only four ordained members—McGee, Ewing, King, and McAdow. McAdow was in feeble health, and had not been meeting with the council. The name of Rankin never appears on the rolls of the council at all. He went off to the Shakers. McGee drew back from carrying out the resolution to organize an independent presbytery. This left them without the constitutional number. They adjourned with the understanding that the solemn obligation into which they had entered to form an independent presbytery should remain in force till the next March, when, if a presbytery was not previously constituted, the council was to be disbanded.

Things looked gloomy. Ewing was willing to constitute with only two ordained ministers. James B. Porter, a licentiate, exerted himself to enlist a third. Ewing and King met together and went to the house of Ephraim McLean to consult with him. McLean's wife joined earnestly in the consultation.[1] This was the second day of February, 1810. The party remained till a late hour that night at McLean's before reaching their decision, which was that they would go next day to the Rev. Samuel McAdow's house, in Dickson County, Tennessee, and ask him to aid in ordaining McLean. It was a long ride, but they were at McAdow's before night. McAdow hesitated. It was a grave step. He spent the whole night in prayer over the case. Next morning his face was all aglow with light. He said God had given him clear assurance that the proposed step was approved of Heaven.

On the fourth of February, 1810, they organized, or reorganized, the Cumberland Presbytery, and ordained Ephraim McLean. Years afterward, on his death-bed, Mr. McAdow spoke of that action, and said that he had never since doubted the rectitude of their course in organizing that presbytery, and believed it was done under divine sanction and direction.

Against these three men no charges had ever been brought by their own presbytery, which was the only ecclesiastical court to

---

[1] Incidents furnished by the Hon. F. E. McLean.

which the written constitution of the church gave the right to originate process of trial against an ordained minister. The Kentucky Synod itself, after the action of its commission had been called in question by the General Assembly, explained that the action of the commission was not meant for suspension in the technical sense of that word.

Dr. Ely, who held a high position in the Presbyterian church, published a long article in the *Philadelphian* in regard to the Cumberland Presbyterians. In this article he uses the following words: "Of these three men (Ewing, King, McAdow) it is admitted on all hands that they were never deposed from the Christian ministry." This whole article is published in the *Revivalist* of May 14, 1834, and brings to light the fact that the General Assembly sent a committee to the Kentucky Synod to remonstrate with that body about the proceedings of its commission. Ah, well! Lyles' tears set that all right afterward.

After the organization of the new presbytery, a judicature of the mother church proceeded to silence or depose these three preachers, but these acts were as harmless as the bulls of the Pope hurled at Luther, after Luther had renounced the Pope's authority. As the new presbytery grew, circulars and other publications were sent out warning the people that the new church had no right to administer ordinances. This provoked a smile from some, and drew forth from others a sharp reply. The reply held up in contrast the ordination of the first Presbyterians by Roman bishops, with the ordination of Ewing, King, and McAdow by a regular presbytery. It pointed to the fact that a large majority of the Westminster Assembly divines got their ordination from a single bishop. It contrasted the first presbytery of the mother church, organized by Viret and Farel, with the organization of the Cumberland Presbytery. It called attention to the fact that neither of these two men—Viret and Farel—had ever been authorized to *ordain*, but only to *preach*, when they proceeded to ordain Calvin. The efforts to break down the young church by this mode of attack utterly failed, and were soon abandoned.

I have used the language of Dr. Davidson in calling this "the Cumberland schism," but this epithet is misleading. Only four ministers came out of the mother church into ours at that time. The first meeting of the new presbytery had no churches represented. The second meeting, regular, had just one. The third meeting had none. The fourth meeting, after a year of wonderful toil, had six. The fifth had eight. Several of these had been organized by the new presbytery. By and by some more of the churches, which had been with the revival party before the split, cast in their lots with the new church, but never enough of them to amount to a schism. The membership of the Cumberland Presbyterian church to-day is, ninety per cent. of it, made up of converts won from Satan's dominion, and not of proselytes won from other churches. In the beginning it was an exceedingly little church.

> "The green tiny pine shrub shoots up from the moss,
> The wren's foot would cover it, tripping across,
> The beech-nut, down dropping, would crush it beneath;
> But warmed by heaven's sunshine and fanned by its breath,
> The seasons fly past and its head is on high,
> And its thick branches challenge each mood of the sky."

Our concern now, and for the remainder of this history, is with the work of the new church. The new Cumberland Presbytery held four sessions the first year. At these four meetings it ordained four men to preach the gospel. Besides these four, William McGee came in. He had been with them in heart all the time. Never was there greater activity and zeal than the new presbytery manifested in trying to carry the gospel to everybody within its reach. Grand meetings were held; new churches were organized, and missionaries were sent into the most destitute regions, even of the mountain districts. Dr. J. Berrien Lindsley has rendered the church good service by publishing all the Minutes of the Cumberland Presbytery, but ecclesiastical records can not be given here. Some important actions of the new presbytery must suffice. One of these was a last effort at reconciliation. Commissioners met for the purpose, but they not only failed, but made the breach wider, because our people refused to surrender their reservations about fatality. Another matter worth mentioning was the purchase of a circulating library by the presbytery for the benefit of its probationers. This was a policy long kept up in all the presbyteries.

Another was the temporary adjustment of the difficulties about "the union" with the Methodists, mentioned in a former chapter. Another, and a very important measure, was raising a fund for the education of some of its candidates for the ministry.

There was in this presbytery, as there was in the other denominations of that day, a mode of dealing with probationers for the ministry which belongs now to the returnless past. The same feeling which gave rise to college laws requiring a freshman when he saw a senior approaching, to stand to one side, hat in hand, till the senior passed, and which required freshmen to black the seniors' boots, showed itself in all the treatment of boys, whether by parents, school-teachers, or presbyters. To curb, to humble, to train to physical endurance, and the endurance of wrongs and outrages, was considered an essential part of the discipline through which a boy had to be taken. Authority was a tremendous thing in those days. A presbyter was an autocrat among the probationers, and woe be to that youth who, in presbytery or out of presbytery, disregarded that autocrat.

While this was the accepted rule in such matters, there were men whose naturally kind hearts made them, in the eyes of their stricter co-presbyters, grave defaulters in enforcing this system. I fear they felt very guilty when they remembered their delinquencies, but those delinquencies left a warm glow of hope and courage in many a poor boy's heart. About the close of this presbyterial period a new order of things came about. Men began to break the old regimen. At a later day still, spirits as sweet as an angel's, even in dealing with boys, were led by such genial souls as John L. Dillard, George Donnell, and James K. Lansden. What a thrill of gratitude comes along with the recollection of these blessed servants of God!

One more item about this first presbytery deserves commemoration. All its preachers had a thorough Presbyterian training, and were scarcely behind the Puritans themselves in their profound regard for the Sabbath. The customs of their families in this matter were regulated strictly by the Jewish law. No wood was gathered or carried, much less cut, on the Sabbath. No visiting, no pleasure-riding, no cooking, no strolling through the woods, no whistling, no traveling, except to church, no conversation or reading, except on religious subjects, was tolerated. If a child committed an offense worthy of stripes the penalty was delayed till Monday morning. Stripes were not scarce in those days, except on the Sabbath. An illustration of this Sabbath observance is here given. In my boyhood I went to Thomas Calhoun's to board. My training on Sabbath observance had been of the modern character. Sabbath morning came, and, seated in "Aunt Polly" Calhoun's room, I picked up a newspaper and went to reading. Mrs. Calhoun stared at me a moment, and then said, "That's a political newspaper, sir." I wondered why she told me that. Did she think I had not sense enough to know what sort of paper it was? I read on. Presently "Aunt Polly" raised her glasses and, with an emphasis that frightened me, she said, "We do n't read political newspapers on Sunday, sir." O I knew then why she told me what sort of paper it was. That was lesson number one in a Presbyterian Sabbath. I counted those lessons by the hundred before my acquaintance with "Aunt Polly" closed. The precious, sterling, kind hearted old Puritan that she was! She used to put sugar in my sweet milk; she used to mend my clothes, and fill a mother's place to me, but she would not let me do wrong. I am thankful for that last item now more than for the sugar in my sweet milk.

There was another candidate for the ministry boarding at Calhoun's, going to school. One Saturday he went visiting, stayed all night, came to church next morning, and then came home. There was nothing said that day, but Monday morning before breakfast the Sabbath-breaker was called. The head of the household then began to clear his skirts of the disobedience to God which one who lived under his roof had been guilty of. That one had been away from home on a visit on the morning of God's holy day, not only sinning himself, but disturbing the Sabbath rest of others, and setting an example of Sabbath-breaking, all the more dangerous because a candidate for the ministry was its author. Worse still, the Sabbath-breaker lived under the authority, as well as under the roof-tree, of an old preacher, and might be supposed to represent the views and practices which that old preacher tolerated.

Turning to the offender with holy indignation, while those eagle eyes blazed with Sinai's fires, he shot words like bullets at the poor fellow till he quailed, and withered, and writhed like a tortured martyr flayed alive. The offense was not repeated by that boarder while he remained at Calhoun's house, although he was a mean man and never came to any good. Calhoun knew him and was intentionally severe.

From the nature of the case the little handful of preachers who composed the presbytery could not settle down into permanent pastorates. In this, as in the matter of education, they wisely adapted their actions to their necessities. In both, that action has since been unwisely urged as a precedent under circumstances wholly different. In the true sense of the word pastor, there was none in the church till many years later. All the ministers of the second period were missionary evangelists. There is no grander chapter in all church history than the record of these evangelistic tours. Their circuits extended over vast fields, some of them five hundred miles in diameter. They were usually sent in pairs, one of the older men and one of the boys. They carried bell and "hobble" for their horses; crackers, cheese, and a tin cup for themselves. To these were added blankets for a bed. If they found lodgings in a house it usually had but one room and they slept on their own blankets. In the morning the owner of the cabin would take his gun and go out to hunt meat for breakfast. Yet in such cabins they held grand meetings and organized churches which stand to-day in the midst of wealthy communities. In many neighborhoods the pioneer farmers were just planting their first crop.

Robert Donnell held a camp-meeting near where Huntsville, Alabama, now stands, before any town was there. Timber grew thick around the great spring, though the camp-meeting was not at that, but at another spring a mile below. Calhoun and others held a camp-meeting at the spring where the town of Monroe, Overton County, Tennessee, was afterward built. None of these men got much, if any, pay at first. They wore homespun clothing made by their mothers or wives, and were at little expense. They often swam the rivers, because there were no ferry-boats except on the thoroughfares.

The ordained missionaries of the presbytery were King, Donnell, Calhoun, McSpeddin, Foster, McLin, Chapman, Harris, Kirkpatrick, Barnett, Bell, and McLean, with large additions to the list toward the close of this presbyterial period. A course of study prescribed by presbytery was regularly kept up by the young men on all these tours of evangelism. They recited to their seniors as they rode along on their horses. This was the normal school of science and divinity for the first Cumberland Presbyterians. While it had its disadvantages, it generally made grand thinkers. Testimonies from the ablest alumni of the old colleges are in existence showing with what a grasp of original thought these men took up an investigation. A college president once sat down with Reuben Burrow to investigate a Bible question. They had gone but a little way in the investigation before the college man saw that he was in the presence of his master. In vigor of original thought, in grasp, and depth, and clearness of discernment, he could hold no hand with Burrow. Dr. Anderson, of the Presbyterian church, warned his friend, Dr. Blackburn, against entering into any controversy with Finis Ewing, on the ground that Ewing would prove too hard for him. He said Ewing had already given Blackburn a Braddock's defeat. [See Life and Times of Ewing, p. 203.]

What heroism it required to enter the ministry under our first presbytery! There were no pastorates, no salaries, no possibility of earthly honors. To travel unpaid on horseback across wild wastes to the homes of pioneers in the new settlements; to swim rivers, and sleep on the bare ground; to go hungry and half clad; to belong to a struggling little church whose doctrines and practices were diligently misrepresented, as they are even to this day; to preach in floorless log-cabins, or gather the rough frontiersmen in camps around some spring, and there labor day and night for a week that poor lost men might be saved, and that our new territories might not all be given over to infidelity; and after all this, to die in poverty at last, was the prospect before that generation of our preachers. Thank God there were men equal to the occasion!

Brief biographical sketches of the ordained ministers of the new presbytery, up to the time it was divided, are here given:

Samuel McAdow was born in North Carolina, April 10, 1760,

and was converted in 1771. He was a graduate of Mechlenburg College; was married to Henrietta Wheatley, in 1788; licensed in 1797, by Orange Presbytery; ordained in 1798 or 1799. He moved to Kentucky in 1799; aided in forming the new church in 1810; moved to Illinois in 1828; and died March 30, 1844.

Finis Ewing was born in Virginia, in July, 1773; was married January 19, 1793, to Peggy Davidson; was a candidate in 1801, receiving licensure in 1802; was ordained in 1803. He assisted in the organization of the new church in 1810, and helped to make the Confession of Faith in 1814; moved to Missouri in 1820; died in 1841.

Samuel King was born in North Carolina, April 19, 1775; was married to Ann Dixon in 1795; licensed in 1802, and ordained in 1804. He aided in forming the new church in 1810; moved to Missouri in 1825; died in 1842.

Ephraim McLean was born June 26, 1768; married Elizabeth Walton Byers, of Virginia; was a candidate in 1802; was licensed in 1803, and ordained by the new Cumberland Presbytery in 1810. He died January 1, 1813.

James Brown Porter was born February 26, 1779, in North Carolina, and was converted in 1801. He became a candidate in 1803; was licensed in 1804, and ordained in 1810. He was twice married. He died in 1854.

William McGee was born in North Carolina, in 1768. He was licensed and ordained in North Carolina before 1796, at which time he was sent West as a missionary. He joined the Cumberland Presbytery in October, 1810, and helped to form the Confession in 1814. He died in 1817.

Robert Bell was born December 16, 1770. He married Grizzell McCutcheon. He was licensed in 1804; was ordained in 1810, and was sent as a missionary to the Indians in 1820. He died October 9th, 1853.

Thomas Calhoun was born in North Carolina, May 31, 1782. He became a candidate in 1803, and was married to Mary Johnson in 1809. He received licensure in July, 1810, and was ordained in 1811. He helped to make our Confession of Faith in 1814. He died in 1855.

Hugh Kirkpatrick, the date of whose birth is not known, was a licensed preacher at the time the commission met in 1805. He was ordained in 1810. He died in 1864.

David Foster was born in North Carolina, May 4, 1780; was licensed in 1805. He married Ann Beard in 1806; was ordained in 1810; moved to Illinois in 1827. He died in 1833.

William Harris was born in 1772, and married Nancy Highsmith in 1797. He was a catechist in 1804, a candidate in 1810, licensed in 1811, and ordained in 1812. He published our first hymn book in 1824. He died in 1845.

William Barnett was born April 24, 1785; was licensed in 1810, and ordained in 1813. He was twice married. He died at a camp-meeting in West Tennessee in 1828.[1]

Alexander Chapman was born in Pennsylvania, January 2, 1776. He married Ann Dixon Carson in 1805; became a candidate in 1805; was licensed in 1811; ordained in 1813. He died in 1834.

David Wilson McLin was born December 24, 1785. He became a candidate in 1810, was licensed in 1811, and married Nancy Johnson Porter in 1812. He died in his adopted home in Illinois, in 1836.

Robert Donnell was born in North Carolina, in April, 1784. (The family records were destroyed by the Indians.) He was a candidate in 1806, was licensed in 1811, and ordained in 1813. He helped to form the Confession of Faith in 1814. He married Ann E. Smith in 1817. His second wife was Clara W. Lindley, to whom he was married in 1832. He died in 1855.

The licentiates under the care of the first presbytery were Philip McDonnold, William Bumpass, Samuel McSpeddin, and Samuel Donnell. The candidates were Robert Guthrie, John Barnett, John Carnahan, Elisha Price, Green P. Rice, Daniel Buie, Robert McCorkle, James Stewart, Ezekiel Cloyd, Francis McConnell, and Elijah Cherry. A few others conversed with the presbytery about their call to the ministry, and were advised to defer their decision. Most of these came into the ministry after the presbytery was divided, and after a melancholy period of doubt and struggle.

---

[1] Some authorities say he was carried home before he died.

CHAPTER XI.

FIRST AIMS—NECESSITY FOR A SYNOD—ITS ORGANIZATION—SKETCHES OF ITS MEMBERS.

> Man is higher than his dwelling-place;
> He looks up and unfolds the wings of his soul.
> —*Jean Paul Richter.*

> "Thine arm hath led us on,
> A way no more expected
> Than when thy sheep passed through the deep,
> By crystal walls protected."

IT is indicated clearly all through the records of the first presbytery that a separate denomination was not at first aimed at, but only an independent presbytery of the Presbyterian church, with reserved hopes that in some unforeseen manner the breach would one day be healed. These hopes were not all given up even when a synod was formed, as the preamble to the resolution establishing a synod clearly indicates; but the failure of all past efforts at reconciliation, and the necessities of the great work committed to their hands, required them to take one more step.

The Cumberland Presbytery, at the meeting held at Lebanon church, Christian County, Kentucky, November 3, 1812, put on record the fact that it had been struggling for a reunion with the Presbyterian church, and that it still desired such reunion. [See Minutes in the *Theological Medium*, October, 1878, pp. 494, 495.] The preamble to the resolution to form a synod is as follows:

Whereas, we, the Cumberland Presbytery, have made every reasonable effort to be reunited to the general Presbyterian church; and, whereas, from the extent of our bounds, the local situation of our members, their number, etc., it is inconvenient to do business in but one presbytery; and, whereas, the constitution of a synod would be desirable, and we trust of good consequences, in various respects, and particularly as a tribunal having appellate jurisdiction; therefore, resolved, etc.

The Elk and Logan presbyteries were formed. The Elk Presbytery extended from the mouth of Duck River northward to Tennessee Ridge, thence east to the Cumberland Mountains in Middle Tennessee. Its southern boundary was indefinite, but extended as far as the white settlements, and followed up the advancing wave of these settlements. Its first members were William McGee, Samuel King, James B. Porter, Robert Bell, and Robert Donnell. Its first meeting was at Mount Carmel, and William McGee preached the opening sermon.

The Logan Presbytery was bounded on the south by the other two presbyteries, but extended northward indefinitely. Ohio, Illinois, and Indiana Territories were in its field, as were also Pennsylvania and New York. Its members were Finis Ewing, William Harris, Alexander Chapman, and William Barnett. At the organization the sermon was preached by Ewing.

The Cumberland (Nashville) Presbytery was composed of the following members: Thomas Calhoun, David Foster, D. W. McLin, Hugh Kirkpatrick, William Bumpass, Samuel McSpeddin, and Ezekiel Cloyd. The boundaries of this presbytery were limited only by the fields assigned to the Elk and the Logan. The first synod was organized on the 5th day of October, 1813, at the Beech meeting-house, in Sumner County, Tennessee. There were sixteen ordained ministers within its bounds. William McGee preached the opening sermon.

There is a pen and ink sketch of the men who composed this synod at its second meeting, when the Confession was adopted. It was drawn by E. Curry, who was present at the meeting described:

The Rev. Samuel King was the moderator, and with modest step advanced to the chair,[1] and with a solemnity and dignity of countenance peculiar to himself, entered upon the duties of his station. Upon the right sat Finis Ewing, with a keen eye, ready to scan every thing that came before the synod. Near him sat Hugh Kirkpatrick, with a heavy brow, prepared to define hard words and sentences. On his right sat James B. Porter, with a pleasing countenance, as though he was delighted that they were about to smite off the old shackles. . . . . On the left of the moderator sat Robert Donnell, writing resolutions to

---

[1] King was only temporarily in the chair; he was not moderator that session.—B. W. M.

offer to synod. Behind him was David Foster, with a critic's eye to detect any error. In this group sat my favorite, Thomas Calhoun, who once spoke terror to my heart and caused me to cry aloud for mercy. Just in front sat Alexander Chapman, with a serene look and attentive ear, that he might be prepared to give a judicious vote. A little back lay Samuel Donnell, brother of Robert (in an advanced stage of consumption), who seemed to be a sort of concordance to whom all applied for scriptural proofs. Farther back in the house William McGee was seen, tossing to and fro with deep thoughts and heavy groans, soon to be vented in a powerful speech. A little in front sat William Bumpass, a man of ready wit and good judgment, who always had language to tell what he knew. In a corner of the aisle stood William Barnett, about to deliver one of his thundering speeches, which made the walls of the church reverberate with his loud, shrill voice. Several more of the fathers of the church took part in the deliberations of that synod.

We regret that Mr. Curry did not continue his picture. At that meeting were William Harris, D. W. McLin, Robert Bell, Samuel McSpeddin, Ezekiel Cloyd, and Philip McDonnold. These men were "the fathers" of the Cumberland Presbyterian church.

I often, in my boyhood, saw McSpeddin. He used to preach at my father's house on his circuit in the mountains. "Uncle Sam," everybody called him. He was a plain, earnest, honest, good man, and a great favorite with the mountain people. His favorite theme was experimental religion. I once heard Dr. Cossitt beg him to leave his thoughts on that subject in writing for posterity. "Uncle Sam" lived to great age and retained his memory fresh to the last. It was customary with all our writers on biography or history to go to McSpeddin for facts. Even his dates were always found to be reliable. Several times they were questioned, but investigation proved them to be right. His youngest son, Judge McSpeddin, of Center, Alabama, still lives.

I also knew William Harris. He presided in the examination when I was received as a candidate for the ministry. Dr. Beard has given us a beautiful biographical sketch of Harris; the most interesting, I think, of all his biographical sketches. Harris has sons and grandsons still living. One of his grandsons was a little child, two and a half years old, when Father Harris died. The dying man had this child brought to his bed, and laying his hands upon his head poured forth a prayer of great earnestness for God's blessings on the life of the boy. That grandson is now the senior editor of the *Cumberland Presbyterian*.

Philip McDonnold died before my day, but as his father, Redmond McDonnold, was my father's uncle; and as his mother and younger brother, Barnett, long survived him, I used to hear his wonderful career discussed very often. The family lived in what was then called Stoglan's Valley, on the borders of what was then Wayne County, Kentucky. I made many a visit to their home, and the name of Philip was spoken with profoundest veneration. By some strange freak the orthography of his name is perverted into McDaniel, even in the published minutes of his own presbytery. The McDaniels were another family and no kin to the McDonnolds, but a noble preacher rose up among them at a later day. I know that Dr. Beard tried to collect material for a biography of Philip McDonnold, but as he never published the biography, it may be that he failed to secure the necessary facts.

McDonnold was an extemporaneous orator and left no writings at all. The old people said that when he came from the woods (which was the closet of prayer in those days) and went into the pulpit, he was often as white as a sheet. When he began his sermon, pouring down torrents of oratory and of fire upon them, there was but one way to resist, and that was to run as quick as possible out of hearing. Wonderful things are related about the effects of his oratory. People said he often made them feel as if the day of judgment had already come. Many of our old people, David Lowry among the number, insisted that the spiritual power of Philip McDonnold's oratory was never equaled on earth. He married a daughter of General Robert Ewing, who was Finis Ewing's oldest brother, and died in 1815, at the close of his twenty-first year. His only son, Philip Monroe McDonnold, entered the ministry, receiving licensure. He married, and then, like his father, died, leaving only one child. After Philip McDonnold's tongue had been dust for more than fifty years old men still wept when some of his thrilling appeals to sinners were mentioned in their presence.

Dr. Beard's Biographical Sketches give pen-pictures of most

Rev. Thomas Calhoun.

Rev. Robert Donnell.

Rev. R. D. Morrow, D. D.

of the fathers of our church. There is need of a few additions. In the sketch given by Mr. Curry of William McGee there is mention made of his groaning and restlessness. McGee had a long, hard struggle about doctrine. He rejected the stern features of the Westminster Confession, but he could not frame another system of theology which left out these objectionable teachings, and at the same time avoided the opposite extreme. He declined to aid in organizing the independent presbytery. He refrained a long time from preaching. Alone in the woods he labored and prayed over the system which was to take the place of the one he had rejected. A little light dawned on him and he went then and joined the independent presbytery. Still it was an unsettled question what new creed would be adopted under the new conditions. This was the pending question when McGee showed the anxiety described by Mr. Curry. He helped to make the new creed and voted for it. It was unanimously adopted. At last McGee's troubled heart had rest.

7

CHAPTER XII.

THE CONFESSION OF FAITH — SYNOPSIS OF DOCTRINES — FULLER CONFESSION — A MEDIUM SYSTEM — DIAGRAM.

> Not to know at large of things remote
> From use, obscure, and subtile; but to know
> That which before us lies in daily life,
> Is the prime wisdom. What is more is fume,
> Emptiness, or fond impertinence;
> And renders us, in things that most concern,
> Unpracticed, unprepared, and still to seek.
> —*Milton.*

> My banner—from my Master was it to me intrusted—
> Before his throne must I lay it down at last.
> I dare display it, because I have borne it faithfully.
> —*Schiller.*

THE Cumberland Presbytery, before the organization of the synod, had felt the need of a more definite creed. Its candidates for the ministry all adopted the Westminster Confession, with exceptions about fatality. This was too vague. At the very last meeting of the presbytery before the organization of the synod, Finis Ewing and Robert Donnell were appointed a committee to prepare a synopsis of doctrines. Their synopsis was reported to the synod and unanimously adopted. The synod ordered this outline statement of its doctrines to be published. It appeared soon after in Buck's Theological Dictionary. It was as follows:

1. That Adam was made upright, pure, and *free;* that he was necessarily under the moral law, which binds all intelligences; and having transgressed it he was, consequently, with all his posterity, exposed to eternal punishment and misery.

2. That Christ, the second Adam, represented just as many as the first; consequently made an atonement for all, "which will be testified in due time;" but that the benefit of that atonement will be received only by the true believer.

3. That all Adam's family are totally depraved, conceived in sin, going astray from the womb, and all children of wrath; therefore must be born again, justified, and sanctified, or they never can enter into the kingdom of God.

4. That justification is by faith alone as the instrument; by the merits of Christ's active and passive obedience, as the *meritorious* cause; and by the operation of God's Spirit as the *efficient* or active cause.

5. That as the sinner is justified on the account of Christ's righteousness being imputed to him, on the same account he will be enabled to go on from one degree of grace to another, in a progressive life of sanctification, until he is fit to be gathered to the garner of God, who will certainly take to glory every man who is really justified; that is, he, Christ, has become wisdom (light to convince), righteousness (to justify), sanctification (to cleanse), and redemption (to glorify) to every truly regenerated soul.

The sixth item asserts the traditional doctrine of the Trinity. Then the synopsis states its dissent from the Westminster Confession as follows:

1. That there are no eternal reprobates. 2. That Christ died not for a part only, but for all mankind. 3. That all infants dying in infancy are saved through Christ and the sanctification of the Spirit. 4. That the operations of the Holy Spirit are co-extensive with the atonement; that is, on the whole world, in such a manner as to leave all without excuse.

After stating this dissent, our fathers then add:

As to the doctrines of election and reprobation, they think (with many eminent and modest divines who have written on the subject) they are mysterious. They are not well pleased with the application that rigid Calvinists, or Arminians, make of them. They think the truth of that, as well as many other points in divinity, lies between the opposite extremes. They are confident, however, that those doctrines should not, on the one hand, be so construed as to make any thing the creature has done, or can do, at all meritorious in his salvation; or to lay any ground to say, "Well done, I;" or to take the least degree of the honor of our justification and perseverance from God's unmerited grace and Christ's pure righteousness. On the other hand, they are equally confident that those doctrines should not be so construed as to make God the author of sin, directly or indirectly, ... or to contradict the sincerity of God's expostulation with sinners, and make his oath to have no meaning, when he swears he has no pleasure in their death; or to resolve the whole character of the Deity into his sovereignty without a due regard to all his other adorable attributes.[1]

On this platform of doctrine they (the fathers of our church) dared spread their banner to the breeze; and we, their sons, hope, through God's grace, to keep it flying till the grand mission of the everlasting gospel is accomplished. This platform came not from human schools. It owes no debt to ancient or modern philosophy. In the great revival men who studied their English Bibles while laboring for the salvation of souls, rejected the medieval fatalism in that system to which their church adhered, and, without being scholastic enough to attempt a theodicy, they confined their creed to the plain middle of the track of revealed truth.

A cold scholastic logic applied to theology always terminates in one or the other of two extremes. Grace and freedom are Jacob and Esau struggling in the womb together. Logic destroys one or the other and ends the struggle. Practical pulpit theology lets both live, and lets the struggle go on, nor makes any effort at reconciling things which, though both clearly revealed, are, in appearance, irreconcilable. We have far more confidence in a system of theology growing out of a revival, than in a system made by scholastics writing in the midst of their books and aiming at logical consistency.

The synod appointed a committee, consisting of William McGee, Finis Ewing, Thomas Calhoun, and Robert Donnell, to prepare a fuller creed. This committee worked first in two sections. They simply read over the Westminster Confession, item by item, changing such expressions as did not suit them. Then the two sections met and all went through the same process. By order of the synod, all the churches were observing a day of fasting and prayer for divine guidance to be given to the committee. Thomas Calhoun gave the writer a history of their meetings. They prayed much and had a clear assurance that divine direction had been granted.

I have Robert Donnell's memoranda of the action of the synod

Smith, p. 646, *et seq.*

of 1814 on the proposed creed. Though there were some amendments made by the synod, yet it is recorded by Donnell that the vote on every item was unanimous. What the proposed creed was before the synod's amendments we have no means now of knowing. Donnell's memoranda state the action in words like these: "Motion to strike out second clause carried unanimously."

The following exhibit of the principal changes made in the Westminster Confession, which I cut from an article published by Dr. C. H. Bell, will place the doctrinal status of our church before the reader:

CONFESSION OF FAITH OF THE PRESBYTERIAN CHURCH (O. S.).

CHAPTER III.

Of God's Eternal Decrees.

God from all eternity did by the most wise and holy counsel of his own will, freely and unchangeably ordain whatsoever comes to pass; yet so as thereby neither is God the author of sin, nor is violence offered to the will of the creatures, nor is liberty or contingency of second causes taken away, but rather established.

3. By the decree of God for the manifestation of his glory some men and angels are predestinated unto everlasting life, and others foreordained to everlasting death.

4. These angels and men thus predestinated and foreordained are particularly and unchangeably designed; and their number is so certain and definite that it can not be either increased or diminished.

CONFESSION OF FAITH OF THE CUMBERLAND PRESBYTERIAN CHURCH. (1814.)

CHAPTER III.

Of God's Eternal Decrees.

God did by the most wise and holy counsel of his own will, determine to bring to pass what should be for his own glory.

2. God has not decreed any thing respecting his creature, man, contrary to his revealed will or written word; which declares his sovereignty over all his creatures, the ample provision he has made for their salvation; his determination to punish the finally impenitent with everlasting destruction, and to save the true believer with an everlasting salvation.

Section 3 omitted in Cumberland Presbyterian Confession.

Omitted.

6. As God hath appointed the elect unto glory, so hath he, by the eternal and most free purpose of his will, foreordained all the means thereunto. Wherefore they who are elected being fallen in Adam are redeemed by Christ, are effectually called unto faith in Christ by his spirit working in due season; and justified, adopted, sanctified, and kept by his power through faith unto salvation. Neither are any other redeemed by Christ effectually called, justified, adopted, sanctified, and saved, but the elect only.

Omitted.

7. The rest of mankind God was pleased, according to the unsearchable counsel of his own will, whereby he extendeth or withholdeth mercy as he pleaseth, for the glory of his sovereign power over his creatures, to pass by, and to ordain them to dishonor and wrath for their sin, to the praise of his glorious justice.

Omitted.

CHAPTER VIII.
Christ the Mediator.

8. To all those for whom Christ hath purchased redemption, he doth certainly and effectually apply and communicate the same, making intercession for them, and revealing unto them, in and by the word, the mysteries of salvation; effectually persuading them by his spirit to believe and obey. . . .

CHAPTER VIII.
Christ the Mediator.

8. Jesus Christ, by the grace of God, has tasted death for every man, and now makes intercession for transgressors; by virtue of which, the Holy Spirit is given to convince of sin, and enable the creature to believe and obey. . . .

CHAPTER X.
Effectual Calling.

All those whom God hath predestinated unto life, and those only, he is pleased in his appointed

CHAPTER X.
Effectual Calling.

All those whom God calls, and who obey the call, and those only, he is pleased by his word and

and accepted time effectually to call, by his word and Spirit, out of that state of sin and death in which they are by nature, to grace and salvation by Jesus Christ. . . .

3. Elect infants dying in infancy are regenerated and saved by Christ, through the Spirit, who worketh when, and where, and how he pleaseth. So also are all other elect persons who are incapable of being outwardly called by the ministry of the word.

4. Others, not elected, although they may be called by the ministry of the word, and may have some common operations of the Spirit, yet they never truly come to Christ, and therefore can not be saved. . . .

Spirit to bring out of that state of sin and death in which they are by nature, to grace and salvation by Jesus Christ. . . .

3. All infants dying in infancy are regenerated and saved by Christ through the Spirit, who worketh when, and where, and how he pleaseth; so, also, are others who have never had the exercise of reason, and who are incapable of being outwardly called by the ministry of the word.

Omitted.

CHAPTER XVII.
Of the Perseverance of the Saints.

They whom God hath accepted in his Beloved, effectually called and sanctified by his Spirit, can neither totally nor finally fall away from the state of grace; but shall certainly persevere therein to the end, and be eternally saved.

2. This perseverance of the saints depends, not upon their own free will, but upon the immutability of the decree of election, flowing from the free and unchangeable love of God the Father; upon the efficacy of the merit and intercession of Jesus Christ; the abiding of the Spirit and of the seed of God within them; and the nature of the covenant of grace; from all which ariseth also the certainty and infallibility thereof.

CHAPTER XVII.
Of the Perseverance of the Saints.

They whom God hath justified and sanctified he will also glorify; consequently the *truly* regenerated soul will never totally nor finally fall away from the state of grace, but shall certainly persevere therein to the end, and be eternally saved.

2. This perseverance depends on the unchangeable love and power of God; the merits, advocacy, and intercession of Jesus Christ; the abiding of the Spirit and seed of God within them; and the nature of the covenant of grace; from all which ariseth also the certainty and infallibility thereof.

The great majority of the chapters in the Westminster Confession were placed in the new creed without any change at all, the changes here indicated being the only vital ones made. The Catechism was also changed in the matter of decrees to correspond with the views set forth in the new Confession. The chapters on faith, repentance, depravity, and imputation, in the new book, are the same substantially as in the old. The new Confession clearly enunciates the truth that "God so loved the world that he gave his only begotten Son, that whosoever believeth in him should not perish, but have everlasting life;" and that "the manifestation of the Spirit is given to every man to profit withal." Through Christ's atoning grace, and by the Spirit's aid, man can be saved. What need have we of more metaphysics in our creed?

Besides these principal changes, the Confession of Faith of 1814 made some additions to the deliverances of the Westminster standards on the subject of sanctification, and about the gift or baptism of the Holy Spirit. On the former, our fathers, after giving all the thirteenth chapter of the old book, just as it stands, added the following words: "Although the remains of depravity may continue to affect the true believer in this life, yet it is his duty and privilege, through grace, to maintain a conscience void of offense toward God and toward men."

Finis Ewing tells us, in substance, that the compilers of our Confession of Faith aimed at medium ground on the sanctification question. He was one of those compilers. They did not believe that sanctification is all finished until the soul leaves the body; neither did they believe that a life of sin is compatible with that Christianity which has received the baptism of the Holy Ghost. They believed that a Christian could and should maintain a conscience void of offense, and so live free from condemnation.

While they retained as true the phrases about the remains of depravity continuing to affect the believer as long as he remains in the body, yet they feared these expressions might be abused so as to "make provisions for the flesh," and they sought to guard against this abuse by two very strong declarations. [Chap. xiii., sec. 4, and chap. xvii., sec. 3.]

It has been shown in a previous chapter that our fathers believed in an abiding baptism of the Holy Ghost as a distinct blessing after conversion. They changed the wording of the seventeenth chapter so as to give emphasis to this belief.

The Westminster Confession reads (chap. xvii., sec. 3):

Nevertheless, they [Christians] may, through the temptations of Satan and of the world, the prevalency of corruption remaining in them, and the neglect of the means of their preservation, fall into grievous sins, and for a time continue therein: whereby they incur God's displeasure, and grieve his Holy Spirit; come to be deprived of some measure of their graces and comforts; have their hearts hardened, and their consciences wounded; hurt and scandalize others, and bring temporal judgments upon themselves.

The book adopted by our fathers reads (chap. xvii., sec. 3):

Although there are examples in the Old Testament of good men having egregiously sinned, and some of them continuing for a time therein, yet now, since life and immortality are brought clearer to light in the gospel, and especially since the effusion of the Holy Ghost on the day of Pentecost, we may not expect the true Christian to fall into such gross sins. Nevertheless, they may, through the temptations of Satan, the world and the flesh, the neglect of the means of grace, fall into sin, and incur God's displeasure, and grieve his Holy Spirit; come to be deprived of some measure of their graces and comforts, and have their consciences wounded; but the real Christian can never rest satisfied therein.

If the quotations from McAdow's sermons, in the chapter on the Paraclete, are compared with this change in the Confession, the reasons for the change will be understood. Of all the doctrines held by our fathers, the one about this abiding baptism of the Holy Ghost was most esteemed by them. Gradually it was allowed to be crowded into the background, after our fathers went to their rest. In nearly all our early judicatures of this period, strong resolutions are placed on record about the necessity of a godly life. It is constantly affirmed by all our early writers that all Christians should live in abiding communion with God. A state of full assurance was insisted on in every protracted meeting which these men held.

But enough of this digression. The Confession, studied as a whole, interpreting the scraps and phrases by the general tenor of the book, and not interpreting the whole tenor of the book by these phrases, teaches "the medium system"—a medium between the old time Calvinism and Arminianism.

It has been so often denied that there can be any medium ground between Calvinism and Arminianism, that a few words on that subject seem necessary. The assertion of impossibility is a father's hat on a boy's head. Originally it was, "There is no medium ground between fatality and freedom." If there can not be a free volition with no antecedent cause outside of the fact that there was a free actor, then fatality follows inevitably. The impossibility, if it exists, applies to God's volitions as well as man's. The claim to medium ground was not to a medium between fatality and freedom, but a medium between the Calvinism of that day and Arminianism.

An attempt is here made to exhibit the representative creeds of Christendom, graded according to the amount of Calvinism or Arminianism which they contain. You begin to read the diagram in the middle. Each step upward is supposed to contain one shade more of Calvinism, till it passes Calvinism into atheistic fatality. Each step downward is supposed to be a step further away from Calvinism. Up and down refer only to the page, and not to any superiority in the creeds. From this diagram, if it be a true exhibit, the justness of the claim to a medium position, which the Cumberland Presbyterians set up, will be clearly seen. The place assigned some of the creeds was determined by averaging, some of their doctrines belonging to a higher grade and some to a lower than the one assigned. The fact that the New School Presbyterians and the United Presbyterian Church of Scotland both adopt the Westminster standards modifies their grading. Private and individual systems give other shades not here noticed. The pulpit theology of the New School Presbyterians was often far more Arminian than the system held by Cumberland Presbyterians; so, too, is the theology of many a modern Congregationalist. A large part of the Baptist churches hold about the same amount of Calvinism that the Cumberland Presbyterians do. While many reference books have been examined, Schaff and Hagenbach have been relied on more than others.

DIAGRAM OF REPRESENTATIVE CREEDS.

9. Atheistic fatality.
8. Theistic fatality.   God under fate.
7. Two-seed Baptists.   Antinomians.
6. Supralapsarian Calvinists.   Dort.
5. Infralapsarian Calvinists.   American Old School Presbyterians.
4. New School Presbyterians.
3. The Savoy Declaration, 1658.
2. The United Presbyterians.   Declaration of 1879.
1. The Baxterians.

English Congregationalists, 1833, ⎫
Evangelical Free Church of Geneva, ⎬ Medium.
Cumberland Presbyterians, ⎪
Reformed Episcopal church, ⎪
Free Italian church, ⎭

1. Lutherans.
2. Freewill Baptists.
3. Evangelical Union of Scotland.
4. Methodists.
5. Quakers, "orthodox," not "Hicksite."
6. Campbellites.
7. Pelagians.
8. Socinians.
9. Atheistic freedom.   No divine influence.

The range of our easy and hearty fellowship in work for the Master's kingdom takes in all the grades from five above to five below, and sometimes stretches over the sixth above and below. The sixth below has two wholly different elements among its membership, one class believing in experimental religion, the presence and power of the Holy Ghost, and in revivals. With them our people can co-operate in Christian work. The other class we can not work with, and might do them injustice if we tried to give their views. There are individual exceptions also in the grades which we fellowship. Men of any grade who oppose revivals can not work well with us, nor we with them.

As to communing at the sacrament of the Lord's Supper, we put no barrier in the way, but refer the question to men's own consciences. I have seen Unitarians communing with our people. It is not our custom to require any test—church membership, baptism, or any thing of the sort. If a man believes that he is a Christian and his own conscience is clear in coming to the Lord's table, we invite him to come. This has always been our custom, and is the obvious meaning of our standards. There have been a few dissenting voices to this interpretation of the standards. These insist on church membership, in some orthodox church, as essential. Baptism is, according to them, prerequisite to communion.

One thing can be clearly proved as a historical fact, and that is that slowly but surely the doctrinal views of the Presbyterian church, so far as the pulpit can be taken as their exponent, have been drawing nearer and nearer, ever since 1814, to this *medium* platform.

CHAPTER XIII.

THE THREE PRESBYTERIES—OLD CUSTOMS NOW DROPPED.

Thou shalt remember all the way which the Lord thy God led thee.—Deut. viii. 2.

FROM the organization of the synod, in 1813, until the organization of McGee Presbytery, in 1819, there were just three presbyteries. These had the whole world for their field. It may be interesting to mention several customs which prevailed among them then, and which have long since passed away. The old custom among all Presbyterians of requiring tokens from communicants was kept up a little while by our people, but, without any ecclesiastical repudiation, was gradually dropped. James B. Porter made the first vigorous denunciation of the system. He had seen Colonel Joe Brown driven by it out of the Presbyterian church, and he ever afterward refused to use tokens. The token was a little piece of metal like a trunk check, given by the session to a church member on communion day. It was his pass to the Lord's table when the sacrament was administered. The communicants took their seats at a long table. They always used real tables in those days. Then one man, appointed for the purpose, went round the table to see that all seated there had tokens. If any one there seated had no token he was pointed out to those who distributed the bread and wine, and they skipped him in their distribution. For many years the mother church withheld tokens from those of its members who had communed with "the Cumberlands," as they insisted on calling the members of the new church.

Colonel Joe Brown gave me, with his own lips, the history of his case. He had communed with the Cumberland Presbyterians, and his pastor ordered the session to refuse him a token. His sympathies were already with the new church both on account of its revivals and its doctrines. When the token was withheld, by

Gideon Blackburn's order, Colonel Brown then and there rose in the great congregation and told them that the Cumberland Presbyterians were God's people; that the attempt to bring them under the *odium theologicum* would recoil on its authors; and that he, for one, intended to cast his lot in with the church under whose ministry his children had been led to Jesus. While Mrs. Frances B. Fogg's little biography of this hero of Nickajack is interesting, it fails utterly to give the thrilling story of his life after his release from Indian captivity. I myself once took down from Colonel Brown's own lips full memoranda of his whole life, but the memoranda were destroyed with most of my library during the war. It is hoped that some of Colonel Brown's family will yet preserve to the church and the world a full account of his wonderful career.

What was called "fencing" the table in the days of our fathers included this business of the tokens, and also the code of rules by which the token was either given or withheld. The preacher who publicly announced these rules, and presided in their application, was said to "fence the table." "A fence for communion," "a good fence for the Lord's table," was often published in church papers—that is, a code of rules which ought to be applied in distributing tokens. I have heard old people regret the laxness of discipline which took down the fence from the Lord's table. Whether this removal was censurable or praiseworthy, our own church was a prominent actor in its accomplishment.

All three of the presbyteries had a custom which lingered a dozen years, and whose origin is hard to trace. A presbytery was composed of preachers, elders, and representatives. As in synod, so also in presbytery, every preacher was expected to have his own elder. Then the churches also were expected to send representatives to presbytery, but as the distance was in some cases five hundred miles, it was the custom of the remote churches to club together and send one representative for several congregations. There were instances where one man represented six congregations, so that there was no superabundance of elders even when both classes, the preachers' elders and the churches', were counted. In the synod the churches had no representatives. The preachers and their elders made the synod; but the preachers' elders were appointed by the church sessions in obedience to a requisition made annually by the presbytery. For example: the Elk Presbytery, at its spring session, would designate what congregation should send an elder with Robert Donnell, and the session of that church was held responsible for the presence of said elder in the synod. The utmost rigor was used at first to enforce this arrangement. The elder appointed and failing to go, unless for good reasons, was to have charges preferred against him. Such was the rule in all the presbyteries.

All three of the presbyteries had vast fields to cultivate, and those fields were continually expanding. The Nashville Presbytery, a few years after it began its separate presbyterial existence, found the whole western end of Tennessee opened by the purchase of the country from the Indians. But this expansion of that presbytery was a little thing compared with the vast fields thrown open on the frontiers of Logan and Elk presbyteries. In the case of the latter, soon after its organization, South Alabama was opened to American settlers, then Arkansas, then North-western Alabama, then Missouri. At one session of this presbytery petitions for preachers were received from five hundred pioneers in the new settlements of Alabama alone, and also from vast numbers in Arkansas and Missouri. Both Logan and Elk presbyteries tried to evangelize Missouri. In the wide bounds of Logan Presbytery Illinois, Indiana, and Ohio were opened to white settlements, and the earnest petitions of emigrants begging for the gospel were part of the stirring business coming up at every session.

In all three of the presbyteries fast-days were repeatedly appointed, and all the churches were urged to pray for more laborers to be sent into the harvest. After these fast-days the presbyteries invariably received large accessions to their number of candidates. Yet the growth of the new settlements and the demands for the gospel kept far ahead of this increase in the supply of ministers. It was folly to talk about settling down into pastorates under these circumstances. Men were called pastors, and they will be so designated in these pages. The name existed, but the reality had no place in all the church till near the close of the second period in this history. Thomas Calhoun is called pastor in the next chapter, but he made frequent tours of evangelism which required six months each. He attended camp-meetings for two or three months every year, and he cultivated a large farm.

The plan which all the presbyteries fell upon was threefold. All the vast fields under their care were districted, and itinerants sent to each district. These itinerants established circuits of preaching places, and made appointments for preaching every day in the week. This was generally missionary work, outside of all organized congregations. If the missionary could collect enough members to organize a church, he took their names, pledging them to form a church as soon as an ordained preacher could be had to organize them. The missionary was not usually an ordained minister. This was the first branch of the system.

The second branch pertained to organized congregations. In these the presbytery appointed sacramental meetings semi-annually, and designated the preachers who were to officiate. The fall meetings were camp-meetings, as well as sacramental, and every ordained preacher, no matter what his pastoral relations might be, was required to attend these camp-meetings during the fall months, and was also required to perform his part of that other work on the circuits which unordained men could not do. The presbytery, at every session, designated what portion of these duties fell to the lot of each ordained minister, and each was held to rigid account for his fidelity in the work assigned him.

The third branch of the system consisted of such features of regular pastorates as could be made consistent with the two preceding branches. In the orders of these presbyteries I find it no uncommon thing for a so-called pastor of this period to be required, in the course of a year, to attend as many as a dozen sacramental meetings, distant from fifty to three hundred miles from his home; and when called on to report at the next meeting of the presbytery, it was a rare thing for any one to report a failure. When failure was reported, the reasons were investigated.

The chief question at every meeting of these presbyteries was about the supply of itinerants and their support. These itinerants were always called missionaries by the Logan Presbytery, but they were frequently called circuit riders in the other presbyteries.

Nashville Presbytery consumed one whole session in 1815 in discussing plans for the support of itinerants. The Elk Presbytery came with shorter steps to decided measures. It required every member of the church to pay one dollar to the itinerant fund. This action was taken in 1816, and for three years produced good results. Afterward we find R. D. King and others traveling under order of the presbytery six months on the frontier, without receiving a cent of pay. Nashville Presbytery tried several schemes. The best one, perhaps, was a central board, with auxiliary societies throughout the presbytery; but in two years' time this plan lost its vitality, and again the wail of "no circuit riders" made the meetings of presbytery a Bochim. This whole system of machinery broke down first in the Nashville Presbytery. It failed in all the presbyteries before any other system was introduced.

The first crash of the falling fabric came at the fall meeting of the Nashville Presbytery, in 1816. No itinerants could be secured, whereupon the presbytery apportioned its field and its churches among its ministers, requiring each one to supply the congregations assigned him as often as the circumstances permitted. The fact that no itinerants could be secured was regarded by the presbytery with alarm. A fast-day was ordered in all the congregations, and, after two years of mourning, the system had another brief resuscitation, only to break down more hopelessly than ever. In the new presbyteries organized from time to time, the original scheme was invariably employed. It was a scheme for planting churches, not for training them after they were planted.

This system of itinerant missionaries followed the system of circuit riding among the Methodists in some particulars, but differed from it in many others. In theory it was voluntary, but sometimes the pressure on a young man to induce him to take the circuit was very great. With shame be it recorded that many a dear boy has left his half-finished course of studies under this pressure, and gone out "to ride the circuit." Many such, when old men, left in writings, now in my possession, their bitter protests against a policy which robbed them of their education and crippled their life-work. Popular usage assigned to these itinerant missionaries the name which the Methodists used, but Logan Presbytery refused to accept the name, and never used it in official records. A part of the church accepted the name with cheerfulness, since it was a true designation of the thing to which it was applied, and since, moreover, it came to us all perfumed with grateful odors from the fields of heroic toil for Jesus by Methodist itinerants.

The name Cumberland Presbyterian originated in a somewhat similar manner. The whole of Middle Tennessee, so far as it was settled, and some of Kentucky, was, in an early day, called Cumberland—not at first "the Cumberland country," but just Cumberland. The settlement in the eastern end of Tennessee was called Watauga. These were germs for two new States, and not till long after were they the eastern and middle portions of one State. Cumberland included all of McGready's field. Here the great revival, which was so bitterly opposed by some, began. Before the Cumberland Presbytery ever existed, the two parties of Kentucky Synod were designated by names which the people saw fit to apply. One was "the Cumberland party," which was also called the revival party. When Transylvania Presbytery was divided, and all that country which was called Cumberland assigned to a new presbytery called Cumberland Presbytery, the epithet "Cumberland Presbyterian" was already in popular use as designating all that part of the Presbyterian church which favored the revival. All this was years before the organization of our church. When the church was organized in 1810, it adopted no denominational name. There was no intention then of starting a new church. It was an independent presbytery of Presbyterians, which still hoped for restoration to its old status in the mother church. The people called its adherents Cumberland Presbyterians. It was not till 1813 that the new church indirectly adopted the name which the people had already given. Associated with all that was most sacred while the new doctrines were costing men their ecclesiastical lives, and endeared on that account to such an extent that no subsequent effort to shake it off could be tolerated by those who knew and held sacred the traditions of our origin, the name remains to this day what the people and God's providence made it. It has been often mocked at, but, by God's grace, the church will **make it as dear one day to all who love true work for Jesus, as it** is now to those whose ears still ring, when it is mentioned, with the holy songs of the great revival and the fearless sermons of those who first proclaimed a general atonement in Presbyterian pulpits.

Another custom originating in the Cumberland Presbytery, and kept up by its three successors for many years, was that of having a presbyterial library whose books were exchanged at every meeting of the presbytery. Each minister paid five dollars into the library fund, and also solicited contributions from the wealthy for the purchase of books, so that the library grew in a few years to a considerable collection. A list of the books allowed each preacher form part of the minutes of every presbyterial meeting. The itinerant system failed first in the Nashville Presbytery; so did the custom of having a presbyterial library. In 1819 that presbytery sold out its books. Cities, dense populations, and schools superseded the itinerant library, as they did all the system with which it stood connected.

Another custom was universal all through this period. At all the camp-meetings there was at least one sermon preached on a call to the ministry. The pressure on the presbyteries for more preachers was perhaps greater than was ever before brought to bear on any church judicatures since the days of the apostles. Several causes co-operated to produce this pressure. The first was the constant opening up of new territories to immigrants; for the period when these presbyteries were the only ones in the church is precisely the period when there was the grandest expansion of our national territory. The second cause was the emigration of Cumberland Presbyterians from Kentucky and Tennessee to these new fields. Let the population of Indiana, Illinois, Missouri, Arkansas, Alabama, and Mississippi be examined to-day, and a very large portion of the people will be found to be descendants of Kentuckians and Tennesseans. These two States were the birthplace of the new church. Cumberland Presbyterian emigrants settled over all these vast fields, and they all wrote back to the presbyteries begging for the gospel. The point of special interest is that all that vast Western and Southern field, which drew its population largely from Tennessee and Kentucky, was opened to white settlers at a time when the Cumberland Presbyterians of those two States were intensely active in sending out missionaries.

Two facts apparently, but not really, inconsistent meet us here. In all the older settlements where other denominations had established churches, and in all large towns, where a settled pastor was considered necessary to maintain the life of a congregation, our first preachers showed great reluctance to organizing churches. As a general rule, throughout this period, they absolutely refused, even when pressed to do so, to organize Cumberland Presbyterian congregations in such places. The other fact is, that in all the wild frontier, in the sparsest and most destitute neighborhoods, their readiness to organize churches, even where there seemed to be very little hope of any permanent supply of preachers, amounted to recklessness. The feeling that it was their duty to look first after the souls of those who were least likely to be looked after by others, no doubt prompted them to pursue this course.

Another custom was universal. Every regular minister was required to assemble the congregations and examine them in the catechism. All the licensed and ordained ministers were called upon at every meeting of the presbytery to report whether they had complied with this requirement, and there were very few cases of failure. Copies of the catechism were in nearly every Cumberland Presbyterian household, and every child, as well as every adult church member, was expected to study it. The old men who survived this custom mourned over its loss, and refused to be comforted, prophesying looseness and instability of doctrines as the fruit of its abandonment. In more than one case among the literary remains of the fathers which have been placed in my hands are found large packages of our first catechism.

The subject of a school for their candidates was discussed by each of the presbyteries. Then Nashville Presbytery (1822) asked the others to meet its delegates in convention to consider the question of a presbyterial school. This action was the forerunner of the synod's determination, in 1824, to establish a school for the whole church.

A prejudice existed all through this early period against statistics. An order requiring statistical reports passed at one meeting of the synod, and was repealed at the next. At some of the sessions of presbytery the missionaries would report the number of conversions and accessions in their districts; but in most of the records no mention of any numbers can be found either in the reports of missionaries or reports of the Committee on the State of Religion. Great and precious revivals, without the mention of statistics, are reported at every meeting of presbytery. The clearest index to the rate of growth is found in the organization of new presbyteries. In sixteen years the three presbyteries grew to eighteen, the least of which was as large as the Logan Presbytery at its organization. It is true that the Committee on the State of Religion, at each session of synod, did report the number of conversions for the year; but the fact that no system of gathering statistics was in use by the presbyteries shows how incomplete these synodical reports must have been.

Dr. Burrow was perhaps foremost among anti-statistical ministers in our church. He entered the ministry in the Elk Presbytery, and was one of the noblest specimens of the itinerant preacher that any church ever had. He believed in reporting only to God. He was afraid of all counting, all sounding of trumpets; and all his life he advocated the "pay or no pay" rule about preaching; and not only advocated, but practiced it till his dying day. There were several thousand converts at his meetings the last year of his ministry.

Another custom in those days was to hold camp-meetings in communities which contained not a single member of any church. Not only were such communities found on all the frontier, but there were many people also who had never heard a sermon in their lives. If a few families of unconverted pioneers could be persuaded to move to the place selected, and there entertain the visitors, the camp-meeting was held. Nor was it a difficult thing to find liberal-hearted men who would engage in this work.

Out of many examples I select one instance of the sort, described by the venerable William Lynn, of Indiana, and published just before his departure to his crown and kingdom. This camp-meeting was in Daviess County, Kentucky. There was not a single church member in all the neighborhood; but men who were willing to camp and feed the multitudes were found, and the camp-meeting was held. At that meeting those twin heroes of the cross, Chapman and Harris, were present, and also several probationers for the ministry. The meeting was greatly blessed of God, and among the converts were three men who afterward entered the ministry. This was a camp-meeting held by those heroic missionaries who are better known by the borrowed name of "circuit riders." But much more remarkable cases are on record. In the tours of R. D. King, Reuben Burrow, and Daniel Patton among the destitute settlements, it was a common thing for them to persuade unconverted men to establish a camp-ground. Indeed, there were fewer and smaller obstacles to success among the rough men of the frontier, where no churches of any denomination existed, than there were where denominational prejudices were active. One thing is worthy of special commemoration: these unconverted campers generally were converted to God in these meetings, and had abundant reasons to rejoice that they had ever undertaken to camp. One dear lady of this class said God had paid her back in her own conversion and the conversion of thirteen members of her family.

In all this period and long afterward the preaching of our ministers belonged to a very *thorough* system. They believed the doctrine that man is spiritually dead. This, to them, was not merely figurative, it was real. They taught that in his natural state there is no element of spiritual life in man. As well talk of cultivating a rose until you make it a bird, as talk of educating and training a man up into spiritual life. In his natural state man is thoroughly hostile to God and all spiritual good. Not only some of the imaginations of the thoughts of his heart are evil, but "every imagination." Not only that, but they are evil continually. These first preachers probed deep, and generally roused opposition and anger at first. Afterward the scales fell from the sinner's own eyes, until he saw his depravity and condemnation, and then cries of alarm and remorse broke forth from his lips.

Concerning the new birth their teaching was equally thorough. Regeneration meant a new creation, not a mere training; not "let the goat run with the sheep till it becomes a sheep;" but divine creative power was first to make it a sheep, and then training was to follow. They were equally thorough in their belief in the doctrine of eternal future punishment, and they preached it everywhere. About the atoning blood—the precious blood of Christ—their preaching was equally unambiguous and emphatic. They taught that our salvation rests on no mere moral influence and example, but on a divine vicarious sacrifice. The moral theory never had any place in the Cumberland Presbyterian system. They believed and taught that the Christian's legal standing before God is exclusively in Christ, and not at all in self—not partly in Christ and partly in works, but all in Christ.

They were equally thorough in their belief of inspiration, even *ad verbum*. In regard to God's indwelling presence, concerning his answers to the prayer of faith, and all similar matters, they held to no shallow system. If a probationer for the ministry in that day had taught any of the shallow systems of modern times he would have been instantly thrown overboard. Yet they insisted upon the necessity for good works, not as a procuring cause but as a fruit of the new life. If the fruit were lacking it was because the life was lacking. Works, out of love to Christ as the motive, they preached with great success.

While I mention the preaching of these doctrines as a peculiarity of our early pulpits, I do not mean to teach that our people have repudiated these fundamental truths. I am quite sure they have not; but I am also sure that these doctrines are not pressed in the pulpits of this day as they were by the fathers. In my opinion we lose by this change. Leave a vital doctrine long silent, and a generation will grow up which will utterly reject it.

CHAPTER XIV.

HISTORIC CHURCHES—PLANTING CHURCHES IN TENNESSEE AND KENTUCKY.

> If called like them to cope
> In evil times with dark and evil powers,
> O be their faith, their zeal, their courage ours!
> —*W. H. Burleigh.*

WHILE it is impossible, as a general thing, to give the history of individual congregations, there are a few whose prominence requires special notice. The churches which existed before the revival, and afterward united with the Cumberland Presbyterians, have necessarily been noticed in the history of the revival. Of this class a few still exist as Cumberland Presbyterian congregations. Red River church, in Kentucky, is a center of historic interest. The old grave-yard, with dates which run back to 1730, is itself a history. Among these graves is that of the eldest brother of the Rev. Finis Ewing—General Robert Ewing—born 1760, a soldier in the revolutionary war, a member of the Kentucky legislature, etc. One of his sons still lives in the neighborhood. The grave of his daughter, Mary B., which is also there, has special interest for Cumberland Presbyterians. Her first husband was the Rev. Philip McDonnold. The parents of the Rev. A. M. Bryan lived and died in this neighborhood. When their old house was newly roofed, the old shingles were found to be pegged on. There were no nails in the country when that house was built, and iron was ten dollars a pound. Near this church the ruins of the old fort which protected the pioneers from the Indians can still be traced. It was called Mauldin's Station. Red River is still a revival church. The old log house is superseded by one of modern construction, but the old fire still burns on its altars. This church is an exception, too, among the old churches, in another respect. It does not cling to the old programme of taking a preacher's labors without pay.

The Beech church and Gasper River church are two more of our historic congregations. Gasper was for a time abandoned, its members going to Pilot Knob, but, since the war, it has been again revived, and still works for Jesus. The dates and names on the tombstones in its grave-yard form a precious record.

The Beech church[1] was organized in 1800. Its first house of worship was a union meeting-house. The Rev. William McGee was its first pastor. In 1810 this church joined the new denomination. After McGee died this congregation had no regular pastor, but was supplied by Hugh Kirkpatrick and other itinerants. After many years they built their present stone church near the site of the union church, not being willing to leave the old grave-yard. In 1832 they organized their first Sunday-school, the Rev. John Beard officiating. One hundred and twenty pupils were enrolled. Annual camp-meetings, great revivals, with many ministers rising up from among the converts, make part of the history of the Beech church.

When camp-meetings and itinerant supplies were given up, the Beech church, in spite of its Presbyterian origin, utterly failed to adopt the new programme of settled pastors in the true sense. By supplies and annual revival meetings it did, however, manage to keep alive. Like all the churches which pursue this course, it is sadly suffering, in spite of the "old fire" which is still there.

Of the churches planted by the revival party before the division, there are several still in existence as Cumberland Presbyterian congregations. Among these are Smyrna, Goshen, and Big Spring in Tennessee, and Piney in Kentucky. There are several others, in Alabama, and in other places, but I can mention only a few prominent churches of this class.

Perhaps the most interesting of these is Big Spring, Wilson County, Tennessee. In 1801 some of the revival party who lived too far from Bethesda to attend regularly there, resolved to have services at the Big Spring. They secured a monthly appointment from the Rev. William Hodge. The next fall they held a camp-

---

[1] *Revivalist*, November 28, 1832. Hugh Kirkpatrick's sketch.

meeting on the original plan, without tents or cabins.[1] This meeting was not held on the spot now occupied by that church, but just at the head of the great spring which gave its name to the congregation. The reasons for moving the camp-ground years afterward to a smaller spring in the same neighborhood are unknown to the writer. In 1802 they built open sheds to camp under. These sloped to the ground.[2] When the Cumberland Presbyterian church was organized, the Rev. Thomas Calhoun was called to be pastor of this congregation. The word pastor must, however, be understood in a modified sense. It was in 1810 that the final location of a permanent encampment and the erection of a house of worship took place. The site was then changed to its present position.

When the father of the Rev. Thomas Calhoun had finished his log-cabin, where the new camp-ground was located, he stuck his sycamore handspike down in the ground, and it took root and grew to a great tree which still stands. People used to go to the Big Spring camp-meeting from neighborhoods a hundred miles distant. Twenty of our most efficient ministers were converted at that camp-ground. Its first camp-meetings were glorious visitations of God's power, sending out all over the State an influence which will live forever. All the Western States owe some of their noblest church officers to the Big Spring camp-meetings. I have heard many of the orators whom this nation and Europe loved to honor, but, in my humble judgment, Calhoun surpassed them all. If Moody has a special baptism of power for his peculiar work, in a far higher sense did that baptism rest on Calhoun. Many a time at old Big Spring camp-ground have the vast assemblies gathered there felt and acknowledged that God spake to them through human lips.

Thomas Calhoun lived near this church, and was pastor of this and Smyrna congregations from the time of his ordination till the close of his ministry—forty-five years. After his death, emigration to Texas seriously crippled Big Spring. The Lone Star State has drawn to its bosom nearly all the strength of many a Tennessee congregation. When the people of Big Spring sold their homes,

---

[1] MSS. of Alec. Aston.   [2] The Calhoun MSS.

Baptists and others were the purchasers. Yet there have been great revivals among our people there in more recent times, and there is a respectable number of members now; but the very nearest of these live two miles from the church. It has, at last, been agreed to build a new house nearer the congregation. The old house of cedar logs, and those raised seats, and that pulpit with its "sounding board," and its clerk's seat, will not be left intact.

The Smyrna church, in Jackson County, Tennessee, also has an interesting history. In the private houses of two old men, Williamson and Sadler, meetings were held by Alexander Anderson, William McGee, and Samuel King, in 1800. The next year a church was organized, a spot selected for a camp-ground, and Thomas Calhoun, then only a candidate, held a meeting on this spot. Colonel Smith, the father of the Rev. Robert Donnell's first wife, lived there. People used to go a hundred miles to attend the Smyrna camp-meetings.

Calhoun's life-work as a pastor was in Big Spring and Smyrna congregations. All of Smith County and part of two other counties lay between his home and Smyrna church. A large part of this distance was filled with dense canebrakes. When there was snow, the high cane overhung the narrow path until it was difficult to travel on horseback. Yet he never missed his appointments. Colonel Smith has left us a written statement about several of the thrilling sermons preached there by Calhoun, and about the far-reaching revivals which often resulted from the camp-meetings.

I clip from the *Banner of Peace* the following notice of another historic church:

In 1799 a few persons, members of the Presbyterian church, mostly from North Carolina, agreed to meet every Sabbath to read the Scriptures and pray with and for each other. They afterward constituted the Cumberland Presbyterian church which was organized at New Hope, Wilson County, Tenn. Their names are William and Catherine Gray, James and Margaret Stewart, Andrew and Elizabeth Bay, Alexander and Jane Kirkpatrick, John and Ann Kirkpatrick, David and Rebecca Kirkpatrick, Samuel and Sarah Motheral, Elias Morrison, Joseph Kirkpatrick, and Margaret Motheral. "These all died in the faith." The same year (1799) the Rev. William McGee preached the first sermon in the bounds of this congregation. From this time until 1810 they enjoyed occasional circuit preaching by Samuel King, Alexander Anderson, Hugh Kirkpatrick, Thomas Calhoun, Alexander Chapman, James B. Porter, and David Foster—all of whom have joined the sacramental host beyond death's stream, where parting is no more.

In the fall of 1810 this congregation, afterward noted for camp-meetings, held their first camp-meeting near the "Double Islands," on Cumberland River. At this meeting they were much revived and encouraged; so much so, that the next year (1811) they purchased a lot of ground, erected camps, and held a second camp-meeting one mile above their first encampment. The Rev. William McGee, who was present, called this new camp-ground New Hope. Here, in 1812, the Rev. Hugh Kirkpatrick, with the names designated above, organized a Cumberland Presbyterian church, and preached once a month till 1816, when he was succeeded by the Rev. John Provine, who preached monthly until 1830. From this date to 1843 they were supplied with preaching by the Rev. George Donnell and the Rev. John L. Dillard. The former served four, the latter nine years. The Rev. M. S. Vaughan then accepted the charge and preached until 1850, when he was followed by the Rev. J. E. Davis, who continued two years.

In the fall of 1852 the Rev. William D. Chadick was regularly installed pastor of this church by the late Rev. F. R. Cossitt, D.D., and continued his labors till 1855, when the Rev. J. C. Bowden supplied the congregation one year.

The Rev. M. S. Vaughan again received a call to this congregation and preached until 1859, when he was succeeded by the Rev. William A. Haynes, who served as pastor, with the exception of two or more years during the late war, till the spring of 1866. The Rev. W. W. Suddarth succeeded Mr. Haynes, and labored till the fall of 1867, at which time he received a call from Lebanon congregation, and the Rev. M. S. Vaughan was called for the third time to New Hope.

From these facts, which I find in the church records, we learn that New Hope has enjoyed the means of grace from 1799, and an organized existence of fifty-six years' standing. During this time the church held and supported fifty-three camp-meetings. At these meetings hundreds, if not thousands, of sinners were brought to a knowledge of the truth as it is in Jesus, and obtained through grace a good hope of a happy immortality beyond time. Among these are many able ministers of the gospel. Some of them have laid down the gospel trumpet for glittering crowns in glory. Others, trembling under the effects of age and hard service in their high vocation, are yet preaching Jesus to a perishing world, each cheered on in his "labor of love" with this most precious promise of his divine Master, "Be thou faithful unto death, and I will give thee a crown of life." FELIX H. TAYLOR, Clerk.

HISTORIC CHURCHES.

The first church organized as a Cumberland Presbyterian church was Mt. Moriah, in Giles County, Tennessee. The Rev. C. N. Wood, lately gone to his reward, secured for me the historical sketch of this congregation which is here used. He was converted at one of the meetings at Mt. Moriah, and became a member of that congregation. This church was organized in March, 1810, by Rev. James B. Porter. A very full history of its work, written by one of the elders, is before me. This congregation has had fifteen "pastors." Mr. Porter served from 1810 till the death of his wife in 1815, when he resumed the life of an itinerant preacher. There was one year in Mr. Porter's pastorate of wonderful religious interest. The camp-meeting was unusually successful. The people carried the interest home with them. The earthquake (1812) filled all the country with great solemnity. Mr. Porter knew how to follow up these impressions, and the whole year round there were conversions all through the neighborhood. The interest in the private houses resembled that in the Gasper River neighborhood fourteen years before.

Carson P. Reed served this congregation as pastor sixteen years. After Reed came J. N. Edmiston who served three years. When he resigned, the church fell upon the miserable expedient of itinerant supplies. One thing the session put on record in their history which deserves emphasis. The church, they say, did not prosper under preaching from itinerants as it did under permanent pastors.

The Rev. G. W. Mitchell became pastor of this church early in the year 1867, and served until the close of 1871. During this time the congregation enjoyed its greatest prosperity. The session testifies that the whole membership was quickened into new life and activity. This church has tested three systems: it has had regular pastors, it has depended on the ministrations of itinerant preachers, and at other times it has employed temporary supplies. Its highest success has been attained under the labors of regular pastors. During the five years in which the Rev. D. S. Bodenhamer (now of Trinity University) served as pastor, there were ninety-six accessions to the congregation. Twenty-two converts of this church have become preachers. There are some noted names on the list, such as N. P. Modrall, C. P. Reed, W. S. Burney, LeRoy Woods, C. N. Wood, all now gone to their reward, besides a noble band who still labor for Jesus.

The venerable Joseph Brown, one of our old preachers, made his home near this church, and was buried in its cemetery. When he was nearly a hundred years old he would ask permission to stand in the pulpit beside the preacher, in order to catch every word. As his hearing was bad, he would hold his ear close up to the preacher, and occasionally cry out "Glory to God!"

This congregation has now a large brick church, built in 1856, and is in a prosperous condition. Its camp-meetings were kept up, with one intermission, until 1853, when they gave place to protracted meetings.

Another one of our first churches is Goshen, in Franklin County, Tennessee, on the Boiling Fork of Elk River, near the Cumberland Mountains.[1] Its site is beautiful. Nearly all the first settlers here were Scotch-Irish Presbyterians. In 1811 the Rev. Samuel King and the Rev. William McGee persuaded the people to hold a camp-meeting. A shed and camps were built, and King and McGee held the meeting. There were hundreds of conversions, and a Cumberland Presbyterian church was organized. An incident of this meeting is characteristic of the times. King preached on the Sabbath. As the sermon progressed the solemnity grew oppressive. The mighty power of God rested like a weight upon the people. Men almost held their breath. The preacher felt it as well as the others. By and by the solemnity grew so great that even the preacher's tongue was silent. He stood a moment with looks of unutterable awe, and then went down from the pulpit and started to the woods. When he had gone about a hundred yards, he turned abruptly back, and entered the pulpit. There was no longer any look of awe, but a holy, rapturous light on his face, and he resumed his sermon with a thrilling power which swept every thing before it. From that day on that congregation has been noted for its revivals. Several of its converts have become ministers.

---

[1] The facts concerning this church were furnished by Dr. J. B. Cowan, of Tullahoma, Tennessee.

HISTORIC CHURCHES.

In 1813 Robert Donnell began preaching in Nashville, Tennessee. Mr. Craighead was then in charge of a small church in Nashville, and he exerted himself to keep the people from hearing the new minister. At first neither preaching place nor hospitality was extended to him. He preached in the court-house, and boarded at the hotel. The court-house was afterward closed against him, but the mayor offered him the city hall. After Donnell had filled a few appointments in this hall, the mayor died, and the hall also was closed against the preacher. So great was the opposition in town, that he consented to move his appointment to the dwelling-house of Mr. Castleman in the country. Here several distinguished Tennesseans were converted. Donnell's tour in East Tennessee, described a little further on in this book, interrupted his Nashville work. By and by he secured the assistance of the Rev. James B. Porter, and held a protracted meeting in the court-house. He and Porter lodged at the hotel, but when they once got a hearing, hospitality was extended to them by various families. The preaching in this meeting stirred all Nashville. Under one of Donnell's sermons Felix Grundy, an unconverted man, afterward United States senator, sprung to his feet, seized his friend, Colonel Foster, also a United States senator, by the hand, exclaiming, "That is the truth, Foster, every word of it, and it will stand at the day of judgment." Donnell and Porter organized a church at this meeting, and raised funds for a building.

CHAPTER XV.

EARLY MISSIONS TO THE INDIANS.

> Hark! from the West a voice is heard,
>   A voice beyond the mountain's side;
> It breaks along the deep, dark wood
>   Where roams the savage in his pride.
> A star appears, its cheering ray
> Dawns on the red man's darksome way.
> —*S. O. Wright.*

THE house of Samuel McAdow, in which our first presbytery was organized, was not more than thirty miles from the Indian territory. These Indians were still in their wild and savage state. There were, it is true, a few exceptions, but only a few. Most of these red men were as far away from civilization or Christianity then as the naked sons of the forest who first greeted Columbus over three centuries earlier. Some of the Mississippi Indians of that day wore no clothing, and kept up all the habits of savage life. There is a testimony of great significance from the Presbyterian General Assembly to the effect that the revival of 1800 produced new interest in the evangelization of the red man and the negro. The facts abundantly sustain this testimony. Gideon Blackburn belonged to the revival party in East Tennessee. He planted a mission among the Cherokees, and devoted years of toil to that interest. None of the anti-revival party of that day ever became missionaries.

In Thomas Calhoun's first evangelistic tours he entered the newly settled portions of Tennessee before the whites raised their first crop, and before the Indians ceased to roam over the country. He and others held a camp-meeting at the spring where afterward Monroe, the county town of Overton County, Tennessee, was built. Roving bands of Cherokee Indians attended the meeting. One of these became greatly impressed, and there are reasons to believe he was there converted. He went home and named an Indian town after Calhoun. This was before the organization of the Cumberland Presbyterian church. In talking to Calhoun about these early days, I once expressed some surprise at his frequent mention of Indians attending his meetings. His reply was, "Why, the Indian line was just over here on Duck River."

In Calhoun's and Donnell's tour in East Tennessee (1815) they held two protracted meetings for the Indians. One of these was at Pumpkin Town, and there was deep interest manifested by the hearers. The Rev. James Stewart also preached to the Indians before the existence of our first missionary board.

All three of the presbyteries which composed our first synod began early experimenting on plans for missionary work in their own vast bounds. Missionaries were sent to our new territories as fast as these territories were opened, but societies formed with a special view to work among the Indians and the heathen originated in 1818, and were organized in all three of the presbyteries in the spring of that year. The missionary impulse in the three presbyteries was simultaneous, and the indications are that it started with Samuel King, James Stewart, and Robert Bell. All of these men belonged to the Elk Presbytery. A constitution[1] for a ladies' missionary society was drawn up by Robert Bell, and submitted in March, 1818, to the congregations of Elk Presbytery; and that plan is the same one on which the missionary societies in all three of the presbyteries were organized. This points to Elk rather than Logan Presbytery[2] as the first to move in this work. But its priority, if it existed, was one of only a few days at most, for the 9th of April[3] of that year was the birthday of the ladies' society in Russellville, Kentucky. One thing can be fairly claimed by the Elk Presbytery: its missionary board (there was a central board for the presbytery) was the first to send missionaries to the Indians. In October, 1818, the Elk missionary board sent Samuel King and William Moore to a work which lay along the borders of the Indian country on the Tombigbee River.[4] When these two men returned,

---

[1] The Bell papers. [2] This honor has been claimed for Logan Presbytery.
[3] *Medium*, 1846, p. 326.
[4] Minutes of Elk Presbytery, Vol. I., p. 40.

in the spring of 1819, and reported to their presbytery,[1] they made a strong appeal in behalf of the red men, representing them as eager to hear the gospel, and to have a missionary school located among them. The language of this appeal would indicate that the schools under the American Board in Mississippi were not yet in existence. The missionary board of Elk Presbytery[2] then sent Samuel King and Robert Bell, in the fall of 1819, to travel as evangelists among the Chickasaw and Choctaw Indians. On their return Mr. King brought a young Indian convert with him, intending to educate him for the ministry. He kept this boy at his own house, and sent him to school.

These missionaries made arrangements in the Choctaw Nation to secure a location and money for a missionary school, but their plans were thwarted. Then the missionary society of Elk Presbytery sent Mr. Bell to establish a school in the white settlements close enough to the border for the Indians to patronize it. Accordingly in May, 1820, Mr. Bell opened a school on the east side of the Tombigbee River, nearly opposite the dividing line between the Chickasaws and the Choctaws. He taught here only four weeks, when the missionary board of Elk Presbytery directed him to move the school into the Chickasaw Nation, the board having sent men thither to negotiate a treaty for that purpose.

The Chickasaw Nation had never been at war with our people. It had just sold out to the whites all that portion of Tennessee and Kentucky lying between the Tennessee River and the Mississippi, a delta far better known in early times for David Crockett's bear hunts than for its cotton. The Chickasaws, so long the near neighbors of Tennesseans, were still neighbors to the white people farther south. Only the Tombigbee River (Indian name Itomba Igoba) lay between them and the white settlements.

The Chickasaws of Mississippi, at the time our first mission was opened, were in advance of other Indians. Many of them had built cabins to live in. These were plastered tight with mud. The door was in the back part of the hut. There was no floor but the ground, and the cabin had but one room. The dead were

---

[1] Minutes of Elk Presbytery, Vol. I., p. 45.   [2] Ibid., p. 49.

buried in the cabin under the bed. The corpse was doubled up before it was buried, and the vault, after receiving the mortal remains, was closely plastered over with mud. When the body was buried the squaws present took down their hair and wore it dishevelled around their faces for one whole moon. During sickness they had what was called a sick dance. They laid the sick out wrapped in blankets, and danced around them. Some of these Indians raised patches of corn and sweet potatoes; only a few raised cotton. [See *Ladies' Pearl*, November, 1860, p. 76.]

The traditions of the Tombigbee River surpass in thrilling interest those of the Mississippi. At no spot do more of those traditions center than at Cotton Gin Port. Here at an early day the United States government established a cotton gin among the Indians to induce them to engage in the cultivation of cotton. Levi Colbert, the most enlightened of all the Chickasaw chiefs, moved to the neighborhood and devoted himself to persuading his people to raise cotton, he himself setting the example. Here at Cotton Gin the United States government had a post-office. The country on the eastern side of the Tombigbee, in Robert Bell's day, belonged to the white people, and some families lived there, the father of Dr. C. H. Bell among them. Cotton Gin Port as early as 1800 began to be a shipping point for emigrants to the Tensas and other new countries. Canoes lashed together and covered with a floor of cane made the boats. The wreck[1] of one such boat at night, just below Cotton Gin, furnishes one of those thrilling traditions of the Tombigbee of which there are so many; but this tradition is eclipsed in interest by the more recent one of the burning of the Eliza Battle, and the fearful loss of life on that bitter night in March, 1858. A beloved Cumberland Presbyterian minister, A. M. Newman, was among those who perished when that steamboat was burned. Many of the passengers escaped on cotton bales. A gentleman who was on the boat gave me an account of that catastrophe. Newman threw a bale of cotton into the river and placed his wife and child upon it, and then leaped in himself without any cotton bale. Mrs. Newman and daughter were

---

[1] Picket's Alabama, Vol. I., pp. 187–189.

taken up by my informant and saved, but Newman perished in the waves.

When Robert Bell's two comrades (the commissioners of Elk Presbytery) arrived at Cotton Gin Port, they went to Levi Colbert's house. Bell had preached in that house on his former visit. Colbert was eager for the establishment of the school, and to have it located near him. He assembled the king and chiefs of the Nation at his house, where the three commissioners of the Board of Missions of Elk Presbytery entered into treaty with them. The commissioners promised instruction in mechanic arts and agriculture, as well as in the literary course. They promised, also, within the limits of their ability, to teach, board, and clothe the indigent gratuitously. The chiefs promised protection, and the free use of land for cultivation. This treaty was signed the 11th of September, 1820, the names of the white commissioners standing on the right and those of the king and chiefs on the left. The names affixed to this agreement are: Robert Bell, Samuel King, and James Stewart, for the mission. On the part of the Indians the names are: Shako Tookey, king of the Nation; Tisho Mingo, Appa Suntubba, Samuel Sealy, William McGalba, James Colbert, and Levi Colbert, chiefs.

Three miles below Cotton Gin Port, at the base of the bluff, were some springs of pure water. This spot was selected for the school. It is seven miles from what is now the town of Aberdeen, Mississippi.

At the same time that the Elk Presbytery was taking these steps for an Indian mission, it was also urging upon the General Synod the propriety of having a board of missions for the whole church. Elk Presbytery was not alone in this view of the case. In the fall of 1819, at the meeting of the synod, it was resolved to have one central board, and to make all the others tributary. The arrangement made was certainly novel. The ladies' missionary society of Logan Presbytery, without ceasing to be a presbyterial society, was also made the general society of the church, and all the ministers of the church were appointed trustees. Robert Donnell, of Elk Presbytery, became the president of the general board at Russellville, and Bell's mission was turned over to this board.

The antecedents of the Russellville board deserve a passing notice. In September, 1817, H. A. Hunter, of Russellville, Kentucky, professed religion at Liberty church, near Russellville. His mother also became concerned about her soul. The young convert, Hunter, with one other Christian to aid him, began a weekly prayer-meeting in his father's ball-room. This was with the consent of his parents. Then the Rev. Finis Ewing and the Rev. William Barnett[1] came and held a meeting in that ball-room. There was no meeting-house then in the place. The town had been nick-named "The Devil's Camp-ground." This meeting in the ball-room was greatly blessed. The whole town was revolutionized, and several of the converts entered the holy ministry. At the close of the meeting Finis Ewing organized a ladies' missionary society in that same ball-room.[2] By request of the ladies of this society, the Logan Presbytery[3] became its board of directors. After the action in 1819, consolidating the missionary work of the church, this society had two boards of directors. As the society of Logan Presbytery it had the ministers of that presbytery for one of these boards; as the general missionary society of the church it had all the preachers in the church for the other. Cumberland Presbyterians had no chartered board of missions until 1845. Men even opposed chartered boards as savoring of Church and State.

It was under this curiously organized society that Mr. Bell's mission was placed soon after the school began. The site chosen for Bell's mission was in a beautiful country; but in the early settlements there was a good deal of sickness. Bell and his wife opened their school in the fall of 1820, in Levi Colbert's house, which he generously tendered for that purpose.

Robert Bell was one of "the young men" (licentiates) arraigned before the commissioners in 1805. A memorial for his ordination was pending when his presbytery was dissolved. His heroic wife belonged to the McCutcheon family of Logan County. Bell professed religion at McGready's meeting, September, 1800. When he felt himself called to preach he commenced a thorough classical

---

[1] Dr. Cossitt's Life and Times of Ewing, p. 253.
[2] *Medium*, 1846, p. 326.
[3] Minutes of Logan Presbytery, May, 1818.

course of study; but under the heavy pressure of calls from the destitute regions, and by the advice of the old preachers, he abandoned his studies and took the circuit. In his later writings he expresses his profound conviction, based on a life-time of close observation, that it would have been better for him to have completed the required course of study. Bell's manuscript autobiography is thoroughly interesting. He was living in Logan County, Kentucky, when McGready's great meetings began. He attended every one of them. His account of the commission and the council is also deeply interesting.

Robert Bell was the grandfather of the Rev. Dr. C. H. Bell, so well known in the church as general superintendent of missions. The father of Dr. C. H. Bell superintended the erection of temporary buildings on the site chosen for the mission, while Robert Bell and his wife taught temporarily in Colbert's house. In four weeks these temporary buildings were ready, and the school was moved into them.

In 1823 the Rev. John C. Smith and his wife were sent to assist in the mission. With a variable amount of hired help a tan-yard was built, a farm cleared and fenced, and a blacksmith shop and a saddler's shop established. Much of the manual labor was done by the missionary himself. With a family of thirty boarders, Mrs. Bell often had less, never more, than two assistants in the cooking and washing departments, though she generally had some ladies to aid her in the work of teaching the girls to spin and weave.

Government aid, under a general regulation of the United States, was secured for Bell's mission. The United States was aiding schools, under certain restrictions, in all the Indian tribes within our domains. Often, however, rivalry sprung up in the struggles of different churches to secure this aid. It was thus our first bargain for a school among the Choctaws was lost, and thus other far darker wrongs blackened the annals of our Indian schools in the North-west. Mr. Bell's mission secured government aid to the amount of about three hundred dollars per annum. This is the average, for there was an unaccountable irregularity both in the government aid and also in the contributions sent by the missionary board. The latter amounted, in 1824, to over a thousand dollars, but sunk to $272 in 1826, and to $142 in 1830. Until the last two years of the mission's life, during which no help was sent, the annual receipts from both these sources ranged between $367, the lowest, up to $1,494, the highest. The average, omitting the two years just mentioned, was $640. Out of this Mr. Bell paid all his assistants, and boarded, taught, and clothed gratuitously an average of twenty indigent students annually. His chief reliance for support was on his farm, which the students helped him to cultivate. There were also ten or twelve students who paid their own way. The assistant teachers were often changed. I find half a dozen persons mentioned at one time or another as assistants, who had grown weary of the hardships and the poverty, and left the institution; but Mr. Bell could not be driven away by hardships. If his meat gave out he mounted his horse, rode back to Tennessee, and begged hogs from his old acquaintances, and drove them himself to the mission. If the money gave out, he drew on his own little estate, hoping perhaps to be repaid, but if he had such hope, he had to wait till he got to heaven for its fulfillment. If his teachers left him, he put his son and daughter in their places, and doubled his own labors until other help could be had. He was farmer, preacher, traveling agent, government agent, with orders to collect information in philology, Indian archæology, Indian traditions, and to report in detail on the ornithology, zoology, and all the other "ologies" of the land he lived in.

It was hard enough to struggle as he had to do, without having burdens of heart-ache superadded by opposition from ministers of his own church. One of the dark backgrounds to every beautiful picture of the Cumberland Presbyterian ministry is the element of opposition to foreign missions which has always been found among the preachers. It is never opposition to foreign missions *per se*, but opposition on the plea of some fancied inexpediency. This element has never been very large, but it exists even to-day in all its mischievous power. It is no native growth. Its fitting home is with the Antinomians.

At the close of the late civil war, while the South was still a smoking ruin and the people impoverished, the General Assembly of the Southern Presbyterian church had one man who raised the question of expediency in regard to foreign missions. Then there rose in his place a man who still wore his army suit because too poor to buy any other, and uttered a sentence which deserves to be written in gold. He said: "To debate whether we shall now undertake missions to the heathen is to debate whether we shall now do what the Lord Jesus told us to do." There was not another voice raised in that Assembly against the expediency of foreign missions.

A suggestive history showing how a strong man was cured of his opposition to Bell's mission is found in a letter written by the Rev. Thomas Calhoun. This man was the Rev. William Barnett. The missionary society fell upon the expedient of sending him to inspect the mission for them, and report its condition. He accepted the appointment, and made his tour of inspection. Mr. Bell showed him all the exercises of the school, and had the children sing for him. This completely won him, and from that day onward the mission had no warmer friend than William Barnett. It would be well if all opposers of foreign missions could be brought into contact with those who are now laboring among the heathen, and see the fruit of missionary work. There were at least half a dozen cases of opposition to Bell's mission cured by visiting the institution. Opposition to missions, by good men, only needs to have the light shine on it, and it dies.

There is another interesting case. The Rev. William Moore, who was one of the first advocates of a mission school, removed, before Bell's school was established, to South Alabama, where at that time we had no organized churches. A few families of Cumberland Presbyterian immigrants were scattered in the vast whirlpool of new settlers from different countries, like Virgil's wrecked Trojans in the boiling waves of the ocean.[1] He wrote to Mr. Bell that he could do nothing in that new field for the mission. Mr. Bell made a vigorous presentation of the laws of success in home work, and their relations to a faithful discharge of our duties to the heathen; and Mr. Moore became a regular contributor himself, and collected money also from that pioneer people for Bell's mission.

Among Mr. Bell's papers are letters from nearly all the minis-

---

[1] "Rari nantes in gurgite vasto."

ters who belonged to the synod at that day. Bell's correspondence with the Hon. John C. Calhoun, Secretary of War, is in these files. A copy of a letter from the Indian chief, Levi Colbert, is here given:

CHICKASAW NATION, September 25, 1822.

Friend and Brother of the Cumberland Missionary Board:

I suppose you wish to know what the people of this Nation think of your missionary school, and what encouragement they seem disposed to give it. They talk favorably of the school, and are well satisfied with the manner in which it has been conducted. They wish it to be continued and carried into full operation, so that our poor people who are not able to board their children can have them educated. The more wealthy part of our Nation will give some assistance. . . . I have talked to the chiefs in council two or three times, and have met but little opposition. . . . We want our Nation to be enlightened, and to understand that gospel which you missionaries preach, and we wish all our good friends among the white people to pray for us.

I am your sincere friend,

LEVI COLBERT.

Mr. Bell, like all our first preachers, considered camp-meetings an indispensable part of the church machinery. We are not surprised, therefore, at finding annual camp-meetings at the mission mentioned in these records. Among the names of men who assisted in these meetings I find Alexander Chapman, David Foster, James S. Guthrie, James Stewart, and William Barnett. At one of the camp-meetings held at Bell's Mission Station was a convert whose name afterward became a household word in West Tennessee. I mean the Rev. Israel S. Pickens. He and his wife had been employed to assist in the establishment. Several of the Pickens family had, from time to time, been employed as assistants in some of the many departments of work about the mission, and thus it came about that Israel Pickens was at one of the camp-meetings.

Some extracts from Mrs. Bell's diary will now be given. The first is for 1823:

June 11.—Mr. Blair left us this morning on his way to Florence, after supplies for the use of the school.

June 14.—Received a letter from the sub-agency of this Nation informing us that the United States government had appropriated the sum of four hundred dollars for this institution this year, for the payment of the tuition of poor children; also informing us that five hundred dollars had been sent us last year, of which we never before heard. This was owing to the absence of the agent. We humbly trust that this assistance, when obtained, will enable us to bring a number more of these poor destitute heathen to a knowledge of the gospel.

June 15.—Mr. Smith, with most of the mission family, crossed the river to preach to the white people, just on the margin of a Christian land, where we had the inestimable privilege of worshiping God along with a respectable congregation.

It must have been sweet, after so long a time spent with uncivilized heathen, to meet a congregation of at least nominal Christians; but Mrs. Bell and the mission family were just as eager to attend meetings among the red men.

She says, in another place:

Mr. Smith preached at Cotton Gin Port to-day, from Matt. xvi. 26. There was a good audience, and they gave uncommonly good attention. Two of our scholars left the station to-day without leave, or any known cause. We suppose they have gone home to see their friends. They have been but a short time in school, and were greatly attached to their old habits.

June 20.—Attended to our weekly examination, which was satisfactory. The exercise in vocal music made us hope for the day when Indian congregations, instead of engaging in war songs and superstitious dances, will join in singing the songs of Zion.

June 21.—Received a letter from Mr. Bell, dated Limestone County, Alabama. He is well, and has encouraging success in raising funds for the mission.

Thus often did the missionary have to leave his work and go out to raise funds.

June 22.—For lack of an interpreter, Mr. Smith was prevented from filling his appointment to-day at Mr. James Wolf's, three miles distant.

Complaint about the great difficulty in securing regular and persevering attendance comes up in all Mr. Bell's reports, as it does in all the accounts which I ever saw of schools for Indians. The wild, free sons of the forest will not be bound down to hard study. They can learn well enough while they are at it, but they will not stick to their task. Of the twenty Indians sent to Cumberland University during my connection with that institution, only one was graduated and he only in the scientific course.

Chapter XV.] EARLY MISSIONS TO THE INDIANS. 139

June 26.—Mr. Smith saw four white men on their way to see a dance among the Indians. These white men were all drinking, and some of them were already drunk. It is bad enough for white people to encourage the superstitious dances of the Indians, but to carry drunkenness among them is too bad. It is this which makes the chief obstacle to the success of missions.

July 16.—We were visited to-day by Colonel G——, who has been bitterly opposed to our mission. The children read and sang for him. He is completely won over. O that all our people who oppose the mission would make us a visit!

The mission boarded, taught, and clothed the pupils. Over half of these were charged no fees at all, they being too poor to pay. By order of the board the free list was limited to twenty. The school usually numbered thirty-five. A touching case is given in Mrs. Bell's diary of two bright Indian children below the regulation age, who were brought to the school by their parents. They were very poor. The school was overtaxed and oppressed by the number of beneficiary pupils, which was already two more than the board's limit. But these naked children of the forest were specially bright, and Mrs. Bell determined to take them.

The hardships and sufferings of these missionaries were equal to any borne by missionaries to distant heathen lands. Often the money sent the mission was so greatly under par that it was difficult to use it. Mr. Bell, besides all his other labors, cultivated a considerable farm, and in this way helped to keep the establishment from starving. Many of the Indians who paid either all or part of their boarding, paid in cattle, and the supply of milk was largely depended on as a means of support. The contributions from the churches were a curious medley. Cotton cloth was a chief item. Raw cotton, beeves, socks, flax cloth, and jeans were also among the contributions.

At different times persons sent by the missionary board to visit the mission made stirring reports of the hardships and privations suffered by the missionaries. At no time was there a sufficient supply of either money, clothing, or provisions sent to them. The Rev. David Foster and the Rev. James S. Guthrie, after a visit to this mission, wrote to the board as follows:

Mr. and Mrs. Bell have more labor of different kinds than their strength can stand, and unless they have in future some assistance their days must be shortened.

An extract from Mrs. Bell's journal will show how painful it was to the missionaries to reject the applications of the destitute:

January 4, 1823.—Mr. Pitchland has visited us again this day, soliciting us to take under our care another little son, ... but we were obliged to turn him off; and, with hearts full of regret, we informed him that we were obliged to circumscribe our wishes for want of funds to furnish the necessary support.

It was the custom of Mr. Bell and his assistants, one of whom was always a preacher, to go out into the Indian country and preach. Levi Colbert, the chief already mentioned, opened his house on such occasions as a preaching place.

Regular quarterly reports of the work done by this mission were sent to the missionary board. The average number taught per session was about thirty-five. The programme for daily duties in the mission was reported to the board. It was as follows:

At daylight the trumpet is blown, the signal for all to rise. In half an hour it is blown again, the signal for family worship, which all, black, white, and red, are to attend in the dining-room. After worship Mr. Bell and the boys go to the farm and Mrs. Bell and the girls to spinning and weaving. At eight o'clock comes breakfast; then come school hours till twelve; then an hour's interval for dinner and rest; school again from one till four; then labor in field and loom till six; then supper and worship. All the students share alike in the manual labor, which amounts, in summer, to four hours daily.

Manual labor schools for white people as well as for Indians had just come into fashion.

Two or three years before the purchase of this country from the Indians its cession to the whites was agitated to an extent that seriously interfered with the mission. Then came the startling tidings that the chiefs had signed a treaty with the United States government agreeing to vacate all the soil of Mississippi. Although the promised exodus from the State dragged its reluctant fulfillment through many bitter years, yet even the prospect of a treaty two years before its ratification terminated all aid for the mission, both from government and church.

Mr. Bell tried for two years to carry on the school without aid, relying on the farm, tuition fees, and his own private funds for support; but the excitement among the Indians over the sale of their country, and the clamor of government agents who were struggling to remove the Indians, made it absolutely necessary to close the mission. Mr. Bell's final settlement with the board was made in 1832, but he remained in the same country the rest of his days, preaching to the white people. The fruits of this mission are abundant to-day among the Indians of the West, as well as among the redeemed in glory. As the second period of this history extends only to 1829, all further discussion of the church's work among the Indians belongs to a later chapter. A noble biographical sketch of Mr. Bell has been published by Dr. Beard, to which sketch the reader is referred. It is evident, however, that Dr. Beard never saw Mr. Bell's autobiography. It is in manuscript and will be placed in the Cumberland University library. It deserves to be published.

CHAPTER XVI.

PLANTING CHURCHES IN THE NEW TERRITORIES OF EAST AND WEST TENNESSEE AND THE KENTUCKY PURCHASE.

> Far off on the desert mountains
>   To wandering souls it came,
> That sound of a tender message,
>   That pleading in Christ's name;
> It followed the sorrowful path they trod,
> Till the wandering spirits were turned to God.
> —*A. A.*

IN the very States where the church originated there were new fields opened to white settlers after the church was organized. These were the Hiwassee Purchase, in East Tennessee, all of what is now called West Tennessee, and all that portion of Kentucky lying west of the Tennessee River. All of East Tennessee up to 1815 was unbroken soil, so far as our people were concerned. Long before our evangelists went to this field pressing demands for the revival preachers to visit East Tennessee had been made. Early in 1800 visitors to the camp-meetings had carried the revival spirit over the mountains and spread it among the churches. Opposition arose there, as it did in McGready's field. The ministry were divided there too on the revival question. The doctrine of a general atonement began to stir the Presbyterian churches there also. The cry for more preachers rang through those mountains as it had rung along the banks of the Cumberland. From Mr. McMullen's MS. we learn that all the presbyteries of East Tennessee were stirred on the question, "Did Christ die for everybody?" The revival awakened that question wherever it entered Presbyterian communities. The cry for more preachers also arose wherever the revival went. This, while historically a fact, was also a logical consequence. Itinerant preaching also followed wherever the revival entered new settlements.

The outcry against disorder in church was raised by the Old Side party in East Tennessee, as it had been in Cumberland. Dr. Henderson led one party and Dr. Blackburn the other. But justice to Dr. Henderson requires me to state that his opposition to the revival never went to such extremes, nor resorted to such ecclesiastical violence as characterized the anti-revival party in the Kentucky Synod.

We have preserved to us a letter of remonstrance written by Mr. McGready to his Old Side brethren in East Tennessee. He says:

Tell my brethren to let the Lord choose his own way of working; to bid the Spirit of God welcome, even though he should choose to work among them as he does among the Methodists. Tell them to be more afraid of sinners being damned for want of religion, than of what they call disorder when sinners cry out for mercy.

Before our church sent any evangelists into East Tennessee, an ecclesiastical barrier was interposed between them and even the revival party of that country. The Presbyterian church had forbidden its clergy recognizing as ministers any of the Cumberland Presbyterian preachers, and had also forbidden its members communing with the members of our church at the Lord's table. Therefore our first missionaries there had to encounter the open opposition of one party and the lack of co-operation from the other. Our first evangelists in that field were Thomas Calhoun and Robert Donnell. The published dates of this first mission to East Tennessee are all wrong. I have before me Calhoun's written history of it, and I also have Robert Donnell's diary, kept throughout that whole tour. That diary says: "Through the mercy of God we met in McMinnville, Tennessee, the last day of June, 1815, according to agreement."

They began their meetings in Sequatchie Valley first, where they had good success; and then they crossed the mountains to the field which they had chosen. Their first work was at Washington. Then they went into the Hiwassee country, though Indians still occupied large portions thereof. They next visited Morganton and Maryville. They expected to preach in the Presbyterian church at Maryville, as its pastor, Dr. Anderson, was one of the revival party. They had sent their appointment to him, but the ecclesiastical interdict was not to be trampled on. When they entered the church, though a little in advance of the preaching hour, Dr. Anderson was up preaching. At the close of his sermon he called on Donnell to conclude. "Donnell gave an exhortation which set the house on fire."[1] The soberest of Dr. Anderson's members, and even his elders, went to shouting. The people rose to their feet and crowded around Donnell, begging him to stay and protract the meeting. Dr. Anderson took the evangelists home with him to dinner. At the table he said, "The Methodists (!) gave Mr. Donnell a very hearty welcome to-day." The evangelists then left an appointment for a meeting to be held at the seminary, and went to some of Dr. Blackburn's churches, where they were kindly received. The doctrines they preached were indorsed by Dr. Blackburn's members, and his congregations received some valuable accessions. No effort was made to take advantage of his courtesy by organizing a Cumberland Presbyterian church. Then they returned to Maryville and held their meeting in the seminary. Dr. Anderson not only attended that meeting, but followed them to one they held in the country. At the country meeting Donnell's sermons set the people to shouting, old Presbyterian elders being the chief performers. Dr. Anderson caught the fire and leaped over rigid boundaries for a moment, but, recollecting himself, he returned to the order required by his church. Thus the evangelists went on through all of East Tennessee, helping to build up the congregations of the revival party, but refusing in all cases throughout that tour to organize any Cumberland Presbyterian church. They held a meeting in a grove near Kingston, and there Calhoun was taken sick. Thus ended this campaign.

The next year an unconverted man by the name of Miller came all the way from East Tennessee to Smyrna church, Jackson County, Tennessee, to beg Calhoun to make another visit to his country. Calhoun gave him a long list of appointments. One of these was at the Indian town named Calhoun. Another was at the Indian agency, now Athens. In this trip Calhoun met with, and preached to, W. C. McKamy, who afterward became a very

---

[1] The Calhoun papers.

efficient minister. All through East Tennessee the solitary evangelist went, preaching where Miller had previously published his appointments.

The next account we have of preaching in East Tennessee by our people is in the records of Nashville Presbytery, spring of 1818, in which David Foster is ordered to a regular circuit in East Tennessee, to spend his whole time there till the next meeting of the presbytery. He complied with the order. In 1821 J. S. Guthrie was sent to the Hiwassee circuit. It is to be regretted that we have none of the details of these two tours of evangelism, but what we know about the two noble evangelists leaves us no room to doubt that their work in East Tennessee, as in all the other places where they labored, was abundantly fruitful. The language used by the presbytery in Foster's and Guthrie's appointment to this field would indicate known and established circuits, on which former missionaries had labored. It is quite likely that evangelists were sent thither the next year after Calhoun's voluntary mission (1816), or that such evangelists went voluntarily to that field, but if this is so we have no record of the fact.

J. S. Guthrie was a "rough ashlar," just out of nature's quarry, but he had an intellect full of native vigor, and was well versed in Scripture and in the doctrines of his church. His work was everywhere owned of God, and its results still abide. All the numerous anecdotes about Guthrie have something ludicrous mixed with an awful solemnity. He was continued in East Tennessee till 1823.

The same year Robert Baker and Abner Lansden, two men like minded, both sweet spirits, were sent to that country. In 1824 George Donnell and S. M. Aston were also sent thither, and for many long years these two noble spirits preached Jesus in that field. They were very unlike in many things, yet they were deeply devoted to each other. We have a grand biography of George Donnell, written by President T. C. Anderson. It would be an effort "to paint the rose" should I try to add to that truthful picture; but we have no biography of his noble fellow-laborer. S. M. Aston was a strong thinker, outspoken, independent, rather blunt in his utterances, fearless, and fully persuaded that God was with him. While Donnell could make the people weep and win the enemies' hearts, Aston could wield strong arguments that would convince the gainsayers. Abner W. Lansden was often sent to this field. Once S. Y. Thomas was sent to assist in this work. All these were then young men and not ordained. The anti-revival party of the Presbyterian church mocked at their youth, their homespun clothing, and their lack of classical education; yet these young men gradually made their way, winning the hearts and confidence of even the Old Side party.

One little sketch, taken from President Anderson's excellent biography of George Donnell, is here given to illustrate how these "boys" overcame prejudice:[1]

> You may have some idea of our meeting if you will fancy yourself looking over the weeping congregation, and beholding here an Old School man on his knees bending over four children, all come to years of maturity, and all crying for mercy; and there an old gray-headed sire, with streaming eyes, in great agony for a whole family of children; and yonder a mother in Israel on her knees, bending over a husband and four grown children, all unconverted.

The meeting here alluded to was held in the midst of an Old Side community, and these parents were Old Side in their antecedents. But their prejudices were swept away when all their children found Jesus and salvation.

Many Presbyterians offered their private dwellings for these missionaries to preach in. One case of this kind deserves special notice. Thomas Gallagher was an elder in the Presbyterian church, and had a son who was a faithful minister in that church. Yet he, like many others, offered the use of his house to George Donnell for regular circuit appointments. Four of Mr. Gallagher's children afterward claimed George Donnell as their spiritual father. Thus the Lord compensated the old elder for his liberality to a youthful missionary of a proscribed church.

There are many accounts of bitter prejudice against the missionaries among those belonging to the Old Side party in that day, but it is a source of great comfort to know that no such prejudice is to be encountered in that country now. In a long preaching

---

[1] Life of George Donnell, pp. 190, 191.

tour among the people of East Tennessee a few years ago, I met nothing but kindness and co-operation from the ministry of the Presbyterian church.

The first camp-meeting which our people held in East Tennessee was at Low's Ferry, in 1823. The second was at a spot long ago endeared to a thousand hearts. This meeting was held in 1824, at Concord, in Knox County, by the missionaries, assisted by two of the old men who came across the mountains for this purpose. These old men were Thomas Calhoun and Samuel McSpeddin, and along with them came Robert Baker. The meeting was a great victory, and laid the foundation for several churches.

In 1826 a curious spectacle greets us. The Lebanon Presbytery crossed the mountains and held its meeting in a private house belonging to Mr. Cowan, in Grassy Valley, East Tennessee. This fact indicates the deep interest felt for that field, and will do so all the more when we remember that "horseback" was the only mode of travel.

The next year (1827) Knoxville Presbytery was organized. Its original members were George Donnell, S. M. Aston, Abner W. Lansden, and William Smith. These four men were our ministers in that field till about the close of this period, when another noble band took their places.

It ought to bring a blush to the cheeks of East Tennesseans even to this day to know how poorly all these early missionaries were paid. That George Donnell should be laughed at for his homespun coat, worn out at the elbows, is no credit to our people, especially when we remember how unspeakably precious the labors of this man of God were. In a MS. history of the Presbyterian church in East Tennessee I find the same kind of bitter complaints. These early preachers were not paid. Great improvement has been made in this respect, but there is room for yet further progress. Nor is East Tennessee the only field needing such improvement.

In Thomas Calhoun's manuscripts are several glimpses at the hard life which pioneer preachers encountered in East Tennessee. Once in his journey he stayed all night at the house of a preacher. There were cracks or openings between the logs of the cabin through which the hogs passed in and out with uninterrupted freedom. Often his meals consisted of nothing but hominy. Bridges and ferry-boats were a luxury reserved for the great thoroughfares or for later times. Swimming rivers was a pastime whose attractions would meet small appreciation in our day.

In Hugh Kirkpatrick's manuscripts he speaks of his feet being frost-bitten in one of his preaching tours. His meetings were eminently successful. At a camp-meeting held by him in East Tennessee there were two hundred conversions. In such a sparse population that was a great number. He says of this meeting: "We worked up all the material."

The country west of the Tennessee River was bought from the Indians in 1819. It was settled very rapidly. Many Cumberland Presbyterians were among its pioneers. An anecdote of the Rev. N. I. Hess, a Cumberland Presbyterian minister, who had explored all of West Tennessee before it was bought from the Indians, is here given. When the friends of the Mobile and Ohio Railroad were making a canvass to secure subscriptions to its stock they employed two orators, one a distinguished congressman and the other Mr. Hess. At each barbecue Hess would tell some incident of his early travels and adventures in that very neighborhood before the country belonged to white men, and would so adroitly use it as to leave the congressman clear behind in popularity. The congressman chafed at this and resolved on a remedy. He determined to transfer their canvass to the other side of their field, where, he supposed, the pioneer tours of Hess had not extended. The plan was agreed to and a barbecue was prepared at a big spring on the other side of the district. The congressman spoke first, and being confident of victory he made a great effort. When Hess arose his first sentence was, "Just forty years ago, in company with two red men of the forest, I drank water out of that spring;" and then, with more than his wonted felicity, he painted the wonderful progress and grander destiny of West Tennessee.

The Nashville Presbytery established circuits in West Tennessee just as soon as that country was settled by white people. The first itinerants sent thither were John L. Dillard and James McDonnold, and they began their work in 1820, less than a year after the purchase of the country from the Indians. In 1821 Richard Beard was sent to the "Forked Deer" circuit. Dr. Beard, to his dying day, loved to talk about his experience on this circuit. There were no bridges. The country is flat and its water-courses spread for miles over the bottoms in the rainy seasons. Some of these bottoms are three miles wide, with sloughs at intervals over all their extent. When the water covered all the bottom there were stakes or blazed trees to indicate where the road was. Between these stakes, in water often coming up to the horse's sides, the missionary would make his way until a deep slough was reached, into which he plunged without warning, and across which the horse had to swim. Nor were water-courses the only difficulty. There were quicksands. A crust over these would bear a horse safely one time, and perhaps the next trip the crust would break, and horse and rider would then be fortunate if they ever got out alive. Besides all this, a large part of the pioneer population was shaking with the ague. The missionaries shared in this affliction, but were not thereby kept from filling their appointments.

Robert Baker, J. S. Guthrie, and J. W. Rea (1823) were also sent by the Nashville Presbytery to this land of cypress knees and quicksands. Thomas Calhoun made a brief tour through this region on his own responsibility, and was so delighted with the country that he determined to make it his home. He secured a tract of land for this purpose, but finding his congregations arrayed against his removal, he sold his West Tennessee land, and never again tried to leave his first field of labor.

Camp-meetings came, of course. Other preachers besides Calhoun bought lands in this splendid cotton delta, and were not dissuaded from settling on them. At Robert Baker's camp-ground, Old Shiloh, in Carroll County, David Crockett, the bear killer, would sometimes attend the meetings, dressed in homespun shirt and without any coat. This camp-ground could itself furnish ample material for a volume. It has ever been famous for its precious revivals. The name of Robert Baker is a household treasure in all West Tennessee. Having known him well in my boyhood, I think I could give an epitome of his biography in one sentence: He was noted for sweetness of character, holiness of life, and a loving earnestness in the pulpit which never failed to win the hearts of his hearers.

The Rev. S. Y. Thomas, of precious memory, was another pioneer in this field. At the old Yorkville camp-ground many were converted under his ministry, and his name and memory are still fresh in all that country.

The Rev. William Barnett was among the preachers who took up their permanent abode in West Tennessee. He immediately established a camp-ground and a church. From Dr. Beard's biographical sketches I extract an item about Barnett's preaching in this country. He was at a camp-meeting at McLemoresville, and the sermon here spoken of was on Monday. Dr. Beard was present, and gives the description from his own observation. We all know that Dr. Beard did not at any time make his statements too strong. He says: "On Monday he preached on the subject of the judgment. It was a sermon of great power. . . . It was terrific. The crowd trembled under the influence of its awful and overwhelming appeals. Such appeals are seldom heard, and such impressions are seldom made now. He closed with a great movement in the congregation. Many were convicted and hopefully converted that evening." By universal consent William Barnett was called the Boanerges of the church.

In 1824 the order for the organization of the first presbytery in that field was issued. It was called Hopewell, and still bears that name. Its original members were William Barnett, Richard Beard, Samuel Harris, and John C. Smith. The first meeting of this presbytery was at McLemoresville, in Carroll County. West Tennessee soon became one of the great strongholds of the church, and remains so to this day.

What was called Jackson's Purchase in Kentucky now contains seven counties of that State. This country and the Forked Deer region of Tennessee were opened to white settlers about the same time. Cumberland Presbyterians in both Tennessee and Kentucky seemed to feel some responsibility for the religious cultivation of this field, but it was many years before our people in either of these States assumed the sole oversight of this work. Lying in Kentucky, it was separated from the circuits of our missionaries in that State by two great rivers, which flow only twelve miles apart. The inconvenience this caused will be better understood when we remember that the lower Tennessee River is too wide to swim, many horses utterly failing to reach the farther shore when they are made to try the dangerous experiment.

An illustration of the trouble a Kentucky missionary had on account of these rivers is here recorded. The Rev. B. H. Pierson, D.D., now of Arkansas, was one of the pioneer preachers in this field. He is now (1886) in his eighty-third year. He says:[1]

We traveled with but little if any remuneration. . . . My circuit was arranged so that I had to ferry the Cumberland four times each round. Once I came to the bank of this stream without a cent. How I would get over the river I knew not; but having to call on a brother who lived close to the ferry, when I started from his house he, without knowing the state of my finances, handed me a "bit"—twelve and a half cents—remarking, "This will pay your ferriage."

Still there were other ferriages to be paid, but the preacher went on his way. He says: "I had the altar and the wood, but where was the sacrifice?" God provided it. He preached that day, and after the benediction was pronounced, and he was ready to set out for the next ferry, a lady in shaking hands with him left a whole dollar in his hands. With overflowing thankfulness of heart the preacher went on his way, with money enough in his pocket to pay eight ferriages. This was the amount received for a whole year's labor.

Dr. Pierson says there were no meeting-houses in this region at that day. All the preaching was done in private houses, or out under the trees. He speaks of a two days' meeting in a private house where there were seventeen conversions. In this year's work in this new field Mr. Pierson had for his associate in missionary labor the Rev. Adlai Boyd, of Kentucky.

I have been able to secure only very meager accounts of the church's early work in Jackson's Purchase. This mention of Dr. Pierson's experience will have to suffice for a sample, and it is doubtless a fair sample of what all our first missionaries in that field could relate, were they still living.

---

[1] Dr. Crisman's "Our Old Men," p. 76.

The Logan Presbytery, when its territory included what are now five States, could not cultivate all its field. It sent men to Indiana, Illinois, Ohio, and Missouri, when, if a selfish localism had governed it, it might have employed every preacher it had in its home field. Yet that noble presbytery, though it was sending so many missionaries to the West, still struggled to build up the church in Kentucky. The whole State was divided first into two districts, and later into four. In each of these districts evangelists preached every day in the week. The biography of those evangelists would include the whole history of our church. Chapman, Harris, Hunter, Lowry, Bryan, Knight, Delany, Johnson, Philip McDonnold, John and William Barnett, McLin, McDowell, Lynn, and many others, were on the roll of evangelists sent out in that day. Stirring accounts of their meetings come to us in great numbers.

In the later years of this second period the number of noble workers in our Kentucky pulpits grew to such proportions as to render it impracticable to give special individual descriptions. Only sample incidents can be indulged.

The Rev. Matthew Houston Bone, began his career in Kentucky. At one camp-meeting where he expected to have the assistance of several older preachers, he being then only a licentiate, he found himself to be the only preacher in attendance. He spent nearly all the first night in prayer. His soul was distressed not only about the overwhelming responsibility which had fallen upon him, but he could decide on no text for the morrow's sermon. However, a text on which he had no sermon was impressed on his mind, and he accepted it as from the Lord. He preached next day from this text with wonderful freedom and power. The whole vast audience was deeply moved, and a work of grace began which resulted in a great number of conversions.

"Scotch" Smith and Dr. Cossitt both entered the ministry in our Kentucky pulpits during this period. One was a camp-meeting preacher, the other made his grandest record in connection with our educational enterprises.

The incident in the life of Mr. Bone just cited, is characteristic of our early preachers. They believed not only that God guided them in the selection of their texts, but they earnestly believed that on some occasions he gave the whole sermon as well as the text. An incident in point is given from the autobiography of the Rev. H. A. Hunter. It was at a camp-meeting at Mt. Moriah, near Russellville, Kentucky. Hunter was to preach, but could think of no suitable text or sermon. He was just beginning his ministry, and had but few ready-made sermons. In those days the senior minister who managed such matters often issued his orders to the young preacher only a short time before he required him to begin his sermon. Hunter, receiving orders thus, fled in dismay to the woods. Falling prostrate there he poured out his complaints to the Lord. There were only a few moments for prayer. The time to preach came, but there was no light, no text, no sermon. He rose and went to the pulpit. They sang a hymn, and while they sang, text and sermon too were impressed on the young preacher's mind. He rose and read, "Ye have said it is a vain thing to serve God." He testifies that each successive sentence came like an inspiration, until, the sermon over, he "called for mourners," and more came than could find room to kneel. That was at the nine o'clock morning service. The usual second sermon had to be omitted, and all the rest of that day was spent instructing and praying for anxious souls. Many were made glad in Jesus that day. Many cases in which the Holy Spirit did undoubtedly guide the minister in his arguments have occurred among the truly consecrated preachers of the Cross in all churches and all ages. These cases have by no means been confined to ignorant and visionary men; but in instances coming within my own observation, men of the profoundest scholarship and severest habits of study have been led out beyond all their accustomed fields of research into arguments and illustrations not their own—arguments whose divine origin was abundantly vindicated afterward when the preacher discovered their exact fitness to a state of things of which he was profoundly ignorant at the time he delivered the sermon. The writer, in his own experience, has seen and felt and known enough of this truth fully to convince him of the fact of the Holy Spirit's presence and power in such cases.

The Rev. G. W. Reynolds, of Berdan, Illinois, describes a Kentucky camp-meeting in which the Rev. Henry F. Delany set forth in a sermon the contrast between the eternal future destiny of the saved and the lost. The two worlds were so vividly painted that they seemed to be right before the people. An awful sense of their reality filled all hearts. The sermon closed, and the preacher took his seat without "calling for mourners" or asking any one to conclude the services. In silence and tears all sat for ten minutes, when M. H. Bone rose to his feet and without uttering a word walked slowly down from the pulpit and out to the woods. The congregation followed his example. In the woods, that universal resort for private prayer in those days, more than a thousand people were soon prostrate before God. No dinner nor supper was eaten that day. At night the praying multitude gathered at the place of public worship, and the Holy Spirit was poured out in converting power to the salvation of great numbers. Mr. Reynolds thinks that this was the meeting which the Rev. Dr. Samuel Miller attended when he got those impressions about Mr. Delany's preaching which he described in the letter spoken of in a previous chapter.

Mr. McGready's field of labor was in Logan County, Kentucky, and the history of the origin of the Cumberland Presbyterian church in all the older portions of the State belongs to the first period of this history. Two things conspired to prevent our church from gaining that pre-eminence in this field which seemed at first to be its heritage. One was the bitterness of the anti-revival Presbyterians, and the other was the immense emigration of Kentuckians to the new territories. In most cases these emigrants sold their Kentucky lands to Baptists from Virginia. The Cumberland Presbyterians had no churches in Virginia, from which State nearly all these land buyers came. Still the church grew in Kentucky. Before the close of this second period, Cumberland Presbyterians had three strong presbyteries in this State, all remarkably like their mother—old Logan Presbytery. They all held special fast-days to pray for more ministers to be called into the great harvest, and sent many of these ministers, when they were called, to labor among the destitute in the new countries. They also tried, so far as they could by the itinerant system, supplemented by camp-meetings, to cultivate their home field.

CHAPTER XVII.

PLANTING CHURCHES IN ALABAMA.

> Now the training, strange and lowly,
> Unexplained and tedious now;
> Afterward the service holy,
> And the Master's "Enter thou."
> —*F. R. H.*

A GLANCE at the history of Alabama is necessary to a correct understanding of the church's work in that State. The country was all claimed by Georgia under its original charter from England. Several efforts were made by Georgia to place colonies on this soil, but as the whole land was in the hands of Indians and Spaniards, who also claimed the country, it generally cost the Georgians their lives to settle there. Those who escaped did so by promising allegiance to the Indians or the Spaniards.

Then the United States bought Georgia's claim to this country, but Spaniards and Indians still had not only their claims, but also what is called "nine points in the law"—possession. A territorial government was however established, and all the country was called Mississippi, and continued to be so designated till 1817.

In 1805 the Indian claim to a small portion of what is now Madison County, Alabama, was purchased, and settlements were established and the Indians withdrawn in less than two years afterward. In 1813 the long-promised, long-delayed evacuation of South Alabama by the Spanish was accomplished. In 1814 the Creek claim to that portion of Alabama was extinguished, but hostile Creeks still roamed over it and made it unsafe for Americans.

In 1816 the country east of Cotton Gin Port, on the Tombigbee River, was bought from the Chickasaw Indians. In 1817 the first Territorial legislature assembled, Alabama being then severed from Mississippi. In that legislature there was but one senator. Some of the counties represented had in their elections cast but ten votes.

There were just three settlements of Americans in the Territory—one centering at Mobile, one at Huntsville, and one on the Tombigbee River. There were hostile Creek Indians, and a Creek war on Alabama soil as late as 1836. The way to the American settlements in South Alabama was open and free from danger only by the sea, though Georgians and Carolinians sometimes took their chances and traveled along the land route from the east. Travel from Tennessee and Kentucky was sometimes accomplished on rafts down the Tombigbee, but there was very little emigration by that dangerous route.

When the country about Huntsville was first settled, and before the organization of the Cumberland Presbyterian church, "the council" sent Robert Bell to the new settlements around Hunt's Spring. The next year, 1808, the council sent Thomas Calhoun to the same field, and he preached in Hunt's house before that house was finished. The next year (1809) the council sent Robert Donnell to that field, and kept him there till the new denomination was organized. It was a favorite field with him all his life. His ashes rest in North Alabama. Our old churches all over that country were planted by him.

In 1817 a family that had just arrived from South Carolina visited Donnell's camp-meeting at the Meridian church, and several of its members were converted. One of these was a boy seventeen years old, who from that day to this has been helping to preach Jesus to the people of North Alabama. His name is A. J. Steele. John Carnahan[1] and he rode the circuit together, in 1819, through North Alabama, attending all of Donnell's camp-meetings. A little later John Morgan and Albert Gibson joined the band of Alabama preachers. Then came other noble laborers, and North Alabama bloomed like the garden of the Lord.

In John Morgan's diary he states that the distance around his circuit was four hundred miles. From Steele's autobiography (MS.) we learn that three new camp-grounds were established on his circuit the first year. This was everywhere the order of things. The young men, as soon as they were received as candi-

---

[1] Carnahan's home was then in Arkansas, but he was under the orders of Elk Presbytery.

dates, were sent out as evangelists on circuits; and they went, too, pay or no pay. The old men attended the camp-meetings, and occasionally made tours of evangelism, but sustained also, in some cases, the nominal relation of pastor to some congregations. This relation, in many cases, was so loose, that any preacher of the church living within reach of a congregation which had one of these nominal pastors might, without asking the pastor's or the session's consent, send an appointment for regular monthly preaching on any unoccupied Sabbath. While all the work of the church was devoted to planting congregations, the absurdity of such Presbyterianism was not keenly felt. There came a time, however, when it sent a wail of woe throughout the denomination.

The Elk Presbytery, in 1820, ordered two of its members to establish a circuit in South Alabama, but for satisfactory reasons they both failed to comply. In 1821 the General Synod appointed certain preachers to go to South Alabama and organize a presbytery. There were candidates for the ministry who wanted to settle in that field, and it was believed that a presbytery might soon secure a local supply of ministers; but this attempt to form a presbytery composed entirely of non-resident ministers was a failure. A quorum never met. This, as will be seen elsewhere, was not the only instance in which the church sent non-residents to such a work.

In 1817, just one year from the time the country east of Cotton Gin Port was purchased from the Indians, we find Cumberland Presbyterian pioneers from that region petitioning Elk Presbytery to send them a preacher. The presbytery requested Robert Donnell to go to their relief, but for satisfactory reasons he failed to do so. The next year (1818) the ladies' missionary board of Elk Presbytery sent Samuel King and William Moore to that field, and to a portion of the Indian country west of the Tombigbee. From the autobiography of the Rev. R. D. King (son of the Rev. Samuel King), there are indications that these two men labored more among the Indians than among the white emigrants; but they reported at the next meeting of presbytery that they had complied with the instructions of the missionary board.

The manuscript autobiography of the Rev. R. D. King says:

In April, 1821, I was ordered by the presbytery to form a circuit on the south side of Tennessee River, in the counties of Morgan, Lawrence, and Franklin, in Alabama. I had to hunt my own preaching places, and make my own appointments. The country was all newly settled, having been lately purchased from the Indians. Here I found many good Cumberland Presbyterians. I formed a circuit of four weeks' extent, with regular daily appointments. I succeeded in getting up three camp-meetings, one in Morgan County (then Cataco County). Here I was assisted by the Rev. James Stewart, the Rev. James Moore, and my father. . . . The results of those three camp-meetings were one hundred and fifty professions. Besides these, there were a good many professions at my circuit appointments. I never failed to reach my appointments. I received in compensation from the people sixty dollars. During all this time I was only a candidate.

In the fall of 1821 Elk Presbytery ordered R. D. King, then a licentiate, and Daniel Patton, then a candidate, to go to South Alabama and form a circuit. They began their work on the head waters of the Black Warrior. The Pleasant Valley, Jones Valley, and farther south to Cahawba were their fields of action. King's manuscript says:

South Alabama was newly settled, mainly with people from the Carolinas and Georgia. They had never seen a Cumberland Presbyterian before our visit. What they had heard of us was from our enemies; so we had to fight our way against prejudice and opposition. We traveled separately, and never failed, either of us, to reach our appointments. We often had to swim the rivers. We preached every day. God blessed our labors. We gathered societies under a written compact to organize regular congregations as soon as an ordained minister could be had for the purpose. This was the beginning of the church in South Alabama. On our way to the meeting of presbytery in the spring we swam five streams in one day. Hundreds of persons petitioned for us to be sent back. For this winter tour I received nothing.

These evangelists were not sent back, however, but sent to other destitute fields, and for a little season the seed planted in South Alabama was left to grow without cultivation or to perish.

The Tombigbee Presbytery, organized in 1823, extended partly into Alabama: but the first successful effort to form a presbytery in the southern portion of the State was made in 1824. The manner in which the new presbytery was organized is typical. The Rev.

Benjamin Lockhart and two licensed preachers had settled in that portion of the State. The Rev. William Moore declared himself ready to move to South Alabama for the sake of the church. The Tennessee Presbytery, which was cut off of the Elk Presbytery in 1821, resolved to hold an intermediate session in South Alabama for the purpose of ordaining the two licensed preachers who had settled there, and in this way to provide a quorum for the organization of Alabama Presbytery. All this was in obedience to an order of synod. It was a long journey for a whole presbytery to make, but men did not shrink from such journeys in those days. Hostile Indians roamed between Tennessee Presbytery and South Alabama, but a quorum was present at the appointed time. At this meeting the presbytery ordained John Williams and James W. Dickey, the two licentiates. William Moore attended, and he and Benjamin Lockhart, together with the two newly-ordained ministers, constituted the Alabama Presbytery, and made that field their permanent home.

This presbytery had a strange, hard field. With hostile Indians near at hand; with a population mainly from States where Cumberland Presbyterians were unknown; with one of its members already past the period of life for much active labor; with the bitterest misrepresentations, both of its doctrines and its practices, actively circulated; with a location isolated from all the rest of the church: it is not strange that this presbytery did not grow as did some others.

It has been my aim to avoid the discussion of all those prejudices which once embittered the spirit of many in the Presbyterian church; but the history of the early struggles of our own church absolutely requires some mention of these things. An incident taken from the manuscript autobiography of the Rev. R. D. King will suffice to illustrate the state of things in South Alabama when Cumberland Presbyterians began their work in that field. The State legislature then met at Cahawba, and it was in session while King was there. Several of its members knew King, and invited him to preach for them, which he did. As there was no house of worship in the place, the three denominations of the town each had procured the use of the State-house for one Sabbath per month.

This left one Sabbath unoccupied. By a formal and official resolution the legislature invited King to take possession of the house for that vacant Sabbath. He accepted their invitation, and left an appointment. When the time for his appointment arrived, and he was on his way to the place of preaching, the resident minister of the Presbyterian church came driving rapidly past him in his buggy. When King, who was walking, entered the hall, which was then thronged with people, this Presbyterian preacher, whose name was Sloss, was up lining out a hymn. After song and prayer, Mr. Sloss announced a text and proceeded to preach. The sergeant-at-arms of the legislature came to King and said: "Sir, with your permission, I will put him out." King, however, begged him not to interfere. Mr. Sloss gave a horrid caricature of the doctrines, the practices, and the ignorance of the Cumberland Presbyterians, and warned everybody against having any thing to do with them. After the benediction, King announced preaching for the afternoon. When the hour arrived, he had a crowded hall, and there was a solemn and precious meeting without the least allusion to Mr. Sloss or his caricature of our people. When Mr. Sloss came to his own appointment the next Sabbath, his wife was his only auditor. He tried one more time to fill his regular day, and again his wife was his only hearer, the members of his own church reprobating his conduct as much as others. Then he closed out his work in Cahawba.

The Rev. Gibson W. Murray, whose parents were South Carolina Presbyterians, was brought in early life to South Alabama. While visiting relatives near Elyton, this young man attended the first Cumberland Presbyterian camp-meeting he had ever seen. It was all new and strange to him, and the newest and strangest thing of it all was the preaching. He says in his manuscript autobiography, which is before me, that the preaching he had been used to from childhood was about the decrees, about the absolute certainty of all the elect being saved, and that all this had never in any way disturbed his conscience. He felt that nothing he could do would in anywise change his predetermined destiny. The religion upon which he had been brought up consisted in keeping the Sabbath sacred, and in being whipped on Monday for any failure in his catechism lesson the day before. But this camp-meeting opened up a new world to him. A preacher of splendid figure and lovely countenance rose in the stand, and with a voice which won its way right into his heart, began to discuss the text, "What is truth?" This preacher was the Rev. William Moore; and this remarkable sermon, though it continued four hours, Mr. Murray says, held the whole congregation spell-bound to the last, so that they were sorry when it ended.

In that sermon Mr. Moore stated that there were so many misrepresentations abroad as to what his church believed, and his denomination as yet had so few books, that he felt it to be his duty to give, that day, a synopsis of the doctrines which his people held as the system of Bible truth. Mr. Murray says that from that day on he was a believer in the Cumberland Presbyterian system. He went home and re-preached Mr. Moore's sermon to his father's family, and the result was that the whole family joined the Cumberland Presbyterian church. Mr. Murray had impressions from that sermon which he never shook off. His own heart was laid bare to his gaze; his own responsibility was revealed, and he found no rest until he cast himself irrevocably upon the crucified Redeemer. He immediately began to plead with sinners to flee from the wrath to come, and spent the remainder of a long life in work for Jesus.

The Alabama Presbytery had eleven candidates for the ministry in five years. Only one of the eleven ever made a preacher. Five of these candidates were dropped from the roll at one session of the presbytery. This, like all the other presbyteries of this period, had pastorates only in name, for all its so-called pastors were really evangelists. After several years the Rev. William Moore took regular pastoral charge of one of its churches. The Rev. J. S. Guthrie came into the presbytery at an early day, and made a live evangelist of the original type. He became an efficient instrument in carrying the gospel into many destitute places, and in planting new congregations.

South Alabama is one of the most beautiful countries in the world. In 1860 I was traveling among its churches, and wrote some sketches, historical and descriptive, from which I here make a few extracts:

"In company with the Rev. Wiley Burgess I visited the site where long ago our people had a camp-ground. 'Fallen, fallen, a silent heap of ruins now!' Here I saw the old Bible which once belonged to Canaan pulpit. On a fly-leaf were the notes of a sermon preached at the opening of presbytery by J. S. Guthrie long ago." At Canton Bend, in the house of the Rev. J. C. Weir, this was written: "Mr. Weir is one of our pioneers in this field. He has held on to his post for more than thirty years, begging all the time for more men, more help. Alabama has not fallen below the third State in rank for contributions to our missions, yet she has never received any aid from our missionary board. It is a newer State than either Ohio or Illinois, but the general church gives no help to this frontier field. At Pleasant Hill, Alabama, one of our oldest ministers sleeps—the Rev. William Moore. I often hear him mentioned in the South. His work here was for many years a difficult one. Sometimes the wicked threatened to kill him. Lawlessness and violence were quite common in this town at that early day, and the minister of Jesus was looked upon as a dangerous intruder." Often while Mr. Moore was engaged in family prayers, sons of Belial would stand outside mocking and making disturbance. Meeting no check in their lawlessness they were encouraged to continue it, and finally they fired a whole volley of balls and shots through the window into the room where the family were kneeling in prayer. Two of the household were wounded, and the indignation of all the better class of settlers was so aroused that they organized a vigilance committee, and gave notice to the leaders among these desperadoes that the very next time Mr. Moore was molested every one of these leaders would be hanged. Mr. Moore had quiet after that.

There are names of other ministers now gone to rest that are uttered amid grateful tears in these Alabama homes. Old men, in the shady portico, talk while the winds bring spices from the groves of magnolias: and in their talks their voices grow husky, and their eyes glisten with tears while they speak of Wayman Adair. Adair was the only one of the first eleven candidates for the ministry in that field who persevered in the work.

South Alabama has from the first been a field beset with trials to our preachers. The early developed tendency to gather all the white people into towns, leaving the rural districts to immense cotton plantations cultivated by negroes, was the death of most of our rural churches throughout the beautiful land of the magnolia and the cape jessamine. A people relying on camp-meetings and circuit riders found their occupation gone when there was no place to preach in except towns.

CHAPTER XVIII.

PLANTING CHURCHES IN INDIANA AND ILLINOIS.

> Now the long and toilsome duty,
> Stone by stone to carve and bring,
> Afterward the perfect beauty
> Of the palace of the King.
> —*F. R. H.*

THE Rev. William Harris was the first Cumberland Presbyterian preacher to visit Indiana. In a letter to him, written by Mrs. Lindsey, of Indiana, in June, 1812, she says: "We have had but one sermon since your visit to this country. One Sabbath after another comes, but all is silent—the glad news of salvation is never heard."[1] The date of the visit by Harris alluded to in this letter can be only proximately determined. As Mrs. Lindsey moved to Indiana in 1810, and the visit was prior to 1812, we may fix its date as probably in 1811. Her pleadings finally induced Harris, accompanied by Alexander Chapman, to make a second preaching tour in that country. The date of this second visit is also uncertain, but it preceded the tour which Chapman and Barnett made by order of Logan Presbytery in 1817.

What the Methodists called circuits, Logan Presbytery called districts; and what the Methodists called circuit riders, Logan Presbytery called missionaries. Nowhere in the Minutes of the early meetings of Logan Presbytery have I found the missionary called a circuit rider, though he had regular rounds of "appointments" like a Methodist itinerant. One of the districts of Logan Presbytery at first took in several counties of Kentucky[2] along with all of Indiana; but when ministers multiplied Indiana became a separate district.

During Harris's tour through Indiana the claims, wants, and earnest pleadings of those pioneers made a deep impression on his

---

[1] Beard's Harris, p. 129.   [2] H. A. Hunter's MSS.

heart. At the next meeting of his presbytery he preached a sermon on the need of more laborers. In this sermon he gave a description of the West and its wants. His feelings became so deep that he could not talk, and, sinking down in overwhelming emotion, he wept and prayed, but could not finish his sermon. Several preachers date their call to the work of the ministry from that hour and that sermon, and several of these made that same western country their life-time field of labor.

The presbytery named one of its districts Wabash and one Indiana, and sent missionaries to both every year. The older preachers generally attended the camp-meetings in Indiana. There is something sublime in the struggles of Logan Presbytery to supply all this vast field with the gospel. As the number of its ministers was wholly inadequate to meet the ever-increasing demand for the grand work, a fast-day was appointed for special prayer to God for more called laborers. At the very next meeting of the presbytery David Lowry, Aaron Shelby, William McCord, and William Henry were received as candidates, and before another year four others were received—H. A. Hunter, W. M. Hamilton, A. Downey, and Thomas Campbell. Six of these men were, at one time or another, sent to the vast districts of Wabash and Indiana. At subsequent meetings, within a few months, another long list of names was added to Logan Presbytery's roll of preachers, among others Henry F. Delany and Joel Knight. These men, along with others, helped to plant the churches in Indiana and Illinois.

When Anderson Presbytery was organized Indiana and Illinois were included in its bounds. Before this Logan Presbytery had extended over this vast field. The first mention of any representatives in Logan Presbytery from the churches in either of these States is found in the Minutes of the fall meeting of 1819. The Black River congregation of Indiana and the Seven Mile Prairie congregation in Illinois both had representatives in that meeting. The Rev. Dr. Darby and the Rev. J. E. Jenkins in their pamphlet history of our church in southern Indiana give the probable order of date for our first churches there as follows: Mt. Zion, McAlisters, Shiloh, Milburns, White Oak Springs, Lester's, Osborne's, Mt. Pleasant.

The manuscripts of the Rev. H. A. Hunter give some touching accounts of the hardships which the first missionaries in the Indiana district endured in their winter tours. To swim rivers in midwinter in such a climate as that of Indiana was a trial to Southern men even when they were of that hardy type which was so common in those early times. Over half the first preachers of Indiana were natives of Tennessee, where the winters are mild. Others were Kentuckians, and one was from South Carolina. None of these men ever missed an appointment. If there was any exception, sickness and not the weather or the hardships was the cause.

These early preachers had other things besides weather to try their courage. Their work in this field began before Indiana was a State, and before Indian troubles ceased to fill the land with midnight alarms. The great Indian war, in which General Harrison led the American troops to victory on Indiana soil, did not end until after Cumberland Presbyterian pioneers began their work for Jesus on that same soil. Harrison's victories live in the annals of blood; the victories won by Harris and Chapman live in the annals of eternal life.

The following account of the organization of Mt. Zion congregation is from the historical pamphlet already mentioned:

This congregation was organized by the Rev. William Barnett in August, 1817, at a Methodist place of worship known as Shiloh, in Gibson County. The elders were James Knowles, Samuel Montgomery, and Alexander Johnson, the two former having been elders in the Presbyterian church. It is probable that this was the first Cumberland Presbyterian congregation in the State. At first the name of the congregation was Hopewell, and the members were accustomed to worship and hold their camp-meetings at the same place with the Methodists. Thus two camp-meetings were held each year on the same spot conjointly for a number of years. Finally, under circumstances which need not now be mentioned, the two meetings having been announced to take place at the same time, the Cumberland Presbyterians withdrew, and, with the aid of many sympathizers in the community, established a camp-ground one half mile from Shiloh, and held their meeting at the appointed time. When Messrs. Downey, Lynn, Hunter, and others were assembled at the time of meeting, the question arose as to what name the new place of worship should bear. Father Downey said: "Call it Mt. Zion, for it shall never be removed." [Ps. cxxv. 1.]

There are other historic churches in Indiana, but the interesting details of their history must be left for some larger book, or for some local State history of our people. The Evansville and Newburg congregations belong to later periods, and deserve more space than I can give them. The former is now the largest church in our denomination.

Two incidents of the early Indiana camp-meetings are here given on the authority of the Rev. H. A. Hunter, who witnessed them. They are clipped from Dr. Darby's pamphlet:

A man of considerable prominence in the estimation of some, particularly of himself, who claimed to be a Universalist, heard a sermon on Monday of the meeting, and became the subject of such conviction that with many others he came to the altar for prayer. The preacher went to him and endeavored to encourage him to believe and be saved. "O Mr. ——," said he, "I can believe that Christ died for and will save the whole world, but I am such a sinner I fear he will not save me."

At a camp-meeting near Mr. Lester's, in Daviess County, a young man and his bride were in attendance. The lady became exceedingly concerned about her soul, and came forward for the prayers of the church. Being deeply affected, her weeping and praying excited the sympathy of her husband, who came to her, not to encourage her in her purpose, but to oppose it. He bade her arise and go out of the congregation. She entreated him to stay with her, saying, "Let us go together to heaven." Becoming enraged, he refused his assent to her course, and threatened to leave her there if she did not come out. Then throwing her arms around his neck, she exclaimed: "I will go with you, my husband, if we go to hell." They left the congregation, and went home together. They were never in another congregation alive, but within a few weeks were both dead.

It is to be regretted that Mr. Hunter did not leave us accounts of many other thrilling camp-meeting incidents witnessed by him not only in Indiana but in other States. Such incidents show that the preaching of these Western missionaries produced results similar to those seen under the ministry of McGready and others at the beginning of the great revival in Kentucky and Tennessee. There are traditions of a wonderful character about Hunter's camp-meetings. Interesting details of Chapman's work in Indiana are given in Dr. Bird's Life of Chapman, a book that all Cumberland Presbyterians ought to read. The following account of a camp-meeting held by Chapman and others just on the borders of the white settlements, and near to the Indians, is given by the Rev. William Lynn:

> They commenced their operations. The Lord was present, and worked with power. Many fell to the ground under the power of the gospel. Some lay helpless for a long time, which caused a great talk among the people. There was a very strong, rough-looking man who said they could not make him fall. The meeting passed on till Monday. Mr. Chapman preached, and just as he commenced his discourse he noticed this man come into the edge of the congregation and stop and look at him very steadily. Directly the man drew nearer the stand, and as Mr. Chapman advanced in his sermon the man came still nearer, and about the close of the discourse he was trembling in every joint. Discovering that he had lost the use of his limbs, and the people refusing to carry him away, he grasped a small tree that stood near, and cried out, "I won't fall, I won't," still hugging the tree; but at last he fell full length on the ground before the stand.

This falling helpless continued to mark the work of the great revival till about the year 1840. It was common at most of the camp-meetings where the fathers of our church preached. It disappeared gradually as the power of the great revival waned and the men of 1800 passed away.

Illinois was not a State till 1818, but daring emigrants settled there before the French and Indian titles to that country were extinguished. The father of John Crawford moved to Illinois in 1808 and settled in sight of a camp of Indian hunters. This was the first family connected with our history that became settlers in this territory. Crawford's parents were anti-revival Presbyterians, but their children heard the revival preachers in Kentucky and all sooner or later became Cumberland Presbyterians. John Crawford was one of the pioneer preachers of our church in that State. He lived to a good old age and left a treasure in the form of a brief manuscript autobiography which is now before me. The first sermon in this State by a Cumberland Presbyterian minister was preached in 1815, near Golconda, by the Rev. John Barnett, at the house of Mr. Glass, whose children were Cumberland Presbyterians. These children were the first members of this church in that territory.

Chapter XVIII.] INDIANA AND ILLINOIS. 169

In Mr. Crawford's autobiography he says in reference to the early experience of his family in Illinois: "We were in constant fear of Indians, beasts of the forest, and river desperadoes." He gives an interesting picture of the impressions produced on a youthful mind by prejudice. He says he heard so much about the horrible Cumberland Presbyterians that he concluded there must be something of demoniacal nature and power in them. Finally he had an opportunity to hear one of them preach. He went on foot twelve miles to see and hear the dangerous preacher. He studied the preacher's looks, but saw no ferocious beast but a kindly looking human face. He watched his movements but saw neither the spring of a tiger nor the antics of a monkey. When the sermon began he studied every word, but he then found something else to do besides studying the preacher. His own life began to stand out before him all covered with sin. His own heart began to be revealed to him as he had never seen it before. His own startling relations to God and eternity swallowed up his thoughts till all other things were utterly forgotten. As his smitten soul found no relief that day, and as there was no other appointment for the strange preacher in the neighborhood, Mr. Crawford went twenty miles on foot to a camp-meeting in Kentucky, but he found no relief there. Then these dangerous strangers came again to Illinois, and under their ministry Mr. Crawford found Him of whom Moses and the prophets did write, and from that day onward he proclaimed the truth of the gospel and pointed the people of Illinois to the Savior.

There were many similar instances of early prejudice and its cure. Although the one here added was not located in Illinois it took place under the ministry of the same men who participated in the Crawford incidents. A young lady who was reared by Roman Catholic parents came from her home in the city of New York on a visit to relatives in Kentucky. A Cumberland Presbyterian camp-meeting was held in the neighborhood. Like young Crawford, her information about this church led her to expect something unutterably monstrous at one of its camp-meetings. She resolved, however, come what might, to see for herself. She attended the meeting and then wrote an account of it to her mother. After telling about the antecedents of the case, she says:

I just went to see and be seen and, mother, I did both as never I did before. I saw, not some inhuman monster in the shape of a preacher, but my own lost, ruined self, stripped of all my hollow pretenses, guilty, and naked, and condemned before God. I saw beneath me eternal perdition and my poor soul about to plunge into its fathomless depths. I was seen, too, in all my guilt by the piercing eye of God. I felt its withering gaze and shrieked with condemnation while I felt it. Then, mother, I saw the most glorious sight any poor, lost sinner ever gazed upon. I saw the Son of God bearing *my* sins on the cross. I saw *my* Savior reconciling me to God's law and God's kingdom. O mother, I know you will be angry, but I must tell you all. I, even I, am now a happy member of the Cumberland Presbyterian church; and I thank God that I ever heard one of their faithful, honest, scriptural, and fearless sermons. Mother, they are God's people.

John Crawford, from Illinois, and the Roman Catholic woman, from New York, have gone home now, whither their spiritual guides preceded them. They see and are seen without any obscuring veil to shut out part of the glories; and among the things there to be seen are a great company of redeemed ones from the early camp-meetings of the Cumberland Presbyterians.

After John Crawford's trip to Kentucky an incident occurred which deserves a place here. Notwithstanding the bitter prejudices which Mr. Crawford's parents had against the Cumberland Presbyterians, they yielded to the wishes of one of their sons who had professed religion under the preaching of James Johnson, in Kentucky, and with many misgivings agreed that this son might invite Johnson to preach at their house. The appointment was made and Johnson came and preached. At the close of the sermon there was deep feeling and the preacher began to shake hands with those present as he went singing through the congregation. The parents of Mr. Crawford could not stand this, but springing to their feet they left the room. When, however, God used these same Cumberland Presbyterians in bringing their other children to Jesus their prejudices all gave way.

In 1817 the Rev. Green P. Rice moved to Illinois and settled not far from St. Louis, which was then a meager village of Frenchmen. In the vicinity of Edwardsville there was a Methodist camp-ground but no preacher. Methodists, Presbyterians, and Cumberland Presbyterians united in holding prayer-meetings.

There was deep and solemn interest in these meetings, but no preacher of any church could be secured. Finally the people entered into a solemn agreement to invite the first preachers they could get of any evangelical church to come and hold them a camp-meeting. Mr. Paisley, a Cumberland Presbyterian pioneer, originally from Finis Ewing's congregation in Kentucky, was the first to succeed in securing a minister. He wrote an earnest appeal to the Rev. William Barnett setting forth the great need for gospel work in that new country. Barnett had no horse, but he took the letter to Finis Ewing. Ewing read it to his congregation and they raised money and bought Barnett a horse and sent him on his way to Illinois. Green P. Rice met him, and he and Rice, at this Methodist camp-ground, held the first Cumberland Presbyterian camp-meeting in Illinois.[1] This was in 1817.

In 1818 the Rev. D. W. McLin settled in this State. He was a preacher of the original type. He organized the first regular congregation of our people in the State. This was the Hopewell[2] church (now Enfield), in White County. In 1819 the camp-meeting at this place was very precious. Among its converts was Joel Knight, whose career in the ministry has left its mark for all time on the church in Illinois as well as elsewhere.

The second Cumberland Presbyterian camp-meeting in this State was held by R. D. Morrow, John Carnahan, and Green P. Rice at Elm Point, in Bond County. A pleasant fact about all the first work of the church in Illinois is that it still abides. The churches first organized continue yet in existence.

In 1820 the Board of Missions of the church sent the Rev. Alexander Chapman on a missionary tour through this State. This was a winter tour, beginning in December, and was one of no little hardship, but the missionary reported good results. He says that the destitution of the means of grace and the great desire of the pioneers for the gospel were enough to melt the hardest heart.

Though Illinois abounded in soil of surpassing depth and fertility, yet there were so many new territories thrown open to settlers

---

[1] Dr. J. B. Logan's History, and other authorities.
[2] Called, at first, Seven Mile Prairie.

simultaneously that the prairies were for a long time sparsely settled. In the manuscript autobiography of the Rev. Joseph M. Bone, he tells us that when he moved to Illinois and settled in Moultrie County his nearest neighbor lived five miles distant. Yet this was in 1829, a period much later than the principal events of this chapter.

A manuscript history of the Cumberland Presbyterian church in Illinois, by the Rev. H. H. Ashmore, has been very helpful to me in preparing this chapter. Speaking of the hardships of pioneer work on the prairies, he says:

The pioneer preachers rode over the prairies in summer traveling sometimes twenty and thirty miles without passing a house. There was danger of getting lost in the rain and fog and they were sometimes thus forced to spend the night in the open prairies without food or shelter. Wherever there were a few cabins along the skirts of the timber they were ready to preach at any hour of the week-day. On Saturdays and Sabbaths the people for miles around attended the meetings, and earnest efforts were put forth to build up congregations. Many of the early settlers lived ten miles from their place of worship, yet they were rarely absent on Sabbath. The week-day appointment was a sort of skirmish line to find a suitable place for the Sunday services and for protracted efforts. The meetings were held in school-houses, groves, or private residences. In the winter and spring, though the circuits were long and the appointments numerous, the preacher had to be at each place rain or shine. If high waters were in the way the preacher would place his saddle-bags, inclosing his Bible and hymn book and extra linen on his shoulder, and, in less time than a ferry could cross, his faithful horse would carry him over by swimming. No one who has not seen a snow-storm on the bare prairie can comprehend its driving fury. If the winds were changeable, as was often the case, the danger was great. At one time a terrible storm overtook three teams on the prairie. The wind changed. The horses could only go with the driving snow. The travelers were separated and lost. The same day my father was to cross that thirty-mile prairie on his way home. After the storm three awful days of suspense passed before we heard from him. At the edge of the timber and along the lanes near the timber lines the snow was too deep for man or beast to pass. Every man that could muster a strong horse was searching for the lost. They were brought in one by one, some with fingers frozen and foot-sore. At last our eyes were gladdened when my father rode up with his great buffalo coat making him look three times his usual size.

Besides the owners of the three teams lost near my father's many other people were lost in that storm. All business throughout that whole country was suspended while people searched for the lost. Roads were blockaded for weeks, and only at great risk could men mounted on the strongest horses go from one house to another. Our pioneer preachers passed through just such scenes as this. The common people in these early days were glad to have the privilege of going to church, or "meeting," as they called it. There were no railroads and but few post-offices. Newspapers were a rarity. They were glad to meet and hear the preacher and enjoy the privilege of comparing notes. People would sometimes sit and listen to a sermon two or three hours long without growing weary. If our people of this generation could go back to the days of Isaac Hill, Joel Knight, James Ashmore, William Finley, R. D. Taylor, Cyrus Haynes, J. M. Berry, Daniel Traughber, and Archibald and Neil Johnson, they would learn how the seed of the Cumberland Presbyterian church was sown in this State. These men were giants in their day. Lincoln University is largely the result of their labors.

The first presbytery organized exclusively in Illinois was in 1822. But McGee Presbytery, which was organized in 1819, included in its bounds part of Illinois. In 1822 the order for the organization of Illinois Presbytery was passed. Its original members were to be Green P. Rice, D. W. McLin, John M. Berry, and W. M. Hamilton. Rice did not attend; all the others were present. This presbytery immediately organized a presbyterial board of missions. Nine probationers for the ministry were transferred to its care. That meant circuit riding. In 1829 this presbytery had ten members in good standing. It had been obliged to silence some of its ministers. One of these cases of discipline was mixed up with the great slavery question, and shows that the church in Illinois at an early day took a decided stand on that subject.

There is a wonderful difference between the growth of the Cumberland Presbyterian church in the two States to which this chapter is devoted. In Indiana there are now (1885) but three presbyteries; in Illinois there are ten. There is one thing indicated both by recent statistics and by this early history which may help to explain the difference. In Illinois from the beginning there was a vigorous struggle to raise up a home supply of preachers. Fast-days were appointed on which all the congregations joined in prayer that God would call and send forth men of his own choosing to preach the gospel. God answered these prayers, as he will do to-day in all our frontier presbyteries if, instead of clamoring for more preachers to come from the older States, they will ask God to call their own sons into the work.

Another fact doubtless had its influence in causing this superior growth in Illinois. At an early day some of the oldest ministers of the church made this State their permanent home. Among these were Samuel McAdow, one of the three men who formed the first presbytery of the church. David Foster and D. W. McLin also cast their lots permanently with the pioneers of Illinois. The first preachers of the church made preaching tours in Indiana, but none of them settled in that State; and when a later generation of Cumberland Presbyterian preachers made their homes there a large portion of the ground was preoccupied. From the first it was a maxim of our people not to build on other men's foundations, but to go among the destitute. With very few exceptions our preachers have conformed to that maxim in the past, and do still conform to it.

CHAPTER XIX.

PLANTING THE CHURCH IN MISSOURI AND ARKANSAS, 1811 TO 1829.

> So willing to toil and travel,
>   To suffer and watch for all,
> So near in heart to the Master,
>   So eager to hear his call,—
> *They* spent *their* souls in the service sweet,
> And only in death could rest at his feet.
> —*B. M.*

THE first great tide of American emigrants to Missouri Territory began in 1816. There were Cumberland Presbyterians in that first tide, and the usual cry soon began to come, "Send us a preacher." In 1817 the first Cumberland Presbyterian sermon was preached in the Territory by Green P. Rice at the little French village of St. Louis. The first Cumberland Presbyterian preacher to settle in Missouri was Daniel Buie. He was a citizen already established in Howard County and had regular preaching places when R. D. Morrow made his visit to that country in 1819. In a graphic history of Buie's emigration to Missouri we are told that he made the journey in 1818 in a one-horse cart.

In April, 1819, the ladies' missionary society at Russellville, Kentucky, requested the presbytery to send the Rev. R. D. Morrow on a preaching tour through Missouri Territory. The presbytery agreed to the plan and the missionary board fixed his salary at twenty dollars per month. He had to make his own appointments and "blaze his own way" in more senses than one. A letter of instructions was placed in his hands and he was commended to God and sent forth on his responsible mission. Mounting his horse, equipped for travel through the wilderness, he started on his long, solitary journey. Could he have foreseen the glorious work for Jesus to which God was leading him his heart would have leaped for joy. He carried bell and "hobble" for his horse and rations for himself. Besides these things there were a few books in his saddle-bags. The wilderness between Logan County, Kentucky, and Alton, Illinois, was passed with only his horse for a traveling companion. Crossing the river he proceeded up to what is now Pike County, where he preached to a few settlers, among whom were three Cumberland Presbyterians. Proceeding westward he held his next meeting in Callaway County. At that meeting were grown men who had never heard a sermon in their lives. Many such there were in that territory—children of pioneers who penetrated the wilderness long in advance of the general tide of emigration. Settling down on some rich prairie perhaps ten miles from the nearest neighbor, these pioneers brought their children up without schools and without churches.

In just such a home amid just such destitution was our now venerable brother, the Rev. J. T. A. Henderson, reared. His rich manuscript autobiography, now before me, describes the joy of the whole family when they heard of a Methodist preacher making an appointment for occasional preaching within reach of their home. When this family and one other settled near Round Prairie, Missouri, there was no other family within a circuit of ten miles. It was many a long year before there was any school within reach. Having neither post-offices, newspapers, nor stores, the pioneers lived a lonely life. There was plenty of game and plenty of prairie grass. In some parts of the territory the grass grew higher than a man's head when he was mounted on his horse. At a later day this grass teemed with a species of flies so numerous that they sometimes killed the traveler's horse as he rode across the prairies. It is a touching thing to read Mr. Henderson's account of his rapture when at last his home was surrounded with neighbors who employed a school-teacher. Into such sparse settlements of pioneers Mr. Morrow penetrated, proclaiming the gospel and planting the standard of our King.

When time for the meeting of Logan Presbytery drew near, Mr. Morrow saddled his horse and made the long journey back to Kentucky. He was one of those who never failed to be present at the judicatures of his church. At this meeting he was pitied and criticized for his emaciated appearance. The long journey, the arduous labor, and the indescribable hardships, had well-nigh cost him his life. Yet at that meeting of the Presbytery he made an appeal for the spiritually destitute pioneers of Missouri which melted the people to tears. His whole heart was enlisted for that field, and his wonderful career afterward was but an outgrowth of his deep earnestness.

Again Mr. Morrow was sent to Missouri. The orders under which the missionary went on this second trip required him to remain a year. Although Missouri now had a presbytery, and Mr. Morrow's membership was in it, yet he still worked under the missionary board at Russellville, Kentucky. His report to that board in the fall of 1820 deserves to be handed down as a precious record. Here it is, copied from the manuscript history prepared by Logan Presbytery in obedience to the order of the General Synod:

I traveled as a missionary in Missouri nine months. I passed through all the counties in the Territory except two. I rode horseback upwards of three thousand miles; have enjoyed pretty good health. I was kindly received by the people. My congregations were large and attentive. The desire for preaching from our body surpasses any thing I have ever before witnessed. Everywhere the people were pressing me to return and preach for them again. Often I left them with tears streaming down their cheeks, while they said, "You are going away, and we shall have no more preaching. Our children are growing up in a strange land, without having any one to show them the way of life." Mothers would follow me to the gate, begging me to pray for them and their children in that wild wilderness. Young people would mount their horses and ride with me five or six days for the sake of instruction in spiritual things. Among these were many poor sinners seeking salvation, many of whom were grown men and women who had never heard a sermon in their lives till I came among them. During my tour I preached one hundred and sixty sermons. The Lord was with me, and applied his own truth to the hearts of my hearers. Sixty-five professed to find Christ precious to their souls. I received forty-nine dollars for your missionary board.

Mr. Morrow was continued in Missouri. He was now connected with another presbytery, but he wrote a letter to Logan Presbytery the next year (1821) pleading with undiminished fervor for the destitute. In that letter he says he finds that good fruits have followed his former visits, and that there have been several conversions among those whom he left in tears. He had held four camp-meetings since his return to Missouri, all of which were successful. Then he adds:

> Brethren and fathers, permit me, through you, to address the Ladies' Missionary Society under your care. I want them to know that their labor of love in the cause of God has not been in vain. The great Head of the Church has condescended to bless the weak efforts of their missionary far beyond what I had any right to expect. Precious souls in great numbers have been brought to the knowledge of salvation. But past success greatly increases the demand for more missionaries. O that you and they could hear the cries of the destitute which are coming up from all quarters of this wilderness, cries for the gospel of our salvation, cries for more preachers, coming up, too, from the unconverted as well as from lambs of the fold, who have no one to guide them in the way of life.

The order for the organization of McGee Presbytery was passed in the autumn after Morrow was first sent to that field (1819). Its original members were Green P. Rice, Daniel Buie, R. D. Morrow, and John Carnahan. Rice lived in Illinois, and Carnahan across the wilderness, five hundred miles away in Arkansas; yet all these men were at the organization.

The next year (1820) Finis Ewing moved to Missouri and settled in Cooper County among his old neighbors from Kentucky who had preceded him. He soon had an organized congregation, a meeting-house, and, of course, a camp-ground. This church, New Lebanon, has had a remarkable history, and has shared largely in the work for the Master in that State.

In 1821 R. D. Morrow and Finis Ewing opened a school of the prophets. Morrow taught science and Ewing theology. No charge was made for the young preachers' tuition or boarding. McGee Presbytery had already enrolled a large number of candidates for the ministry, and these eagerly availed themselves of the advantages here offered. There was a long summer vacation which was spent in preaching tours and camp-meetings, Morrow and Ewing accompanying the young preachers.

In all the history of our church there is no more interesting work than that done by this school. It was a pioneer theological seminary conducted by live men who loved souls and knew how to work for them. Morrow was a man of good scholarship, and presided over a college in later years; but this pioneer theological school stands pre-eminent among the good results of his and Ewing's noble work for the Master. The roll of young men here taught includes many cherished and honored names, and one must read the history of the whole Cumberland Presbyterian church to appreciate the precious fruits of this school. There were features about the school which deserve to be copied by our later and stronger theological seminary. It combined theory with practice, not that stupid moot practice before a professor in the recitation room, which always seemed to me to be a good way to teach lifeless routine and make hypocrites, but practice under the eyes of the professors out in the real harvest-field where souls are perishing, and where trophies for the eternal crown of glory are won by the young laborers. The teachers went along with their pupils, and held meetings during their long vacation.

In the spring of 1822 the Rev. R. D. King, a licentiate, and the Rev. Reuben Burrow, a candidate, were ordered by Elk Presbytery to travel and preach in Missouri. I am fortunate in having a full account of this tour from both the actors in it. They started on horseback from Tennessee just after the April meeting of the presbytery. Their first entertainment was swimming water-courses. After this followed a much more protracted entertainment in the form of chills and fever; yet they missed no appointments until long after, when sickness of a more stubborn nature caused a few failures. Burrow says:

> I was placed on a circuit with John Morrow. The circuit was in western Missouri, including the country where Lexington and Independence have since risen up. . . . About the fourth day, after Brother Morrow had preached rather a dull sermon, I was invited to conclude the services; and while trying to talk, ere I was aware of my own condition, God had raised me higher and filled me fuller of heaven than ever before. The people present were deeply moved by the power of the Almighty. . . . In the course of about two weeks the most of them made profession of religion. Captain William Jack became awakened on this occasion, and covenanted with others to seek life, but did not find peace till two weeks afterward.

A camp-meeting was held not far away. Captain Jack took his family and attended. It was there he found Jesus, and his after life was full of usefulness to the church. There were over three hundred converts on that circuit that year. Burrow states:

> The people were kind to us, and gave us some clothing such as they could make, and I received eight dollars in money for the year, and felt very well contented and thankful for that.

At one time during this missionary journey Burrow's horse got out and ran off, but he was not to be thwarted by a little thing like that. He shouldered his saddle-bags and started around his circuit afoot. He had eighty miles to travel over the prairies. He says:

> My feet became very sore from travel. The second day about three o'clock I entered the last stretch of my journey. It was a prairie of more than twenty miles. Here I toiled in weariness and pain until midnight before I reached a house where I could quench my thirst and rest my weary limbs.

Here Captain Jack overtook him, bringing his horse. An incident in Dr. Burrow's later life has the same ring. He was regular supply for a church fifteen miles from his home. On one occasion he had no horse to ride to his appointment. He made no effort to borrow, but taking his staff in his hand (he was an old man then) he walked to his appointment.

While Burrow rode the circuit with the youthful John Morrow, King was taken under the guardianship of the Rev. R. D. Morrow, to travel with him and hold meetings. They spent the summer holding camp-meetings in the bounds of McGee Presbytery. In the fall, when Morrow returned to his work in the school, King was placed on a circuit in Ray and Clay counties. He kept up his work on this circuit until February, when he was prostrated by sickness. In the spring he traveled one hundred miles to be at the meeting of McGee Presbytery, although he had a chill every other day on the whole trip.

Next year Mr. King returned to Elk Presbytery, but was sent back to Missouri in company with his father, the Rev. Samuel King, on another missionary tour. Then he and his father both moved to that State, where his father spent the remainder of his life in earnest labors, preaching to the very last. Among the converts of R. D. King's meetings in various fields were LeRoy Woods, T. M. Johnston, and many others, who afterward became efficient ministers. King's ashes rest in Texas, where he closed his life of toil.

While these missionaries from a distance planted the church in Missouri, it was the home supply of ministers who grew up in that pioneer school taught by Ewing and Morrow that carried on and established the work. In a careful study of the whole field from Pennsylvania to California I find no section or State where the church has become a strong, established power without this home supply of pastors and evangelists. Looking to distant fields for missionaries instead of praying God to call our own sons to the holy work is the road to failure. It is the sons of Texas who are taking that great State for Jesus. It is Pennsylvanians who are making the church strong in western Pennsylvania. It was the sons of Missouri who, in the early history of the church, gave Missouri such a prominent place among Cumberland Presbyterians. But no native Californian is leading our forces on the golden shores. Other parts of the church supply ministers to bear our banners in Ohio. Preachers from other States are chiefly depended on to fill our pulpits in Louisiana and Georgia. We need the return of the spirit of the olden times. We ought to go with fasting, and humility, and humble prayer to God, pleading with him to call men, to call our own sons, to the gospel ministry.

In 1823 the Rev. Robert Sloan was one of Missouri's circuit riders. One of his camp-meetings, in Chariton County, was the means of bringing many of the prominent settlers into the fold of Christ. That meeting is spoken of even yet in Missouri as a wonderful work of God among the pioneers. Several of the converts were men who in after years made a deep impression on the public affairs of that country. In 1824 Mr. Sloan spent six months on what was then called the "hard circuit." For this six months' labor he received one white cravat. Mr. Sloan continued his faithful pioneer labors till the close of his life. His noble wife, who was a daughter of the Rev. Finis Ewing, still survives.

Among the faithful workers for Jesus in this field, as in all others were noble women not a few. Those who would like to read the life of one of the noblest of these are referred to the biography of Mrs. Margaret Ewing—"Aunt Peggy," as she was called—written by her gifted son, Judge R. C. Ewing.

Among the hardy pioneers of the Missouri churches the Rev. Archibald McCorkle fills an honorable place. He traveled through the wilderness from one new settlement to another. He carried his own provisions, slept on the ground, and turned his hobbled horse on the grass at night. He faced the beating rains and the bitter snow-storms in order to preach Jesus to men living in the destitute regions of the frontier. In one of the camp-meetings on Mr. McCorkle's circuit there was such a general victory that, like Hugh Kirkpatrick in the meeting in Tennessee, described in a former chapter, he reported "all the material worked up"—that is, all the unconverted people present became Christians. The work at this meeting began under the preaching of the Rev. Finis Ewing. During one of Mr. McCorkle's tours over a hundred persons claimed to be converted in his meetings, and yet for that six months of successful work among the scattered pioneers he received just eight dollars; the same salary which Reuben Burrow received a few years before for six months of arduous toil with the grandest results on the records of the church's pioneer work.

Burrow and McCorkle both furnished their own horses and paid their own unavoidable traveling expenses. But eight dollars was more than the pay many another missionary received, not only in Missouri but even in the oldest parts of the church. R. D. King preached two years in Maury and Giles counties, Tennessee, before he moved to Missouri, receiving for his services neither money nor any other kind of compensation from the people to whom he ministered. He lived on the small estate which his wife had inherited till that was exhausted, and then sold his little farm for money enough to take him to Missouri.

The Rev. Hugh Robinson Smith was among those who took the infant churches of Missouri by the hand and rendered them great service. He also sought out the homes of the destitute and planted churches among the scattered cabins on the prairies. He carried Hebrew and Greek books in his saddle-bags and pursued a full course of study while on his circuits. His career, says Judge

Ewing, was full, complete, finished. In all its parts he accomplished his mission, and was wanting neither in literary preparation nor in soundness of doctrine, neither in unction of the Holy Ghost nor in fidelity to perform the work committed to his trust. Judge Ewing speaks also of Frank M. Braly as a representative of the best type of Missouri's circuit riders. He was among the hardy pioneers of an early day. His father went to Missouri in advance of that great wave of emigration which set in toward that territory in 1816. He was brought up in that wilderness, and to the circuit on the frontiers and to camp-meetings he devoted all the days of his manhood. For one whole year devoted exclusively to the work of an itinerant evangelist he received nine dollars and fifty cents.

Judge Ewing relates a characteristic incident of Mr. Braly's career. On his way to the meeting of presbytery, accompanied by several others, one of the young preachers was taken suddenly sick so that he could not travel. Mr. Braly remained with him. Their stopping place was a cabin in the wilderness. Neither doctor nor drugs were to be had, but Mr. Braly believed that God healed the sick in answer to the prayer of faith; so he and his friend resorted to the great Physician and his friend recovered in time to reach the presbytery. Another incident from the same authority illustrates the manner in which opposition and prejudice were often overcome. A Calvinist of the most rigid type undertook to prove to Mr. Braly that missionary work and all revival meetings and camp-meetings were uncalled for and wrong, because God would save his own elect in his own way and time. He seemed to be sorry for Mr. Braly personally, and to wish to dissuade him from undergoing all the fatigue and hardships which he was encountering. He tried to convince the preacher that no amount of exertion which he could make would change the final results. It is not claimed that this man was a fair representative of genuine Calvinism, but his perversion of the doctrine was a very common one among its professed adherents. Mr. Braly, however, went on with his meeting. Several members of the Calvinist's family were at the "mourner's bench" weeping and crying for mercy, and soon they were filled with joy and peace in Jesus.

Their faces shone with a heavenly radiance as they told what God had done for them. Then this man's prejudices all vanished.

Judge Ewing in his sketches gives a touching picture of Braly's faithfulness and self-denying consecration. At one time he had traveled among the destitute, holding meetings and receiving no pay until his clothing was almost worn out. His boots especially were unfit to wear and he had no money to buy new ones, yet he made a long journey through a strange land in order to attend the meeting of synod, and in spite of his worn garments he was in his place in that body. Nor were the rough frontier regions of Missouri alone in leaving their missionaries thus to suffer. There was a man, now aged and infirm, who traveled in West Tennessee in 1846 holding meetings among a prosperous people. For six months he preached nearly every day, and more than three hundred persons professed conversion at his meetings. In all that time he received no compensation, either in clothing or in money. A rich elder said to him, "Go down to the shoe shop and get your boots mended." The young man went, but having no money he borrowed tools and tried as best he could to do his own repairing. He adopted the old programme of saying nothing about money or pay of any kind to anybody. The Cumberland Presbyterian church had its beginning under this mistaken plan, and the example of "the fathers" is still the argument which is everywhere used by those church members who want their pastor to serve them for naught.

We must remember how scattered and sparse were the settlements in all the new territories before we can appreciate the victories won in these early meetings. An account of a camp-meeting held in Missouri in 1821 will illustrate this point. It is taken from the published biography of the Rev. A. A. Young, who was one of our early preachers in that State: The people in this sparsely settled region (now Saline County) had no Sabbath-schools, no churches, no preaching, no prayer-meetings. They determined to secure some preachers to hold a camp-meeting. Their efforts were successful, and they selected a spot about equally distant from several settlements, but five miles from the nearest house. When the camps were erected and all the population of the adjacent settlements were gathered together there were just twenty-five persons present. Yet that meeting was perhaps as fruitful in the long run as some in later times in which the converts are counted by the hundred. At that meeting A. A. Young, whose after life in the ministry was greatly blessed, found the preaching just what John Crawford, of Illinois, found it a few years before. The mask was torn off his heart, and he saw himself helpless and ruined and condemned before God, and cried earnestly for help to Jesus, who alone could save, nor did he cry in vain.

The Rev. Daniel Patton, who was one of the most useful Cumberland Presbyterian pioneers in Missouri, is still living, and though now over eighty years of age, he still takes his horse and his saddle-bags and goes out on an old-time circuit as an itinerant missionary in that field. He rode the circuit in South Alabama in 1821. His history of our church in Missouri is before me. He begins with Barnett Presbytery, which was organized in April, 1828, at Lexington, Missouri. The ministers composing this presbytery were Samuel King, R. D. Morrow, Daniel Patton, and Henry Renick. Under its care were Clemens Means and William Horn, candidates, and Robert Renick, a licentiate. Of the early work of this presbytery Patton says:

To know man perfectly you must see him under the pressure of the varied phases of human life. You must see the pioneer preacher in his log-cabin built by his own hands. In frontier settlements in an unbroken wilderness of more than five hundred miles north and one thousand miles west, our first Missouri preachers with their families found their homes. In a few years other settlements are formed beyond. The cry comes up from the new settlements, Come over and help us. To answer this cry wide-spread prairies without roads and deep creeks without bridges had to be crossed. None of these things deter the pioneer preacher.

The same writer gives a sketch of the early preachers of Missouri. Of Samuel King he says:

He was preaching in my father's house, in Bedford County, Tennessee, to a crowded company, when my father professed faith in the blessed Savior. I saw father passing through the crowd clapping his hands and praising God, and many others doing the same. I was then eleven years old. I record this incident not only as a grateful remembrance of the past, but to present an instance of the power manifested in all the public ministrations of Samuel King. He was pre-eminently a man of prayer. He lived more on his knees than any man I ever knew, hence his power in the pulpit. I believe that God gave him more seals to his ministry than to any other man since Whitefield's day. I heard Finis Ewing say more than once, "I would rather preach after any other man." He said it seemed to him that King always said all that could be said to profit, and the state of feeling was so high that it would only be lowered by his effort. I am sure no man was a better judge of preaching than Finis Ewing.

It was Patton himself who was preaching at Bee Creek campmeeting, Missouri, when the people rose to their feet and unconsciously pressed toward the pulpit till they were densely crowded around the preacher. There was no more preaching for two days, "altar work" taking up all the time.

Another glimpse of Patton's work is found in his history of Barnett Presbytery. He says:

The writer husked corn which grew from the soil where Richmond, the county seat of Ray County, now stands. He helped raise the first log-cabins to make it a town. He made the first wagon road running north from Richmond, crossing the west fork of Crooked River on his land one mile from town. He drove the first four-horse team that crossed this stream after digging the bank to ascend. This road was for many years the highway of emigration north. As much of this northward travel was directly by my cabin I was much questioned as to the country beyond. I entertained many weary travelers, always free. You see by these means many formed my acquaintance, so that I was known to almost all the new settlements north. As soon as little settlements were formed it was but natural for them to ask me to come out and preach for them. I well remember my first tour to the forks of Grand River. Some of my old Ray County friends had settled there and thereabouts. The presbytery had sent out William Clark, a good young man, just licensed to preach, to form a sort of circuit to suit the frontier settlements. I was to follow, preach, and administer ordinances as needed. The first day's travel I swam two considerable streams on the back of my horse, and then steered for a "deadening" in a little grove of timber. I found a kind family in a new cabin, nature's floor and nature's fare, fat venison and good cheer. The next day with difficulty I found the place for preaching. Mr. Clark had preached in the forenoon and the people were gathering for the three o'clock service.

In a little grove between Shoal Creek and Grand River, Patton held a camp-meeting. He does not give the date, but he says of the meeting:

I was conducted to the place by an old hunter who knew the country and led the way "by course," as we used to travel in the unbroken wilds. My guide and myself were the first to reach the place. I examined the ground with a feeling of interest which no man can realize who has not been placed in a like position. The lonely place, the hastily-raised pulpit, the rude, narrow "slab" seats, a narrow path cut through the brush to a good spring at the base of the hill, called to my mind Isaiah's prediction of the gospel's spread and conquests, "The wilderness and solitary places shall be glad for them: yea, the desert shall rejoice and blossom as the rose." Strange but true, whilst I call up the glorious scenes of the past I live over the emotions of soul of which I certainly was the subject at that time! I involuntarily and most earnestly asked, Will this solitary place be made glad to-day because of thy presence, O God? The answer in my poor heart was, It will. And so it was.

Most of Mr. Patton's history belongs to a later period.

Some facts recorded in the history of the Cumberland Presbyterian church in Missouri, written by the Rev. P. G. Rea, are here given. Jacob Ish, a Cumberland Presbyterian elder, was the first man who drove a wagon into Big Bottom, near the place where Glasgow, Missouri, now stands. This was in 1816. New Lebanon church was organized by John Carnahan in the house of Alexander Sloan, father of the Rev. Robert Sloan, in 1820. Among the children and grandchildren of the members of the first session of this church there have been twelve preachers. It was here that the school of Ewing and Morrow was located.

Where pioneer settlers in the wilderness were destitute of the gospel, there the early Cumberland Presbyterian preachers preferred going. In a great many instances they declined to organize churches in North Carolina, South Carolina, Virginia, and New York, saying that every preacher our people had was needed in the West by those who had no minister of any church to break to them the bread of life. That there was no sectarian ambition among our people then is not asserted, but that there was far less of it then than now can be maintained.

A pioneer scene in Missouri is here sketched. When Mr. William Blackwell, a Cumberland Presbyterian elder, moved to Missouri, in 1827, and settled in the wilderness, wolves and Indians were no rarity in his neighborhood. In 1829 Mr. Blackwell was living in what was then Randolph County, when tidings of an Indian invasion and of murders in the region where Kirksville now stands reached him. Joining a band of volunteers he hurried to the relief of the invaded settlements. A battle followed. The whites fought fiercely, but were compelled to retreat. In the retreat Mr. Blackwell came up with a wounded man afoot. He placed this man upon his own horse, and continued his retreat. Farther on he came upon another comrade who had stopped from exhaustion. While Mr. Blackwell was trying to help this comrade on, a shot from the Indians killed the poor fellow, and Blackwell continued his retreat. Farther on he found another comrade lying fast under a dead horse which had been shot, and although the Indians were coming, he waited to extricate him, and then again continued his retreat. His rescued comrade was soon shot down, but Mr. Blackwell escaped. It was for the sake of such men and their families that our first preachers longed to labor in these pioneer fields.

Mr. Blackwell helped to organize the first congregation of Cumberland Presbyterians in that part of the country. The preacher who held the meeting out of which that church grew was the Rev. James Dysart. The church was called Liberty.

While the French title to what is now Arkansas was transferred to the United States in 1803, yet Indian claims and Indian inhabitants long interposed other obstacles to its settlement by white people. Arkansas had its separate organization as a Territory in 1819, and was admitted into the Union as a State in 1836. Before the organization of its territorial government, and while the Indians were still in the land, the country furnished a retreat to those hardy and daring young men who loved adventure and wanted to secure good lands in advance of the inevitable white settlements. Several of these had young wives as daring as their husbands; and there yet live old ladies who on the long winter evenings tell the throng of happy children that gather around them in their now prosperous and elegant homes about their wonderful adventures.

In 1811[1] some families of Cumberland Presbyterians, converts of the great revival, moved to Arkansas. James and Jacob Pyatt and their wives, and two young Carnahans, James and Samuel—sons of John Carnahan, the preacher—embarked in a flatboat and floated down the Tennessee, the Ohio, and the Mississippi, to the mouth of Arkansas River. Though they were all Kentuckians, yet it was from northern Alabama that they emigrated. Like many others, they had rushed to Alabama when some of the Indian titles were extinguished, only to find others still in force, and to be driven off as intruders. It took them from January to May to make this journey to the mouth of the Arkansas River. Then they went up that river in a keel-boat to Arkansas Post—the oldest settlement in the territory. Here they expected to make their homes, but they soon found that the only religion there was Roman Catholicism. The population was French, Indians, and a few Americans. Things did not suit them, so they determined to go farther up the river. In 1812 they went past the spot where the city of Little Rock now stands to a bluff fifteen miles above, where they established their homes. The name of the place was Crystal Hill.

The same year (1812) the father of the two Carnahans moved to Arkansas. He had been riding the circuit as a licensed exhorter before. In the house of Jacob Pyatt he preached the first Protestant sermon ever preached in Arkansas territory. In those days our people licensed a man twice: first as exhorter, or lay evangelist, and, if "he purchased to himself a good degree," they afterward licensed him as a probationer for the full work of the ministry. At the meeting of the Cumberland Presbytery in October, 1812, John Carnahan was ordered to form a circuit on the Arkansas River, "among the people where he lived."[2] When the synod was formed (1813), Carnahan was placed on the roll of Elk Presbytery. He attended its meetings regularly till a presbytery was organized in his own field. In 1814 he was licensed in the regular way.[3] The presbytery ordered him back to his old circuit on the Arkansas River, and also addressed a circular letter to the people

---

[1] The Pyatt MSS. Secured for me by President F. R. Earle.
[2] Minutes in the *Quarterly*, 1878, p. 496. [3] Elk Minutes, Vol. I., p. 8.

of those settlements, commending Mr. Carnahan to them as an excellent man and a worthy minister. This solitary standard-bearer determined to make this new country his permanent home, and for nine years he was the only Cumberland Presbyterian preacher in all that field. In October, 1816,[1] the pioneers petitioned for his ordination, and their petition was granted. During all the years of his lonely toil on the frontier, he was in the habit of attending every meeting of his presbytery. The place of meeting was often more than five hundred miles from his home, and he traveled all the distance on horseback. Once the presbytery kept him six months in Tennessee and Alabama for his health's sake, and then sent him back to Arkansas.

It is claimed in papers left by the Pyatt family that Carnahan held the first sacramental meeting ever held by Protestants on Arkansas soil. In all the western territories opened up between 1800 and 1840 Cumberland Presbyterians were pioneers in gospel work. God raised them up for frontier missions. Carnahan's sacramental meeting was at the house of one of the Pyatts, and he baptized a daughter of the family. Then there were five persons who joined him in celebrating the Lord's Supper. This was twenty years before Arkansas was a State, and three years before it had a territorial government. Away in this wilderness the Carnahans and the Pyatts had erected the family altar, and now they provided also for the ordinances of God's house. These families were noted for liberality. There was but little money circulating in any of the pioneer settlements, but where the heart is right liberal souls will find ways of doing liberal deeds. In 1823 Pyatt's little boy, seeing Reuben Burrow nearly shoeless, made the missionary a pair of shoes with his own hands. The pioneers had to perform such tasks as the making of their own shoes.

Another incident is here given illustrating the character, habits, and adventures of these pioneers. Jacob Pyatt kept a ferry-boat. One day there came a weary pedestrian, stating that he had met with misfortunes and had no money to pay his ferriage. Pyatt took him over the river, and kept him at his own house a week; then he mounted him on one of his horses, and, sending a boy

---

[1] Minutes of Elk Presbytery, Vol. I., p. 25.

along with him to bring the animal back, thus conveyed him home to Little Rock. That young man was a nephew of the Rev. Thomas Calhoun. He graduated at Princeton College, Kentucky, and finally became governor of Arkansas.

Crystal Hill settlement was a center for Cumberland Presbyterian immigrants. Among others the Blairs, two of whom afterward became ministers, made that neighborhood their home. John Carnahan was still with them, devoting himself to the work of an evangelist, and traveling all the way to Tennessee every six months to attend the meetings of his presbytery.

After a few years Carnahan's membership was transferred to the McGee Presbytery, which included Arkansas in its bounds. That body became deeply concerned about the organization of a new presbytery in Mr. Carnahan's field. As there was a prospect for a supply of candidates for the ministry from that territory, the presbytery determined to hold an "intermediate" meeting in Arkansas. The distance was great, and much of the intervening country an uninhabited wilderness. The route was partly through Indian neighborhoods, and none of the rivers had either bridges or ferries. The young and active men of the presbytery were therefore to be pressed into this distant mission. It has already been noticed that Reuben Burrow, then a candidate, and R. D. King, then a licentiate, were traveling as missionaries in Missouri. Both were at the meeting of McGee Presbytery in 1823, though King was sick in bed. The presbytery, however, licensed Burrow and ordained King in order to send them to Arkansas. King, though very sick, was held up, a good lady plying camphor in the meantime, while they ordained him. Then the moderator resigned, and King was chosen moderator in his stead, so that he might preside at the intermediate meeting of the presbytery. It was five hundred miles to the place of meeting, and one third of the way was a wilderness. Most of the nights had to be spent without shelter, but King, Long, and Burrow were with Carnahan at the appointed place on the appointed day.

The presbytery at this intermediate session received three candidates for the ministry. Two of these were James H. Black and J. M. Blair, men whose names were afterward well known throughout the Arkansas churches. After the close of the meeting, which was held at the house of John Craig, on White River, Mr. Long returned to Missouri, while Burrow and King remained to do mission work in Arkansas. These missionaries held two camp-meetings that same year in Mr. Craig's neighborhood, both of which were greatly blessed. Carnahan and King went to the Arkansas River, while Burrow formed a circuit among the White River settlements.

In King's autobiography he says there were grown men at his meetings who had never heard a prayer, much less a sermon. The settlements were few and far between. The largest crowd of people which even a camp-meeting could draw together might possibly reach, in extreme cases, a hundred and fifty persons. Great gaps of unpeopled wilderness stretched between the settlements; and of the one hundred and fifty persons who might possibly be at a camp-meeting, some had to come from a distance of more than a hundred miles. When forty or fifty converts are reported at one camp-meeting, we are to understand that from fifty to eighty per cent. of the entire assembly were converted.

King and Carnahan being ordained ministers, took special charge of the camp-meetings. The camps were built of rails, and covered with bushes or the leafy boughs of trees. The preaching places were not covered, except the stand or pulpit, which had over it a shed of leafy branches. In these rude frontier tabernacles God was pleased to display his converting grace, and many a church grew up where these rude encampments were erected.

After several months of circuit work Burrow joined the camp-meeting corps at Fort Smith; but before he reached the meeting he was attacked with chills. The first two camp-meetings which he attended were crowned with gracious results; but Burrow grew worse, until he was unable to preach, and finally became delirious with fever. Then Carnahan was also taken with fever. King found himself alone. Another camp-meeting, one hundred and fifty miles farther down the river, had been appointed. Neither Burrow nor Carnahan was able to sit up, but King was not to be thwarted. He bought a very large canoe, or pirogue. In this he placed dried prairie grass for beds, and put a cover on bows over the beds. He then laid in a supply of provisions, hired young men to help row, and others to take the horses through by land, and, placing his two sick brethren feet to feet in the pirogue, started on his journey. The second day all the provisions were found to be spoiled, and they made the rest of their journey without food. They, however, reached the appointed place in time for the camp-meeting. Neither Burrow nor Carnahan was able to assist. Both, indeed, were delirious.[1] One day, after King had preached on the text "the harvest is past," a lady in the congregation repeated the text and fell shrieking to the ground. Others instantly fell; then others, until all over the congregation prostrate penitents were pleading for mercy. For several days King had felt his frame burning with fever; but as both his comrades were prostrate, he determined not to acknowledge that he was sick. Standing in the midst of this throng of weeping sinners, and trying to instruct them in the way of salvation, he fainted and fell to the ground. He was taken up and borne to one of the camps, bled, and put to bed in an unconscious state. There was no more preaching at that meeting, and neither of the missionaries was ever able to tell how the meeting closed. They were both carried along with Carnahan to private houses. King remained delirious eleven days, and kept his bed five weeks.

The hardships of the journey of these two missionaries back to Missouri may be taken as a type of what our pioneer preachers endured. We have a full account of this journey from both King and Burrow, and the narrative is here placed before the reader with the greater pleasure because both of these missionaries were among the very noblest specimens of true manhood that any church in any age ever enrolled among its heroes.

Dr. Burrow was a man of great physical power. He had a compact, heavy, muscular frame, and heavy eyebrows. His black hair grew low down on his forehead, and his accent betrayed just a little his German extraction. The working of his mind was like the heavy and powerful movements of some ponderous machine.

---

[1] In this account of the river trip I follow the King manuscript. Burrow's is slightly different; but Burrow was delirious or unconscious throughout the trip, and wrote from memory long afterward.

His eye and countenance slowly kindled as he advanced in his sermons, until at last his homely face grew beautiful with the glow of intellect set on fire by the Holy Ghost.

King was a fine specimen of the pioneer preacher. Trained in pioneer work by the Rev. Samuel King, his father, and all his life keeping on the frontier, he delighted in hardships and sufferings for Jesus with something of the same spirit which the first century witnessed in those who earnestly coveted the martyr's crown. He closed his career, at last, on the Texas frontier, leaving it as his dying testimony that, if he had his life to live over again, he would wish it to be just the kind of life which he had already passed through.

When the time came to go back to Missouri, King was still unable to travel, and Burrow set out without him. There was an appointment for a camp-meeting on the road one hundred miles distant. Eighteen young people, most of whom were unconverted, mounted their horses and accompanied Burrow to this meeting, and almost all of these souls were there blessed. After this camp-meeting Burrow resumed his journey. He was now alone, and what was worse, his horse was sick; but we have already seen that he never allowed such things to interfere with his work. Placing his saddle-bags on his shoulder, and driving his sick horse before him, he pursued his journey. Then his horse died, and he plodded on afoot, having an appointment one hundred and fifty miles ahead. It was often from twenty-five to thirty miles from one house to the next. How he crossed the rivers without a horse, in a land where there were neither bridges nor ferries, and where the settlements were twenty-five miles apart, is left to conjecture.

He reached St. Michaels, Missouri, in time for his appointment, and there with great joy he grasped by the hand his beloved fellow-laborer, the Rev. W. C. Long. But the end was not yet. The presbytery was to meet at Finis Ewing's church, near Booneville, Missouri. He and Long, placing their baggage on Long's horse, both started afoot. On the way Mr. Burrow was again taken very sick, and was unable to proceed. Not willing to miss a meeting of presbytery, Mr. Long, although he believed Burrow to be in a dying condition, continued his journey. But Burrow's work was not done. He recovered partially, borrowed a horse, and was at the appointed place in time for the presbyterial meeting. Being unable to sit up, he was carried to Finis Ewing's house, and cared for until his recovery by that queen of nurses, "Aunt Peggy" Ewing.

In the meantime King recovered sufficiently to sit on his horse. Worn with sickness, and all alone, he set out on the long journey "to presbytery." His first stretch of houseless wilderness was thirty miles across. It was dark when he closed that dreary ride, and he was burning with fever. At every house he was urged not to try to travel while in that condition; but, says he, "I was going to presbytery." The fifth night the family where he stayed were all sick—no one able to sit up. King himself was in a raging fever, and too weak to climb up to the loft where the fodder was kept, but he managed to give his horse some corn; and then, being wet to the skin from rain and crossing rivers, he spread his blanket before the fire and passed the night in sleep. Toward morning he awoke greatly improved, his fever all gone. He says that he felt willing to die for the sake of reaching that meeting of presbytery, and there representing the interests of the destitute people along the banks of the White and the Arkansas rivers. Indeed, by some means the report had reached the members of McGee Presbytery that he was dead; and when he entered the house in which the presbytery was sitting, the Rev. R. D. Morrow was on his feet reading a preamble and resolutions in relation to the death of their beloved brother, the Rev. R. D. King. When they saw him enter, the whole presbytery rushed to meet him with tears of joy and exclamations of thanksgiving to God.

The Rev. Hiram McDaniel, of Kentucky, spent the winter of that same year (1823) as missionary in Arkansas. He found trials, too. Once when he swam the Arkansas River his horse was all covered with ice before he reached the farther shore. Such things came in as a matter of course in the work of these pioneer preachers, not only in that day but for many years afterward.

On the fourth Thursday in May, 1824, according to the order of the synod at its preceding session, the Arkansas Presbytery was constituted in the house of John Craig, in Independence County.

Robert Stone, one of the men appointed to assist in the organization, was absent. The ministers who were present were John Carnahan, W. C. Long, and William Henry. They lived at great distances from each other, but that was the usual state of things in the new presbyteries. They at once turned their attention to raising up a home supply of preachers. There were four candidates for the ministry to begin with. Prayer, beseeching God to call more men to preach the gospel, made part of the business of every meeting of that little presbytery in the wilderness.

At the time for the second meeting of this presbytery, in the fall of 1824, a quorum was not present, but Andrew Buchanan presented himself to the committee as a candidate for the ministry. He afterward became a leading preacher, and his name fills a large place to-day in the history of our church in Arkansas. From 1824 until he was an old man he was an active missionary among the Arkansas people. An old lady who long knew him and held him in very high esteem said to me: "He did n't preach at all; he just talked as if he were speaking to little children, and made every thing so plain. But I tell you Uncle John[1] preached." A natural, simple manner was a rare thing in those days of pulpit thunder.

In the spring of 1825 the Arkansas Presbytery again failed to hold its regular session, as no quorum was present. The following autumn a similar failure occurred for the same reason. Several probationers were ready for licensure. It was a distressing case, and was brought before the synod. The synod sought to remedy the trouble by extending the bounds of Arkansas Presbytery far into Missouri, so as to include the homes of several preachers of that State. A quorum was thus secured, and licensures and ordinations followed.

By this extension of the bounds of Arkansas Presbytery several names were placed on its roll which do not belong to the history of the church in that State. Robert Sloan, however, who lived and died in Missouri, and who for a while held his membership in Arkansas Presbytery, did labor nobly as a missionary among the

---

[1] The Rev. John Buchanan was familiarly spoken of as "Uncle John," and the Rev. Andrew Buchanan as "Uncle Buck."

people of Arkansas. Once while traveling in that territory his horse died; but he was more fortunate in this emergency than Reuben Burrow had been in similar circumstances. The people remounted him, and he went on his way rejoicing. Judge Ewing's excellent little volume of "Historical Memoirs" contains a biography of Mr. Sloan.

At the meeting of Arkansas Presbytery in the spring of 1826, Jesse M. Blair, J. H. Black, W. W. Stevenson, and Andrew Buchanan were all licensed to preach. In the fall meeting that year J. A. Cornwall and W. W. Stevenson were ordained. Black and Blair were ordained the following spring. In the records of this presbytery for 1827 there is an item characteristic of the men and the times. The Rev. James H. Black, who had been appointed to one of the oldest circuits, reported his failure to carry out the appointment, giving this as his reason: a Macedonian cry from the new settlements on Red River, where the people had no preaching of any kind, had greatly touched his heart. He therefore left his old circuit, where there were some other preachers of other churches, and spent his whole time in the newer and more destitute field. He said the success of that work had convinced him that the call came from God, and he hoped his brethren would excuse his failure to comply with their order. He was excused, "Red River circuit" established, and in a few more years we find Red River Presbytery organized.

In the Minutes of the Arkansas Presbytery the boundaries of the congregations are defined. These boundaries were frequently as large as a whole county. In some instances, indeed, a circuit was established exclusively within the limits of a single congregation. Of course the meetings were held in private houses. During this first period there seem to have been no meeting-houses in the territory.

In 1827 Arkansas Presbytery called on all the churches to unite in a day of fasting and of prayer to the great Head of the Church for more ministers to be called and sent into that needy field. There were four immense circuits in the Territory, yet the missionaries did not reach one half of the destitute. Camp-meetings and circuit appointments were here, as everywhere else, the chief reliance for supplying the country with the gospel. At least once a year every congregation was to be examined on theology (the catechism) by one of the ordained ministers. This universal custom of all our presbyteries in that day was not forgotten in Arkansas. Another characteristic item appears on the records of this presbytery. An order was passed requiring every minister to preach to each church which he visited one sermon on "the support of the ministry," and report results to the presbytery. At the next meeting five reported that they had not complied with the order. One who reported compliance said that the people on his circuit had pledged sixty-eight dollars and fifty cents for this purpose. Another reported that he complied with the order, and that the people on his circuit all said they could not pay any thing for preaching.

In 1827 all the country around what is now Cane Hill College, Washington County, was opened to white settlers, the Osage Indians having sold their lands and moved farther west. A goodly number of the Crystal Hill people moved to this new field, and among them were two Cumberland Presbyterian preachers, Carnahan and Blair, and also two elders. They organized Cane Hill church, which has been from that day to this a center of spiritual power for all Arkansas. It soon "swarmed," and the new hive was called Salem, which still lives and works for Jesus.

Before the Crystal Hill people reached Cane Hill, another Cumberland Presbyterian family had settled there. This was James Buchanan and his household. Around the Pyatts, the Buchanans, and the Blairs clusters a large part of the history of the Cumberland Presbyterian church in that field.

One thing about Cane Hill congregation deserves to be specially mentioned — the large number of noble ministers it has sent forth, and the very high positions of usefulness which these ministers have filled. Among its converts are found not only ministers, but noble men in other callings, as, for example, Prof. A. H. Buchanan, of Cumberland University. Many of our large churches never send out any preachers. Numbers and wealth do not constitute spiritual power. Alas, no! oftener do they co-exist with a godless worldliness which causes parents to shrink from the thought of giving their sons to be preachers.

Cane Hill church founded Cane Hill College, stamping upon it the image of its own deep spirituality, which that institution still bears and impresses on its pupils. A school for Jesus—what a precious thing it is!

"Not more than one third of the people of Arkansas have any opportunity to hear the gospel,"[1] said a writer in 1831. "There are only three Sabbath-schools in the Territory," he adds. He pleads with the Cumberland Presbyterian church not to send men East, where other churches are supplying the people with the word of life, but to follow up the great wave of western emigrants. At the close of the period ending in 1829, when the Cumberland Presbyterian General Assembly was organized, Arkansas was still a sparsely settled territory, with wide areas between the settlements, and with the Indians still on the soil.

There were also two desperate bands of robbers in Washington County, of this Territory, and many of the pioneer families, and especially the noble women whose husbands traveled as missionaries, lived in constant dread of these desperadoes. These robber bands were especially troublesome about Cane Hill. All efforts to reach them through the courts failed. Finally, after whole families, including little children, had been murdered, a vigilance committee took the matter in hand and made quick work of the whole business. To this committee the Rev. Andrew Buchanan gave his hearty support. There was no other way to rid the country of these robbers.

There are many traditions concerning Andrew Buchanan and his adventures. A cool, fearless hero; never excited, never losing self-possession, never shrinking from any duty, however hard, he was well fitted for the field in which his lot was cast. Two of his favorite sayings are still quoted in Arkansas. One was, "I take no more trouble on my hands than I can kick off at my heels;" the other, "I never let my feelings stick out far enough for people to tramp on them."

One of the pioneer workers in Arkansas camp-meetings, Mrs. Mary Marshall, formerly Mrs. Moore, died in Williamson County, Tennessee, in 1886. She and her husband settled in Arkansas in

---

[1] *Religious and Literary Intelligencer*, May 12, 1831

1822. Both were converted in one of the early camp-meetings in that Territory, and from that day on were very active in all the meetings within fifty miles of their home. Mrs. Marshall furnished me several incidents illustrating the eminent piety of our first Arkansas preachers. On one occasion she and others were talking to the Rev. Guilford Pylant about religion. It was at night after services. So absorbed were they in this spiritual communion that the day began to break before they noticed how long the conference had been protracted. Mrs. Marshall says Mr. Pylant was always "in the Spirit." He is one of the surviving pioneer preachers of Arkansas.

At another time the Arkansas Presbytery held its meeting in Mrs. Marshall's parlor. After the presbytery adjourned those who remained, Andrew Buchanan among the rest, engaged in religious conversation. In a short time the whole assembly was so filled with religious ecstasy that the house rang with loud shouts of "Glory to God." Such was the confidence which our young preachers had in this woman's piety and good sense that they even went to her to read, for her criticism, the trial sermons which they prepared for presbytery.

CHAPTER XX.

THE COLLEGE—THE GENERAL ASSEMBLY—SUMMARY OF WHAT HAD BEEN DONE.

> The old order changeth, yielding place to new,
> And God fulfills himself in many ways.
> —*Tennyson.*

THE Cumberland Presbyterian church at an early period in its history recognized the necessity of establishing a school for the education of its preachers. When there were but three presbyteries this question was discussed in each of them. In 1822 commissioners from the Elk, the Nashville, and the Tennessee presbyteries met in convention to consider this subject. Again in 1823 a more vigorous discussion of the subject ended in the determination to bring the matter before the synod with a view to co-operation in one school for the whole church.

At the meeting of the General Synod, in Princeton, Kentucky, in 1825, the final plan for the contemplated school was adopted, and commissioners appointed to receive bids and locate the institution. It was to have a department of arts and also a department of theology. The highest judicature of the church was to be its board of trustees. The whole country was at that time taking up with Fellenberg's theory of manual-labor schools, and the synod caught the infection and resolved that their college should be conducted on that plan.

A novel spectacle greets us here. The synod, composed of all the ministers of the church, prescribes a course of study, selects the text-books, and makes a code of by-laws to govern the students; more than that, it undertakes to direct in the habits of the students about dress and other personal matters. It prohibits the use of feather beds; it requires from every student two or three hours' labor daily on the farm: it directs also about the management of the farm and the boarding-house. That race of hardy pioneers, brought up in a life of hardships on the frontier, undertook to train up another generation of men for the same rough work.

The synod also directed the commissioners to connect a printing establishment with this manual-labor enterprise, and to provide thereby for a church paper. It is manifest from all their proceedings at this time that the members of the synod expected large results from the cultivation of the farm by the students, but they were not wholly forgetful of the necessity for endowment. Agents in large numbers were appointed to solicit donations and remit to the commissioners, but no salary or other compensation was to be given to these agents.

The history of this college is reserved for another chapter. It was located at Princeton, Kentucky. The Rev. Franceway R. Cossitt, D.D., who came to the Cumberland Presbyterian church from the Episcopalians, was its first president. He was also the first president of the college afterward established at Lebanon, Tennessee. His appeals in behalf of education deserve to be collected in a volume, both as a memorial of a noble life of toil and to keep forever ringing in the ears of our people the important truths which Dr. Cossitt so earnestly pressed upon their attention—truths which will live forever, and which are for all countries and all churches, but especially for this young church of the frontier. If God, in his providence, raised up and fitted McGready and Ewing to lead in a special work for the great West, much more did his fatherly care show itself in training up a special leader for the first educational work of the church. Bred in New England, taught in her best schools, graduated in one of her best colleges, brought to Christ according to the Cumberland Presbyterian ideas of "time and place" and conscious conversion, trained in a regular theological school, drilled, too, in the work of teaching, Cossitt came West and cast in his lot with this new church. From that day until the day of his death he was an active worker for our educational enterprises.

The last days of the General Synod were chiefly occupied with the various questions which the college originated, but there were also several minor matters which received attention, among other things the publication of a hymn book for the church. The Rev. William Harris, on his own responsibility, had brought out a little book of hymns suited to camp-meetings, but the synod wanted a larger book and appointed men to prepare one. It also made arrangements to publish the lectures which the Rev. Finis Ewing had delivered in his theological school in Missouri. A college, a theological school, a church paper, and the publication of books were all partially provided for by the synod before the formation of a General Assembly.

The expediency of organizing a General Assembly began to be discussed as early as 1823. The question was debated and deferred at each successive meeting of the synod for five years. Two things seem to have caused delay. First, some members feared that the expansion of the church when proclaimed and acknowledged by the organization of an Assembly would cause some of our people to rely on their numbers and forget the true source of all their strength. Finis Ewing especially feared this, and while his fears did not lead him to oppose the steps of progress which it was necessary to take, yet at every such advance his voice of warning was heard pleading with his brethren to keep humble at God's feet and to remember that all their power came from him. There seems also to have been a lingering hesitation even yet about accepting the situation of a permanently organized separate denomination. A conference with commissioners from the Tennessee Synod of the Presbyterian church was looked to with strong hopes by some, but it ended without giving any ground to expect reunion. This conference originated with the Presbyterians and only proposed friendly relations, not organic union. The right of a synod to enter into such negotiations was, however, questioned by the Presbyterian General Assembly and the whole matter was dropped.

All of the preachers had to ride on horseback to attend the annual meetings of the General Synod. Daniel Patton, who is one of the three surviving members (1887) of that synod gives an interesting account of its last meeting. He had traveled seven hundred miles to attend, and traveling expenses had become a burden. He, therefore, laid ten dollars on the clerk's table to start a permanent fund, the interest of which should meet such traveling expenses. His example was followed by many others. Four hundred dollars for this fund was secured at that meeting. But the requisite number of presbyteries sent up their responses in favor of organizing a General Assembly. It was, therefore, no longer necessary that all the preachers of the church should attend every meeting of its highest judicature. So responses to Mr. Patton's proposition were never carried beyond the four hundred dollars. A very strong feeling in favor of a delegated synod, and no higher court, existed, but those maintaining this view were outvoted. The organization was to be Presbyterian in all its details.

Some of the minor rules and transactions of the General Synod deserve to be noticed before we pass to the next period. There was, for instance, a standing order requiring every presbytery to furnish from time to time a full history of its work and progress, to be filed with the stated clerk of the synod. The Rev. David Foster was appointed general superintendent to see that this rule was complied with. While many of these histories are lost, there are enough of them still in existence to render valuable aid in the preparation of this volume. Why could not this old rule be revived, and precious material be thus preserved? Not a mere digest of ecclesiastical records, but a photograph of the work in all the churches of the presbytery is what is needed. The synod, in its official action, took high ground on the subject of temperance. It placed itself on record as in favor of all the great benevolent enterprises of the day. It was recognized in all the West as foremost in work for the Bible Society and the Tract Society.

New presbyteries were organized from time to time, and when the General Synod finally adjourned *sine die*, there were eighteen of these presbyteries. The date of the order for the organization of each, and a list of the original members, are here given:

Nashville,[1] 1813: Hugh Kirkpatrick, Thomas Calhoun, David Foster, D. W. McLin.

Elk, 1813: William McGee, Samuel King, James B. Porter, Robert Bell, Robert Donnell.

---

[1] The Nashville Presbytery was what was left of the original Cumberland Presbytery after Elk and Logan were stricken off in 1813 It was still called the Cum-

CLOSE OF SECOND PERIOD

Logan, 1813: Finis Ewing, William Harris, Alexander Chapman, William Barnett.

McGee, 1819: Green P. Rice, Daniel Buie, R. D. Morrow, John Carnahan.

Anderson, 1821: William Henry, John Barnett, D. W. McLin, Aaron Shelby, W. M. Hamilton, James Johnston, William Barnett.

Lebanon, 1821: Thomas Calhoun, William Bumpass, John Provine, J. L. Dillard, Daniel Gossedge, Samuel McSpeddin, James McDonnold.

Tennessee, 1821: A. Alexander, Albert Gibson, R. Donnell, James Stuart, James Moore, John Molloy.

Illinois, 1822: Green P. Rice, D. W. McLin, John M. Berry, W. M. Hamilton.

Tombigbee, 1823: Robert Bell, John Molloy, John C. Smith, John Forbes.

Arkansas, 1823: W. C. Long, William Henry, John Carnahan, Robert Stone.

Hopewell, 1824: William Barnett, Richard Beard, Samuel Harris, John C. Smith.

Alabama,[a] 1824: William Moore, Benjamin Lockhart, John Williams, J. W. Dickey.

Indiana, 1825: Aaron Shelby, H. A. Hunter, A. Downey, William Lynn.

Barnett, 1827: Samuel King, R. D. Morrow, Daniel Patton, Henry Renick.

Knoxville, 1827: George Donnell, S. M. Aston, Abner W. Lansden, William Smith.

St. Louis, 1828: F. M. Braly, John R. Brown, John W. McCord, John H. Garvin.

Princeton, 1828: F. R. Cossitt, David Lowry, John W. Ogden, James Johnston.

Sangamon, 1828: David Foster, John M. Berry, Thomas Campbell, Gilbert Dodds, John Porter.

The synod resolved to divide itself into four synods preparatory to the organization of a General Assembly. These new synods were named Missouri, Franklin, Green River, and Columbia. There were six presbyteries in Missouri Synod: McGee, Barnett, Sangamon, Illinois, St. Louis, and Arkansas. Franklin Synod had four

---

berland Presbytery till 1814, when its name was changed. Elk, Logan, and Nashville were the presbyteries composing the first synod.

[a] The order to organize in 1821 failed for want of a resident quorum.

presbyteries: Nashville, Lebanon, Knoxville, and Hopewell. In Green River Synod there were also four presbyteries: Anderson, Princeton, Logan, and Indiana; and four in the Columbia Synod, viz.: Alabama, Tombigbee, Elk, and Tennessee. The General Assembly was to hold its first meeting in Princeton, Kentucky, the third Tuesday in May, 1829. Such changes in the Form of Government as the organization of a General Assembly necessitated were made by the synod, and, without any reference to the presbyteries, were accepted by common consent, and became part of the laws of the church.

This synodical period, from 1813 to 1829, was one of unsurpassed activity and spirituality on the part of our ministry. Taking it altogether, the world has never witnessed its equal; certainly the Cumberland Presbyterian church has not witnessed any thing like its equal in the two particulars specified. I am sorry to add that there are no statistics to show even the number of ministers in the church, much less the number of members, at that time. There were eighteen presbyteries, and we know who their first members were; but what names had been added to their rolls after their organization can not now be ascertained. There were thousands of conversions every year, but God kept that roll; and the fear of "counting," which still exists among our people, did not cause one single genuine convert to be omitted from the family record in our Father's book of life. On Monday, October 27, 1828, at Franklin, Tennessee, the General Synod, composed of all the ministers of the church and their elders, adjourned to meet no more on earth.

THIRD PERIOD.

CHAPTER XXI.

GENERAL SURVEY.

> And now with voices soft, mysterious, low,
> The phantoms whisper round me, and I seem
> To hear life's blended memories come and go
> In strange ethereal music fitfully.
> —*Paul H. Hayne.*

THE third period, from the meeting of the first General Assembly in 1829 to the removal of Cumberland College in 1842, is the great transition period in the history of the Cumberland Presbyterian church. It seems proper, before taking up any thorough notice of details, to sweep over this period with a sort of general survey.

When the first General Assembly met at Princeton, Kentucky, the church extended into only eight States, six of which had become States since the church was organized. The other two States had both acquired large areas of Indian territory since the organization of the church, and even in these two older States work among the pioneer settlements had constituted a large part of our denominational activity, while all the work in the new States had from necessity been accomplished by missionary evangelists. Born on the crest of the great wave of emigration which was rolling into the immense western territories, as one after another these territories were thrown open to white settlers, this church was specially raised up and fitted by a wise Providence for pioneer work in this field. The ministry of the new church filled this pioneer mission nobly; but the time came when all the circumstances were changed, and Providence pointed to other missions.

That period begins with the meeting of the first General Assembly. There were still new territories acquired by the nation on the western frontier, but there were also many old established communities in which our people had churches that needed training.

There were eighteen presbyteries at the time this period began, sixteen of which were represented in the first General Assembly. Not one of the preachers who attended this General Assembly had ever been a pastor in the true sense of that term. Missionaries who had borne great hardships all their lives, who had shown themselves ready and willing to suffer for the sake of leading souls to Jesus, but had little or no experience in the management of financial affairs, found themselves in charge of all the great enterprises of the denomination. It is not to be wondered at that they made many a blunder in the business department of their transactions. We know not whether smiles or tears are most called for when we see the General Assembly year after year appointing agents to travel over all the United States for the college, without any salary whatever. Were they not ministers who were thus appointed? Had they not all been thoroughly trained in working without any pay? But our smiles turn to admiration when we find that the Rev. Matthew Houston Bone, the Rev. Franceway R. Cossitt, and the Rev. John W. Ogden did all three comply with this appointment made by the first General Assembly, and make extensive tours in the interest of the college through half a dozen States. We are not surprised, however, to find in their reports the next year much more about the number of poor sinners converted at their meetings than about the amount of money secured for the college.

Much of the business of the General Assembly during this transition period had reference to the difficulties and the struggles of the college. Another matter of a most embarrassing nature, over which there was much trouble, was the church paper. A third source of trouble and loss was "the book concern." There were also heart-burnings and distress over the case of the Rev. John Barnett, who was financially wrecked while trying to carry on the business department of the college under contract with the General Assembly. Another source of embarrassment was a difficult and protracted discussion about the pastoral office. The home missionary work in Pennsylvania, Texas, Louisiana, and other fields was a hopeful feature of the church's progress during this period.

While the General Assembly uniformly indorsed the American Board of Missions, and recommended the churches to contribute to that board, it also clung to the theory of having a missionary board of its own both for domestic and foreign missions. The General Assembly of 1836 resolved to co-operate with the American Board in the foreign work. The Cumberland Presbyterian Board of Missions, which originated in the second period and continued through the third, never had any charter. While voices in favor of a chartered board of foreign missions were heard at every General Assembly, still no such board was created. The unchartered board was considered sufficient. Expecting neither legacies, law-suits, nor defalcations, a majority thought a charter unnecessary. All the congregations were required to have auxiliary missionary societies, tributary to this board.

At all the General Assemblies during this period the great benevolent enterprises of the day received hearty indorsement, and the churches were urged to co-operate with them. The Colonization Society and Tract Society seem to have been favorites, though the Bible Society, Temperance Society, and Sunday-school Union were never forgotten.

While the General Assembly declared itself in favor of full statistical reports from the presbyteries, and, with constantly diminishing opposition, resolved at every annual meeting that these reports must be sent up, yet up to the close of this period only about half the presbyteries complied with the order. There was a strong feeling against statistics among some of our best men. The first synod to make a full statistical report, accompanied with a directory of its ministers, was the Synod of Missouri, in 1836.

At every General Assembly the reports on the state of religion speak of extensive revivals, but do not give full statistics of conversions. At one meeting half the synods sent up statistics. The number of conversions in their bounds for that year was a little over eight thousand. In 1835 the Committee on the State of Religion reported that secularization of the ministry prevailed to an alarming extent. At two meetings the General Assembly held a fast-day in the midst of its sessions, the members gathering at six o'clock in the morning for prayer. General fast-days for the whole church were twice appointed during this period, and the people called on to pray for more men to be called to the ministry. Camp-meetings were still universal, and the General Assembly constantly gave them its official indorsement, and urged the churches to hold them. Even in the very few old churches which, after the middle of this period, had settled pastors, nobody thought of abandoning the camp-meeting. The church papers teem with accounts of revivals at these meetings. Nowhere else did the preachers of this period appear to such advantage, or preach with such power. It was customary to hold the sessions of the church judicatures during or immediately preceding a camp-meeting.

The General Assembly solemnly declared holy living on the part of God's people to be greatly needed and sadly lacking. In 1836 it declared it to be part of the policy of the church for presbyteries to license lay exhorters. It is a pity that the church ever departed from that policy.

It is remarkable how very few appeal cases came up from the lower church judicatures, and what a mild nature characterized those which did come. The first appeal case was at the fifth General Assembly, and the question was whether Hiram McDaniel belonged to the Princeton or to the Anderson Presbytery. Nor were there any appeals or any graver questions during all this period. Questions about the right way of appointing elders to attend synod were constantly coming up. Occasional memorials to abolish the synod were laid on the table, or voted down.

Two of the early ministers of the church were superannuated and in destitution. The General Assembly at every meeting made some provisions for these sufferers and their families. For one of them it bought a little farm.

The first part of this period presented few exciting debates. There were no great speeches. Oratory found its field in the pulpit, especially at the camp-meetings. The last Assembly of this period (1842), however, was more like one of our modern judicatures. There were animated debates and long and earnest speeches on the question of removing the college from Princeton. Local and party feelings made their first decided exhibition in this Assembly. According to all accounts the speeches in all the former sessions were short, and utterly destitute of any ill-feeling. This was true even in the discussion of the questions about which it is known that there were bitter heart-burnings. The peace and harmony of the church were at that day held in very high esteem.

In 1833 the General Assembly resolved that it would be a gratifying thing to have the three men who organized our first presbytery visit all the churches. The Rev. Samuel King, therefore, after some preparation, took with him his son, the Rev. R. D. King, and started in April, 1834, on the grand tour. His first year was spent in the South-west, during which time he aided in organizing the Louisiana Presbytery. He reported good meetings all through the year. The next General Assembly asked him to continue the work, which he did, and reported to the Assembly of 1836. He visited Logan, Kentucky, and Knoxville presbyteries, the Creek and Cherokee Indians, and the Elyton, Alabama, and Mississippi presbyteries, holding meetings all along the journey. He says that he everywhere found the old preachers more zealous than their juniors. Several precious revivals and other good results of the mission are mentioned. For the whole two years he and his son received compensation nearly equal to their traveling expenses.

In 1836 the General Assembly declared that making, selling, or giving away ardent spirits was an offense requiring discipline. It put on record a declaration about fraternal intercourse with all orthodox churches, and directed its preachers to maintain this intercourse so far as possible with all God's children. The same Assembly formed a society for the purpose of aiding candidates for the ministry in securing a thorough education.

Owing to the financial embarrassments into which the college was plunged at the very beginning of its career, the first General Assembly decided to defer indefinitely the scheme of establishing a theological department in that college. The church, however, was clamorous for a theological school, and the General Assembly of 1834 submitted the question to the presbyteries whether it would be better to have one school under Assembly auspices. or several schools under synodical control. The replies from the presbyteries were not in harmony: some wanted presbyterial, and some synodical schools, and some one school under the Assembly. Others thought that the time for action had not yet arrived. Under this state of things the whole question was again postponed. The General Assembly of 1838 resolved to try the plan of holding biennial instead of annual sessions; therefore no Assembly met in 1839.

During this period the number of synods in the church grew from four to twelve, and the number of presbyteries from eighteen to fifty-three. The period began under the dispensation of missionary evangelists; it closed with a recognized pastoral system thoroughly indorsed by church authority, but not yet established in the hearts of the lay members. This was in some respects the darkest epoch of the church's history, the war period itself not excepted. The darkness arose from troubles over the college, the paper, and the publication of books, and from the transition from missions to pastorates. A list of the new presbyteries established during this period, with the dates when they are first mentioned on the rolls of the Assembly, is here given: Kentucky, 1830; Elyton, Forked Deer, Hatchie, Mississippi, Vandalia, and Wabash, 1832; Lexington, New Lebanon, Obion, Pennsylvania, Salt River, and White River, 1833; Jackson and Red River, 1834; Louisiana and Richland, 1835; Chapman, King, Rushville, Shiloh, Talladega, and Wolf River, 1836; Athens, Hiwassee, Mackinaw, Neosho, Ohio, and Uniontown—now Union (Pennsylvania)—1837; Oxford, Texas, and Washington, 1838; Columbus and Union (West Tennessee Synod), 1840; Charity Hall, Foster, McGready, and Memphis, 1841; Ewing (Illinois), Mound Prairie, and Ozark, 1842. Several of these, however, were not new presbyteries, but new names for old ones. The new synods added in 1832 were Mississippi, Illinois, and Western District, afterward called West Tennessee. In 1834 Arkansas Synod was created, and the name of Missouri Synod changed to Washington, but the original name was soon after resumed. Union (now Alabama) Synod was organized in 1836; Indiana in 1837; and Pennsylvania, McHaca, and Middle Tennessee in 1838. The name McHaca was afterward changed to Sangamon. The Franklin Synod was dissolved, and its presbyteries attached to other synods. Finis Ewing, David Foster, David W. McLin, William Barnett, Alexander Chapman, and H. F. Delany died during this period, and the Rev. Samuel King just at its close.

One thing is fully manifest from the study of this whole period: At the bottom of all the financial trouble about the printing of books, about the paper, about the college, and about John Barnett's embarrassments and losses, lay one and the same foundation of rottenness—the credit system. Let the church heed the danger signals which its past experience has raised so high over the wrecks of its early enterprises.

The same period furnishes another danger signal demanding present and perpetual attention: No body as large as the General Assembly is competent to manage financial enterprises. A small board of experts selected for this special work may do so; no General Assembly in any church has ever done so successfully. During this period the whole church, through its General Assembly, entered into half a dozen or more business contracts, making solemn pledges which it did not and could not keep. Trouble and disaster came from every one of these contracts. The inconsistency of attempting the direct management of financial enterprises by so large a body is well illustrated in the history of the church's first general Board of Missions. This board was composed of all the ministers of the church. Among them were a considerable number of men who were opposed to foreign missions; yet they helped to manage our first foreign mission!

What then is the conclusion? "Look ye out seven men" fit for such business, and leave its management to them. What if they prove false? Then the immorality, not the business management, is a fit subject for ecclesiastical reckoning. Unfitness for the trust may call for a change of men, but it never justifies an Assembly in taking into its own hands the financial direction of any business enterprise.

CHAPTER XXII.

THE FIRST CUMBERLAND PRESBYTERIAN COLLEGE.

"Si monumentum queris circumspice."

A CHURCH college necessarily has two histories—one outward and ecclesiastical, the other internal and domestic. The first Cumberland Presbyterian college has been very fortunate in the writer of its outward history, but much of the material for a record of its internal workings has forever perished. Dr. Richard Beard's article, secured by Dr. J. Berrien Lindsley, and published by Dr. M. B. DeWitt in the *Theological Medium*, April, 1876, is a full and reliable presentation of the official and ecclesiastical side of the history of this college. With all the official records of the college and the General Assembly to guide him, besides a personal connection with most of the events he recorded, there could not have been found a more accurate historian than Dr. Beard. One of his dates is no doubt a misprint. It was not 1844, but 1842, when the General Assembly forever severed its connection with Cumberland College.

The antecedents of the action establishing the college were given in a former chapter. The following reasons were urged in favor of a manual labor institution: Health will be promoted, economy will be secured, the poor will have a chance for a collegiate education, and the ministry will thus be trained for that life of hardships which pioneer missions call for.

The commissioners appointed by the synod in 1825 to arrange for the location and establishment of the college visited Hopkinsville, Elkton, Russellville, and Princeton. The synod felt obliged to locate the school in Kentucky. The people of Princeton made the largest bid ($28,000) *in subscriptions*, and the college was located there, and a board of trust chartered. A large farm was bought on a credit, tools and stock were bought with borrowed money; buildings were erected on a credit. "Here beginneth our morning lesson." Less than one fourth of the subscriptions made by the people of Princeton were ever paid. Thus the institution was born in embarrassments. The conditions on which the location at Princeton was made were thus violated at the beginning, and the church began immediately to regret that some other place had not been selected. There were many strong men in the church who from the first seriously doubted the fitness of the location at Princeton. Prominent among these was the Rev. Robert Donnell. He predicated his doubts solely on the weakness of the Cumberland Presbyterian church in that town. He said that a temporary interest aroused among members of other churches by local considerations could not be relied on for a long struggle. To all this he gave utterance before Princeton was selected, and while different locations were under discussion. The results showed that Donnell's doubts were well founded. A few men of other churches were true helpers to the last, but there was lacking that strong local support which every college imperatively requires. Cumberland College was my own *alma mater*, and for half of my lifetime Princeton was the dearest spot to me on the earth. No community anywhere could have shown more kindness to the students. The trouble did not lie in that quarter.

The college opened on the first of March, 1826, with six students, but the number soon increased. The large, hewed log house, which afterward was Dr. Beard's residence, now burned, was the college building. Dormitories, some good and some rude, were on the other side of the street. The refectory was a little nearer the town. Before the institution was a year old the farm was mortgaged to raise money to meet the most pressing debts. In 1831 debts had accumulated until the institution was about to be sold. Several agents had been sent out, but very few of them secured any thing more than traveling expenses. The Rev. John W. Ogden, who canvassed the churches in South Alabama, paid over to the trustees seven hundred dollars, but that was "only a drop in the bucket." The others altogether paid just seventy-eight dollars and forty-seven cents. Debts to the amount of twelve thousand dollars were then pressing. The case was pronounced hopeless. When the General Assembly met that year, many people thought it would be better to abandon that enterprise, and start a college in some community which had never arrayed the prejudices of the church against it.

The Rev. John Barnett and the Rev. Aaron Shelby, both possessed of considerable estates and both warm friends of the college and of its location also, made a proposition to lease the institution for four years. Their proposition was accepted. Its terms and conditions are here briefly stated: (1) The lessees assumed all the debts and all the expenses both of college and refectory; (2) They were authorized to charge eighty dollars a year for boarding and tuition, instead of sixty dollars, the former price. There were four conditions: First, It was stipulated that the individual members of the General Assembly should give their notes for $2,400, due in one and two years. Second, It was agreed that the General Assembly should keep an agent constantly in the field soliciting aid for the college. Third, All the net profits from the church paper were to be given to the lessees. (This item was changed afterward.) Fourth, All the assets of the institution of every description, and all its net income, were to be given to the lessees. After this contract was entered into, the trustees, whose chartered existence and general oversight of the college still continued, agreed to extend the lease to Barnett and Shelby to twelve years in payment for a large brick building to be erected by them. They erected the building which was so long the chief home of the institution.

The details of the trouble and complaints which grew out of this lease would be neither interesting nor profitable. Shelby was shrewd enough to get his head out of the halter while the rope was slack. Young, who bought out Shelby, died of cholera, and the trustees bought his half of the lease. Both the lessees and the General Assembly failed in part of their pledges. The lessees never paid off the debts against the institution, and the General Assembly failed to pay the $2,400 pledged to the lessees. Crimination and recrimination followed. The cholera visited Princeton year after year. There was great dissatisfaction among the students with the labor requirement, and with the refectory. These things combined to make Barnett's connection with the college disastrous to him. Some thought the General Assembly ought to indemnify him, but a majority voted against such a proposition. Many hard feelings and heart-burnings there were, but it is needless to follow the subject further.

When the General Assembly of 1836 met, Barnett proposed to surrender his lease; and declared himself unable, by reason of many losses, to carry out his contracts. The General Assembly then asked the trustees to form a joint-stock company. They failed to do so, and bitter complaints were made in the church paper about this failure. Some of the trustees replied, representing the condition and prospects of the college as utterly hopeless. The General Assembly of 1837, which met at Princeton, urged the formation of the joint-stock company. The trustees replied that the property of the college was all under the hammer, and no joint-stock company was possible. Thereupon various members of the Assembly agreed to become stockholders, and these members, aided by a few citizens of Princeton, formed the company and Barnett surrendered his lease.

This company was to be independent of the Assembly and to relieve the church of all responsibility for the debts of the institution. It had its own chartered board of trust chosen by itself. The main consideration in view of which the Assembly agreed to surrender all control of the institution and all title to its property of every description was that the Association should pay off all the debts against the college. A two years' breathing spell was gained by the new arrangement and money enough was secured to stave off the most pressing debts, but not enough to liquidate them.

An Episcopalian minister was placed in the faculty, and people thought it was through his influence that the new board of directors began to talk about transferring the college to the Episcopal church. To the General Assembly in 1840 the college authorities reported their determination to transfer the college to some other church unless that Assembly would make reliable provisions for endowment. They told how much the people of Princeton had done for the institution, and lectured the Assembly about its failures. A new plan was then adopted. On condition that all the property, real and personal, should be transferred back, free from debt, to a board of trust to be appointed by the General Assembly, that body undertook to raise an endowment of fifty-five thousand dollars.

In 1841 the college reported that the charter for the new board had been secured and that the institution had better patronage. The agents reported fifteen thousand dollars subscribed for endowment. Hopes began to revive. In 1842 the new board reported to the General Assembly that the property was not turned over to them free of debt according to the contract, but was then levied on for debts far exceeding in amount what the real estate was worth. A large number of those who had subscribed to the endowment were at this Assembly, and with great unanimity they declared themselves absolved from the payment of their subscriptions.

The Committee on Education then reported in favor of selecting a more eligible site for the church college. Their report was adopted, it is said, with only three dissenting voices. It recommended the appointment of a commission to receive bids, to locate the school, and to make arrangements for buildings and for all other necessary things, so as to enable the new college to begin its work in September; but with the distinct understanding that the commission was forbidden to contract any debts. The General Assembly had sufficiently tested the credit system, and was thoroughly sick of being in debt. After this motion was carried, it was resolved to allow Princeton also to put in its bid. Other and different statements concerning this final action have been published, but the original records of the General Assembly are followed in this account. The removal of the college had long been spoken of, and for some time had been distinctly foreseen by leading men of the church.

The commission met in Nashville, July 1, 1842. It was composed of the ablest and purest men of the church, among them Robert Donnell, Reuben Burrow, and James B. Porter. The bid of Lebanon, which was by far the best, was accepted, and the school was located there. The history of this college belongs to another chapter, but one item deserves to be put on record here. Every dollar of Lebanon's bid was promptly paid. When the commission met a vigorous protest from the Cumberland College Association against the attempt to remove the college from Princeton was presented.

To the next General Assembly, May, 1843, the commissioners made their report, announcing that they had located the college at Lebanon, Wilson County, Tennessee, and that the school was already in successful operation. This report referred to the remonstrance of Cumberland College Association against the removal of the college from Princeton, but declared that since "the General Assembly had decided on a removal of the college, and appointed commissioners to locate it, the Association's remonstrance, unaccompanied by any proposition or any guarantee that the institution would be disenthralled from its pecuniary embarrassments, did not present sufficient reasons to the commissioners to justify their departure from the instructions of the General Assembly."

It set forth four reasons which had influenced the Assembly to provide for the removal of the college: First, Many had been led to regard the location at Princeton unfavorable because less than one fourth of the subscription originally made by the citizens of that town had been paid. Second, During several years after the location of the college at Princeton, agents appointed by the General Assembly had traveled in different directions soliciting and receiving donations. An impression had gone abroad that a large amount had been received, and this impression, though to some extent erroneous, had, when viewed in connection with the continued pecuniary embarrassments of the college, created in many minds a prejudice against the location. Third, The report declared that the disastrous failure to relieve the institution of debt by leasing it to individuals, and its continued and augmented indebtedness in spite of all measures for its relief, had done much to alienate the minds and feelings of the people from Princeton as a suitable location for the college. Fourth, The final effort to relieve the institution from its embarrassment by the formation of the Cumberland College Association was also described, and the failure of this effort, the report said, had tended still more to discourage the church with regard to the success of the college at Princeton.

The commissioners then gave their reasons for selecting Lebanon as "a more eligible site" for the church college. The citizens of that town proposed the erection of a large and commodious edifice for the school. Lebanon was known to be a healthful place, and was one of the most flourishing towns in the State. A large number of its citizens were intelligent and energetic members of the Cumberland Presbyterian church, who were interested in the college and able to help it. The people generally were well disposed toward the church, and in Wilson and adjoining counties there was a strong Cumberland Presbyterian influence. The society of Lebanon was refined and moral; its people were hospitable; dissipation was banished from the town.

The Lebanon people had promised to build an edifice two stories high and one hundred feet long; but this report informed the General Assembly that the building actually erected was "three stories high, one hundred and ten feet long, and forty feet wide," conveniently constructed of substantial materials, and covered with cedar shingles, and that "the comb of the roof" was about fifty-five feet from the foundation, and the highest part of the dome seventy-five feet. This building, the report said, was to be completed in July. There were then forty-five students in attendance. The trustees had made arrangements by which young men preparing for the ministry might be educated without the payment of tuition.

The report explained that the General Assembly did not have or claim to have any right or title to the incorporated powers or privileges, or the property of Cumberland College Association, or contemplate the removal of any of these. It said that the Assembly's trustees, an incorporated body entirely distinct from the Cumberland College Association, held, and were intended to hold, the endowment of the college, of which the interest alone could be used. All that was understood or intended by the removal of the college was the appropriation of this endowment at another place. The report expressed the opinion that the General Assembly had the right "to direct the application of the endowment to such place as the college might be removed to," but suggested that for the sake of peace subscribers who had pledged money to the endowment fund should be allowed to pay it for the use of either the college at Princeton or the one at Lebanon, at the election of such subscribers. It also declared that, should the General Assembly desire to endow a college at Princeton, the commissioners were assured that the friends and patrons of the Lebanon school would make no objection to any equitable arrangement; but denied that the resolves of former General Assemblies to raise an endowment for Cumberland College were legally binding on the Assembly then sitting or on the church.

The ground taken by the friends of Princeton was that the General Assembly had no power to sever its connection with the college at Princeton, and that that connection still existed. They presented these views in a communication to the General Assembly. The decision was against them, the vote being thirty-six to twenty-eight. This decision is embodied in the report of the Committee on Education, to which this question was referred, and of which Richard Beard was chairman. After declaring that the committee "entered into the investigation with a settled determination most rigidly to follow truth and justice to whatever decision their consciences and their judgment might be conducted," this report goes on to say that, after an elaborate review of the facts, the committee but yielded to the overwhelming weight of these facts and the clearest convictions of justice in coming to the conclusion that the action of the General Assembly in dissolving its connection with Cumberland College Association "was not only altogether justifiable, but imperiously demanded by a proper self-respect and the dearest interests of the confiding community for whose good that high judicatory is appointed."

The report continues:

What loss has that Association sustained by the action of the General Assembly of 1842? All the debts against it are understood to be now paid by the sale of the college property. Not a dollar is pointed out to as actually lost by the Association on account of that action. The pretended wrongs complained of seem to be a withholding of the prospective munificence of the General Assembly from them.

After declaring that the General Assembly and not the Association was the injured and suffering party, the report closed with two resolutions:

Resolved, In view of the premises, and in the exercise of the rights recognized in the amended charter of 1841, that the General Assembly of the Cumberland Presbyterian church, in the exercise of its just rights, and in view of the facts which in its opinion at the time fully justified that action, did on the 22d day of May, 1842, intentionally dissolve its ecclesiastical connection from Cumberland College Association thereby leaving the property and rights of said Association to revert to the same, according to the provisions of its charter.

2. That in view of the rights and interests of all concerned, the present subscribers to the endowing fund be authorized and advised at their own discretion to determine the place to which they will pay over their subscriptions, they being fully competent to act for themselves.

Dr. Beard did not vote for his committee's report, but joined in the strong protest against it, which was put on record.

This protest denied that the General Assembly of 1842 did sever its connection with Cumberland College Association, or that the General Assembly had fulfilled all obligations to that Association. It claimed that a more vigorous effort should have been made to endow the college, that the zeal and unanimity of the General Assembly in 1840 had led to hopes that had not been realized, and that if the members of the Association had expected so sudden an abandonment of the institution they would have preferred to look elsewhere for endowment and patronage. The protest further expressed the belief that the Association had sustained losses through the General Assembly's action; that "if the affairs of the institution had been wound up in 1840 the property would not only have paid the debts but returned to the members of the Association their original stock." This, however, was charged not to any wrong intention on the part of the General Assembly, but to hasty and unadvised legislation. The protest admitted that the General Assembly had been injured and had suffered from its connection with Cumberland College Association, but denied that the injury and suffering originated with that Association.

Dr. Beard, and the minority of the Committee on Education, had presented a plan for the settlement of these difficulties, in which it was proposed to transfer the General Assembly's legal powers and responsibilities in relation to Cumberland College, and the control of the Board of Trustees, to an association composed of eleven individuals, and to bind Cumberland College Association to relinquish its claims on the General Assembly and to allow the moneys subscribed to the endowment to be invested at Princeton or Lebanon, or elsewhere, as the donors might direct. The protest expressed the solemn belief that this plan would have met the views and wishes of the Cumberland College Association, and that it would have effectually disencumbered the General Assembly of the affairs of the college without compromising any essential or important principle.

Any wish to embarrass the General Assembly was disclaimed, and it was declared that those who made this protest were the fast, unwavering friends of the church, and that they wished the General Assembly to be freed as far as possible from all causes of agitation and confusion. This protest was signed by Robert Sloan, Caleb Weeden, Elam McCord, James Smith, William Henry, G. A. Fleming, Joel Lambert, F. C. Usher, David Negly, H. McDaniel, A. H. Dudley, Richard Beard, Milton Bird, James Ritchey, William Halsell, James Ashmore, A. Shelby, and P. G. Rea. John S. Sawyer appended a personal protest in which he added other reasons for objecting to the action of the General Assembly.

After the adoption of the report and the presentation of this protest against it, the friends of Princeton introduced a resolution declaring it inexpedient for the General Assembly to have control of any financial enterprise. Dr. Cossitt, Robert Donnell, J. S. McClain, and the friends of Lebanon generally supported the resolution. Only six negative votes were cast, while fifty-nine voted in the affirmative. The resolution was in these words:

Resolved, That it would be unwise, impolitic, inexpedient, and contrary to the genius of presbyterian government for the General Assembly to enter into connections of a pecuniary nature giving it the supervision of any literary institution or newspaper, or otherwise to become embarrassed by the control of pecuniary matters, so as to give occasion for its moral integrity and good faith to be called in question.

When the General Assembly severed its connection with Princeton College, the authorities of that school resolved to keep it alive. They allowed the farm to be sold, reserving the buildings and ten acres of ground. After a brief suspension they reorganized a faculty, and spread the banner of the college again to the breeze. The Rev. Richard Beard was elected president, and accepted the position. The career of the college after its abandonment by the General Assembly was happier and more useful than ever before. It kept clear of debt. It secured the services of that excellent agent, the Rev. W. G. L. Quaite, who, in spite of all the limitations placed upon him by the unfortunate history of the school, succeeded in securing considerable subscriptions to the endowment. Green River Synod took the cast-off child under its care. A good faculty was secured, and the existence of the institution was protracted till 1858. At that time it ceased to be an institution of the Cumberland Presbyterian church.

The outward history of the college has thus far been followed. A few words are added about its inner domestic history. Let us go back to the origin of the college in 1826, and take glimpses only, until the close in 1858.

Economy was a standing text of the General Assembly, on which it annually preached the college a sermon. The faculty began their administration in cap and gown *a la mode*, but the General Assembly notified them that it wished both faculty and students to dress in home-made clothing from head to foot. The order was obeyed, and Dr. Beard says his jeans suit was made too large for him, but he wore it obediently. The students were required to have long linen aprons to wear while working on the farm. Many of the Southern boys, reared where slaves did all the work, met the labor requirements with bad grace, but there were no exemptions. Difficulties between students and the overseer of the farm were very frequent. The daily college routine had many details which would seem strange now. Every two hours a horn was blown for a new section of laborers on the farm. This horn and the ringing of recitation bells made the place seem quite lively. Those recitation bells were unlike any others I ever heard. A big bell hung near by. Each professor did his own ringing in his own peculiar way, so that his bell could be distinguished from all the others. One gave three clear taps, another gave two clear taps, another gave one tap and a jingle. When the hour was out it did not follow that the class would be dismissed, even if it had a recitation in some other room, until the professor who had possession got ready to let it go.

Every student was required to board at the refectory and sleep in the college dormitories. The spiciest part of this history belongs to the refectory. The pigeon-holes in the old library used to be full of documents about that department of the college. Poetry, records of trials, testimony of committees sent to examine the fare, memorials of students praying for changes, complaints—sometimes by the students, sometimes by the managers—were all filed there. The students used to express their dissatisfaction with their fare in doggerel verse, and these satirical effusions were filed with other refectory papers. When it is remembered that the college undertook to furnish boarding at forty dollars a year, we need not wonder that the fare was often complained of.

Concerning those honored gentlemen who served as presidents of this institution a goodly volume might be written, and no doubt will be at some future time. Under the five different presidents there were five administrations of the college, each deserving a much longer notice than can here be given. The first president was Dr. Cossitt. His management of the young men was wise and fatherly. There were precious revivals of religion among the students at different times during his administration. Dr. Cossitt's sermons were one of the chief agencies used of God in bringing these revivals about. For many years the graduates and foster children of this school who were trained under Dr. Cossitt's influence were the noblest workers for education in the Cumberland Presbyterian church, and among them were many faithful and efficient laborers in other departments of the work.

The men who at one time or another assisted Dr. Cossitt in the work of instruction were James L. Morrison, Bertrand Guerin, David Lowry, T. C. Anderson, Livingston Lindsay, Richard Beard, F. C. Usher, and C. G. McPherson. Several of these became distinguished teachers, and their record is well known. Dr. McPherson has spent a large part of his life in educating young ladies. Mr. Lindsay went early to the practice of law, which he still pursues. Anderson and Beard will come before us in other connections, as will David Lowry. But it is proper to introduce here an interesting item about Lowry's dwelling-house. When he was elected professor in the college ten acres of the college farm were allotted for his cultivation, and *fifty dollars* were appropriated to build him a house back of the camp-ground spring. In that fifty dollar house, the man who afterward spent the best years of his life as missionary among the Indians, lived without murmuring.

Of the next administration, under the presidency of the Rev. Richard Beard, D.D., I can speak with the confidence given by personal knowledge. Dr. Beard took charge of the college in 1843, after the Assembly abandoned it; when it was officially pronounced dead; when its faculty had transferred their labors to the new institution at Lebanon, Tennessee; when, indeed, it was said and thought too that the college itself had been removed to Lebanon. Finding itself abandoned by the church, Princeton rallied and called Dr. Beard to the presidency. The loss of the farm and the manual labor feature proved to be a good riddance.

The administration was all new. There was no more refectory; no more restrictions laid on a student in selecting his boarding-house; no more laws requiring students and faculty to dress in home-spun. It was like passing out of Mosaic rigor into Christian freedom. True, there was still a printed code of by-laws nominally in force, but the example of Dr. Beard's holy and dignified life, and his appeals to the young men's sense of right were more effective than all by-laws. The students respected, honored, and loved their president, and were proud of being under such a leader.

They were like a family of brothers with Dr. Beard for their father. Each one felt that he had a friend and counselor in the president. Never under any circumstances laying aside his dignity, never tolerating any lack of respectful demeanor in his presence, he yet was felt and known to be the true friend and counselor of every one of his pupils. When these young men left college they never ceased to write back to him for advice in every perplexity. Of the thousands of old letters which he carefully kept, a large part are from his old students asking his counsel in some emergency. None ever asked in vain.

All through the college life of his students there was a silent, invisible influence, a subtle, indescribable power going out from Dr. Beard's life and impressing all around him with the truth of Christianity and the high destiny of cultivated, sanctified, immortal manhood. Scholarship put on a new aspect under this influence; an undersong awakening thoughts of personal responsibility and immortality blended with every lesson and recitation. This influence soon spread over the whole church. Noble men, trained under Dr. Beard and his colleagues, carried this power with them wherever they went, and the precious fruits of his administration are earnest and consecrated men in the pulpits and colleges in all parts of the church.

Those habits of severe study which Dr. Beard formed while a student of this institution, and which were a part of the town-talk for thirty years afterward, were strictly kept up by him all through his life. An idle student, strolling about at night, always met a silent rebuke when he turned his eyes toward Dr. Beard's library where the inevitable lamp burned on until late bed-time. His lectures in the chapel were one of the potent moral and educational resources of his administration. With an equanimity of temper rarely equaled, with a clock-like regularity of life which governed even the length of his footsteps, his uniform faultless precision was the talk of all the students.

The faculty who labored with him in the work of instruction at one time or another were the Rev. F. C. Usher, the Rev. J. G. Biddle, Philip Riley, W. S. Delany, and the Rev. Azel Freeman, D. D. Except Dr. Freeman, these were all alumni of Cumberland College. Mr. Usher had also been graduated in the Theological School at Princeton, New Jersey. Riley and Delany were graduated under Dr. Beard. Mr. Delany soon turned his attention to the legal profession, to which he is still devoted. Professor Riley spent his life in teaching. He was one of the purest and truest of men. His memory and his very looks are still enshrined in many hearts. One incident will illustrate his conduct toward his students: A young man who was very poor, and often unable to buy text-books, went one day to Professor Riley to borrow a copy of Smellie. He was told to come back next day. That evening Professor Riley went to town and bought a copy of Smellie, and when the student returned he loaned him the book. An accident revealed the fact that he had bought the book specially for this student.

Mr. Biddle remained only a short time in Princeton College, and then took charge of the school for young ladies at Winchester, Tennessee, devoting the remainder of his life to teaching in this school and to preaching the gospel. He labored as both teacher and preacher even while at Princeton. He has a son now in the ministry, the Rev. A. C. Biddle.

The Rev. Azel Freeman, D.D., afterward president of three of our colleges, was for a while professor of mathematics in Cumberland College. The closing years of his life were spent in pastoral work in Pennsylvania and Ohio. He died at Cumberland, Ohio, December 3, 1886. Dr. Beard closed his connection with the institution in 1855. That was its death blow. The church everywhere so felt. Still three good men struggled, each for a short period, to save the dying institution, and some noble alumni were sent out by them; but the three administrations averaged only a year apiece. Then the institution was given up by Cumberland Presbyterians and other churches tried for a year or two to sustain it, but finally abandoned it. Princeton still has a college on another site and under new auspices, but it is in no sense the successor of old Cumberland College. The latter has utterly passed away, every vestige even of the old buildings having disappeared.

Of the alumni of Cumberland College, the Rev. W. G. L. Quaite once said: "I can track every one of them by a path of light." This dear old college, even in its mistakes, bore good fruit. Our people had to learn by experience. Cumberland Presbyterians will hardly attempt another manual labor college. They have seen and felt the curse of the credit system. They will not be likely to locate another college where the church is weak, expecting the members of other churches and outsiders to give the institution the necessary local support. Nor will they again make the fatal blunder of placing the financial management of such an enterprise in the hands of the General Assembly. Even these mistakes bear fruit; but the grand and deathless fruit which outweighs all else is found in the men who were trained in this institution, and in the souls that have been won through their labors.

CHAPTER XXIII.

THE CHURCH PAPER.

"Away with distrust and away with despair,
Beyond all my thoughts and above all my prayer
Exceeding abundantly Jesus will prove,
The power and grace of his wonderful love."

"*Mente manuque potens.*"

THE chapter now to be written is the darkest one in all the history of the Cumberland Presbyterian church; and, perhaps, the very hardest to write correctly. Two parties, with wholly different views of what was right, and also with different views about what were the facts, have left us their conflicting testimony.

The formidable difficulties which grew out of the church paper can not be explained without a general sketch of that paper's history. At Princeton, Kentucky, early in the year 1830, Dr. Cossitt, aided by the faculty of Cumberland College, started a weekly paper called the *Religious and Literary Intelligencer*. There had before this been several abortive attempts to start a church paper, but this was the first Cumberland Presbyterian paper which was really published. It was purely a private enterprise. The press was owned by the Rev. David Lowry, who at that time was one of the faculty of Cumberland College, and who was Dr. Cossitt's chief assistant in the editorial work.

The General Assembly of the church met in Princeton that year, as it had done the year before. A strong feeling was manifested in favor of a church organ, whose editor should be under the control of the General Assembly. When the men who were publishing the *Religious and Literary Intelligencer* met this General Assembly, they submitted to that body a proposition to have their paper made the recognized organ of the church. In consideration of this advantage they agreed that the Assembly should have the exclusive right to appoint the editor. The records show that the proposition was accepted with the understanding that the General Assembly should neither own the press nor assume any financial responsibility in the matter. The Rev. David Lowry was chosen editor, it being understood that he should resign all his former relations to the college and devote his whole time to the paper. He proved to be well suited to the place. His administration was a good one. His financial management was wise. His editorials were able and his spirit Christ-like.

In 1832 he moved the paper to Nashville, changed its name to *The Revivalist*, and made the Rev. James Smith his partner. This was not exactly authorized by the contract under which the paper became the organ of the General Assembly, but it was allowed to pass. The publication had prospered under Lowry's editorial and business management until he felt able to have an assistant. Smith was a Scotchman of great learning, and a preacher of strong influence throughout the West. He, however, liked to lead and expected others to follow.

Before a year passed away Lowry sold out to Smith, leaving the latter in sole management of the paper. It is by no means certain that the Assembly, if left untrammeled, would have chosen Smith for its editor, but when it met in 1833 and found him already in possession, it "accepted the situation" and continued him in this position. In business matters Smith carried far more sail than ballast. He issued his paper to subscribers on a credit. He borrowed money extensively and gave his brethren in the ministry for security. When he was "in funds" instead of paying off these debts and saving his securities, he started new enterprises and made more debts. He contracted to publish all the books of the church, and these books were generally sold on a credit. He edited and published a monthly magazine of his own. He was "pastor" of the Nashville church. He published books, too, of his own, large works which required the best energies of his strong manhood, so that, in his own editorials, he tells us the paper was neglected on this account. Nor were these all the labors which he undertook. He was stated clerk of the General Assembly; he was treasurer of the church fund, and he taxed himself with various smaller matters.

In 1834 the name of the paper was changed to the *Cumberland Presbyterian*. When the General Assembly met that year, Smith was hopelessly in debt. He laid all the blame of his embarrassment on the church because the people had not patronized the paper as he expected. The Assembly resolved to do two things for his relief. First, to raise twelve hundred dollars then and there, to be loaned to Smith or exchanged for unpaid subscription bills. Second, to extend the patronage of the paper during the next year to four thousand subscribers. The first resolution was carried out, but the second was never fully made good.

On this action was based the best semblance of just ground for complaint which the editor ever had against the General Assembly. The subscription was never raised to four thousand. While some exerted themselves to secure new subscribers, old ones were constantly withdrawing. There were several reasons for these withdrawals. One of them is greatly to Smith's credit. He kept up incessantly the cry for reform in paying preachers and in having settled pastors. He was sometimes very severe; the facts called for severity, but subscribers grew sore under it and discontinued their subscriptions. Another source of dissatisfaction was the multiplied engagements of the editor, and his frequent and protracted absence from the office. But greater than all other causes of trouble were the alienations which grew out of his business management.

For two years the Rev. T. C. Anderson was employed by Mr. Smith as assistant editor. In his manuscript autobiography, written from time to time long before he began to fail in his memory, is an extended account of Smith and his paper. Dr. Anderson says that he himself, though working for a definite salary, and in nowise sharing in any profits which the paper might realize, was obliged to bring in all his own funds, and all his own credit, and to draw into the same snare all his personal friends who were willing to loan money or indorse Smith's notes; and that he retired from his connection with the paper because he saw clearly that Smith's management would bring bankruptcy, no matter what help the church might be able to render. He also states that Smith was often absent from the office three or four months at a time engaged in selling his books.

In 1835 the General Assembly renewed its determination to secure the four thousand subscribers. The list still fell six hundred short of that number. In 1836, in spite of the renewed exertions, the number of subscribers had declined rather than advanced. Bitter attacks had been made on the paper and on Smith. The General Assembly declared that so long as the paper was the church organ, those attacks were really on the church and not on Smith. The members renewed their pledges to struggle for an increase of the subscription list, and struggle they did, but it was like pouring water into a sieve.

In 1837, when the General Assembly met, Smith resigned. He stated in his resignation that when he was elected editor it was understood that the church would buy the press, own the paper, and indemnify him for all the losses he might sustain in the business. The General Assembly did not so understand matters. The official papers are preserved, and have been searched in vain for any hint of such an agreement. The records of the General Assembly show that Smith was to publish the paper *on his own responsibility*, so far as its finances were concerned. Smith stated in editorials, year after year, that he was publishing the paper on his own responsibility, except that the church had chosen him as editor, and his paper as the church organ. He had simply, of his own accord, stepped into Lowry's place, and the church allowed him to continue in it. That individual members had assured Smith, on their own responsibility, that the church would buy the press and indemnify him for any losses which he might sustain is quite likely; that the General Assembly never gave any such assurances is absolutely certain. He had often urged the church to buy his subscription list and his press and pay him a salary as editor. His failure to secure the adoption of this policy had long chafed him.

The committee to which Smith's resignation was referred, submitted two plans for the publication and management of the paper. The first recommended that a joint stock company should be formed to own the paper and the press, and that the General Assembly should still elect the editor. The other plan was for the General Assembly to buy the paper and the press and conduct the enterprise through a publishing committee. Investigation showed that both schemes were impracticable. Then the General Assembly appealed to Smith to state the conditions on which he would be willing to continue the publication of the paper. He named three conditions. (1) That the members of the General Assembly should individually pledge themselves to help collect unpaid subscriptions. (2) That the members should pledge themselves to use all practicable exertions to bring the list up to four thousand subscribers. (3) That the General Assembly should publish a circular calling on all the members and friends of the church to aid in carrying out these pledges. All of these conditions were unanimously agreed to. Smith then pledged himself to carry on the work until the volume then commenced should be completed, and then either to hand the paper over to an association or continue it himself, or else cease to publish it.

When the General Assembly met in 1838, Smith, without any conditions, asked to be continued as editor, and his request was granted. It was decided at this time that the next General Assembly should not meet until 1840. Therefore, the dissolution of the General Assembly of 1838 was equivalent to an adjournment for two years. The first of January, 1839, Smith began a series of editorials on reformation in the church. The pastoral relation, the pay of preachers, the mode of raising money for preachers, and the education of the ministry were the themes. While justice requires it to be said that the evils which he denounced were beyond the possibility of exaggeration, and the excoriations which he gave the church were all richly deserved; yet the terrible denunciations were not always of a nature to be endured, even by those who believed about those matters as the editor did.

After all, it may have been necessary to make the crew angry and bring the ship within an inch of hopeless wreck in order to insure better navigation in after years. God's merciful and overruling hand was doubtless in it all. Men began to reply to Smith's severe denunciations of the church in his own columns. Several of Smith's editorials had prophesied secession. All the best ministers, he predicted, would be driven out of the church, unless certain reforms took place. As there was to be no General Assembly that year, he called for a convention. His call was seconded, and a convention was agreed upon to meet in Nashville at the time usually appointed for the General Assembly's meeting. A year before Smith had sold his printing office, and agreed to take his pay in printing. Before the convention met the publication of the paper was suspended, and the closing editorial, as well as several previous editorials, declared in the most unequivocal manner that Smith was forever done with all connection with the church paper. He urged the church to have an organ, but declared his purpose to be unalterably fixed not to be its editor.[1] The last issue of the paper at Nashville was dated April 30, 1839. If editorial declarations could settle any thing, it was settled that Smith was, under no conditions, ever to be church editor again.

Although Smith was not appointed by his presbytery as a delegate to the convention, yet he was allowed to take his seat as a member, and he occupied one whole day in a set speech on the necessity of reforms. He published this speech afterward in a pamphlet. I have only some extracts from it, not being able to secure a copy. He said: "The ministry of the Cumberland Presbyterian church are a mass of ignorance, heresy, and fanaticism." He charged lying and fraud upon the General Assembly, and other pleasant little compliments to the denomination inflated his sails in that wonderful harangue. But all this was mild compared to the wormwood, the gall, the *pus atque venenum*, which his private letters for the next few years poured forth. Several hundreds of these letters have been placed in the hands of the writer of this history.

The convention passed resolutions in favor of reform. It appointed a committee to form a stock company to continue the publication of the *Cumberland Presbyterian*. It decided to have this paper issued from Lebanon instead of Nashville. The Rev. George Donnell was chosen editor. Its publication was to be delayed till the fall meetings of the presbyteries. At this point in the history some conflict as to facts begins. Members and friends of the convention say that Smith asked such an enormous price for his subscription list that no one could think of paying it. Smith denies that any conference with him on the subject of his subscrip-

---

[1] See editorials January 22, January 29, and April 30, 1839.

tion list was ever sought. T. C. Anderson is very positive on the other side. One thing all are agreed upon, the subscription list of Smith's *Cumberland Presbyterian* was not purchased; but the convention resolved to start a paper with the same name to be the organ of the church. It was at this point in its action that the convention proved afterward to be vulnerable. The committee which reported the plan of action which was adopted by the convention was composed of Hiram A. Hunter, J. S. McClain, Carson P. Reed, George Donnell, T. B. Wilson, Jesse Ford, and George Williamson.

The first of September, just before the fall meetings of the presbyteries, lo! Smith's paper reappeared! This time it was issued at Springfield, Tennessee, and some brethren, who had plenty of money, were meeting its financial wants. It claimed still to be the organ of the church, and the only organ. It explained its reappearance as a necessity, since the Lebanon committee had neither bought out its subscription list, nor made any provisions to supply the paper to subscribers whose time had not expired. It denounced the convention as a clique, and declared the action of that body in assuming to publish an organ for the church unconstitutional and seditious.

The defense made by the friends of the convention is all summed up in a few words. They said that the convention claimed no power to make any paper a church organ, but met and acted simply to keep alive the organ which the General Assembly itself had started; that it had the strongest evidences that Smith was forever done with the paper; that it met on Smith's call, without any hint or dream of any conflict like the one which had arisen; and that Smith himself coöperated heartily with the convention until he found that another man was to be chosen editor, and that his subscription list was not to be bought at an extravagant price. They said further that the convention had resolved to do its utmost in the next General Assembly, and before the meeting of that body, to have Smith indemnified for all the losses he had sustained through any fault of the church. They showed that the convention was composed of fifty delegates, among them many of the purest men of the church, appointed by the presbyteries in obedience to a public call; and that if any presbyteries were not represented it was their own fault; that the convention acted in an emergency, under the pressure of a great necessity; and that the changes made in regard to the business management were such as the imperative necessities of the case required, and such as the General Assembly resolved on in 1837, when Smith first tendered his resignation.

That Smith had the legal right to resume the publication of his paper and call it the organ of the church was generally conceded; but the propriety of his course, after his unequivocal declaration, in April, was questioned. Parties rapidly formed. Angry feelings were stirred up. The presbyteries nearly all took action in favor of one party or the other. Finis Ewing and John L. Dillard, both threw their great influence on the side of Smith's paper. Logan Presbytery passed resolutions condemning the convention, and declaring Smith's paper the true organ of the church. Alabama Presbytery did likewise. Richland Presbytery and all of Columbia Synod, with Robert Donnell at their head, took the side of the convention and requested the members of their congregations not to take Smith's paper.

Secession, division, disruption were the words floating in the air. After nearly all the presbyteries had arrayed themselves as partisans in the contest, and many of our best men had utterly despaired, a synod in Illinois passed resolutions calling on all parties to agree to submit the whole question to the next General Assembly, and to forbear all further discussion of the merits of the case till that Assembly should meet, and urging all true lovers of Jesus to join in prayer to God for the peace of the church.[1] That voice for peace and prayer, without taking either side, was surely a voice from heaven.

The committee appointed by the convention to issue a paper from Lebanon resolved to delay this publication until the meeting of the General Assembly, and to refer the whole matter to that body, but this wise decision of that committee was robbed of some of its peaceable fruits by the course of Smith's paper. In October, 1839, the Rev. George Donnell wrote a private letter to the Rev. John W. Ogden, who was corresponding editor of Smith's paper,

---

[1] It is said that Rev. Joel Knight was the mover of these resolutions.

correcting the rumors which even then were afloat that the Lebanon committee had declined publishing a paper. This letter, with no dates affixed, was kept standing in the editorial columns of Smith's paper until the Assembly met, in May, 1840.

I have not felt at liberty to quote Smith's private letters, but have used them in investigating questions about which the other authorities are in conflict, especially when the evidence of these letters is on the side of the convention. These private letters shed much light on various editorials about "The Union College," and other cognate subjects which appeared in the paper while it was published at Springfield, Tennessee. Their contents, moreover, are a complete vindication of the people of Lebanon from some of the charges which the friends at Princeton made at the time the "removal" of the college took place. While Mr. Smith had all the time ably advocated an educated ministry, he seemed to have a deep-seated dislike to Cumberland College. His bargain with the General Assembly, in 1833, taxed him ten cents on each subscriber, for the benefit of that institution; and although John Barnett, after his lease began, voluntarily released the paper from all tribute to the college, yet there was a sting left. Editorials in the paper declared the college to be of little or no benefit to the church. Mr. Smith visited Lebanon, Tennessee, in 1839, for the purpose of inducing the people of that place to establish a church college. The account of his conference with R. L. Caruthers, under Smith's own signature, is in my possession. Caruthers took just the ground which his known loyalty to the church would have led us to expect. He thought the college at Princeton a doomed enterprise; but so long as it continued to be the college of the church, he would do nothing in conflict with the General Assembly's plan. Smith's account of that conference is dated September 10, 1839. At Springfield his persuasions proved more effective than at Lebanon. Here he not only found men to set his paper going once more, but he secured subscriptions amounting to six thousand dollars for a church college. Through his influence the school and buildings then in use in that town were transferred to this new "college." He urged the presbyteries to send their candidates for the ministry to Springfield, promising every presbytery fifty dollars on each two hundred subscribers for the paper, the money to be paid in tuition at Springfield. He afterward made extensive tours among the southern churches, raising money to endow his college. He always speaks of it as "my college." He says, in one letter, that he secured several thousand dollars from the Cumberland Presbyterians of Mississippi for his school. He never raised a farthing for Cumberland College.

Smith was ubiquitous. He traveled, he wrote letters, he delivered lectures, and in all places he struggled to stir up the church against the convention and its proposed paper. He visited the presbyteries at their spring meetings in 1840, calling attention to his sufferings and arousing sympathy. Some presbyteries which had shown strong aversion to him and his course as editor turned over under his vigorous speeches, and passed resolutions indorsing him and his paper, and denouncing the convention. It was evident to all true friends of the church that there was danger ahead. Smith had an army of old camp-meeting friends; for his camp-meeting preaching had been, from the first, his most powerful work. But there was another army, made up of sufferers from his financial recklessness, who said that every enterprise of the church which had ever been touched by him had either been injured or ruined by the contact.

There were still alarming symptoms of approaching schism, when, in March, 1840, the Rev. F. R. Cossitt, President of Cumberland College, commenced issuing a monthly pamphlet, which he called *The Banner of Peace*. He made no charges for this periodical, but sent it, at his own expense, throughout the church. He declared his aim to be the peace and unity of the church. He said that this monthly would be published until the meeting of the General Assembly as a free magazine, but if continued longer a subscription fee would be charged. His editorials were powerful appeals to all parties for peace. He showed no leaning, in his paper, to either party; but he published an article for Smith which declared the church to be in its death agonies.

True friends of the church rallied to the support of Cossitt's views, and many a noble plea for peace appeared in the columns of the *Banner of Peace*. To F. R. Cossitt, more than to any other human agency, does the church owe its escape from wreck in the General Assembly of 1840.

When that Assembly met the mind of the majority was made up to leave both Smith's paper and the proposed Lebanon paper without either recognition or condemnation, and for the time being to have no church organ, but to settle on something like liberal terms with Smith, and to be forever done with him. Smith claimed large things, especially on account of his losses arising from the failure of several General Assemblies to secure the promised four thousand subscribers. He proposed arbitration, but the General Assembly declared this unnecessary, as a satisfactory settlement seemed practicable without it. A committee was appointed to investigate the matter. This committee reported that a patient inquiry into all the facts had satisfied them that the General Assembly did not owe Mr. Smith any thing; but, as he made a large claim, and as some of the members of the church believed his claim to be just, they recommended that nineteen hundred dollars be paid to him as damages.

The recommendation was adopted. The nineteen hundred dollars were paid before the Assembly adjourned, and Smith's receipt was spread on the Minutes.

After this Smith's course was a strange medley. While the General Assembly maintained control of the college at Princeton, Smith wrote the most abusive private letters against that institution and all connected with it. But when the Assembly abandoned that school, and Smith was forced also to abandon *his* college, then he became a very earnest partisan of the college at Princeton and against the college at Lebanon. All through his editorial career he had been an advocate of a church organ, to be owned and controlled by the General Assembly. When the Assembly failed to continue him as editor, he at once suspended the publication of his paper, and warmly denounced the policy he had defended before, declaring that the church should not own or manage either college or newspaper. This he did through the columns of Milton Bird's paper. There were two weekly newspapers now published—one by Dr. Cossitt, and one by Milton Bird. Bird was then a young man. Smith, it is said, did his utmost to array

Bird's paper against Cossitt, and against the college at Lebanon. In this way alone is it possible to account for some of Mr. Bird's editorials, they are so unlike all that noble man's record before and afterward. Smith had been stated clerk of the General Assembly; but he did not deliver the records over to his successor till three years after his resignation, though he was twice ordered to do so. He came very near involving Milton Bird in a serious difficulty by inducing him to make a proposition to publish these old records, and sell them as private property. Not friendship to Bird, but schism in the church was thought to be his aim. Once he talked of forming a church of his own.[1] He tried to enlist various parties, but could not secure the followers that were necessary for such a scheme. Then he struggled to persuade many of our best men to go with him into the Presbyterian church; but his only success was in the case of John W. Ogden.

The evils growing out of the lack of proper compensation to ministers, of which Smith so bitterly complained, had already driven out of the church several strong men. Among these the strongest, perhaps, was the Rev. W. A. Scott, D.D., who recently died in San Francisco. Mr. Ford, of Louisiana, who also left the church about the time Scott did, was influenced by purely doctrinal considerations, so he declared in a letter to Dr. Beard. Smith was very confident that he would take Dr. Beard with him. He told various persons that Dr. Beard was going to leave the church. Beard wrote to Smith calling him to task for these reports. Smith defended his statements as a prophecy based on the nature of the case. He said to Beard: "You will be obliged to go; they will drive you out as they are driving me."

It was once generally believed among Cumberland Presbyterians that W. A. Scott tried to induce Dr. Beard to leave the church. There was not a particle of foundation for this belief. All Dr. Scott's letters to Dr. Beard have been examined, and there is not the remotest hint at any such thing. While there were tempting offers made to Dr. Beard, most of them originated with Smith.

---

[1] Proofs of all this are among many of the literary remains in my hands, especially those of the Rev. Isaac Shook.

Rev. F. R. Cossitt, D.D.

Rev. A. M. Bryan, D.D.

Rev. Milton Bird, D.D.

The impression was long current among our people that systematic and unlawful means were resorted to to entice our educated men to join the Presbyterian church. Careful examination of private diaries, correspondence, and other records, reveal no trace of any such efforts. Had the facts been as our people once thought they were, the evidence would inevitably exist in some of the documents now in my hands. The main motive for withdrawing from the Cumberland Presbyterian church and joining the Presbyterians is correctly stated in a letter to Dr. Beard, written by one who had taken this step. He says: "There is no hope of my ever getting a living as a pastor in the Cumberland Presbyterian church. Between being secularized and false to my ministerial vows, and adopting the Westminster Confession with such mental reservations as I know to be made by many of the Presbyterian ministry, I chose the latter as the far lesser evil."

CHAPTER XXIV.

THE TRANSITION FROM MISSIONARY EVANGELISTS TO PAID PASTORS.

A library imitated in wood.
— *Vinet.*

THE learned Erasmus declared that no king's office is equal in dignity to the office of the humblest pastor. In a heathen country, under peculiar circumstances, it was all right for Paul to work with his own hands to earn his own bread, and preach without any pay. Likewise the state of things in the new settlements to which the self-denying missionaries went, made it absolutely necessary for them, at first, to earn their own bread by some secular pursuit. It is not to be wondered at, therefore, that there should have grown up in the Cumberland Presbyterian church, all of whose preachers were at first missionaries, loose views about the pastor's office and pastors' salaries. Indeed, many of our preachers and people came to think that pastorates were invented by self-seeking men who dreaded the hardships of an itinerant life and wanted big salaries. An element of positive opposition to the office of settled pastor, in the true Presbyterian sense of that word, sprang up. There was, along with this, a disposition to apply the name pastor to any minister who had regular appointments, however rare, to preach in any one congregation.

When the second Cumberland Presbyterian General Assembly met, 1830, this opposition to the pastoral office had reached its zenith. That General Assembly, by a large majority, voted to submit to the presbyteries the question of striking out of the Form of Government the whole section recognizing the pastoral office.[1]

---

[1] It may be well to note that the chapters and sections were then numbered differently from their later form. The numbering was changed by the Rev. James Smith, publisher of the book.

The General Assembly not only submitted this question but declared the change desirable.

There were then only eighteen presbyteries: of these, only two voted for striking out that chapter. Thirteen voted no. Three made no report—perhaps did not meet—as there were often failures to secure a quorum in the new presbyteries. The effort was never renewed, but year after year the feeling grew in the General Assemblies that the regular pastoral office, in its true sense, would have to be established. In 1835 a faint utterance in favor of settled pastors was given by the General Assembly. In 1836 an unequivocal declaration of the importance of the pastoral office was placed on record.

The first battle was won; but let it not be supposed that all opposition to the pastor's office had disappeared. I give one example: At the meeting of the West Tennessee Synod in 1849 the Committee on the State of Religion brought in a report which contained a paragraph about the deplorable lack of settled pastors. This report was met with the most uncompromising opposition. Earnest and eloquent speeches were made against it by some of the oldest ministers present. The chairman of this committee and the Rev. Samuel Dennis, D.D., then pastor of the Cumberland Presbyterian church in Memphis, were the only men who stood up in that meeting in favor of the regular pastoral office. Yet, in that synod, the largest in the church, there was not at that time any genuine evangelist, and not as many as a half dozen men devoted exclusively to the work of the ministry. A system of supplies, on Sabbaths, by preachers who through the week earned their bread in secular callings, was depended on in that synod, and is, alas, the system by which many of our churches are still kept up.

Very few of the early Cumberland Presbyterian ministers had any correct idea of the true nature of the pastor's office. When the necessity for real pastorates was urged, many seemed to think that installation was all that they lacked. The people soon understood, however, that he who served them under the name of a pastor, was in fact but a secularized supply who preached on the Sabbath and then went back to his worldly pursuits. In many cases these preachers rode eight or ten miles on Sabbath morning to their appointments, and rode back Sabbath evening. Thus an utter lack of any correct knowledge of what a true pastor is, was a serious difficulty in the way of introducing true pastors.

Even now the truth is but slowly dawning upon our people that pastor and evangelist belong to two very different vocations; so different, indeed, that fitness for one is presumptive evidence of unfitness for the other. The standards by which the churches have usually judged of a man's fitness for the pastor's work, or of his success when in that work, are standards which belong rather to the other vocation, that of the evangelist. To preach thrilling, popular sermons, to attract a great crowd, to gather in many wealthy members, to build a fine meeting-house—such things as these have been regarded the *ne plus ultra* of pastoral success. There may be no systematic beneficence in the congregation, no entire personal consecration to Christ's service in the daily practical life of any member; the missionary spirit may be wanting in both pastor and people; no child of the church may ever go to labor among the heathen or enter the holy ministry; family prayers may be neglected in the households, and the members be untaught in the great fundamental truths of Christianity; there may be as little separation from the ways of a godless world as the devil himself could wish—still if the attractive sermons draw great crowds and a handsome salary is paid, the man who occupies the pulpit is regarded by many as a successful pastor. Ah! the great day will reverse many a human verdict.

The long-established custom of looking upon thrilling popular sermons as the sole test of a pastor's fitness has built up a stubborn barrier against right measures. Let a man who knows what real pastoral work is studiously avoid all sensational discourses and all mere spasms, and set himself to work earnestly to organize, drill, train, and indoctrinate his flock in real, personal consecration to Christ; let him strive to cultivate love to Jesus by enlisting every member of the flock in a thorough study of the Bible and in active efforts to do good and win souls, and in a large majority of cases, the church will rebel. That is not what they want; they want to be thrilled with eloquence on the Sabbath and left to themselves through the week.

That the pastor's office is the most difficult and important of all human callings can be easily proved. It is a calling from God, yet those who engage in it need special training, more careful than that required in any secular employment or profession. But when the transition from circuit preaching to settled pastorates became a necessity, there were in the Cumberland Presbyterian church no men trained to the pastoral office. Our people had no school to teach the theory of pastoral theology; no experienced pastors to lead and train the rising ministry, and there were no churches willing to sustain a pastor decently. It is a wonder, under all the circumstances, that the preachers of that period succeeded as well as they did.

Men who know nothing about a difficult calling generally underestimate the labor required to master it. Many of the preachers failed to understand the difficulty and importance of pastoral work. A leading minister, one of the most beloved and successful pioneer missionaries in the church, declared in a public discourse that the whole science of pastoral theology could be mastered in two hours! Even yet few among us know what careful and extensive preparation is needed for the pastor's work. Discussing the extreme difficulty of a true pastorate the learned Bengel said: "Many things are needed in order to create a true community." The care of individual souls is like preparing the individual stones for a temple. To create a true spiritual community — the temple in its finished state — is a life work. It is never done by any one great revival or under frequent change of pastors. As well talk of one painter beginning a painting and a whole "apostolical succession" of other painters carrying out the original design. A true pastor, by a whole life-time of toil, may accomplish the work, but even then the inner fountain of power must be the Lord of glory himself dwelling in the pastor. When one such spiritual community is secured the results are abiding.

The pastors in this transition period had to unteach some wrong lessons which the church had learned. The silence of the pioneer preachers about money had created a strong opposition to paying preachers. This existed not only among the covetous and the worldly, but among people who had considerable reputation for piety. Indeed, congregations which were celebrated for demonstrations of religious fervor were often the very ones which gave the least money.

All the first Cumberland Presbyterian preachers started wrong. Bitterly did our old men regret their failure to teach and train the people in this duty, but their regrets came too late. It will take several generations yet to get rid of the leaven of their example. In the midst of the great congregation at Big Spring, Thomas Calhoun, near the close of his life, used substantially these words: "I am now old, and must soon go to meet my Judge. I have been one of the actors in establishing the Cumberland Presbyterian church, and in all that pertains to its early history. I have a clear conscience save only about one thing. We have all failed to do our duty in training the people to pay their preachers. I have lived to see the ruinous consequences of that failure, and I don't want to die without confessing my sin in this matter in the most public manner possible." So too, did Ewing and others make public confession, but it came too late. The evil continues.

In several instances synods sent men to preach on this subject throughout their bounds, the order in one case extending to a whole State. One can not, however, help doubting whether any man of the class and type to which the first Cumberland Presbyterian preachers belonged, would be likely to accomplish much in such a mission. That whole generation of preachers had false views on this subject. "Supporting the gospel" was the text; a pitiful hat collection, which furnished the ministers who held the meeting from one to three dollars apiece for a week's labor, was the application. The men who gave the money were, in their self-complacent views, "supporting the gospel." Many of the efforts of the presbyteries to remedy the difficulty were as pitiful as these hat collections. One presbytery[1] resolved that every member of the church ought to give twenty-five cents a year to "the support of the gospel;" another, that all church members should give fifty cents apiece annually for this purpose, and another had the daring to ask every member of its congregation to pay a dollar a year to secure the means of grace. In one of the oldest and richest por-

---

[1] I have all these presbyterial records before me.

tions of the church, a presbytery named ten dollars per annum as the amount which each of its congregations ought to try to pay its "pastor."

Now place by the side of these "heavy burdens" which the presbyteries were laying upon the churches, the burdens which these preachers were themselves patiently bearing. From a number of examples recorded in the church paper, one is selected. In the spring of 1832, when a minister of good talents was ordained, he volunteered to go as a missionary to a new State. He had fifteen hundred dollars in money and no family. He went on his mission without any provision for compensation. He traveled and built up several small churches, paying his own way, until all his money was gone. He had said nothing about compensation, though the people he preached to were generally getting rich; but the time now came when he could no longer pay his own way and travel as a missionary. He went into secular business, and continued to preach on Sabbath without one cent of pay. The church paper commenting on this case and others like it, calls them cases of necessity. But did not the neglect of duty have something to do with creating this necessity? The ministers of that day were too sensitive and timid about preaching on the duty of giving. What they did say often made matters worse.

At a later day there were a few men in the church who knew how to present this subject. Dr. A. J. Baird was one of these. There was a church in one of the wealthiest portions of Middle Tennessee whose pastor had resigned because his salary could not be raised. Dr. Baird visited this church with a view of bringing it up to its duty in this matter. He first conferred with the session and learned that the difficulty was not about the man, but only about the salary. The people could not raise enough money to support that man or any other, and had decided to dismiss the pastor and depend on monthly supplies from some non-resident minister. Baird plead and argued, but the session finally told him that he would not even be permitted to canvass the congregation for subscriptions. All this was on Saturday. On Sabbath Dr. Baird preached, discussing the whole subject in that practical and common-sense way of which he was a master. At the close of the sermon he described his interview with the session. Then he added, "I am not going to ask either this session or these church members to give one cent; but I am going to raise the pastor's salary here to-day among the unconverted people. These sinners have a higher appreciation of the blessings which stand forever connected with the regular means of grace than this session has. I want some of these rich old sinners to start the subscription. Who will pledge a sum bearing some little proportion to the inestimable worth of the gospel?" In less than a half hour the whole salary was raised, and that without the name of a single church member. Dr. Baird then delivered a scathing lecture to that session, and proceeded to *install* the preacher as pastor for those sinners.

Dr. Baird was often called to present this subject, but in no two cases did he use the same methods. Once at Lebanon, Tennessee, where the congregation had generally maintained a standard of liberality above the average, they fell sadly behind in the pastor's salary, and sent for Dr. Baird to help them. He came and met the congregation, making just a little talk in which were only three points. In the first he assumed that the people of Lebanon would not consent to be left destitute of the means of grace. In the second he discussed, very briefly, one way of supplying this acknowledged necessity—the old scriptural way of having one man exclusively devoted to that work and paying him for his labors, as we pay lawyers, doctors, and others. Thirdly, he stated that this scriptural method had been tried in Lebanon, and had broken down, and he had been sent for to help devise ways and means to meet the emergency. He said, "Sometimes when people want a new meeting-house, and can not raise money enough to hire a carpenter, they divide out the work among the members and do it themselves. Inasmuch as we can not raise money enough here to have one man do all the preaching and pay him for it, we shall have to divide out the work among the members and not try to have any pastor. I have made," said he, "the best distribution of the labor I can, and will now proceed to read the appointments. 'Squire McClain, you will preach next Sunday morning and Sunday night." "No I won't," said the 'Squire. "No dodging," answered Baird, "there will be some rare head-scratching in 'Squire McClain's office the next few days. It is not quite as easy as it looks to prepare two sermons in one week." "I am not going to prepare any sermons," said McClain. "What will you do then? Are you going to do without the gospel?" "No," he answered, "I am going to pay my full share of the salary and have a pastor to do my part of the preaching." The pastor was retained, but we are not told whether he was adequately paid or not.

To go forward and preach the gospel, pay or no pay, is certainly right. In that, the example of our fathers is worthy of all commendation. But there is also another line of duty. To be silent about money, to say nothing about consecration to God in pocket as well as profession, to leave unrebuked a habitual course of conduct which robs God and robs his own called ministers who stand before the church in his name and by his authority as his own ambassadors—this is a criminal neglect of part of the very work committed to those ambassadors. It is useless to try to conceal the fact that our fathers were sadly delinquent in this part of their duty. This is a blot on the record of their heroism and their spirituality which we can not wash off. The heroism and spirituality are with the dead past. Old established communities, crystallized into a life devoted mainly to worldly things, is what we have now. This silence on the subject of money which was persisted in by the first Cumberland Presbyterian preachers even while actual want pressed upon some of them and their families, and the general secularization of the ministry which followed it, suited well the carnal hearts of nominal church members who gloried in a "free gospel." As a consequence, it is hard now to find any church which is willing to pay a pastor a living salary. Our churches have been trained to take a preacher's labor without pay.

Grave as was the fault of the ministry, a far more grievous complaint is recorded in heaven against the churches. With some honorable exceptions, they stand charged before God with robbing their own pastors, and that, too, where there is no chance to plead any lack of plain teaching from the pulpit as an apology for the robbery, nor any lack of ability on the part of the robbers. A painful array of historical facts might be here presented, but to publish the details, with the names of the preachers and of the churches which took their services without pay would, perhaps, give offense and not cure the evil. An old preacher, in extreme poverty, and utterly helpless in body, says "I spent forty years giving my whole time to such and such churches." The list is omitted. "In no one of these churches" he continues, "did I ever receive more than half the salary which they promised to pay me. If I had these unpaid balances, I would now be in easy circumstances." This man was an able preacher in his day, and there were many conversions under his ministry. The position taken here is indorsed by the authority of one of the noblest servants and truest friends the Cumberland Presbyterian church ever had. In Dr. Beard's diary for September 18, 1855, is the following entry: "Went to Brother Mansfield's; found him in his field at work. He is a good and useful preacher, and yet is laboring on a farm to support his wife and children. Will not the church have to render a fearful account for her treatment of such men?"

The reports of several hundreds of circuit riders show that about one third of them received no pay at all. Perhaps another third received some socks, and from five to twenty dollars a year in money. The largest salary reported by any one of them was eighty dollars a year. Only one reports so large a sum. The compensation of the first "pastors" in the church was still more meager. It was not expected that men who did not travel would be paid any thing for preaching. It was said that the church to which a leading minister devoted the best years of his life did not, during the whole time, pay him as much as twenty dollars. But we are improving; people and preachers are improving. Perhaps when all the formidable obstacles which had to be overcome are taken into the account, the improvement ought to be considered remarkable. One of the largest and most central presbyteries may perhaps be taken as an average sample of what the whole church is now doing. It has forty ministers. Three of these are entirely supported by their congregations. Two others, whether supported or not, give their whole time to the work of the ministry. Six others are devoted to church work under some of the boards, and twenty-eight are secularized, though they preach on Sabbath and get some little compensation. Now that circuit riding is no more, and camp-meetings are generally abandoned, our churches must employ regular pastors or cease to exist. The chief hope of the church is with the young men who take a regular course of theological studies and enter the pastoral work. Every true pastor is a light-house among the churches. The work of many such in town and country stands as the strongest argument in favor of permanent pastorates.

The sermon which this chapter preaches needs to be followed by an exhortation. The credit system, pledges forfeited by church judicatures for future payment of money, the failure to pay subscriptions and even notes given to church enterprises, the injustice and robbery of neglecting to support pastors and evangelists, or of refusing to pay the meager salaries promised them, are all forms of financial mismanagement and wrong-doing. From just such things as these the greatest dangers and losses of the church have come in the past. It will be well if such causes of trouble are avoided in the future.

Not only to Barnett and Smith did the General Assembly make pledges which it had no power to fulfill, but there were other similar cases. The particulars of one such instance are found in the manuscript autobiography of the Rev. R. D. King. When the General Assembly of 1834 asked the Rev. Samuel King and his son to go on their long evangelistic tour among the churches, it included in the request a solemn pledge that the evangelists should be compensated for their services. R. D. King took his wife to the home of her relatives in Kentucky, where she and her children remained during the twenty months of her husband's absence. When these evangelists made their final report to the General Assembly, they stated that their compensation had been one hundred and fifty dollars less than their unavoidable traveling expenses. One member then arose in the Assembly and moved that steps be taken to redeem the pledge for compensation made to these evangelists. Another member made a speech against the motion, declaring that neither he nor the Assembly then sitting had ever made any such pledges. "This Assembly," said he, "is not the same body which pledged compensation, and we are not bound either morally or legally." The matter dropped there. There being no second to the motion, no vote was taken. When the clerk read in the Minutes the words, "compensation nearly equal to their traveling expenses," Samuel King objected. But being appealed to to let this record stand "for the sake of the church," he withdrew his objection. R. D. King had to borrow money to remove his family back to his little home in Tennessee. On his arrival he found that his note for the borrowed money had preceded him and was in the hands of an officer. His property was sold under the sheriff's hammer. He says that for a considerable time after that his purpose remained fixed to preach no more for Cumberland Presbyterians. In that state of mind his communion with God was cut off. Heart-searching followed, and the conclusion was reached that his preaching was for Jesus and not for any denomination, and he girded on his armor once more. There have been many other cases like R. D. King's, belonging to all the periods down to the present day.

There are scriptural methods of transacting financial affairs, but the credit system forms no part of these methods. Church debts are unscriptural, and whether they be contracted by congregations, or church judicatures, or chartered boards, they are always a curse. A chapter might be devoted to the history of such debts. It would tell of college buildings which have been sold to meet the claims of creditors; of houses of worship mortgaged, and at last forfeited; of pastors disappointed and crushed; of good men alienated from the church because its pledges were not redeemed; of donations from the wealthy turned away from our institutions by disaffection and want of confidence caused by financial failures. The materials for such a chapter are at hand. Among other things is the record of a consecrated pastor, an able and holy man, who in his last illness, only a few years ago, was kept from starving, not by his congregation which still owed him large balances on his salary, but by unconverted men whom God sent, like the prophet's ravens, to feed his servant. But let these sad records of failure and wrong rest in oblivion till the great day of reckoning shall bring them to light.

CHAPTER XXV.

THE CHURCH IN MISSISSIPPI AND LOUISIANA

> Thy mighty river yet shall know
> A gracious stream of grander flow.
> —*Anonymous.*

IN the chapter on Bell's Indian mission, notice was taken of the first work of Cumberland Presbyterians in the territory which now forms the State of Mississippi. That work was exclusively among the Indians, who throughout that period occupied the northern portion of Mississippi. The condition of things south of the Indian country presented few attractions for Cumberland Presbyterian preachers. The settlers did not come from the field occupied by this new church; they sent no pressing calls for its missionaries, while far more such calls than the presbyteries could possibly respond to came from other fields. The Tombigbee Presbytery, organized in 1823, included Bell's mission, but there were then in Mississippi no congregations of white people belonging to this church.

White people, and some of them Cumberland Presbyterians, had penetrated the Indian country, and were making their homes there, the treaty of 1816 having opened the door for such settlements. Robert Bell, John C. Smith, and James Stewart, all connected with the Indian mission—Stewart only a short time—preached to these pioneers. But the whites who settled in the Indian country were, with some noble exceptions, people of bad character, and their influence was a serious barrier to the success of the gospel among the Indians. One of these white men was a slave trader from Princeton, Kentucky, who circulated slanderous reports about a mission which the American Board had established in Mississippi. This negro trader, on his purchasing tours, frequently visited Kentucky, and spread his slanders against the missionaries wherever he went. These missionaries held antislavery views, and were sadly in his way. F. R. Cossitt and David Lowry, knowing the vileness of this man's character, publicly denounced his slanders, and warned the people of Kentucky against him. They also wrote to the Cumberland Presbyterian missionaries, begging them to furnish the means of vindicating their brethren in the Monroe mission. This Mr. Bell did in such a thorough manner that the neighboring mission was not again assailed. This generous interference against a dangerous ruffian in behalf of a mission planted by another board illustrates the magnanimous spirit of the Cumberland Presbyterians of that day.

One of the men who settled in Monroe County, Mississippi, long before the Indians moved away, was Colonel John S. Topp, an elder in the Cumberland Presbyterian church. Among the anecdotes told by him is one connected with the final removal of the Indians from this territory. Various pretexts for delay had for years retarded this promised removal. Finally, all things were supposed to be ready, but still the Indians failed to assemble for their journey. The agent inquired, "What is the matter now?" They told him that their chief, Tisho Mingo, was in prison for debt. This was strange, for Tisho Mingo had been rich. It seems, however, that he had been robbed while preparing to move, and could not pay his debts. Colonel Topp suggested to the agent that the old chief should take the insolvent debtor's oath. This was done, and Tisho Mingo released. The Indians, who stood around when the oath was administered and their chief released, exclaimed in wonder: "Talk a little on the book, talk a little off the book, and Indian's debts paid." This was the last obstacle of any serious character to their removal.

The agent who removed the last company of the Chickasaws completed his task in the spring of 1839. Only a few wealthy families of this tribe remained till a later period. The Choctaw country was opened in 1833. The sudden opening to settlers of all the vast cotton lands vacated by the Indians, synchronizing with that wonderful inflation of the currency, together with the fabulous stories of vast fortunes to be accumulated in Mississippi, caused an immense rush to that territory. It was said, and perhaps with some truth, that a man without one cent of capital could go there, buy land on a credit, and negroes with borrowed money, and make enough on his cotton to meet every payment. Speculation ran wild. Many preachers of different churches went to Mississippi under its promptings. Others who went there to preach were told by older settlers to seize the golden opportunity to make themselves independent first. "We will loan you money. Get you a plantation and hands to cultivate it; get them paid for; and then you can go and preach as much as you please." One preacher writes in the church paper that he was told that Mississippians would not listen with any respect to a preacher who let "this golden opportunity for independence slip, and then expected the people to support him." Thus it came about that most of the preachers of all the churches were secularized. The statement was published at that time that nine out of every ten ministers in Mississippi were secularized. From a long series of letters in the church paper on the condition of things in Mississippi between 1832 and 1834, we learn that the capital of the State for fifteen years had neither church-house nor school-house. Ten whole counties in the poorer regions east of Pearl River had only one preacher who could read and write. The richest county in the State had neither bookstores, academies, nor pastors. According to this writer, people going to Mississippi caught the mania for speculation, and lost all concern about books, schools, churches, or any thing else. He wrote over a fictitious signature, and his statements are perhaps exaggerated.

Other writers, who do not use fictitious names however, give a sufficiently dark picture of the wild spirit of speculation which prevailed for five or six years after the Choctaw country was opened. The Clinton Presbytery (Presbyterian) sent forth a strong protest against this state of things; and inasmuch as it had previously given official indorsement to the zeal and consecration of the few Cumberland Presbyterian preachers in that field, it now published through our church paper an earnest protest against the course which some preachers of our church in Mississippi were then taking.

In the diary of the Rev. Isaac Shook is an account of a visit to a Mississippi town in 1834. There were seven hundred inhabitants, and among them five Protestant ministers all secularized. One was a merchant, one a school-teacher, one a lawyer, and two "slave drivers," as Shook calls them. They were "seizing the golden opportunity to secure independence." Shook began a series of meetings. By and by the school-teacher began to attend. There was a revival. Then the merchant, who also sold whisky, came of nights, and grew wonderfully zealous, but he still sold whisky. The others would drop in occasionally, but took no special interest. The meeting closed. One of these preachers afterward was silenced; all of them utterly lost the confidence of the people. The town became noted for its contempt of Christianity.

In 1836 the church paper stated that all the Cumberland Presbyterian congregations in Mississippi had been organized in the preceding five years. At the meeting of Columbia Synod, in the town of Pulaski, Tennessee, on the fourth day of November, 1831, the order was passed for the formation of Mississippi Presbytery. Its limits on the south-west were indefinite; on the south it extended to Mobile. Its original members were to be Thomas J. Bryan, Robert Molloy, Samuel W. Sparks, and Isaac Shook; and its first meeting was to be held in the town of Gallatin, Copia County, Mississippi, the fourth Thursday in April, 1832, Thomas J. Bryan to be its first moderator.[1] Different statements as to who were the original members of this presbytery have been published, but this is the correct list as ordered by the synod. These varying accounts are thus explained: Several ministers from different synods were living in Mississippi, but not enough from any one to form a presbytery. The Rev. S. W. Sparks and the Rev. Isaac Shook, both of Columbia Synod, volunteered to go at their own expense to Mississippi and co-operate with Molloy and Bryan—who also belonged to that synod, but lived in Mississippi—in the formation of a presbytery. As soon as the presbytery was organized it received as members the other resident ministers, and then Shook and Sparks returned.

In going to Mississippi they had traveled on horseback to Memphis, thence by boat to Vicksburg, and thence on horseback

---

[1] See records of Columbia Synod, in the church paper, November 17, 1831.

to Gallatin. They expected to return by the same route, but God, in his providence, had other plans for Shook. He was induced to visit some old friends in Mississippi and hold meetings for them. He afterward made arrangements to go all the way back to Huntsville, Alabama, by stage. Saturday, May 19, 1832, Mr. Shook was traveling homeward in the stage. He would not travel on the Sabbath, and his only alternative was to spend two days at the hotel in a strange town, which had the reputation of being a very wicked place. Stages passed only on alternate days, and hotel bills in Mississippi were very high. Late Saturday night Shook put up at the Columbus hotel. Sunday morning he found the hotel keeper to be an old acquaintance and a special friend. Through him an arrangement was made for Shook to preach that day in the Baptist church. Shook says that he preached with the feeling that he would never see his congregation again till the great judgment-day, and he prayed God to enable him to be faithful. Early Monday morning he was waited on by the pastor and one elder of the Presbyterian church who urged him very earnestly to remain till the next Sabbath, when their communion meeting was to begin. He hesitated, but said he would give them an answer before stage time. In the course of the day, he found that his sermon the day before had awakened several sinners. He resolved to remain. Mr. Byington, of the Choctaw mission, came and assisted in the meeting. At the close of Shook's first sermon, he "called for mourners," and two ladies, who were leaders in society, came forward. At the close of his second sermon, the school-mistress and nearly all her school came forward. The interest spread to the country, where it seemed to be greater than in town. It was finally decided to hold meetings at different points all around Columbus. On, till the first of August, over two months, Shook continued preaching every day. In Columbus and the surrounding country, three hundred persons claimed to be converted at these meetings. Of these, Shook took *twenty* into the Cumberland Presbyterian church. He says he encouraged no one to join the Cumberland Presbyterians because he saw no prospects of any reliable supply of the preached gospel from our ministers. He even apologizes for receiving the twenty, but says they would not agree to belong to any other church, and were willing to put up with sermons by occasional circuit riders. The Rev. Samuel Nelson rode that circuit and supplied this little flock with the gospel for a few years. In 1839 this little church at Columbus called Mr. Shook as their pastor at a salary of $800. He served them faithfully for many years. The war came near destroying this and many other Southern congregations, but in spite of the war and of other hindrances, this faithful band still perseveres in the work.

A member of the Mississippi Presbytery, rather short of funds, rode one hundred and fifty miles to attend one of the early meetings of that body. He found the members all quartered at the town hotel, each paying $3 a day for himself and horse. There was no meeting-house in the town, but the forest was near by, and the presbytery convened under the trees. The clerk wrote on his hat crown. The largest Cumberland Presbyterian congregation in the State in 1836 numbered only twenty-eight members. Small as was this beginning our membership in that State at a later day was among the foremost in the whole church in every good work. This is especially true in reference to the payment of pastors' salaries. In all the important financial enterprises of the church from 1840 to 1860, Mississippi and Alabama took a leading part. They were favorite fields for agents appointed in any part of the church to raise money. Before the war the contributions of Alabamians and Mississippians to the endowment of the colleges of the church far exceeded those made by the people of any other two States. Notwithstanding the losses caused by the war, Mississippi still stands among the foremost States in supporting all church enterprises.

In 1832 the Mississippi Synod was organized. Its presbyteries were the Mississippi, the Alabama, and the Elyton. This synod extended its jurisdiction into Louisiana and over all Texas. By it Louisiana Presbytery was organized in 1835, and Texas Presbytery in 1837—(ordered in 1836). Three new presbyteries created by Mississippi Synod were soon dissolved. These were named Columbus, Charity Hall, and Shiloh. Two other presbyteries were organized in this State during this period, which still exist—Oxford and New Hope. The efficiency and energy of the New

Hope Presbytery, its admirable organization, and the consecration of its preachers and people, deserve special commendation.

In 1832 the Rev. H. H. Hill traveled in Alabama and Mississippi, holding meetings. His work was greatly blessed. The Rev. R. L. Ross was a convert of these meetings, as were his father and nearly all the family. In 1834 the Rev. W. S. Burney was engaged in holding camp-meetings in Mississippi. He was assisted by the Rev. A. P. Bradley, and their work was abundantly successful. Jefferson Brown, Joseph Harrison, and Cyrus Wilson all labored in this field about this time. Wilson was afterward a candidate for governor of Arkansas, but was defeated. Elam Waddell, Jabez Hickman, and F. M. Fincher came next. In 1838 the Rev. Richard Beard took charge of the Sharon Academy in Mississippi, and his influence and labors were a great help to the church in that State. James Mitchell, Andrew Herron, J. B. Jopling, Wayman Adair, and John P. Campbell, all preached in Mississippi during this period. Of all this list, only a very small number were free from secular pursuits. The New Hope Presbytery (1838) was united with the Columbus Presbytery in 1840, and then had among its members, Wayman Adair, Thomas Tabb, Joe Bell, James W. Dickey, W. C. Ross, F. E. Harris, Isaac Shook, and some others. Perhaps W. C. Ross is the only one of the list who still lingers on earth.[1]

The Rev. R. L. Ross entered the ministry in Mississippi soon after his conversion in 1832. He has always been a liberal helper in church work. By good management and rigid economy he has been enabled to give more money to our church enterprises than any other preacher in the denomination. He has often aided Cumberland University, in some cases "just in the nick of time," when his contributions saved the institution from disaster. There are some touching incidents of his early work in the ministry, one of which deserves to be recorded here. There was in Mississippi a neighborhood made up of Scotch emigrants, and Mr. Ross became very much attached to them and married one of their daughters. They were all Presbyterians, and had brought their Scotch pastor along with them. This pastor, whose name was McDonald,

---

[1] The united presbytery was called New Hope.

was an earnest Christian but very much afraid of "disorderly" revivals, and especially afraid of Cumberland Presbyterian revivals. Still he became attached to Ross, and finally consented to have Ross and Leftwich, both Cumberland Presbyterian preachers, hold a camp-meeting for him. It was not long before the Scotch pastor was startled by loud shouting from some of his "orderly" members. Throngs of penitents were at the "mourner's bench," and the conversion of some of them made parents and relatives forget all about "order." The pastor, along with the elders, looked on with great displeasure. One of these elders was named McKee. The pastor soon discovered, to his great disgust, that McKee's little daughter, only eleven years old, was one of the mourners. He advised the father to take her away, saying they would "frighten her to death." The father acted on the advice immediately. She was taken to a tent and put under medical treatment. She was given a camphor bath, then a strong *toddy* was administered, and she was put to bed. The pastor and elders then decided to put a stop to such a disorderly meeting, and so announced to Ross. The latter, believing the pastor to be a sincere Christian, asked him first to go alone to the forest and spend a season of earnest prayer for divine guidance. The old Scotchman was a believer in divine guidance, and he took Mr. Ross' advice. When he returned his mind was made up to let the meeting go on one more day and see what the results would be. In his prayer he said he had asked God if there was any good in such meetings to let him see convincing proof of it that day. That night a curious spectacle was presented. The Scotch parents, with their children seated by them, all occupied the outside seats as far away from the pulpit as possible. They had all given orders to their children not to go to the mourner's bench. Ross preached with great power, and then "called mourners." The pastor stood leaning on the pulpit. Mourners came in great numbers, among them Elder McKee's son, thirty years old. His two married daughters also came. Mr. Ross then went to Mr. McKee's wife and insisted that she should go to her children who were seeking salvation and give them instruction. She went and commenced talking to her daughter about "waiting the Lord's own time." But just as the mother began her instructions the daughter rose shouting. Her face shone with heavenly light, and the mother then and there acknowledged that the work was from God. She went and knelt by her son, and began a silent prayer for him. Her prayer soon grew audible. Then it was poured forth with all the ardor of a Methodist. The son was soon rejoicing. Then another son; and then the mother was on her feet preaching Jesus and crying "glory to God." By this time every doubt vanished from the pastor's heart, and mounting a chair he gave a thrilling exhortation to all sinners to come at once to the arms of the Redeemer. He told them all that he was now fully convinced that this was God's work, and that resistance to it was resistance to God's Spirit. All barriers were now swept away and many were gathered into the fold. Several of the converts joined the Cumberland Presbyterians. The Rev. J. F. McDonald, of our church, is a descendant of this old Scotch pastor. It is gratifying also to know that the little girl who was dragged away from the mourner's bench was, in after years, converted. She became the Rev. R. L. Ross' second wife.

The Cumberland Presbyterian church was never strong in Louisiana. At a camp-meeting held by Rainey Mercer and Robert Molloy, near Springfield, on Lake Pontchartrain, in St. Helena Parish, October, 1831, the first congregation of our people in that State was organized. Here, as everywhere else, the pioneers formed a temperance society when they organized a church. The next account we have of the work of Cumberland Presbyterians in that State is from John W. Ogden, March, 1832. He had organized a church at Opelousas, with forty members; and another at Alexandria. Each of these congregations began at once to build a suitable house of worship. Ogden also reported great revivals at his meetings throughout his circuit, especially in Bayou Cotile and Bayou Rapide. In 1835 the Rev. Samuel King and his son, R. D. King, rendered some valuable assistance to the church in Louisiana. W. A. Scott, then a licensed preacher, was also in that field. So, too, was the Rev. Thomas B. Reynolds, and probably Wiley Burgess. The Louisiana Presbytery was organized March 13, 1835. Its original members were John W. Ogden, Rainey Mercer, and Thomas B. Reynolds. At this first meeting it ordained W. A. Scott, P. M. Griffin, and Sumner Bacon.[1] This presbytery had a hard struggle. After many vicissitudes, it was finally dissolved. Of its ministers, Scott, Ogden, and Ford left the church. Thirty years later, October 19, 1872, a new Louisiana Presbytery was organized, which, in spite of discouragements, maintains its organic life. Its preachers and congregations are accomplishing a good work. They deserve help.

---

[1] Minutes of Louisiana Presbytery, in *Revivalist*, Vol. I., No. 31.

CHAPTER XXVI.

PLANTING THE CHURCH IN TEXAS—1828 TO 1842.

The Holy Ghost said, Separate me Barnabas and Saul for the work whereunto I have called them.—*Acts xiii. 2.*

WHILE Texas was a part of the constitutional and federal Republic of Mexico, various colonies of people from the United States settled in that province. Most of these colonies obtained large grants of land from the Mexican government. In 1834 it was said that sixty thousand of these colonists were living on Texas soil. Though all these Anglo-Saxons were from a Protestant country, yet they lived under laws which forbade all public Protestant worship. There was at first no Protestant preacher in all the province.

In 1826 Sumner Bacon, an unprepossessing son of Massachusetts, living then in Arkansas, presented himself to Arkansas Presbytery of the Cumberland Presbyterian church as a candidate for the ministry. He was dressed in buckskin clothing. His manners were rough, like his dress. He gave a very unusual account of what he considered his call to the ministry. He said he was only called to one special work, and not to the general work of the ministry. He was called to go to Texas, where there were no Protestant preachers. On account of the strange appearance and strange call of this young man, the presbytery declined to receive him. At a subsequent meeting of the same presbytery he presented himself again, and was again rejected[1] How blind we all are! God had specially trained up a man of his own choosing for a special work which no ordinary man could do. As a soldier in camp, then as a surveyor on a dangerous frontier, with Yankee energy and Cumberland Presbyterian zeal, this rough man was furnished for his wild, hard, dangerous, but exceedingly important

---

[1] History given by the Rev. J. A. Cornwall, who was present.

mission. Because he was rough, wore buckskin, and had a special call, the dear brethren of Arkansas rejected him; but God will not be thwarted if men are blind.

At the same time that Bacon was receiving these impressions, a Cumberland Presbyterian lady living in one of the Anglo-Saxon colonies in western Texas was daily making it a matter of special prayer that God would send to her neighborhood a preacher of the everlasting gospel. Meantime Bacon, nothing daunted by rebuffs, gathered up what means he could control, and in 1828 set out to perform his mission to Texas, without human authority. At his own expense he managed to secure some Bibles and tracts, and began his work as an independent lay evangelist among the people of western Texas. He was the first Protestant who ever preached on Texas soil. As it was dangerous for people to open to him their houses, he held his first meetings under the trees, near the house of that praying lady.

But Bacon encountered far greater danger from ruffians than from Mexican laws. If there had been any very great rigor in enforcing those laws his out-door meetings could not have been held. Only a small part of the population were Catholics. The priests were generally extremely ignorant.

Bacon was acquainted with a regular agent of the American Bible Society in Louisiana, the Rev. Mr. Chase, and often obtained Bibles from him. Chase was a minister in the Presbyterian church, and took great interest in Bacon. The question of lay ordination had been pressed upon Bacon, as there was no ordained preacher of any Protestant church in Texas. His friend, Chase, did not favor this plan, but urged him to wait and trust God to open up the way for ordination in some regular channel. In 1832 Mr. Chase obtained for Bacon a commission as agent for the American Bible Society, which he accepted with the distinct stipulation that he was to receive no salary.

Sometime in 1833 Bacon's life, which had often been endangered and often threatened, was nigh being taken by some desperadoes of western Texas. There are some variations in the many different accounts of this adventure, but the authority here followed is the church paper, whose editor compiled his statements from correspondence with Bacon at the time.[1] Bacon was informed, before starting to an appointment to preach, that he would certainly be waylaid and killed if he went on that journey, and earnest efforts were made to dissuade him from going. Failing in that, the man who warned him against attempting the journey, and who some say was a Texas ruffian won over to be Bacon's friend, armed himself, saddled his horse, and went along with the preacher. Passing a narrow ravine, in which it was necessary to ride single file, the armed friend saw two men rush upon Bacon and knock him from his horse at a single blow. His companion fled, and reported that Bacon was killed. It seems, however, that he was not dead. The assassins dragged him into the thicket for the purpose of concealing their bloody deed, when they discovered that their victim still lived. They were proceeding to complete the work, when Bacon asked them to allow him a few minutes for prayer. This was granted. The man of God knelt and poured forth a most earnest prayer for his murderers. When he rose, the assassins were in tears, and declared to him that they could not kill so good a man.

Sometime afterward Bacon was to hold a camp-meeting. His first camp-meeting,[2] and the first ever held in Texas, was in Sabine County, in 1833. It is not certain whether it was at this or some other camp-meeting in the same year that his life was again in jeopardy. Ruffians went to the meeting armed, declaring their purpose to kill him. On the appearance of these desperadoes, one of the men who had been prayed for in the former attempt on Bacon's life, rose with his gun in his hands, and, planting himself in front of the preacher, told the people that he was there to defend Bacon. He stood guard while the minister delivered his sermon, and no violence was attempted. Amid scenes like these the Cumberland Presbyterian church, the first Protestant church of Texas, was planted.

Bacon kept a book in which he took the signatures of all those who claimed to be Christians, and of all others who were willing

---

[1] See *Cumberland Presbyterian*, April 25, 1835.
[2] A Methodist minister aided in this meeting. See Bacon's own letter in the *Cumberland Presbyterian*, October 23, 1833.

to enter into a solemn pledge to live a Christian life. As yet, he had no human authority to preach, nor was there in Mexico any Protestant church court to give such authority. Mr. Bacon's work, as Bible agent, was characteristic of pioneer life. He had a pack-horse to carry his books, and bear skins to cover them in rainy weather. His chief difficulty was in crossing the watercourses. When he reached a deep river he went into camp and remained till he could construct a raft which would bear him and his books. That done, he swam his horses over beside his raft, and went on his way again. A number of his private letters written to friends "in the States" show that he made earnest appeals for help. In these letters he says that he found the Mexicans destitute of the Scriptures, and generally eager to be supplied. He seemed to feel no fears of being arrested for distributing the word of God, and always spoke in terms of tender interest about the immortal souls of the people among whom he labored. His circuit was from the Gulf of Mexico to the western border of Texas. He preached and scattered Bibles as he went. The heavens were the roof over his head at night. The prairie grass furnished him forage. Indians, Mexicans, persecuting priests, and rigid laws, bloody assassins, and wild beasts, were all in the hands of his God who sent him to that special field.

Arkansas Presbytery had refused to recognize his special call, but the Great Head of the church raised up another presbytery to enjoy the honor of commissioning him to preach. In 1835 the Rev. Mr. Chase wrote to Mr. Bacon that a Cumberland Presbyterian Presbytery was to be organized at Alexandria, Louisiana, in March, and urged him to attend. Bacon did so. Mr. Chase also attended and made a statement to the presbytery of the peculiar and pressing nature of the case, whereupon the presbytery received Bacon as a candidate for the ministry, licensed, and ordained him all on the same day.[1] Mr. Chase preached the ordination sermon. God not only raised up the man of his own choosing for this work, but he raised up also, in the bosom of the Presbyterian church, a friend to stand before a Cumberland Presbyterian judicature and

---

[1] Minutes of Louisiana Presbytery, in *Cumberland Presbyterian*, April 15, 1835, and April 22, 1835; also, editorial in it.

plead for a suspension of the educational rules in that particular case. It was with some difficulty that Mr. Chase succeeded in this matter, and the presbytery spread on its minutes a declaration that this case was not to be a precedent in the future. Ah, God rules!

Before Bacon's ordination, some two or three other ministers of other churches had penetrated the wilds of Texas and lent their aid to the good work. They and Bacon often met at camp-meetings, and through their united efforts many souls were brought to a knowledge of Jesus.

Meantime, other features in the plans of the heavenly Father were slowly brought to light. The usurpations of a military despot drove the Texans into revolt. Men from the States rushed to their assistance, and among these was Andrew Jackson McGown, a son of one of Andrew Jackson's old colonels. His parents were then living in Texas, and though he was a probationer for the ministry, going to school, when he heard the cry for help he left school, and books, and native land, and went to join the patriot Texan army. He reached Texas in the darkest period of the revolution. Citizens fleeing in wild dismay from the cruel invader first met him; next the retreating army. All the woe and alarm which such things always involve, greeted him. Casting in his lot with the army he gave his whole heart to the struggle. The books, the songs, the histories, and the oratory of Texas, all dwell fondly on the name of A. J. McGown. One of the Texas poets represents it as the loftiest achievement of any man to pass through such a war with both a soldier's heroism and a Christian's integrity unsullied by a single spot, and then ascribes this high honor to McGown.

His service with the patriots of Texas was in the providence of God a means of fitting him for his special work afterward. The fact that he had shared in the dangers and triumphs on the battle-fields of 1835 and 1836, appealed, as nothing else could, to every Texan patriot's heart. All the rest of his days, in his work in the ministry, McGown used the influence thus acquired with wonderful effect. Many a time he visited neighborhoods where mob violence had been used against preachers, but an appeal to his comrades of San Jacinto never failed to call forth daring friends who would protect him from all attacks. On one occasion, in a thrilling appeal to his army comrades while "calling mourners," he saw a man who had been an officer in his regiment, rising, and as he advanced saying, "I'll come, Andy, for your sake." McGown cried out, "Stop, stop, not for my sake, but for your poor soul's sake, and for Christ's sake." That day was one of great victory for Christ and his cause. Not even the historic fields of the 21st of April, 1836, can compare with it. The books of earth keep one record, the archives of eternal glory keep the other.

McGown traveled and preached with as much zeal and energy as he had manifested in the struggle for Texan independence, laboring as all other Cumberland Presbyterian preachers on the frontier had to do, without any pay. On one occasion he came to a ferry, but had no money. He told the ferryman that he had a pair of new socks which he would give him for his ferriage. The offer was accepted, and the preacher went on his way rejoicing. On another occasion, his clothing was worn and threadbare. The Rev. S. W. Frazier, who was traveling with him, was also in need of clothing. A gambler, who saw their need, went into a store and bought a suit of clothes for each of the preachers. Thus they were supplied.

In 1836 McGown and Bacon first met. Both of them had their hearts earnestly set on the interests of Christ's kingdom in the Republic of Texas, for the Lone Star banner then floated over that field. A presbytery, a newspaper, and a school were three things which they agreed to work for. To secure the first they attended the meeting of Mississippi Synod, whose jurisdiction extended indefinitely to the south and west. At their request this synod authorized any three ordained ministers of the Cumberland Presbyterian church who could be got together on Texas soil to organize a presbytery. McGown was not yet ordained. Next year, November 27, 1837, the Rev. Amos Roark of Hatchie Presbytery, and the Rev. Mitchell Smith of Talladega Presbytery, met at the house of the Rev. Sumner Bacon of Louisiana Presbytery, and there constituted the Texas Presbytery.[1] At this first meeting R. O. Watkins was received as a candidate for the ministry. The

---

[1] Minutes published in *Cumberland Presbyterian*, February 20, 1838.

organized churches of our people then in the Republic were but four in number. One was in eastern Texas, then supposed to be in Arkansas, and was organized by Milton Estill, in 1833, the first in the State. Another was in Sabine County, where the first camp-meeting was held. It was organized by Bacon, in 1836. A third was in the Watkins neighborhood (Nacogdoches) and was organized in 1837. With war still raging, with only three ordained preachers, and four churches, the first presbytery had a dark prospect before it. It however adopted brave and decided measures. It resolved to establish a school and a religious paper, and seek help from the church in the United States. It adopted the platform of total abstinence. Its memorial to the General Assembly asking help, was a document of great ability and earnestness. It sent Amos Roark to the next General Assembly (1838), and that body resolved to send the Rev. Samuel Frazier as missionary to Texas. Roark, accompanied by Frazier, returned to Texas overland, on horseback, holding meetings along the way. In a letter to the church paper, written on this long journey, they say that in every place people bade them farewell with tears, imploring God's blessings on their labors in that distant field.

Before the Texas Presbytery was organized, the Rev. Robert Tate, one of the most devoted of Tennessee's young preachers, resolved to make Texas his home. This young man had property enough to enable him to preach without pay, and it is said he uniformly refused to accept any compensation for his preaching. His was a wonderful religious experience. After thrilling adventures in a life of sin, he had been almost miraculously rescued by divine grace. He went to Texas in 1835. He spent less than a year preaching as an itinerant missionary in that country when his financial interests called him back to Tennessee. After transacting this business he started on his long journey back to the land of his adoption, but died on his way, September 17, 1837. Tate was not the only pioneer preacher in that field who was called to heaven after a very brief season of toil. Samuel W. Frazier entered on his work there, and died the same year at Houston, December 9, 1838.

That year also witnessed the accession of two more ordained

preachers to the Texas Presbytery. These were James McDonnold and Milton Moore. In those days the journey to Texas from any of the Eastern States was a very different thing from what it is to-day. There were two routes, one by river and Gulf, and then by ox wagons; the other overland in ox wagons all the way. Emigrants generally chose the latter route. Santa Anna, while a prisoner, had acknowledged the independence of Texas, but Mexico refused to abide by the acts of a prisoner. War was not over. Indians and Mexicans made common cause, and the Comanches were more dreaded than the Mexicans. When James McDonnold started from Tennessee to Texas great crowds of people gathered to see the family take their departure. He had a large circle of kin besides numerous church friends whom his preaching had won. His eldest son was with Houston's armies, and stories of battle and blood were still coming from that land which was farther off than British India is to-day. When the ox wagons began to creak along the highway, bearing our friends away, it was to us who were left behind very much like seeing them led to execution. Everybody was weeping. On McDonnold's arrival in Texas he entered on his old life—"a circuit rider." With a large family to support, he yet managed to give himself to the work of the ministry.

One measure adopted by the Texas Presbytery at its second meeting had in it the ring of 1800. In the vast destitution which that pioneer field presented, the presbytery resolved to send out elders to help to organize churches. Another fact shows the character of the times and the dangers to which these pioneers were exposed. At one time the place appointed for the meeting of the presbytery was invaded by the Indians, and the whole settlement broken up, so that a called meeting had to be held to select another place. Along with this fact is another of similar significance. R. O. Watkins had a regular circuit assigned him. The whole circuit was invaded by Mexicans and Indians and the settlers all driven off. Watkins being unable to pursue his circuit work, went to Mississippi and entered school. Still another incident sheds light of the same character. In 1840 the presbytery was to meet at Fort Houston. When the time for the meeting arrived, it was considered necessary for all the members to arm themselves and travel in a body, like a band of soldiers, for mutual protection. At this meeting of the presbytery, R. O. Watkins was ordained. This was the first ordination of a minister by Protestants on Texas soil. At the same meeting Watkins' horse got away and he had to walk home, a distance of eighty miles, through a country over which hostile Indians were constantly roaming. He traveled mostly by night.

Meantime, other valuable men were joining the ranks of Texas Cumberland Presbyterians. The Rev. J. M. Foster, and the Rev. F. E. Foster, natives of Wilson County, Tennessee, but Missourians by adoption, arrived in Texas in 1841, and spent the rest of their days in labors for the church in that country.

There was a period of great darkness to the members of this solitary presbytery. Warlike invasions, and other difficulties, drove them to the verge of despair. Roark went back to the United States. A. J. McGown went also, but expected to return. His mission was to seek aid for Texas, and especially to try to raise money to start a newspaper. Some powerful appeals for help were at that time published by Texas preachers. They said that other churches were sustaining several missionaries there, while the little band of Cumberland Presbyterian pioneers were left without help. They did not complain of their own hardships, but pleaded that others should be sent and sustained. Very little, however, was ever done by the church through its boards or General Assembly toward planting missions in that country.

In 1841 McGown returned to Texas. God wonderfully blessed the meetings held by Cumberland Presbyterians in different parts of that Republic. It was like life from the dead. The Texas Presbytery, after being ready to disband, was now ready to extend its work. In 1842 it asked for and obtained the order for the formation of Texas Synod. This synod was organized in March, 1843. It was made up of the Texas Presbytery, whose members were Sumner Bacon, Milton Moore, Milton Estill, and R. O. Watkins; the Red River Presbytery, whose members were Mitchell Smith, James McDonnold, Robert Gilkerson, and Samuel Corley; and the Colorado Presbytery, whose members were A. J.

McGown, J. M. Foster, and F. E. Foster. In 1837 our people had three preachers and four churches in Texas. In 1842 there were three presbyteries and eleven ministers; and churches, which had been planted amid the horrors of a civil war, had grown up in all parts of the Republic.

It will be seen from this little sketch that Cumberland Presbyterians had the start of all other Protestants on Texas soil. They had the first preacher, the first camp-meeting, the first church judicature, and the first religious newspaper in that field. Texas, made a State of the Union in 1846, with a territory sufficient to sustain over thirty millions of people, with soil of unsurpassed fertility, and resources varied and inexhaustible, with a rapidly growing population, is an inviting field for our people. Among the martyrs who died to rescue this country from Mexican misrule were the sons of the Cumberland Presbyterian church; and the ministers of this church were with the patriots at San Jacinto. Our people have historic and traditional advantages which ought to give them ready access to the hearts of Texans as long as the Alamo and San Jacinto are remembered.

Table of Texas Dates.

1821 to 1827. Colonization by Missourians and other Anglo-Saxons.
1828. Bacon preaches the first Protestant sermon in Texas.
1833. Bacon, assisted by a Methodist preacher, holds the first camp-meeting.
1835. Bacon ordained in Louisiana. The revolution begins.
1836. Independence declared. McGown arrives.
1837. Texas Presbytery organized. Arrival of Roark and Smith.
1838. McDonnold, Frazier, and Moore arrive. Frazier dies.
1839. Dark period. Invasions.
1840. Roark returns to the United States. Watkins ordained.
1841. The Fosters arrive. Great revival.
1842. Organization of Texas Synod ordered.
1846. Texas annexed to the United States.

CHAPTER XXVII.

ORIGIN OF THE CHURCH IN PENNSYLVANIA.

> My presence shall go with thee. 'Tis enough!
> Lead on, my heavenly guide;
> . . . . . .
> Enough for faith to hear thy voice, and see
> Thy own right hand in love upholding me.
> —*Anna Shipton.*

IN 1829 a Presbyterian minister who held and taught the doctrine of a general atonement lived on Ten Mile Creek, Washington County, Pennsylvania. His name was Jacob Lindley. In the same presbytery was another minister with equally liberal views about the provisions of divine grace. His name was Cornelius Loughran. The churches of these two men shared in these views, as did several other Presbyterian churches in western Pennsylvania. When the outline of Cumberland Presbyterian doctrines appeared in Buck's Theological Dictionary, many of these people read it with intense interest.

Two agents for Cumberland College, the Rev. M. H. Bone and the Rev. John W. Ogden, whose commission embraced the whole United States, extended their labors into western Pennsylvania. They began their mission in June, 1829. Smith's history says of them:

They spent the following summer and autumn in the State of Ohio and in western Pennsylvania, preaching with power and demonstration of the Spirit, especially in Ohio, where through their instrumentality many souls found redemption. Their mission paved the way for the opening of a door for extensive usefulness to the church in Ohio, western Pennsylvania, and New York. In January, 1831, by request of a congregation of Presbyterians in Washington County, Pennsylvania, five of its members wrote a letter to the president of Cumberland College, stating that they had lately heard of the existence of the Cumberland Presbyterians in the West; that they had examined, in Buck's Theological Dictionary, the brief exposé of their doctrines and discipline, which the congregation sincerely approved; that although they were members of the Presbyterian church, they could not adopt the whole of its Confession of Faith, and were solicitous to become better acquainted with the Cumberland Presbyterians, who were viewed by them as their brethren in Christ Jesus. They requested that the president should adopt some measures to provide them, at least for a short time, with the ministrations of a Cumberland Presbyterian missionary. Mr. Cossitt informed them that he would lay their case before the next General Assembly, and urge upon that body to meet with their wishes on the subject. To this the committee replied: "Immediately on the receipt of yours, we called a meeting of the congregation, and, having read your letter to them, they expressed their gratification at the prospect of becoming better acquainted with the Cumberland Presbyterian ministers. They entreated us to continue our correspondence with you, and to renew the request that your Assembly would send us a missionary for a short time. Should you succeed, we wish you to inform us as early as possible; and, if practicable, we are solicitous for him to reach here by the first of June, which will enable us (should we agree with you in faith and practice) to obtain our dismission from the Presbyterian church at the session of presbytery which meets about the middle of that month. We are also authorized to state that our minister heartily approves of our procedure, and will with us attach himself to your body as soon as an opportunity offers.[1] We think that nine tenths of our sister congregations of the Presbyterian church believe as we do, and for some time, especially since two of your preachers were in Washington, an anxious desire has been manifested by them to become better acquainted with your ministry. Many who make no profession of religion are solicitous for your ministers to operate in this country; and we believe that if your Assembly will send us one or more zealous preachers, they will prove a great blessing to the church of Christ. We do request that you will press the matter upon the General Assembly with as much ardor as possible."

These documents, together with others of the same nature from the western section of the State of New York, were laid before the General Assembly of 1831. The Assembly viewed these pressing calls as an intimation that the Head of the Church was opening a more extensive field of labor to the Cumberland Presbyterian ministry, and appointed Alexander Chapman, Robert Donnell, Reuben Burrow, John Morgan, and A. M. Bryan missionaries to visit the congregations that had applied for the ministrations of Cumberland Presbyterians. Imme-

---

[1] This congregation was without a pastor when the missionaries arrived

diately after their appointment, Chapman, Morgan, and Bryan proceeded to western Pennsylvania. Donnell and Burrow passed through North Carolina and Virginia, and in the autumn met the others in the vicinity of Washington, Pennsylvania. An extract from a letter to Mr. Cossitt from a member of the Pennsylvania congregation that had applied for a Cumberland Presbyterian missionary, exhibits the reception of the missionaries by that people, and the success of their first labors: "Messrs. Chapman, Bryan, and Morgan reached us about three weeks ago, and were received with joy and thankfulness. Their first business was to declare their doctrinal views. This they did with such clearness and perspicuity, that almost all who heard them appeared to be convinced that their peculiarities were founded on the word of God, and none were disposed to controvert. Having declared their peculiar views, they dropped non-essentials, and commenced preaching Christ and him crucified. This they did with such power and demonstration of the Spirit, that many were cut to the heart. At the close of the sixth sermon preached by them, Mr. Morgan invited all who desired to obtain an interest in the blood of Christ, to distinguish themselves by meeting him before the stand, and to our astonishment forty-two went forward, and at this time more than a hundred have thus distinguished themselves. God has often revived his work among us here, but we have never before witnessed any thing to compare with the blessed work which is now in progress among us through the instrumentality of these missionaries from the West."

John Morgan gives this account of the work:

Messrs. Bryan and Morgan, after visiting and preaching at many points on the way, reached Washington, Pennsylvania, July 14, 1831. At this time there was not a member of the Cumberland Presbyterian church in any part of the State of Pennsylvania. The Methodist brethren received us kindly, to some of whom we had introductory letters from the Rev. C. Cook, a Methodist preacher then stationed in Wheeling, Virginia. We preached several sermons in the Methodist Episcopal church in Washington, then under the pastoral care of the Rev. John Waterman, who received and treated us in a most courteous and Christian manner. Nothing of special interest occurred at this time under the preaching at Washington. In a few days a committee from those persons who had written to Dr. Cossitt asking for missionaries waited on us, and told us an appointment had been published for one of us to preach on Wednesday, the 20th of July, in the afternoon, at a small church belonging to the Methodists, called Mount Zion, about twelve miles from Washington. Mr. Bryan was now quite unwell. Mr. Morgan accompanied the committee to the place appointed, where we found a large and promiscuous crowd of people, all anxious to hear what these Cumberland Presbyterian preachers would say. The Rev. Jacob Lindley, then pastor of a Presbyterian church in that neighborhood, was present, and after receiving an introduction to "the strange preacher," was invited to take a seat in the pulpit, which he did very cordially. During the sermon there was nothing remarkable but a fixedness of attention on the part of every hearer, and many tears from many eyes, which bespoke the searching influence of gospel truth. Mr. Lindley closed the meeting with an unusually feeling and powerful prayer, the tears streaming from his eyes all the time.

An appointment was then made for preaching the next Sabbath in a sugar camp in that neighborhood. We had no meeting-houses of course; and, indeed, if we had had, unless they had been large enough to cover from a half acre to an acre of ground, they would have been of but little use to us, so large were the crowds that attended. Sabbath came, and the people from all directions came pouring into the sugar camp, a most delightful and beautiful spot, and one now dear to many hearts from the recollection of what it pleased the Lord to do for them in that place.

By this time Father Chapman had reached us, who was a most precious instrument in the hands of God in winning souls to Christ. Our hearts were cheered by this valuable accession of ministerial help. Mr. Bryan was still unable to preach, though convalescent, and in a few days was able to join our feeble band.

The hour for preaching arrived. Mr. Morgan preached, and was succeeded by Mr. Chapman immediately with another sermon. During the preaching a deep solemnity pervaded the vast assembly. All was still and orderly however, only that one lady fell from her seat as if she had fainted. Dr. B——, being on the ground, was called to her, but was unable to determine the nature of her disease—a strong mark of the doctor's discriminating medical judgment—for, indeed, it was a case which demanded the presence and skill of the Physician of souls, to whom she made fervent application in prayer, and was made every whit whole.

In the afternoon of that day we preached at a private house (Mr. Marsh's), where the mighty power of the Holy Ghost was realized by all present. Christians were melted into penitence and thankfulness, many of the unconverted were cut to the heart, and some cried out, "Sirs, what must we do to be saved." It was manifest the Lord had begun a great and good work among the people. We continued preaching from house to house and grove to grove every day during the whole week, and convictions multiplied daily in every direction.

The people in the neighborhood had enjoyed religious instruction under Presbyterian influence during all their lives. No people could be more opposed to noisy excitements than they were. . . . Their exercises were not the result of education in favor of such things, but of the mighty power of the Holy Ghost sent down from heaven.

Many of the ministers and members of the Presbyterian church had received information that we were coming to this country, and had taken timely measures to prevent their people from hearing us preach. But this only increased their anxiety to hear what we had to say, and go they would. One would be the means of another's going. All who went seemed to have their prejudices greatly abated, and became more and more anxious to go again, and to have others go. The very means intended to hedge up our way only tended to build us up, and taught us this very important lesson, that gag laws and proscriptive acts will never answer the purposes of those who enact them among a free people. They tend directly to promote the things they are intended to defeat.

The first Presbyterian minister to open his church to the missionaries was the Rev. Mr. Dodd, of "the Brick church." He had heard them preach, and he gave them a hearty invitation to hold a meeting in his congregation. Many members of this church afterward joined the Cumberland Presbyterians. Philip and Luther Axtell, both faithful and beloved ministers of our church in western Pennsylvania, were sons of one of these members.[1] It is said that when a large part of this flock joined "the heretics," and the Presbyterian congregation ceased to exist, the remnant preferred tearing down the house to letting the Cumberland Presbyterians use it.

The next invitation came from Jacob Lindley, of Ten Mile. The meeting in Mr. Lindley's congregation is minutely described by Mr. Morgan. When "mourners" were called for, seventy-five responded. Some of the old elders began to oppose the work, but the pastor encouraged the missionaries. Mr. Morgan says:

In the arrangement for preaching on Monday Mr. Chapman was appointed to occupy the pulpit at 11 o'clock A.M. He preached from the text, "Strait is the gate and narrow is the way which leadeth unto life, and few there be that find it." His manner was naturally agreeable, his person dignified and commanding, his voice clear, strong, and musical. He seldom preached without leaving a deep sense of religious

---

[1] Luther Axtell died March 23, 1886.

awe upon the minds of his hearers, but on this occasion he far surpassed himself. He became awfully sublime in his descriptions of the sinner's danger and of the love of God in Christ to a perishing world. The house was large, and crowded full of people. Every eye was fixed on the preacher during the whole discourse; every heart melted; not one careless person could be seen in all the crowd. The service closed very happily, leaving a favorable impression on every heart.

After a recess of thirty minutes or more the people came together again. Mr. Morgan was to preach. After reading a hymn he remarked that some thought the anxious had been called forward the evening before under too much excitement; and to prevent this charge being made again, he was going to invite them forward at the very commencement of the service, before singing or prayer, and without making any appeal to their feelings. The seats being prepared, one hundred and two came forward. A more moving scene has seldom been witnessed. When their sons and daughters and neighbors of all ages, from the children of but ten to men and women of seventy years of age, from the most intelligent and moral down to the most ignorant and profligate, were seen deliberately coming forward in the public assembly deeply affected with a sense of their lost condition, even many of those who had found fault before now melted and said, "It is the Lord, let him do what seemeth him good." A most powerful and general revival of religion ensued. Hundreds were hopefully converted to God, and Christians of different sects were revived and stirred up to take a deep and lively interest in the promotion of the Redeemer's kingdom.

In regard to the formation of the first Cumberland Presbyterian church in that State Mr. Morgan says:

After having preached some time, and the work having progressed to a considerable extent, those individuals who had applied for missionaries to be sent desired the formation of a church. To this the ministers replied, "We do not expect to remain in this country; we wish to return South." This, however, was strongly objected to, and the strongest appeals made to induce them to remain. To this they did not consent until late in the fall of 1831.

The first church was organized on the 18th of August, 1831. The appointment had been previously made for preaching and the organization of the church. Many people came, some from a considerable distance: some to join the church, and others to see who would join. The service was held in a beautiful grove on the premises of William Stockdale, Washington County, Pennsylvania. The minister arose and read this beautiful text, "For I am not ashamed of the gospel of Christ, for it is the power of God unto salvation to every one that believeth."

When he closed his sermon, it seemed that all present had imbibed the sentiment expressed by the apostle. I do not now remember the number who associated themselves together at this meeting as a church, but the number was large, and the promptness and zeal manifested showed that they were in good earnest, and understood what they were doing. This little band grew rapidly in numbers, zeal, and usefulness.

The circumstances under which this church was organized were truly trying. Think of a people publicly adopting the religious views of a denomination which they had but very recently known, and against which rumor, with her ten thousand tongues, was scattering abroad every kind of slander that prejudice and bigotry could invent. Add to this the fact that there was not another congregation of the same church within five hundred miles, and it will be plain that it required strong faith and unshaken confidence in God, and in the power of his truth, which they believed they were adopting, to enable them to take the step they did.

Mr. Morgan describes the first camp-meeting held by our missionaries in Pennsylvania in these words:

Cases of deep awakening had become so numerous, and the subjects were so remote from each other, that the missionaries thought best to propose holding a camp-meeting as the best method of getting them together, and of bringing them more directly and effectually under the influence of the means of grace. But the idea of a camp-meeting was shocking to most of the people in that neighborhood. They urged that it would be impolitic—look too much like the Methodists. Such meetings, in their opinion, were calculated to produce disorder in worship, and bring religion into disrepute. To this the missionaries replied that there was nothing peculiar in camp-meetings further than the fact that the people stay on the ground and do not return home after one service is over; that there was nothing in this calculated to produce disorder, that it was this remaining on the ground, secluded from domestic and worldly cares, worldly company and influences, which give camp-meetings their chief advantage over other meetings; that more people could be thus brought together and kept on the spot where the means of grace are brought to bear directly and continuously upon the mind. They insisted that, under proper regulations, camp-meetings might be conducted with as good order and as much religious dignity as any other. After many meetings and much conversation on the subject, it was decided to hold a camp-meeting. The first Sunday in September, 1831, was the time agreed on. The people went to the ground to make the necessary preparations. The pulpit was erected of boards, and made large enough to contain nearly a dozen persons. Before it seats for the accommodation of many hundreds were arranged. Tents made of logs, boards, and canvas were arranged so as to form a hollow square of about an acre of ground. Two hundred and fifty families tented on the ground, one hundred wagons and carriages stood round the encampment. The services commenced on Thursday evening with a lecture on the duties of Christians on such occasions. Friday was observed as a day for fasting and prayer. The services from the beginning were unusually interesting and solemn. Christians were in the spirit, and abounded in prayer. The irreligious were attentive, and scores of anxious souls who had been awakened before came here to ask what they must do to be saved, and to seek an interest in the blood of Christ. The power of the Lord was present to heal, and there were happy conversions at the commencement of the meeting. The concourse grew larger every day until Sunday, when the number present was estimated at from five to seven thousand people. We have attended many meetings, but this surpassed any we had seen. Several times when the anxious were invited forward, two hundred and fifty were counted on the seats at one time. Not one light, trifling countenance was to be seen in all the crowd. Convictions for sin were more general, deeper, and more rational than we had ever before noticed, and conversions were the clearest, and attended with the most overwhelming joy and peace. It was common to see persons of age and intelligence, overwhelmed by a sense of their sins, in the deepest anguish of soul as if they could not possibly live. From this sad and affecting state they would seem all of a sudden to awake into light and life and joy the most ecstatic and indescribable. We can never recur to those blessed scenes but with the deepest emotions.

Three hundred conversions were reported to the church paper at the time. Jacob Lindley, who was a Presbyterian, says[1] that the missionaries had such a hold upon the sympathies of the young converts that nearly all of them would have joined the Cumberland Presbyterian church had the opportunity then and there been given; and that, in view of this fact, the missionaries proposed the plan of waiting four weeks, and then having the officers of all the coöperating congregations meet the converts at Mr. Lindley's church for the purpose of receiving members. As a large number of the converts were members of Mr. Lindley's Sunday-school, this measure saved his congregation from heavy loss. In four weeks all had time to think soberly, and Mr. Lindley received one

---

[1] Manuscript autobiography, p. 221, *et seq.*

hundred of the converts into his church. According to Mr. Lindley this was not the only time that these missionaries might easily have taken advantage of the tide of popular sympathy and carried whole congregations into the Cumberland Presbyterian church. He mentions four other instances in which they refused to take such advantage, and he testifies most earnestly to their disinterested love of souls, and their freedom from all partisan and sectarian motives. He wrote this testimony while he was still a member of the Presbyterian church, and he says that he had no expectations at that time of ever becoming a Cumberland Presbyterian.

The foregoing description of this first Pennsylvania camp-meeting was published by Mr. Morgan in 1840. There is another account of these events which was written by Mr. Morgan, and published in the church paper the same year in which they occurred. There is also a manuscript account of this meeting written by Reuben Burrow. From these sources we learn that the meeting continued seven days, and that such crowds of people gathered on Sunday that no one man's voice could reach them all. Though the services were out of doors, yet two sermons were preached simultaneously. Donnell preached at the stand where there were seats, and Morgan under the trees where no seats were prepared.

Among other interesting incidents Mr. Morgan tells about the conversion of an old man who just before the beginning of this camp-meeting became so violent in his opposition to the missionaries, and so enraged because some members of his family had joined the Cumberland Presbyterians, that in a drunken fit he attempted to kill his wife. With his gun in his hand he drove the family away from home, and remained for three days alone in his house raging and blaspheming. But at the end of this time he sent for his family to return, and, to their astonishment, they found him praying. He asked to be taken to the camp-meeting, which was to begin the next day. He was unable to walk, but supported by his two sons he appeared on the camp-ground early in the morning before the services began. He went to the preachers' tent and implored their forgiveness, begging them to pray for him. He professed conversion that day, and soon afterward joined the church, and continued a consistent and worthy Christian until his death.

This first camp-meeting was held in the neighborhood of the church now known as Concord. When this camp-meeting was just beginning, Burrow and Donnell arrived. Burrow was sick, but Donnell preached throughout the meeting. There are old people still living who describe his wonderful discourses, quoting the very texts and giving many of the main points of the sermons. Several of these aged members seem to be deeply imbued with the spirit which reigned in that first camp-meeting. This church is not on the same spot where the meeting in the grove of sugar trees was held, but is in the same neighborhood. This first camp-meeting silenced all the objections to such meetings, and another was soon held in another neighborhood.

This incident is related about Burrow. He and Donnell made an agreement that if either one felt specially impressed to preach on some particular subject when the other happened to be the one appointed to preach, the fact was to be made known, and the one appointed to preach was to give way. While they were in Pennsylvania, Burrow was appointed to preach on a certain day. All the morning, in prayer and study, he had struggled in vain to get hold of some text, some old sermon or new sermon which he could take an interest in, but everything was dark. He could not decide on any text. In this state of mind he went into the pulpit. The introductory services were over, and he rose to his feet, but still utterly in the dark as to what his text or sermon should be. He opened the Bible and began reading a chapter, his heart crying meanwhile to God for some gleam of light. While he was reading, Donnell pulled him by the coat, and said: "Reuben, I think God wants me to preach to-day." Burrow said afterward that if ever his heart went out to God in thanksgiving it was then; and that of all the many powerful sermons he had heard Robert Donnell preach, that was the most powerful.[1] All the first Cumberland Presbyterian preachers believed that God gave special indications of his will in such matters, and they were very careful to obey those indications.

---

[1] Conversations with Dr. Burrow.

There were enough of the missionaries to hold meetings simultaneously in different places. The Rev. A. M. Bryan was the first to work in Pittsburg. No church was opened to him; but he preached on the streets and elsewhere, and soon won many friends. In the church paper, *The Religious and Literary Intelligencer*, the missionaries gave regular reports of their work. There were reported by them for the whole period of their first mission, June to November, 1831, about eight hundred conversions. These letters state that the only obstacle in the way of forming Cumberland Presbyterian congregations throughout that field was the impossibility of supplying them with preaching. Two of the missionaries had made up their minds to make Pennsylvania their permanent home, and the number of churches was limited by this scanty prospect for the means of grace. The congregations organized were one at Washington with fifty members, one twelve miles from Washington with two hundred members, another in Washington county with forty members, and another in the town of Jefferson with fifty-two members.[1]

The Rev. Mr. Loughran, who preached the doctrine of a general atonement, had ministered to the Presbyterians of Waynesburg. He afterward became a Cumberland Presbyterian. In November, 1831, Mr. Morgan, just before he returned temporarily to the South, and after the other missionaries had gone, assisted Bryan in a meeting in Waynesburg, and they organized a small church in that place. It had but twenty-two members.

In the autumn of 1831, Burrow, Donnell, and Chapman returned to the South. Morgan remained till late in December, and then he returned. Bryan was now alone, but before December passed away the Rev. Milton Bird arrived. The reports published by the missionaries had stirred the whole church. Mr. Bryan had made up his mind to make Pennsylvania his permanent field of labor, and although Morgan went South in December, it was only to make his arrangements for a permanent settlement in Pennsylvania.

All the missionaries jointly addressed a letter to Green River

---

[1] This is taken from the official report of their work, made by the missionaries. The names of the churches are not given in that report.

Synod, whose jurisdiction extended indefinitely northward, praying for the organization of a presbytery in Pennsylvania. This letter was sent to the synod before the missionaries left that State. It was published October 20, 1831. In the same month Green River Synod passed the order for the formation of the presbytery. It was at first called Washington, and included the States of New York, Pennsylvania, and Ohio. Its original members were to be William Harris, Alexander Chapman, A. M. Bryan, and Milton Bird. Friday before the first Sabbath in May, 1832, was set for its first meeting. That Chapman and Harris went horseback from Kentucky to Pennsylvania, simply to constitute this presbytery, and that they did so at their own expense, was nothing at all remarkable *then*. The Rev. S. M. Aston was also at this meeting with his letter ready to join the presbytery as soon as it was organized. It was his purpose, also, to make this field his permanent home.

In the manuscript autobiography of the Rev. Le Roy Woods is an interesting account of Mr. Morgan's efforts to secure help for Pennsylvania. Morgan visited the presbyteries pleading for men. His zeal was a flaming fire. He had long private conferences with the young preachers on this subject. With arguments, appeals, and tears he labored to enlist recruits for the Pennsylvania work. The Rev. S. M. Sparks and the Rev. Le Roy Woods finally consented to accompany Mr. Morgan. The Assembly of 1832 commissioned all three of these men to go as missionaries to Pennsylvania.

We have in Mr. Woods' manuscript another glimpse of the habits of that time. He bought horse, saddle, and bridle on a credit, borrowed money for traveling expenses, and, on the 4th day of June, 1832, he and his comrades set out on their long journey. They reached their destination on the 7th of July. Mr. Woods was appointed to preach to the Greene County churches, and he puts on record his grateful acknowledgment of the liberality of this people—especially those of Carmichaels. His debts back in Tennessee were promptly paid, and all his financial wants fully provided for. Mr. Woods also puts on record a noble tribute to his wife's helpfulness to him in all his ministerial life. She was a daughter of the Rev. Jacob Lindley. Mr. Woods married her after he went to Pennsylvania. He gained that, as well as other benefits, by his mission.

The manuscript autobiography of the Rev. Jacob Lindley shows what were his own relations to this mission. He had been president of the University of Ohio; but in 1831 was the pastor of a very large country church in western Pennsylvania. He says that he had heard the statement often that the "Cumberlands" and "Schismatics," or "New Lights," were the same body. He had met with the Schismatics, and had no use for them. When, therefore, he learned that missionaries from the Cumberland Presbyterian church were to hold meetings in his country, and within reach of the lambs of his flock, he was filled with alarm. That the missionaries were men of power only increased his apprehensions. He determined to prepare for battle. First, he took up the records of his own General Assembly and other works, and studied the history of the case. This study amazed him. The "Cumberlands" and "New Lights" had nothing in common. They originated in different parts of the country, at different times, and had never affiliated. They were not alike in doctrines, polity, or history. The Cumberland Presbyterians, he was surprised to find, had a Confession of Faith. He had been told that they denounced all human creeds. What still more surprised him was that they held that very same system of doctrines which he had avowed to his presbytery, at the time of his ordination, thirty years before, and which he had been preaching ever since without any charge of heresy being brought against him. Still more, he saw clearly that the final cause of the separation of the "Cumberlands" from his church was an unconstitutional usurpation of a presbytery's rights. He was puzzled.

When he met the missionaries and heard them preach he could find nothing to condemn in their doctrine or their methods, but was, on the contrary, fully convinced that they sought only God's glory, and would never harm a single lamb of his flock. Morgan especially won him. He took the missionaries to his own house and joined his session in inviting them to preach in his church. He gives us a full account of the meeting which they proceeded to hold, and mentions some gray-headed infidels who were brought under the power of the gospel. After the camp-meeting, in which Mr. Lindley coöperated, the missionaries held a second series of meetings in his church, in which there were nearly a hundred converts.

When Mr. Lindley went to the meeting of his presbytery that fall he took Mr. Morgan with him. The presbytery gave him and Morgan both the "cold shoulder." When ministerial reports were called for, Mr. Lindley was questioned very closely about his coöperation with "excommunicated heretics." When he, in his answers, quoted a passage from the Cumberland Presbyterian Confession of Faith, the moderator stopped him, saying, "They have no Confession of Faith, but denounce all such things." Mr. Lindley produced a copy, greatly to the moderator's confusion. When attention was called to the action of the Presbyterian General Assembly of 1825, in which intercourse with Cumberland Presbyterians was placed on the same footing as intercourse with other evangelical denominations, the moderator and the members generally denied that there had ever been any such action. Mr. Lindley then produced the Minutes of that Assembly, and had the words referring to this subject read. The moderator said he felt it to be the duty of all good Presbyterians to scout those heretical fanatics from the face of the earth. The presbytery then passed an order directing "the session of Upper Ten Mile congregation to close the doors against Cumberland preachers." A committee was also appointed to visit this congregation with a view to bringing it to order.

Mr. Lindley says he still had not formed the purpose of joining the Cumberland Presbyterians, but was in favor of appealing to higher courts, feeling sure that the General Assembly would set matters right. The course pursued by the committee which visited his church, taken in connection with the fact that there were among his people many anxious inquirers after salvation, finally led both him and his congregation to go together into the Cumberland Presbyterian church. That church is now called Bethel. The fruit of its Presbyterian training is still seen in Bethel congregation, as also in Concord. They keep a pastor, and pay him.

But they show also the true revival spirit which belonged to Morgan and Chapman. Old Presbyterian training, grafted on Cumberland Presbyterian zeal, makes the very best church members. Pennsylvania and Ohio furnish examples of our noblest congregations. These are, all of them, of Presbyterian antecedents.

Jacob Lindley found in the Cumberland Presbyterian church his own sphere of usefulness, and he worked among the people with marked success until the day of his death. The second wife of the Rev. Robert Donnell was his daughter. Dear "Aunt Clara," loved by many in all parts of the church, sought by the young people for her genial company, sought by true Christians for her holy counsels, sought by ministers for her wide knowledge of church affairs, has bequeathed a sacredness to the name of Athens, Alabama, where she lived and died, and has left a pattern from which Christian womanhood may take many a lesson. Mr. Lindley's other daughters were all noble Christian women. His son went to Africa as missionary. Mr. Lindley's book called, "Infant Philosophy," is a valuable treatise on the right mode of training children. It ought to be republished.

The church at Carmichaels, organized August 20, 1832, has ever been one of the most active of our congregations. Greene Academy, the first Cumberland Presbyterian church school in Pennsylvania, was located there. This congregation has from the first kept its own pastor. It has done much for missions, and is still liberal in its gifts for this purpose. An exceptionally long pastorate, for Cumberland Presbyterians, was that of the Rev. I. N. Carey. He served this congregation for sixteen years.

The missionaries who remained in Pennsylvania soon had encouraging intimations of accessions to their force, and they went on organizing churches all through the western part of the State. Uniontown was one of these pioneer congregations. It was a sort of mother of churches. It still flourishes. The dust of John Morgan sleeps there. A college, once under the control of our people but never owned by them, was located there. Many of our good men have served that church as pastor.

Rev. J. T. A. Henderson[1] relates the following incident which

---

[1] Henderson's MS. autobiography.

occurred while he was serving as pastor here: He frequently visited in the home of an infidel whose family attended the church. This man would leave the house whenever he saw the preacher coming, but finally his poor health made it necessary for him to stay in the room during these visits. The preacher came and went several times without saying any thing to him on religious subjects, but at last ventured to ask him his views. The reply was that there was no truth in Christianity. The Bible, he said, was full of contradictions. Tom Paine had proved that abundantly. Mr. Henderson asked him to point out some of these contradictions. He replied that he would hunt them up and show them at the preacher's next visit. The next visit came and the contradictions had not yet been found. The man was confident, however, that he would find them by the time the preacher came again. At the next visit the preacher asked him if he had yet found them. He said he had not, but he had found out that the Bible was a searcher of men's hearts and lives. It had shown him that he was a miserable, lost sinner. He was sure now that the book was from God. In a short time this man became an earnest Christian.

This account is given of the origin of Hopewell congregation, Fayette County. The Methodists had a church named Hopewell, and they invited the missionaries to preach there. Bryan and Bird sent an appointment, and great multitudes attended. The pastor of a neighboring Presbyterian congregation was present, but refused to be introduced to the missionaries. Several sermons were preached, and very pressing invitations were given the missionaries to make another visit. In about six weeks two of them came back, and their preaching was so popular that the Presbyterian elders felt constrained, by public opinion, to invite them to preach in their church. When the hour came for this service in the Presbyterian church the pastor took a back seat and still refused to be introduced to the visiting preachers. After some moments of painful suspense, Aaron Baird, uncle of A. J. Baird, whispered to one of the missionaries, "you had as well be killed for an old sheep as a lamb. Knock all the hard points of Calvinism to pieces to-day." Then Mr. Ebenezer Finley, one of the elders, took Mr. Bryan by the arm and led him to the pulpit, and placing a silver dollar in the preacher's hand said, "We want you to preach your own doctrine to-day and not feel the least restraint about it." An old man, describing that sermon many years afterward, said that although he had been reared a "Seceder" of the straitest pattern, he was fully convinced before Bryan closed that discourse, that Christ died for every man. In a short time the missionaries were urged by the new converts to organize a church in that neighborhood. This was done; and, in honor of the liberality of the Methodist Hopewell, the new Cumberland Presbyterian church was named Hopewell also.

The Rev. J. T. A. Henderson, who served as pastor of the Hopewell church for many years, states in his manuscript autobiography that his relations with this congregation were ever pleasant, and all his salary was promptly paid. He names, also, some men in this and the Salem congregation who, he says, were the purest men and the best Christians he ever knew. This he writes after a sojourn on earth of over eighty years.

While the revival in which the Hopewell church had its origin was in progress, the missionaries were invited to hold meetings in the neighboring town of Brownsville. Bryan and Bird accepted the invitation, and spent two days there. Bird preached in the forenoon of the first day in the Methodist Episcopal church; Bryan preached in the evening. Crowds of people left their work to attend the services. A large number of penitents crowded the altar. The next day the services were held in the Episcopal church. During these two days many of the leading people of the town professed faith in Christ. No effort, however, was made to organize a congregation. The Cumberland Presbyterian church at this place was not organized until more than twelve years afterward, September, 1844.

In his missionary work, the Rev. A. M. Bryan[1] visited Meadville, Pennsylvania, to hold meetings. Not only were the churches and other public buildings closed against him, but the Presbyterian minister and some others canvassed the town from house to house to persuade the people not to give the "heretic" a hearing. They denied that Bryan had any right to preach or hold

---

[1] The church paper, February 12, 1833.

services. Not at all moved by such opposition, he held his meetings, partly on the streets, and partly in a private house. There were a great multitude of conversions, and Bryan organized a church with ninety-three members. Unfortunately, however, there was no preacher to place in charge of such a flock.

The Pittsburg church was organized by the missionaries in 1833, John Morgan officiating. The Rev. A. M. Bryan spent the best part of his life as pastor of this church. His ashes sleep there. From time to time Mr. Bryan reported in the church papers interesting revivals in his congregation. At one of these there were two hundred converts. If it be true that the poet is born, not made, it is equally true that A. M. Bryan was born a preacher and not made one. It is wonderful how any man, with no broad scholarship, could have had the pure style, the clear thoughts, the fine resources which Dr. Bryan always had in the pulpit.

An anecdote, which still lingers about the home of Bryan's boyhood, is pertinent in this connection. When, as a candidate for the ministry, he was called on for his first trial discourse, he stated that he had no sermon, that he could not write one. That was in the days of authority, and the brows of the grave fathers portended a storm. It was expected that the boy would be treated as the sailors treated Jonah. Before the fatal vote was taken, his mother, who sat looking on with alarm, said to one of the preachers, "I tell you the boy can preach if he can't write. Appoint a time and hear him try." It is said that the appointment was made, and the boy preached with such earnestness and fervor as to make all the reverend ecclesiastics weep. So he was retained on the roll of candidates. From that day to the day of his death A. M. Bryan never lost his power to move the hearts of all his hearers, old or young, lay or clerical. The Pittsburg church was his life's best work.

When the Pennsylvania Presbytery met in October, 1833, it had twelve ordained ministers, three licensed preachers, and seven candidates. It had seventeen congregations and two thousand eight hundred members. Every preacher belonging to the presbytery was then "living of the gospel." The records of no other presbytery in the church furnish an instance like this. In the minutes of some of the presbyteries the record might be truthfully made that none of their preachers have ever lived of the gospel.

On the 17th day of October, 1841, in the thirty-sixth year of his age, and the fourteenth of his ministry, the Rev. John Morgan passed through the golden gates to his Father's house. Of his work in Pennsylvania, Dr. Bird says "he traveled through the country like a flame of fire." Aged Christians who were converted under Mr. Morgan's first preaching in Alabama, still live and hold his memory in a reverence as sacred even as that felt for him in Pennsylvania. To the young churches in Pennsylvania the death of Morgan seemed an irreparable loss, but the great Father still led them on. Other good preachers were raised up, but among them all there was no other John Morgan. It was in 1840 that Mr. Morgan began the publication of *The Union and Evangelist*, at Uniontown, Pennsylvania. It was a valuable little semi-monthly paper, but before he had been long in that work he received his summons from the King. After his death the Rev. Milton Bird took charge of the paper.

At the close of this period Cumberland Presbyterians had two presbyteries in this State. This was the growth in ten years. The Union Presbytery was organized at Uniontown, Pennsylvania, April 14, 1837, the Rev. John Morgan being the first moderator. The Pennsylvania Synod, which was at first made up of Pennsylvania, Union, and Athens presbyteries, was organized at Uniontown, October 11, 1838. Allegheny Presbytery was not formed until 1847. In mission work and in sustaining regular pastorates these Pennsylvania churches rank among the first in the denomination. They had to work throughout this first decade like Nehemiah's builders on the wall, sword in one hand and building implements in the other. Those who assailed them were, however, the losers by this policy. Various slanderous misrepresentations of the doctrines and practices of Cumberland Presbyterians were published in Pittsburg during this period. That they were slanderous was triumphantly proved then, and there is no need of reviving the old bitterness.

CHAPTER XXVIII.

ORIGIN OF OUR CHURCH IN OHIO.

"And a little picture shall meet the eye,
That dear hands painted in years gone by."
—*S. G. Prout.*

THE same agents of the church college who were the first Cumberland Presbyterian preachers in Pennsylvania also traveled through portions of Ohio in 1829 and 1830 holding meetings and soliciting help for the college. We have no history of their work except the general fact that their meetings often resulted in many conversions. It is known, also, that they did not, during this tour, attempt to organize any Cumberland Presbyterian church.

The first Presbyterian church at Athens, Ohio, was organized by the Rev. Jacob Lindley. The college over which Mr. Lindley long presided was also at that town. His interest for this community was so great that he entreated Mr. Morgan to visit Athens while on his way South in 1831, promising to accompany him thither. To this Morgan agreed. They both met a warm welcome from the Presbyterian church at Athens, and also from its pastor, the Rev. Mr. Spaulding. Mr. Lindley speaks in strong terms of Mr. Spaulding's liberality.[1] Mr. Morgan tarried nine days, and preached eighteen sermons. Although it was winter, and bitter cold, the house was crowded, and there were forty-three professions.[2] Here again, as Mr. Lindley testifies, Morgan resisted the young converts who wanted to be organized into a Cumberland Presbyterian church.

Before Mr. Morgan's departure, pastor and people united in importuning him to come by Athens when he returned to Pennsylvania in the spring. He gave his promise, and kept it, too; but on his arrival he found a very great change. Mr. Spaulding called

---

[1] Lindley's MS. autobiography, from which this whole account is taken.
[2] Fifteen of these afterward entered the ministry.

on him and told him with deep mortification and sincere regret that his session had become alarmed at the outcry for a Cumberland Presbyterian church, and had resolved to close their doors against Morgan. A leading layman in the Presbyterian church then informed Mr. Morgan that the members of his church had secured the court-house for him to preach in. It was evident that a movement was on foot among these members to secede and join the Cumberland Presbyterians. Mr. Morgan at once declined to preach for them. He was then invited to preach in the Methodist church, which he did, and nearly all of the Presbyterians attended. At the close of his sermon that Sabbath, he was requested to attend a temperance meeting ten miles from Athens. To this request he acceded. The Rev. Mr. Hibbard, a Presbyterian, whose church was six miles distant from Athens, also obtained a promise from Mr. Morgan that he would attend his sacramental meeting, which was to be held the next Sabbath. Morgan left Athens Monday and held his temperance meeting in a grove. An immense concourse of people was gathered. A new distillery owned by two brothers was situated right at the place where this meeting was held. The lecture, though on temperance, was all of it intensely religious. The vast crowd was in tears, and Morgan, at the close of the lecture, called mourners. Many came. He appointed preaching for the next day on the same spot. Before he closed the meeting one of the owners of the distillery and the wives of both of them were converted. The distillery was forever closed. O the power of God's Spirit is the true source of victory against rum and all other works of Satan. Instead of the distillery there arose a house of worship in a community where there had never been one before.

At the meetings in Mr. Hibbard's church the usual blessing of Heaven followed Mr. Morgan's preaching. About seventy souls professed to be saved. Mr. Morgan had some difficulty in convincing the young converts that no Cumberland Presbyterian church could be organized for them. After he went on to Pennsylvania a large number of people who had attended the two meetings just described, wrote to him to come back and hold a camp-meeting. This he did, Mr. Lindley and his daughter accompanying him.

This camp-meeting was held in Alexander township, six miles from Athens. It was here that the first Cumberland Presbyterian church in Ohio was organized. At this camp-meeting the Rev. Mr. McAboy, of the Presbyterian church, saw his two sons converted. They both entered the ministry afterward, and their father from that camp-meeting till the day of his death, without changing his ecclesiastical relations or having any charges preferred against him, not only adopted Cumberland Presbyterian measures, but preached Cumberland Presbyterian doctrines. His ministry was far more fruitful after he made these changes.[1] This first Ohio camp-meeting was prolific in its results. There were over a hundred conversions, and calls for Morgan's and Lindley's services poured in upon them from all the adjacent counties. Mr. Lindley relates several touching incidents of this camp-meeting. A certain militia captain, who was also dissipated, conspired with a number of rough men to break up the meeting. They entered into a regular organization for this purpose, and elected this militia officer as captain of their band. At the hour for services these men gathered under the trees near the place of worship. Mr. Morgan, before he began his sermon, invited penitents to come forward. Many Christian people rose to their feet and went out through the congregation trying to persuade their relatives to go to the mourner's bench. While this was going on, the brother-in-law of "the captain" came to Mr. Lindley and requested him to go to that promoter of mischief. Mr. Lindley went, accompanied by the brother-in-law. On seeing those Christians approach him, the captain straightened himself up with a defiant look. Mr. Lindley says that at that moment his own soul was overwhelmed with sympathy and an awful sense of this poor sinner's perilous state. So great were his emotions that utterance failed him, and for some time he could do nothing but weep. At length, finding the use of his tongue, he struggled with all his soul to warn the poor captain of his danger. Finally the hardened sinner burst into tears, fell upon Mr. Lindley's neck, and asked that his wife should be brought. When she arrived she also burst into tears, and soon both husband and wife agreed to go to the mourner's

---

[1] Lindley's MS.

bench. As Mr. Lindley led them up to the place of prayer several of the gang of desperadoes followed. The captain had a hard struggle, but he and his wife both found peace in Jesus before the meetings closed.

Another case deserves mention. An aged infidel attended the meeting, sitting afar off and watching. Finally his favorite son was converted, and with a face beaming with the light of heaven, started to find his father. When the old man saw his boy approaching, and looked into his illumined face and heard his tender, loving appeals, he was utterly broken down, and, falling to the earth, began crying aloud for mercy. Nor were his cries in vain. After some delay, and after a beloved minister had patiently instructed him in the way of salvation, he sprang up from the ground where he was lying and told to all around what a glorious light had dawned upon his soul.

There was in this neighborhood a skeptic of unusual bitterness toward Christianity. He had an interesting daughter who was very anxious to attend the camp-meeting, but he would not permit her to do so. Mr. Lindley's daughter, Louisa, who had accompanied her father to this community, where she was well acquainted, visited this skeptic with a view to gaining permission for his daughter to attend the camp-meeting. After many failures she finally won a conditional consent. The condition was that Louisa would solemnly promise him that his daughter should not go to the mourner's bench. The promise was made, and the young lady attended. Under Morgan's preaching she became overwhelmingly convicted, and when the call for mourners was made she wanted to go. Louisa went to Mr. Morgan for counsel. He told her to keep her promise, and to take the young lady off to some private place and pray with her there. This was done, and in a few moments the poor girl was rejoicing in the hope of glory, and ever afterward lived a consistent Christian.

When a church was organized, at the close of this meeting, a congregation of Presbyterians in the neighborhood, who were without a pastor, formally seceded from the Presbyterians, and proposed to unite with this new congregation. Mr. Lindley received them, and became their temporary pastor, arranging with Mr. Morgan to take care of Ten Mile until some permanent arrangement could be made for the Ohio flock. This was in the fall of 1832. The next spring Mr. Lindley returned to his Pennsylvania church. The Pennsylvania Presbytery supplied the Ohio congregations with itinerant preaching. These itinerants were changed frequently. The records show that nearly all the members of that presbytery were at one time or another appointed to this Ohio work.

Mr. Lindley had been pastor of the Presbyterian church at Beverly, Ohio, before he took charge of the college at Athens. On his journey to his home in Pennsylvania, in the spring of 1833, he stopped at Beverly, and held a meeting. Great interest was manifested in his preaching, and fifty persons professed conversion. The Presbyterian church at Beverly, which Mr. Lindley had organized long before, was at this time without a pastor, and its members passed a formal act, by unanimous vote, withdrawing from the Presbyterian church, and unanimously resolved to join the Cumberland Presbyterians, and call Mr. Lindley for their pastor. He accepted the call, and, after a brief visit to Pennsylvania, returned to Beverly, where he spent four years in charge of his old flock, preaching, as his elders put on record, the very same doctrines which he had preached thirty years before.

Mr. Lindley said he found a state of moral death in all the country surrounding Beverly. The people had little or no preaching, save in Marietta, the county town. Country pulpits were all vacant, and Sabbath-schools had been abandoned. He therefore arranged with the Beverly church to be allowed to spend one fourth of his time as missionary to the surrounding country. Within a circle of thirty miles he established a round of appointments for preaching. He tried to do pastoral work in all this vast district, as well as to preach regularly. He passed none by, calling at great houses and small. He says his sole aim was the salvation of these destitute souls. He took no written sermons. He went forth with his Bible and with a loving heart. He says he looks for sheaves from many a humble home which he visited in this strange field.

In these missionary tours Mr. Lindley visited Senecaville, thirty miles from Beverly. There was a Presbyterian church there, but for a long time it had been without preaching. Mr. Lindley held an eight days' meeting, and had a great revival. The interest stirred the whole country for fifteen miles around. There were great numbers of conversions. The Lancaster Presbytery (Presbyterian), of which Mr. Lindley had been one of the original members, took the alarm. Mr. Lindley says all the members of this presbytery had the same false views about the identity of the Cumberland Presbyterians and the New Lights which he himself had before he investigated the matter. Lancaster Presbytery sent a man to Senecaville to warn the people against the heretics. But he did not investigate the subject before commencing the battle. His attacks were against a man of straw. The good people of Senecaville were much better informed about the Cumberland Presbyterians than he was, and they were disgusted at his ignorance and offended at his injustice. The members of that congregation felt themselves outraged by the severe censures poured out upon them. They met together and formally seceded from the Presbyterian church, and declared themselves Cumberland Presbyterians. This was in the summer of 1835. Mr. Lindley agreed to give one fourth of his time to this church until better provisions could be made.

His first meeting under this new arrangement was to begin on a Friday. It happened that the circus was to be there that day. The gaudy show bills covered walls and fences. The show arrived on time. The great tent was stretched, the brass bands played, flags waved, and mottled harlequins danced on spotted animals as the procession moved around town. But the door-keeper who stood at the entrance of the tent took in not even one single ticket. Mr. Lindley had the crowd. After a little delay the circus tent was taken down, and managers and harlequins went on their way in great disgust, cursing Cumberland Presbyterians.

An elder of the Presbyterian church, near the village of Cumberland, attended the great revival at Senecaville. He earnestly pressed Mr. Lindley to hold a meeting in his town. This elder said the church at Cumberland was in a state of spiritual torpor. The house of worship was out of town, built there before the town existed. Mr. Lindley sent an appointment for a meeting in the town. A large unfinished dwelling-house, whose partitions were not yet erected, was used for this meeting. God revived his work. Many souls were converted; but the Presbyterian pastor stood aloof and opposed. Mr. Lindley visited him, and tried to win him, but failed to elicit the slightest expression of concern for the salvation of the unconverted; though the pastor did try to be polite, and played the violin beautifully for the entertainment of his visitor. Other engagements calling Mr. Lindley away, he sent the Rev. Isaac Shook to Cumberland, in 1835, and the latter organized a church of our people in that town.

One of the towns in which the Rev. M. H. Bone (one of the college agents) preached was Lebanon, Ohio. He had a very interesting meeting there. The people begged him to remain and organize a church. This he could not then do. In 1835 he was earnestly importuned by letters from the Lebanon people to return. They had seen and learned still more of the ways and doctrines of the Cumberland Presbyterians, and were anxious to be identified with them. Mr. Bone, therefore, made another visit to that town. A congregation was organized, and he consented to remain one year as their pastor. The same year he appointed a camp-meeting, and wrote for Hugh B. Hill and T. C. Anderson to assist him.[1] They both lived in Tennessee, but they responded promptly to Mr. Bone's appeal. Owing to failure in boat and stage connections they arrived too late for the camp-meeting.

Mr. Bone started a movement for building a meeting-house at Lebanon, but for some reason he gave up his charge and returned to the South. Before doing so, however, he obtained the consent of the Rev. Felix G. Black to take charge of the little church. Black was a pastor in the true sense, and did good service in this congregation. From eleven original members the church in three years grew to one hundred and thirty-eight. This growth was all under systematic and steady pastoral work. Mr. Black, in 1838, published a good report from that congregation, showing its progress in all the departments of its work. It contributed systematically to all the benevolent enterprises of the church. It paid its pastor's salary in full, and was spiritually alive and active.

The old church bell at Lebanon has a curious history. When

---

[1] Manuscript autobiography of T. C. Anderson.

Spain confiscated the property of the convents this bell was sent to New York and sold at auction. It brought two hundred dollars. It was cast in 1636 for a convent. It was the first church bell ever rung in Lebanon, but it now calls not nuns but Cumberland Presbyterians together. It has a Spanish inscription upon it calling on the Virgin to "pray for us."

In 1833 there were supplies appointed by the Pennsylvania Presbytery for two Ohio churches—Waterford and Athens. In 1834 supplies were appointed for four Ohio congregations—Athens, Alexander, Waterford, and McConnellsburg. The Rev. James Smith and the Rev. Joseph A. Copp, made a preaching tour through that State in the winter of 1833-4. Smith says the Presbyterian pulpits were everywhere closed against them. In 1835 a grand forward movement was made by Cumberland Presbyterians in Ohio. The Rev. Isaac Shook spent that year in this field. T. C. Anderson and Hugh B. Hill were also there, as was S. M. Aston. Three or four of the ministers of Pennsylvania Presbytery were also working part of their time in this field. Aston held a good meeting at Jacobsville, and organized a church there.

The Covington congregation has an interesting history. When the Rev. F. G. Black succeeded Mr. Bone as pastor at Lebanon he found on the church-book the name of Benjamin Leavell. There was no such man living in Lebanon. On inquiry he learned that this was Judge Leavell, who lived fifty miles away. Owing to his dissatisfaction with the hard points of Calvinism he had withdrawn from the Presbyterian church and joined the Lebanon congregation, there being no other Cumberland Presbyterian church nearer his home. On receiving this information, Mr. Black mounted his horse and started on a pastoral visit fifty miles. He had to swim one canal before reaching his parishioner. The Judge told Mr. Black that before he heard of the Cumberland Presbyterians he had made out a system of theology for himself. On a business trip to Cincinnati he stopped to spend the Sabbath at Lebanon. Bone and others were holding a meeting there. He went to hear them. To his surprise and delight they preached his system of doctrine, a medium system between Calvinism and Arminianism. He therefore joined the new church. Then the

Judge told his pastor about a town called "Rowdy," noted for its drunkenness and other vices, and induced him to visit the place and hold a meeting. The first services were in a little schoolhouse. Other visits followed, and finally in 1838, Mr. Black organized a congregation. "Rowdy" is now Covington. The church there to-day numbers four hundred and nineteen members. It contributed to church enterprises last year (1885) ten thousand dollars. It keeps a regular pastor. Two faithful ministers have grown up among its members, the Rev. W. H. Black, of St. Louis, and the Rev. J. A. Billingsley. It has just built an elegant house of worship, and it maintains a high standing for liberality and efficiency in church work.

The Cumberland Presbyterian church in Ohio has never been strong in numbers. There are at this time (1886) only three presbyteries in the State; one with eight ordained ministers and no candidates, another with five ordained ministers and one candidate, and a third with four ministers and no candidate. Preaching on a call to the ministry, and praying the great Head of the church to call *their own sons* to this holy work, are clearly the urgent duties of our Ohio ministry and people. A home supply of preachers and provisions for their education, would certainly improve the prospect of the church in that State. In this field, as well as several others, we have this strange phenomenon: Much larger donations have been made by some of our own members to the colleges of other churches than have ever been made to our own institutions.

CHAPTER XXIX.

MISCELLANEOUS SKETCHES AND INCIDENTS.

"There is no wind but soweth seeds
Of a more true and holy life,
Which bursts, unlooked for, into high-souled deeds,
With wayside beauties rife."

AN account of the great revival at Bowling Green, Kentucky, deserves a place at the beginning of this chapter of miscellaneous sketches. There was no Cumberland Presbyterian church at Bowling Green in 1833, and the presbytery refused to organize one, even when pressed to do so, because no preacher could be spared from the itinerant work and located there; and it was understood that a church in a large town could not be sustained by itinerant preaching. Some of the preachers were willing, however, to hold a meeting there for the sake of souls; but it was announced beforehand that they would attempt no organization. Chapman, Lowry, Harris, and Lewis began meetings in the First Baptist church. Lowry did most of the preaching. By Monday the whole town was so stirred that shops, business houses, and law offices were spontaneously closed for each service. There were three services a day. At these meetings some strange results, similar to those which so startled the people of Logan County, Kentucky, in 1799, manifested themselves. Men of strong frames fell to the ground and lay motionless for hours. One man was carried out and his friends sent for a physician. Mr. Lowry, however, told them that he had seen many such cases and never knew any dangerous consequences to result. After a long delay the man rose with rapturous exclamations of joy and trust. An infidel attended this meeting and was seized with deep convictions. He went to the mourner's bench and offered up this prayer: "If there be any such person as the Lord Jesus Christ, I want him to have mercy on me, and save me." He at last found the Savior.

These meetings continued seventeen days, and their influence swept over all the town and the surrounding country. All the Bowling Green churches received many valuable members. Mr. Lowry was urged to organize a Cumberland Presbyterian church, but as he steadfastly adhered to his refusal many who would have entered into such an organization went into other churches. The now venerable Judge Burnum, of Bowling Green, was one of the converts at this meeting. The father of the Rev. J. M. Halsell was also among the converts.

The Rev. J. B. McCallan, of Illinois, relates the following incident: In 1833 he was living in Calloway County, Kentucky. No religious services were held in all his neighborhood. He and his wife were both unconverted. A camp-meeting was to be held ten miles away. He and his wife both attended, walking all the way, and both were converted. On their return home they set up the family altar. Then Mr. McCallan began holding prayer-meetings in the neighborhood. A revival soon followed with numerous conversions. Then circuit riders were induced to make regular appointments for preaching in that neighborhood. In a short time the character of the whole community was changed. C. E. Hay was the first circuit rider who preached there, and he organized a congregation and ordained Mr. McCallan as one of its elders.

A fair sample of the best Cumberland Presbyterian churches under the old supply system was the Concord congregation, West Tennessee. The boundaries of this congregation extended from Trenton, Tennessee, to the Mississippi River—sixty miles. The Rev. S. Y. Thomas was its preacher. His financial necessities once caused him to change his field, but the Concord people loved him, and they wrote to him proposing to give him a deed to four hundred acres of good land if he would come back and stay with them, and preach regularly one Sabbath in each month. He accepted the offer. Including his work before this arrangement was made, he served this church thirty-nine years, farming and preaching. A number of ministers have grown up in this congregation, among them several members of the Thomas family. Its camp-meetings were great occasions, and people attended from all parts of West Tennessee. Converts of these camp-meetings are found in all parts of the church.

The Oak Grove congregation, Sumner County, Tennessee, organized 1836, which had Hugh B. Hill for its regular pastor, long kept up its annual camp-meetings. At one of these one hundred and seventy-five conversions were reported, and at another three hundred. At the camp-meeting held in 1840, Robert Donnell and several other ministers from a distance were assisting. Of course the pastor did not expect to preach. Mr. Hill's father-in-law, then quite old, was not a Christian, and several members of his very large family were also unconverted. After the meetings had continued several days, Mrs. Hill saw her husband come into the tent "pale as a sheet," and evidently in some deep soul-struggle. She went to him and asked what it was that troubled him; but he begged her to leave him alone, and fell upon the bed groaning. Mrs. Hill inquired of others, and learned that her father and another very old gentleman, both unconverted, had sent a special request for Mr. Hill to preach at the next service. Mr. Hill remained lying on his face till the hour for service, and then went to the pulpit. The two old men who had made the request sat in front near the pulpit. The realities of the eternal world were face to face with the preacher. Something more than that was with him. God's irresistible Spirit breathed through his lips and quivered in his words. Hill always had a holy power in the pulpit, but this sermon, it is said, surpassed all his other efforts. The two old men, both past their threescore and ten, were brought into the joyous liberty of the sons of God. So, too, were many others.[1]

Hill devoted the whole of his life to the ministry, and owing to the meagerness of his salary and misfortunes brought on by the war, he died in comparative poverty. Loving friends erected a monument over his grave, near Murfreesboro, Tennessee. The Middle Tennessee Synod, while in session at Murfreesboro soon after his death, held a memorial service at his grave. Hill's life was the text for an address on consecration in the ministry by Dr. A. J. Baird. The Rev. M. H. Bone, the life-long associate of Hill, said in the obituary notice which he published: "I never

---

[1] Facts furnished by Mr. Hill's daughter.

knew Hill to utter a sentence which I wished unsaid, or to do a deed which I wished undone."

In the autobiography of the Rev. Isaac Shook is recorded a notice of the "stars falling" in 1833, which is worth quoting. Shook was holding meetings in Huntsville, Alabama, and there was considerable interest in the services. One morning at early dawn he was awakened by sounds of shouting and prayer over all the town. He rose and dressed himself, and on going out discovered the whole horizon ablaze with what seemed to be stars falling. Advent teachers had been through the country proclaiming the speedy end of the world, and this looked very much like the accomplishment of their proclamation. All over town negroes and white people, too, were either praying or shouting. It was five o'clock in the morning. Presently the church bell began to ring, and soon the house was filled with people. When Shook entered he found nearly a hundred unconverted men and women on their knees, pouring out earnest prayers to God for pardon and salvation. It is a curious fact that there were no conversions among all that number of frightened mourners. The meeting, however, continued many days with good results, not from the fright, but from the blessed gospel of the Son of God.

The 28th of October, 1834, a meeting of the Cumberland Presbyterians of Washington County, Arkansas, was held in the Cane Hill meeting-house for the purpose of taking the necessary steps to establish a school. This was two years before Arkansas became a State of the Union, and six years before Cumberland University at Lebanon, Tennessee, was born. The Rev. Samuel King, then traveling as evangelist at large, was called to the chair, and presided over the meeting. A board of trust was chosen, and the Rev. B. H. Pierson, D.D., was elected president, and Ezra Wilson, clerk. This school was opened April, 1835, and was probably kept up in some form until seventeen years afterward, when Cane Hill College was chartered. Cane Hill was only about ten miles from the Indian country. The tracks of the red man were scarcely gone from the spot. The three men who organized the first presbytery of the Cumberland Presbyterian church were all living, and one of them presided over this meeting. This school in the wilderness, some say, was the first institution of learning ever established on Arkansas soil. Its prime object was to educate young men preparing for the work of the ministry.

Dr. Pierson, both the Buchanans, and the Pylants were all active movers in inaugurating this pioneer educational enterprise. Of John Buchanan's education it has been said: "He was like a grindstone; if not very sharp himself, he was specially useful in sharpening others." The fruit of his work in aiding young preachers to secure an education will endure forever. John Buchanan's name everywhere in Arkansas calls forth exclamations of praise and affection. He spent many years as Bible agent. The salary offered him was more than he was willing to accept. He had it reduced two hundred dollars per annum, and out of the remainder he regularly gave a tenth to the Lord's cause. He devoted all his days to the Lord's work. Once he stopped at a blacksmith shop and had his horse shod. When he asked, "What is the bill?" the answer was, "Pray for me." "Uncle John" replied: "I am in the habit of paying as I go, so we will kneel down here now and have the prayer." There in the way-side shop the two men knelt, and a soul-stirring prayer went up to God for the blacksmith. Buchanan rode the circuit ten years without pay. He worked as colporteur one year for one hundred dollars and his traveling expenses. He was Bible agent five years on a salary of five hundred dollars per annum. He collected money for the society equal to six times his salary.

In 1834 President T. C. Anderson and the Rev. J. M. McMurray were traveling in Missouri. They put up at a private house on the way-side—strangers in a strange land. At table the landlady kept gazing at Anderson. After a while she heard Mr. McMurray call his name. Immediately she asked, "Are you any kin to the Rev. Alexander Anderson?" When she was told that her guest was his son, she sprang to her feet, seized Mr. Anderson's hand, and related the touching story of her conversion under the ministry of his father. The travelers yielded to a pressing invitation to remain and preach in the neighborhood. President Anderson says, they had great difficulty in getting away from this dear lady. She clung to the son of her spiritual father with a touching tenderness, and begged him to remain in that field and be their preacher.

Some of the people's favorites in the political horizon of Missouri, in 1831, had been fighting duels. Resolutions were brought before the Missouri Synod, not only condemning duelling, but earnestly advising all members of the church to vote for no man who ever gave or accepted a challenge. This was bringing matters to close quarters. Andrew Jackson and Thomas H. Benton would be proscribed by that action. Fiery Democrats in the synod declared that these resolutions were introduced for political purposes. The debate was very warm, but the resolutions passed. The minority appealed to the General Assembly, but their appeal was not sustained. A hard case. Loyalty to party or loyalty to the church courts was the question to be decided. Perhaps General Jackson did not lose many votes by the decision.

When Jackson was elected President of the United States, one of his old soldiers, the Rev. J. M. Berry, then of Illinois, was heard to say, "The 8th day of January made Andrew Jackson President and me a preacher." He said he had long felt it to be his duty to preach the gospel, but had rebelled. During the fiercest portion of the battle, on the day of Jackson's great victory, Mr. Berry found himself in a very exposed position. The prospects were very poor for escaping all the deadly missiles. In view of almost certain death, his rebellion against the duty of preaching came up before him as a very solemn matter. It seemed a fearful thing to go into the presence of the Judge from a life of disobedience! With these thoughts he there vowed to God that if he should be spared he would rebel no longer. He kept his vow, and was an ordained preacher when Jackson was elected President. He then made the remark here quoted, adding, "I would not swap places with him to-day."

In that beautiful valley which lies south of the great bend in Tennessee River, there lived, far back in the days of slavery, a wealthy doctor. He and his wife were both infidels; and what was worse, they had propagated their views far and near, especially among the young people. In their large parlor had been held many a dancing party, where ridiculing the Bible and Christianity was one of the chief sources of amusement. By and by the doctor was taken very ill, and saw that his illness was unto death. Summoning a servant he sent him in haste after the Rev. W. D. Chadick, of the Cumberland Presbyterian church. When Chadick arrived the wife of the sick man met him at the gate and said to him, "Mr. Chadick, if I had known in time I would have prevented the messenger from going and so saved you a useless ride. I am not going to allow you to see my husband." The preacher mounted his horse, and returned to his home. The sick doctor, finding himself thwarted in his efforts to secure Chadick, determined on another scheme. He owned a negro, who was a preacher. This old man was called "Uncle Dick." The doctor sent for Dick, and told him that he wanted to be taught the way of salvation. Dick replied "O Lord a mercy, massa, I can't help you. If de Lord hisself don't help you, you 're gone." The doctor then asked Dick to kneel and pray for him. With fast streaming eyes the old negro knelt and poured out a most earnest prayer for divine help. The prayer continued long, and contained in it the simple lesson of trust in the Redeemer alone for salvation. The doctor grasped the blessed truth, and when Dick rose to his feet, the sick man was clinging to Christ, the one hope for lost souls. He died and was buried, and after the funeral the infidel widow returned to her home. Alone and desolate she walked through her large rooms and elegant parlors, absorbed in earnest thought. She was an educated woman, and in her sorrow she felt the truth of what Christians had always told her about the emptiness of worldly pleasure. If they were right about that might they not be right about a future state? She could not believe that her husband was only dust and ashes. Then she sent for old Uncle Dick, and after hours of earnest prayer she became a rejoicing convert. She joined the Cumberland Presbyterians. As she had been a propagandist of unbelief, she now resolved to devote her life to the work of leading souls to Christ. Accompanied by Uncle Dick, who drove her carriage, and assisted by his prayers, she often went from house to house laboring for souls. The good fruits of her Christian influence and efforts are still found in that valley. Old Uncle Dick went to his reward long ago, but she, though now quite old, still gives her strength to the service of her King.

In 1825 the Rev. R. D. King was "riding the circuit" in Tennessee, when a man described to him a wonderful prayer which he had overheard a woman offer up to God. The woman was living in a new settlement where infidelity abounded, and her husband and sons were coming under its influence. The neighborhood had no regular preaching of any sort, and this Christian woman had tried in vain to secure some one to preach the gospel to her family. In her prayer, which was by accident overheard, she opened up her heart's deep troubles to the Lord, laying before him the whole dreadful condition of the community in which she lived. She told the Lord how infidelity was making its way into her own family, and, finally, in all her helplessness, she laid the case down at the Master's feet. On further inquiry, King learned that this woman lived only eighteen miles from his usual route, and he determined to send an appointment for preaching at her house. This he did; but he happened, in the meantime, to meet with a Methodist minister who warned him not to visit that neighborhood because personal violence had been threatened against any preacher who might venture to preach there. When the day arrived the people at whose house King had spent the night, tried hard to dissuade him from going. King yielded, put his horse back in the stable, and sat down to try to study. But he could not study. He had an appointment to preach and was playing coward. Never had that been the case before. Again he brought out his horse, and this time no persuasion could stop him. When he reached the place, though it was not Sabbath, the whole yard was thronged with people. Three rooms were packed full. King preached; and began singing, "Hark, my soul, it is the Lord." As yet there was no violence, no interruption; but some frowns and scowling faces were seen, and King was not yet free from apprehension. When he was singing the second verse, a beautiful woman cried out, "Glory to God." "That," says King, "was one of the sweetest interruptions ever a preacher suffered.'' Rising to her feet, this woman made her way toward a man who had been looking defiance all through the sermon. When the happy woman drew near him, stretching out both her arms toward him she exclaimed, in thrilling accents, "O father." The man fell prostrate. He was the husband of the woman who prayed that wonderful prayer, and he proved to be the key-stone of the arch, and all the arch came tumbling down. This was one of the day's of the Son of man. They had services again that night. Next day when King started on his way sixteen of the young people were at the gate, mounted and ready to go with him to his next place of preaching; and every one of these sixteen professed conversion that day. The woman who had prayed the wonderful prayer also went along with King to that next day's meeting.

The results were so different from all his apprehensions that Mr. King was puzzled to understand the case. Inquiring into the matter, he learned that after the woman had prayed so earnestly she began the regular practice of gathering all her children into her private room, every Sabbath, and there reading a portion of Scripture and trying to expound it, after which she knelt with them in prayer. A change came over these children, especially in their Sabbath habits. Their comrades, who visited the family, noticed the change, and asked the cause of it. Learning about the Sabbath lessons in that private room, they obtained permission to attend. The little private room was crowded at every recitation, and there, under the teaching and prayers of that humble woman, God was sapping the foundations of infidelity, and preparing the way for his gospel. When King next passed that way on his circuit, he again preached at this good woman's house, and then organized the Lasting Hope congregation, Maury County, Tennessee. The name was appropriate to the long clinging, and finally gratified, hope of that mother. At that second service this mother saw her husband and children become members of the church. This account is taken from King's manuscript autobiography.

FOURTH PERIOD.

CHAPTER XXX.

A GENERAL SURVEY.

> Already, laboring with a mighty fate,
> She shakes the rubbish from her mounting brow,
> And seems to have renewed her charter's date,
> Which Heaven will to the death of Time allow.
> —*Dryden.*

AT the beginning of this period of eighteen years there were twelve Cumberland Presbyterian synods and fifty-three presbyteries; at its close there were twenty-seven synods and ninety-seven presbyteries. The average increase was not quite one synod each year; and considerably over two presbyteries a year, not quite three. When this period began the church had just emerged from great internal trials; at its close the whole country was just plunging into the fiery external ordeal which the civil war was bringing on. It was well that the church had this breathing spell of eighteen years between these two ordeals.

True, the bitter strifes of the third period projected their waning shadows into this fourth period. The Rev. James Smith remained a member of the church several years after his resignation of the office of stated clerk, and after the beginning of this period. He refused to hand over the Minutes of the General Assembly to his successor, but, after many calls and some threats of legal process, the Assembly finally got possession of its own records. The Minutes of three meetings of the General Synod, 1821, 1823,[1] and 1826, however were lacking, also the Minutes

---

[1] I have found the Records for 1823, since I began to write this History.

of the General Assembly for 1838. The Assembly called on all the ministers of the church to help find the lost records. The Minutes for 1838 were partially recovered through the newspaper reports. The others remain lost.

The opening sermon of the General Assembly of 1843 was preached by Milton Bird. The text was Acts vi. 4. Two great evils had been crushing the very life out of the church: A secularized ministry and a secularized General Assembly—that is, an Assembly embarrassed by financial enterprises, all of which had proved disastrous. Various writers had been pointing out the evils arising from this secularization of preachers and church courts; but the most forcible and effective of all these protests was this opening sermon by Milton Bird. He argued first against a secularized clergy. He showed what was the voice of both history and Scripture on the subject, and dwelt with power on the high and holy nature of the minister's calling. He showed next that the mission of the church courts was like the mission of the ministry, exclusively spiritual; that both the Old and New Testament Scriptures laid down rigid laws excluding these courts from the management of secular affairs. Other and wholly separate organizations were required by Scripture for the transaction of financial business. Boards of experts could manage these things far better than any General Assembly, while the spiritual oversight of the churches far exceeded in importance all secular business, and was work enough to fill the hands of any Assembly. From that day onward Milton Bird's high rank among the ministers of the church was recognized. The Assembly passed resolutions declaring itself forever divorced from all management of financial affairs, whether connected with newspapers, colleges, the publication of books, or aught else.

Inasmuch as there were still found in the Assembly of 1843 men who kept alive the strife about the colleges and the papers, those who were for peace determined to have no Assembly in 1844. Their views prevailed, and the Assembly adjourned, requiring the next Assembly to meet in 1845, at Lebanon, Tennessee.

The General Assembly of 1845 was a most interesting convocation. The great speech of that occasion was made outside of

Assembly hours by the Rev. A. M. Bryan, D.D., of Pittsburg, Pennsylvania. His theme was the great fire which had lately swept through Pittsburg. At the close of that speech Judge R. L. Caruthers gave Dr. Bryan a thousand dollars for the sufferers. Dr. Beard's address on education was also deeply impressive.

The missionary work of the church had almost entirely passed into the hands of presbyterial and synodical boards of missions. The Ladies' General Board at Russellville, Kentucky, had ceased to exist, and the church at that place had declined much in numbers and influence. The Assembly of 1845 proceeded to organize a Board of Domestic and Foreign Missions, and located it at Lebanon, Tennessee. For a few years it carried on its foreign work as an auxiliary to the American Board. The Rev. Thomas Calhoun was its first president. After his death the Rev. F. R. Cossitt was president.

A curious complication arose in connection with the church's mission work. The presbyterial and synodical boards had extended their operations far beyond their own boundaries. Some of them were slow to yield their independent work and become auxiliary to the general board. The men in charge of the general board had a hard struggle to get all this machinery adjusted; but through a wise and prudent administration of the board's affairs, harmony was secured.

The board at first had no paid officers. The whole receipts would not have paid one salary. When at last, in 1851, the Rev. Isaac Shook was employed as secretary, the receipts were only a little more than the salary. In 1853, after this secretary had held his office for two years, the entire receipts were $2,953. It was a curious view of this responsible work which allowed the only paid officer of the board to live on his farm fifty miles away from Lebanon. This state of things, however, was not permitted to continue long. Mr. Shook moved to Lebanon in 1852, and put forth all his strength in the work. In 1853, by the direction of the board, and with the approval of the General Assembly, he began the publication of a monthly missionary magazine. Shook was a holy, earnest man. His heart was in his work. He stirred up new interest for the Indians, and made some progress in enlisting the whole church in the great work of missions. He was all his life an invalid.

After Mr. Shook's resignation, in 1854, there was an interval without a secretary. Then the Rev. T. P. Calhoun was elected. He was a young man just out of college, a son of Thomas Calhoun so often mentioned in the preceding chapters of this history, and a son-in-law of the Rev. David Lowry. In the collection of missionary funds he relied largely on traveling agents, but the results of this whole system were unsatisfactory. In 1857 Mr. Calhoun resigned, and there was considerable difficulty in securing another secretary.

The Rev. T. C. Blake was secured for this position in December, 1857, and to him the church is indebted for the first successful attempt to dispense with traveling agents in the work of collecting money for missions. When he announced that the preachers throughout the church would be solely relied on to do the work hitherto done by agents, many were the prophesies of disaster. But the secretary adhered strictly to his programme. In two years, without paid agents, the receipts of the board were increased from five thousand dollars to fourteen thousand dollars. Notes on hand were regularly reported by Mr. Blake, but these were notes taken under former secretaries. The cash receipts were fourteen thousand dollars. The receipts by States for 1860 were, in round numbers, as follows: Tennessee, $5,235; Alabama, $2,251; Arkansas, $1,595; Mississippi, $1,460; Kentucky, $1,135; Indiana, $925; Missouri, $562; Texas, $302; Kansas, $181; Louisiana, $106; Illinois, $90; Iowa, $75; Pennsylvania, $53; Ohio, $48. There were small contributions from several other States.

For several years each synod made its own arrangements about having the Confession of Faith and Catechism published. The propriety of having some general and central committee of publication had often been discussed, and at the Assembly of 1845 such a committee was appointed. The scheme contemplated proved impracticable. The members of the committee lived in different States at great distances from each other. A joint stock company was to be formed, and all the presbyteries were asked to become stockholders in the enterprise. Thus the mania for joint stock companies which prevailed during the preceding period had not wholly disappeared. Speculation in Western lands, in gold mines, in insurance companies, in various other schemes, have all been tried by our boards, and have all left the marks of God's displeasure upon the past records of the church. Giving money for God's cause is an act of worship and a means of grace, and all schemes to supplant God's established method are theoretically false and practically disastrous. Under a new disguise the Assembly of 1845 fettered itself again with the halter from which the Assembly of 1843 had freed itself. Financial speculation was to be embarked in, not this time by the Assembly itself, but by the presbyteries. The Committee on Publication at the next two meetings of the Assembly reported nothing accomplished.

In 1847 the programme was changed. The General Assembly appointed a publishing committee whose members lived near Louisville, Kentucky. This committee was instructed to secure a charter, and to appoint financial agents to solicit donations, to keep clear of debt, and to make no sales on a credit. Like little boats, they were to keep near shore. The Rev. Milton Bird was at the head of this enterprise. It was on a sound basis, though its lack of capital was a great embarrassment. For several years it issued Confessions of Faith and hymn books, and seemed to be doing well. This board sent out traveling agents, and thus secured means to begin its business. Its books were published under contract, by the house of Morton & Griswold, which was then the best publishing house south of the Ohio River.

The administration of the board's financial affairs frequently changed hands, and there grew up at last general dissatisfaction with the management. In 1857 the General Assembly declared the report of the board both vague and unsatisfactory, and called for a final settlement of its affairs. The next year (1858) the board made no report, but A. F. Cox, financial agent, attended the Assembly, and answered the inquiries made by the committee appointed to investigate the case. The result of this investigation was that the Assembly appointed a new committee of publication, to be located at Nashville, Tennessee, and ordered the Louisville board to transfer all its assets to this Nashville committee. The Rev. W.

M. Reed was chairman of this committee. The Rev. W. S. Langdon was the first financial agent, and he began his services soon after the committee was organized, but resigned after a few months.

The Nashville committee obtained from the Louisville board a lot of badly damaged books, the manuscript for a hymn book, a number of old notes, and a few stereotype plates. Along with these it received another inheritance, the debts of the Louisville board. The books and old notes, however, paid off these debts, and furnished besides about nine hundred dollars capital. The committee then secured a regular charter. After the confusion attending the removal of the effects of the board from Louisville, the stereotype plates of "Infant Philosophy," "Ewing's Lectures," "Donnell's Thoughts," and "Porter's Foreknowledge and Decrees," were found to be missing. The Louisville board in 1853 had reported all these plates except the last as assets, mentioning the recent purchase of the copyright of "Infant Philosophy." When the plates were missed, a man was sent from Nashville to search for them. He succeeded in tracing them from Louisville to Philadelphia, but failed to find them. They will probably never be recovered.

In the second year after the removal to Nashville this board secured the Rev. Isaac Shook as its general financial agent. The last year of this period it reported books and plates on hand amounting in value to thirty-seven hundred dollars. Ten thousand copies of the Hymn Book had been sold. The board owed one debt of one hundred and sixty dollars. The report to the General Assembly declared that no church could carry on its publication work on any other plan than strict conformity to sound business principles.

Cumberland Presbyterians have a curious hymn book history. Several small collections of camp-meeting hymns were published by individuals, but the church for a long time had no recognized book of its own. On the pulpits could be found the hymn books of Methodists, Baptists, and other churches. At a Sunday service in a church where a Methodist book was used a minister who had but lately preached a series of sermons on the final perseverance of the saints hurriedly selected a hymn. Beginning without noticing the import of the words, he read:

> " With shame of soul I do confess,
> A real saint may fall from grace."

In 1845 a manuscript hymn book was adopted by the General Assembly, and afterward published by the Board of Publication. In 1858 this book was revised by a committee appointed by the Assembly, and then stereotyped under direction of the board at Nashville. This was that board's first work of this kind.

The Assembly of 1855 organized the Board of Education at Nashville, Tennessee. The Rev. M. H. Bone was its president, and the Rev. J. C. Provine, D.D., secretary and treasurer. This board's receipts averaged about one thousand dollars a year in cash, while the notes it annually took ranged from six hundred to five thousand dollars. It was interrupted by the war, but is still at work. The aid it has given annually to young men preparing for the ministry does not, however, equal the tenth part of what is done by the church, because many individuals and even some societies prefer to report only to the Lord what they give for this purpose. It is very important that the receipts of this board should be greatly increased.

The Board of Church Erection, organized by the Assembly of 1856, was located at St. Louis, Missouri, with the Rev. J. B. Logan at its head. This board was instructed to secure donations, and to loan, not give, the money to weak churches for building purposes. At no time did its receipts amount to three hundred dollars per annum. One year it received only seven dollars; another year it reported no receipts at all. Let it not be supposed, however, that our people turned a deaf ear to all calls for help in building churches. At Philadelphia, St. Louis, and Cincinnati, at Austin, Texas, Burlington, Iowa, and Murfreesboro and Jackson, Tennessee, and at other places, comfortable houses were erected with money given by distant congregations. It is not known why these handsome donations to church erection were not given through the board or reported to it.

From an early day the highest judicature of the Cumberland Presbyterian church kept renewing its declarations of readiness for friendly correspondence with other evangelical churches. The General Assembly appointed a standing Committee on Fraternal Correspondence. In 1845 several articles from members of the New School Presbyterian church appeared in the papers, advocating closer union with Cumberland Presbyterians. One New School synod passed some resolutions calling for such union. The New School General Assembly of 1846 passed the following paper:

WHEREAS, there is a spirit abroad that seeks to unite in closer bonds the different divisions of the Christian church; and whereas, there prevails extensively in some parts of our country an impression that a union between the Presbyterian church and the Cumberland Presbyterian church would be very desirable; and whereas, the General Assembly of that body did, at its session in May last, at Lebanon, Tennessee, appoint a committee of correspondence on the subject of union; therefore,

Resolved, That this Assembly now appoint a committee to correspond with the aforesaid committee on the subject, to obtain all necessary information, and to present it to this Assembly at its next stated meeting.

Although this action was not known to the Cumberland Presbyterian Assembly of 1846, yet there had been so much written by members of the New School church about union with our people, and so many friendly signals had been held out by synods and presbyteries, that this Assembly felt itself authorized to take some steps toward responding to these friendly expressions. It therefore appointed Dr. Richard Beard a corresponding delegate to the next New School Assembly. In 1847 our Assembly met at Lebanon, Ohio, while theirs met in Cincinnati. Their committee came to Lebanon, and there held a conference with our standing committee while the two Assemblies were in session. These two committees entered into an agreement not only for correspondence, but much more. The items of their agreement were in these words:

Resolved, Provided both Assemblies shall agree thereto, that the following plan of correspondence be adopted, viz.: The General Assembly of each of these churches shall receive and appoint two delegates to each stated meeting of the General Assembly of the other church, who shall possess all the powers and privileges of other members of such Assemblies, with the exception of the right of voting. 2. It is hereby recommended that the synods and presbyteries of these churches which are contiguous, or which occupy the same territory, appoint and receive delegates to one another in like manner, and that they endeavor to cultivate a spirit of friendly correspondence and extended toleration, mutually to increase in courteous and fraternal feelings toward each other. 3. Vacant churches belonging to each denomination may at their own discretion, and under regulations to be provided by the presbyteries to which they belong, employ the ministers connected with the other body as temporary supplies for their pulpits, without a change in the ecclesiastical relations of such ministers or churches.

The Rev. Milton Bird, chairman of our standing committee, submitted this report to our Assembly immediately. The first item was unanimously agreed to. The second and third items were indefinitely postponed. The New School committee hastened to Cincinnati and submitted their report. There was considerable debate. The large slave-holding element in the Cumberland Presbyterian church constituted the only objection. One prominent doctor said in his speech[1] that the Presbyterian church owed the Cumberland Presbyterians an acknowledgement for the wrong which drove them into a separate organization. The chairman of the committee said that he had found no difference between the two churches in doctrine. Finally the whole matter was deferred till the next General Assembly.

Dr. Beard, as corresponding delegate to the Cincinnati Assembly, found himself in an awkward attitude. He was present and heard this discussion on the question of receiving corresponding delegates from the Cumberland Presbyterians. He declined to press his case on the attention of the Assembly, but after spending one day as a private spectator only, he returned to his home. He felt mortified and humiliated, and said he would never again allow himself to be placed in so embarrassing an attitude.

The New School Assembly of 1848, to which this report of the Committee on Fraternal Intercourse was referred, adopted the first item of this report, and appointed a delegate to the next Cumberland Presbyterian Assembly. Action on the second and third items was forestalled by what our Assembly had done the year

---

[1] *The Texas Presbyterian*, July 17, 1847, quotes these speeches at some length.

before. In spite of ecclesiastical marriages, fraternal correspondence has been kept up in some form between the two churches ever since. In 1850 the Rev. Edward McMillan, D.D., delegate from the New School church, closed his address to the Cumberland Presbyterian Assembly with these words:

The literary institutions of your church, with the divine blessing, will prove a most effective instrumentality for promoting that enlargement of mind and vigor of thought which, when united with evangelical piety, form such important qualifications for doing good on a large scale. We congratulate you most heartily in your success in securing the endowment of your university, and the encouraging prospects before you of establishing schools for your sons of the prophets. May Christ conduct your efforts in this undertaking to a prosperous termination. I would not fail to assure you that we rejoice much in the decidedly evangelical character of your religious periodicals.

Finally, brethren, I testify that I have with much happiness witnessed the excellent spirit with which you have conducted the business of your present sessions, and the tender regard continually shown by all your speakers for the feelings of their brethren. I shall long cherish the fondest recollections of this beginning of fraternal correspondence between these kindred branches of the church of Christ. May it be long continued, and, as it continues, may our mutual love, attachment, and co-operation in every good work be increased till the Master comes and finds us so doing.

It was not till 1860 that the Old School Assembly took steps toward an exchange of corresponding delegates with our Assembly. While Cumberland Presbyterians naturally waited for Presbyterians to move first in this matter, yet they hailed this movement with great joy.

At different times official efforts have been made to secure a complete history of the Cumberland Presbyterian church. The Assembly of 1847 appointed Dr. Cossitt to write such a history. This, like other similar appointments, came to nothing.

Two general fast-days were appointed in this period: one to pray for peace with England, in 1846, the Oregon difficulties being then portentous of war; and the other, in 1853, to pray that more preachers might be called and sent into the ministry. All through this period the Assembly kept up its efforts to secure full statistics, and a complete ministerial directory, but at no time were there full reports from more than half the presbyteries. Not until after the war did all opposition to counting cease to show itself.

In 1855, while the General Assembly was in session at Lebanon, Tennessee, it received a letter from the Rev. Robert Donnell, written from his death-bed. It was a tender, fatherly letter, full of love and full of hope for the future of his church. He urged the importance of securing a full history of our church. He remonstrated against revising the Confession of Faith. He said of the Confession: "Though it is not perfect in phraseology, yet it has system and perfection enough to make us all think alike." The General Assembly appointed a committee to respond to this letter, and thus closed forever the church's earthly intercourse with one of the noblest of all its servants.

Memorials proposing to change the name of our church to American Presbyterian were voted down in 1850. Discussions about baptism were brought before the Assembly of 1857, and the traditional position of the church was steadfastly maintained.

In 1860 there were fifteen chartered Cumberland Presbyterian colleges, and thirteen academies and seminaries. Many other matters of vital importance which occupied the attention of the various Assemblies, having special chapters devoted to them, need not be now discussed. In 1855 the day of meeting for the General Assembly was changed to the third Thursday of May instead of the third Tuesday. In 1850 Milton Bird was elected stated clerk, C. G. McPherson having resigned. The synods that were formed in this period, or whose organization was ordered by the General Assembly, were: East Tennessee, 1843; Texas (recognized as existing), McAdow, Kentucky, Hernando, 1845; Cumberland (dissolved in 1852), 1848; Brazos, 1849; Ozark, Ouchita (incorrectly spelled Washita), 1852; Ohio, 1853; Colorado, 1854; Iowa (failed to organize), 1855; Mississippi, 2d (name changed to Iowa afterward), 1856; White River, Central Illinois, 1859; Sacramento, 1860. The presbyteries named in the following list are mentioned for the first time in the Minutes of the Assembly at the dates here indicated:[1] Madison, Trinity, Yazoo, 1846; Allegheny, Springfield (Missouri), 1847;

---

[1] Several of these presbyteries were doubtless organized at earlier dates than those here assigned.

Hodge,[1] Charlotte, Independence, 1848; Frazier, Ouchita, Marshall, 1849; Chillicothe, Ewing (Missouri), Harris, 1850; Ewing[2] (Arkansas), Union (Mississippi), Bartholomew, Brazos, Foster, and California, 1852; Oregon, Muskingum, 1853; Guadalupe, Little River, 1854; Tehuacana, Pacific, McMinnville, Waxahachie, West Iowa, 1855; Searcy, Kansas, White Rock, Greenville, 1856; Monroe, 1857; Frazier (reported dissolved), 1858; Mount Olive, Red Oak, Georgia, Davis, West Prairie, Decatur, Bacon, White Oak, Colesburg, Central Iowa, 1859; Kirksville, Sacramento, 1860.

---

[1] Name changed to Springfield (1849).
[2] The other Ewing Presbytery (McAdow Synod) was dissolved in 1852.

CHAPTER XXXI.

MISSIONS—1843 TO 1860.

> But through the clouds and through the flame
> And flowing floods as on I went,
> A voice of hope and cheering came,
> Fear not to go where God hath sent.
>
> —*Upham.*

IN all the territories which were opened to settlement during this period, as well as in all the new States mentioned in former chapters, Cumberland Presbyterian missions were planted, some under the general board, but a larger number under the care of presbyteries and synods. Church judicatures had long arms when it came to missionary work. A presbytery in Tennessee had a missionary in Texas. Most of this work by synods and presbyteries will have to be passed over in silence. However precious it may have been, it is only traceable now in the fruit which still abides. The special chapters devoted to the new States will bring to our notice some of these fruits, as well as some account of the general board's work in those States.

One feature of the home missionary work of this period was city missions. There were a great many of these, some under the general board and some under local boards. In Tennessee, missions were established at Chattanooga, Murfreesboro, Clarksville, and Jackson. These have all become self-sustaining churches, with good buildings finished and paid for.

In Kentucky the city missions of the period were Louisville and Paducah. At Louisville a good house was built and paid for, and a little congregation organized; but the house was lost during the war by processes which it is not now worth while to discuss. This mission has been revived, and now has a new house almost completed. Paducah became for a time self-sustaining.

In Missouri the city missions were at St. Joseph and St. Louis.

There were two at the latter city, one for the Germans and one for the Americans. These missions, especially the one for Americans, passed through many struggles and reverses, and will claim attention in another chapter of this history.

In Indiana our only city mission was at Evansville. It grew steadily, and is now one of the strongest congregations in the church.

In Illinois our people had missions at Peoria and Alton. At Peoria a church was built, but the mission failed to be sustained, and Cumberland Presbyterians have no congregation there. At Alton, after a long struggle, a self-sustaining church was established.

In Cincinnati, Ohio, our people attempted a mission, and succeeded in building a house. The Rev. F. G. Black, the missionary, spent one thousand dollars of his own money while struggling to establish this enterprise, but it was at last abandoned.

In Philadelphia, Pennsylvania, there was a Cumberland Presbyterian mission. A good house was built and paid for. Over a hundred members were gathered into the congregation, but on account of its isolated condition the little church was peculiarly tried every year. As our people had no churches on that side of the Alleghenies, this congregation had no tributaries. Every member that moved out of its bounds to some distant part of the city was lost, and those who rented houses near the church could always find in the neighborhood a church of the same denomination to which they had before belonged. There was thus a constant drain on the membership. This forlorn outpost was finally abandoned.

In Texas there were missions at Austin, Jefferson, and San Antonio. The first two were in due time self-sustaining; the last, after being long abandoned, has in recent years been revived.

During this period there were successful missions at Little Rock, Arkansas; Corinth, Mississippi; Waukon, Iowa; and Shelbyville, Tennessee. All these are now self-sustaining churches. To the mission at Burlington, Iowa, the church paid more money than to any other city mission except St. Louis. In spite of this large outlay the work there was an entire failure.

There were missions in various smaller towns, which can not be enumerated here. City missions were a prominent feature of the work of the church in this period. During former periods towns and cities had generally, from the necessities of the case, been shunned. In spite of losses and failures the city mission work during this period yielded permanent results of good, far outvaluing the labor or the cost.

In 1834,[1] under what he considered divine leadings, the Rev. David Lowry undertook a mission to the Winnebago Indians. He had no church appointment, but he had pledges from the Indian agent that the usual aid from the United States government would be given him if he established a school among the Winnebagoes. Mr. Lowry first made his home at Prairie du Chien. On his arrival the Indians were celebrating a funeral with drunken orgies. Naked savages were lying prostrate on the ground and some of them howling like wolves. Their annuity had just been paid them, and this enabled them to buy whisky. The missionary says he felt very much like he had undertaken to evangelize a herd of wild animals. The agent was absent. The promised school-buildings were not ready. It was a dark day. Mr. Lowry had his family with him, and they were filled with dismay.

The inhabitants of the town of Prairie du Chien were mostly French Catholics, but Mr. Lowry says they were but little better than the Winnebagoes. At first the Indians would not allow their children to attend Mr. Lowry's school. His first session was without a single pupil. But with unshaken courage and unyielding devotion the missionary persevered. In 1837, after three years of apparently fruitless struggle, the obstacles began to yield. That year the school had forty-two pupils. Mr. Lowry's preaching also bore good fruit. Doubtless many converts of this mission greeted him when he passed from earth to dwell by the side of the river of life.

In 1844 Mr. Lowry lost his appointment. He and others attributed this loss to the intrigues of Catholic priests. In 1846 his appointment was restored and he immediately returned to his mis-

---

[1] The arrangements for the school were made in 1832, and a Cumberland Presbyterian elder, General Street, appointed agent.

sion. An official report of the Indian sub-agent, J. E. Fletcher, after sketching the condition of the tribe, their crops, etc., speaks thus of the school:

The Winnebago school is in successful operation under the superintendence of the Rev. David Lowry. I have frequently visited the school and inspected the boarding and clothing departments. I find that the children in attendance are well supplied with wholesome food, and are suitably clothed. Neatness, order, and cheerfulness are apparent throughout the establishment. Mr. Lowry's management of the school is, I think, judicious. Patience and kindness are substituted for passion and severity. The general system of education adopted in the school is similar to the system ordinarily adopted in primary schools. The capacity of the scholars to learn is similar to that evinced by white children of the same age. The progress of the scholars attending the school is not equal to the progress usually made by white children. This difference on the part of the Indian is accounted for by his irregularity of attendance and the influences to which he is subject when not at school.

Believing that a practical knowledge of agriculture, and the formation of industrious habits is to the Indian youth of at least equal importance to the acquirement of literary knowledge, I recommended to the principal of the school that the boys of suitable age should be employed in manual labor a part of every day. The plan met his approbation, and was acted upon, and it is understood that manual labor, both in the field and in the shop, will be a part of the system of instruction in the school. There are at present three female and two male teachers employed. If it was considered probable that the Winnebagoes would long occupy their present home, I should deem it my duty respectfully to suggest to the department the expediency of establishing branches of this school or the establishment of additional schools at a point on the Iowa River, and also on the Red Cedar. Three bands of the Winnebagoes have concentrated on the east fork of the Red Cedar and built the best village in the nation, and have upward of one hundred children of a suitable age to attend school.

Mr. Lowry, in his official report to the United States Indian agent, dated Winnebago school, August 15, 1846, says:

I entered on the duties of superintendent of the Winnebago school on the first day of May last. Eighty-five children were found registered on the daily list; but as usual at all Indian schools, the whole number were not in constant attendance. Twenty new scholars have been added in the course of the summer, making one hundred and five now connected with the institution.

This report goes on to state that some of the pupils had acquired "a respectable knowledge of figures, geography, etc.," and were learning to write. There were a few more girls than boys in attendance. The girls were taught to sew, and with the assistance of the lady in charge made all the clothes worn at the school, while the boys were "called out at regular periods to labor on the farm." Mr. Lowry stated that the condition of the Indians was greatly improved through the influence of the school. They owned more property, their physical sufferings were much diminished, there was a growing disposition to cultivate the soil, they employed horses to draw plows and wagons. The missionary adds: "They would live in houses, but have been discouraged by the government, owing to their unsettled state." He goes on to show that the great obstacle to the progress of the tribes was the want of a permanent home. This state of uncertainty prevented the erection of additional buildings needed by the school. The pupils returning to their houseless and homeless people, found their education of but little service. Mr. Lowry spoke of "whisky and intercourse with the whites" as "the stereotyped curse of the red man," and insisted that a people could not be raised from a savage to a civilized and happy state without religion. He suggested "the propriety of sending off, with the consent of their parents, a few of the most promising children of the school, to complete their education in some religious community." He also suggested the purchase of a printing-press for the use of the school.

In May, 1848, Mr. Lowry published in the *Cumberland Presbyterian* a brief history of this mission, showing the evils of the liquor traffic among the Indians and the wrongs they suffered from the vices and greed of the whites. He says: "Sixteen years ago a government school was established among these Indians, under the care of a Cumberland Presbyterian minister. Buildings were erected on the west side of the Mississippi, in the interior of the country, teachers were employed, land plowed and fenced for them, and other advantages held out to induce them to settle in the vicinity. In 1837 they ceded all their country east of the Mississippi to the government, and in 1840, according to the stipulations of the treaty made at that time, new buildings were erected and the school and agency removed fifty miles farther into the interior, that the Indians might be farther away from whisky and the contaminating vices of the frontier. It was not long, however, before the intervening forests and prairies began to be filled with rapidly growing settlements of whites. Whisky traders soon came with their red-stained barrels to engage in their murderous traffic." With whisky came drunkenness among the Indians—quarrels, fights and depredations. The people of Iowa soon began to clamor for the removal of the Indians from their boundaries. The government sent a commissioner, and the Winnebagoes were told that "the Great Father, the President," was pained to hear of their difficulties and depredations and thought his red children too near his white children, and wished them to go out farther, where game was plenty, and where they would be away from whisky and could live in peace. It was several years, however, before these negotiations were successful. At last, in 1846, the Indians ceded all their lands in Iowa to the government; but the government did not purchase for them the country promised, and they refused to move.

In 1848 the treaty was enforced, the government agreeing to obtain other lands for the Winnebagoes. The Indians were not satisfied with the treaty, and it took something like military force to induce them to accept its conditions. A letter written by Mr. Lowry from Fort Snelling, to his son, June 28, 1848, shows how reluctantly this treaty was complied with, and what embarrassments the missionary suffered on that account. This letter shows that Mr. Lowry's family, with other white families living among the Winnebagoes, foreseeing the trouble which was likely to result from an attempt to enforce the treaty, removed to Fort Snelling before the time appointed for the removal of the Indians. The result proved that this precaution was necessary. The Indians refused to move, and two hundred and fifty of their warriors armed themselves for battle. Sylvanus Lowry was sent for. He went immediately to the scene of trouble and threw himself between the Indians and the dragoons. The cry, "shoot him down," was heard, but he continued his appeal, and the Indians at last agreed to disperse. Some days of disputing followed, and then they took up their line of march.

But after they began their journey they held a council and a large majority declared against removing. All but about six hundred refused to proceed. The great majority did not remove until forced to do so.

Mr. Lowry and his son often interposed to prevent bloodshed. He followed the Indians to their new home in the far north-west. Here he again opened his school and had it well under way; but after a few years of successful labor he was again the victim of intrigues, and lost his appointment.

Many of the older members of the church remember with what earnest words David Lowry used to plead in the pulpit for the perishing heathen. The years sweep on, Lowry has gone to his Father's house; a generation of heathen has also gone to eternity since those thrilling appeals were made, but still the church doles out its poor little pittance of men and money to Foreign Missions. And yet the thrilling interest at stake in the work which our King has commissioned us to do is far greater than all the earthly interests to which men are so ready to devote their money and their lives. "Go ye into all the world, and preach the gospel to every creature."

Two noble young ladies, members of the Cumberland Presbyterian church in Philadelphia, went, in 1853, under the direction of the American Board of Missions, to work among the heathen. We know in a general way that they were successful missionaries, but we have no details of their work. They both belonged to that class of real Christians who give Christ the supremacy in all things. Their family name was Diamont, and their native State was New Jersey.

In 1854 David Lowry visited the Cumberland Presbyterian Board of Missions and appealed to its members for more help for the Indians. The board resolved to send him to the Indian country on a tour of inspection, clothing him with authority to appoint missionaries if he could find men suitable for the work. He made a very thorough investigation and submitted a report to the board. Some extracts from this report are here appended:

I traveled several hundred miles through the Choctaw Nation and preached wherever opportunity offered. The Rev. S. Corley, of Texas, was appointed to ride and preach in this country one half of his time.

His appointment and acceptance are herewith submitted. He is well known among the Indians; and no preacher could exert a stronger influence over them. He resides within thirty miles of their country, and his circuit will embrace a few congregations on the border of Texas, west of Red River. In preaching to the Indians he may have to employ occasionally an interpreter, and in view of such contingency his appointment permits him to draw on the board for a sum not exceeding fifty dollars. Two native Cumberland Presbyterian preachers, Israel Folsom and Payson Wiliston, have been appointed to ride and preach as extensively as their circumstances will permit, and report to the board quarterly. Their appointments are herewith submitted. Mr. Folsom is an ordained preacher, and his ministerial services among his people have been greatly blessed. Mr. Wiliston is a licentiate and full Indian. He is a man of much promise, and capable of doing great good; but he is poor and has a family depending on him, and can not preach extensively without aid from the board. He was in debt for a horse, and twenty dollars of missionary funds were appropriated to liquidate this debt.

Some preparatory steps were taken for the purpose of establishing schools and permanent missions in the Indian country, but no final action was taken. Although it is desirable to locate schools for the intellectual improvement of the Indians, yet my conviction is that itinerant preaching is more loudly called for now among the Choctaws than any other service the Cumberland Presbyterian church can render. Many of their children have gone through the ordinary course of education at the schools and academies, and have returned to their homes without any deep religious impressions and are now entirely destitute of religious instruction. Their former teachers (though most of them ministers of the gospel) being confined to their schools, can not follow them with the word of life; therefore, unless itinerants can be introduced, it is difficult to see how they can be brought under the power of the gospel. They have abandoned the heathen religion, but they have not yet embraced Christianity, but it is believed that no people are more accessible to the truth than the educated Choctaws, could they be blessed with a zealous ministry.

Under the act of the late Choctaw legislature, ten boys were sent by me to Tennessee, to learn trades, and one came on his own responsibility to study law. Six of these boys have been bound as apprentices in Nashville and two in McMinnville. One is preparing for the ministry, and another has been put to school. I am happy to learn that thus far these boys are well pleased, and that they are receiving sympathy and encouragement in the communities where they reside. I shall confidently expect another company of boys to enter the university in the course of the winter.

Mr. Lowry's report gives also a brief history of all the missions under other churches throughout the Indian country. The Cumberland Presbyterian Board pressed the work begun by Lowry. The Rev. R. W. Baker was added to the corps of itinerant preachers. He proved a faithful and successful missionary. Corley also was a true and noble Christian minister. They by their joint labors, aided by the Rev. Israel Folsom and other native preachers, brought into the church that year over six hundred members.

In 1855 Baker was placed by the board over Armstrong Academy, Choctaw Nation. In 1859 this school had one hundred pupils. Baker, while managing this mission school, still kept up his preaching, though within a smaller circle. The same year the board resolved to have a school for the Chickasaws. This was called Burney Academy. Its opening was delayed by the tardiness of the builder. The Chickasaw Nation furnished the buildings, and the board furnished the teachers. The Rev. F. D. Piner was appointed the first superintendent. In 1859 the Rev. R. S. Bell and his wife were sent by the board to teach the Chickasaw girls. Bell remained at his post all through the war, though all help from the board was cut off. All our Indian missionaries were exposed to hardships, but perhaps none of them suffered so much as R. S. Bell.

Israel Folsom was a strong man and a genuine Indian. He manifested a most touching devotion to the interests of his people. The writer of this history can never forget his last interview with him. If one could write an accent, or put the modulation and the emotional vibrations of the voice into a written sentence, then might the full meaning of Folsom's words about that portion of the Indian population which he, with flowing tears, said was rapidly lapsing back into barbarism be expressed on a printed page. One of his appeals to the board deserves a place here. The letter is addressed to the secretary of the Board of Missions.

NEAR FORT WASHITA, CHOCTAW NATION,
December 30, 1852.

BROTHER ISAAC SHOOK:—I hope you will not become tired of me. Will you once more listen to my words as I speak? A child starving for want of bread can not be satisfied with any thing short of it. Here are people starving for the lack of the bread of life, and they will not be satisfied with any thing else. I have been called upon again and again to go and preach to the people living twenty, forty, eighty, and one hundred and forty miles off. Not that I was any better than other preachers, but they hunger and thirst after the bread of life, and many of them tell me they want a Cumberland Presbyterian minister to preach to them. They reject no minister of any name. They would be glad to hear any preaching. I am speaking for those who spoke to me desiring to hear Cumberland Presbyterian preaching as their choice. It has been impossible for me to go and preach to them. We want help. We need it right now. Can you not send us one young minister, full of the Spirit of God, to preach to these people? By this way he could acquaint himself with the real wants of this Nation, and furnish your board with important information in reference to establishing a mission.

I have a complaint in my body which disables me from riding out and preaching. I also have a large family to provide for. It is out of my power to labor as much as I did formerly, and I do need help. Can you do any thing for us? I believe you can; I believe you are willing. The prayers of a righteous man availeth much, and through your prayers we may expect help in due time. Send a missionary to my house, and let him make my house his home; he will be boarded and have his washing done for nothing, and his horse fed free. And I will also instruct him in acquiring the Choctaw language, that he may preach in the native tongue.

In going out to preach through different parts of the country where he is known as a preacher, the people will not charge him. But there are some who care very little for the gospel, that would no doubt charge. The missionary sent should have a good English education, at least. . .

Yours in Christ, ISRAEL FOLSOM.

Here is a letter from an Indian chief to the Board of Missions:

CHOCTAW NATION, May 13, 1853.

BROTHER SHOOK:— I never saw you, but have often heard of you. It would give me much satisfaction to see and speak with you about the salvation of my people. I understand you have labored to send a man among my people to teach them the way of life. I thank you. I trust God will bless your labors. I once thought of going to the General Assembly, but have failed.

The word of God says, "The Son of man is come to seek and to save that which was lost." If any could be said to be lost whom the Son of man came to seek and to save, I think the poor red man may truly be placed among them. God did not reject us, but came to seek and save us. We hope that his friends will not reject us. I hope that your board will soon send a man in the name of Christ to come, and seek and save the poor lost red man. Our foes are many and powerful. Our woes are heavy on us. We are distressed on every side. We want friends and help. Shall we find them in the Cumberland church? It seems now that the last and only hope for aid to be relied upon is the church of Christ. Shall we hope that the Cumberland Presbyterian church will send us help? Brother, pardon me for the liberty I take to write to you. I desire only the good of my people.

Your brother in Christ,   GEORGE FOLSOM,
Chief of Pushimataha District.

Besides the earnest old Choctaw, Israel Folsom, who was the first native Cumberland Presbyterian preacher, and to whom the Missionary Board gave some small salary, several other natives also entered the ministry during this period. Several Indians, both Chickasaws and Chocktaws, came to our church schools in Tennessee. Among them there was occasionally found a young man preparing for the ministry.

Though these missions were more recent than Robert Bell's in Mississippi, yet none of the missionaries preserved for us journals or other data for a full history, as Robert Bell did. We see now only the fruits of their toil, in native preachers, churches, and presbyteries.

Besides the regular native preachers who co-operated with Corley and Baker, they also called to their aid a considerable number of Christian laymen from the native churches. These traveled with them during "the camp-meeting season" each year. One of these whom they called Frazier, was especially valuable to the missionaries. He could interpret for them. Occasionally when translating the preacher's words he would break forth in an exhortation of his own. Mr. Corley, who was more dependent on the interpreter than any of the other missionaries, became greatly attached to Frazier. The board often called for more men for this work, but failed to get half the number called for. Still the work done and the results obtained were of great and lasting importance.

Though the voice of every General Assembly recommended co-operation with the American Board in foreign work, yet there was a growing feeling in favor of having our own foreign missionaries under the Cumberland Presbyterian Board. It was argued that the strength of the church could not be brought fully into service for the Master until our people engaged directly in the foreign work. It was said also that the church had no means of knowing what its congregations were doing for Foreign Missions, that it was not known whether our people were asleep or awake. It was urged, too, that the church and the ministry needed the inspiration and the training which nothing but work in the foreign field could give. These and many similar arguments finally prevailed. But the relations with the American Board were not at once severed. Our congregations were left free to contribute to that board. For many years our people continued to send help to the foreign work through that channel.

The first Cumberland Presbyterian missionary to a distant land was Edmond Weir, whose work was in Liberia, Africa. This mission was opened providentially. Weir was a young colored man, who was licensed to preach and afterward ordained by Anderson Presbytery, in Kentucky. Though a slave, he had succeeded in securing a good education. The American colonization movement was then enlisting many in all the Southern States. Many slaves were manumitted and sent to Liberia. Among these were two older brothers of Edmond Weir, who had secured a good education. They studied law, and on their arrival in Liberia entered the practice of this profession. Edmond Weir wanted to go to Africa as a preacher of the gospel. He was manumitted and sent to Liberia for that purpose. Through the influence of his brothers he was elected sheriff. From this office he secured a living and preached without salary. In 1857, five years after his removal to Africa, he came back to America in order to secure missionary help. He wanted money and men. The board commissioned him as missionary, and sent him out among the churches to raise funds to build a house of worship.

The *Watchman and Evangelist*, published at Louisville, Kentucky, mentions Weir's visit to that city, and says that a large audience greeted him at the Cumberland Presbyterian church, and that his address was listened to with great attention, and that a liberal collection was taken up for the mission. The ladies of the First Cumberland Presbyterian church of Louisville organized a society "for the purpose of affording such aid as the Liberia Mission might need in the way of clothing and school books."

The Board of Missions, through its president, the Rev. F. R. Cossitt, published a stirring appeal to the ministers and members of the church in behalf of this mission. In this appeal the board urged upon our people the force of Christ's command, "Go ye into all the world and preach the gospel;" and pointed out the crying need for missionary work in Africa, declaring that no church which neglected the Lord's great commission could long live and prosper. It called attention to the providential circumstances which led the board to undertake this mission. On going to Liberia, Mr. Weir had found a number of people who had been Cumberland Presbyterians before their removal from the United States. While some of these had joined other churches, there were many who had preferred to wait for the providence of God to open the way for them to unite with a church of their own faith. This mission seemed to be God's appointed means of opening the way. It was proposed to establish the mission at Cape Mount, a thriving sea-coast town, near which Weir had settled, and where there was no church. The board stated in its appeal that the missionary had already received six hundred dollars for his building, and that this was not quite half the sum needed.

He was finally successful in raising the money, but the board's call asking those who owned colored Cumberland Presbyterian preachers to set them free so that they might be sent with Weir to Liberia, was not successful. Weir returned alone, and amid many discouragements, carried on his solitary work in Africa. At one time he received a request from the king of a neighboring tribe to send Mrs. Weir to be governess for the king's daughters. The proposition was not according to Mr. Weir's fancies. Mrs. Weir had her heart set on other things, as an extract from a letter written by her to Mrs. Hunter will show. In this letter she describes the kind of clothing needed by the boys in the mission —"trousers and shirts made of any kind of cloth." She speaks of her desire to help the native girls as well as the boys, and of the pleasure she would take in making clothes for these poor heathen children if the material could be furnished her. She adds with touching simplicity:

"You do not know how glad I am to help in the work of God among the heathen in this dark part of the world." Her letter continues:

My health is indifferent, and has been for some time. I need the prayers of all the praying friends in America. I expect to open a regular day school for the native children. All that I ask of my friends is a few common books. I beg the friends not to deny me these. I know that I can't do this work of myself, but I know that God can and will help me. He has helped me. About one year and six months ago we had a small boy given to us out of the Goler country. When he came he had no clothing, and I gave him a piece of calico to put around himself; he went so about a month. I could not bear that. Mr. Weir told me to take some of his garments and make clothes for the boy. I did so. We named him Willa. It was a long time before I could get him to understand. I tried and tried until I thought my work was in vain. But at last his stammering tongue was loosed. On the 26th of July was our day of celebration, and we also examined our Sabbath School. Willa was in the midst and recited some verses which he had committed to memory.

The voice of the board was in favor of China as a field in which to begin work for the heathen. To this, however, there was one exception. Dr. Cossitt, while saying nothing against other fields, kept pleading the cause of Japan. Meantime four young men in Cumberland University offered themselves simultaneously to the board for the foreign work. The General Assembly was consulted, but there was unaccountable delay. These four young men made other engagements. Then the Rev. J. C. Armstrong, a graduate of the theological school at Lebanon, Tennessee, felt special impressions to go to Turkey as a missionary. In 1859 he offered himself to the Board of Missions for this special work. His offer was accepted, and the board sent him out as an agent to raise funds for his mission. He was quite successful in this agency and by the General Assembly in May, 1860, he was specially consecrated to his work as a missionary to Turkey. The story of this mission belongs to the next period of this history.

CHAPTER XXXII.

PLANTING THE CHURCH IN THE NORTH-WEST. IOWA AND OTHER FIELDS.

> Through ways we have not known,
> We pass yet not alone
> From height to height,
> To dwell with Him in light.
> The Lord shall lead us on.
> —*Miss Lathbury.*

THE beginnings of the work of Cumberland Presbyterians in Iowa before the close of the third period (1842) were so small that it has seemed best to reserve the history of the origin of the church in that State for this chapter.

When David Lowry, in 1834, planted his mission in Iowa, the whole of that country except some small settlements was occupied by Indians, though treaties for its cession had been agreed upon. There were no Protestant churches on Iowa soil. At the points where Indian agents were stationed there were United States troops and some French families.

Mr. Lowry organized the first church of our people, and the first Protestant church in Iowa, in 1834. It was composed of soldiers, officers of the United States army, government employes, and a few Indians. When the Indians and soldiers were removed that was the end of the organization.

Iowa was organized as a separate Territory with its own Territorial government in 1838. Three years before this a Cumberland Presbyterian minister, the Rev. Joseph Howard, settled among the emigrants in Iowa. The next year, May, 1836, the Rev. Cyrus Haynes traveled in this country and organized a church in Mr. Howard's house. Counting Mr. Lowry's organization at the mission, this church in Mr. Howard's house was the second Cumberland Presbyterian congregation in Iowa. At the organization of this church Mr. Haynes baptized Mr. Howard's infant son. That son is now the Rev. J. S. Howard, of Oxford, Mississippi.

In 1853 the Rev. J. G. White was laboring in Iowa as an independent evangelist, that is independent of any salary from church boards. The first camp-meeting of which mention is made was held by him and B. B. Bonham, August 1843, at Mt. Pleasant. Thirteen professions were reported.

Like all the pioneer congregations in the new Territories, each of these Iowa Cumberland Presbyterian churches embraced a large area, requiring several preaching places. In 1844 the Sangamon Synod ordered J. G. White, B. B. Bonham, Joseph Howard, and J. M. Stockton to constitute the Iowa Presbytery. In 1846 there were nine congregations represented in this presbytery.

In 1848 the Rev. Neil Johnson rode the circuit in Iowa, and received from the settlers two hundred and fifteen dollars for his services. There were then six ordained ministers (one had been deposed), and twelve congregations in Iowa Presbytery.

All through this early period there were in Iowa many Mormons and Catholics. Ruffianism was everywhere. Whisky and pistols, outlaws and murderers, mingled with the heterogeneous mass of emigrants. It required preachers with sterling courage to make their way in the midst of such a population. Men like J. G. White seemed to enjoy such hardships and perils. The Rev. John Cameron and the Rev. Wm. Lynn are also mentioned among the pioneers of Iowa,[1] but no facts or incidents connected with their work have been secured. The Rev Benjamin Hall was among the successful laborers in that field.

It was a favorite scheme of David Lowry to concentrate in Iowa, Wisconsin, and Minnesota a strong home missionary force. One of the warmest debates ever heard in the rooms of the Missionary Board at Lebanon, Tennessee, was on that question. That debate is mentioned in Dr. Richard Beard's diary, and he speaks in terms of the deepest mortification and regret about the failure of Mr. Lowry's plans. Several of his letters, written to Lowry, on this subject are preserved.

---

[1] The Rev. R. A. Ferguson's MS. Ferguson himself has spent most of his life in that field.

In 1856 the board commissioned the Rev. J. C. Armstrong to go as missionary to the North-west. It was Mr. Lowry's wish that the missionary should begin his work at Prairie du Chien. Taking letters of introduction, this young man, just out of the theological school, set out for his first field of labor. The Rev. J. M. B. Roach, who was appointed to accompany him, failed in health, and Armstrong went alone. On his arrival at Prairie du Chien, he found little but ruins. The town and Fort Crawford were gone. The church where General Zachary Taylor had regularly attended Mr. Lowry's preaching was gone. Only a few settlers remained.

A citizen of Iowa, named P. C. Balsinger, was a sporting gentleman, who kept race-horses, and who was wealthy. Armstrong had a letter of introduction to C. C. Balsinger, and, supposing this person to be the one intended, he presented his letter. Mr. Balsinger read it with a look of scorn and wrath, then tossed it back to Armstrong, saying: "Sir, I am not the man; this man lives away down on Turkey River." Armstrong, after some further conversation with him, set out for Turkey River. He found the right Balsinger this time, and met a most cordial welcome. This man was the father of the horse-racer, and was a Pennsylvanian who had been converted at one of John Morgan's meetings.

The missionary appointed a camp-meeting at Mr. Balsinger's. When this meeting began the races at Colesburg were going on. Great crowds of people passed the encampment, going to the races. Armstrong, though without ministerial assistance, went bravely on with the daily services. Monday, the fourth day of the meeting, a strange scene was witnessed. Loaded wagons began coming in from Colesburg, and kept coming. All these wagons brought tents, provisions, and families, coming to attend the camp-meeting. Among others who came was the sporting gentleman, P. C. Balsinger, with his family. When the call for mourners was made, Mr. Balsinger, the horse-racer, rose and made a talk. He said he had been under conviction ever since he read Armstrong's letter of introduction, and was now determined to seek his soul's salvation. Then, turning to his seven sons who had come with him to the camp-meeting, he asked the people to pray for him and his boys. He found the Savior that day, and his conversion gave new life to the meetings. A great revival followed. The converted horse-racer was a man of great liberality. Each day he would mount the pulpit and invite everybody to come and eat with him at his tent.

Out of this meeting grew the Hopewell church, which Armstrong organized, making P. C. Balsinger an elder therein. This elder made a large-hearted and faithful worker for Jesus. At this meeting the wife, daughter, and two sons of a Roman Catholic were converted. Almost at the risk of their lives by the enraged drunken husband and father, they joined the Cumberland Presbyterian church.

On an Indian pathway, at some springs in the prairie, there had grown up a little village called Waukon. Thither Armstrong next directed his steps. His work there was owned of Heaven, and many souls were converted. In September, 1856, he organized the Waukon church with thirty-one members. When the missionary left this field in 1859, Waukon congregation had built a house of worship, and paid for it.

In July, 1857, through Armstrong's importunities, the Rev. P. H. Crider was sent by the Missionary Board to his assistance, Armstrong guaranteeing missionary money enough from Iowa to meet the salary. In this arrangement his trust in the pioneers was not disappointed. The following letter gives a glimpse of Mr. Armstrong's labors in this field:

WAUKON, IOWA, Sept. 15th, 1856.

The prospects are still bright here. My strength failed after I wrote last, and I closed the meetings. But as the interest was still great in the town, I afterward resumed the work, and we had meetings four nights, resulting in five conversions, making in all twenty-nine. Our little band, organized the 21st of August, now numbers forty-four members. Owing to the want of a house, we have not had our meetings regularly, but will resume them again to-night.

On Thursday next I will start again for Colesburg, sixty miles distant, and will hold a meeting in that town. . . . .

Waukon is improving very rapidly. Our Sabbath-school is ably conducted. The number in attendance yesterday was 114, with increasing interest. The Maine Law is enforced to the letter in town. The Temperance Association has 200 members. We have a joint stock of seven thousand dollars to enforce the Liquor Law. Nearly sixty houses were built in all in 1856.

Colesburg is a larger town than Waukon, and much older, but Satan has had almost supreme dominion in that community. The Protestant churches there are not much more than a name. They have been daubed with untempered mortar. The truth startles them, enraging some, and breaking down many. Members of the different churches were seen crowding to the anxious seat, and crying for mercy at our late revival. Pray for us, for we are a needy few, often assailed and persecuted.

J. C. ARMSTRONG.

In 1857, Armstrong and Crider, and the Rev. Joshua Loughran, of Wisconsin, organized the Colesburg Presbytery, extending from forty degrees north latitude to the North Pole. In 1858 the Rev. D. A. Houghton came into the Cumberland Presbyterian church from the Congregationalists, and took charge of the upper Iowa mission.

In these missions the pioneer preachers suffered many privations, and were often exposed to danger. Once Armstrong was shot at while in the pulpit preaching. At a camp-meeting a mob came to kill him, but others gathered to his defense and he was unhurt. He says he often went where there was danger of being killed, but God took care of him. He was never harmed. The pioneers contributed liberally to his support.

In Iowa at this time (1886) there is one small Cumberland Presbyterian synod composed of three small presbyteries, with an aggregate of seventeen ordained ministers and six licentiates, but *no candidates*. In that field, and everywhere, the perpetuation and growth of the church demand that the money and the prayers of our people be devoted to raising up a home supply of preachers.

There have been Cumberland Presbyterian missions in several other north-western States. Michigan, Wisconsin, and Minnesota have all been visited by individual enterprise. In 1859 the Missionary Board reported that the Rev. A. H. Houghton had been commissioned to travel and preach in northern Iowa and southern Minnesota. There is no record of the extent of his success in Minnesota. In 1860 the board's report again mentioned Houghton as missionary in this field, and adds, "He is doing a good work." In 1857 the board resolved to establish a mission in St. Cloud, Minnesota. Some money was raised for that purpose, but no missionary was sent. The work dragged along till the war put an end to such enterprises. Good meetings were held in several of these north-western States, and some feeble churches were organized, but the population being made up of emigrants from States where there are no Cumberland Presbyterians, it was the more difficult for our people to gain a permanent foothold. Among the early settlers in Kansas, Nebraska, Colorado, Oregon, California, and Washington, there was a large Cumberland Presbyterian element, therefore these States and Territories offered more inviting fields for our ministers.

Our Church has sometimes tried to press its way into fields where there was no providential opening, but the results have never been satisfactory. There are fields where others are manifestly chosen of God to bear his name to the perishing, and where Cumberland Presbyterians are not so chosen; and there are other fields where our people have a high mission to fill simultaneously with others. Let us follow the divine leading.

CHAPTER XXXIII.

OREGON AND CALIFORNIA—1844 TO 1860.

> By dust of earth encumbered,
>   None prized the precious stone;
> Christ looked on it and loved it:
>   How fair his gem hath grown!
>   —*Anna Shipton.*

CALIFORNIA gold was not the precious stone, but the dust which encumbered it. God rules, and he has used even man's lust for riches as a means of carrying the gospel to multitudes of perishing immortals. The work of the Cumberland Presbyterian church on the Pacific coast began in Oregon, and extended from that field to California.

Oregon was disputed territory till 1846. The claimants had been Spain, England, and the United States, but in 1818 Spain relinquished all her claims in favor of the United States. Both Great Britain and America, knowing the great difficulties which beset this question, shrank for many years from attempting a settlement of boundaries. Fur companies with their employes were there from both nations, and with no kindly feeling toward each other. The first meetings of commissioners to settle the boundaries ended in nothing but an agreement to postpone the difficulty, and leave the pioneers to joint occupation of the country. While treaties in 1846 averted a war and settled the boundaries, yet it was not till 1848 that Oregon was organized as a Territory of the United States with regular territorial government.

The difficulties in the way of colonizing Oregon by the Americans were so great that prominent writers in British quarterlies prophesied that it would never be done.[1] The route by sea around Cape Horn, and the route overland across the great desert and the Rocky Mountains, were alike appalling. In spite of these difficul-

---

[1] See *Edinburgh Review*, 1843.

ties two Methodist preachers (Lee and Shepherd) took a colony of Americans to Oregon in 1834, twelve years before the boundary question was settled. It was a daring thing, but it was done. This colony of Methodists went by sea, and settled in Willamette Valley.

Fur traders and government expeditions began to call attention to the overland route. Mr. Parker, the missionary, led a band over the dreadful desert and across the Rocky Mountains in 1835. Next year the ill-fated mission of Whitman, Gray, and Spaulding (American Board) was planted in Oregon.

All this time American settlers in Oregon had to encounter hostile Indians and unfriendly English fur traders. They settled, too, on soil whose ownership was still in dispute. They reached their destination through dangers, trials, and losses rarely paralleled. In 1839 the following list of prices on Green River was published for the information of emigrants. Whisky (of course this came first), three dollars a pint. Dogs (for food), fifteen dollars apiece. Tobacco, five dollars per pound. Flour, none to be had. Whisky, dogs, tobacco—that was the bill of fare!

The first Cumberland Presbyterian who undertook to plant a colony in Oregon was the Rev. J. A. Cornwall. He made his call for colonists in 1844, two years before the war-cloud which grew out of the boundary question passed away. It was 1846 when his colony reached Oregon. The Rev. J. E. Braly and his family went in 1847. Long afterward Mrs. Braly ("Aunt Sue") often recited the story of this daring journey. They started in 1846, but halted on the Platte till the next year. Indians dogged their steps, and sometimes stole their cattle. One favorite method with the red men was to stampede these animals. Overland emigrants relied mainly on cattle. Every family took as many oxen as possible. Cows, too, were sometimes yoked to draw the wagons, or driven in herds. Cattle not only endured the journey better than horses, but they constituted the most desirable property after the journey was finished. For mutual protection large numbers of families formed a company, elected a captain, gave him almost military authority, and traveled in one band or "train." Thus an army of cattle was brought together. These animals in vast herds, frightened and stampeded, became as destructive as a tornado. After they were thus scattered they could never all be gathered together again. A stampeded train meant the death of many an emigrant during the stampede, and starvation to many another afterward.

On his arrival in Oregon Mr. Braly stopped with his family at Whitman's mission. There he found a most welcome rest for himself and his family, and he felt disposed to remain till thoroughly recruited. To this, however, there arose an obstacle. Mrs. Braly told him one day that she felt an overwhelming presentiment of evil, and could not consent to remain at Whitman's any longer. Mr. Braly expostulated, but "Aunt Sue" said, "I'll die if I have to stay one day longer." The result was that Braly took up his line of march for other portions of Oregon. He was just in time, for soon after his departure the whole country was ringing with the tidings of the horrid massacre by the Indians of all the people at Whitman's Station.

It was generally believed by the Protestants that this deed was instigated by the Jesuit priests, who were exceedingly averse to having Protestant missions established in that country. There was an independent provisional government in the territory belonging to no nation, but watched by English and Americans alike. The militia under the control of this government went in pursuit of the murderers of the missionaries. Mr. Braly's horses were pressed into the service by these militia-men, but he afterward recovered them. There was an official investigation of the charges against the Jesuit priests, but the story of this massacre does not belong to this history.

Some facts concerning emigration to Oregon at this early period will be of service in explaining the work of the first Cumberland Presbyterian preachers in that country. Some statements about a body of eight hundred emigrants (1843) are quoted from the *Overland Monthly:*

Successful as the first large emigration was in safely reaching eastern Oregon, the emigrants found one of the most difficult portions of their journey would be the passage of the Cascade Mountains with their families, household stuff, wagons, and stock. Upon arriving at the Dalles, very few of these eight hundred people had any provisions left. Neither had the colonists made any preparations for them. Many of them had left their exhausted cattle in the Walla Walla country to recruit until spring. Others expected to drive theirs into the Willamette Valley by a narrow pack-trail, over which it was impossible to take the wagons. In this extremity the very corporation they had been taught to fear and dislike came to their assistance, with food for the starving families and boats for transportation down the Columbia. Those who could not pay fared as well as those who could. The colonists had made no preparation for the reception of the eight hundred new settlers; neither was there food nor shelter for all these people, nor teams to break up the sod, nor seed to put in the earth for the next year's provisions. Credit had to be extended to large numbers of these people, whose little all was exhausted by the long and wasting journey from the Mississippi to the Pacific Ocean. The colonists themselves could not relieve such a number. The mission store had no authority to give credit; the few small traders already in the country would not. Dr. McLaughlin alone was both able and willing. Thus none of the immigrants suffered as they must have suffered without this assistance.

Dr. McLaughlin was the agent of the Hudson Bay Fur Company (British), and for this kindness to American emigrants he was deprived of his office.

One of the keen disappointments which immigrants encountered was that which they met after reaching Oregon. They reached the high mountains of Oregon with exhausted and starving teams. To their amazement and horror they often found it impossible to cross these mountains before another year. Thus the Rev. J. A. Cornwall and his party were forced to tarry through the winter of 1846. When spring came nearly all the cattle and other property belonging to these suffering immigrants was gone, and they made their way to the settlements under difficulties which no pen can describe.

The Rev. Neil Johnson went to Oregon in 1851, and the Rev. J. H. D. Henderson in 1852. Johnson lost nearly all his earthly possessions on the journey. Many emigrants in 1852 perished on the way. Johnson, while on his journey, writes thus to one of the church papers:

There are a few things connected with the journey that are far from being pleasant. The first is the weather. Scarcely a day passes without a storm of rain and hail and thunder and lightning all combined, and sometimes these continue for many hours together. This, combined with a scarcity of fuel, often makes the emigrant feel any thing but comfortable. The scarcity of fuel is quite an inconvenience. What there is in the way of wood consists mainly of cottonwood and willow. These are generally found on islands in the river, and may be obtained by wading from fifty to one hundred yards. But for days together you will travel and not see so much as a riding switch. Then your alternative for fuel is "buffalo chips"—a very poor substitute, especially in wet weather. Or drift-wood may be found in some places along the margin of the river; or occasionally the remains of an emigrant's wagon. But little calculation can be made on the latter, from the fact that when a wagon is to be left it is nearly all burned by the company before leaving camp. . . . The abundance of alkali water has caused many a poor ox to leave his bones to bleach on the prairie. This extends at intervals for a thousand miles of the journey all along Platte River, and until you reach Big Sandy. Should you get along early in the season the danger is not so great; but when the dry season sets in, and the ravines cease to run, then look out for poison. The common remedy when cattle are poisoned is lard, fat bacon, or citric acid. These, if administered in time, generally give relief. . . . .

Another Cumberland Presbyterian emigrant while on this dreary journey writes about the cholera thus:

The dead are disposed of in a summary manner. The grave is dug as soon as the breath leaves the body. This occupies about half an hour; not that graves are dug so shallow, but the earth is so sandy and soft that the work is soon accomplished. The corpse is then borne upon a blanket, or some of the bed-clothes upon which the person died, and let down into its final abode, this blanket answering for winding-sheet and coffin. The sand is then replaced, the name, residence, date of death, etc., inscribed upon a board placed at the head, and the train is all probably under way again in thirty minutes. In such graves hundreds are sleeping.

In 1852 the emigration was so large that the grass was exhausted, and the emigrants who started late not only lost all their cattle and other property, but a great many of the men and women perished on the journey. Through such difficulties as these the first Cumberland Presbyterian preachers made their way to Oregon. Our first congregation in Oregon was organized by Mr. Cornwall, aided by J. E. Braly. The Rev. Neil Johnson has published a historical sketch of our church in that country, which shows that the organization of the Oregon Presbytery was ordered in 1847, and this order was carried out November 3, 1851. The members present were Neil Johnson, J. A. Cornwall, and Joseph Robertson. The Rev. A. W. Sweeney was present as a visitor. Licensed preachers present: B. F. Music and John Dillard. Four congregations were represented. A great revival was reported. Braly had gone to California, as had many private members.

In 1853 this frontier presbytery resolved to have a college. It raised the money and built a house. It secured a $20,000 scholarship endowment. It employed a graduate of Waynesburg College for president, and opened the institution. The infidels of Eugene City, where the school was located, were its bitter enemies. In a few weeks some incendiary burned down the buildings. A hall was rented for temporary use, and other buildings erected. The teaching force was enlarged, and the school had one hundred and fifty pupils when the buildings were again destroyed by fire. Then our people erected a fire-proof building, but unfortunately went in debt for a large part of the work. The infidels started a rival enterprise, and struggled to alienate those who had promised to contribute for the erection of the fire-proof buildings. By reason of accumulated disasters payments were not met, and the buildings were sold for debt. This ended the college enterprise. Private schools, however, were kept up by our people in different parts of Oregon with good results.

A manuscript sketch of the history of our church in Oregon, prepared by the venerable Jacob Gillespie, gives some additional particulars about the fire-proof college building. It seems that a storm came and swept away the roof after the building was nearly completed. Mr. Gillespie also mentions some other struggles of the Oregon churches to secure educational facilities. Surely they have had to brave many difficulties. Gillespie gives a graphic picture of the scattered condition of our people in that country. Oregon included at first the whole of what is now Washington Territory, and was once thought to extend to 54° 40' north latitude. In a territory large enough for an empire a half dozen preachers and a few feeble churches were scattered here and there.

The Rev. T. H. Small and the Rev. Jacob Gillespie were among these pioneer preachers in Oregon.

All these men had to earn their own bread. The immigrants were generally poor, and could not sustain pastors. There was no Cumberland Presbyterian minister in all the territory whose hands were freed from secular pursuits. Yet our preachers planted churches and worked patiently on. How valuable a consecrated minister, sustained by the Missionary Board for a few years, might have been! The church did not have even one such helper on any part of the Pacific coast.

Gillespie was one of the original members of Willamette Presbytery. He has been in the ministry over fifty-six years. He organized a congregation in Oregon thirty-seven years ago. He calls attention to the fact that the Cumberland Presbyterian ministers in Oregon are nearly all old men.

Our church has three presbyteries in what once was Oregon Territory. The Oregon Presbytery has six ordained ministers and one licensed preacher. Walla Walla Presbytery has twelve ordained ministers and no probationers. The Willamette Presbytery has nine ordained ministers and two licentiates. This lack of a home supply of rising ministers is startling, and ought to send all the surviving pioneers in that field to God in earnest prayer that their own sons may be called into the ministry.

It was not till 1859 that Oregon became a State in the American Union. It is still a new field with ample room for growth.

The acquisition of California by the United States, and the discovery of gold there immediately afterward (1848), produced a rush of population from all parts of the world, such as perhaps never had a parallel. All the tongues of the earth mingled in the jargon that babbled about the mines. All grades of scholarship and culture, as well as all grades of ignorance and vice, were represented among the gold diggers. A desert, waterless, treeless, foodless, stretching wider than Sahara, could not check the great rush from the States. The way was paved with skeletons, but the gold hunters pressed on. Men perished in the snows of the Sierra Nevada Mountains, but other parties still kept coming with larger forces. California was peopled at once.

The change from the sluggish progress under the padres, which had marked the last three hundred years of California life, was like waking from a vague dream and a quiet sleep in your own chamber to find yourself in the midst of a city which infuriated armies are sacking. Among these wild and motley masses at the mines, as well as among the dead who fell on the journey, were many members of the Cumberland Presbyterian church. Some of our ministers were also among these transient multitudes.

All was transient. A city of tents would spring up where gold abounded, and if "better diggings" were discovered elsewhere, the city would vanish in a week, leaving perhaps a dozen Chinamen to rewash "the tailings." Four hundred thousand letters were returned from California to the dead letter office in a single year. The soldiers in our great civil war were more permanent and far more readily found than were these mining populations.

Ruffians and Christian gentlemen, preachers and people, all alike went to California to dig gold. The scholarly clergyman girt himself with a revolver and shouldered his spade. Alas, too, that it should be necessary to add that some of these clergymen became notorious gamblers before they left the mines. A young minister was fitted out by the Rev. Hugh B. Hill and furnished money to go to California and preach to the miners. This was in the beginning of the great rush thither. This young man made his way to the Golden Gate, and there, after six months among the pioneers, set up a gambling saloon. Nor was his the only case of this kind. This unfortunate feature of the history of the church in California is mentioned that it may be known that our true men in that field had such traitors in their camp, and were crippled in their work for Jesus by their evil example.

But some true men went with their families to California in 1849, aiming to preach as much as was consistent with their circumstances. They all had their own families to support. Our board sent no missionary to California until ten years later. The only men who remained true to their calling among the first Cumberland Presbyterian preachers in that country were those who received no help from the Church.

The first of these to arrive in California was Rev. John E.

Braly.[1] He went from Oregon and settled first at Fremont. Putting up a canvas structure, he established a Christian boarding-house for the miners. He was then without property, but he soon made money. On the 4th of July, 1849, he began his ministry to the gold diggers, Indians, and heathen. Some say his was the first Protestant preaching in California.

Another true man and faithful minister in that field was the Rev. T. A. Ish. In a letter dated Sacramento City, March 25, 1850, which was published in the *Cumberland Presbyterian*, he says he "left the land of civilization" on the 5th of May, 1849, and arrived in California September 12. In the latter part of the journey the cattle grew so weak that they had to be abandoned, and were left to perish in the desert. The letter continues:

When I arrived here I was worn out with the fatigue of the journey and much debilitated by an attack of fever. In a short time, however, I recovered my health, and it has been unusually good ever since. For a time I stopped in the vicinity of Fort Sutler, a town of four or five thousand inhabitants, mostly intelligent and energetic men. I afterward came to Sacramento City, and will probably stay here during my residence in California. I, with many others, had something of the gold fever, yet I could not content myself to sit down as an idler in the Lord's vineyard. After consulting a few of the brethren and friends, I resolved to make an effort to have a house of worship erected. The house is now completed, in good order, and is a comfortable room, well furnished, where some three or four hundred persons may comfortably sit and hear the gospel of peace. The city has so enlarged that we want several churches. You can not imagine how much good it did us on last Sabbath week, and yesterday, to meet in our church to worship together. The Rev. J. M. Cameron and myself have both preached each Sabbath since the completion of our room. He came to this city a few weeks since with his family, but he is talking of leaving this place and going lower down in the country.

There are several substantial members of our church here, and I think we could after a while organize a tolerably respectable congregation. We have enough ordained preachers in this country to form a presbytery, but gold has such a distracting influence that I do not know whether they can be got together or not. The Rev. J. E. Braly is in the town of Fremont, twenty-five or thirty miles above Sacramento

---

[1] Some say the Rev. J. M. Small was first, but give no dates. I believe Braly was first.

City. Brothers Mansfield and Moore are in the mines. These, as far as I know, are the only Cumberland Presbyterian preachers in this country.

Here are people from every nation under heaven who much need the gospel. The harvest is white, but the laborers are few. Strikingly was my mind impressed last night at our prayer-meeting by the petition offered in every prayer, "Lord, send more laborers into thy vineyard!" This was sanctioned by hearty amens from all the praying band. It is only now and then, amidst the busy throng, that I am permitted to see the face of a minister of the gospel. The Methodists have a good church here, and a faithful man to preach to them. The miners in many parts are said to be doing very well, obtaining from $16 to $50 per day.

The Rev. Cornelius Yager has long been a faithful Cumberland Presbyterian minister in California. With six motherless children he arrived in that country in 1850. He had a hard journey across the plains, and had to go immediately to work to earn bread. At first the only opportunity open to him for work and wages was to do hauling with his ox teams. From that day to this Mr. Yager has labored with his own hands for bread, preaching regularly on Sabbaths. Once, for the sake of sacred interests, he consented to represent his fellow-citizens in the legislature. A man of peace, a hard worker, a safe counselor, he has been of great service to our little churches in his adopted State.

In 1854, Linville Dooley, a married man, and a candidate for the ministry, arrived with his family in California. He had been there as a gold miner before he made up his mind to enter the ministry. This time he went to this country exclusively to preach Christ. He went at his own charges, with the deliberate purpose of bearing any and all privations that might come to him in the prosecution of his chosen life work. He has never swerved from this purpose. Receiving less than three hundred dollars annually for his labors, and supporting a large family in a land where meat was at first a dollar per pound, he has gone faithfully on in his work for thirty-two years. He has organized a number of congregations and received many converts into the church. Much of his time has been spent "on the circuit" among the miners. Through all these years he has faithfully kept a diary. He has preached on the streets, in drinking saloons, in dance-houses, in gambling dens, in hotel dining-rooms, and in other strange places. Some idea of the character of communities in which he has held meetings may be gathered from the names of the towns mentioned in his diary. Samples of these are Humbug, Red Dog, You Bet, Poker Flat, and Gouge Eye.

Although Mr. Dooley is now old, and of course has accumulated no worldly wealth, he says he expects to pursue the same calling till the Master takes him home. He says he has no regrets over his long years of privation, but would bear it all over again if he had to start at the beginning with a full knowledge of all the hardships. Regrets? ah no! Let those have regrets who have been false to their Lord and their high calling.

A description of a California meeting held by the Rev. E. C. Latta, another faithful Cumberland Presbyterian pioneer on the Pacific coast, will give the reader an idea of the difficulties under which the first preachers in that country sometimes labored. Latta was earning his bread by hunting. A hotel at which he boarded bought his venison. He got permission from Jim, the hotel keeper, to have preaching in the bar-room. When Sabbath came the only two women in all the country came to the meeting. Gamblers, too, were there, busy at their cards. Latta interrupted their games, saying, "Boys, it's my put in now. Jim says I may preach in this room. Just mark your place and wait till I preach." And then, without preliminaries, he began his sermon. When the sermon was over the gamblers returned to their cards.

It was difficult to determine what synod had jurisdiction in California. The Cumberland Presbyterian preachers in this State wanted to form a presbytery, but no order had been passed authorizing such an organization. In this emergency they resolved to organize without any formal order, and to ask the General Assembly to recognize the new presbytery and attach it to some synod. In the house of J. E. Braly, on the 4th of April, 1851, Cornelius Yager, W. Gallimore, James M. Small, and John E. Braly, all ordained ministers, constituted the California Presbytery. The next General Assembly approved their action, and attached the presbytery to the Missouri Synod, whose jurisdiction extended also to Oregon.

So long as the great mass of the population had less local permanency than a great army in the midst of war, church organizations were also without permanence. In traveling over this State one may hear the history of such mushroom churches in almost all the counties; and yet who shall dare say that the results were not permanent? "By Yuba's red waters" the grave of the miner who died three thousand miles from his mother's fireside is all unmarked and unknown; but amid the blessed spirits of light and glory who gather along the banks of the river of life, the immortal soul saved in the mushroom church now reigns in deathless glory. Not lost were those transient labors among those transient peoples.

One of the pioneer churches which did not melt away like morning mists was the Mountain View church, in Santa Clara County. It was organized in 1852 by the Rev. J. E. Braly. Mr. Braly long ministered to that flock.

In the very beginning of our denominational work in this State the Rev. J. M. Small planted a church and built a house of worship in Napa City. In the neighborhood of one of Mr. Small's congregations, in 1852, some young unmarried men sustained a camp-meeting. The same year Mr. Small and others held a meeting in Sonoma, and secured money to build a house of worship.

The Pacific Presbytery was organized in 1854, in the house of the Rev. J. M. Cameron. This presbytery established an academy at Sonoma, which in 1860 was turned over to the synod and called Cumberland College. It had a short but useful career. It was the first Cumberland Presbyterian school in California. There was wrangling over the location, and this, according to Mr. Dooley, was ultimately the cause of its death. Another, or at least an auxiliary cause can be found in the flitting away of all the first population of Sonoma. German wine growers now own the principal part of the beautiful country around the old college buildings. That rivalry and divided counsels injured not only Cumberland College at Sonoma, but other church work in California, is however a painful fact. The history of these differences and disputes would make a long chapter, but it would be useless to record it here.

The Board of Missions was instructed by the General Assembly (1855) to send a man to California before opening any other new mission. For years the board reported that all efforts to secure a man for that field had failed. Finally, in 1859, the Rev. W. N. Cunningham was sent to Stockton, California. Nothing more was done, however, than to pay the missionary's way to his field of labor, the board seeming to have the impression that he could live on what our people in Stockton could pay him. On his arrival he found in that city a few members of our church, but no organized congregation. He received such small compensation for his labors that he suffered for the actual necessities of life. He struggled alone and in destitution till he secured money to build a church, but was driven at last by sheer starvation to seek other work.

He next took charge of Sonoma College. This institution was overwhelmed in debts when he entered upon its management. He labored till these debts were paid off. He raised twelve thousand dollars to build a new college edifice, remaining twelve years in all at Sonoma. He has since combined some secular business for the support of his family with his work of preaching. This he did not do till he had been driven to it by the most pressing necessity. In this combined work he has built up and helped to build up several churches. Mr. Cunningham has suffered long from hope deferred. The church did just nothing to help the struggling few who went to California to preach the gospel. Had even one missionary been sustained in that field the case would not be so bad; but while other churches were paying salaries and building houses of worship in California, the pioneer preachers of the Cumberland Presbyterian church had to earn their own bread and preach without pay.

Speaking of the paper started by Rev. T. M. Johnston in 1860, and of the college at Sonoma, the Rev. D. E. Bushnell, D.D., says in a published article:

Both of these enterprises have been connected with nearly all of our subsequent history, though both have ceased to exist in fact though not in influence. When the full history of the Cumberland Presbyterian church on the Pacific slope shall have been written, there will be found two enterprises inseparably connected with its record, and the forces that have contributed toward the results already achieved, viz.: Cumberland College and the *Pacific Observer*. And indissolubly connected with these invaluable agencies for Christ and his cause are the names of the sainted Johnston, the founder and for ten years the proprietor and editor of our church journal, who has gone to reap the reward which was wholly denied him in this life, and the indefatigable and heroic Cunningham, whose indomitable will and lofty courage bore up the cherished college enterprise when the hearts of others failed them. . . . Working in the same general direction, but resulting from an unfortunate and ever-to-be-regretted division and diversion of the energies of our little band of builders in the spiritual wilderness, so sadly common in such cases, were the Union Academy at Alamo, and the San Joaquin College near Stockton. After short careers of struggle, though at times well manned and liberally patronized, and accomplishing no little good for the communities in which they were located, these institutions lost all their property by accidental fires, and having no endowment, ceased. No well-defined effort has since been made to establish a church school in the name of the Cumberland Presbyterians of California.

What a pity that our people could not concentrate their college work even in that feeble frontier! They tried to have three colleges, and ended in having none at all.

The Rev. T. M. Johnston was an earnest preacher, a sound theologian, a safe counselor, and an indefatigable worker. When others wrangled, he wept. When others sought self, he toiled for Jesus. When it was attempted to involve him in these unfortunate disputes, he removed to another presbytery. He was a peacemaker, ready to bind up the wounds of those that had been wronged or injured, ready to pray with them and remind them of what Jesus suffered while achieving the world's redemption.

The fascinating opportunities to acquire wealth both in farming and in mining were a snare in which many a preacher became involved. Many of these opportunities bore a striking resemblance to gambling. One year a single crop would yield net profits sufficient to buy a ranch. Another year, in some parts of the State, the crop would not repay what the seed cost. There were many ministerial wrecks, caused in most cases by an undue haste to be rich.

The difficulties in the way of faithful Cumberland Presbyterian evangelists in this State were at first appalling. Besides the transient nature of the population, the mixture of nationalities and creeds was a serious obstacle. Educated infidels abounded.

As late as 1877 infidel lecturers were ready to confront the earnest advocates of the gospel in nearly all the California towns. But above all else, the mad rush for wealth was and is the thing most unfriendly to the development of spiritual life. Steady honest toil is mocked at by men who ride horseback eighty miles a day, who feed three hundred hands all through harvest, who talk only about hundreds of thousands when speaking of their future expectations.

But there are for Cumberland Presbyterians advantages of no mean character in that field. Of all the States, California is the most thoroughly national. It is neither Northern nor Southern; or rather it is both. So, too, is our church, and so was it even while the war was at its worst. California is constantly receiving emigration from our churches. Some of our best men go there. With a delightful climate, a wonderful soil, an invigorating atmosphere, and a world of natural wonders; with a grand system of free schools, and throngs of the world's ablest scholars and thinkers constantly pouring in among its motley society—it is by all odds the most fascinating as well as the most difficult field our church has ever undertaken to cultivate. They do nothing by halves in California—at least not in the financial world. Small, slow-going enterprises are not likely to live in that country. Other churches send large sums of money and strong missionaries; Cumberland Presbyterians send one man at a time for a whole State, and have but recently done that.

Our people have now in that State three presbyteries. The directory for 1886 shows that the California Presbytery has fourteen ordained preachers, three licentiates, and one candidate. The Sacramento Presbytery has seven ordained ministers, two licentiates, and no candidate. The Tulare Presbytery has twelve ordained ministers, one licentiate, and one candidate. A home supply of preachers is one of the great wants of our church in California and everywhere.

Some of the same men who planted the Cumberland Presbyterian church in California also organized a few churches in Idaho, but our people never had strength enough in that Territory to call for any separate history.

CHAPTER XXXIV.

SUNDRY SMALL BEGINNINGS—NORTH CAROLINA, WEST VIRGINIA, GEORGIA, KANSAS.

> All the lessons He shall send
> Are the sweetest;
> And his training, in the end,
> Is completest.
> —*F. R. H.*

THE history of the Cumberland Presbyterian church in North Carolina is soon written. Before 1842, under church direction, missionary tours were made through this State by Reuben Burrow and Robert Donnell. They held meetings for the revival party of the Presbyterian church. They had gracious revivals, but they uniformly declined to organize churches. At a later day our church in East Tennessee began to extend a little into North Carolina, and a few zealous men thought the way was open to push the work far into that State. Young men pressed beyond the borders, organized some feeble churches, and published appeals for help; but the church did not respond, and these little picket stations were abandoned.

Cumberland Presbyterians have penetrated into West Virginia through the natural expansion of the church in western Pennsylvania, and mainly under the ministry of Pennsylvania pastors living near enough to give a part of their time to the work beyond the State line. One congregation in West Virginia has considerable strength, but our people have no presbytery in that State, and never had any missionary in that field.

It was by the natural expansion of the forces of the church that Cumberland Presbyterians extended their boundaries into Georgia. In East Tennessee and in Alabama, all along the Georgia border, there are congregations of our people. Members of these churches were constantly moving to Georgia, and writing back to their pastors to come and preach for them. Prominent among the ministers who responded to this call was the Rev. A. Templeton, then of Chattanooga, Tennessee. Finally one of our preachers settled in Georgia. This was the Rev. Z. M. McGhee. The war made Georgia the temporary home of many a Cumberland Presbyterian minister, the Rev. A. Templeton among the rest.

An anecdote of Templeton taken from the papers is here condensed. He was preaching at a Georgia meeting-house at a time when either blue coats or gray might be expected at church. Sure enough at one meeting the gray coats were there. The services began, and were progressing quietly, but with deep interest, when up rode a company of blue coats. Mr. Templeton turned to the Southern soldiers and said: "Keep your seats. If you really want to worship God, he will not allow you to be hurt." They remained in their seats. The Federal soldiers then entered. Mr. Templeton said to them: "Please be seated, gentlemen, and let us all worship God a few moments together." They did as he requested. In a few moments the whole house was in tears. The petty contests of this little life were all forgotten. Eternal things pressed every heart. There were that day souls born of God. When the benediction was pronounced, each company of soldiers followed its own leader and went quietly away without any fighting.

Cumberland Presbyterians have in Georgia one little presbytery with nine ministers, four licentiates, and two candidates. We have no missionary in this field, though precious interests are at stake there. At Rome there are several valuable members, but they have no house of worship and no minister. In Atlanta our people once had a mission, but it was allowed to die, although the influx of members from Alabama and Tennessee might in a few years have made it self-sustaining.

Kansas was settled amid scenes of blood, not blood shed by Indians, but brothers butchering brothers. There were Cumberland Presbyterians in both the angry parties which struggled for supremacy in that State. The repeal of "the Missouri compromise" and the law leaving the first settlers to decide for themselves whether Kansas should be a free or a slave State opened the gates of civil war. No full history of that bloody struggle has ever been written. It was crowded back into forgetfulness by the greater contest which so soon followed. Nevertheless it was really a war, with armies, battles, and campaigns—war to the knife between two parties coming to live in the same Territory.

Kansas was opened to white settlers late in 1854, under an act that led slave and free States alike to send armed emigrants thither, each aiming to keep out the other party by force. The rush of emigrants was stimulated by the angry political strife of the day. To gain in Congress the votes of a new State was the aim of each party; to use force in keeping out emigrants from States unfavorable to the schemes of its partisans was the policy of each.

A peaceably disposed Cumberland Presbyterian emigrant, while on his way to Kansas in 1854 to preach Jesus to the settlers, wrote a letter which was published in the church paper. He thus describes the scene at the ferry across the Missouri River at Weston, Missouri:

The crowd of passengers wishing to cross had become so great that we were somewhat doubtful of the safety of embarking on so crazy a craft with so large a number of passengers. The ferryman assured us, however, that there was no danger, and that if we waited until the next trip we would only find matters worse, as the crowd would probably be greater than it now was. We, therefore, ventured on his boat, but such cramming and jamming of buggies, wagons, horses, mules, and footmen on a little crazy steam ferry-boat we have never seen, and do not care to see again soon. We took the pains to count them and found that there were about eighty persons on board, most of whom were going over into the new Territory to stake out their claims and take possession of the soil. They were generally equipped according to border life, having a set of camping furniture, besides axes, hatchets, butcher and Bowie-knives, guns, pistols, and other weapons of the chase and of warfare, offensive and defensive. We began to feel as if we had got into the wrong crowd, being entirely unarmed, whilst every one about us seemed to be armed to the teeth. A more daring, resolute, reckless set of men we have scarcely ever looked upon. Each man seemed to say by his airs and gait, "I am able, single-handed and alone, to vindicate my rights against all intruders." Still we found that beneath this rough and forbidding exterior there was generally a current of warm and genial feeling.

The river once passed, they branched off in every direction, each in search of some spot on which to locate his claim. As we rode off we saw on the other bank another company equally large awaiting the return of the boat. The ferryman assured us that he had been kept busily engaged from morning till night for the last two or three weeks in ferrying immigrants. Most of those whom we saw were from upper Missouri, but they were already beginning to arrive in considerable numbers from all the Western States, though but a single month had elapsed since the opening of the country.

Kansas did not become a State of the Union till 1861, but soldiers of the Cross were as ready to rush thither in the beginning as the soldiers of political parties. Early in 1855, under the ministry of the Rev. C. B. Hodges, the Round Prairie church was formed. This, it is claimed, was the first Cumberland Presbyterian congregation organized on Kansas soil. According to an order of Missouri Synod, Kansas Presbytery was organized November 16, 1855.[1] The original members were W. W. Bell, Benjamin McCrary, C. B. Hodges, A. A. Moore, Thomas Allen, and O. Guthrie. The two last named were not present at the organization. The presbytery met in a school-house in Leavenworth County, near the dwelling of the Rev. B. McCrary. A. A. Moore was moderator. There were some licentiates and candidates from the first, and one of the licentiates, A. P. Searcy, was ordered to prepare for ordination at the next meeting.

This presbytery had all of Kansas for its field, though a large portion of the territory was without a single inhabitant. All of its ministers lived north of Kansas River, while settlements abounded south of the river, and earnest appeals came up from that region begging for the bread of life. The presbytery took the very best steps in its power toward responding to these appeals, urging all the churches and every member to contribute money to secure preachers. At its very first meeting it passed strong resolutions against whisky. Of the original members two still live, Moore and Hodges.

Leavenworth Presbytery was next organized, and then followed two others. The territory assigned to these new presbyteries was all carved out of the field first assigned to Kansas Presbytery. The

---

[1] Valuable extracts from the Minutes and other items were furnished me by the stated clerk, the Rev. William Spencer.

original Kansas Presbytery now has twenty-five congregations and nine hundred and eighteen communicants. There is still great need of more preachers in that country. There are Cumberland Presbyterian families scattered over all the State. The Rev. W. Spencer and the Rev. R. H. Shearer are the only Cumberland Presbyterian ministers in Kansas who are natives of that State.

In 1857 the Missionary Board at Lebanon, Tennessee, commissioned the Rev. A. A. Moore to travel as missionary in Kansas. He spent several years in this work and had good success. In 1859 the board sent the Rev. J. B. Green (now the Rev. Dr. Green, of Nebraska) to travel as missionary in the country around Fort Leavenworth. He had some very fruitful revivals and did valuable service.

The Directory, 1886, shows that Kansas Presbytery has thirteen ministers, two licentiates, and one candidate; Leavenworth Presbytery five, and Republican Valley Presbytery eight ministers; and Wichita Presbytery, twelve ministers and one candidate. The members of the church in Kansas should ask the Lord to call their own sons to preach the gospel.

CHAPTER XXXV.

MISCELLANEOUS.

Hush, my troubled heart be still,
God is faithful come what will.
—*Anna Shipton.*

THERE has always been a party in the Cumberland Presbyterian church opposed to concentration, and another party which has believed it necessary to combine the forces of the church in some of the greater enterprises, especially in our denominational schools. Milton Bird and F. R. Cossitt, as editors respectively of the two leading church papers, took opposite sides of this question. The policy advocated by Dr. Cossitt was concentration on one or two colleges, one or two papers, and one theological school. Though Robert Donnell and many other thoughtful men gave their voices on this side of the question, their views did not prevail. The church had to learn by experience, and this period, from 1842 to 1860, was full of lessons on this subject.

It was no uncommon thing for a single presbytery to resolve to have an endowed college of its own. Thus, Tennessee Presbytery, in 1850, resolved to establish and endow a college. Purdy College had a still smaller ecclesiastical backing. Such efforts showed clearly that many of our people had no correct idea of what constitutes a college. We had at one time in this period fifteen chartered colleges for young men, besides several similar institutions for young ladies. Fifteen does not exhaust the list for the whole period, but this is the largest number that simultaneously existed. Some of the schools did not live five years.

But, in the course of time, these evils began to correct themselves. Young men who went from these mushroom colleges to real ones had their eyes opened. The little school which suddenly sprung up as a rival of an older institution and called itself a college, soon found some other little college springing up in its field, rivaling it, until, sooner or later, came the death agonies of both. Of the fifteen Cumberland Presbyterian colleges which, in 1859, had a name to live, only three now survive. Each of these three had secured some little endowment, though by no means enough.

For more than twenty years the General Assembly tried to obtain harmonious reports from the presbyteries in reference to a theological school. Some of the presbyteries favored presbyterial, and some synodical, and some General Assembly schools. There was no harmony, and the Assembly waited, declaring meantime its opinion that it would be wisest to establish one school for the whole church. At different times this question was sent down to the presbyteries; but while the responses showed a steady increase in the number of voices in favor of giving the exclusive control of such schools to the General Assembly, there was still too much conflict to allow that body to establish such an institution.

The last reference of this question to the presbyteries was made in 1848, and when the response came back in 1849 with something like unanimity in favor of a theological school under the control of the General Assembly, there was great rejoicing. Steps were taken at once toward the establishment of such a school. At first the rival claims of two colleges made the Assembly agree that there should be two schools; but this matter was soon adjusted, and one school for the whole church, to be located at Lebanon, Tennessee, was undertaken.

There were some delays in getting this school into successful operation. Meantime the Assembly of 1852 was thrown into confusion by the action of Bethel College, in West Tennessee. Before the charter of this college was a year old it resolved to establish a theological school and send out agents for its endowment, appealing to the whole church for contributions. This had the appearance of an attempt to head off the General Assembly. West Tennessee Synod, under whose control Bethel College held its charter, had many members who opposed this measure. So, too, had even the Board of Trust and Faculty of Bethel College. There were, however, three controlling spirits who advanced the scheme and carried it through the synod. These were Reuben Burrow, J. N. Roach, and C. J. Bradley.

Three years prior to this action Mr. Roach had been in charge of a flourishing school for young ladies at Lebanon, Tennessee. When the school was in its greatest prosperity grave charges were made against Mr. Roach, of which he was afterward fully acquitted; but although he was doubtless innocent of the things charged against him, yet the tide of public prejudice ran high enough to break up his school. Deeply hurt, he left Lebanon and went immediately to West Tennessee and set to work to establish a college there. As West Tennessee lay between Lebanon and the field from which the university at Lebanon drew its principal patronage, many questioned the wisdom of this course. Mr. Roach, though not a thorough scholar, was a man of splendid natural abilities, and he had an amazing capacity for hard work. He had, too, a commanding influence over the common people, and his plan for the establishment of a college was carried through the West Tennessee Synod mainly by his personal influence. He next planned a theological department, naming Dr. Burrow and the Rev. C. J. Bradley as prospective professors.

West Tennessee Synod was then in a sharp controversy with Lebanon men about the revision of the Confession of Faith. Dr. Burrow was not only a leader in advocating revision, but, on various points, he held doctrines which were not in strict harmony with the creed of the church, and he seemed to feel under solemn obligations to propagate his peculiar views. A theological school would enable him more effectually to do this, therefore Mr. Roach easily won him to his plans. Burrow's voice carried the measure through the synod.

When the General Assembly of 1852 met severe resolutions of condemnation against this project of Bethel College were offered, and after hot discussion were in a fair way to pass, when the Rev. C. J. Bradley rose in his place and warned the Assembly that the passage of these resolutions would be the signal for the secession of West Tennessee Synod. That was then the largest synod in the church. Mr. Bradley's announcement checked proceedings. The Assembly adopted pacific measures, simply entreating the lower judicatures to co-operate with the Assembly's school, and left Bethel College to pursue its course. For many years Dr. Burrow's theological pupils adopted the Confession of Faith only in part, openly stating their partial adoption of the book at their ordination.

This case suggests a very different matter. One of the living questions now pressing on all the denominations is how to protect their theological schools from teachers who change their views after their appointment to professorships.

In the chapter on missions it was seen that it was with difficulty that co-operation with a general board was secured. There were fears by some that the general board would become a pope. But the danger in the Cumberland Presbyterian church has never been in the direction of the pope, but in the other direction. Independence, which regards neither session, presbytery, assembly, nor the general welfare, has more frequently paralyzed our enterprises. There is a medium between the centralization which makes a pope and the private independence which makes anarchy. God in his providence is slowly leading the church to this medium ground.

One of the measures often proposed in the General Assembly in this period was the consolidation of the church papers. There were at one time seven of these weeklies. It cost a preacher not less than fourteen dollars to secure the news from all parts of the field, while a communication intended for the whole church had to be sent to seven editors. Each of the seven had a circulation mainly local, and the support of each was too meager to command first-class facilities. To have one paper owned by the church, or the presbyteries, was one of the plans proposed. It is a curious fact that the *New York Observer* took a special interest on the negative side of this discussion. Its objection was that the scheme put too much power into the hands of one editor.

A sample of the arguments used by those who favored this plan is found in the following extract from a communication published in the *Watchman and Evangelist:*

A change has come over me in regard to the church paper which has been so much talked of. The arguments in favor of one paper for the whole church preponderate in my judgment. A like change is discoverable in those who, in this region, take any of our papers.

"In union there is strength," is an indisputable maxim. Had the church adhered to this in all its important undertakings, our spiritual momentum would have been greater than it now is. Had no more literary institutions been planted than the pecuniary ability of the church could have amply furnished and rendered potent, our educational facilities would have been far in advance of what they now are. Mere local interests have operated against the general good, and originated, here and there, schools of various grades until they have become so numerous as to be burdensome and meagerly supported. A similar error has been committed in our publishing enterprises. Local interests have been regarded as the *sine qua non*, until blindness to the general well-being of the whole body has come over our eyes.

One presbytery or synod conceives it to be important that a paper should be published within its bounds to advocate the cause in that quarter. Another, in another portion of the body, is actuated by a similar reason, and so on until the patronage of the church is cut up into small sectional divisions, and none of the papers sufficiently well supported to give us even one of the right character. By this division of our strength, our name and influence evidently suffer. The Cumberland Presbyterian church has had experience of this kind to its sorrow. Why should we support this evil policy in regard to an enterprise which affects so directly the vital interests of the whole church? Or will we continue to disregard those lessons of wisdom to be learned from our past history?

Another evil growing out of the strenuous advocacy of these local publishing interests is strife. An attempt to originate a paper and support it in a body already too feeble to maintain well what it has, curtails the patronage of those of prior existence. But each watches its own interests with a jealous eye, and upon the first appearance of infringement upon its dominions takes up the sword, and the result not unfrequently is the disturbance of the peace of the church by a newspaper war. Has there not been sad experience in this very thing?

This writer also pressed two other arguments: the cost to one person who desired to take all the papers and secure the news from the whole church, and the fact that all seven of the weeklies copied from one another, so that such a subscriber got much of the same matter in all of the seven papers.

On the negative I find all the arguments are capable of reduction to these: It was claimed that local interests in remote parts of the church would suffer under the one paper plan, and that more people can be induced to take a paper published in their own locality than one from a distant part of the church.

One writer pressed another and a strong argument in these words:

Should controversy arise on important subjects, under the trammels of the "one paper" system the editorial authority would have the right to sit in judgment upon the propriety of admitting or not admitting articles on either side in controversy, which might unknowingly be productive of much ill-feeling, and do great injury to certain brethren and some portion of the church. Should the editorial authority come to the conclusion, as has once occurred, that nothing should be published until the judicature had taken action, then the whole church must abide the decisions for the time, or appear in the unenviable attitude of scattering church dissensions in secular newspapers.

The one paper scheme failed, but the Assembly appealed to the editors to combine and reduce the number of papers. In this way, and still more by the failure of several of the weaker publications, the number was considerably diminished. There was a deeper lesson from financial failure than from the voice of the Assembly.

The books published by Cumberland Presbyterians in this period were neither many nor large. It was a time of too great activity in planting churches and inaugurating new enterprises to allow much book making. One of the most valuable books ever published on the subject of training children was Dr. Lindley's Infant Philosophy. The stereotype plates for this book were lost in 1858, and it has never been republished. The copyright was bought by the Cumberland Presbyterian Board of Publication at Louisville in 1853. Dr. E. B. Crisman's little volume, "The Origin and Doctrines of the Cumberland Presbyterian Church," met a demand which was keenly felt prior to that time. The Rev. John L. Dillard published a little book in reply to Lewis A. Lowry, who left the Cumberland Presbyterian church and bitterly attacked it in a volume which was brought out by the Presbyterian Publishing House. It was the general opinion among our people that Dillard gave the young man a well-deserved castigation. Various newspapers of other churches expressed the same opinion. Mr. Lowry's book was in the form of letters addressed to his father, the Rev. David Lowry. The latter, it is said, never read a line of these letters.

One of the most scholarly books of this period was, "The Life and Times of Ewing," by Dr. Cossitt. The very nature of the subject made the book necessarily controversial. At the close of the book is a severe but able review of Davidson's History of the Presbyterian Church in Kentucky. But most of our people have grown tired of fighting over the old battles with the Presbyterian church, and such is their lack of interest in this subject that they will not buy books devoted to that old contest. The writer of these pages has been entreated by many of the purest and best men in the Cumberland Presbyterian church to pass over all that old bitterness just as lightly as the truth of history will permit. This he has done.[1]

President Anderson's Life of George Donnell was published in this period, and is generally regarded as the best biographical book in our church. It would be hard to find a better biography in any church.

Dr. Beard began the publication of his great work on systematic theology in this period. These lectures present the genuine original Cumberland Presbyterian system of doctrine. There is more Calvinism in the book than some of our modern theologians like, but not more than the whole of the first generation of our ministers preached. This book will stand as a landmark from which we can measure from age to age any drifting away of our theology from orthodoxy.

While Dr. Beard was never brilliant, and never relied on any extemporaneous afflatus, his profound and patient research always went to the bottom of any subject which he investigated, and then swept around all the adjacent field before he attempted to write his lecture. Loyalty to Scripture, without a particle of ambition for originality, marked all his work. From first to last there is in his book no harsh word about other theological systems or teachers. He labored simply, by prayer and severe study, to give God's system as it is found in the Bible. With a profound knowledge of the original Scripture, with a world-wide acquaintance with theological writers, he devoted the best years of his noble life to the preparation of his lectures. If his church ever fails to appreciate this

---

[1] It is necessary to know something of the number of false charges made against our people before the extent of my forbearance in this matter can be appreciated.

Rev. R. O. Watkins.

Rev. Reuben Burrow, D.D.

Rev. J. B. Logan, D.D.

book, so much the worse for the church. There are so many *original* thinkers in modern times that it is hard to find among them one who is willing to draw all his theology from God's own revelation. Human philosophy must shape and square and trim and smooth the Scripture system, eliminating here, supplementing there, until with great truth the original thinker can at last say, This is my system.

About twenty other books were brought out by Cumberland Presbyterians in this period, but none of them call for any special notice in this history. There was not a single devotional book published by any of our people, nor has there been to this day any great amount of devotional literature among our publications. Controversial writings, *usque ad nauseam*, we have had, but very few works which would ever lead a soul to Christ. The second period in the history of the church presented better things in this respect than the fourth.

In this period there were long controversies on doctrinal questions. One of these questions was whether or not faith should ever be called the gift of God. On both sides in this controversy there seemed to be fears that the other party held doctrines which it not only did not avow but indignantly disclaimed. A patient study of all the long controversy has satisfied the writer that there was no difference at all between the parties about the real nature of faith. Both said that the sinner could not believe unto salvation without the Holy Spirit's aid, and that the act of believing was the act of the sinner thus aided, and not the act of the Holy Spirit. The disputants agreed, too, as to the manner in which the Holy Spirit aids the sinner—that he sheds light on the way of salvation, on the wonderful love and the gracious words of Christ to all who seek him, until the heart is won to trust him. The real question was whether this assistance thus given by the Spirit justifies us in calling faith a grace—a gift of God. One party charged the other with holding that faith is created in the sinner's heart by a divine act. The other party retorted: "You hold to an unaided human faith, merely historical." Neither charge was just.

There was also a long controversy about sanctification. One party, led by Dr. Reuben Burrow, advocated the Zinzendorfian view of sanctification. The other party, and by far the larger one, held to the doctrine of the Confession, which is the same as the doctrine of the Westminster Confession. There were also sharp controversies between Dr. Burrow and his brethren generally on various doctrines wherein Burrow differed from the Confession of Faith. Infant justification was prominent among these subjects of controversy. Dr. Burrow held that infants are born in a justified state.

There were so many points in which Burrow departed from the traditional teachings of the church, and he pressed his views so persistently in the church papers, that one presbytery finally took official action, warning its young preachers against these doctrines. This warning was published in the papers. Then came a sharp controversy about the rights of presbyteries. Burrow said that though he was not a member of this presbytery, nor amenable to it, yet it had assumed to try and condemn him. In answer to this it was said that the presbytery did not try men, but doctrines; that the Book of Discipline made it the duty of presbyteries to condemn erroneous doctrines which were injuring the peace of the church. Burrow's friends then pleaded his noble service as an evangelist on our frontiers as proof of his soundness in doctrine, and with that the controversy closed.

Another controversy was about abolishing the synod. S. G. Burney, D.D., led the affirmative in this discussion. Many of the old men of the church took the other side. The synod was not abolished. A proposition to revise the Confession of Faith was also discussed. Some of the papers declined to publish any thing on this subject. Others opened their columns, but men hesitated to discuss general questions in local papers.

The tone of church controversies has greatly improved since 1842. The Rev. W. S. Langdon, while editor, announced this as his rule: "No writer shall publish in these columns any thing about his brethren which I would be unwilling to have him publish about me."

In this fourth period camp-meetings in all the older portions of the church died a lingering death. Of the later meetings of this kind only a few were equal in results to those of earlier times. At

Bethel church, Carroll County, Tennessee, there were three camp-meetings between 1846 and 1850, all of them like the old gatherings of other days. John Barnett attended one of these meetings. Besides preaching with holy power, he went from camp to camp, and from person to person, preaching Christ in private interviews as well as from the pulpit. At one of these meetings two hundred mourners bowed simultaneously in the great congregation. The mighty power of God was present.

An unusually large number of church trials occurred during this period. Some men of the highest standing were arraigned on the gravest charges before their presbyteries. The verdict in most cases, not all, was "not guilty," and after years approved these verdicts.

A long and profitless controversy over the restoration of J. A. Dewoody to the ministry by one presbytery after he had been deposed by another, though always decided against, this restoration kept finding new methods of getting before the General Assembly and annoying that body.

There was a fierce controversy between Hopewell Presbytery and a Methodist presiding elder over the reception by the presbytery of a minister who had been deposed by the Methodists. The members of the presbytery claimed that they had evidence that it was personal spite in the elder which caused this man to be deposed. There have been sundry instances of preachers coming to the Cumberland Presbyterian church from other denominations to escape some difficulty with their own churches, but no such accession to our ranks has ever proved valuable.

There were long newspaper debates during this period between our people and the Baptists. These discussions were not always conducted in a Christian spirit, and were injurious to both churches. Dr. Burrow published a book on baptism full of hard sayings against the Baptists. This book was fiercely assailed by Dr. J. R. Graves, of the Baptist church. Then there were oral debates between him and Dr. Burrow, and between Burrow and the Rev. James Hurt. Bitter personal charges and a long and acrid newspaper controversy followed. All through West Tennessee Cumberland Presbyterians and Baptists became like Jews and

Samaritans. The cause of the Master suffered in both churches. May no such unseemly strife ever occur again!

There was also a protracted controversy on doctrines between Dr. Cossitt and the Presbyterians. It was conducted with ability and in a Christian spirit on both sides, but there is no proof that the doctrinal views of any one were changed by this discussion. However, one good thing at least came of it. People saw that two strong men could differ and discuss their differences without transgressing the rules of Christian courtesy, or departing from the spirit of the Master. Such a lesson was needed.

CHAPTER XXXVI.

SKETCHES AND INCIDENTS.

> All things are His, and all obey
> His wonder working will;
> E'en common things have life and speech,
> And His command fulfill.
> —*Anna Shipton.*

THE church at Memphis, Tennessee, was organized in 1830, in the house of the Rev. Mr. Whitsett. For ten years preaching was kept up by Mr. Whitsett, W. A. Bryan, Robert Baker, H. A. Morgan, and Samuel Dennis. In 1840, Mr. Dennis was assisted by Reuben Burrow in a meeting held in the Methodist church. At this time elders were chosen and the organization perfected. Mr. Dennis was commissioned to travel and obtain funds to build a church. Robert Donnell, who afterward was pastor for a time, aided in raising money to complete this work. This house stood till about 1860, when the building now in use was erected.

Matthew H. Bone and Hugh B. Hill were boys together. Their associations were of the most intimate character. They were converted about the same time. One day Hill said to his dear young friend: "If you will never tell any one I will communicate to you a secret." Bone promised not to betray this confidence, whereupon Hill said: "I believe God is calling me to preach the gospel." Bone replied: "I believe he is calling me to the same work." The two boys were alone together in the woods, and they wept and prayed together there. Months passed away, and Hill had another confidence to repose in his friend. It was that he had concluded that it was all a mistake about God calling him to preach. To his surprise he found his friend had also reached a similar conclusion. So they both agreed to abandon all thoughts of preaching and turn their attention to something else. It happened that they went together soon afterward to a camp-meeting. The leading preachers of Kentucky were present. Barnett preached, Chapman preached, Delany preached. God's spirit was poured out. Again Hill sought his friend and told him that all his old impressions had come back stronger than ever. Bone made similar statements about his impressions. Before the meeting closed one of the ministers asked the two young men to go with him to the woods. It was the daily custom at the camp-meetings to go to the woods for secret prayer. The two young men were surprised on reaching the retreat in the grove to find all the preachers there together. It was a preconcerted arrangement. The old men wanted to talk to these two young men about preaching. The result was that Hill and Bone were advised to attend the next meeting of the presbytery and become candidates for the ministry. After that these two friends traveled together on the circuit. All their lives they worked together at camp-meetings. Once they went together on a voluntary mission to Ohio, and the origin of the Cumberland Presbyterian church at Lebanon, Ohio, is due to that mission. In Bone's manuscript he says that Hill in his riper years bitterly regretted that the old men forced him away from school and put him on the circuit before his education was completed.

An aged minister, the Rev. Benjamin Watson, who began life as a Methodist, but joined the Cumberland Presbyterian church afterward, gives at the close of his manuscript autobiography some interesting reflections. He says his long experience has taught him that the church's best members and most of its converts come from the Sabbath-school; that giving to the poor is lending to the Lord, and that only out-and-out consecration to the ministry has any right to claim the gracious promises which God makes about the preacher's temporal necessities. He tried teaching and preaching, but could not claim these promises and did not realize their fulfillment. For sixteen years he tested the other plan. He cast himself upon God to preach even if he starved. Then he did claim the promises and did realize their fulfillment.

Mr. Watson's history is interesting in many particulars. His father bitterly opposed his entering the ministry, and to prevent his riding the circuit attempted to shoot his horse, but, just as he fired, the gun was thrown up and the ball passed over the animal.

Then the enraged father took his knife and cut his son's saddle, bridle, and saddle-bags to pieces. Not content with that, he gathered up all the young man's Sunday clothing, books and money, and burned them. Then he struck his son with a walking-stick, and seized his watch chain, and jerking the watch out of his pocket broke it against a post. The boy was then told to choose between giving up circuit riding and leaving his home forever. Benjamin took his final choice then and there. He bade mother and sister good-bye, and went to a neighbor's house. Next morning a merchant called and invited him to go home with him. On his arrival he found a number of ladies assembled for the purpose of making him a suit of clothes. Bridle, saddle, clothing, and money were all furnished him, and his own horse was brought from his father's, and the young man went on his way preaching the gospel.

The Rev. P. G. Rea, in his manuscript history of the New Lebanon Presbytery of Missouri (organized 1832) gives some interesting facts. He says: "Since its organization to 1885 this presbytery has ordained thirty-two ministers, licensed forty-eight, and has had under its care eighty-six candidates. Eight thousand one hundred and eighty-eight accessions, and over eleven thousand conversions have been reported." Some samples will show how the preachers of this presbytery were compensated for their services: "John Reed and W. B. Wear, as missionaries for six months, each received four dollars and twenty-eight cents, and A. McCorkle, twenty-three dollars and ninety-five cents. J. M. Foster, for six months, received thirty-three dollars and twelve cents, and F. E. Foster the same amount. P. G. Rea, for six months, received fifteen dollars and forty-three cents, and W. F. Lawrence, fifteen dollars and twelve cents. M. Neal, for one month, received two dollars and thirty-seven cents, and Moses Allen, for three months, twelve dollars and twelve cents."

In 1853 this presbytery indorsed "the Maine law." In Mr. Rea's manuscript is a melancholy notice of the last days of the Rev. Daniel Buie. He became insane while presiding as moderator of the presbytery, in 1834, and died years afterward in the Fulton asylum. Mr. Rea corrects a few of R. C. Ewing's dates.[1] In making

---

[1] Ewing's Memoirs.

these corrections, which have been adopted in this work, he had before him the records of the presbytery. Mr. Rea is now an aged man, and looks back upon a long life of usefulness as he lingers waiting the signal to call him home.

From a manuscript autobiography of the Rev. James Johnson (who was born in 1803) we learn that after he began the ministry in Ocoee Presbytery, Tennessee, he attended a protracted meeting held in connection with the meeting of East Tennessee Synod. The leading preachers of the synod all seemed to fail in the pulpit. A Presbyterian minister said: "You will have no revival so long as you rely on your big preachers. Pick out the least and humblest man you have and let him do the preaching, and let your big men go to praying." Johnson naively tells us that they selected him. He replied that he would preach if they would have Hiram Douglass follow with an exhortation. He said: "Let Douglass follow a poor sermon, and he has never been known to fail." The arrangement was made. Johnson preached, Douglass exhorted, and when the call was made crowds pressed to the mourner's bench. A great revival with scores of conversions followed. Johnson's humorous estimate of Douglass's talent is correct. Douglass excelled in tact, in ability to meet emergencies, to lead forlorn hopes, and turn defeats into victories.

Ten years ago there lived in the Choctaw Nation an aged Indian named Durant. He was an elder in the Cumberland Presbyterian church. He wrote for Dr. Crisman a sketch of his life, which contains some interesting facts. He says he was born in Mississippi, in 1798. In his childhood there were neither schools nor books, neither churches nor preaching anywhere in his country.. He never heard of such things till he was fifteen years old, and when at last a missionary school was established near his home, he was afraid of it. He did not understand what kind of a thing it was, and the mere thought of going to it frightened him. He says his people wore no hats, and instead of shoes wore moccasins. Very little was said or thought about any Supreme Being, though they did believe in a Great Spirit. Finally, however, he heard the gospel in his own language and became a Christian. He claims Cyrus Kingsbury as his spiritual father.

Chapter XXXVI.] SKETCHES AND INCIDENTS.

In West Tennessee there was, in 1845, near the home of a pious Cumberland Presbyterian mother an extensive neighborhood in which there was neither church nor Sunday-school. This was a source of great grief to this dear lady. Finally she found an earnest Christian man, Wm. Moore, who was willing to join her in an effort to establish a Sunday-school in the neglected neighborhood. Engaging the little log school-house, they published their appointment for a Sabbath-school. Neither of them had any knowledge of modern methods of Sunday-school work, but they both had a deep love for souls. The school at first was composed mostly of grown people, some of them gray headed. Their method was to read a chapter, talk about it a little while, then pray. After the first prayer came personal conversation with the unconverted about their souls, then another prayer. It was not long before a most gracious revival began in the log school-house, and it continued for months, until many of the married people, as well as a number of the young people, were counted among the converts. This incident, taken along with another now to be related, may serve to encourage some earnest worker in the Sabbath-school. The other instance was at Bowling Green, Kentucky. One of the teachers in the Cumberland Presbyterian Sabbath-school at that place went to her pastor and said, "I want to give up my class." He asked her why, and she answered: "I am no scholar. I can't understand all these new methods. I can't keep up with all these learned teachers or with my class. Everybody has got so far ahead of me. I am not fit to teach." He asked her how many of her large class of boys were Christians when she took charge of it. She replied, "None of them." "How many do you believe have been converted since you took charge of them?" "All but one." The pastor then asked her if she thought she had learning enough to pray earnestly for the conversion of that one. With tears she said, "Yes, with my whole heart." He then said to her, "I would not give you for fifty learned teachers who never led a pupil to Jesus."

The following incident is found in the manuscript of the Rev. M. H. Bone: The Missionary Board desired to secure the services of the Rev. F. G. Black, of Ohio, to take charge of a new mission in the city of Cincinnati; but the members of his congregation were not willing to let him go, and he would not leave them without their full consent. The board employed Mr. Bone to visit Black's congregation with a view to persuading them to yield their interests to the demands of the general cause. He made the visit, and on Sabbath he delivered an address on the great claims of Christ's kingdom, and showed how we ought to yield our local interests to larger general interests. Seeing the whole congregation in tears, he thought the time had come to have the question decided. Turning to the elders, he asked them if they would consent to give up their pastor. The elders asked: "What does Brother Black say? Does he want to go?" Mr. Black replied: "I believe it is my duty to go." Then Mr. Bone asked: "How many elders and members are there who are willing to let Mr. Black go where he feels that the Lord is calling him?" To this the only answer was increased weeping throughout the congregation. Still the agent of the board persevered in private till he accomplished his mission. Mr. Bone, when he was an old man, and long after Mr. Black had lost his wife and another member of his family by the cholera in Cincinnati, and after the Cincinnati mission had been for many years abandoned, put on record, concerning his visit to Mr. Black's church and his efforts to sever that holy pastoral relation, these words, "It was not of God."

The Rev. R. A. A. Moorman, of the Cumberland Presbyterian church, stammers badly; yet, strange to say, he has no impediment in his utterance while praying. In the beginning of his sermons this infirmity is often very embarrassing, but when he advances and becomes absorbed in his discourse, all traces of it vanish. Once at a large camp-meeting Mr. Moorman was to preach at eleven o'clock Sunday morning. He tried hard to begin his sermon, but his stammering was worse than usual. He sang a stanza, then tried again to preach, but he could not finish a single sentence. Falling upon his knees he poured forth a touching prayer for divine help. He asked the Lord that he might be rid of all concern about himself, and have grace that day to preach the simple gospel. He confessed before God and the people that his heart had been set on preaching a great sermon. He prayed God to forgive him and enable him to preach a little sermon that should lead souls to Christ. Long before he rose from his knees the whole congregation was melted to tears, while many earnest Christian hearts were joining in the preacher's earnest prayer. When he rose at last and began his discourse there was no more stammering. The sermon was soul-stirring and convincing, full of the power of the gospel. One who heard it testifies that it was the most powerful presentation of the truth he ever listened to. Scores owe their salvation, under God, to that prayer and sermon.

FIFTH PERIOD.

CHAPTER XXXVII.

TEN ASSEMBLIES—1861 TO 1870.

Per mare, . . per saxa, per ignes—Horace.

OF the ninety-seven presbyteries with which the Cumberland Presbyterian church began this period, sixty-nine were in the slave States. Fifty Southern and thirteen Northern presbyteries were each entitled to four representatives in the General Assembly. In a full Assembly there would have been two hundred and thirty-eight commissioners from the Southern States, and eighty-two from the Northern. The Board of Church Erection was located at St. Louis, Missouri; the Boards of Education and Publication at Nashville, Tennessee; and the Board of Missions and the Theological School at Lebanon, Tennessee—all on Southern soil, though St. Louis was far more under Northern than Southern control. It was generally claimed as a Northern city, but as it had but two congregations of Cumberland Presbyterians, both of them feeble and struggling missions, it was not a favorable location for a church board.

When the crushing weight of the war rested on the Southern States, it rested on and paralyzed over two thirds of our people, so that our General Assemblies, which all met north of the military lines during the whole war, were greatly weakened. When the Assembly of 1861 convened in St. Louis, Missouri, there were twenty-nine delegates from Southern presbyteries, and twenty-one from Northern presbyteries: fifty out of three hundred and twenty. Sixty-one out of ninety-seven presbyteries had no representative at the organization. The question was seriously debated whether or not those present should try to transact business for the church when so large a number of the presbyteries were not represented. It is well, however, that they decided the question affirmatively, for no better representation was secured until the great military struggle was over.

The church boards all managed to have their reports before the Assembly of 1861, and though the state of the country had already diminished their prosperity, yet they all showed a slight gain upon the preceding year's work. The Theological School had been suspended. The Missionary Board reported twenty-two thousand dollars receipts, fifty-five hundred dollars of it being a legacy. Only one hundred and thirty-three dollars had been paid to agents. In the ten Assemblies now under discussion much time was occupied in considering questions growing out of the war, but all that is reserved for the next chapter.

The General Assembly of 1862 met at Owensboro, Kentucky. The selection of that place was made in the spirit of conservatism. It is on the line between the two great sections then at war with each other, but the state of the country was such that no representatives of the Southern presbyteries were in attendance. When the Assembly was organized, sixty-nine presbyteries were unrepresented. It is not difficult to understand the reason why the Southern presbyteries were not represented. It was either wholly impossible for delegates to cross the military lines, or altogether too dangerous to be undertaken. The chances of being treated as a spy, or of being sent to a military prison, awaited any man from either section who crossed the lines without a pass; and passes for such trips to go and return were not granted.

The boards located in Tennessee had no representatives and no reports before this Assembly. These boards were, in fact, wholly unable even to have a meeting. All such operations were suspended. In this emergency two temporary committees were appointed by the Assembly, one on missions, and another on publication, to take charge, for the time, of these interests. The Committee on Publication was composed of men living far apart. They were to act in co-operation with the board at Nashville, if that was practicable, but independently of that board if they found it necessary. The Committee on Missions was composed of men living in three different States. We are not surprised, therefore, at the nature of the reports made by these committees to the next Assembly.

When the General Assembly of 1863 met at Alton, Illinois, sixty-nine presbyteries were still without representatives, and none of the boards located in the South sent any report or representative. The two committees appointed to co-operate respectively with the Board of Missions and the Board of Publication, or to supplement their work, reported nothing done. These committees were then both re-organized. The one on missions was located at Alton, Illinois, and the one on publication at Pittsburg, Pennsylvania. Neither the Board of Missions at Lebanon nor the Board of Publication at Nashville was disbanded, but these new boards were organized for existing emergencies.

When a committee appointed by the General Assembly went to Nashville to take charge of the books, plates, and other property of the Board of Publication, with a view to removing these effects to Pittsburg, they encountered one serious obstacle. There was a debt against the board, and the creditors interfered to prevent the removal of the property. The committee returned without the books. They then raised money to pay off the debt, and when it was paid the books were safely shipped to Pittsburg. P. G. Rea and Frederick Lack were the committee. During their visit to Nashville no unpleasant word passed between them and the representatives of the Nashville board.[1]

In 1864 the General Assembly met in Lebanon, Ohio. The times were stormy, and the Assembly spent much of its session in discussing questions connected with the great national struggle.

The General Assembly of 1865, which was held at Evansville, Indiana, was more conservative than its predecessor. Owensboro, Kentucky, was nominated by the Rev. J. W. Woods, a Federal chaplain, and chosen as the place for the next Assembly.

From 1862 to 1865 the state of things in the Southern portion of the church was distressing beyond all description. No delegates could reach the General Assembly. No Cumberland Presby-

---

[1] Private letter of Dr. W. E. Ward to Dr. Beard, written at the time.

terian paper was published in the South after the fall of Fort Donnelson, February, 1862. Papers from the Northern part of the church very rarely reached Southern readers. Even the proceedings of the General Assemblies were unknown. Synods and presbyteries could seldom meet except at called sessions, the regular meetings being prevented by military events. The records of some of these Southern presbyteries show failure after failure in their efforts to hold even called meetings. The place appointed might be accessible enough when the call was made, but not accessible when the time for meeting arrived.

In view of these things it was resolved to try to hold annual conventions to be composed of delegates from all the Southern presbyteries. Several unsuccessful attempts to bring such a convention together to consult about the church's interests were made prior to 1863. Finally calls for a convention to meet in Chattanooga, Tennessee, were published in the secular papers. The time set for this meeting was August 10, 1863. As far as possible private letters were also sent to all the Southern presbyteries. The convention was to be composed of delegates from the presbyteries, the same ratio of representation being adopted as that observed in regard to commissioners to the General Assembly. In the organization of the convention, however, some elders and preachers who were not commissioned by any presbytery were present, and were admitted to seats. The convention was composed of over sixty members. Its Minutes were never published; therefore in giving a synopsis of its proceedings reliance is placed on private memoranda taken down at the time. There were only three important measures adopted. The first was the appointment of a missionary committee located in the army, with General A. P. Stewart chairman. The second was to resolve to hold annual conventions at the same time that the General Assembly met. The third was the adoption of a resolution steadfastly to resist any movement which looked toward the division of the church.

The largest Cumberland Presbyterian convention of this period met in Selma, Alabama, May, 1864.[1] It had about one hundred and fifty delegates. A most touching letter from the Rev. Milton

---

[1] My own memoranda, and papers furnished by N. Waller, of Selma, Alabama.

Bird, D.D., was received by this body. Bird lived north of the military lines, and his letter pleaded for the unity of the church. Many present were moved to tears while they listened to this letter. The convention changed the membership of the Committee on Missions from army men to citizens with a fixed residence. The new committee was located at Selma. But those were times when Southern citizens as a rule were almost as destitute of a fixed residence as were the soldiers, and in a short time it was proved that the members of the Selma committee were no exceptions. This committee, however, did good work so long as it had power to meet.

Inasmuch as the Cumberland Presbyterian papers in the South were all suspended, the Selma convention resolved to publish a religious weekly, and elected the Rev. L. C. Ransom editor. A copy of the *Southern Observer* would be quite a curiosity now. The same edition would be partly on foolscap paper, partly on brown wrapping paper, and partly on wall-paper. The coming of the United States troops to Selma put an end to its career.

A very small convention met in Memphis, Tennessee, the next year. But the church throughout the South thought the time for conventions past, inasmuch as the way promised to be opened for all sections to be represented in the next General Assembly.

In 1866 the way was open for delegates from the Southern as well as the Northern States to attend the General Assembly, and there was a very full delegation from both sections. The Assembly met at Owensboro, Kentucky. It appointed a general fast-day to pray for more preachers. A very large number of the young ministers of the church had been killed in the war. This Assembly recognized both the Board of Missions at Alton and the one at Lebanon as legitimate boards of the church. The Committee on Missions which had long been at work on the Pacific coast was also at this time taken under the care of the General Assembly. The board located at Lebanon made its first report since 1861. It had held no meeting during the war, neither had it established any missions or collected any money. It gave the Assembly its reasons. Those who have lived in a country overrun by armies and blazing with battles will readily guess what the reasons were. Others could never understand them.

The next General Assembly, 1867, met in Memphis, Tennessee. There was a very full attendance. A sermon about the church as the body of Christ, which was preached at this Assembly by the Rev. L. C. Ransom, deserves to be specially mentioned. The preacher spoke of wounds in the body. He said every thing depended on the state of health. The forces of nature could soon overcome wounds in a healthy body, but a weak, sickly condition might make even small wounds fatal. The healthy condition of the church, Christ's body, was a state of vigorous spiritual life, and depended on daily communion with Jesus. Such a state would insure the rapid healing up of any wounds which it was possible for the body to receive. He said there were no wrongs which could possibly separate true Christians hopelessly, no wrongs which such Christians could not adjust. He based his hopes for preserving our church unity on the vigorous spirituality which Cumberland Presbyterians still preserved as a heritage from their fathers, and which, by the wonderful grace of God, had been maintained through all the trying contest which had deluged our land in blood. This Assembly resolved to discontinue the Committee on Publication located at Pittsburg, and to re-organize the board at Nashville, and directed that the assets should be transferred from Pittsburg to Nashville. Motions looking to the re-organization of this board at Nashville had been made in a former Assembly, but owing to the impoverished condition of all the Southern States the measure had been delayed.

The corresponding delegate representing the Cumberland Presbyterian church in the General Assembly of the Presbyterian church (Southern), had on his own authority stated in his speech to that body that he believed the time for steps toward organic union had come. That Assembly thereupon (November, 1866) appointed a committee to meet a similar committee from our church. The Cumberland Presbyterian committee was appointed by our Assembly in 1867. The two committees met in Memphis the following August. A long and pleasant conference was held. At the first meeting a resolution was adopted expressing the belief that the strengthening and edification of the church and the salvation of sinners would be greatly promoted by the union of the two churches. Each of the two committees, after consulting separately, presented a statement of the conditions upon which it was thought possible to effect an organic union. The Presbyterian committee proposed that the union should be formed "on the basis of the old Standards as they were held by the fathers previous to the separation." The committee representing the Cumberland Presbyterian church agreed to give up our church name; to surrender our Standards and accept those of the Presbyterian church in the matter of ministerial education, and to adopt the Presbyterian Standards, or such modifications of them as might be mutually acceptable, on all other points of difference in Form of Government and Discipline. But they asked that the Confession of Faith and Catechism of the Cumberland Presbyterian church should be adopted instead of the Presbyterian Confession and Catechism; or, as an alternative, they agreed to adopt the doctrinal Standards of the Presbyterian church with the modifications of the third, fifth, eighth, and seventeenth chapters of the Westminster Confession of Faith indicated on pages 69 and 70 of this History. In case this should not be satisfactory, the Cumberland Presbyterian committee expressed their willingness to accept a new compilation on the basis of the Westminster Standards which should exclude all phraseology and modes of expression which might plausibly be construed as favoring the idea of fatality or necessity. The conference closed, and these propositions were referred to the General Assemblies of the two churches. The Presbyterian Assembly met first (November, 1867), and voted down the proposed union, adopting the following deliverance on this subject:

The Assembly hereby records its devout acknowledgement to the Great Head of the church for the manifest tokens of his presence with the committees of conference during their deliberations as evinced by the spirit of Christian candor, forbearance, and love displayed by both parties in their entire proceedings. The Assembly regards the object for which the committees were appointed as one fully worthy of the earnest endeavors and continued prayers of God's people in both branches of the church represented in the committees. But at the same time it is compelled, in view of the terms for effecting any organic union suggested by the committee of the Cumberland Presbyterian church, to declare that, regarding the present period as one very unfavorable for making changes in our standards of faith and practice, it is more especially so for effecting changes so materially modifying the system of doctrine which has for centuries been the distinguishing peculiarity and eminent glory of the Presbyterian churches both of Europe and the United States.

This was equivalent to a decision by the Presbyterian church that doctrinal differences are the one bar to union with Cumberland Presbyterians.

Delegates appointed by the Cumberland Presbyterian General Assembly for the sole purpose of bearing fraternal greetings to other churches have several times abused their official positions by inaugurating negotiations looking toward organic union with these churches. This has been done at least four times since the war. The Assembly of 1886 adopted a resolution requiring corresponding delegates to refrain from all such unauthorized officiousness.

The General Assembly of 1868 met at Lincoln, Illinois. The Board of Publication at Nashville had been organized by the election of the Rev. A. J. Baird, president, and the Rev. J. C. Provine, financial agent. Its receipts for the year were $12,208. The previous Assembly had appointed a committee to revise the Form of Government (not the Confession of Faith), and the report of this committee occupied a large part of this Assembly's time. This revised discipline was on hand for several years. It was referred to the presbyteries three times, but their responses not being satisfactory in any case, it was finally abandoned.

The General Assembly of 1869 met at Murfreesboro, Tennessee. Various matters in the action of these Assemblies, it will be remembered, are reserved for special chapters. Except such reserved items, the chief work of this Assembly was the consolidation of the three missionary boards into one. The *Cumberland Presbyterian*, then published in Pennsylvania, had been earnestly urging this consolidation. The Theological School, the Board of Publication, and the Board of Missions were regarded as the three most important denominational enterprises, and there was among the delegates in this Assembly a general feeling in favor of establishing one of these in the Northern part of the church. A movement with this end in view was inaugurated by representatives from the

South, and at the suggestion of Northern representatives the consolidated Board of Missions was located at St. Louis, Missouri. The wisdom of this selection needs no vindication. A point farther north than St. Louis would have been too near the outer border of the church. Under this new arrangement it was understood that the whole church was to co-operate with the Board of Missions at St. Louis, and also with the Board of Publication and the Theological School located respectively at Nashville and Lebanon, Tennessee. With only such exceptions as all human affairs abound in, this pledge is still kept in good faith.

Between the Assembly of 1869 and that of 1870 a sharp discussion arose over the plans of the Board of Missions. The Assembly had divided the ecclesiastical year into quarters, assigning to each of the four principal enterprises of the church one quarter for its financial collections. The aim of this quarterly system was to avoid conflicting calls upon the congregations, and, by having all the pastors take these regular quarterly collections, to supersede the employment of agents by the boards. As soon as the consolidated Board of Missions at St. Louis was organized, it decided to adopt a system of agencies similar to those employed by insurance companies. There were two obligations which, some people thought, were violated by this scheme. The Assembly's plan for quarterly work by the pastors would be virtually set aside, and the pledge of co-operation with the other church boards would be infringed. If agents were to be sent out to canvass the churches all the year round as proposed, working only for missions, there would be conflicts, and, it was feared, very little co-operation. Long articles on both sides of the question appeared in the church papers.

The Board of Missions argued that the pastoral system of the church was as yet too imperfect to justify the abandonment of agencies. The other side replied that all ministers, whether pastors or supplies, were expected to work under the quarterly system, and would in time all fall into line. When the Assembly of 1870 met at Warrensburg, Missouri, the Board of Missions proposed as a compromise that its agents should be intrusted with all the collections for all the boards of the church. The Assembly referred the whole matter to a committee composed of representatives of all the boards. None of the other boards agreed to the proposed compromise; but they submitted another plan which was accepted and approved by the Assembly. The substance of this compromise was that the quarterly system should be suspended for one year, and that the missionary board and all the other boards should be allowed to work on their own plans. The friends of the missionary board felt confident that one year's test of their plan would demonstrate its utility. But their expectations were not realized, and the system of quarterly collections was subsequently restored.

There was a long and able discussion in the church papers between Dr. S. G. Burney and Dr. Milton Bird on the proposition to abolish synods, Dr. Burney taking the affirmative. The matter was brought before the General Assembly, but the proposition met with but little favor. It was not referred to the presbyteries, though most of the presbyteries discussed the question, and gave utterance to their views on the subject. Much interest was awakened throughout the whole church by this discussion, not only because both the disputants were men of marked ability and used very able arguments, but also because the question really had two sides, with a long array of facts favoring each side.

The church periodicals of this period were numerous, but most of them short lived. The *Cumberland Presbyterian*, in Pennsylvania, was published all through the war. The *Banner of Peace* was suspended from 1862 till the war closed, and then revived. With various changes of name and auspices, a weekly paper was kept up either at St. Louis, Missouri, or at Alton, Illinois, throughout this period. After the war *The Ladies' Pearl* and the *Theological Medium*, the former a monthly and the latter a quarterly, were revived, and Dr. T. C. Blake established the *Sunday-school Gem*. This was the first Sunday-school paper ever published in the interest of the Cumberland Presbyterian church. This little paper has been the means of leading many a child to Jesus.

The new presbyteries appearing on the Minutes of the Assembly in this period are: Huntsville (1866), Leavenworth (1867), Guthrie (1868), King, Bethel, and Tulare (1869). The work of consolidating the synods began in this period, so that there were fewer synods in the church but much larger ones in 1870 than in 1860. Through such consolidation the Kentucky Synod disappeared from the roll in 1865, and the Ozark Synod in 1866. The latter was re-organized in 1871. The name of Union Synod was changed to Alabama (1867), and that of Sacramento to Pacific (1863).

CHAPTER XXXVIII.

THE WAR RECORD.

> They strive alike for truth's behoof,
> For God and country, right and roof.
> —*J. G. Holland.*

IN this period several General Assemblies were held which were not accessible to Southern representatives, and there were also conventions of delegates from Southern presbyteries not accessible to Northern men. Then after the war closed there were several Assemblies in which the representatives of the church from both sections met and deliberated together. The deliverances of these several Assemblies and conventions concerning subjects connected with the civil war are now to be considered. It seems most impartial to give the full text of these deliverances, as it is possible to make a wrong impression by omissions, or to change a fair history into a partisan one by omitting portions of the record.

Before proceeding to these deliverances let us read the opening sermon of the Assembly of 1861 as it was reported in the papers at the time. This sermon was preached by the Rev. Milton Bird, D.D., from Hebrews xiii. 1: "Let brotherly love continue." The speaker introduced the subject with the inquiry, Who are brothers? and then proceeded to say:

In the most comprehensive sense of the word, all men are brethren, being made of the same blood. In its most limited signification those who are born of the same immediate parents are brethren. In the Bible sense of the term, Christians—those who are born of God, adopted into his family, and made partakers of his Spirit—are brethren. It is of this great brotherhood in Christ that the apostle speaks when he says, Let brotherly love continue.

1. It is a fact that Christians love one another. The spirit of Christianity is a spirit of love; faith works by love; pure Christianity is the strongest bond of friendship and kindness. That religion which is

not so is unworthy of the name. It is sounding brass or a tinkling cymbal. 1 John v. 12; iv. 7, 8, 9, 16; and iii. 14, 15.

2. The continuance of brotherly love is the true apostolic succession. There is but this one sense in which there is a regular line, descent, or succession from the apostles. All who are regenerated by the Holy Spirit and built together upon Christ, the corner-stone, are in the regular line—no others. Any other succession than this is a gross delusion. They who set themselves up as the only church in virtue of a regular line of popes, or apostolic ordinations, or water baptisms, deceive themselves and others. The true church of Christ is made up of all regenerated persons of all ages, nations, and denominations. All who have been born of the Spirit are brethren; they are one, and should love one another as God has commanded. The true line of succession revealed in the gospel is the law of life in Christ Jesus, which makes us free from the law of sin and death. All in whom this law abides recognize the same Spirit in each other by his outgoings from their hearts; and with a pure heart they fervently love one another as brethren. Judas was an apostle, and Simon, the sorcerer, was baptized; but outward ceremonies and rites were not sufficient to place them in the true line of succession; they were without the spirit and law of life in Christ Jesus; their hearts were not right in the sight of God.

Trusting in barren ordinances and rejecting the vital spirit of Christianity has perverted and poisoned the church. Ecclesiastical bodies without the renewing life of the Holy Spirit are not the habitations of God. They are not built upon the corner-stone, nor cemented together by brotherly love in the unity of the spirit and the bonds of peace. They conform to the world, and are attractive to the carnally minded because such can live in their communion without any restraint upon their follies and lusts. The current of the world has set so strongly into the true and living church, that multitudes make profession of religion and connect themselves with the visible church who are little if any better than before. They are often full of envy and strife among themselves, being desirous of vainglory, provoking one another, envying one another; and they often have more bitter prejudices and less charity for those who do not agree with them about some rite or minor point of doctrine than the people of the world. Alas, for such Christianity as does not change the carnal mind, and turn the heart from hatred to love, and prove itself genuine by yielding the fruits of the Spirit—"love, joy, peace, long-suffering, gentleness, goodness, faith, meekness, temperance." Such a religion is not worth the name. It had been better, infinitely better, for the cause of truth and the world, had it never existed. "They that are Christ's have crucified the flesh with the affections and lusts." "If we live in the spirit, let us also walk in the spirit.' "Let brotherly love continue."

3. When is brotherly love in danger of being lost?

At the time when it was said to the Hebrews, "Let brotherly love continue," the Jewish people were divided and distracted among themselves about matters of State and religion. Both the church and State were greatly corrupted and demoralized. So it is now in our nation. This fact can not be disguised; we all painfully feel it. Most of our old men, great men and good men both in church and State, have died. The rude blast was permitted to shake them like ripe fruit to their fall. Our beloved country is now convulsed with civil war. Why and how this was brought about, and who is to blame for it, is not for me to say in this place. Of the fact I speak, and a lamentable fact it is to every patriot, to every Christian heart. In such times as these brotherly love is in great danger of being lost.

Brothers in Christ, though our country is divided and engaged in fratricidal war, we are brethren still, we can not afford to separate. Pure religion changes not. Its life is love, its atmosphere peace. As soon could heaven sink into hell, or hell rise up to heaven, as a change come over the pure principles and spirit of Christianity. Love can not become hatred; it always endeavors to keep the unity of the Spirit in the bonds of peace. If we are the followers of the meek and lowly Jesus, we are the subjects of a kingdom not of this world. The weapons of our warfare are not carnal, but spiritual; we wield the sword of the Spirit. The more we love one another with a pure heart fervently, the better we can fight the battles of the Prince of Peace. If the spirit of Christ is in us, we will let brotherly love continue. We will not dishonor the white flag of heaven, nor give aid to the black flag of hell by strife and division. A pure and honest Christian is just and true still, though the heavens fall. He will not desert the standard, nor give aid and encouragement to the enemy of God. He will not wound the Captain-General of his salvation in the house of his friends. Brethren, we are in the midst of temptations; and motives to disobedience, alienation, and division present themselves on every hand. Let us, as Christians, prove our faith and love and verify our profession by abiding in love and in obedience to the laws of God and man in humble imitation of him who was obedient unto death.

In our organic relations as brethren let the pure spirit and principle of Christianity continue to connect us as one body. Christ is not divided, why should we divide? There is no sufficient cause. That which can not divide Christ should not be permitted to divide his people. A double guard and a most rigid scrutiny are required of every Christian who would do his duty in times so perilous as these upon which we have fallen. We find alarming developments in the tone of some of the secular and so-called religious journals which profess at once to express and guide the public mind. These openly evince an utter disregard for truth and right, of constitution and law, and do their utmost to marshal North and South against each other in the most bitter malignity.

In these times of serious religious apostasy and general political corruption on which we have fallen, city and State and nation are tainted with the virus of loathsome disease; magistrates take bribes, legislators are more selfish than patriotic, and rulers are oftentimes demagogues instead of statesmen. It is easy to do wrong in matters which seem insignificant, owing to the circumstances which have brought other things into greater prominence. It is very easy, in a time of general defection and excitement, to lose sight of those fundamental principles of right by which we are bound to act at all times. It is very easy to loosen the restraints which God's law, conscience, and good government impose for our welfare and to keep us in unity as brethren. It requires genuine faith in God to stand firm in these times of general defection of church and State. The pulpit has been perverted and the church prostrated. The standard of morality has been lowered, and the nation so demoralized that God and the Bible have been repudiated, passion and lust have been enthroned. The nation has defied the binding force of the law of the Sabbath. The country has been ruled by the passion of avarice. God will humble the pride of the nation. Sectional war has fallen upon the land as a just judgment of the Almighty. It is a punishment for the ingratitude and guilty delusion, folly, and blindness of the people. Let the church and the nation humble themselves beneath the rod, and, in penitential confession and earnest supplication to God, seek deliverance from the most terrible calamity and threatened destruction.

Beloved brethren, we must not allow ourselves to be drawn into disputes about the things which belong to Cæsar, and so become divided in things which belong to God. Each must allow others to follow their convictions of right in regard to the unfortunate condition produced by the Northern and Southern extremists who have dismembered our once happy and prosperous Union. Before this rupture our religion was not geographical or sectional, nor is it so since the rupture. If a sectional religion divides us here, and destroys brotherly love, it will exclude us from heaven. There is no Northern or Southern religion there, but God's redeemed in heaven come from the north and the south, from the east and the west. Disputes about religion should never be suffered to cool our Christian affection. Christians should always love and live as brethren. Without regard to name, denomination, or peculiar views, they should recognize each other as members of the same great spiritual family. More especially should those who agree in doctrine and practice cultivate friendly relations, and remain one. The sea is rocking, the waves are rolling, great is the necessity therefore that we should stand firm in this perilous hour, and show that our church has enough of the life and power of godliness to be capable of braving the storm and guiding the ship. We must look to Jehovah, who is the God of the rainbow as of the deluge. He reigns in the storm as in the calm. How appropriate and how full of comfort the language of the Psalmist, as read in your hearing in the introduction of these exercises, "God is our refuge and strength, a very present help in trouble. Therefore, will not we fear though the earth be removed, and though the mountains be carried into the midst of the sea, though the waters thereof roar and be troubled, though the mountains shake with the swelling thereof. . . . He maketh wars to cease unto the end of the earth; he breaketh the bow, and cutteth the spear in sunder; he burneth the chariot in the fire." We are in the hands of the Lord. Only let us do our duty and put our trust in him and all will be well. He will protect his people and save his church. As we have loved each other heretofore, so let brotherly love continue until all men shall be constrained to cry aloud, "Behold, how good and pleasant it is for brethren to dwell together in unity."

Through all these bitter years the voice of Milton Bird rang out on the same key, nor did it ring in vain.

The Assembly of 1861 met at St. Louis. After a preamble deploring the war, it put on record the following resolutions:

Resolved, 1. That we recognize the good providence and rich grace of Almighty God in bringing our General Assembly together in the present fearful crisis in the unity of the Spirit and the bond of peace, and in giving us to experience "How good and how pleasant it is for brethren to dwell together in unity."

2. That while we regret the circumstances which have prevented the attendance of commissioners from some of the presbyteries, we do now and hereby record our sincere thanks to our heavenly Father that brethren have met from north and south, east and west, and that brotherly kindness and love have continued from the opening to the close of our present meeting—nothing occurring to disturb in the least the warm and brotherly spirit of unity and peace.

3. That, the grace of God assisting us, we will always endeavor to cherish the true principles and pure spirit of Christianity; that, with this enthroned in our hearts, we can and will walk in love and live in

peace; that thus we may walk and live in the bonds of unbroken brotherhood, we do hereby recommend that unceasing prayer be made throughout the whole church for the guidance and blessing of Almighty God through these times of great peril and trouble.

4. That the General Assembly do now and hereby recommend to every person, family, and congregation composing our church the observance of the twenty-second day of June as a day of humiliation, fasting, and prayer before and unto that God who has said, "Be still, and know that I am God," for the deliverance of his church out of her fiery trials, and for a righteous and peaceful solution of the troubles and fratricidal war that now curse our common country.

The General Assembly of 1862, held at Owensboro, Kentucky, adopted the following report:

The committee submit the following report: Since the last meeting of this body the church has been passing through a severe ordeal. No small injury to her spiritual and temporal interests has resulted from the crisis of public affairs, religious and civil. While in some portions of the church there have been precious revivals of religion, still there is an evident want of an earnest-hearted Christianity. . . . Our church in its teachings on the subject of our duties to the civil government has in its doctrines (drawn, as we believe, from the word of God) set up a pure and lofty standard of Christian morality, included in which is the doctrine that government is God's institution, not a mere human regulation, and that obedience in its constitutional sphere is a religious as well as a civil obligation. This doctrine is particularly set forth in our Confession of Faith, chapter 23, section 4: "It is the duty of the people to pray for magistrates, to honor their persons, to pay them tribute and other duties; to obey their lawful commands, and to be subject to their authority for conscience' sake. Infidelity or difference in religion does not make void the magistrate's just and legal authority, nor free the people from their due obedience to him, from which ecclesiastical persons are not exempted."

Chapter 20, section 4: "And because the powers which God hath ordained and the liberty which Christ hath purchased are not intended by God to destroy, but mutually to uphold and preserve one another, they who upon pretense of Christian liberty shall oppose any lawful power, or the lawful exercise of it, whether it be civil or ecclesiastical, resist the ordinance of God. And for their publishing of such opinions, or maintaining of such practices as are contrary to the light of nature or to the known principles of Christianity, whether concerning faith, worship, or conversation, or the power of godliness, or such erroneous opinions or practices as either in their own nature, or in the manner of publishing or maintaining them, are destructive to the external peace and order which Christ hath established in the church, they may lawfully be called to account, and proceeded against by the censures of the church."

Regarding our duties to civil government, we refer our ministers and people to the aforementioned article of our faith as the utterance of the Assembly on the subject. In connection with this we invite their attention to, and strict observance of, chapter 31, section 4: "Synods and councils are to handle or conclude nothing but that which is ecclesiastical, and are not to intermeddle with civil affairs which concern the commonwealth, unless by humble petition, in cases extraordinary, or by way of advice for satisfaction of conscience, if they be thereunto required by the civil magistrate."

Resolved, 1. That in the teaching of our Confession of Faith, as well as in our admirable civil constitution, church and State are wisely kept apart, and the principle established that ecclesiastical legislation is not needed for the State, nor civil legislation, except for security of person and property, which is a political right, for the church.

2. That in this time of trial we approve and re-indorse unequivocally the above-mentioned article of our faith, and agreeably thereto we at all times hold ourselves accountable for our ecclesiastical relations and conduct to the church.

3. That we deeply deplore the carnage and demoralizing tendency of a war of brothers.

4. That in the present crisis of our public affairs we regard the church and the nation especially called upon to humble themselves before God for their many and grievous sins, imploring his assistance in bringing the war to a speedy conclusion in a righteous peace.

5. That in this time of confused passion we will, so far as in us lies, endeavor to allay and not exasperate the feelings of those who differ from us, and we most earnestly and affectionately advise our ministers and members to cultivate forbearance and conciliation; to avoid partisanship and sectionalism in church and State; and to evidence their loyalty to Cæsar by their loyalty to Christ in following his example and teaching, and thus continue in brotherly love, and stand before the world a united brotherhood, walking in the comfort of love and in the fellowship of the Spirit.

6. That we deeply sympathize with those stricken families in our several congregations now mourning the death of loved ones fallen in the bloody strife, and we commend them to the tender compassion of the God of all consolation who is good, a stronghold in the day of trouble, and who knoweth them that trust in him. (Nahum i. 7.)

Adopted unanimously by the committee.

This report was signed by Milton Bird, *Chairman*, W. F. Baird, Archibald Johnson, A. B. Brice, H. C. Read, F. A. Witherspoon, J. B. Green, J. B. Logan, J. H. Nickell, J. M. Gill, and I. N. Cary.

The General Assembly of 1863, at Alton, Illinois, adopted the following:

Your special committee to whom was referred the memorial from the Synod of Ohio touching the morality of political secession and the institution of American slavery, have had the subject assigned them under prayerful, protracted, and patient investigation, and in answer to the memorial before us, and, also, in order to present a paper that will embody a deliverance from this General Assembly touching these subjects, we submit the following preamble and resolutions:

WHEREAS, This General Assembly of the Cumberland Presbyterian church in the United States of America can not conceal from itself the lamentable truth that the very existence of our church and nation is endangered by a gigantic rebellion against the rightful authority of the general government of the United States, which rebellion has plunged the nation into the most dreadful civil war; and, whereas, The church is the light of the world, and can not withhold her testimony upon great moral and religious questions, and upon measures so deeply affecting the great interests of Christian civilization, without becoming justly chargeable with the sin of hiding her light under a bushel; therefore,

Resolved, 1. That loyalty and obedience to the general government in the exercise of its legitimate authority, are the imperative Christian duties of every citizen; and that treason and rebellion are not mere political offenses of one section against another, but heinous sins against God and his authority.

2. That the interests of our common Christianity, and the cause of Christian civilization and national freedom throughout the world, impel us to hope and pray God (in whom is all our trust) that this unnatural rebellion may be put down, and the rightful authority of the general government re-established and maintained.

3. That we deeply sympathize with our fellow-countrymen and brethren who, in the midst of great temptation and sufferings, have stood firm in their devotion to God and their country; and, also, with those who have been driven, contrary to their judgment and wishes, into the ranks of the rebellion.

4. That in this time of trial and darkness we re-indorse the preamble and resolution adopted by the General Assembly of the Cumberland Presbyterian church at Clarksville, Tennessee, on the 24th day of May, 1850, which are as follows:

"WHEREAS, In the opinion of this General Assembly the preservation of the union of these States is essential to the civil and religious liberty of the people; and it is regarded as proper and commendable in the church, and more particularly in the branch which we represent (it having had its origin within the limits of the United States of America, and that soon after the blood of our revolutionary fathers had ceased to flow in that unequal contest through which they were successfully conducted by the strong arm of Jehovah), to express its devotion on all suitable occasions to the government of their choice; therefore,

"*Resolved*, That this General Assembly look with censure and disapprobation upon attempts from any quarter to dissolve this Union, and would regard the success of any such movement as exceedingly hazardous to the cause of religion, as well as civil liberty. And this General Assembly would strongly recommend to all Christians to make it a subject of prayer to Almighty God to avert from our beloved country a catastrophe so direful and disastrous."

The General Assembly of 1864 met at Lebanon, Ohio. The momentous events then transpiring and the perilous and excited state of the country doubtless had much influence in shaping the deliverance of this Assembly. It adopted the following:

The special committee appointed to consider the memorial from the Presbytery of Indiana, and to which was referred the communication from the Presbytery of Richland, would respectfully report that the questions brought under consideration in the memorial and communication are of deepest interest to the church at the present time. This is a season of extraordinary events and unusual responsibilities. God, the Maker of the world, the Governor of kingdoms and States, who will be known by the judgments he executes, seems now to be dealing with the nations in his displeasure, and in dignity and majesty he is marching through the land, while the foundations of society are breaking up. Then, it is a time when we should look to the wrong that we may forsake it, and inquire diligently for the truth that we may embrace it as a precious thing that can not be disregarded without offending the Most High.

The question intended to be brought to the consideration of your reverend body by the Presbytery of Indiana is contained in the fourth resolution of its memorial, which is as follows:

"*Resolved*, further, That in this great crisis of our church and nation we memorialize the next General Assembly of the Cumberland Presbyterian church to set forth still more fully and more clearly than it did last spring, the social and moral evils inherent in the system of slavery as it exists in the Southern States; and that it urge upon our Southern brethren, in all Christian faithfulness, that the time has fully come, in the providence of God, when they can, and therefore should, without delay, abandon a system which is a reproach to our holy religion, and which has so imperiled our beloved church, our free government, and our national union."

On this memorial we propose the following deliverance:

Resolved, 1. That we regard the holding of human beings in involuntary servitude, as practiced in some of the States of the American Union, as contrary to the principles of our holy religion; and as being the fruitful source of many evils and vices in the social system.

2. That it be recommended to Cumberland Presbyterians, both North and South, to give countenance and support to all constitutional efforts of our government to rid the country of that enormous evil.

The business intended to be brought before your reverend body in the communication from the Presbytery of Richland, is contained in the following resolutions:

Resolved, 1. That as a presbytery we do not desire the dissolution of our church whether our government be permanently divided or not.

2. That as a Presbytery we wish to cultivate the same feelings which have ever existed between this presbytery and the brethren of the whole church.

3. That we do not think political differences a sufficient ground for the dissolution of any church.

4. That this presbytery instruct her delegates to the General Assembly, to study the interests of the whole church, leaving out of view any sectional feeling or interest.

In response to which your committee would say that we regard the preservation of the integrity of the church as of great importance, and we hope that all will be done that can be done to preserve it whole, without conniving at sin and sacrificing the principles of truth and justice, but to these we must adhere. The great Master said: "I came not to send peace, but a sword; for I come to set a man at variance against his father, and the daughter against her mother, and the daughter-in-law against her mother-in-law, and a man's foes shall be they of his own household." Not that such was the design of his coming, but that such would be the effect, in that conflict that must go on between truth and falsehood, holiness and sin. In this conflict we must stand by our Master, though it require us to sever the dearest ties of time. And as this General Assembly has twice declared that obedience to the civil magistrate is a Christian duty, therefore we must regard those who are, or have been, voluntarily in rebellion against the government of these United States, as not only guilty of a crime against the government, but also guilty of a great sin against God; and with such, without repentance and humiliation before God and the church, we can desire no fellowship. But to all such as have stood true to God and the government of the United States, and prove their loyalty by their works, we extend the cordial hand of a brother's greeting and a brother's welcome, saying let us live in peace, love as brethren, and toil together under the banner of our common Master, until we shall be called from labor to the refreshing rewards on high.

[The committee which submitted this report consisted of W. S. Campbell, Illinois; Le Roy Woods, Ohio; J. L. Payne, Tennessee; Jas. Ritchey, Indiana; Geo. S. Adams, Iowa; J. M. Gallagher, Pennsylvania; H. W. Eagan, Illinois; J. B. Logan, Illinois; P. G. Rea, Missouri. The first item was signed by all of these, and the second item by all except J. L. Payne.]

Against this action the following protest was entered:

We protest against the action adopting the report: 1. Because the principle of action is erroneous, and its spirit secular and sectional. It makes, or seeks to make, an issue that is not made in the fundamental law or doctrine of the church. The point involved subverts our ecclesiastical law, by inaugurating a radical course of action tending to revolutionize and destroy. The principles of the constitution of the church and teachings of the word of God, point out an open way, wherein all must walk, who avoid revolution and destruction produced by radicalism, in its opposite types; it is erroneous in principle and fanatical in spirit, producing alienation, division, and ruin.

2. The fundamental law of our church organization can not be changed, nor a new one introduced, either directly or indirectly, by any person in this Assembly; any action it may take overstepping this law or tending thereto is of no binding force, and is, in fact, merely the opinion of those voting for it.

Those who demand that the time of this Assembly shall be occupied in the unceasing agitation of slavery, to the neglect of its legitimate business, say they want and must have a full and clear expression of the whole church. Now if such expression was not given in 1851 and 1863, it is certain that it is not given in 1864, when the country is in such a state of excitement as it never was before, and this is the smallest Assembly that ever has taken action on the subject. (Here follows a comparison of figures to show that the Assembly of 1864, which had representatives from but twenty-six presbyteries out of ninety-seven, and had only fifty delegates present when the vote was taken, was not able to give the "full and clear expression of the whole church.")

The action of the previous Assemblies was sufficiently plain and full to satisfy all reasonable persons, and as for others they will continue to clamor for increased and continued agitation.

3. Intelligence, order, piety, justice, and benevolence do not consist with agitation and violence, or the result thereof. Indulgence sharpens the appetite for agitation and makes it more craving. In the incipient stages of it, few if any look to the final result. It is a chronic nightmare, varied with periodical spasms, until its normal state is convulsion, and it enters upon a revolution, the radicalness of which becomes every day more apparent. The ever-restless and clamorous agitation is destructive in its tendency; it generates an atmosphere of alienation and bitterness in which the genius of cohesion dies and union crumbles away. When the creed of the church or its fundamental law dies, or sectional hatred becomes stronger than love to that creed and that law and their sacred associations, then fanatical sectional agitation dismembers the church and makes its continued unity impossible, by having no common ground for a truce to conflict of opinion; the spirit of fanaticism not being less intolerant than that of the Spanish inquisition.

4. The perpetual agitation is aimless, if its end is not to introduce a condition of communion such as is not made by our Savior and his apostles, and the framers of the constitution and discipline of our church. The agitation is not demanded by a type of piety and benevolence above that professed by others, but by a strange mania that is abroad, which seems to operate alike in scoffing infidels, corrupt and babbling politicians, and such professors of religion as are led or driven by the pressure of any peculiar circumstances which may surround them. They who would make the church conform to the outside secular, sectional pressure of the times, under the idea that if they do not do so, that pressure will crush and kill the church, take the most effectual course they could to destroy the spiritual life, strength, and moral influence of the church. Do they follow the example and believe him who said, "I will build my church upon this rock, and the gates of hell shall not prevail against it?"

God and his word do not change. What is our duty *now* was our duty in the past, and will be our duty in the future. Changing circumstances are not the standard of duty.

5. The adoption of the report arrives at no finality on the subject. The presbyteries have not had it before them, as the issue is sought to be made here, and therefore any action of the Assembly amounts to nothing more than an expression of the private opinion of those sustaining it. Present action will be no more a finality than past action, if we may judge the future by the past. Those voting for the report simply express their opinion, and that opinion neither becomes the word of God nor the principle of the Constitution and Discipline of the church; it is merely agitation for the sake of agitation, and the appetite for it becomes more clamorous by indulgence, and it is not even satisfied when it has produced alienation, division, and ruin.

6. We protest against the adoption of the report, because we are opposed to that which in effect leads to secession in church and State. It is a historical fact that church secession opens the way to, and was auxiliary to, secession and division in the State; that which carries forward the former aids the latter.

There is an *abolition type of disloyalty* as well as a *secession type;* the latter is the offspring of the former, and there is a sympathy between them, both operating as a unit in effect. If the end aimed at in ecclesiastical secession is to strengthen good government, then it is commendable, but it is not attained in so cheap a way. They do greatly deceive themselves who think to establish a character for extraordinary patriotism and loyalty, by delivering themselves of preambles, and resolutions, and wind, in ecclesiastical bodies. If they would take their position with the suffering soldier in the front ranks under the lead of the true and earnest generals, then they would obtain credit for patriotism and loyalty, by showing that they had a heart to serve the country in its trials. It is an old but true maxim that "actions speak louder than words."

7. We can not countenance the work of alienation and disorganization in the church, because faith and liberty suffer equally from it. The course of action against which we protest, we regard as unwise, especially in the present condition of the country. There is no precedent in the primitive church for the policy of this action. While it does no good, it will do harm. In our judgment, its advocates are under some bewildering influence, and strangely misconceive the question which they undertake to settle, and the bearing of their action upon it. The chapter God has written upon the heart and animus of the Assembly, he will cause to be respected, and each one of us must meet it for himself at the judgment seat of Christ.

This protest was signed by Milton Bird, Minor E. Pate, E. Barbour, M. T. Reed, J. W. P. Davis, J. B. Green, W. B. Farr, M. V. Brokau, S. A. Ramsey, R. A. Reed, Ezra Ward, and Jesse Anderson.

Thirty-eight votes were cast in favor of the deliverance adopted by this Assembly, and twelve against it.

The Assembly of 1865, at Evansville, Indiana, made no new deliverance, but passed the following resolution:

Resolved, That we are apprised that in all the States lately in rebellion against the government of the United States, there will be difficulties to encounter in re-organizing churches and presbyteries, on account of the fact that many of our ministers and members have been involved in the rebellion; some perhaps willingly, and many from force of circumstances. Therefore we recommend to all our brethren in those States, in re-constructing the churches, to adopt the action of the last General Assembly, touching that matter, as a basis, believing that said action after showing true devotion to civil government, is according to the principles of God's holy word and our Confession of Faith, and that no further legislation is necessary on the subject.

A full report has now been given of deliverances made by Assemblies inaccessible to the Southern presbyteries. We are next to look at the action of the Southern Cumberland Presbyterian conventions. These conventions refused uniformly to give any deliverance on these questions. This was not because there was on the part of those composing them any lack of earnest conviction, nor because there was any less outside pressure on them than on the Assemblies. The convictions of rectitude, and the feeling against what was regarded the outrages of "the enemy," were, if possible, even deeper with Southern than with Northern Christians. The pressure on the conventions for some "deliverance" condemning "the sectional usurpations of the Northern States," was very great. The Oxford Presbytery seceded from the denomination because the church still held to its "union with the enemy." Members in the extreme South were withdrawing for political reasons.

When the Chattanooga convention met in 1863, there was one member who thought that the Southern churches would be compelled to yield to this outside pressure, and he moved that steps be taken in that direction. Then the Rev. W. M. Reed, a rebel colonel, rose in his place and made a most thrilling speech. In substance, among other things, he said: "They taunt us with treason. Very well. Let those whose ecclesiastical skirts are red with the blood of this fratricidal war taunt on. I would rather go before my final Judge with our record than with theirs. Mr. Chairman, at this solemn hour, when Jehovah is dealing with our people, it is a source of unspeakable comfort to me that our church has always been conservative. The outside world demands that we come out. They call for deliverances. Well, sir, the whole manhood of our Southern churches is giving its deliverances, with muskets in the trenches, not on paper in church judicatures. Those who are not satisfied with the form of our deliverances, but ask in addition that we put Cæsar above Christ, and rend Christ's body, in order to show our patriotism, are not entitled to our respect. We want to please God, not politicians. Mr. Chairman, let us wait, and pray, and hope. I believe our church will remain undivided, no matter what comes of this bitter civil struggle."

When the vote was taken not one single voice was heard in favor of the motion. Even its mover voted no. No such motion ever again came up in this or any subsequent convention held by Southern Cumberland Presbyterians. A persistent determination to avoid schism was both expressed and maintained.

We are now to consider the deliverances adopted by the representatives of the two sections in General Assemblies held after the close of the war. The first Assembly in which Northern and Southern delegates met after peace was established, was held at Owensboro, Kentucky, May, 1866. This appointment, by Northern votes, to meet on Southern soil, looked like holding out the olive branch of peace. Still there were many fears of division. There were extreme men on both sides who wanted partisan action, but there were also many who were earnestly praying for the unity of the church. The question was, What shall be done about the deliverances of 1864? If they were enforced, some said, the Southern delegates would not be entitled to sit in the Assembly. The stated clerk, however, enrolled all the regularly commissioned Southern delegates. They were then, of course, largely in the majority.

This Assembly of 1866 was the first in which the voices of all the presbyteries had a chance to be mingled into one expression. Its deliverance, which was written by the Rev. J. C. Provine, D.D., then editor of the *Banner of Peace*, and offered by Milton Bird, was as follows:

WHEREAS, According to the plain teaching of our Confession of Faith, "synods and councils are to handle and conclude nothing but that which is ecclesiastical, and are not to interfere with the affairs of the commonwealth;" and,

WHEREAS, It is of momentous interest to the church to recognize practically, as well as in theory, the great truth taught by the Savior, viz.: That his kingdom is not of this world; therefore,

Resolved, 1. That this General Assembly is opposed to every movement, coming from any quarter, that looks to a union of church and State.

2. That we are opposed to the prostitution of the pulpit, the religious press, or our ecclesiastical courts to the accomplishment of political and sectional purposes.

3. That any expression of political sentiment made by any judicatory of our church, north, south, east, or west, is unnecessary, and no part of the legitimate business of an ecclesiastical court.

4. That nothing in the foregoing shall be construed into an expression of opinion upon slavery and rebellion.

There were 112 votes in favor of this deliverance, and 40 against it.

The next fall the Pennsylvania Synod passed the following resolutions asking the General Assembly to explain or modify this action:

WHEREAS, The Cumberland Presbyterian church did, in the adoption of its form of government and discipline under the title of "The Form of Government and Discipline of the Cumberland Presbyterian church in these United States, under their care," recognize the duty of submission to the general government, as the supreme civil power; declaring also that "they who, under pretense of Christian liberty, shall oppose any lawful power, or the lawful exercise of it, resist the ordinance of God," and that such persons "may lawfully be called to account and proceeded against by the censures of the church;" and,

WHEREAS, The General Assembly of 1864, in the exercise of its declared authority for "reproving, warning, or bearing testimony against error in doctrine or immorality in practice," did declare those voluntarily engaged in the late rebellion against the government of the United States to be guilty of great sin, and the General Assembly of 1865 reaffirmed this deliverance against the sin of rebellion; and

WHEREAS, The late General Assembly which met at Owensboro, Kentucky, passed certain resolutions, sometimes styled the "final action," which are now claimed by many who voted for them to be, in effect, a repeal of the deliverances of 1864 in regard to the sin of rebellion; and,

WHEREAS, These resolutions, from their own ambiguity as to their intended bearing on the deliverance of 1864, are the occasion of much difference of view as to their import, engendering strife and confusion, and threatening to divide the church; and,

WHEREAS, The late General Assembly, which met at Owensboro, Ky., is considered by many of our people not to have been a constitutional Assembly, in that it admitted to seats, as is alleged, certain members who had not a constitutional right to membership in that body because of the disorganized condition of the presbyteries from which they came, the action of the Assembly of 1865 respecting the re-organization of such presbyteries being, as it appears, entirely disregarded; therefore,

Resolved, 1. That we respectfully memorialize the General Assembly, to meet in 1867, and that it is hereby memorialized to investigate the question of the legality of the representation from disorganized presbyteries in the General Assembly of 1866.

2. That the action of the late Assembly is in effect a nullification of the deliverance of 1864, leaving the church without any record against the sins of slavery and rebellion, and justly chargeable with approving slavery and rebellion, both because it has nullified a deliverance *against* these sins, and because that nullification was demanded by its advocates on the ground that slavery is right in itself and that the rebellion was not wrong.

3. That as a synod we hereby solemnly and unequivocally declare our adherence to the deliverence of 1864 against the sins of slavery and rebellion.

4. That we hereby memorialize the General Assembly which is to meet in 1867 to declare unequivocally whether or not the deliverance of 1864 still stands as the declared and unmodified position of the church on the question of slavery and rebellion.

5. That should the next Assembly refuse to reaffirm the deliverance of 1864, or to adopt such an expression as will fairly and unequivocally recognize that deliverance, in its substance, as the record of the church against the sins of slavery and rebellion, that we will then, in common with others who adhere to that deliverance, claim to be the true Cumberland Presbyterian church in the United States.

This called forth from the Assembly of 1867, at Memphis, Tennessee, the following deliverance:

WHEREAS, There exists some doubts about the bearing of the last General Assembly's utterances on those of former Assemblies on the subjects of slavery and rebellion; therefore,

Resolved, That while the decisions of the General Assembly are of high authority, they can not become a law, binding upon all the churches, so as to set up a test of church membership, unless they are referred to the presbyteries, and there approved. Hence, such decisions are not subjects of repeal, and the decisions of last Assembly did not repeal the decisions of former Assemblies on the subjects above named, nor did they acknowledge their authority, but simply disclaimed all jurisdiction over such questions.

There were only two dissenting voices to this resolution, and they afterward withdrew their opposition. So, with the full consent of all the Southern members, the deliverances of 1864 stand on the records as the opinion of all those who voted for them, and all who chose to conform to them. Their moral force, whatever it may be, is not a subject for repeal. They are a part of the history of the times, and, like all other utterances, a part of the records which are to come before the last appellate court, when the final Judge assembles the universe to the last assizes.

But some in Pennsylvania and elsewhere were still dissatisfied, and a memorial called up the subject in the Assembly of 1868, at Lincoln, Illinois. That Assembly adopted the following report:

Your Committee on Overtures have had under serious and prayerful consideration a memorial, signed by a number of brethren of the ministry and eldership, asking of "your reverend body to declare and affirm the following propositions as the principles taught in our Confession of Faith, and the word of God:

"1. That things secular and civil belong to the State.

"2. That things moral and ecclesiastical belong to the church.

"3. That in regard to things which are mixed, being partly secular and civil, and partly moral and ecclesiastical, the secular and civil aspects belong to the State, but the moral and ecclesiastical aspects belong to the church.

"4. That it is the prerogative of the church of Christ to sanction correct morals, to express its views through the pulpit, the press, and the various judicatures, on all moral questions, regardless of civil codes or political creeds."

While your committee appreciate fully the sincerity and earnest desire of your memorialists, we can not recommend the adoption of the precise language of said memorial, as being in harmony with your Confession of Faith, and the word of God. At least it is so liable to misconstruction that it would be unsafe as the form of a rule of practice.

We respectfully recommend the adoption of the following answer to said memorial:

1. The Confession of Faith is a much clearer statement of civil jurisdiction than the first proposition of the memorial. See chapter 23, section 3. "Civil magistrates may not assume to themselves the administration of the word and sacraments, or the powers of the keys of the kingdom of heaven; or in the least interfere in matters of faith. Yet as nursing fathers, it is the duty of civil magistrates to protect the church of our common Lord, without giving the preference to any denomination of Christians above the rest, in such manner that all ecclesiastical persons whatever shall enjoy the full, free, and unquestioned liberty of

discharging every part of their sacred functions, without violence or danger. And, as Jesus Christ hath appointed a regular government and discipline in his church, no law of any commonwealth should interfere with, let, or hinder the due exercise thereof among the voluntary members of any denomination of Christians, according to their own profession and belief. It is the duty of civil magistrates to protect the person and good name of all their people in such an effectual manner as that no person be suffered, either upon pretense of religion or of infidelity, to offer any indignity, violence, abuse, or injury to any person whatsoever, and to take order that all religious and ecclesiastical assemblies be held without molestation or disturbance." See also accompanying scripture, 2 Chron. xxvi. 18.

2. Your committee are of opinion that the second proposition of the memorial is not respectful to the State, as a power ordained of God. For while the pulpit, press, and ecclesiastic courts have jurisdiction over all moral and ecclesiastic questions, there are many moral questions over which the State has jurisdiction also.

3. Many questions have arisen and doubtless will arise, which must be divided, the church considering and acting upon such parts of said questions as come within her jurisdiction. And while she is to be free and untrammeled in her teaching and adjudication, she must be wise and prudent, and will find ample instructions in her just and scriptural standards. See Confession of Faith, chapter 31, sections 2, 4. "It belongeth to synods and councils, ministerially, to determine controversies of faith and cases of conscience, to set down rules and directions for the better ordering of the worship of God, and government of his church, to receive complaints in cases of mal-administration, and authoritatively to determine the same; which decrees and determinations, if consonant with the word of God, are to be received with reverence and submission, not only for their agreement with the word, but also for the power whereby they are made, as being an ordinance of God, appointed thereunto in his word." "Synods and councils are to handle or conclude nothing but that which is ecclesiastical; and are not to intermeddle with civil affairs, which concern the commonwealth; unless by way of humble petition, in cases extraordinary, or by way of advice for satisfaction of conscience, if they be thereunto required by the civil magistrate." See also Luke xii. 13, 14; John xviii. 36. Also, Form of Government, chapter 7, section 2. "These assemblies ought not to possess any civil jurisdiction, nor to inflict any civil penalties. Their power is wholly moral and spiritual, and that only ministerial and declarative. They possess the right of requiring obedience to the laws of Christ, and of excluding the disobedient and disorderly from the privileges of the church."

4. Your committee agree fully with your memorialists in the expressions of the fourth proposition, except the phrase, "of civil codes." Your committee are of opinion, that while it is the prerogative and duty of the church to reprove and rebuke sin, and approve and establish all righteousness and true holiness, she should not put herself in an attitude of defiance, or disregard for the civil laws of the land.

This was the last action on the war issues, and seems to have given universal satisfaction.

Before closing this chapter it seems proper to speak briefly of the relations of Cumberland Presbyterians to slavery. Though the church had its origin in a slave State, and though its greatest strength has always been in the South, yet the author of this book never knew an extreme pro-slavery man among its members. There were doubtless some before the war who believed that slavery was justifiable; but most of these looked upon it as a means of educating the negro and preparing him for ultimate freedom, and all held that it was a solemn duty to labor for the spiritual salvation of the slaves. Much the larger number believed slavery to be an evil and a curse which had been at first thrust upon the people without their consent, and against their protest, and then handed down from father to son. But they denied their responsibility for the deeds of a past generation. They believed in restoring the negro to his rights, but they held that the whole case, with all its surrounding facts, should be considered, and that method of restoration selected which promised the least mischief and the largest advantages to both races. Many advocated the gradual colonization of the slaves in Liberia, or elsewhere. Nearly all admitted that there were under the existing laws, cases in which humanity and religion both made it necessary to hold men in bondage, and that in such cases, if the slaves were properly treated, there was no sin involved. But a majority of our people, South as well as North, would have rejoiced to see all the negroes peacefully emancipated.

Of the three ministers who organized the first presbytery of the Cumberland Presbyterien church, Ewing was the only one who owned slaves, and he *emancipated them*.[1] Besides this noble act, he also boldly wrote and preached against "the traffic in human

---

[1] The laws where he lived permitted that to be done.

flesh." He lived all his days in the slave States, and was the leading spirit in the first generation of Cumberland Presbyterians. In a published sermon[2] he says:

> But where shall we begin? O is it indeed true that in this enlightened age, there are so many palpable evils in the church that it is difficult to know where to commence enumerating them? The first evil which I will mention is a traffic in human flesh and human souls. It is true that many professors of religion, and I fear some of my Cumberland brethren, do not scruple to sell for life their fellow-beings, some of whom are brethren in the Lord. And what is worse, they are not scrupulous to whom they sell, provided they can obtain a better price. Sometimes husbands and wives, parents and children are thus separated, and I doubt not their cries reach the ears of the Lord of Sabaoth. . . . Others who constitute a part of the visible church half feed, half clothe, and oppress their servants. Indeed, they seem by their conduct toward them, not to consider them fellow-beings. And it is to be feared that many of them are taking no pains at all to give their servants religious instruction of any kind, and especially are they making no efforts to teach them or cause them to be taught to read that Book which testifies of Jesus, whilst others permit, perhaps require, their servants to work, cook, etc., while the white people are praying around the family altar.

The church papers also contained many communications of a similar character from his pen. He says:

> I have determined not to hold,[3] nor to give, nor to sell, nor to buy any slave for life. Mainly from the influence of that passage of God's word which says, "Masters give unto your servants that which is just and equal."

McAdow was not an aggressive man, but he was thoroughly opposed to slavery; and, lest his own family should become involved in it, he moved away from Tennessee to Illinois. While always charitable toward Southern people, he hesitated not to speak out against the institution which so long oppressed the country.

That there were individual members of our church that may have been guilty of all the unholy practices which Finis Ewing here condemns is not called in question. There have also been members of all churches guilty of adultery and of other great crimes,

---

[2] Life and Times of Ewing, page 273. [3] Ib.

but that is a very different thing from advocating and defending such crimes.

Some Cumberland Presbyterian preachers who inherited slaves were greatly perplexed to know what was their duty. Ephraim McLean, the first minister that was ordained in the church, believed his negroes incapable of freedom, yet desired to be rid of slave-holding. He laid out a farm, built a house, gave his negroes stock and tools and told them to go free. In a few years, drunkenness and idleness brought them to suffering, and they came to McLean, begging him to take them back, which he did.[1]

Robert Donnell puts on record a prayer and a vow,[2] in which he asks the Lord to let him know what is his duty in regard to the negroes, whom he has inherited; and he solemnly promises, no matter what the sacrifice, faithfully to perform the Lord's bidding. During his whole life he gathered all his servants at family prayers daily; and spent a season in instructing them in spiritual things. His negroes were unwilling to be sent away to Liberia. The laws of his own State did not allow emancipated slaves to remain there. In just such straits were thousands of conscientious men who became slave owners without their own consent. Some kept up the outward appearance of saintliness by selling the poor negroes, perhaps to heartless slave drivers, but a far better class did as Donnell did; kept the negroes and treated them as a Christian should. Donnell's overseer used regularly to complain that Donnell stood between him and the negroes under his charge, and kept the whole plantation waiting morning and evening for his protracted family worship.

In Dr. Beard's diary I find many antislavery records. He declares it to be his opinion that his negroes (inherited) were incapable of taking care of themselves. He thinks them a trust committed to his hands for whom he will be held responsible as much as for his own minor children. July 11th, 1855, he makes this entry: "About ten o'clock word came to me that one of my servants, who is hired out, was lying out. This is one of the curses of slavery, and the longer I live the more deeply I regret that I ever became

---

[1] Items furnished by Hon. F. E. McLean.
[2] Donnell's manuscript to be filed in Cumberland University.

involved in it. My heart always hated it, and now loathes it more and more every day."

There were many cases in which the demands of humanity and religion forced antislavery men living South to become slave owners. Take one case. A Southern preacher of the Cumberland Presbyterian church, who had resolved never to become mixed up with the curse, saw the day when his own father's slaves were levied on for his father's debts. These negroes were the playmates of his childhood. His old father was heart-broken about the matter. While this preacher had money enough to pay for the negroes, he did not have enough to meet any thing like all his father's debts. To pay out what money he had on these debts and leave the negroes still the property of his father would leave them to fall again into the hands of the sheriff and the negro trader. The horror with which slaves generally regarded negro traders passes all description. In this case the laws of the State did not allow the emancipation of slaves unless they could be taken out of the State. These negroes were consulted, and declared that they would rather die than be taken away, either to Canada or Liberia. What they longed for and prayed for was to be allowed to remain with their old master. So the preacher bought them and left them living in their old home with his parents, where they remained till the end of the war, and longer too. This case, which is no fiction, is a typical one. Many Southern men similarly situated, are now, with a quiet conscience, awaiting the awards of the last solemn tribunal.

From 1830 to 1836 our church paper at Nashville not only denounced slavery and the rigid legislation of some of the Southern States, but it was also fiercely attacked by the political papers of the South on this account. The paper was the *Revivalist*. Some extracts will show what was its attitude on this question. Lowry, Smith, and Anderson all wrote editorials for it.

SHAMEFUL LEGISLATION.

The legislature of South Carolina, at its last session, enacted a law imposing a fine of not more than one hundred dollars, and imprisonment not more than six months, upon any person who shall be found guilty of teaching a slave to read or write! Or if a free person of color be convicted of the like crime, he must be whipped not exceeding fifty lashes, and fined not more than fifty dollars! It further provides, that any person employing a man of color as a salesman or clerk, shall be subject to a fine of one hundred dollars and six months' imprisonment! Such enactments are foul blots upon the records of a free people, which our posterity will blush to behold. They are not only unjust and cruel but actually impolitic—such laws do not even deserve the name of time-serving policy. We are aware that the notion prevails to some extent that it diminishes the value of a slave to teach him to read; and some are so credulous as to believe that religious instruction, yea, the possession of the spirit of Christ, will injure slaves. Those who entertain the latter sentiment, it will be granted, are themselves ignorant—grossly ignorant—of the nature and tendency of the religion of Christ, and we must think that those who oppose teaching servants to read the Bible and other religious books, are equally ignorant of the influence of such instruction upon their minds. The extensive slave-holder is at too great a remove from the slave to learn the workings of his mind and the feelings of his heart. There is no contact of feeling, no interchange of sympathies between most Southern planters and their servants. They govern, control, and direct their labors by proxy; and too many masters are dependent upon the representations of heartless overseers for a knowledge of the character and disposition of their own slaves. Southern planters who govern by proxy, are, therefore, unprepared to do justice to the African character. Men who have, through life, been in more immediate contact with the slave, are better qualified to render an impartial judgment. And, notwithstanding all that has been or may be said or enacted to the contrary, from long acquaintance with educated and uneducated slaves, from experience in imparting instruction, from extensive observation, from all the facts we have been enabled to collect, we are fully persuaded that ability to read, and especially a disposition therewith to read the Scriptures, so far from diminishing, adds to the value of a slave.

This position is tenable from principles of sound reason. Any gentleman wishing to purchase a slave with the design of retaining him as a servant, would give ten per cent. more for one of good moral character, in whose integrity he could confide, than he would for another possessing equal bodily powers and dexterity, yet destitute of moral character. Well, what is so well calculated to improve and mature the morals as ability and disposition to read the volume of inspiration, and other religious books? It would be most impious infidelity to deny the adaptedness of divine truth to induce and confirm moral habits. In fact it is the only antidote to corruption, the only conservator of personal or public morals; and as slaves are most exposed at least to certain descriptions of vice, they most need its restraining and conservative influence.

Teach your slaves to read, and give them moral and religious instruction, and they will not only be better men but better servants. We speak what we know, and have seen demonstrated by actual experiment, and in the assertion we are sustained by reason and revelation. To assume the opposite is a departure from reason, and an approach to infidelity. If indeed slavery is incompatible with the ability and privilege of reading the Scriptures and receiving religious instruction, then it is as heinous in the sight of Heaven as idolatry or priestcraft. No circumstances whatever can justify the master in withholding from his servants a knowledge of the Scriptures; wherein alone life and immortality are brought to light. Doubtless, it was for this very purpose that God, in the depth of his councils, suffered the poor African to be brought into bondage, intending by the subjection of his person to bring him under the influence of the gospel, and thereby free his immortality from the dark cloisters of gross superstition, and if so, woe to that man or legislature that denies the African the light and hope of the gospel. If you would not provoke the God of heaven to entail upon us worse than Egyptian plagues, and lead out the oppressed by the hand of a second Moses, don't withhold from the African religious instruction.

Later the same paper contained the following:

THE GOSPEL CAN NOT INJURE SLAVES.

Some time since, we published, without note or comment, a communication from a "Mississippi Planter," calling for a reputable evangelical preacher, of any denomination, to be sent to that State, to itinerate and preach the gospel to the slave population. The planter pledged himself for fifty dollars, and gave some assurance that five hundred could be raised for the support of such a missionary. We find the said communication in a recent number of the *Western Weekly Review*, preceded by the following editorial:

SLAVERY—MOVEMENTS AT HOME.

"We quote the following article from the Nashville *Revivalist* for the purpose of raising a warning voice against the proposed measure. Far be it from us to say aught against the diffusing of light and intelligence, or against ameliorating the condition of any of our species, but let it be remembered that there is a time and place for all things; and circumstances to be considered in all cases. The "Mississippi planters" have no desire to see the terrible tragedies of St. Domingo and Southampton re-enacted amongst themselves; and to such a result the mission proposed below must inevitably lead. We speak what we know."

We think that, for once, the editor of the *Review* has gone a little too far and spoken more than he "knows." How does he "know" that the "proposed mission" would "inevitably lead" to such results in Mississippi as the "terrible tragedies of St. Domingo and Southampton?" Does he "know" that the gospel of peace will produce strife, excite discontent and rebellion? Will that gospel which teaches servants to obey their masters, prompt them to rebellion? Were the terrible tragedies of St. Domingo and Southampton the results of the gospel? Does not universal experience prove that when a slave becomes truly pious, he is ever afterward a more obedient servant than he was before. Does not the editor of the *Review* know that missions among the slave population in South Carolina and Georgia have been and are now being attended by the best of consequences? That the slave-holders in those States testify to their good effects upon the slaves, and that such missions have received their decided approbation? Many Southern planters have erected meeting-houses for their slaves, and solicit preaching every Sabbath, or as often as they can procure the services of the missionaries. The editor does not "know" that preaching the gospel to the slaves in Mississippi will lead to such results as the tragedies of St. Domingo and Southampton. We believe he is sincere, but think his fears have outrun his knowledge, and therefore he has been induced to lift up his "warning voice." We apprehend no such bloody results, but believe that the gospel is the best and only sure preventive of rebellion; and in our estimation the Mississippi planters would promote their own interests and security by employing all judicious means to evangelize the slave population.

The *Cumberland Presbyterian*, of Nashville, Tennessee, August 19, 1835, says: "We proclaim it abroad we do not own slaves. We never shall. We long to see the black man free and happy, and thousands of Christians who now hold them in bondage entertain the same sentiments." The same editor constantly advocated gradual emancipation, and urged on masters the duty of preparing their servants for freedom.

It is proper, however, to state that all these things underwent great changes after slavery entered into the bitter political struggles of the country. Just what the feelings or views of Cumberland Presbyterians were during the years just preceding the war, or what their relations were to the bitter political questions of the times, this history does not undertake to discuss. Two of the General Assemblies held during the period named, one at Memphis, Tennessee, in 1848, and the other at Pittsburg, Pennsylvania, in 1851, adopted reports directly relating to slavery, and these two deliverances perhaps indicate what was at that time the prevailing sentiment of our people.

The action of 1848 was called out by the minutes of the Pennsylvania Synod. That synod, at its meeting in 1847, had rescinded "a resolution passed at the preceding session declaring the relation existing between the synod and American slavery to be such as required her to take no action thereon," and had proceeded to take action in these words.

Resolved, That the system of slavery in the United States is contrary to the principles of the gospel, hinders the progress thereof, and ought to be abolished.

The synodical minutes containing the resolution came up in the Assembly of 1848 for review, and were referred to a committee, consisting of the Rev. Hiram A. Hunter, of Kentucky, the Rev. A. H. Goodpasture, of Illinois, and Ruling Elder J. S. McLean, of Tennessee. This committee's report, which was concurred in by the Assembly, expressed regret at the synod's action, and disapprobation of "any attempt by judicatures of the church to agitate the exciting subject of slavery," closing with these words : "The tendency of such resolutions, if persisted in, we believe is to gender strife, produce distraction in the church, and thereby hinder the progress of the gospel.[1]

In the General Assembly of 1851 "the moderator announced the reception of six memorials from persons residing in Ohio and Pennsylvania, numbering, in the aggregate, about one hundred and fifty, upon the subject of slavery."[2] The Committee on Overtures, to which these memorials were referred, submitted the following report :[3]

The church of God is a spiritual body, whose jurisdiction extends only to matters of faith and morals. She has no power to legislate upon subjects on which Christ and his apostles did not legislate, nor to establish terms of union, where they have given no express warrant. Your committee, therefore, believe that this question on which you are asked by the memorialists to take action, is one which belongs rather to civil than ecclesiastical legislation ; and we are fully persuaded that legislation on that subject in any of the judicatories of the church, instead of

---

[1] Assembly's Minutes, 1848, pp. 12, 13.   [2] Ib. 1851, p. 16.   [3] Ib. pp. 56, 57.

mitigating the evils connected with slavery, will only have a tendency to alienate feeling between brethren; to engender strifes and animosities in your churches; and tend, ultimately to a separation between brethren who hold a common faith, an event leading to the most disastrous results, and one which we believe ought to be deprecated by every true patriot and Christian.

But your committee believe that members of the church holding slaves should regard them as rational and accountable beings, and treat them as such, affording them as far as possible the means of grace. Finally, your committee would recommend the adoption of the following resolutions:

Resolved, 1. That inasmuch as the Cumberland Presbyterian church was originally organized and has ever since existed and prospered under the conceded principle that slavery was not and should not be regarded as a bar to communion ; we, therefore, believe that it should not now be so regarded.

2. That, having entire confidence in the honesty and sincerity of the memorialists, and cherishing the tenderest regard for their feelings and opinions, it is the conviction of this General Assembly that the agitation of this question, which has already torn in sunder other branches of the church, can be productive of no real benefit to master or slave. We would, therefore, in the fear of God, and with the utmost solicitude for the peace and welfare of the churches under our care, advise a spirit of mutual forbearance and brotherly love; and, instead of censure and proscription, that we endeavor to cultivate a fraternal feeling one toward another.

The members of the committee, all of whom signed the report, were: the Rev. LeRoy Woods, of Indiana; the Rev. A. J. Baird, of Kentucky; the Rev. J. J. Meek, of Mississippi; the Rev. N. P. Modrall, of Tennessee; the Rev. J. H. Coulter, of Ohio; the Rev. S. E. Hudson, of Pennsylvania; and Ruling Elder J. C. Henson, of Indiana.

As to the present attitude of our people in regard to the now old and thrice-dead slavery issue, the writer does not know a Cumberland Presbyterian of any section who is not heartily glad that the negro is free.

The fact that the church did not divide, even in those bitter times, when all the other Protestant churches of America were rent asunder, speaks with great power in favor of the Christian and conservative spirit of our people. The Cumberland Presbyterian church is now, was during the war, and we trust will always be, national, not sectional; and it has to-day no members who look with more pride on our ecclesiastical unity than do those who fought under Lee and Bragg in 1863.

In one view of the case the church is specially indebted to its Southern membership for this unity. Most of the strength of the church was in the South, and neither in members nor church property would Southern Cumberland Presbyterians have been very great losers by setting up an independent establishment as the Southern Presbyterians did; but there were other things which they prized far more than members or property. One thing more is claimed to their special credit. When they were in the majority in the Assembly, and able to carry things their own way, they unanimously granted terms to our Northern membership, such as the Southern wing of the Presbyterian church has steadfastly refused to accept from Northern Presbyterians. At no time in the last fifteen years would the Presbyterian church have continued to be rent asunder, had the Southern wing thereof declared its willingness to accept a similar compromise.

CHAPTER XXXIX.

PREACHING TO SOLDIERS.

"Like Him, through scenes of deep distress,
　Who bore the world's sad weight,
We, in their crowded loneliness,
　Would seek the desolate."

THIS book has little to do with military records, but the history of the work of Cumberland Presbyterians for the salvation of souls, whether in Northern or Southern armies, ought to be interesting to us all. The man whose soul is too narrow to believe in a conversion because it was in the army which he called "the enemy," would do well to pass over this chapter. God loved the souls of men, whether they wore blue coats or gray, and who can doubt that there were earnest Christian men in both armies who fell in battle and winged their flight to heaven together? The heroism of Americans from both sections has become part of our common national heritage of glory.

The principal strength of our church lay in the South, and almost all the men in that section went to the army. Nearly all the youthful ministers from one section, and only a few comparatively from the other, marched with the soldiers during the four years of civil strife. There was, therefore, a much larger number of Cumberland Presbyterian chaplains in the Southern than in the Northern army. Of the services of the latter, only a meager account can now be obtained. It will, therefore, require more space to sketch the work of Southern than that of Northern chaplains. The limits of this volume do not permit the description of all the worthy actors, or important events. Only selections, and not a full history, can be given.

In one single Southern army—Bragg's—there were twenty Cumberland Presbyterian chaplains. All the other Southern armies also had a considerable number. So far as the personal history of these men is known, they were every one faithful in the perilous duties which they had undertaken. Much of the material which has been collected for a history of their work can not be used in this short chapter.

No army missionaries were sent out by our church Boards of Missions. There might have been embarrassing questions attending any such an effort at that time. There was, however, a missionary committee in the South, organized after the war began, for the special purpose of prosecuting missionary work among the Southern soldiers. In the North the Christian Commission superseded the necessity for any special denominational organization for this kind of missionary effort. In both sections there was earnest work done by the Cumberland Presbyterian church for the evangelization of the soldiers.

The call to preach to a regiment was sometimes made by the colonel, and sometimes by the united voice of the men composing the regiment. There were two very different methods pursued in taking converts into the church. The Northern chaplains and the chaplains in Lee's army had what they called an "Army Church." All except Catholics and Episcopalians co-operated in this organization. Converts became members in this undenominational church. "The Army of Tennessee" had a different arrangement. If there were under the charge of a Cumberland Presbyterian chaplain converts who wanted to join the Baptists, he sent for a Baptist chaplain to come and baptize them. Their names, with a certificate of the facts, were then sent to the home congregation. So of the adherents of all other churches, except Roman Catholics and Episcopalians. These generally refused to co-operate with the other chaplains.

The programme for work among the soldiers had to be shaped to meet the nature of the case. If a chaplain was a true man, he was to all intents the pastor of his regiment. All the spiritual oversight and care of persons which any pastor ever had at home, fell to his lot. He visited the messes. He held prayer-meetings for the regiment. He held private conferences with individuals about their spiritual interests. He distributed tracts and books.

He preached at regular times. But there were other spheres of duty peculiar to his station. During a battle his usual place was at the field hospital, or along with the litter corps, who carried the wounded back to the field hospital. To take down from the lips of the dying their last message to loved ones was a large part of his work in the midst of a battle. To point suffering and dying comrades to the Friend who was wounded for our transgressions was a still larger part of his work on those fields of blood. Then the chaplains had another and broader field of operations. There were chaplains' associations, where all consulted together about the general interests of the work. These associations had regular officers and regular meetings; and ministers of our own church took a prominent part in nearly all of them. The permanent chairman in the very largest of these associations was a Cumberland Presbyterian. Another duty which some of the chaplains felt called upon to fulfill, was to preach against "official sins"—not the sins of "the enemy," but the sins of their own generals, and even of the official head of the government which they recognized. In the South, at least, there were instances in which Cumberland Presbyterian chaplains took such a bold stand in the presence of the very parties arraigned, that their friends expected to see them put under arrest or punished in some still severer manner. On one such occasion, after the chaplain had boldly denounced, in the presence of all the leading generals of "the Army of Tennessee," some of the official sins of those very generals, and had taken his seat in the pulpit, General Leonidas Polk rose to his feet, walked up to the pulpit, seized the chaplain by the hand, and said, with deep feeling: "Sir, I thank you for your fidelity this day."

It was next to impossible for a chaplain to do denominational work in the camps. A few tried it and came to grief. The soldiers would not tolerate any man who undertook sectarian work among them. No other work of the churches, not even missions to the heathen, has ever been more efficient in breaking down sectarian feeling. Two chaplains had worked side by side for twelve months when one of them, a Cumberland Presbyterian, learned with surprise that the other was a New School Presbyterian; up to that time he had thought his companion a Methodist. A chaplain

(Cumberland Presbyterian) was sent for by a wealthy lady of the Episcopalian church. Her words to him were substantially these: "I have seen the time when I would have preferred risking the death of my boy out of the church to having him placed under the instruction of any minister who is not an Episcopalian; but I have got past that. My son is in your regiment. I am looking daily to hear of his falling in battle. He is not ready to die. I want you to see him and talk to him about his soul's salvation, and I ask you to press the matter upon him at once."

Some samples of the work of Cumberland Presbyterian ministers in connection with the Union armies are presented first. The Rev. A. W. White and the Rev. G. N. Mattox, of Pennsylvania, spent a brief period working under the United States Christian Commission. Their brief services produced very valuable results. It is recorded of these two men that, among other good deeds, they interposed to prevent mistreatment of prisoners. They preached Jesus to prisoners as well as to the soldiers in blue. At Decatur, Alabama, they secured a room and raised their flag. Here they held regular prayer-meetings with good results. There were inquirers after the way of salvation, and conversions in considerable numbers in this room under the preaching of these missionaries. Mr. White mentions with gratitude the fact that those who had been out on picket duty came in and reported at the prayer-meeting that a great revival was going on at the same time in the Confederate army. Thus God was at work on both sides of the hostile lines.

One day Mr. Mattox found in the hospital a little boy whose right shoulder was shattered by a piece of shell. Talking with this child about his soul, he soon learned that the boy had run away from a Christian mother in Vermont. Mattox prayed with him and labored for him till he saw bright evidences of conversion. The child's first desire then was that Mattox should write the good news to his mother. This was done. For a wonder the boy recovered apparently, and for a while made a hearty worker for the souls of other soldiers. He then relapsed and died, and his death occurred about the same time that Mattox also sickened and died. This was the introduction to a warm correspondence between the boy's mother, in Vermont, and the preacher's mother, in Pennsylvania. A volume might be filled with similar incidents. In many cases, too, the parties who were brought into communication by such incidents belonged to different sides of the great contest. Among Dr. Beard's literary remains are several intensely interesting letters of this class.

A curious thing about Mattox is that he had felt himself specially called to the work of a foreign missionary. It does not detract any thing from our confidence in the divine origin of the call, to see that God himself thwarted its accomplishment. God called Abraham to offer up Isaac, but God never intended to let Abraham carry the work farther than a certain fixed point. God calls men to preach, and sometimes takes them home to heaven before they deliver their first sermon.

Chaplain A. G. Osborn, of Pennsylvania, published a letter addressed to Union Presbytery, from which this extract is made:

> I can, through the mercy of God, my dear brethren, assure you that the great Head of the church has not left himself without witnesses even here, amid army scenes and battle strife. During nearly the whole of this winter there have been reviving influences in our camps. About three hundred persons have professed faith in Christ. I can say that a great change has taken place in my own regiment. Our camp, it is true, has a great deal of wickedness in it yet; but, thank the Lord, many who but recently were numbered among blasphemers and Sabbath-breakers, are now enrolled among the names constituting our regimental church, or "Christian League," as it is more fitly denominated. One remarkable feature in the case is the fact that nearly every one in the Fourteenth Regiment that has made a profession, has taken up the cross, and prays in public. I know of but one or two exceptions. We now have a chapel tent erected. The Christian commission on my application, furnished the canvas to cover it, and our soldiers labored with a good will to get it built. It is comfortably seated, and has a stove in it. There has been meeting in it nearly every night since it was built, and every Sabbath we have two services. A. G. OSBORN,
> Chaplain Fourteenth Pennsylvania Cavalry.
> Martinsburg, West Virginia, March 21, 1864.

The Rev. H. H. Ashmore served long and faithfully as chaplain in an Illinois regiment. He furnishes some interesting incidents. He says that in all the protracted intercourse with Cumberland Presbyterians, which the long sojourn of his regiment in the South enabled him to hold, he met with no one of them who did not earnestly desire the preservation of the ecclesiastical unity of the church. That his observations on this subject were in keeping with the general facts in the case will be seen from the proceedings of the conventions discussed in a former chapter. This fact, and that other precious fact that we stood undivided through the war which rent other churches asunder, is a valuable proof of the power of that spiritual legacy which has always constituted our noblest denominational heritage. It was Milton Bird who, in a sermon in 1864, after pointing out the evils of disruption, uttered the following noble words: "If, on the other hand, we can show to the world a church which is able through divine grace to rise above all the passions of this furious war, and stand bound together in holy unity by a divine bond which no national strife can sunder, then truly may we put forth an argument for the divinity of Christianity which infidelity can not overthrow."

At the battle of Pea Ridge, Arkansas, Chaplain Ashmore was worn down by work with wounded men. Late at night, utterly exhausted, he sank down upon a log, rested his head upon what he supposed was a fallen limb of a tree, and sank to sleep. On awaking in the morning, he found that his pillow was the amputated leg of some poor soldier. Ashmore testifies that the dying soldiers, however wicked they had been in life, died calling on the name of God. "My mother," "my wife," "my country," "my God," were the words oftenest on the dying lips of those over whose last moments the army chaplains kept watch.

While Ashmore's regiment was at Murfreesboro, Tennessee, some very sore trials pressed upon the chaplains. They met together once to consult about disbanding and going home in a body, but the proposition was not carried out. Instead of going home they began a series of meetings. God blessed their efforts. A revival began and spread far through that portion of the army. Ashmore was an active worker in this revival, and it was estimated that one thousand persons were converted before this series of meetings closed.

The venerable Hiram A. Hunter, who had been a member of General Andrew Jackson's body-guard in the war of 1812, and was in his sixty-first year when the late civil war began, was a chaplain in the Federal army. Neither in his diary nor in his very full autobiography (MSS.) does he give any details of his work as chaplain, except the texts he used, and the dates of certain transactions.

The Rev. J. W. Woods served as chaplain of the Fifth Illinois Regiment from September, 1861, till the close of the war. Like many others he was regularly elected by the men of the regiment before receiving any military appointment. For several months he was detailed to special work among the colored people who flocked to the army. He diligently circulated Bibles, tracts, and papers among the soldiers, besides doing all the other regular work usually done by chaplains. He was with his regiment at Vicksburg, and his labors there resulted in many conversions. Three of these converts afterward entered the ministry.

The Rev. S. Richards, D.D., was also chaplain throughout the war, but no account of his labors has been secured.

As to the work in the Southern army, a few selections carefully made are here presented in order to illustrate different features of that work. A large volume would be needed to furnish a full history.

About the time the chaplains of the army under General Rosecrans were consulting as to the propriety of disbanding and going home, the chaplains in Bragg's army were in consultation over the same kind of a proposition. A meeting of all the chaplains in that army had been called to consider the question of resigning and going home *en masse*. The feeling was quite common that war and religion were incompatible, and that no good could be accomplished by preaching to soldiers. A few of the chaplains responded to the call. After the proposition to abandon the chaplains' work had been made and discussed for a few minutes, the Rev. Mr. Milligan, of the Baptist church, offered some resolutions to the following effect:

Resolved, 1. That the souls of this vast multitude are too precious to be abandoned to perdition.

2. That God is able to give his own called ministers the victory even among soldiers.

3. That the chaplains should enter into a covenant to pray for each other, and that all should at once begin protracted meetings in their several regiments, claiming this whole army for the King of kings.

These resolutions were adopted. One week from that day the chaplains met again to report results. The number present was much larger than on the former occasion. The bowed heads were lifted up. Every chaplain who had entered into the covenant one week before, reported that a revival had already begun in his regiment. This work of grace went on till the armies of the Confederacy were disbanded.

One of these chaplains was the Rev. George L. Winchester, of the Madison Presbytery, of our church. He was eminently fitted for a chaplain's work. After entering into this covenant, he went back to his regiment and began his series of meetings. The next week he reported a wonderful revival in progress, with great demand for more preaching. Various regiments were destitute of chaplains. Winchester began a series of services in one of these, besides continuing the meetings in his own regiment. Forgetting that his body was mortal, or ceasing to care for its mortality, he carried on this double service for a considerable time, until, in the midst of his labors, he suddenly fell and was gone to heaven before his fellow chaplains knew that he was ill. His regiment was like a family of orphans, mourning a father's death. Nearly all of them had been led to Jesus by Winchester. When they selected a new chaplain the principal point was to find a man whom Winchester had loved and indorsed.

An exchanged prisoner who had belonged to that regiment returned to it after Winchester's death. He took out his deck of cards, and went to some of his old companions to have a game. They all declined, stating that they had become Christians. He went to others with the same result. He made the trial in every mess of the whole regiment, without finding a single one to join him. With a bitter oath he said: "The whole regiment has got religion."

Mention has been made of the Cumberland Presbyterian Southern Committee, on army missions. This committee resolved to raise a salary to secure a general missionary for "the Army of Tennessee," to whose hands they might commit a sort of supervision of missionary work among the soldiers. Three failures were made before a suitable man was obtained; and finally one of the chaplains was induced to resign and take this missionary work instead of his chaplaincy. Under his management, after he entered on this general work, money was raised to secure the Rev. J. L. Cooper, of Mississippi, as a general army missionary, and Cooper accepted. Besides this, several other arrangements were made for missions among the soldiers. The location of the missionary committee was changed from the army of Tennessee to Selma, Alabama, in 1864, and under its direction, aided by the superintendent, money was raised and still other missionaries secured.

Mr. Cooper was pre-eminently fitted for the missionary work, and he devoted himself to it from 1863 till the end of the war with an energy and fidelity that were never surpassed. For four months and five days he held meetings on the lines, under fire, every night except one. At every meeting his congregations were measured only by the compass of his voice. When men could not approach near enough to hear they would go away. This was during Joe Johnston's retreat through North Georgia. The one night when there was no meeting the army marched all night. Nor was Cooper the only one who had services every night. The work was general along all the lines. There were fourteen miles of revivals nightly and multitudes of conversions.

The programme of exercises agreed on by all the co-operating chaplains in this army was as follows: First, at the opening of the services all those who had found the Savior were called up to ascertain what church they desired to join. At Cooper's meetings the number responding to this call was about one hundred per night. The next item in the programme was to call up all who were seeking salvation. To this invitation a still larger number always responded. Then a sermon of instruction was preached, specially to the seekers. Then the congregation was dismissed. At every service during this bloody retreat, some were present who would be killed before the next meeting. Many found Jesus during the sermon; some after they went out into the picket holes. These holes were very near the enemy, and the pickets had to be relieved at midnight, and there were always men killed in this work of relieving pickets. One poor fellow gave the following account of his conversion. He went from the preaching service to picket duty. Getting down into his picket hole, still thinking of the sermon, still eagerly seeking salvation, he felt the light dawn upon his soul. Forgetting all about war and its dangers, he raised himself up and shouted, "Glory to God." Just then a minie-ball cut away a lock of his hair, grazing the scalp. Down into his hole he crept again, but his soul was too full of joy to suffer him long to keep in mind minie-balls, and in a little while he again rose up shouting. Another bullet went through his clothing. So he said he "spent the night alternately praising God and dodging the devil." On being questioned what he meant by "dodging the devil," he said: "It is my opinion that his satanic majesty was angry about losing my soul, and I believe he rode astraddle of every one of those balls, but the Lord would not let them hit me."

The Rev. Mr. Baker, of Missouri, a Cumberland Presbyterian, was standing on the breastworks preaching. In his sermon he was crying, "Glory to God," when a ball struck him and killed him instantly. Old men, past military age, were army chaplains. Rev. J. F. McCutcheon, of the Cumberland Presbyterian church, was one of these. I saw this old man when his garments were riddled with bullets, for he always went along with his men wherever duty called him, but bullets were more merciful than some other things. General Bragg, a few days before he was removed from the command of "the Army of Tennessee," issued an order to have all his chaplains' horses pressed for military uses. Ministers of the gospel were exempted from conscription in "Dixie," but men who were far past the military age were in the chaplain work. The Confederate government furnished no horses to chaplains. Bragg's order paid no respect to age. Old men like McCutcheon were robbed by it of their private property, except where some generous officer, like George Johnson, who was allowed several horses, claimed the chaplain's horse, and kept it for its owner. Ah well! the way Bragg left Missionary Ridge, a few days after that order about the chaplains' horses, always seemed to me to be a special retribution.

One little incident connected with this missionary work is too good to be lost. A pocket-book was sent to our missionary committee accompanied with the following statement: "The good sister who sent it is a widow. Her husband was killed by the fragment of a shell at the battle of Chickamauga. The deadly missile struck his pocket first, and drove the pocket-book into his body. The surgeon extracted it with its contents. The widow says these blood-stained bills are too sacred for any common use. She sends them to the missionary board."

The trials of Southern chaplains were very great. The mess tax, which was imposed to eke out sufficient rations, was generally larger than a chaplain's salary. It would require a month and a half's wages of a chaplain to buy a pound of coffee; and about two years' wages to buy an overcoat. The price of a good horse was more than any chaplain earned during the whole war. Yet there were chaplains who wore out as many as five horses while they were in the service. The Southern government furnished neither horses nor clothing to chaplains. It was not an uncommon thing for chaplains and soldiers to be brought to great suffering both for rations and for clothing.

Chaplain M. B. De Witt, now the Rev. Dr. De Witt, of Nashville, Tennessee, had some severe trials. The country where his home had been, and where he had left his wife, was invaded. When the state of things became unbearable there, Mrs. De Witt, like thousands of others, became a refugee. Having no other place to fly to, she went to the camps, and remained near her husband through all those dreadful last struggles of the Confederate army. De Witt was one of that class of chaplains whose call to the work came first from the men of the regiment, not from the colonel. Of course his official nomination had to be made by the colonel.

Chaplains with the cavalry had a peculiar lot. Their only place during a battle was with their regiments. Chaplain A. G. Burrow was one of these. He was wounded, and came to the writer's tent. It was winter and bitter cold. The wounded chaplain had no overcoat. His other coat was thin and ragged. All his clothing was worn out. His wound was in his head, and his skull had just been trepanned. His face was the color of a corpse. He staggered as he walked. His voice, once so quick and cheerful, was faint and faltering. The wound was four inches long. Yet this man, who might have had a comfortable home under his father's roof—who, both by reason of his profession, and on account of his wound, might have found exemption from further service—chose rather to remain as chaplain with the soldiers, and continue his efforts to lead them to their Savior. (Acts xx. 24.)

Many other chaplains deserve as favorable notice as those mentioned in the foregoing sketches, but as it would require a large volume to give a full history of all, only such illustrations have been selected as the most reliable materials at hand furnish. There were other Cumberland Presbyterian preachers who gave their lives up, as G. L. Winchester gave his, a willing sacrifice for the salvation of the soldiers. Sharing the privations and dangers of siege or battle, eating mule beef at Vicksburg, or marching all night in the mad raids, and, when the fight came on, following along the battle's fiery front to pick up the wounded and carry them back to the field hospital; then returning to the line to bend over the dying, and there, on the bloody field, to write their last message to loved ones at home, while shells hurtled and minie-balls whistled thick around them, were some of the tasks and duties which fell to the lot of our army missionaries.

In the wonderful revival in the Southern armies the number of conversions must have reached an aggregate of more than a hundred thousand men. Dr. Felix Johnson, now gone to his rest, once said, while this work was going on: "God is going to answer all these prayers and fast-days which the people of the South are having—not by setting up a new Republic, but by converting all the Southern soldiers." At two different times, by two different men, an extensive history of this great revival was prepared, many years ago, but, for unknown reasons neither of these works was ever published. No history of the great conflict can be complete without an account of this wonderful work of grace.

CHAPTER XL.

COLORED CUMBERLAND PRESBYTERIANS.

<blockquote>
Let us have faith in God's all-wise intention,
  His plans will never fail;
Though far beyond our feeble comprehension,
  We know it must prevail.
—*S. A. Stoddard.*

O stranger, with all your wealth,
Do you 'spect to buy heaven and keep it for yourself?
—*Negro Melody.*
</blockquote>

BEFORE the war there were twenty thousand colored Cumberland Presbyterians. These all belonged to the same congregations of which the white people were members, and were under the ministrations of the same preachers who served the white congregations. While there were instances in the South in which white men built separate churches for their slaves and hired for them separate pastors, yet there were no such instances among the Cumberland Presbyterians. In our church colored members everywhere attended the same services with the white people. It is true that separate seats were appropriated to them, but white people and black were taught the way of salvation by the same pastors. In addition to this privilege of attending services along with the white people, the colored people had preachers of their own race, and held their own special services, occupying the same houses which were owned and used by the white congregations. State laws generally required that some steady white man should be present at these meetings. This requirement was always complied with.

An illustration showing the nature of pastoral work in a congregation made up of white people and their slaves will doubtless be of interest. In a town in Middle Tennessee the pastor of such a church had under his charge one hundred and fifty colored members. He was as much the pastor of the humblest of these as of the wealthiest and most influential white member. Common sense, if nothing better, required that his pastoral labors among these people should conform to the wishes and interests of the owners. Many a time was he taken by the mistress into the negro cabin to minister to some afflicted servant. Many a time, too, under similar direction, did he go to the negro cabin to pray for some penitent sinner, and try to lead him to his Savior. While he was the pastor of these colored people he had a colored assistant, "Brother Jim," the property of one of the elders. It was Jim's custom regularly to bring the notes of his sermon to the white pastor Saturday afternoon for criticism; and when something was pointed out to be corrected he never failed to make the suggested changes. Jim preached at three o'clock Sunday afternoons in the same pulpit which had been occupied by the regular pastor in the morning. It was the pastor's duty and pleasure as a Christian to be present at these three o'clock services, and he testifies that he has heard no preaching from our colored brethren since the war which was as near the pure gospel as Jim's simple and earnest discourses. There were many converts at these meetings. This is a sample of the general order of things with Cumberland Presbyterian pastors throughout the Southern States before the war.

At the camp-meetings there were some special arrangements for colored worshipers. A shed in front of the pulpit was built for the white people, and another in the rear for the colored people. When the call for mourners was made at the close of the sermon, seats next the pulpit both front and rear were reserved for the penitents. There were many conversions in the rear of the pulpit as well as in the front; but the negroes never seemed to feel entirely free to work in their own way until the white people closed their services and went to their tents. Then began a scene of wild excitement and wonderful interest which no pen can describe. The singing at such a time was specially interesting. Nothing in the meetings of the colored people at the present day makes any approximation to these revival melodies. The camp-meeting songs of the negroes, like the corn songs of that period, were rich, original, and genuine African productions. When a thousand negroes, keeping time with foot and head, with arms and body, poured out all their souls upon the night air in a camp-meeting chorus suited to their voices and their culture, the weird and solemn grandeur and grotesqueness were indescribable.

Our colored ministers sometimes preached to white audiences. There was a colored Cumberland Presbyterian preacher in Missouri who often preached at camp-meetings to the white people. It was everywhere the custom among Cumberland Presbyterians to ordain white and colored preachers in precisely the same way and by the same presbyters, except that the necessities of the case made it necessary to use leniency about literary requirements. The education of the colored preacher in the days of slavery was secured under no little disadvantage. Generally his teacher was his "young master," usually a lad of from twelve to eighteen. His theological instruction was obtained partly at church, partly at the meetings of the presbytery, where he was catechised, and partly in private interviews with his pastor.

The old order of things broke down during the war. The origin of this change has often been misunderstood. It was by their own choice, and without any promptings by their former masters, that the colored members of our church ceased to attend services with the white people. The change was universal, and in all the denominations. A state of things sprang up during the war which not only led to this result, but also closed their ears for a time against all white preachers of Southern antecedents.

After the war, in October, 1868, the colored people of the Cumberland Presbyterian church held a convention at Henderson, Kentucky, to decide what steps should be taken. The convention was not large, but the prevailing voice was for ecclesiastical separation from the whites. A call for another convention to meet in Huntsville, Alabama, January, 1869, was responded to by only a few. Those who met decided to defer all action until the next May, and endeavor to have a full delegation of colored ministers in a convention to be held at the same time and place at which the next General Assembly was to meet. The *Banner of Peace* joined heartily in the call for a full convention. Dr. W. D. Chadick, pastor of our church at Murfreesboro, where the Assembly was to meet, published assurances that all the colored delegates would be entertained free of charge. A full delegation was present. After this convention had held several meetings, the Rev. Moses T. Weir, brother of our African missionary, went to one of the members of the General Assembly and requested his co-operation in obtaining the consent of the Assembly to the organization of a separate African Cumberland Presbyterian church. In a long conversation on this subject Weir said that colored men would never learn self-reliance and independence in the same church judicatures with the white people. It seemed evident that much larger financial assistance for the work among the negroes could be secured by Mr. Weir's plan than by any other.

In a short time the convention sent in to the General Assembly its official action. That action declares that "it would not be for the advancement of the interests of the church among either the white or colored people for the ministers of the two races to meet together in the same judicatures." The convention therefore asked the Assembly to adopt a plan by which, under the superintendence and by assistance of the whites, they might be organized into separate presbyteries and synods. It asked also for financial aid in setting up the new organization.

To all of this the Assembly gave its consent, and appointed the necessary committees for carrying out the plan. Under this plan several colored presbyteries were organized that same year. The committee to co-operate with the colored people in this organization, and in establishing a school for the education of their ministers, was composed of the Rev. J. C. Bowden, D.D., the Rev. Barnett Miller, the Rev. Thomas E. Young, together with ruling elders A. M. C. Simmons and A. J. Fuqua. This committee, besides such aid as it was practicable to give in organizing presbyteries, also appointed the Rev. Moses T. Weir agent to secure funds for the establishment of a college for colored people.

In the organization of the colored presbyteries others besides the committee rendered valuable assistance. The Rev. M. B. De Witt, D.D., was perhaps the very first to aid in this work.

All seemed to start off with the utmost harmony. No jar had occurred up to 1870. In May of that year, when our General

Assembly met at Warrensburg, Missouri, the Rev. Moses T. Weir appeared with a commission from the Greenville Presbytery (colored), asking a seat as a member of the Assembly. Fears were entertained by Southern members that somebody was trying to use Weir for political purposes, and there were in the Assembly indications of serious trouble about this matter. The commission which Mr. Weir presented was read by Dr. Bird, the stated clerk, and action concerning it was deferred until after the committee appointed the year before at Murfreesboro, Tennessee, to co-operate with the colored people in their efforts to establish an institution of learning should make its report. The matter came up several times during the first four days of the Assembly's meeting, and there were some exciting discussions. Finally, the Rev. W. S. Campbell, D.D., of Illinois, called attention to the fact that there was no proper information before the General Assembly touching the organization or existence of Greenville Presbytery, and on his motion Mr. Weir's informal commission was almost unanimously laid on the table. A similar case was before the next Assembly, with similar results. Since then all strife about the relations of our church to the colored people has ceased.

The colored Cumberland Presbyterians have continued their work with varying prosperity, but their success has been far beyond what the many discouragements would have led us to expect. They now have a General Assembly, a Board of Missions, a Board of Publication, and other boards. The increase in the number of their ministers has been wonderful. They have five synods, nineteen presbyteries, two hundred ordained ministers, two hundred and twenty-five licensed preachers, two hundred candidates for the ministry, and fifteen thousand members. Although there were about twenty thousand colored Cumberland Presbyterians in 1860, only a very small portion of them were gathered into this independent denomination. The Rev. Robert Johnson, corresponding delegate sent from that church to our General Assembly in 1874, made the following statement:

MODERATOR AND BRETHREN: Believing that more good would be accomplished by a separate organization, the body which I have the honor to represent hailed with pleasure the action taken by the General

Assembly of the Cumberland Presbyterian church in Murfreesboro, Tennessee, in May, 1869. With the assistance and co-operation of presbyteries under your control, a number of colored ministers have been from time to time set apart to the whole work of the ministry to labor among their own people. These ministers have formed themselves into presbyteries and synods, and on the first day of May, 1874, commissioners from the various presbyteries met in the city of Nashville, Tennessee, and formed a General Assembly. That body determined to appoint a corresponding delegate to represent them in this meeting of your reverend body, and that duty devolved upon me. Under the control of the body which I represent, there are now seven presbyteries, viz.: Huntsville, Elk River, Farmington, Hiwassee, New Hopewell, New Middleton, and Springfield. The first four constitute the Synod of Tennessee, and the last three the Synod of Huntsville. In our communion we number now, as nearly as can be ascertained, 46 ordained ministers, 20 licentiates, 30 candidates, and 3,000 communicants. The value of church property is about $5,000. We earnestly desire, moderator and brethren, to have your assistance and co-operation. We are weak, you are strong; we are young as an organization, you are old. We need the benefit of your experience. Above all, we need your prayers. For these things I confidently ask, and may the great Head of the church accept you and us with all true believers into his holy keeping always.

In twelve years the growth in numbers in the ministry and membership of this church has been five hundred per cent.

The school for colored Cumberland Presbyterians at Bowling Green, Kentucky, has never received any considerable assistance from the wealthy. Perhaps the whole church has not contributed as much as ten thousand dollars for its establishment and support. It is a struggling enterprise, yet it has done some good work in spite of its disadvantages. At the meeting of our General Assembly at Covington, Ohio, May, 1887, nearly $2,700 was raised for the benefit of this institution, thus freeing it from debt.

We all acknowledge our obligation to send the gospel to Africa, and think it a noble work of Christian heroism to go to that dark land and win souls to Christ; but the Africans here at our doors have still stronger claims on us. In spite of past difficulties and theoretical fears, it stands to-day as a demonstrated fact wherever tested that labors in the interest of the colored people by Southern white men are not only acceptable, but also fruitful of good results.

The Rev. J. L. Cooper, who was army missionary, furnishes an account of his work among the negroes of Mississippi since the war. In the field where he labored the "prohibition" ticket triumphed through negro votes, and that, too, when the advocates of the liquor traffic with money and whisky sought to corrupt these voters. Mr. Cooper had his hands full of other work, but he made occasional tours among the negroes, and he testifies that these occasional visits yielded better fruits than his labors among the white people. He says that the negroes of Mississippi are everywhere accessible if Southern white preachers approach them in the right spirit. This is the testimony of a man born and reared in Mississippi—a man who was a missionary in the rebel army.

There ought to be an organized system of evangelistic work among the negroes by Cumberland Presbyterians, and Southern white men should lead in this work. There ought to be ministers and lay workers in the South noble enough and with enough of the spirit of Christ to trample under foot all foolish prejudices, and render personal assistance in the meetings and the Sabbath-schools of the colored people. Why should a young man who had a negro nurse for daily companion and instructor through all the tenderest and most impressible years of childhood, now be thrust out and lose caste because he tries to instruct a class in the colored Sabbath-school, or leads the worship in a meeting of colored people?

The religious interests of the colored Cumberland Presbyterians will no doubt be best developed in a separate denomination of their own, where the whole responsibility of their ecclesiastical affairs is placed in their own hands. Yet who can doubt that it is our solemn duty to help them establish a school for the instruction of their preachers? And when this school is established, one of our educated white men who is sound in the faith should be secured for its theological department until the time comes when enough of scholarship and enough of soundness in the faith are found among the colored preachers to enable them to teach their own candidates for the ministry.

As a fitting close to this chapter, the appeal of the Rev. J. F. Humphrey to our Assembly in 1879 is inserted:

FAYETTEVILLE, TENN., May 14, 1879.

To the General Assembly of the Cumberland Presbyterian church, Memphis, Tenn.

The General Assembly (colored) of the Cumberland Presbyterian church, which convened at Bowling Green, Kentucky, May 1, 1879, conferred the honor upon me to address your reverend and honored body, to set forth our warm sympathies and Christian love. We look upon you as our fathers and our refuge in time of need, and feel assured that you will hear the cries of your poor, humble, destitute children. We have been set apart only a few years, and through much prayer and hard struggles we have been able to sustain the doctrine of our fathers, which is as dear as life itself to us. As children, you have our prayers that all the proceedings of your body may be guided by the unerring counsel of the God of our fathers. We pray that the day may not be far distant when our poor young preachers shall be imbued with the spirit and wisdom which distinguishes your noble body. You have our sincere and heartfelt thanks for your liberal donations to our young preacher at Lebanon, Tennessee, at your last sitting, and we humbly solicit and pray that you will still remember us, and provide some means to aid us in the publication of our little paper, which we desire to issue in the interest of our church. I herewith send you a circular letter, which will set forth our desires and intentions. Should it trespass upon your precious time and suspend your business to read this article, please allow your minds to reflect upon our deplorable condition when we were set apart, by our own request, expecting, after we had made earnest endeavors to help ourselves, that you would extend the aiding hand to succor your child that looks to its father for assistance.

We truly regretted that we were deprived of the counsel of your corresponding delegate at Bowling Green, as he did not appear or send any communication whatever. We value your prayers for the fulfillment of our desires, and shall ever expect your earnest petitions to ascend to the throne of grace in our behalf. If nothing else is done but the offering of your prayers in our behalf, the dark cloud will be dispersed, and then we shall be able to rejoice in the God of our fathers.

Please remember the colored Cumberland Presbyterians in your devotional exercises. If you do this, we feel confident that the obstacles will be removed, and we shall be able to advance in our work, ever holding up the Cumberland Presbyterian banner, with the precious name of Jesus inscribed upon it. May God be with you and conduct the business of your body to the approval and approbation of the Supreme Moderator of the universe.

Yours fraternally,

J. F. HUMPHREY,
Stated Clerk Cumberland Presbyterian Assembly.

CHAPTER XLI.

MISSIONS—1860 TO 1870.

"Sow in faith through joy and sorrow,
Lo, the promise standeth plain,
There shall dawn a harvest morrow,
Seeds that die shall live again."

IN 1860 there were in the United States fourteen Cumberland Presbyterian missions in cities and larger towns. So far as can be ascertained, self-sustaining churches have been established at all these points, except in Louisville, Kentucky, San Antonio, Texas, and Burlington, Iowa. The work at Burlington has been finally abandoned. At Louisville and San Antonio promising mission churches are now growing up.

While the war raged, mission work was prosecuted at Mattoon, Macomb, Atlanta, Winona, and Jerseyville, Illinois; Leavenworth Kansas; and Waukon, Oskaloosa and Nevada, Iowa. Most of this work was under the charge of the Board of Missions at Alton, Illinois. The churches at Waukon, Nevada, Mattoon and Atlanta have become self-sustaining.

In the years immediately succeeding the war missions were reported at Austin, Texas, and Bowling Green, Kentucky; also at Paducah, Kentucky; Clarksville, Chattanooga, and Shelbyville, Tennessee; and Helena, Arkansas. The first two advanced rapidly to a self-sustaining strength.

On the Pacific coast no new missions in cities or towns were undertaken during this period. Some active country missions and valuable itinerant work were reported. The missionaries of this period in California were D. E. Bushnell, E. C. Latta, O. D. Dooley, E. J. Gillespie, C. H. Crawford, L. Dooley, W. N. Cunningham, and C. Yager. Some of these labored in local missions, and some traveled only for a short period. There was a missionary board, or committee, in California. But little or no help was sent from the older portions of the church to any part of the Pacific coast.

In other States, itinerant missionaries were not numerous. The Rev. Benjamin Hall was kept at work in Iowa part of the time as missionary evangelist, and part of the time in charge of the Waukon mission. He gave frequent accounts of precious revivals. The Rev. P. H. Crider was missionary in the same State, devoting himself partly to a local field and laboring also as an evangelist. He, too, reported gracious revivals. The same statements apply to the Rev. A. H. Houghton, who was laboring in Iowa and Minnesota. At the beginning of this period the Rev. J. B. Green was working in Kansas as an itinerant missionary under the direction of the Board of Missions at Lebanon, Tennessee. He had remarkable success. The Rev. A. M. Wilson was employed as a missionary in Kansas during part of this period. The board says of him: "He is a faithful, self-sacrificing brother."

The principal new territories entered by our people between 1860 and 1870 were Nebraska and Colorado. This work began through the immigration of Cumberland Presbyterians into these Territories, but so little was accomplished in these fields that it is best to reserve it to be placed along with the events of the next period.

Although the entire work of the Board of Missions at Lebanon, Tennessee, was suspended by the war; and although the intervening military lines prevented any communication between the board at Alton, Illinois, and our Indian missions, yet these missions stubbornly refused to die. The Rev. R. S. Bell and his wife, with the native preachers to aid them, determined to keep the churches alive. All through the war, without any salary from the board, Bell labored on. The Indians helped to feed him; but it was by a hard struggle, and through much privation and self-denial, that the work was sustained. The fruits of this self-sacrificing toil will endure forever. When the war closed and mails were re-established, it was with feelings of amazement that the church found this missionary hero still at his post. He continued in this work till 1880.

The foreign missionary work of Cumberland Presbyterians during this period was in three fields: the Indian country, Liberia, and Turkey. The work of Edmond Weir in Africa was continued through all these dark war years. From 1861 till he came back to America, in 1868, his letters grew more and more gloomy. Writing to the Rev. J. B. Logan, from Cape Mount, Liberia, September 11, 1861, he says:

This morning I must confess that I am at a great loss to know how to write these lines to you in the United States. . . . . I think that my good Brother Logan will drop me a few lines and let me hear how stands the case with the board and its foreign fields of labor. I know, from what I read, that it can not do much at present toward paying us off. But when will it? I am bare for clothing—indeed I may say that I have but one coat; . . . . and I don't know what I will have to do, seeing those who have such things for sale, say: "I can not credit you, for I think that your board will not do any thing more." . . . . Now, if any member of the board were to drop me a line, saying, "The board will send you some money in a short time," I could get credit, and not suffer so much. Will you please let me know how stands the case at this time. Please write as soon as you get this letter, so that I can know what to do.

I am your most humble servant, E. WEIR.

While the war progressed, and the Board of Missions at Lebanon was inoperative, the Alton board took charge of this Liberia mission, but could send Weir only a very meager support, and utterly failed to secure any other preachers to join him. When the board at Lebanon resumed operations in 1867, the missions were divided between the boards, and the work in Liberia fell to the Alton board. Weir's letters were gloomy; his wife's still more so. In 1868 he left his family in Africa, and came to America to see what was the matter. He attended the meeting of the Alton board, but was not much encouraged by what he there learned. That board was in debt, and had no money for him. It, however, gave him permission to canvass its field and collect all the help he could. After a brief and very unprofitable canvass, he was requested by the board to take a mission to the freedmen of the Southern States, instead of his African mission. This he declined. The board then asked the advice of the General Assembly, and was instructed to abandon the Liberia mission.

This is a sad record to make, but it will be borne in mind that all the Southern States, where two thirds of our people lived, were in a state of extreme financial prostration. North as well as South the absorbing interest in the war, the excitements and distractions, the sore losses and bereavements, had long interfered with missionary collections and hindered all church operations. Every department of the work was crippled for the lack of money. Time was needed for our people to recover their strength and for those who had been separated during the years of the great struggle to re-adjust themselves to one another and to the work. While the church was in this crippled state, it was found impossible to do much for foreign missions, and so the Liberia mission failed.

As for Mr. Weir, he quit the Cumberland Presbyterian church and joined the Congregationalists.

The Rev. J. C. Armstrong's mission to Turkey had, in some respects, a sadder history than the Liberia mission. His Southern birth and Southern sympathies involved him in a class of difficulties which need not be discussed. He was sent by the Lebanon board, which became inoperative before Armstrong had been in Turkey twelve months. This board was crippled almost to its death before Armstrong set his foot on Asiatic soil.

In the summer of 1860, supplied with numerous letters of introduction, the missionary and his wife, and their three-months-old babe set sail from New York in the Golden Rule, Captain Mayo. This was a sail ship, bound for India *via* London. It was overladen, and had a poor crew, though a good captain.

They were becalmed for a week near the banks of New Foundland. After this, late one night when they were under full sail, near the middle of the Atlantic, they were overtaken by a sudden storm. Every sail was spread when the hurricane struck them. The ship was thrown on its beam ends, and when the captain ordered the sails to be furled, he found the crew in mutiny. Not a man obeyed the order. It was perhaps due to this mutiny that the watch had not been faithful to report the approaching storm. The captain, however, was equal to the emergency. He managed by the assistance of the officers to capture and lock up the crew, and take in the sails. Presently the ship was found to be leaking rapidly. The pumps were resorted to, but it was ascertained that the mutineers had intentionally spoiled them. After much trouble and alarm, the pumps were repaired and officers and passengers were set to pumping; but in spite of their utmost efforts, the water gained on them. Wild alarm now reigned. The captain said that the vessel would not keep afloat fifteen minutes longer. Death was the accepted issue. True, there might be some faint hope of escaping in the boats, if the officers could manage to launch them. Before this was undertaken, however, the captain remembered that the vessel was still on its side, and that the leak might be in the side, and not in the hull. Instantly he called every body to aid in righting the ship. That was a supreme moment of peril and suspense. Should all the time remaining be spent in righting the vessel, and the leak still continue, it would then be too late to lower the boats. Every energy was taxed to its utmost, and the ship was righted. It was then found that the leak had entirely ceased. The injury was in the side of the ship, above the water-line. After much vigorous pumping they succeeded in emptying the vessel of water, and finally reached London in safety.

In London, the missionaries utilized their many letters of introduction in a social and pleasant manner. Here, too, tidings reached them of "the Syrian massacre." This was a trial to missionaries bound for Damascus. The different missionary societies of London advised them to abandon the mission to Syria. From London they went to Paris, where they again made pleasant use of their letters of introduction. From France they sailed on a French steamer to Constantinople. They came in sight of this city the morning of the 22d of September, 1860.

Armstrong says that he had from his boyhood felt a special call to preach to the Mohammedans, and when he reached Constantinople, he felt as if his life's mission lay before his eyes. Engaging boarding with the Rev. Wm. Goodell, D.D., the missionaries set to work immediately to study the Turkish language. After six months they rented a house, moved into it, and then began in a small way to work among their neighbors. In the meantime they had cultivated the acquaintance of all the Protestant missionaries then in the city.

In the latter part of the year 1860, a delegation from Brusa, a populous city seventy miles westward, visited the missionaries at

Constantinople. This delegation represented two thousand people who had revolted from the Greek church. They proposed to turn over their houses of worship, membership, and other interests to any Protestant missionary board that would immediately supply them with preaching. Two Protestant preachers, one an editor and a native Greek, proposed to Armstrong that they three should unite and form a Cumberland Presbyterian presbytery, and take charge of this work in Brusa. Here was a conflict between what seemed a clear call of divine Providence, and a long-cherished impression that he was especially called to work for the Mohammedans. He had made good progress in the Turkish language, but he could already speak modern Greek.

Two things, however, were necessary in order to carry out the Brusa enterprise — authority from the Cumberland Presbyterian Board of Missions, and more money. If the two Greek preachers entered the work with him, they, as well as he, would need a small advance from the board. He wrote, but received no reply. He waited and hoped till the opportunity was gone forever.

There were other similar offers, however, from the Greeks—one from the islands of the Greek Archipelago, but they were all declined. Armstrong studied several languages simultaneously with the Turkish. Mrs. Armstrong studied these languages with her husband, and one (Armenian) which he did not. She and her husband still use the Turkish language in their family, being great admirers of that conglomerate tongue.

When the war grew to a white heat in America, the American missionaries in Constantinople became intensely wrought up concerning the war issues at home. Armstrong's position became perilous. His supplies from America were all cut off. His political antecedents prevented him from obtaining any loans from the other American missionaries. He saw before him no prospect but starvation. He says: "I called my faithful servant and his wife, and told them we could no longer afford to keep a servant; they would have to go." He then had prayers with them. When they rose after prayer, the man said: "God do so to me and more also if we leave thee." He then ran down stairs and brought up his earnings, amounting to a hundred dollars, and placed the money in Armstrong's hands. This kept them from starvation a little while longer. Then their rent was due, and their provisions exhausted. The landlord gave them notice to vacate the house in twenty-four hours. In that burning heat they could not live twenty-four hours outside of shelter. Human help there was none. The night was spent in looking to a higher source of help. The next morning there was a vigorous knocking at the door. They supposed their landlord had come to put them out, but, when they opened the door with fear and trembling, it was not the red turban, and big breeches, and bloated face of their landlord which met them, but a young Frenchman in European costume. He seemed excited, and handing Armstrong some money, said hurriedly that the Lord had impressed it on his heart in the night that Armstrong was in want, and had sent him with relief. He told Armstrong that he had just seen the dreaded landlord, and settled the rents for the past, and for six months in advance. He refused to give his name, but said, with tears: "I belong to your King; never doubt that a gracious Lord is watching over you. Good-bye." From that day to this Armstrong has neither seen this timely messenger nor received any tidings from him. He found his rent all paid, as the Frenchman had told him.

That night the chaplain of the British embassy, the Rev. Mr. Gribble, came and loaned Armstrong some money. Next day Mr. Gribble and his wife called, bringing various articles which the missionaries greatly needed. By invitation, formally made, Armstrong began making translations for the seven pastors of the Reformed Armenian church, who about that time had declared themselves independent of the American Board, and set up an organization of their own. The manuscripts of their leader were a mixed mass of English, Turkish, and French, as confused in matter as in language. They desired Armstrong to arrange this mass in one language, and from it to formulate their system of theology for them. To this work he devoted three months, and when he had digested, arranged, and translated the matter placed in his hands, he found it to be a system of doctrine almost identical with that taught by Cumberland Presbyterians. This creed, he says, is no doubt still held and preached by these oriental pastors.

Another work now opened up for our missionary. It was the translation of the Scriptures into the Roumanian language. He accepted this work, and expected to travel to the capital city of Roumania. Here a new difficulty met him. American citizens who were suspected of rebel sympathies had trouble about securing passports. Armstrong took Turkish protection; but he did not, after all, embark in this new work, or need his Turkish passport. An attack of typhoid fever kept him in Constantinople. The illness was long and severe, but all his wants were supplied. The missionaries sat up with him, nursed him, and when he was able to travel loaned him money to the amount of six hundred dollars to come home on. The voyage back to America restored his health and closed his missionary career.

His wife was a Canadian, and he sailed from Asia to Canada, where he remained teaching school until after the close of the war. He greatly longed to return to Asia, but the way has never been opened. The Board of Missions at Lebanon, Tennessee, when it resumed operations, paid off the debts which he had been forced to contract. "God sometimes sends his servants a long way to do what seems to us a very little thing." No matter, if he sends us, it will all be right.

SIXTH PERIOD.

CHAPTER XLII.

SEVERAL GENERAL ASSEMBLIES.

> Return to thy fortress
> That can not be taken,
> And rest on thy rock
> That no earthquake hath shaken.
> —*Anna Shipton.*

THE earthquake was past, and our temple stood without a rent in its walls. We had felt the shock only to learn new lessons about the firmness of that Rock on which our house is builded. After 1870 the spirit of unity and fraternity in the Cumberland Presbyterian church grew rapidly, and there is more union of heart among our people now than ever before.

The General Assembly of 1871, which met at Nashville, Tennessee, was harmonious and full of hope. The quarterly system of collections by pastors, which had been suspended for one year, was by this Assembly promptly, and with great unanimity, restored.

The Assembly of 1872, at Evansville, Indiana, appointed a day of prayer for colleges, and called on the whole church to join in its observance. The great want of the church was men. All keenly felt this want; and the struggle to train men for their work in the ministry was embarrassed by the overwhelming bankruptcy of all the Southern people. Besides this general bankruptcy, which surpassed all description, there was in the Southern States a sad lack of young men. Many from both sections who had been the hope of church and State were sleeping in coffinless graves on the myriad battle-fields of the civil war. Our church was very weak in the Northern States, and the hope of a supply of recruits for the broken ranks of the ministry was but faint. Hitherto, the most of our preachers, even in the Northern States, had come from that South which was now to a large extent demoralized and in ruins. The day of prayer was well timed and was generally observed, and as the history of our colleges will show, it was not observed in vain.

At this Assembly the announcement was officially made of the death of the Rev. Milton Bird, D.D., the stated clerk. Dr. Bird is one of those characters that will grow in our esteem as the years sweep away and all littleness and party prejudices die out. He belonged to no section, no party; and because he would not bow down and worship at any partisan shrine, the true grandeur of his soul was not appreciated in the days of mad partisan extremes. Ruling Elder John Frizzell was elected stated clerk in Dr. Bird's place. Mr. Frizzell had special adaptedness to this work, and the announcement that he could be secured to fill this vacancy gave universal satisfaction.

This Assembly warned our churches and people against bad books. Most of the session was occupied in considering the revised Form of Government, which had long been under discussion, and which, after three references to the presbyteries, was at last laid on the table indefinitely.

The Assembly of 1873 was held at Huntsville, Alabama. One matter of special interest came before this body. Dr. A. J. Baird, who had been sent as corresponding delegate to the General Assembly of the Northern Presbyterian church, in session at Baltimore, Maryland, telegraphed that a committee to consider organic union with Cumberland Presbyterians had, at his request, been appointed by the Presbyterian Assembly, and he asked our Assembly if it would appoint a similar committee. Dr. Baird had, on his own responsibility, made this proposition, and the Presbyterian Assembly had acted on it. Our Assembly appointed the committee asked for, and thus another fruitless movement looking toward organic union was inaugurated.

The two committees thus appointed had a very pleasant and fraternal conference at Nashville, Tennessee, beginning February 25th, 1874, and continuing through the next day. The members of the Cumberland Presbyterian committee present were Drs. Richard Beard, J. B. Mitchell, A. J. Baird, and A. B. Miller. Among the members of the Presbyterian committee were Drs. H. A. Nelson, of Cincinnati, Ohio; Joseph T. Smith, of Baltimore, Maryland; and Charles A. Dickey, of St. Louis, Missouri. But in this case, as in the conference at Memphis six years before with the committee of the Southern branch of the Presbyterian church, the only basis of union submitted by the Presbyterians was the Westminster Confession of Faith. In the Nashville conference the Presbyterians did not even promise to submit to their Assembly the plan of union proposed by the Cumberland Presbyterian committee, but recommended that negotiations should be continued. As in the conference at Memphis, so at Nashville the Cumberland Presbyterian committee went to great lengths in trying to devise a plan upon which the two churches could unite. The plan proposed in the latter case was as follows:

We, the committee on the part of the Cumberland Presbyterian church, submit the following as a basis of union between our church and the Presbyterian church here represented:

1. That both Confessions of Faith shall be retained as they are, and shall be regarded as of equal authority as standards of evangelical doctrine; and hereafter in the licensure of candidates, and in the ordination of ministers or other officers of the church, or on any other occasion when it shall be necessary to adopt a Confession of Faith, it shall be left to the choice of the individual as to which of these he shall adopt.

2. That the Form of Government and Discipline of the Presbyterian church shall be the Form of Government and Discipline of the united church.

3. That the united church shall be known as the Presbyterian church of the United States of America.

The impression went abroad that the joint committee had agreed to this plan of union, and such an impression prevailed among the members of the next Cumberland Presbyterian Assembly; but neither the published records of the joint committee nor the original manuscript minutes of its meetings justify any such conclusion.

To the plan of union proposed by our committee the Presbyterian committee responded in these words:

The committee on the part of the General Assembly of the Presbyterian church having considered the paper presented by our brethren, cordially respond:

1. That this paper and our familiar conference of this morning confirm the impressions and hopes indicated in our previous paper, and our desire for the continued and increased intercourse, co-operation, and united prayer of the ministers and people of both churches which that paper recommends.

2. That in our judgment it is desirable that such intercourse be continued, and the mutual acquaintance of the two churches become more extensive and intimate before their General Assemblies shall be called upon to act upon any plan of union.

3. That in submitting the proceedings of this joint committee to our respective Assemblies we recommend the appointment of a joint committee for continued conference and for promoting intercourse and acquaintance between the two bodies during the next year.

The one thing which the joint committee agreed upon was that the negotiations should be continued. This was the only question connected with this matter which the Cumberland Presbyterian Assembly of 1874, at Springfield, Missouri, was called upon to decide. The discussion of this subject, however, which was not free from ill-feeling, took a far wider range. The Assembly finally adopted a resolution which, without expressing any opinion on the proposed plan of union, declared it inexpedient to continue the negotiations. This forestalled the action of the Presbyterian Assembly, and the whole matter was dropped.

There are two false ideas that ought never again to deceive us or our Presbyterian brethren. One is the hope on their part that our people will sometime adopt unchanged the Westminster Confession of Faith. The other is the belief among Cumberland Presbyterians that Presbyterians are ready to accept our doctrinal platform. Both parties are honest and conscientious, and so long as there exist such important differences in doctrinal views, they can work with more harmony and love in separate ecclesiastical organizations. The union which Christ prayed for is not an outward visible union, else we would all be driven back into the Roman Catholic church. Outward union is vain and worthless when union of heart and spirit do not accompany it. Union of heart often binds Christians of different churches closer together than brothers of the same family. We should cultivate this loving spirit, and wait till God's providence prepares the way for outward oneness. We can cordially co-operate in promoting such preparation, but we can not force it.

All the propositions made by Presbyterians for conference about union with Cumberland Presbyterians have contained evidence that the union to be taken into consideration was, according to the Presbyterian view, to be on the basis of the Westminster standards. Thus the Presbyterian Assembly (Southern), in appointing a committee to meet a similar committee from our church, used this language:

In practically carrying out this idea [viz., of a union], the Assembly, laying aside ecclesiastical etiquette, would affectionately say to their brethren of the Associate Reformed Synod, that they may pull the latch-string of our dwelling whenever they may choose, and may be incorporated with us upon the simple adoption of our standards, whenever these may happen to differ from their own; and to our brethren of the Cumberland Presbyterian church, we respectfully suggest whether the time has not come to consider the great importance to the kingdom of our common Master of their union with us by the adoption of the time-honored standards to which we adhere.

In the conference with the committee of the Southern branch of the Presbyterian church their only proposition was that we should take the Westminster Confession unchanged. In the conference with the representatives of the other branch of the Presbyterian church six or seven years afterward, nothing was offered our committee but the Westminster Confession unchanged. In a movement originated by individuals in California, the Presbyterian synod on the Pacific coast proposed that the Cumberland Presbyterian synod be consolidated with it on the basis of the Westminster Confession unchanged. What ground individual members of our church gave our dear Presbyterian brethren to encourage them to make such offers is an inquiry whose investigation would not be for our edification.

The Assembly of 1874 was rendered memorable by the visit of Dr. James Morrison and Dr. Fergus Ferguson, corresponding delegates from the Evangelical Union Church of Scotland. The profound scholarship of Dr. Morrison made him a fitting companion for Dr. Beard, and it was interesting to see how these two scholars "took to each other."

Ferguson is a genial, witty man, and a thorough Scotchman. A preacher who had been chaplain in the Southern army was Ferguson's room-mate. General Holland, at whose house they were quartered, had been a commander in the Northern army. The two army men became warm friends at their first meeting, and they showed great fondness for talking over war experiences. Ferguson listened in amazement. At last he broke forth with his strong Scotch accent: "I don't understand it, General. Just a little while ago he was preaching to the soldiers, and you were shooting at him. Now here you both are cheek by jowl together, like the best friends in the world." Yes, and the best friends in the world they are still, whether a Scotchman can understand it or not. But they are not any warmer friends to each other than they both are to that quaint, original, genial son of Caledonia, who published a pleasant little book about his trip to Springfield.

The custom of sending corresponding delegates to bear fraternal greetings to General Assemblies and conferences was then at its zenith. For fourteen years it had been growing. The churches which generally had representatives on the floor of our Assembly were the Presbyterian (both branches), the Lutheran, the Evangelical Union, the Colored Cumberland Presbyterian, the Congregational, and sometimes others.

The address of the Rev. J. S. Hays, corresponding delegate from the Presbyterian church in the United States of America to the Cumberland Presbyterian Assembly of 1874, is here presented:

For two reasons no service could be more agreeable to me than that of being the bearer to you of the Christian salutations of that branch of the church to which I belong. In the first place, after observing the spirit and temper of my church toward you as manifested in our General Assembly one year ago, I am able to present these greetings without a single misgiving as to the sincerity and cordiality of those for whom I speak. And then the old animosities that were engendered by the separation which took place before we were born have all been happily buried and forgotten. There is but little diversity and much in common in our history and doctrines and discipline. We serve the same Master and fight against the same enemy in the hope of the same glorious reward.

In a communication received by the Presbyterian General Assembly a year ago, you were pleased to speak of us as the mother church. I am happy to reciprocate the compliment and assure you, in return, of the mother's great pride in recognizing her daughter. It is true, I presume, that some of our very proper people regard the daughter in her religious enjoyments sometimes as a little demonstrative, as possibly some of your more demonstrative people regard the mother as a little too sedate. It is also true, perhaps, that some of our very orthodox people regard your belief as a little flexible, as doubtless some of your flexible people regard the mother a little rigid. Such differences we may expect, but I assure you that there is on our part a deep, strong current of respect, affection, and love such as a mother feels for her child.

When your representative, Dr. A. J. Baird, one year ago in our General Assembly, expressed a desire for the formation of a stronger bond of union between us—a desire, indeed, for organic union if it could be satisfactorily accomplished—his words were met in our Assembly with a round of applause, the meaning of which it was impossible to misunderstand. Upon the spot and without a dissenting voice a committee was appointed to meet and confer with a similar committee from your own body for the purpose of ascertaining if such a union could be effected. We have not yet heard the report of that committee; but it is understood that it was only a royal courtship, not a wedding nor an engagement for a wedding. Perhaps the committees were right about it. We have had a wedding of that sort in our house recently. There are those among us—and I am free to confess that I am one of them—who have never been able to see any indispensable necessity for organic union in order to genuine co-operation and the most cordial fraternal relations. I understand that many of you hold the same opinion.

Now, what sort of unity in the church of Christ would be productive of the greatest amount of efficiency and fraternity, is a question that can not be passed over lightly or easily by our corresponding committees. No more important or delicate question is now before the church. However it may be settled, I am sure that there is a deep and wide-spread desire in my own church for some such organic union as that which was suggested to you by the memorial of Drs. Crosby, McCosh, and others in regard to union among Presbyterians. For such a union, especially with your church, we are ready to labor and pray. If at any future time a full organic union can be effected on terms alike honorable and agreeable to all, we will thoroughly rejoice. If not, we will still stand side by side and shoulder to shoulder with you in the strife against evil, and we will defer our little differences about election and other matters until we pass beyond the vale and sit at the feet of Jesus, where we will enjoy better instruction than that which we now receive from the lips of a Beard or a Hodge.

I was intensely interested yesterday in hearing your educational and missionary reports read. With many of the statements I was highly gratified, and when I make my report to my own General Assembly I shall try to convey to them the same impression that was made upon my mind while I listened.

When we, as Presbyterians, look out upon this broad land and observe the millions that are swarming into it, and when we look out upon the broader field, which is the world, and hear the cries that come to us for help which it is impossible for us to give, it is with the profoundest interest that we watch the increasing strength and hail the rising power of vigorous young churches like your own, marching under the same banner, calling themselves by the same name, and proclaiming substantially the same faith.

Laying upon your table the minutes of our last General Assembly, in which you will see an exhibit of our present condition and future prospects, permit me to close as I commenced, by tendering to you the fraternal greetings and the cordial sympathies of the Presbyterian church in the United States of America.

The Presbyterian church (Old School) sent its first delegate to the Cumberland Presbyterian General Assembly in 1860. Delegates came regularly after that. By and by the churches generally concluded to convey these fraternal greetings by letter, and not send delegates in person. Only the colored Cumberland Presbyterians now send corresponding delegates to our Assembly, and there exist special reasons in their case for still keeping up the old custom.

The Assembly of 1875 met at Jefferson, Texas. An interesting item in the business of this meeting was the presentation to the Assembly, by Joseph W. Allen, of Nashville, of an elegant gavel, made from wood which grew on the McAdow farm near the spot where the first Cumberland Presbyterian presbytery was organized.

The Assembly of 1876 met at Bowling Green, Kentucky; that of 1877 at Lincoln, Illinois. At the Assembly of 1878, which was held at Lebanon, Tennessee, Caruthers Hall, one of the buildings of Cumberland University, was dedicated.

The Assembly of 1879, at Memphis, Tennessee, introduced one new feature. It set apart a whole day for the discussion of topics connected with Sunday-schools. In actual Sunday-school work our people were doing far too little, and though we have since then made decided improvement, yet the statistical report for 1886 shows only a little over half as many Sunday-school scholars as members of the church. Not until 1883 was it decided to have a general superintendent of Sunday-schools for the whole church. Dr. M. B. DeWitt was elected to this office, but as no provisions were made for his salary, and as his time was fully employed with his duties as a pastor, he was unable to devote himself to this work. He resigned in 1886. The Rev. J. H. Warren, his successor, has done good service, collecting many valuable statistics and preparing the way for a greater work in the future. One collection each year from all the congregations in the church, to be taken up on a Sunday designated as "Children's Day," is hereafter to be devoted to the payment of the salary of the general superintendent and the support of Sunday-school interests.

Dr. E. D. Morris, corresponding delegate from the Presbyterian church (Northern), delivered an address in the Cumberland Presbyterian Assembly of 1879, at Memphis, Tennessee, which for sound sense and a rare combination of unflinching fidelity to his own church, along with the noblest liberality toward others, is deserving of special mention. While he called in question the wisdom of any attempt to unite all Presbyterians in one organic body, and expressed doubts about the utility of such large bodies even were they one in faith, calling them "too unwieldy to be efficient, too proud to be endured," he yet declared it desirable for all Presbyterians to "think less about their differences and more of their vital points of agreement in doctrine and order."

The Assembly of 1880 was held at Evansville, Indiana, and by a sort of averaging of dates it was agreed to celebrate this as its semi-centennial meeting. Our first Assembly was organized in 1829, but there had been two years in which no Assembly met. This semi-centennial celebration called forth numerous historical addresses. These were published in a neat little pamphlet prepared by the stated clerk, the Hon. John Frizzell.

The Woman's Board of Foreign Missions was organized at this meeting. While there had been suggestions and resolutions looking toward such an organization years before, such propositions had until 1880 ended in words yielding no positive results. Our missionaries in Japan at last kept the subject ringing in the ears of our people, and Dr. W. J. Darby, of Evansville, helped to press the matter until the organization became an accomplished fact. This board was located at Evansville, Indiana. Just as soon as it was organized, a young lady from Missouri offered herself as a missionary to go to Japan, and was accepted. No part of our ecclesiastical machinery works more successfully or yields larger results of good than this board with its numerous auxiliaries and children's bands. Its annual receipts have increased from a little over $2,000 for the first year, to almost $6,800 for the year ending May, 1887. It has now five missionaries in Japan. It has established a school for the education of Japanese girls. It also assists in mission work in Mexico and among the Indians, and is steadily extending its operations and influence.

The first Cumberland Presbyterian Board of Missions ever organized (1818) was a woman's board, and at different times there were local boards of the same character. One such organization is mentioned in the following letter found in the *Watchman and Evangelist*, a Cumberland Presbyterian paper published at Louisville, Kentucky, thirty years ago:

LEBANON, TENN., November 25, 1857.

MR. EDITOR—I am pleased to read in your paper—nay, the expression does not do justice to my feelings—I am delighted, overjoyed, at the movement of the ladies, members of our church in your city. Indeed, they have set a noble example, which I trust may be followed by the ladies of many other churches. "A female foreign missionary society" according to the plan of that lately formed in Louisville, and for the object there specified, as well as other similar objects which will doubtless be presented, might be formed in every congregation. This would rejoice pious hearts, be approved by the great Head of the church, and, being crowned with the divine blessing, might accomplish results the extent and glory of which eternity alone would reveal. What is more natural than to see the followers of Jesus Christ laboring to advance the great object on which his heart is set? As workers together with him, and loving him who has loved them and saved them

from sin and the wrath to come, it is to be expected that they will desire to please him and exert themselves to save those for whom he shed his precious blood. The Savior, it is true, is able to convert the world without human instrumentalities; but it has pleased him to employ his people in the glorious work. The church is the grand instrument by the labors and sacrifices of which the Son of God is to have the heathen for an inheritance and the uttermost parts of the earth for a possession.
F. R. COSSITT.

The custom of organizing and maintaining such societies had fallen into neglect. The Assembly's action in 1880 gave it new form and new life.

Growing out of a resolution presented to the General Assembly of 1880, which was referred to the standing committee on fraternal relations, a correspondence sprung up on the subject of organic union with the Evangelical Lutheran church. Committees were appointed, but they did not meet for a joint conference. The correspondence between the Rev. F. Springer, D.D., chairman of the Lutheran committee, and the Rev. J. P. Sprowls, D.D., chairman of the Cumberland Presbyterian committee, developed the fact that while both churches desired closer and more hearty fraternal relations, neither of them was ready for organic union.[1]

By the Assembly of 1881, which met at Austin, Texas, measures of far-reaching significance were adopted. The constitution of the Presbyterian Alliance was approved, and "our Confession of Faith was submitted as indicating our harmony with the Consensus of the Reformed Confessions." Committees were appointed to revise the Confession of Faith. The Board of Ministerial Relief was organized. The national council of the Cherokee Indians was memorialized to set apart lands for a Cumberland Presbyterian mission school. A memorial page in the Assembly's Minutes was set apart to the memory of Dr. Richard Beard. This was the first time in the history of the Cumberland Presbyterian church that such a tribute was paid to one of its members. A similar memorial has since been accorded to the Hon. R. L. Caruthers.

The next Assembly, 1882, which met at Huntsville, Alabama, elected delegates to the General Presbyterian Alliance, leaving that

---

[1] See Minutes of General Assembly, 1880, p. 38; 1882, pp. 30, 96; 1883, pp. 30, 31.

council to decide concerning the harmony or want of harmony of the Cumberland Presbyterian creed with the Consensus of the Reformed Confessions. A new committee to co-operate with the colored Cumberland Presbyterians in establishing and endowing a school was appointed.

This Assembly spent most of its sessions in considering the proposed new Confession of Faith, which was submitted to it by the committees appointed the year before. After thoroughly reviewing the work of the committees, and making various changes and amendments, this General Assembly approved the revised book and transmitted it to the presbyteries for their action.

At the Assembly of 1883, held at Nashville, Tennessee, it was announced that one hundred of the one hundred and sixteen presbyteries had approved this revised Confession. In sixty-one presbyteries the vote was unanimous, and in seven there was but one dissenting voice. One presbytery protested against the revision; a majority in nine presbyteries voted against its adoption; three did not report, and three presented memorials suggesting changes or asking postponement. The new "Constitution and Rules of Discipline," and the "General Regulations, Directory for Worship, and Rules of Order" were approved by one hundred and six of the presbyteries. The General Assembly then declared that "the Confession of Faith and Government of the Cumberland Presbyterian church had been constitutionally changed," and that the revised Confession should thereafter "be of binding authority upon the churches."

In 1883 the Hon. John Frizzell, stated clerk, resigned, and T. C. Blake, D.D., was appointed in his place. The Assembly of 1884, which met at McKeesport, Pennsylvania, chose Mr. Frizzell as its moderator, he being the first ruling elder ever elected to that position.

At the next Assembly, which convened at Bentonville, Arkansas, after the opening sermon, which was preached by J. M. Gill, D.D., Mr. Frizzell, on retiring from the moderator's chair, delivered an address abounding in valuable suggestions about the business affairs of the Assembly. He took strong ground in favor of some provisions for regulating the work of evangelists, condemning all that class of lay evangelism which is under no regular ecclesiastical appointment.

At different times in this period, as well as in former periods, the General Assembly bore strong testimony against card playing, theater going, and dancing. The language of one deliverance on dancing was as follows:

Resolved, by this General Assembly, as expressed by former Assemblies, That the practice of promiscuous dancing as an amusement by professed Christians, as well as attendance upon such places of amusement, is hereby declared to be inconsistent with Christian profession and the pure and sacred obligations of our holy religion; and that presbyteries and church sessions are advised that members persisting in such a practice are proper subjects of church discipline.

The meaning of "promiscuous" dancing was discussed at the time, and was defined to be dancing in which both sexes participate.

In 1874 the Board of Publication bought the *Banner of Peace* for $10,000, the *Cumberland Presbyterian* for $13,000, and the *Texas Cumberland Presbyterian* for $2,500, filling out the unexpired subscriptions of each. The *Sunday-school Gem* and the *Theological Medium* had been purchased in 1872. All the weekly papers were consolidated under the name of the *Cumberland Presbyterian*. The consolidated organ was located at Nashville, and the Rev. J. R. Brown, D.D., was appointed editor.

The Board of Ministerial Relief, though not organized until 1881, has done valuable work in providing for the wants of men who have worn their lives out in half-paid labors for the church. The self-sacrificing services of these veteran soldiers of the Cross have been worth a thousand times more than all the pay they ever received or can ever receive from man. This board was located at Evansville, Indiana. The Rev. W. J. Darby, pastor of the Cumberland Presbyterian church in that city, was the prime mover in securing its organization. Articles of corporation were obtained for it in October, 1881. Its receipts during the first year were less than $600. Its total receipts for the year ending May, 1887, were nearly $5,500. It has a permanent fund of $3,500. The number of persons receiving aid has increased from four, who were helped during the first year, to forty-three now on the roll of beneficiaries.

SEVERAL GENERAL ASSEMBLIES.

The boards of the church all made good progress in this period. The Board of Publication, through the aid of contributions from the churches, paid off the immense debt created by purchasing papers and periodicals published by individuals, as well as all the debts for presses and fixtures. It also gave, by order of the Assembly, one thousand dollars to meet expenses incurred in connection with the revision of the Confession of Faith.

The new books written and published by ministers or members of the Cumberland Presbyterian church in this period are not numerous. The themes of the volumes issued are theological, biographical, educational, and practical. No devotional books have made their appearance. There is a wide gap here for our writers to fill. Tracts that will strengthen and build up church members in Christian life are greatly needed. One little book to guide disciples in the Christian life—"Lights on the Way," by Dr. J. R. Brown—was issued in 1879. The work of publishing Sunday-school books has made some little progress. A few religious stories constitute the principal additions. Works to guide the young unto salvation, to train hearts in love to Jesus, to develop the Christian life, to foster faith, and build up souls in real consecration—not works to fascinate by questionable fictions—are what our Sunday-schools need. Such books are likely to find the largest sales. Frances Ridley Havergal's books are an illustration. Of these millions of copies have been sold, and there is no cessation in the demand. At first her publisher protested against the subjects she had chosen, and proposed some world-pleasing substitute, saying that books on the themes she had selected would not be salable. The results show that God still rules. His presence and blessings are with those whose labors are "ever, only, all for Jesus." Let one little book, or tract, or periodical, be so filled with God's truth and God's Spirit that conversions constantly follow its circulation, and no human power can long shut it up within denominational boundaries. To write one such book as "Kept for the Master's Use" is far better than to found an empire, or revolutionize all human sciences.

It remains to speak of the relations of the Cumberland Presbyterian church to the Presbyterian Alliance. The plan for this "general council of all Presbyterian bodies throughout the world" was formed at the meeting of the Evangelical Alliance in New York city, in 1873. In response to a communication from the General Assembly of the Presbyterian church in the United States of America, inviting the Cumberland Presbyterian church to participate in this "Ecumenical Council of Presbyterians," our Assembly in 1874 appointed "a committee to confer with similar committees from other Presbyterian Assemblies to arrange for such a Council." This committee never reported. In 1875 our Assembly appointed the Rev. W. E. Ward, D.D., to attend the "Presbyterian Alliance to meet in London." At this London conference, which began July 21st, 1875, there were sixty-four commissioners present, representing twenty-two Presbyterian organizations; but as Dr. Ward failed to be present, the Cumberland Presbyterian church had no representative in this initial meeting, and, therefore, did not become one of the churches originally composing the Alliance. The commissioners in attendance agreed upon a basis of union, and adopted a constitution, designating the body as "The Alliance of the Reformed Churches Throughout the World holding the Presbyterian System," and providing that "Any church organized on Presbyterian principles, which holds the supreme authority of the scriptures of the Old and New Testaments in matters of faith and morals, and whose creed is in harmony with the Consensus of the Reformed Confessions, shall be eligible for admission into the Alliance."

The first regular meeting of the Alliance under this constitution was held in Edinburgh, Scotland, beginning July 4, 1877, but no Cumberland Presbyterian delegates were in attendance. None had been appointed. Our General Assembly in 1880 appointed nine representatives to attend the Alliance's regular meeting, which was to convene at Philadelphia, September 23d of that year. Only two of these, the Rev. W. H. Black, and Mr. John R. Rush, presented themselves for admission. The Committee on Credentials reported against the admission of the two delegates. The report said:

We are constrained to adopt this resolution by the absence of sufficient evidence that the Cumberland church now accept the doctrinal basis of the Alliance, and by the terms of Article II. of the Constitution, which restricts the Alliance to churches whose creeds are in harmony with the Consensus of the Reformed Confessions.

No one in the Council seemed to comprehend the importance of this report, when it was first presented by the committee, and it was adopted without discussion; but on the following day the question was re-opened, and led to an exciting debate. One leading member argued that these delegates could not be admitted because the church they represented did not accept the whole of the Westminster Confession. Another argued that because the committees on organic union between Cumberland Presbyterians and Southern Presbyterians had, in their conference at Memphis, in 1867, failed to agree, therefore Cumberland Presbyterians had no right to seats in the Council. But many of the best men in the Alliance, representing both Europe and America, argued in favor of the admission of our delegates. After this matter had been before the Alliance for several days, the following was adopted in lieu of the report of the Committee on Credentials:

Resolved, That the Council are unable, *hoc statu,* to admit as members brethren representing churches whose relations to the Constitution have not been explained and can not now be considered.

This, as a leading religious paper remarked at the time, kept the delegates out without committing the Alliance permanently to the rejection of the church they represented. In his report to our General Assembly, the Rev. W. H. Black said:

You are already acquainted with the facts concerning the rejection of your delegates, *ostensibly,* because our Assembly had not taken the necessary regular steps toward admission; but really, as your delegate thinks, because some of the members of the Alliance considered the doctrines of the Cumberland Presbyterian church out of harmony with the Consensus of the Reformed Confessions.

This matter awakened a lively interest, both in this country and Europe, and was widely discussed by the press. There was, among the more liberal members of the Alliance, much dissatisfaction with the result. The Cumberland Presbyterian General Assembly at its next meeting, in 1881, after formally adopting the Constitution of the Alliance, and submitting our Confession of Faith, "as indicating our harmony with the Consensus of the

Reformed Confessions," appointed a committee, "to consider the subject in the light of future developments, and to report to the next Assembly." The report of this committee, which was unanimously adopted by the General Assembly of 1882, stated the particulars[1] in which the founders of the Cumberland Presbyterian church dissented from the Westminster Confession, and then added:

By these exceptions it will be seen that we have an amended form of the Westminster Confession of Faith, and if this puts us out of harmony with the Consensus of the Reformed Confessions, we will be glad to have the fact clearly and unequivocally stated. That this may be certainly done by the next Council, we recommend that you appoint delegates to the next meeting of the Alliance in the city of Belfast, Ireland, in 1884.

The next year our Assembly adopted an address, submitting to the Alliance "Our Confession of Faith and Government," and saying to that Council: "If the difference between our statements of doctrine and those of the Westminster Confession of Faith is inconsistent with our being represented in your body, you will so decide."

Twenty-five delegates had been appointed to attend the meeting of the Alliance at Belfast, which was to convene June 24th, 1884. Twelve of the number were present at that meeting. The first important item before this Council was the report of a committee appointed four years before to define the Consensus of the Reformed Confessions. This committee announced that, after diligent inquiry, the conclusion had been reached that it was inexpedient to attempt a statement of the creed on which the churches composing the Alliance were united. It had been discovered that the Presbyterian churches in Continental Europe were not in harmony with the Westminster Confession of Faith in many important particulars, and it was well known that even the United Presbyterian Church of Scotland had found it necessary to adopt an explanatory clause, to which candidates for ordination were required to subscribe, rather than to the simple Confession.

Much interest was felt in the probable result of the application of our delegates for admission. So great was the demand for Cum-

---

[1] See page 99 of this history.

Rev. R. Beard, D.D.

Rev. A. J. Baird, D.D.

Rev. S. G. Burney, D.D.

berland Presbyterian Confessions of Faith, that a Belfast firm printed a new edition of three thousand copies of that book. The Committee on the Reception of Churches was enlarged from three to seventeen members, representing all shades of opinion and all parts of the world. After due deliberation this committee unanimously agreed upon the following report, which was presented to the Council:

Respecting the Cumberland Presbyterian church in the United States of America, the following deliverance was unanimously adopted:

WHEREAS, The Cumberland Presbyterian church has adopted the Constitution of the Alliance;

WHEREAS, It was one of the churches which was invited to assist in the formation of the Alliance in 1875;

WHEREAS, It has now, as on previous occasions, made application for admission, and has sent delegates to the present meeting;

WHEREAS, Further, as declared by the first meeting of the Council, the responsibility of deciding whether they ought to join the Alliance should rest on the churches themselves, your committee recommends to the Council, without pronouncing any judgment on the church's revision of the Westminster Confession and Shorter Catechism, to admit the Cumberland Presbyterian church into the Alliance, and to invite the delegates now present to take their seats.

The Rev. Dr. Martin, of Kentucky, moved to reject the report, and made a lengthy speech against the reception of our delegates. A heated debate followed which lasted three hours, and in which the representatives from the Southern Presbyterian church took the lead in opposing the report of the committee. Men representing the best thought in the several churches composing the Alliance, took strong grounds in its favor. Among these were Dr. Briggs and Dr. John Hall, of New York; Professor E. D. Morris, of Cincinnati; Professor Calderwood, of Edinburgh; Principal McVicar, of Montreal; and Dr. Brown and Dr. Story, of Scotland. Dr. Monod, of France, warned the Council that if the Cumberland Presbyterians were rejected the continental churches would feel themselves bound to withdraw from the Alliance.[1] Less than twenty members of the Council voted in favor of Dr. Martin's motion. On motion of the Rev. T. W. Chambers, D.D., of New

---

[1] Report in *Cumberland Presbyterian*, July 24, 1884.

York, the closing part of Committee's report, was made to read as follows, and with this amendment was adopted:

The Council, without approving of the church's revision of the Westminster Confession and of the Shorter Catechism, admit the Cumberland Presbyterian church into the Alliance, and invite the delegates now present to take their seats.

Our delegates, in their report to the next Assembly (1885), said:

Dr. Chambers' amendment was carried by a vote of 112 to 78. Those voting against Dr. Chambers' amendment were in favor of admitting our church unconditionally. Those voting for the amendment desired the admission of the church "without approving our revision of the Westminster Confession of Faith." After due deliberation and consultation, we decided to accept seats in the Council and report our action to you. The action of the Council in this matter gave great satisfaction to its members. . . . We take special pleasure in bearing testimony to the cordial and hearty reception our delegates received, both from members of the Council and the citizens of Belfast. . . . We recommend that you continue to fraternize with this great and powerful organization intended to promote the welfare of our common Presbyterianism.

The General Assembly (1885) adopted the following report on this subject:

Your committee has fully considered the report of your delegates to the Pan-Presbyterian Council, also the official communication from the clerk of the Council, and unanimously recommend that you adopt the following preamble and resolutions:

WHEREAS, The Council was neither asked nor expected to express approval of our Confession of Faith, but to decide whether it is in harmony with the Consensus of the Reformed churches; and,

WHEREAS, The Council decided to admit the Cumberland Presbyterian church to membership in the Alliance, and our delegates to seats in the Council, thereby placing the Alliance upon a basis not inconsistent with our creed; therefore,

Resolved, 1. That this new evidence of a growing catholicity among the members of the great Presbyterian family is hailed with pleasure by this General Assembly representing the Cumberland Presbyterian church.

2. That we, as a denomination of Christians, continue to fraternize cordially with the liberal and progressive churches composing the Alliance, endeavoring, in the true spirit of unity, with them to promote the gospel's advancement throughout the world.

Although the action by which our church was admitted to membership in the Alliance was not entirely pleasing to all our ministers and people, yet the General Assembly has shown no disposition to recede from the steps it has taken in this matter. In its latest action the Assembly declared that the connection of our church with the Alliance has brought the system of doctrine taught by our people to the attention of the world as never before, and that the Alliance has become a medium of greater fraternity among the churches, drawing them together, promoting a better understanding among the great organizations constituting the Presbyterian family, and promising to become the medium of practical co-operation in foreign mission fields. While it is felt that co-operation is needed, the indications are strong that the churches which most opposed the admission of Cumberland Presbyterians to membership in the Alliance need us more than we need them. The noble words of Dr. E. D. Morris, of Lane Seminary, Cincinnati, Ohio, uttered in behalf of our people in the Council at Belfast, ought to endear him to all Cumberland Presbyterians forever.

A sad event connected with the journey of the Cumberland Presbyterian delegates to the Belfast Council was the death of the Rev. A. J. Baird, D.D. His health had been failing for several months, but he was unwilling to give up his cherished purpose to attend the Alliance, and he hoped to be benefited by foreign travel. He, however, grew rapidly worse after leaving home, and at New York city, June 15, 1884, the day after his fellow-commissioners sailed, he breathed his last. By his eloquence, his winning personality, and his genial and loving spirit, as well as by his work as a pastor and revival preacher and a writer, he had won a place in the affections of our people which has been attained by few, and his death was mourned as a great loss to the church.

The process of consolidating synods has gone on steadily throughout this period. Presbyteries, also, have in several instances been consolidated. So far as can be learned, the results in all these cases have been favorable. Large bodies are more powerful.

The following new synods have been organized: Ozark (re-organized), 1871; Oregon and Kansas, 1875; Missouri Valley, 1877; Trinity, 1878.

The following new presbyteries have appeared in the Assembly's Minutes:

Ozark (reorganized) and Rocky Mountain, 1871; Nolin, Nebraska, and Louisiana, 1873; Hot Springs and Magazine, 1874; Purdy, Republican Valley, and Bosque, 1875; Kirkpatrick and Hill, 1876; Wichita and Graham, 1878; Springville, Albion, Missouri, Burrow, and La Crosse, 1880; Mayfield and San Saba, 1882; Gregory, 1883; Bonham, Cherokee, and McDonald, 1884; Florida and Buffalo Gap, 1885. Louisiana and McDonald are disbanded presbyteries restored. The dates given are the dates when the first mention of these presbyteries is found in the Minutes of the Assembly.

The following table shows the statistics for different parts of this period:

Year.	Ministers.	Members.	Sunday-school Pupils.	Contributions.
1871	1,116	96,335	26,466	$136,231
1875	1,232	98,242	44,912	$295,886
1880	1,386	111,863	54,813	$329,418
1886	1,547	138,564	74,576	$553,033

The contributions have increased more than four hundred per cent., and the number of Sunday-school pupils nearly three hundred per cent. The progress in other things is also encouraging.

The colored Cumberland Presbyterians have made rapid growth in numbers, but their statistics are not included in this table. One thing which has always been characteristic of the growth of the Cumberland Presbyterian church is that it represents not proselytes from other churches, but souls won from the kingdom of darkness. For the few proselytes coming to us from others we can show a little army of persons who were converted at our meetings, and who afterward joined some other denomination. Such a record is worth more than longer lists of names on the church roll. May God grant us grace in all the coming years to be more in earnest to bring souls to Christ than to build up denominational strength!

CHAPTER XLIII.

MISSIONS.

I gave, I gave my life for thee,
What hast thou given for me?
—*F. R. H.*

WHILE still far behind its duty in missionary work, the Cumberland Presbyterian church has made great progress therein during the last ten years. Private missions, presbyterial and synodical missions, and itinerant missions under the church board have been numerous, and it is not possible to give even in outline the history of all these.

In city mission work the results during the last fourteen years have been far more encouraging than in any former period. Since 1870 a large proportion of our mission churches in cities and towns have grown strong enough to dispense with the assistance of the board. Among these are two in St. Louis, one made up of German-speaking and the other of English-speaking Cumberland Presbyterians. The latter, which, to distinguish it from the other, was designated as the "American" mission, has had a remarkable history. The Rev. J. G. White became missionary at St. Louis, November, 1848, and continued in this work until 1860, when he was succeeded by the Rev. L. C. Ransom. At the beginning of the civil war this mission had a growing congregation and a good house of worship located in a central and desirable part of the city. On the property, valued at $27,000, there was an embarrassing debt of nearly $10,000. Soon after the war commenced the missionary went to Alabama, and the little flock became shepherdless. The regular services were suspended, and the building was finally sold to meet the claims of creditors.

Though the fruit of the toil and sacrifice of more than fifteen years was thus lost, efforts to revive the work were not given up. In the Assembly of 1865 the Committee on Missions recommended

St. Louis as an important mission field, and stated that the congregation then had "an opportunity to purchase a comfortable and well-situated house of worship at reasonable rates." The next year the Board of Missions, at Alton, Illinois, reported that the Rev. F. M. Gilliam had been appointed to take charge of the St. Louis work, and that a plan for raising money by a joint stock company to purchase a house and lot had been adopted and was succeeding admirably. The missionary had been in the field as soliciting agent, and had secured subscriptions enough to pay for this property. He, however, for some reason not stated in the Minutes, resigned in October, 1866.

About this time the board adopted a new, and what proved to be an unfortunate measure. A congregation known as the "First Independent Church of St. Louis," which had grown out of a mission Sunday-school, had a large and expensive house of worship in process of erection. Eight thousand dollars was needed to complete this building, and there was a debt of fifteen thousand dollars on it. The members of this church proposed to become Cumberland Presbyterians, and to convey this property to our mission, on condition that the board would assume the debt. This proposition was accepted, and the property already owned by the mission, as well as this new property, was mortgaged in order to borrow $20,000 to meet the pressing claims of the creditors of the Independent church, and to advance the work on the new building. December 12th, 1866, the Rev. J. H. Coulter, whose ministerial services had been temporarily secured by the mission, perfected the organization of the Cumberland Presbyterian congregation, and the formal union with the Independent congregation was effected February 17, 1867. The consolidated church then numbered one hundred and fifteen members. The property acquired by the Cumberland Presbyterian mission before forming this union was sold, and the proceeds used in prosecuting the work on the new building. The basement was finished October, 1867, but to secure this result two thousand dollars more had been borrowed. Though the property was valued at forty-six thousand dollars, the debts began to be pressing. The Rev. F. M. Gilliam, who had for a time resumed the charge of the work, had again resigned, and the Rev.

William S. Langdon had been appointed temporarily as missionary. In 1869 the board reported unforseen reverses. The payments of interest due had not been met by the board, and a large portion of those who had composed the Independent church had seceded and taken possession of the property. When the Assembly of 1870 met, the "Independent" faction still held the building. To the Assembly of 1872 the board reported that all honorable means to get possession of the property or "to get back the money we had invested over and above the debts of the property," had been in vain. That portion of the congregation which had seceded had taken refuge in the Presbyterian church, and under the sanction of the St. Louis Presbytery captured the house. Both this presbytery and the congregation which held the property acknowledged their moral obligation to repay the money our people had invested; but they not only failed to meet this obligation, but thwarted all the board's efforts to re-imburse itself.

Abandoning all hope of success in this quarter, the board resolved to begin a new work in another part of the city. Efforts were set on foot to secure ten thousand dollars to buy a lot and build a chapel. In May, 1873, the Rev. E. J. Gillespie was already soliciting funds for this purpose. In the summer of 1874 the board resolved to prosecute this work with renewed vigor, but "with no hope of success in a day or a year." The Rev. C. H. Bell, D.D., was chosen to take charge of the work. Before the meeting of the Assembly of 1875, ten thousand dollars in notes and pledges had been secured. Dr. Bell and others diligently prosecuted the work of raising money; and the board, made wiser by its past experiments, promised "to take no step until it had the money to pay for what was done." Through these years the missionary, "when not engaged in soliciting funds, devoted his attention to looking up members and others in sympathy with the church, and to conducting services in various parts of the city." The congregation was organized, and took possession of its new chapel December 1, 1877. In May, 1879, this church had fifty-three in communion; and during the year ending with May, 1880, it not only paid its incidental expenses, but contributed nearly three hundred and fifty dollars toward the missionary's salary. At the close of 1880 Dr. Bell asked leave to retire from the work. His resignation took effect January 31, 1881, and the Rev. W. H. Black succeeded him immediately. This church became self-supporting January 1, 1882, and has since grown steadily in numbers and influence. The Rev. W. H. Black is still its pastor (1887).

The lessons learned in connection with this St. Louis work and from similar efforts elsewhere have borne good fruit. Successful mission churches have grown up in a number of cities and towns, and the missionary work of the church has prospered as never before. Among the city missions that have grown into successful churches during this period are one at Little Rock, Arkansas, one at Kansas City, Missouri, one at Sedalia, Missouri, and one at Logansport, Indiana.

The Little Rock mission became self-supporting in 1875. Of this mission the board, in its report to the Assembly of 1876, said:

> The work at this place has made most gratifying progress spiritually, and also financially, so that it has become self-sustaining as to the pastor's support. . . . The fruits which have rapidly attended this work, undertaken only a few years ago, are most encouraging, and are in large part, under God, due to the zeal and judgment of S. H. Buchanan, D.D., the pastor.

Dr. Buchanan is still pastor of this church.

To the General Assembly of 1870 the Kansas City mission was reported as a new enterprise but lately received under the care of the board. Through the efforts of Lexington Presbytery, a neat and comfortable house of worship had been erected. The Rev. J. E. Sharp was missionary, and through his efficient labors, supported by contributions from the presbytery, the foundations of our church here were securely laid. He resigned in the fall of 1874. Afterward the Rev. C. P. Duvall for a time had charge of this mission. The Rev. B. P. Fullerton was called to this field in 1879, entering upon the work October 1st. He is still the pastor in charge. The church was declared self-sustaining October 8, 1883. A new and commodious house of worship was dedicated the day before. The work of this church continues to be greatly blessed. From the beginning this mission was under the direct care and support of the Lexington Presbytery.

MISSIONS.

The Rev. A. H. Stephens became missionary at Sedalia, Missouri, June 1, 1881. Efforts to establish a Cumberland Presbyterian church in this growing city had been begun several years before. With a view of building a house of worship, a small sum of money had been raised, and was in the hands of a committee appointed by New Lebanon Presbytery; but prior to 1878 all efforts to build up a congregation had failed. In September of that year the Rev. J. T. A. Henderson, then of Knobnoster, Missouri, began to preach twice a month in this city without any appointment from the board or the presbytery, and at his own charges. He continued these services regularly for about two years, his compensation being less than his traveling expenses. During the years 1879 and 1880 a small frame church costing $2,500 was erected with money collected by New Lebanon Presbytery. The work, though under the charge of the Board of Missions after 1881, was sustained by the contributions of this presbytery. This congregation became self-supporting November 29, 1885, at which time it dedicated a new and elegant church edifice. In May, 1886, it reported a membership of one hundred and thirteen, and has since steadily grown in numbers and usefulness under the efficient pastorate of Mr. Stephens. The General Assembly of 1886 was held at Sedalia.

In the fall of 1875 the Board of Missions, at the earnest solicitation of ministers and members of the church in Indiana, and after due investigation, resolved to plant a mission in Logansport, and appointed the Rev. A. W. Hawkins missionary. He took charge of the work November 1, 1875. Twelve or fourteen persons who had once been Cumberland Presbyterians were found in or near the city. A hall was rented and regular services held. Of his work at this time the missionary says: "I made my sermons in the early part of the week, and in the latter part of the week I went out and made a congregation to hear them." In May, 1876, a church with thirty-five members was organized. In 1877 a lot with a dwelling-house on it was purchased, and a comfortable church was built and dedicated. All the money used in erecting this building, except fifteen dollars sent from Pennsylvania, was raised at Logansport by the missionary, who though "cramped by a support far too meager," continued to be "patient, persevering, and successful."[1] In February, 1885, he handed in his resignation, but continued in charge of the work until the 8th of the following April, at which time he was succeeded by the Rev. James Best, who continues to labor successfully in this field. This church was declared self-sustaining Sunday, May 9, 1886.

At the beginning of the war there was at Chattanooga, Tennessee, a flourishing Cumberland Presbyterian mission. In 1860 this congregation reported ninety in membership, and it had "a neat brick edifice, well located, and almost entirely paid for." The Rev. A. Templeton was missionary, and his work here had been most successful; but during the great civil conflict the members were scattered and the house greatly damaged. The work was resumed after the war closed, and in 1868 the little church had thirty members, and regular services were kept up. Rev. N. W. Motheral was then the missionary in charge, but for some reason he did not long continue in the work, and for several years the congregation was most of the time without a pastor. Then Rev. W. D. Chadick became missionary, and under his wise and energetic administration the congregation made gratifying progress for three or four years. By reason of failing health he gave up the work in December, 1877. Then after another period of change and uncertainty the Rev. W. H. Darnall, D.D., was appointed to take charge of this mission, and under his labors, which continued from March, 1880, to the fall of 1882, the work was again prosperous. After his retirement this church seems to have passed from under the care of the board, and was again much of the time without a pastor until April, 1885, when the Rev. E. J. McCrosky entered upon his successful labors in this field. During the time he had charge of the work a commodious and beautiful church was erected, and the congregation entered upon a new career of growth and usefulness. He resigned July 15, 1887.

Many other mission churches not less deserving of mention than those whose work has been thus briefly sketched have, during this period, grown into self-support and extended usefulness. Those described are but selections illustrating the character of our

---

[1] Report of the Board of Missions to the General Assembly of 1879.

home mission work. In the wide field extending from Pennsylvania to California, and from Iowa to Texas, scores of similar missions have flourished, not only in towns and villages but in country places; not only under the supervision of the Board of Missions, but under the direction of synods or presbyteries, or of single congregations, or through the liberality or self-sacrifice of individual church members or ministers.

The following is a list of some of the important and growing mission churches now under the care of the board, with the names of the missionaries: Allegheny, Pennsylvania, the Rev. J. H. Barnett; Louisville, Kentucky, the Rev. B. D. Cockrill; Knoxville, Tennessee, the Rev. J. V. Stephens; Birmingham, Alabama, the Rev. F. J. Tyler; St. Joseph, Missouri, the Rev. Alonzo Pearson; Springfield, Illinois, the Rev. S. Richards, D.D.; Fort Scott, Kansas, the Rev. S. A. Sadler; Garden City, Kansas, the Rev. J. R. Lowrance; Fort Smith, Arkansas, the Rev. S. H. McElvain; San Antonio, Texas, the Rev. W. B. Preston; Stockton, California, the Rev. T. A. Cowan; Meridian, Mississippi, the Rev. R. A. Cody; Walla Walla, Washington Territory, the Rev. W. W. Beck. Of these missions, and others under the care of the board, Dr. Bell says, in a recent address:[1]

Some of these are nearly self-supporting, having good property unincumbered; others have suitable buildings, and the work of gathering congregations is in progress; while some are earnestly seeking funds for the purchase of church homes preparatory to the commencement of preaching services. Never were the prospects so encouraging for obtaining denominational footing in centers of moral and commercial influence.

Much of this increased success in missionary work has been due to the prudence and efficiency of those who have administered the affairs of the board. At the beginning of this period the work was under the immediate supervision of the Rev. R. S. Reed, secretary. He died early in the summer of 1871, and was succeeded by the Rev. J. B. Logan, D.D., who was for two years general superintendent and corresponding secretary. After this, beginning

---

[1] This address was delivered at the Cumberland Presbyterian State Sunday-school Encampment, at Pertle Springs, Missouri, August, 1877.

May 1, 1874, the Rev. E. B. Crisman, D.D., became superintendent and corresponding secretary, and the almost seven years during which he held this office were a period of increasing success in every department of mission work. Since February, 1881, the Rev. C. H. Bell, D.D., president of the board, has devoted his whole attention to the general management of missions, and in these years this cause has flourished as never before.

In no other country on earth is the home missionary work so important as it is in the United States. New States are springing up, new populations are gathering. Vast communities are taking shape and setting into their final type so rapidly that it requires constant reading to keep up with their progress. The opportunity now open to home missions will never return. This is pre-eminently true in regard to the home mission work of Cumberland Presbyterians. We can not shift the responsibility. We stand nearest of all to these new States. The center of our strength and influence is in the West. Our own sons are among the pioneers who are pressing into these new fields. If we fall behind, and leave these rapidly-growing communities to be evangelized by other churches, we must forever stand charged with being false to our own children and our own King.

Cumberland Presbyterians have missions among the Chickasaw, the Choctaw, and the Cherokee Indians. There are two growing presbyteries in this field. Bethel Presbytery has eleven ordained ministers, and ten probationers. All but two of these are natives, and the work in that field is now mainly done by native preachers. This presbytery embraces the country of the Chickasaws and Choctaws, and it has thirty-one congregations and five hundred and forty communicants. These two Nations are closely united, and form one missionary field. The churches in this presbytery are now nearly all self-sustaining. Leading men among the Indians are active members of our church, and attend our General Assemblies as delegates. One of the most interesting features of the Assembly of 1878 was the presence of Judge Chico as a representative from Bethel Presbytery. Our work among the Chickasaw and Choctaw Indians began in 1819, and has been kept up in some form ever since. The Rev. Calvin Robinson, a native, the Rev. J. H. Dickerson, and the Rev. J. J. Smith are now our missionaries in Bethel Presbytery. All three are consecrated and successful workers.

Although zealous Cumberland Presbyterian preachers have often visited the Cherokees and held meetings, yet it was but recently that the board sent permanent missionaries to that field. The first of these was the Rev. N. J. Crawford, in whose veins there is some Indian blood. He determined in 1876 to cast his lot among the Cherokees. More than four hundred conversions were reported as the result of his meetings prior to 1885.

There are curious items about some of our missionaries in that field. The Rev. David Hogan had been preaching fifty years before he determined to become a missionary. He had preached along with Finis Ewing in other days. With his own hands he closed Finis Ewing's eyes when that hero of the Cross fell asleep in Jesus.[1] A most interesting thing it is to hear Hogan talk of his early experiences. He says: "My church is better known and held in higher esteem in heaven than it is on earth." When he was seventy-one years old he said to the Board of Missions: "If you will commission me as missionary to the Cherokee Indians, without salary, I will spend the rest of my days preaching to that people." The commission was given him, and now for more than three years he has been laboring in this mission field.

The first Cumberland Presbyterian church among the Cherokees was organized by N. J. Crawford in 1877. It is in the eastern part of the Cherokee country, and is known as the Prairie Grove congregation. There was a great revival among the Cherokees in 1880 and 1881.

In 1874 a Cherokee boy came to Cumberland University, Lebanon, Tennessee, to prepare for the ministry. He was graduated in 1879, and is now in his native land preaching Jesus. His name is R. C. Parks. His churches now number over a hundred members.

The Cherokee Presbytery was organized in February, 1884, at the residence of the Rev. R. C. Parks, Canadian District, Indian Territory. N. J. Crawford, David Hogan, and R. C. Parks were the original members. J. H. Kelley, licentiate, placed himself

---

[1] Memoranda furnished by Hogan.

under the care of the presbytery at its organization. This presbytery now has five ordained ministers, two probationers, and seven congregations, with nine out-stations. The aggregate number of communicants is four hundred and fifty.

One of the schools in the Cherokee country is partially under the care of our Woman's Board of Missions—that is, this board has been giving it assistance. This school is known as Hogan Institute. Our native members and preachers have also aided in various other schools among the Cherokees. An item of interest connected with this presbytery is that a consecrated Christian young lady, Miss Bell Cobb, is its stated clerk. In the manuscript history of this presbytery, prepared by this lady, the work of N. J. Crawford, R. C. Parks, J. H. Kelley, David Hogan, Laman Carter, and J. H. Pigman is described with a fullness of detail which can not be repeated here. This interesting narrative closes with some statements which are brief enough to be quoted:

In May, 1886, the Rev. Joseph Smallwood, of the Methodist Episcopal church, South, a full blood Cherokee Indian, was, by a commission appointed by the presbytery, received as a minister in the Cumberland Presbyterian church. All the ministers in this presbytery are now in the field and identified with the Cherokee people, and, under God, and by the help of his Holy Spirit, intend to maintain and advance the church's work among them. The Board of Missions has three missionaries in the Cherokee Nation: the Rev. N. J. Crawford, with a salary of $25 per month; the Rev. R. C. Parks, with a salary of $8.33 per month; and the Rev. David Hogan, without a salary. The presbytery has one missionary in the field, the Rev. Joseph Smallwood, with a salary of $12.50 per month.

Special mention must here be made of the Rev. B. F. Totten, of Arkansas Presbytery, who aided the Rev. N. J. Crawford in revival meetings in 1880-1; of the Rev. E. E. Baily, of Pennsylvania, who, at his own expense, labored through several revival seasons, not only among the Cherokee, but other tribes as well; of the Rev. E. M. Roach, of Arkansas Presbytery, who labored three months with the Rev. R. C. Parks and the Rev. N. J. Crawford in the summer and fall of 1885, being employed and sent by the Woman's Home Missionary Society of Boonsboro, Arkansas. We are, also, under many obligations to the Woman's Board of Foreign Missions, Evansville, Indiana, for five hundred dollars kindly sent us in October, 1885, for the purposes of church extension.

We predict a bright future for the Cumberland Presbyterian church in the Cherokee Nation. The intelligence of the people, the self-sacrifice of the ministry, and the leadings of the Holy Spirit all point to the success of the church and the glorification of God in the salvation of this people.

After the Board of Missions recalled the Rev. Edmond Weir from Liberia in 1868, and until it appointed the Rev. S. T. Anderson, D.D., to go to the Island of Trinidad in 1873, it had no foreign mission under its care, unless we except the work among the American Indians. The records during these years show that our people felt dissatisfied with this state of things.

In 1870 the board declared that the time had come when the Assembly should at least "begin to lay plans and devise means for active efforts in re-occupying the foreign field," and the General Assembly of that year adopted a report which, after calling attention to the opportunities for mission work in Mexico and in the South American States, said, "The foreign field is open to us: so far as God enables us we should occupy it."

In 1871 the declarations of the General Assembly indicate that there was in the minds of our people increasing interest in regard to the foreign work. The board was instructed to ascertain if possible the best method of entering upon this work, and was directed to raise funds for this purpose.

During the year following the board corresponded with persons in different parts of the world in order to elicit information to guide them in selecting a mission field. Among those who were thus written to was Dr. S. Irenæus Prime, of New York, who recommended Japan as the heathen country "most accessible and least occupied by Christian churches," and whose, people in spite of "the strange and seemingly paradoxical position of the Japan government against Christianity," were eager to hear the gospel.

The board had also received communications from N. H. McGhirk, M.D., urging the claims of the Island of Trinidad in the West Indies. He was a member of the Cumberland Presbyterian church who had moved from Missouri to that island. He said that country, while nominally Catholic was really heathen, and urged the board to send one or two missionaries thither.

A memorial came from Pennsylvania Synod entreating the Assembly of 1872 to move at once in the work of foreign missions. This synod had already made arrangements by which it was to send the Rev. M. L. Gordon to Japan through the American Board. Increased contributions for the foreign work showed a growing interest in this subject throughout the church. In their report to this Assembly the board expressed their unanimous judgment, "after much reflection on the subject," that union with the American Board in the prosecution of mission work was not advisable on account of the great dissimilarity of doctrinal views between Cumberland Presbyterians and those represented by that board; adding that those united in the work through the American Board had "ever been regarded as strictly Calvinistic, while the very existence of the Cumberland Presbyterian church is a protest against the radical features of Calvinism."

To the Assembly of 1873 it was announced that the Island of Trinidad and the capital of Venezuela, South America, had been selected as the mission fields most easily accessible and promising the quickest and surest results of good. One chief reason which influenced the board in making this choice was the expectation of coming into possession of an immense tract of land in Venezuela. This was part of a still larger tract which had been granted by the government of Venezuela to a company of which Dr. N. H. McGhirk was a member. This company had re-granted eight hundred square miles of their prospective domain to nine trustees for the use and benefit of the Cumberland Presbyterian church for the purpose of establishing and carrying on mission work in that country.[1]

The Rev. S. T. Anderson, D.D., was appointed missionary in November, 1873, and he proceeded at once to the Island of Trinidad. Dr. McGhirk was also appointed as a lay helper. Dr. Anderson soon after his arrival accepted an invitation to supply a vacant Presbyterian mission church in the city of San Fernando. This congregation was under the care of the Free Church of Scotland. It gave Dr. Anderson ten dollars a week for his services and allowed him the free use of the manse, agreeing to continue this arrangement until the Free Church should send a man to fill the

---

[1] Minutes 1873, p. 63.

vacancy. This gave our missionary a home and work at once, but, as it also gave him the largest part of his support, the liberality of the church at home was not developed by this mission as it might otherwise have been. Though there were several thousands of Hindus and Chinese on the Island of Trinidad and sixty or seventy thousand negroes, besides many Spaniards, Portuguese, French, English, and a few Americans, our missionaries and the board regarded this island as but the starting point of their work. They believed Venezuela, among whose two millions of people there was not one Protestant missionary, to be the great mission field for our people.

During the year preceding the General Assembly of 1875 arrangements were made by which Dr. Anderson became agent of the American Bible Society for the distribution of the Scriptures. Dr. McGhirk expected to move to the Continent and thus the work was to be extended to Venezuela. The board had been making diligent inquiry about the half million of acres of Venezuelan land which had been granted to the church, and trying to perfect the title. But any expectations which may have been cherished of securing from this source the means of enlarging the mission work of the church failed to be realized. Though the board in 1876 expressed the opinion that this claim would "some day be valuable," yet neither the church nor the cause of missions has ever received any benefit from it. Missions have seldom been effectively helped by grants of land or princely endowments from States or governments. The preaching of the gospel among the heathen, as well as at home, must be sustained by the self-sacrificing efforts and direct gifts of consecrated Christians.

In 1876 the board reported that the work in Trinidad and Venezuela had not been prosecuted as intended when the mission was undertaken. The reason assigned was that it had been found impossible "to raise the means necessary to send two other men to accompany Dr. Anderson to Venezuela, which was the plan on which the work was begun." After laboring and waiting more than two years Dr. Anderson wrote to the board expressing a desire to return to the United States unless the needed re-inforcements could at once be sent. He stated also that the condition of his own health and that of his wife, as well as the necessity of educating his children made it his duty to return. At his own request his appointment as missionary expired with May, 1876. He returned to the United States, and the Trinidad and Venezuela mission was abandoned.

But the growing missionary spirit of the church was not checked by this discouraging failure. In answer to a paper presented to the Assembly of 1876, "recommending the cessation of all work in the foreign field," that body declared that the adoption of such a resolution would be "unwise and attended with dangerous consequences," and that "we ought not to grieve the Spirit's yearnings for foreign lands." The Rev. J. B. Hail and the Rev. A. D. Hail had already been accepted "as candidates" for the foreign field, and were preparing to enter the work, though it had not yet been decided into what part of the heathen world they were to be sent.

No series of events in the history of the church bears more distinctly the marks of God's providential hand than that connected with the origin and progress of our denominational work in Japan. The seed was sown nearly thirty years before by a dying mother's prayer. It grew in the heart of one young man until other hearts received it, and until a whole church was awakened and blessed by it. The mother of M. L. Gordon died in Greene county, Pennsylvania, when her son was yet an infant. On her death bed she consecrated this boy to the work of foreign missions. We do not know how often through the years of his youth thoughts of this work were awakened in his mind. At the breaking out of the war he enlisted in a Pennsylvania regiment and served three years. He was converted near the close of his term of enlistment on Morris Island, South Carolina, during the siege, under General Gilmore, of the fortifications in the neighborhood of Charleston. In the autumn of 1864 he entered Waynesburg College, Pennsylvania, but afterward gave up his collegiate studies for a time and began the study of medicine. But his impressions that he ought to devote himself to the work of the ministry became so intense that he closed his medical books and returned to college determined to prepare himself to preach the gospel. He had in 1865 joined the Cumberland Presbyterian church, and in 1868 he became a candidate for the ministry in Pennsylvania Presbytery. After his graduation from Waynesburg College, and while he was in the Theological Seminary at Andover, Massachusetts, he decided to enter the foreign field. His mother's prayers were at last ready to ripen into fruit.

The following extract from the Minutes of the General Assembly of 1871 show that he was in correspondence with the Cumberland Presbyterian Board of Missions in reference to the foreign work:

A young brother of the Synod of Pennsylvania is consecrating himself to this work, and is now offering himself to the board and asks to be sent to bear the glad tidings of salvation to poor dying sinners in heathen lands, but owing to our want of means we are not prepared to recommend such decided action on this subject as we would otherwise be pleased to do.[1]

The Pennsylvania Synod, which urged the appointment of Gordon by the board, pledged its members to sustain him with their means and their influence.[2] Without changing his ecclesiastical relations, he was finally commissioned to the work in Japan by the American Board. He received his ordination from the Pennsylvania Presbytery August 6, 1872. The Pennsylvania Synod stood pledged to contribute to his support, and did for six or seven years pay into the treasury of the American Board a sum averaging more than $700 per annum. He and his wife sailed to Japan September 1st, 1872, arriving at Yokohama the 24th of the same month. His going attracted the eyes of the whole church to that field, and marked the way for the missionaries who were sent by our board to the same country more than four years afterward. God has used him as an honored instrument in helping the work, not only of the board that sent him, but also of the church of which he is so worthy a minister. When our own missionaries arrived in Japan he was there in a successful mission. He was an old acquaintance and friend of the Hail brothers, and gave them all the counsel and assistance in his power. Did the limits of this volume permit it would be a pleasant task to take up Dr. Gordon's own labors and their results in detail, nor would such

---

[1] Minutes 1871, pp. 28, 29. [2] Ibid., p. 47.

a history be unprofitable or uninteresting to Cumberland Presbyterians. After nearly five years spent in general missionary work in the city of Osaka, during which he suffered greatly from an affection of the eyes, he and family returned to America in the summer of 1877. They went out again the next year, sailing October 1st in the same vessel that bore A. D. Hail and family to Japan. Dr. Gordon has since labored most of the time in connection with a training school at Kyoto. In December, 1885, he was compelled by failing health to return a second time to the United States. After spending more than a year in this country, most of the time in California, he again sailed for Japan August 23, 1887. Speaking in a late letter of his work in its relations to the Cumberland Presbyterian church he says with characteristic modesty: "I sometimes think that while my going as I did may have been helpful in arousing the board and church to action, and so divinely ordered, yet when an independent mission was to be established that work was in the same divinely wise way given to other and better hands."

The brothers A. D. Hail and J. B. Hail, whose mother is a daughter of Alexander Chapman of precious memory, were fellow-students of Gordon, at Waynesburg College. A. D. Hail was graduated from this institution in 1866, and his younger brother, J. B. Hail, three years later. Both resolved to consecrate themselves as foreign missionaries. We do not know how much Gordon's example did toward turning their thoughts in this direction. God often touches our hearts through the silent influence of our friends, or by their words or actions. An example of consecration and of faithful service can hardly fail to prove God's call beckoning others to similar self-denial and faithfulness. Consciously or unconsciously every life is influenced and molded by other lives. When Gordon gave himself to the foreign work his fellow-students and fellow-candidates for the ministry could hardly fail to feel the influence of his example.

These two brothers began to look about them for an opportunity to enter the work to which they felt that they were called. The prospects of being sent to any part of the foreign field by the Cumberland Presbyterian Board of Missions were at that time very discouraging. Therefore, J. B. Hail wrote to E. B. Treat, corresponding secretary of the American Board, asking an appointment to the foreign field as a Cumberland Presbyterian missionary. In his reply the secretary, after inquiring what he was to understand by an appointment as a "Cumberland Presbyterian missionary," discouraged the application on account of the limited financial resources then at the board's command. The younger Hail then offered himself to our own board. This was early in the year 1875. His brother made a like offer of himself to the Cumberland Presbyterian board in November of the same year. Both were accepted as candidates.

In 1876 Pennsylvania Synod, of which J. B. Hail was a member, pledged $1,000 for his outfit and $300 a year on his salary, on condition that the board would at once send him to Japan. This offer was accepted, and he and his family sailed from San Francisco about the first of January, 1877, reaching Osaka the 30th of that month. There were then not more than fifty native Christians in that great city. But three Protestant churches were represented in mission work: the Congregationalists, through the American Board; and the Episcopalians, English and American. Our missionary and his wife devoted themselves at once to the study of the language and the people, "sometimes exchanging instruction in English for instruction in Japanese."[1] They found a home in that part of the city allotted to foreigners, and known as the Foreign Concession.

There was no money in our missionary treasury, and A. D. Hail, who had for some years been pastor at Cumberland, Ohio, had to wait. At the board's request he studied medicine, attending Cleveland Medical College in 1876 and 1877. A gentleman in Illinois, early in 1878 offered the board $1,000 for Mr. Hail's outfit. At the meeting of the General Assembly at Lebanon, Tennessee, in May of that year, he was solemnly ordained to this work, and he and his family sailed from San Francisco the following autumn reaching Japan October 21st. Up to this time but one inquirer, a man named Yamamoto San, had placed himself under the instruction of our missionaries. When J. B. Hail acquired a sufficient knowledge of Japanese to begin to preach, efforts were made to find

---

[1] See historical sketch of our Japan Mission in Minutes of the Assembly 1887, p. 77.

a place in the city in which to hold services. But there was such a prejudice against Christianity that it was almost three months before a preaching place was found. At last a building on Ruhebashi street was rented and "the first sermon was preached on Sabbath, February 9th, 1879, at 4 P.M., almost the exact time of the sixty-ninth anniversary of our denomination."

There was much interest in the services from the first. In his report to the General Assembly of 1879, A. D. Hail, speaking of these first meetings, says:

> It is a matter of profound interest to witness the attention paid by some of the hearers, and to see others dropping into the passage-way as they are passing, and standing with great burdens of wares upon their backs, and greater burdens upon their hearts, turning their bronzed faces toward the speaker to catch his words. At such times one feels an inexpressible longing for a thorough knowledge of the tongue through which so many deaf hearts must be reached.

The missionaries found that until they became accustomed to the climate they could not work so well as at home. Three years' study of the language was required in order to begin responsible work. They were hindered by the restrictions of the government, and by the circulation of infidel books from Europe and America, as well as by the difficulty of expressing spiritual ideas in the Japanese tongue, and the degrading effects wrought on the people by heathenism. But the Christian homes of the missionaries were already exerting an influence for good. Schools were springing up and the children were receiving instruction in anti-heathen knowledge. Persecutions had measurably ceased. The reading habits of the people and their eagerness to learn afforded constant opportunities to impart the gospel, while the number of native believers and Christian churches was rapidly multiplying.

A Sunday-school, with an average attendance of fifteen, was organized by our missionaries November 2d, 1879, and a weekly prayer-meeting was regularly maintained, out of which grew a weekly meeting for inquirers. Two native helpers, Obato San and Suji San, were assisting in the work, teaching, exhorting, and aiding in pastoral visitation.

Though there were in 1879 a small number of inquirers, one or two of whom the missionaries thought they might "justifiably encourage to become candidates for baptism," yet it was thought "better to err on the side of caution than of haste amongst those having such low ideas of the Christian life."[1] It was not until September 26th, 1880, that the first converts of the mission were baptized. On that day two men, Yamamoto San and Kuzze San, received this ordinance at the hands of the Rev. J. B. Hail, and joined the missionaries in the first communion service of this infant church in the city of Osaka. Of these two men the Rev. G. G. Hudson says in his late report as corresponding secretary of the mission:[2]

These were the first fruits of our mission in Japan. Without special direction from their teachers these men consulted together, and agreeing that as they were the first members of this new church, their conduct would have great influence with those who should join later, they sought help from God to fit themselves for their responsible position, and promised on their part to have a stated time for secret prayer, and to give to the Lord one tenth of their income. Having such a foundation, we may hope that "all the building, fitly framed together, shall grow unto an holy temple in the Lord."

Though the missionaries felt the importance of extending the work to points outside of Osaka, and tours of observation were made to Wakayama, Tanabe, and other important places, the want of men and women to aid in the work prevented them at that time from occupying these inviting fields.

In the meantime the mission was bearing fruit in the church at home. Missionary contributions were greatly increased. The organization of the Woman's Board of Foreign Missions grew directly out of the pressing necessities of this work in Japan. The missionaries made their first official report in 1879. In it they said:

As the work progresses we feel the indispensable need of female helpers. If one was on the ground now and had a thorough knowledge of the tongue she would prove an invaluable adjunct to the preaching place that is now opened. . . . While the labors of the wives of the missionaries are manifold, yet there is a large field that can be successfully worked only by young lady helpers. . . . The work accomplished by the young ladies of other denominations has been very

---

[1] Report to Assembly, 1880, Minutes, p. 80.   [2] Ibid., 1887, p. 77.

great. No denomination can wholly succeed without them. . . . The time has come in the providence of God when he is opening a great door of usefulness to our Christian women.

In the same report it was suggested that "our board and General Assembly call on the ladies of the church to organize themselves for work," and it was urged that if possible at least one young lady should be sent to Japan the following autumn. But as this suggestion was not, that year, carried out, A. D. Hail and his wife, early in 1880, wrote a letter to the ladies of our church at Evansville, Indiana, through their pastor, the Rev. W. J. Darby, requesting, inasmuch as the General Assembly was to meet in that city in May of that year, that these ladies would call a convention of the women of the Cumberland Presbyterian church to meet there at the time of the Assembly's meeting for the purpose of organizing a Woman's Board of Missions. The call was issued and the matter was pressed by the pastor at Evansville and the ladies of his church. The convention was held, and with the unanimous approval of the General Assembly the Woman's Board was organized and located at Evansville.

In 1881 our missionaries began to make extended preaching tours in the country south of Osaka, and the work was thus enlarged. An extract from the report written March 15th, 1881, will show what were at that time the arduous duties of the missionaries:

The work presses upon us so that every member of the mission must labor so constantly as to call for continual care against overwork. In addition to the regular day's work on the language, there are the usual labors of preaching, teaching, and superintending. During the present year prayer-meetings have been maintained Tuesday and Thursday evenings. . . . The average attendance has been larger than it was last year. . . . The wives of the missionaries have also begun a woman's prayer-meeting, which is held on Wednesday evening. . . . Every morning also, at the hour of family worship, which is arranged with that end in view, there is generally a half hour devoted to exegesis which is shared by several of the Japanese. Every evening of the week also has been devoted to teaching a few young men English and science, for the sake of gaining an influence over them, and reaching them with the gospel of Christ. One of the young men thus taught continues to open his house every Sabbath morning for Bible study.

The Sabbath services, preaching and Sunday-school, were kept up with growing interest at the regular preaching place; and an afternoon Sunday-school was opened in another part of the city, where a preaching service was held every Sabbath at 4 P.M.; and Sabbath evening services were held in still another place. Mainly through native helpers the work had begun to extend outside the city. Services were kept up once a month at a mountain village twelve miles from Osaka; and the influence of the mission was gradually finding its way to other places. Three extensive tours into the Province of Kishu were this year made "with the purpose of ascertaining the feasibility of making it an out-station," but in all these efforts the mission was crippled by the lack of an adequate force of men and women, and the want of means to prosecute the work.

The need of a religious, and especially of a denominational, literature in the native language was at an early period recognized. When the entire New Testament was translated and printed, the work of imparting a knowledge of the gospel was made much less difficult. The Scriptures were sold everywhere, in shops, on the streets, at Christian meetings, and at heathen festivals. It was no unusual thing "to see men with a copy of the gospels in one hand, and the image of a fox or of Buddha in the other, returning from their religious gatherings." In some cases those whose only teacher had been the printed word presented themselves for baptism.

In 1881 a beginning in the matter of denominational literature was made. The Confession of Faith was translated by J. B. Hail, who also translated the chapter of Dr. J. R. Brown's "Lights on the Way," entitled "The Doctrines." A. D. Hail translated the Shorter Catechism and the Catechism for Children. He also wrote an expository tract on Luke xv., entitled "The Sinner's Staff," and a Manual of Systematic Theology. The mission that year issued two hundred and sixty thousand pages of printed matter. Some other translations and original works have since been published, but efforts in this department have been much hindered by other pressing demands on the time and energies of the missionaries, as well as by the lack of an adequate fund to be used in the publication of books.

A religious book and tract store was opened early in 1881. While much religious reading matter was distributed gratuitously, the missionaries believed that more good would be accomplished by cheap sales than by the indiscriminate giving away of books and tracts. In the succeeding years book depositories have been established in many places, and colporteurs have been sent forth. This work is placed in the hands of native Christians, who combine its duties with evangelistic labors.

November 21, 1881, Miss Alice M. Orr, of Missouri, and Miss Julia L. Leavitt, of Indiana, the first two missionaries sent out by the Woman's Board, arrived at Osaka. Though they were able immediately to relieve their fellow-missionaries of part of their English teaching work, and as time went on to assist to some extent in imparting instruction in music, sacred geography, and some other branches, yet their time for the first three years was mainly devoted to the study of the language.

A preaching place was opened October 1, 1881, in a part of Osaka hitherto unoccupied by Christian teachers. The native Christians resolved to pay the current expenses of the services held here. They provided a box which, in memory of the widow's mite, they called "the denarii box," and "hung it every Sunday in the front part of the house, so that the people might place in it their weekly gifts." Since then all the preaching places and churches connected with this mission have been provided with denarii boxes.

Under the direction of Mrs. A. D. Hail a "woman's meeting" was inaugurated to teach the Japanese women domestic handiwork by which they could earn money to assist in maintaining the preaching places. These meetings were well attended and grew in interest and good results. In 1882 the native membership increased more than two hundred per cent. Our half-dozen missionaries felt themselves inadequate to provide for the multiplying demands of the work. They pleaded earnestly for re-inforcements. Work "after the manner of circuit-riding on foot," had been prosecuted in the Province of Kishu, and "a catechumenical class" was in process of formation.

All the converts baptized by our missionaries in any part of the empire were at first enrolled as members of the church at Osaka.

This church raised a salary and tried to secure a native pastor. Although there were several young men studying preparatory to taking a theological course no one among them was found "sufficiently acquainted with theology and the holy Scriptures to take the pastoral oversight of the flock." This church "resolved to sustain its own preaching place"—that is, to pay its own rents and relieve the board of all incidental expenses connected with the services. This enabled the mission to rent a new preaching place in another part of the city. Thus at the close of the year, 1882, there were in Osaka three places where our missionaries maintained preaching and Sunday-schools regularly every Sabbath, while private houses in different parts of the city were opened for prayer and other Christian work.

Events of great importance to the cause of Christianity in Japan and to our struggling mission occurred during the year 1883. A missionary conference, in which all the Protestant missions of the empire were represented, was held April 16th–22d. Delegates from eighteen foreign societies, and representing a native church of five thousand communicants, were present. The report submitted to our General Assembly the next year says:

The Conference came together in the spirit of prayer. All shades of Episcopacy, all the various Presbyterian and Methodist bodies, and different nationalities, came together in a oneness of spirit that proclaimed the essential unity of the body of Christ. The influence of this meeting has been, and will continue to be, felt for good along different lines of mission work in Japan. It will give a greater insight into the work to those Christians in America who have the cause of missions in this empire in their hearts and hands, and give ample instruction to Mission Boards as to the kind of persons that should be sent to this field, and of the best and wisest method of dealing with them so as to secure their greatest efficiency as workers at a minimum of expense.

A still more important event was a general revival of religion throughout the Japanese empire. Describing this revival the corresponding secretary of the mission in his annual report, says:

The results of this revival have been such as to call forth the highest gratitude of all who have given to, and prayed and wrought for, the Christianization of Japan. Many of the churches have almost doubled their membership. The Christian life of the believers has been quickened, and has manifested this quickening in a greater consecration to Christian work, and a spirit of greater liberality. It has done much to eradicate from the hearts of native Christians the deep-seated prejudice against foreigners, which oftentimes made itself felt even against missionaries. Thus has the way for a more cordial confidence in, and cooperation with, missionaries, upon the part of the native church, been opened by the Spirit of God. The native Christians of all denominations hold a biennial Conference, composed of delegates representing the respective churches in the land. The object of this meeting is to consider questions which relate to the life of the church and to its successful progress. Meeting, as it did this year, in the wake of the Missionary Conference, and in the inception of the revival which has been spreading throughout the country, the Conference was converted by the Holy Spirit into a daily and hourly meeting of incessant prayer. At the same time, without preconcerted action, all the churches in the various cities began daily prayer-meetings. The spontaneity of the movement was so manifest that none could question that the hand of God was directing it. It was but natural for these various streams of quickened religious life to flow together into one channel of Christian effort. The numerical results, so far as conversions are concerned, while they have been very great, are only one of the minor features of importance in this work. . . . Our own little church has shared with all others in the precious results. Its spiritual condition seems, therefore, to be much better than at any other time in its brief history.

This year the Osaka church selected three men to serve six months as elders. Their re-election was made to depend on the ability and fidelity with which they performed their duties. The church being still without a pastor, these elders were called upon to discharge the duties of the pastoral office in turn, bi-monthly. The members of the congregation, numbering in all about forty-seven, were "scattered over a territory of about three hundred miles. In Osaka, a city of about 600,000 inhabitants, there were thirty-seven members; in Wakayama (out-station), 75,000 inhabitants, one member; in Hikata, a cluster of villages of 5,000 inhabitants, five members; in Tanabe, 11,000 inhabitants, one member; in Shingu, 8,000 inhabitants, three members." In the beginning of their work our missionaries made it their aim to cultivate in the native Christians a sense of responsibility and a feeling of self-dependence in relation to the financial affairs of the church, and the regulation and management of other church interests. The following is a brief statement of the principles governing the mission in its policy:

The leading idea which the mission strives to realize is: *The responsibility of the native church for the conversion of Japan.* This is the principle which is sought to be made prominent, and which has thus far determined the missionaries' plans of work. It has been their endeavor to follow this idea in defining the relation of the foreign church to the church in Japan: (I) It determines the attitude of the foreign missionaries to the native church to be that of co-laborers and advisers, "as being helpers of their joy and not as having dominion over their faith." While, therefore, they are here as members of a church that has a polity and system of doctrine of its own, yet they do not seek to impose these things upon the converts by any exercise of authority. They encourage any movements on their part toward any kind of union with their native brethren, which will aid them most effectively in carrying out the responsibility which devolves upon them—that is, any union within essentially orthodox doctrine and liberal forms of church government. (II) The missionaries have tried to regulate the use of foreign money for native purposes upon the same principle. Believing that the practice of self-sacrifice and a sense of personal responsibility are essential to the cultivation of a true missionary spirit, the use of foreign money has not been encouraged. When used, it has been as an exception only. The mission, therefore, has no schedule of salaries of native helpers, no definite rules as to aid granted to those desiring to be educated as evangelists or lay workers. In cases where aid is granted, other than directly evangelistic work is required as a compensation—that is, they must pay back to the mission monies expended upon them by the mission. When it is necessary to hire preaching places in neighborhoods where no Christians live, the native brethren are expected to aid in the financial maintainance of such stations. In localities where there are native Christians, they are encouraged to rent a small preaching place within their own means, sometimes aided by private contributions from the missionary, or else to open their own houses. (III) The same formative idea we expect to be governed by in any other phase of the work which may arise. Our experience in the work, as thus conducted, encourages us to hope with reference to ultimate results. Our experience thus far may prove to be only the inexperience of a young mission, yet we shall continue to follow out this principle, subject to further light.

This outline was written for the Osaka Conference in the latter part of the year 1882, by A. D. Hail, corresponding secretary of the mission. The test of experience in the years which have followed has demonstrated the soundness of the principle thus laid down, and the wisdom of the policy growing out of it. The native Christians have shown an increasing disposition to sustain their own churches, and to extend help to new places. Their missionary gifts in 1882 equaled thirty-seven cents for each member, and the year following more than fifty cents per member. In 1884 the total collections for all purposes reached an amount equal to six dollars for each member. When we remember that these people make their contributions out of their poverty, that one hundred and fifty dollars a year is counted a large income, that many earn almost nothing, and that the average pay of those who have regular employment or business is not more than eight dollars per month, we see that they show a willingness to give, far in advance of that shown by the church at home.

Nor has the policy of our mission, in allowing the Japanese Christians freedom in choosing their own methods of work and rules of government, been attended with any evil results. The regulations adopted have sometimes been more strict and wholesome than those enforced at home. For instance, we have this item in the report for the year 1882: "The native brethren have established a rule that persons not well known must wait at least two months after their application before receiving baptism." "This," says the corresponding secretary, "has doubtless saved us from some mistakes."[1] A report made three years later informs us that "The [native] church takes very aggressive ground in regard to the use of wine and tobacco. While it has made no formal utterances upon these subjects, yet the use of such things by non-Christians has such associations that persons coming into the church naturally feel that such habits should be renounced as being inconsistent with Christian character. We have not been very solicitous to correct such an impression."[2]

Mrs. A. M. Drennan, the third missionary sent by the Woman's Board, reached Japan May 4, 1883. Early in 1882 the missionaries had called on this board to take steps to lay the foundation of a girl's school and orphanage in Osaka. No Protestant orphanage

---

[1] Assembly's Minutes, 1882, p. 66. [2] Minutes, 1885, p. 81.

had at that time been established in that part of Japan. The Woman's Board was asked to send an educated lady, one with experience in the care of a household, joined to ability to teach and a motherly tact and judgment in looking after the welfare of the young, to aid in this work. In response to this call, the board equipped and sent forth Mrs. Drennan, contributing also three thousand dollars to furnish buildings for the proposed school and orphanage. A lot and buildings were secured in the Foreign Concession, and the school was opened with four pupils, January 8, 1884. It has since been known as the Wilmina school. By June, 1884, it had seventeen pupils. At the beginning of the year 1886, the attendance was forty-one, with an enrollment of fifty-nine. This school is divided into three grades, the primary, intermediate, and advanced. The studies, with but few exceptions, are the same as those pursued in similar schools at home. Japanese composition and history are taught, and the Bible is a daily text-book in all the grades. The first year six of the pupils joined the church, and others were awaiting baptism. There were sixty pupils at the beginning of the year 1887. In December, 1886, there were three graduates who have since taken their places as teachers and helpers in missionary work. With money furnished by the Woman's Board, a new building has recently been erected for this school.

In addition to her regular work Mrs. Drennan has kept up daily and weekly classes for young men. Out of these has grown a Young Men's Christian Endeavor Society with forty-five members. Through Mrs. Drennan's influence and under her direction a Japanese branch of the Chautauqua Literary and Scientific Circle has been organized, which in 1887 numbered fourteen hundred members. She also instructs a class composed of the wives of government officers "in English, the Bible, and household duties."

The year 1884 was one of great fruitfulness in other departments of the work. The attitude of the people and the government was undergoing a change favorable to the propagation of Christianity. Men of prominence were beginning to appreciate the benefits of the new faith. The people were ready and eager to hear the gospel. The impetus given the work by the revival of the preceding year was not checked, but steadily increasing in beneficial results. One of the emperor's privy council had petitioned the government to employ Christian teachers, and give instruction in Christian morals in all the schools from the Imperial University down. Another prominent man, "as the result of his investigations abroad, memorialized the emperor in behalf of the introduction of Christianity." China and other Eastern countries were catching glimpses of the light shed abroad in Japan. Of Corea the report made at the close of this year says:

The "Hermit Nation" (Corea), so recently opened for commerce to the Western Powers through the successful negotiations of Commodore Shufeldt, is looking upon the movements in Japan with profound interest. A few days ago that government sent one of its learned men (its historian) to this land in order to investigate its condition since the introduction of Western arts and sciences. This man, Rijutei, became a Christian, and is now employed by the American Bible Society in translating the gospel into his native language. The account of his conversion and work, as given by the agent of that society, is full of interest. While investigating the subject of Christianity, he dreamed that two men appeared who offered him books, and he was told that these were the most useful of all things for his people. When it was asked, "What books are they?" it was replied, "These are Bibles." So deeply impressed was the man by his dream, and also by the truths he heard, that he soon became a Christian, and from that time has been earnestly at work for the salvation of his people. His growth in grace and in knowledge of God's word has been marked and rapid. Through his labors several other Coreans have become Christians. Some of these are students in some of the Tokio Mission Schools, preparatory to work amongst their own people. A number of other prominent Coreans, in this country for temporary residence, have applied to him to be taught the doctrines of Christ. Certainly in all this there is such a prophecy of what might be in regard to the evangelization of other Eastern nations by the help of a Christian Japan, as to stimulate the Church in Christian lands to devise more liberal things for the speedy conversion of her people.

The preaching of our missionaries was this year attended with gracious results. In February the Osaka church perfected its organization. Two other churches, one at Kuroye (Hikata), a village near Wakayama, and the other at Shingu, "the extremest point of the province of Kishu," one hundred and ninety miles from Osaka, were regularly organized, the former May the 11th, and the latter the month following. The report of the Corresponding Secretary of the mission in the Minutes of the General Assembly for 1887, gives an account of the origin of these and other Japanese churches, illustrating "God's power to use apparently trivial events to produce great results."

The work at Hikata began with one man who, having heard something of Christianity, asked a missionary of the American Board for preaching. This missionary repeated the request to J. B. Hail. "As the interest deepened, the local priest became alarmed, and circulated a pledge against hearing Christianity taught, and against having even business relations with Christians. One man refused to sign the pledge, saying that Christians were the principal purchasers of their manufactures—lacquer work. On inquiry, a number of Bible readers were found in the village, and these formed the 'Society of Brotherly Love' for Bible study. The meetings were at first secret, though largely attended." Thus the church grew up.

The history of the work at Shingu still more strikingly shows how the truth in the heart of one Christian proved the seed of a church:

Some years ago a man living at Shingu sent his sister to a Girls' School of the American Board at Osaka. She became a Christian, and on returning home and observing the rules of a godly life was greatly persecuted by her relatives. To spend the Sabbath in a Christian-like manner, she was compelled to retire to the mountains, where she spent the day in reading and prayer. Some time after this Yamamoto San was preaching through that province, depending wholly upon Providence for his support. He reached Shingu late at night without money or acquaintances, and weary with his march through mud and rain. He met a man who proved to be the brother of the girl referred to, and who inquired his name and business. When told that the traveler was a teacher of the religion of Jesus, he invited him to his own house, saying that he wished to learn of that way. From this grew the Shingu church.

The church at Mitani Mura, a village nine miles from Wakayama, was also temporarily organized in 1884. A young man from one of the families of the village went to America to seek his fortune. "His father warned him expressly against the Christian religion, and was enraged to find on his son's return that he had become a Christian. The son patiently endured his father's wrath until he could be heard in explanation of his course, when the father became interested and afterward a believer. The first baptism was administered in 1884." The church at that place in 1886 reported a membership of thirty-two.

The history of the two churches organized in 1885, one in Wakayama and the other at Tanabe, is equally interesting. The events which led to the formation of the Wakayama church are thus briefly stated:

A youth went from that city to America, and there became a Christian. He wrote to his mother of the new-found faith, and so taught its principles and encouraged her that she also became a believer. He was anxious for her to have a teacher, and learning from an Osaka friend whom he met in San Francisco that a Mr. Hail taught in Wakayama, he wrote the missionary requesting him to visit the mother. When the request was complied with, it was found that she had been praying for a teacher. After a satisfactory examination the mother was baptized, and partook of the Lord's Supper with the missionary and his helper.

The membership at this place is now fifty-nine, and the Sunday-school numbers one hundred and sixty-two. The church supports a day school of more than one hundred pupils.

At Tanabe J. B. Hail began visiting in 1881. "After a year or two there were many reading the Scriptures, but all seemed waiting for some one to make the first profession of faith. On a certain occasion the missionary and his helper were especially burdened for visible results in their work, and without revealing to each other the unusual anxiety felt, they separated for secret prayer. Upon returning to the hotel they met a man who offered himself for baptism." The church thus begun reports a membership of forty-seven.

We will get a better idea of the importance of these mission churches as centers of influence if we remember that Osaka is the "chief commercial center of Japan; Wakayama, forty miles from Osaka, the largest city of its entire province and of its contiguous southern provinces; while Tanabe and Shingu are respectively the sources of supply and trade for several valleys of populous villages. In the first-named city are five different Protestant bodies, besides the Roman and Greek Catholic churches. In Wakayama the American Episcopal and Cumberland Presbyterian missionaries, and Greek Catholic and Roman Catholic church are at work; while in the rest of that and the adjoining state, our missionaries alone are engaged."[1]

Two churches were built during the year 1884, one at Shingu and the other at Osaka. Work on the former was commenced when the number of baptized believers in the town was only four, and none of them well to do in the world. The report adds: "Yet God, who always honors faith in him, blessed them with hearts to expect great things from him and to undertake great things for him. The people of the village came generously to their aid, and a handsome little church was built and dedicated."[2]

The Osaka church was dedicated in October, 1884. The congregations at Tanabe and Wakayama have since built houses of worship. The other churches rent their preaching places. Up to 1887 none of these churches had pastors, because none of the native preachers had attained to the standard of qualification which was thought necessary. The elders and leading members assume the duties and responsibilities of pastoral work.

In October, 1884, the several churches, three of which had up to that time been formally organized, appointed delegates to meet with the Osaka church to take steps for a better organization. "They were in session about one week, and considered such topics as Form of Government, Confession of Faith, Missions, and Educational Work. The missionaries were called on occasionally for advice, but sustained to them no other than an advisory relation." They organized themselves into a temporary body to meet semi-annually, arranging to have representatives from the elders and brethren of the several churches until they should be supplied with pastors and be able to form a presbytery.[3] These meetings are still held regularly, and the body made up of the assembled delegates is dignified with the title of presbytery.[4]

The apprenticeship of Miss Orr and Miss Leavitt in language

---

[1] Report in Assembly's Minutes, 1886, p. 89. [2] Minutes, 1885, p. 80.
[3] Assembly's Minutes, 1885, p. 80. [4] Minutes, 1887, p. 79.

study and other preparatory work had in 1884 proceeded far enough to enable them to enter regularly upon their missionary labors. Miss Orr at first devoted herself to work amongst the women in the out-stations in the province of Kishu, while Miss Leavitt engaged in similar work in Osaka. Both these young ladies have proven most efficient and consecrated workers. Miss Orr obtained a permit from the government to live for three years at Wakayama, with freedom to travel through the province at will. When Miss Bettie A. Duffield, of Missouri, the fourth missionary sent by the Woman's Board, reached Japan, April 24, 1885, the church at Wakayama secured permission for her, also, to live in that city three years. While studying the language she was associated with Miss Orr in a co-educational English day school, which was opened by the Wakayama church in November, 1885. This school, which is established on a thoroughly Christian basis, and which is "exclusively under the control and management of the native Christians," had, besides Miss Orr and Miss Duffield, three native teachers. The number of its pupils grew from forty in 1885, to one hundred and twenty at the close of 1886. During the latter year this school was "so approved by the government officials that they proposed to give a new school building, pay the salary of two English teachers, and continue the management as a Christian school," if Miss Orr and Miss Duffield would devote three hours instead of an hour and a half daily to teaching in it. This proposition was referred to the mission.

Miss Orr's work has not been confined to this school, or to Wakayama. She visits other places, conducting Bible meetings for women, holding prayer-meetings, and instructing inquirers. In 1887 she reported "two growing classes, respectively twenty and ten miles from Wakayama, at Yuwasa and Iwada." At Yuwasa, where the class numbered twenty men and women, it was expected that a church would soon be organized.[1] In a published letter she gives the following account of the origin of this work:

One young man spent a month of successful work at Yuwasa. During his stay, a party of about twelve Christians from here went to the town and held a large meeting in a theater, with an audience of

---

[1] Minutes of Assembly, 1887, p. 86.

about five hundred most attentive and quiet people. Many school teachers and officials came to the hotel to ask us more minutely the way. Many desire to have Christianity.

Speaking further of the missionary labors of these Wakayama converts, Miss Orr says:

The young men took turns in going to a village, about two miles out, one night in every week, and have met with still more encouragement. Two of the women have gone often to still another village, some eight miles away, and two or three persons there have received baptism as the result, and a church is about to be organized. In consequence of this mission work, the Wakayama church is growing stronger in numbers and in spirit.

Miss Leavitt's labors in the city of Osaka included "house to house visitation of women, conducting women's meetings, catechetical teaching in the ragged school, . . . explaining the gospel of Luke in the woman's theological class," and "giving lessons in foreign handiwork." In March, 1885, she began work among the women of the interior at Shingu and Tanabe and other places. In May, 1885, two schools, one for boys and one for girls, were opened by the church at Shingu. A. D. Hail and his wife spent the summer there, and assisted the native church in this work. Miss Leavitt's work now permanently embraces the churches at Tanabe and Shingu. She spent much of the summer of 1886 at Shingu, where she filled "the varied positions of teacher, adviser, class director, and Christian friend." Of this summer's work she says: "It was the hottest, busiest, happiest time I ever spent in Japan." Of a class of five young men, all but one joined the church. These with eleven others made up the largest number ever baptized at one time in the Cumberland Presbyterian church in Japan.

Besides the Wilmina school at Osaka, which is supported by the mission, and the English day schools supported by the churches at Wakayama and Shingu, a kindergarten is maintained by the church at Tanabe. There is also a ragged school at Osaka, in a district full of pauperism, and free night schools at Osaka and Wakayama. Classes and night schools are kept up also at other places.

Several young men who have been won to Christianity by our

missionaries are studying in America. One of these is Miyoshi San, who has been in Cumberland University, Lebanon, Tennessee, since September, 1884. He graduated in the literary department of that institution, and expects to finish the theological course in 1888, and afterward to devote himself to Christian work in his native land.

In May, 1886, sixteen members of the Osaka congregation received permission from the "Presbytery" to take steps looking to the formal organization of a second church in the city. Counting this second church, there are now seven congregations under the care of the Japan mission, viz.: Osaka, First and Second churches, Wakayama, Hikata, Mitani Mura, Tanabe, and Shingu. At the close of the year 1886 the total membership was 275, and there were 302 pupils in the Sunday-schools. During that year there were 157 baptisms. The growth of the church is indicated by the number in communion at the close of each year since the first two young men were baptized, September 26, 1880. In 1880 there were 3 members; in 1881, 8; in 1882, 27; in 1883, 47; in 1884, 124; in 1885, 208; in 1886, 275.

In December, 1886, the Rev. George G. Hudson and wife, and Miss Rena Rezner, all of Illinois, arrived in Japan to join the mission. Miss Rezner is the fifth missionary sent by the Woman's Board, and is associated with Mrs. Drennan in the Wilmina school. A. D. Hail, accompanied by his family, is now (September, 1887) in America on sick leave.

Composing this mission there are eleven persons besides children. The whole list is as follows: J. B. Hail and wife, A. D. Hail and wife, Miss Alice M. Orr, Miss Julia A. Leavitt, Mrs. A. M. Drennan, Miss Bettie A. Duffield, George G. Hudson and wife, and Miss Rena Rezner. All these, except Miss Orr and Miss Duffield, reside at Osaka, on the Foreign Concession. The need of additional missionaries is very great. From the first and through all the years the force has been inadequate to meet the ever-increasing demands and opportunities of the work.

It was a great gain to the church when it at last had its own successful missionaries in the foreign field under the direction of its own board. This was necessary to awaken the activity and call out the strength of the church. Up to 1845, when our General Board of Missions was first organized, and for a number of years afterward, "Cumberland Presbyterians were accustomed to make their contributions abroad, except what was appropriated to Indian missions, through the American Board. The members of the Presbyterian church did the same until the inauguration of their Foreign Mission Board in 1833."[1] From 1810 till the present time two young ladies and one married couple are the only Cumberland Presbyterians who have gone to a foreign field under the American Board. But these did not bring the work home to the hearts of our people. The Indian work under our own board called forth a hundred-fold more interest. The American Board and its missionaries were to Cumberland Presbyterians telescopic, like the faraway splendors of the fixed stars. But now the case is different. When our own familiar acquaintances, our brothers and sisters and sons and daughters, go forth, and are supported by our own gifts, the heroism begins to enter our own homes. Our young men and women begin to ask, If these can go and be missionaries, why may not we also? The stirring power of a heroic example right in our homes is far more precious than all our money. It is that which the church needs. If every large congregation had its own missionary sent from its own Sunday-school to some foreign field, and not only sustained this missionary, but kept up constant correspondence with him, the results would far outweigh all the money ever given to missions. The children in such a Sunday-school would receive new impulses toward nobler things. Selfishness and worldliness would be rebuked. Pastors would find their hands strengthened in every effort they make against worldliness, and every appeal to nobler impulses would meet with increased success. Our own missionaries under our own board, in the very nature of the case, come nearer to our own people. Their work and their support become a part of the work of every congregation.

Our women's missionary societies over the whole church are in correspondence with our own missionaries in Japan. A letter from some of these missionaries is read at almost every meeting of our

---

[1] Address of the Rev. C. H. Bell, D.D., before the Missouri Cumberland Presbyterian Sunday-school Assembly, at Pertle Springs, August, 1887.

numerous societies and children's bands. Thus the missionary spirit is everywhere kept alive.

While Cumberland Presbyterians have found so great a gain growing out of their own independent missionary work, they are not opposed to the closest possible co-operation with other churches in the foreign field. On this subject the General Assembly of 1885 unanimously adopted the following declaration:

We believe union on the foreign mission field is desirable, and will cheerfully enter into whatever measures may seem best looking to that end. Instead of transferring our differences to mission lands, we would join our sister denominations in the plan of establishing one Presbyterian church in each mission field. We regard it as very desirable, if not essential, to formulate a short and simple yet comprehensive creed in harmony with and containing the essential doctrines held by the churches composing the Alliance, the same to be used in ordaining native ministers, elders, and deacons.

By the Assembly of 1887 this action was re-affirmed. Full confidence in our missionaries and in the native members of the churches organized and trained by them was expressed. "The conducting of negotiations for union with other Presbyterian churches in Japan" was therefore intrusted to these missionaries and native Christians, with the stipulation "that in any basis of union that might be agreed upon they were to be careful to preserve untrammeled their privilege to hold and teach such views of the holy Scriptures as are peculiar to the Cumberland Presbyterian church." It was provided, also, that if such a union was entered into, the missionaries of our board were to continue under its direction in their work, and to receive support from its funds; and that these missionaries, while holding their ecclesiastical relations with the union church in Japan, were to be "recognized in all other respects as belonging to us, and when in this country and present at the General Assembly or other judicatures, to be entitled to seats as advisory members." On all parts of the field in all periods of its history the Cumberland Presbyterian church has given its utterances in an unequivocal tone in favor of the utmost practicable union of evangelical denominations.

The-long-talked-of, long-delayed mission to Mexico was regularly opened in 1886. The Rev. A. H. Whatley, of Texas, who was graduated from the Theological School of Cumberland University, June, 1885, was appointed missionary. He was set apart for this work January 10, 1886, at Lebanon, Tennessee. He soon after proceeded to Mexico, where he spent fourteen months "in preparatory work, the study of the language, the people, and the field." At first he lived at Chihuahua, the capital of the State of the same name. He was sent with instructions from the board "to study well the situation, and take ample time for deciding both as to where and how the work should be begun." "After careful investigation during several months, Aguas Calientes was selected as the place for establishing the first Cumberland Presbyterian church in Mexico." This is a city of thirty-five thousand inhabitants, situated about two hundred and eighty-five miles north-west of the City of Mexico. It has seven Roman Catholic churches, but no Protestant church, and is "one of the neediest fields in Mexico." The missionary advised the board to purchase property for a church, and to establish a school. Illustrating the importance of beginning the work in this way, he said in a letter to the board:

In this country the missionary has to meet the people principally in a public place. The customs of the country will not admit of his visiting from house to house, even among the poorer classes, until he is acquainted with them. One does not easily get acquainted with a people some of whom make the sign of the cross when he merely passes the window, that they may be delivered from the power of the devil, whose servant he is supposed to be. There are many people whose curiosity would lead them to church, whom nothing could induce to enter a place of worship in a private house. . . . These people are much more scrupulous about these things than we are. They have been accustomed to magnificent churches, and many of them look with contempt on the feeble beginnings of a Protestant mission. . . . The board is right, too, in its policy of establishing a school in connection with the mission. The importance of this branch of the work can hardly be overestimated. The Mexicans are very anxious to have their children study English. This interest in our language will furnish pupils for our school.

The Board of Missions, in its report, May, 1887, says of this work:

Our missionary to Mexico, the Rev. A. H. Whatley, has already acquired a sufficient knowledge of the Spanish language to enable him to speak and to preach to the people in their native tongue. He recently returned to the United States and took a wife, a devout Christian, intelligent and resolute, who will henceforth share his labors and rewards. Property suitable for a chapel and a school will be bought at as early a date as practicable. A portion of the needed funds has been contributed by individuals. The Woman's Board, ever prompt and cordial in co-operating with your board in aggressive movements, has appropriated one thousand dollars for the purchase of property, and in due time will supply the proposed school with one or more lady missionaries. The total cost of property and improvements will probably amount to three thousand dollars.

At the meeting of the General Assembly of 1887, at Covington, Ohio, the Rev. F. P. Lawyer, of Illinois, a graduate of Lincoln University, and of McCormack Theological Seminary, Chicago, was formally consecrated to the foreign work in Mexico. It is expected that he will soon join Mr. Whatley and his wife in the mission at Aguas Calientes.

In the last ten years new missionary life has been awakened in our Theological School. An annual course of lectures on missions before the students, by Dr. C. H. Bell, has done much to bring about this result. Our school has been well represented in the meetings of the Inter-Seminary Missionary Alliance.

The Board of Missions has for several years been issuing a monthly paper, *The Missionary Record*. Its able editorials and its aggressive yet catholic spirit have made it an increasing power of good to the church and the cause of missions.

The introduction of radical changes, however desirable those changes may be, is always a slow work. The one thing in which the Cumberland Presbyterian church was of necessity deficient at first was systematic giving. It had no pastors: could have none while our fathers were all out planting the church in the wilderness. It had self-forgetting heroism of the loftiest pattern, and these fathers accomplished the mission whereunto God had sent them. Now, the work of patiently training the organized congregations in the systematic consecration of their wealth to God is our most pressing duty. This duty rests on parents, pastors, and church courts. The home, the nursery, is the most important place for this training. Here is the beginning of missionary education—to teach the little ones that deep love to Jesus which can not rest without doing something for his kingdom. How we do miss this high purpose when we put these little immortals on a course of church theatricals and other substitutes for God's plan of training! The cause of missions appeals to the highest motives which can influence the heart. God's plan is to develop in the church a supreme love to Christ, so that it will be more than our meat and drink to work, to give, to suffer, and, if need be, to die for his kingdom.

To secure such training throughout the church will require many things, and require that these things be persisted in a long time. Co-operation among the church boards, the church courts, and the church papers—among pastors, and Sabbath-schools, and parents, in carrying out God's own appointed plan of systematic beneficence must be secured. Let presbyteries beware of nullifying the wholesome plans of the General Assembly. Let patient training go on. We are making progress, but years of labor will be required—perhaps generations must pass away—before we come up to the gospel standard. And while these generations pass away, let us not forget that generations of unsaved heathen are also passing out into eternity.

The most powerful sun-glass will not set fire to tinder even unless you continue its concentrated light on the same spot. You must give it time. Time and persistence in concentrating the missionary spirit upon the rising generation of Christians are needed. Training is never the fruit of spasms and changes. We want a sun-glass in our theological schools, Sunday-schools, and homes. We want the very sun himself in our pulpits, and by and by we shall have a blaze which will kindle and burn throughout the church.

Let it be borne in mind that the church at home can not live without the influence which foreign missions exert upon it. Without this the great swelling floods of worldliness would soon sweep the church away, or make its professions an empty sham. Infidelity is the home product of sham consecration. A whole neighborhood was once rapidly drifting into infidelity. The leading men in the churches were at heart infidels. Men not members of the church openly mocked at the hypocrisy of modern Christians.

While that was the general state of things, Christ had one loyal servant among the mothers of that neighborhood who trained her children to be what they professed. By and by three of this woman's daughters went as missionaries to the heathen. An immediate revolution began in that neighborhood. Infidels ceased to cry out "sham." Three of the leaders among them became Christians, and when they joined the church they stated that it was the going forth of those young ladies as missionaries which annihilated their skepticism.

A Southern presbytery (Presbyterian) was full of dissensions. Its meetings were scenes of wrangling. In the midst of all this, one of the young men belonging to the presbytery returned from the theological seminary to ask for ordination as a missionary to the heathen. At his ordination every heart was melted and every feud was forever healed.

J. B. Taylor tells us that after he saw Mr. Scudder embark for a distant mission, from that day onward his own preaching of the gospel rose to a higher plane. We must have all these elements of the gospel—love, and consecration, and self-denial—or else our home pulpits descend to the plane of mere human entertainments.

The home church will never grasp the real divinity of Christianity till it comes up to the divine pattern of entire consecration to Christ's kingdom. A patient study of the glorious promises which God makes to his people shows that they are all linked with this entire consecration. While God's sovereign grace may extend blessings to churches which are not thus consecrated to him, there are no assurances that such blessings will be bestowed, but many reasons are given why we should cherish no such expectation. On the other hand, it is absolutely certain that the divinity of Christianity will be realized and known by those who are thus consecrated, will be manifested to their children, and will convince even the gainsaying and the skeptical. We have had no missionary work since the days of the apostles. We have only been playing a little at missions. Let the church of this day give men and money as the apostolic churches gave, and thousands of consecrated missionaries will immediately be added to the forces now in the foreign field.

CHAPTER XLIV.

CUMBERLAND UNIVERSITY—1842 TO 1887.

It is not necessary that this should be a school of three hundred boys. . . . It is necessary that it should be a school of Christian gentlemen.—Dr. Thomas Arnold, of Rugby.

WHAT was known as the removal of Cumberland College from Princeton, Kentucky, to Lebanon, Tennessee, in 1842, has already been discussed. Among those who composed the first board of trustees of this institution at Lebanon were some of the best men in the country—men fitted to lead in all noble public enterprises. Deservedly foremost among these was R. L. Caruthers, who was made president of the board. Who can estimate the value of one great-souled leader? In all noble plans for the advancement of the institution's interests, this man led the way. If he had been what the world now calls wealthy, the university would long ago have been fully endowed. His estate was large enough to enable him to place his name at the head of every subscription paper circulated to raise money for the institution. He led not only in liberal giving, but in planning liberal things. He scorned all littleness and meanness of policy in the management of the college business.

Members of the Cumberland Presbyterian church were nearly always selected as trustees. When exceptions were made it was not from any lack of suitable men of our own, but for the purpose of extending the influence and increasing the usefulness of the institution. James C. Jones, who was once Governor of the State, though not a Cumberland Presbyterian, was a friend to the church and made a good trustee.

The members of the board at a regular meeting, in 1842, designated their choice of men to compose the college faculty, as follows: F. R. Cossitt, D.D., President; the Rev. C. G. McPherson, Professor of Mathematics; the Rev. T. C. Anderson, Professor of Latin and Greek; and N. Lawrence Lindsley, Professor of Modern Languages. At a later meeting the same year, T. N. Jarman was appointed tutor. All of these ultimately accepted their appointments, but McPherson alone agreed to enter on his work at once. He, with the assistance of a student as tutor, opened the first term, September, 1842, in the building now known as Mrs. Jones' school-house. At the opening of the second term, February, 1843, Dr. Cossitt, and Tutor Jarman arrived and entered on their duties. The third term, beginning September, 1843, Dr. Anderson entered on his duties; and Dr. Lindsley began his labors in the department of modern languages September, 1844. This was then considered a pretty full faculty.

Meantime it became plain enough to the church at large that in order to make the college at Lebanon a success, it would be necessary to abandon the "removal" idea, and regard this school as a new and original enterprise. To this view of things none gave more cheerful acquiescence than the people of Lebanon. A new charter was obtained in 1844, in which the institution was called Cumberland University, instead of Cumberland College. The trustees had already resolved to secure a university organization, according to the American interpretation of that phrase—that is, they resolved to establish a group of professional schools around a college of arts as a center.

When the fifth term of the college opened, the buildings erected specially for it were ready for occupation. This gave great relief, as the patronage had grown beyond the accommodations.

At a meeting of the trustees, July 29, 1842, they defined the nature of their obligations for teachers' salaries, and declared that definition to be of perpetual application. This action has been repeatedly re-affirmed. In pledging a salary to any professor, they simply pledged to each his part, *pro rata*, of tuition fees and endowment interest, and any deficiency of salary remaining still unpaid was to constitute no debt against the institution, unless in some future session there should be a surplus from this fund after paying current expenses—a thing by no means likely ever to occur. In two cases, after rigid investigation made by disinterested experts, it has been decided that the institution did not owe any debts to professors who had not received their full nominal salary, but had drawn their proportional part of tuition fees and endowment interest. Two faults, however, are undeniable: one, that this law about salaries was not always kept clearly before the professors; the other, that in case of a favorite professor, the trustees have sometimes departed from this regulation.

The year 1845 was marked by several changes. Dr. Cossitt this year resigned, and Prof. Anderson was elected to the president's chair. Prof. McPherson retired from the chair of Mathematics, and was succeeded by A. P. Stewart; and James H. Sharp was appointed to the chair of Physical Sciences. This, too, was the first year in which the institution published a catalogue. The roll of students numbered ninety-six. Of these, twenty-five were candidates for the ministry.

From the very first the institution gave free tuition to all regular candidates for the ministry, without distinction of denominations. In addition to this liberality on the part of the faculty—for the school had as yet no endowment—about fifteen of the citizens of the town entered into an agreement that each would give one young preacher free boarding. Several of the number kept two each. But liberality of soul does not give infallibility of judgment. A few who proved unworthy were cared for and petted, while some of the church's noblest servants, as the after years proved them to be, who were sent here in their plain clothing and poverty, were rejected as unpromising by the good people to whom their presbyteries commended them, and went away deeply mortified and embarrassed to seek their education elsewhere. But the great majority of those who received this generous aid paid back the favor a hundred-fold in usefulness to the church.

As soon as the institution was chartered, it began to struggle for endowment. After various efforts by others, the Rev. J. M. McMurray was appointed agent, and made a most thorough and protracted canvass. The plan which he was instructed to pursue was to take notes bearing interest. The interest was to be paid annually, and the principal to be retained by the donor during his life-time. By this plan, often modified to suit emergencies, McMurray enlarged the endowment to sixty thousand dollars.

It was soon found, however, that the plan did not work well. It required trouble and expense to collect interest every year from men scattered over so vast a field. In the old note bag of the university treasurer there are to-day (1887) a large number of these old notes still unpaid. They keep well—so do Confederate bonds. One thing deserves to be commemorated—the persevering fidelity of McMurray in this work. With his family, in his own carriage, through mud, swamps, and snow, over mountains and rocks, and along all manner of rough roads, he plodded on his patient journeys throughout the church.

During the year 1845 the trustees determined to open a law department in the institution. This determination was condemned by several leading men in the church. It was argued that a theological school should be established before trying to build up any other department; and that this effort to secure a law school would divert interest, distract our forces, and delay the one work which has always been nearest the hearts of our people—the establishment of a theological school. Various private letters of expostulation were written to the leaders at Lebanon. This opposition, private and public, continued and increased till July 26, 1848, when the trustees met and agreed upon a paper to be published to the church, which should quiet all further apprehensions.[1] The substance of this paper was a pledge, to be forever binding, that the law department should never be any tax on the church; that it should forever support itself, without asking the church for any assistance. The publication of this pledge in the church papers quieted the opposition. The organization of this department was delayed by the refusal of men chosen for that work to accept their appointment. At last (1847) Judge Abram Caruthers was secured as law professor, his brother, Robert L. Caruthers, becoming responsible for any deficiency which might arise in the salary. The law school was opened in R. L. Caruther's law office. There were thirteen students the first term, among them the present chancellor of the university.

In 1848 the Hon. Nathan Green, Sr., then Judge of the Supreme Court of Tennessee, and Hon. Bromfield L. Ridley, one of the

---

[1] Minutes of the Board, July 26, 1828.

State Chancellors, were secured to teach in the law school as much of their time as their other engagements permitted. In 1852 Judge Green resigned his position on the Supreme Bench, and devoted his whole time to the law school. This school grew to great prosperity, paying at one time over four thousand dollars per annum to each of its professors.

The other departments of the university also grew and prospered. Prof. Wm. Mariner, was added to the college faculty in 1847, and Prof. J. M. Safford succeeded Prof. J. H. Sharp in the chair of Physical Sciences in 1848. Prof. W. J. Grannis was secured for the preparatory school in 1852. He still occupies this position. Many different persons served as tutors for short terms.

One thing which has made its impression deep on the church and the country is the very high grade of scholarship possessed by the faculty of this institution. In no one thing is there greater verification of the saying that "like produces like," than in the similar grade of scholarship found in teachers and their pupils. In all churches, all countries, all ages, this truth holds good. The scholarship of the teacher is reproduced in the members of the classes taught by him. The records of the English universities kept from generation to generation show that in rigid and impartial examinations, conducted from year to year, the first honors have nearly always been won by students whose professors were first honor men, and very seldom by those taught by professors who had themselves won no honors. If there were some method by which the senior classes of all the colleges of this country could be annually brought to some such test, it would do much toward promoting thoroughness in our institutions of learning.

As Cumberland University grew, its buildings were found to be insufficient. A magnificent extension to these buildings was designed, and T. C. Blake was in 1856 sent out to secure money for its erection. The plan on which the agent was instructed to operate was mainly the sale of scholarships. The building was to include dormitories, and the rent of the dormitories was to pay the interest on the scholarships. In addition to the new donations to be taken on this plan, the agent was authorized in some special cases to convert endowment notes secured by McMurray and others into building scholarships. The needed amount was secured and the new buildings erected. A large part of this sum was contributed by citizens of Lebanon. The rent of the dormitories was for a while a pretty good equivalent for the subtractions from the endowment. The handsome buildings were an ornament to the town, and a great help to the institution. Placing all departments in one building, however, involved some serious disadvantages, and is not likely to be tried again by Cumberland University.

President Anderson's administration was long and prosperous. A man of deep piety, whose heart was set far more on the kingdom of Christ than on any literary fame or earthly interest, he struggled nobly to train up a cultivated army of Christian soldiers. Broken down in health before he became connected with the institution, and continuing an invalid all the remainder of his life, he yet managed to do a noble service for his church in the long years he spent as president of this university.

The long-delayed theological department was opened in 1853. The Rev. Richard Beard, D.D., was its first professor. Dr. Cossitt had been elected, but declined. Dr. Beard, who gave his whole time to this work, was aided in it by the president of the university and the pastor of the Lebanon congregation. As this department had at first no endowment, Dr. Beard's salary was secured by private contributions from citizens of Lebanon. The Rev. W. D. Chadick, D.D., was then sent out to solicit endowment specially for this department. He secured notes amounting to nineteen thousand dollars. Then the Rev. W. E. Ward was commissioned as agent, and he secured nine thousand dollars in notes.

The patronage of the Theological School was small. In 1858 it had its first graduating class, four in number. With but one professor, and no available endowment, the outlook was certainly gloomy. Dr. Beard, however, toiled on, though often greatly discouraged. The entries in his private diary are often very sad. He began to doubt that his church really wanted a theological school. He grew very sensitive on the subject. Some statements in the church paper from one of the older preachers he regarded as an attack upon the whole system of theological schools, and he wrote a long series of articles in reply. Then another aged minister, while on a visit at Lebanon, preached a sermon which Dr. Beard construed as another attack on theological schools, though the preacher afterward disclaimed any such intention. Dr. Beard spent a week in gloomy fastings and heart searchings. "Am I wrong? Have I taken a wrong step? Thou, Lord, knowest my whole heart. If this work is not from thee, Lord, shut the door on it forever." Thus he wrote in his diary. After that his spirit had rest. A sweet assurance of God's approbation filled his soul, and he went on with his half-paid labors all the remainder of his life. His professorship lasted twenty-seven years.

The university grew and prospered. The largest number of students ever reported for one year was four hundred and eighty-one. That was in 1858. Nearly half of these were law students. In that year the Law School reached its greatest prosperity.

Then came the war, closing out all departments and sending members of the same class to fight against each other in different armies. The war wiped out the endowment, burned down the buildings, destroyed the library, and filled all the friends of the university with despair. Stunned, bewildered, heartless, the surviving trustees, after the war, looked on the old columns which marked the site of the burnt buildings, with very little hope of ever seeing another college class taught in their town. About this time the Rev. W. E. Ward, D.D., visited Lebanon. He was an alumnus of all the departments of the university. Walking sadly about the old ruins, he took out his pencil and wrote on one of the then standing columns, "*Resurgam.*" The word was taken up by others, and soon became the watchword for a new struggle. The Rev. T. C. Blake was sent out as an agent to raise money for the erection of new buildings. The whole country was a scene of confusion and desolation; but in spite of the discouragements he secured in notes and cash over thirty thousand dollars.

Dr. Beard and Dr. Anderson secured a hall and proclaimed their readiness to receive pupils in the College of Arts. The two Greens—father and son—in another hall opened the Law School. Very few matriculants were enrolled in either department the first session.

Some of the trustees advocated the policy of abandoning all

the old departments except the Law School. The board resolved to purchase the former residence of Abram Caruthers, deceased, for this school. For the buildings, sixty acres of land, and the work needed to fit up the buildings, they agreed to pay sixteen thousand dollars. Their only building fund was the unpaid notes which had been secured and handed over by Dr. Blake. The aim was to raise half the purchase money by subscriptions from Tennessee lawyers. This plan, however, was not successful, and dissatisfaction about the purchase became general.

The Law School never occupied these buildings, but the trustees turned them over to the College of Arts, hoping in this way to conciliate the people. But this measure had the opposite effect. It was interpreted as a deliberate abandonment of the plan for rebuilding on the old site. A large majority of those who had promised to contribute to the building fund refused to pay their notes, and most of these notes remain unpaid, and will doubtless so remain forever. Much prejudice and ill-feeling were thus engendered.

This was the state of things when the writer of this history became president of this institution.[1] Dr. Anderson had resigned a year before, and the presidency had been offered to Gen. A. P. Stewart, and perhaps to others. Then the school had remained without a head for some time. The prospects were very dark. The condition of things when the new administration began beggars all description. There was deep-seated dissatisfaction about the buildings. There was no hope in the Board of Trustees. There were old debts contracted before the war, and pressing like hungry wolves. There was not an advertisement of the school in any paper. There was no endowment, there was no money belonging to the institution. And worse than all else were those rentable scholarships by whose aid the burnt buildings had been erected. Many of these were sent to Lebanon to be rented to the students at less rates than tuition fees, and there was nothing to compensate the faculty for teaching the pupils who rented these

---

[1] Not being able to secure the history of my own administration from any other pen, I submitted my own account of it to the present chancellor, who was my colleague in toil and trials, and I have made all changes suggested by him.—B. W. M.

scholarships. These and many other equally trying things involved perplexities and struggles which only the Omniscient One and those who grappled directly with these difficulties can understand. No matter, "*Resurgam*" became a fulfilled prophecy.

The plan for work in the institution was, at whatever cost, to secure a full and able faculty. Private subscriptions at Lebanon, supplemented by what was called "the cash endowment," enabled us to accomplish this object. Many of the leading newspapers of the South declared ours to be the best faculty in all the Southern States. A distinguished jurist said, "Cumberland University has shot out of the channel ahead." Not only were our professors able and tried educators, but they had filled high positions of trust, which fact went far toward giving influence and power to the university.

For a few years we were steadily overcoming the difficulties. The institution, for the first time in its history, was out of debt. Endowment, unencumbered and real, was slowly but regularly secured. For this work, reliance was placed on several things. The main one was to enlist the efforts of pastors. This method was extensively successful. Next to that was a series of well studied articles in the church papers. There were also vacation trips and visits and speeches to the church judicatures. The wealthy were called upon in order to secure donations. These methods, combined with "the cash endowment" for immediate use without investment, made up the programme by which the work was sustained.

The Finley Bequest, secured in 1869, now furnishes the best part of the living of the theological professors. A will, made through the influence of one of our pastors at that time, has been changed since into a ten thousand dollar cash contribution. Several small tracts of land were about this time deeded to the university, and turned by it into money to meet some of its pressing wants. Extensive mining lands, which were thought then to be valuable, though nothing has ever been realized from them, were secured; also a tract of land lying between Kansas City and Independence, Missouri, which promises to be very valuable. A dear friend of the university holds a life-time reservation claim on the tract last mentioned, so that it is not now available. This land was donated to the university in 1870. It was then supposed to be of sufficient value to endow a professorship. Its value has since increased greatly, and is perhaps the largest donation ever made to the institution.

The largest gift of books which the university ever received was made in 1869. This is the library of the Rev. James Murdock, of the theological department of Yale College. It is specially rich in patristic and historic literature. This library was donated by the Hon. Abraham Murdock, of Columbus, Mississippi. He is a son of the old Professor, and was at the time the donation was made under the pastoral care of that active friend of the university, Dr. G. T. Stainback.

When the war closed the citizens of Lebanon were no longer able to give free boarding to candidates for the ministry. Dr. T. C. Blake suggested the establishment of "a camp" for them, similar to the quarters or barracks occupied by soldiers. Provisions were to be solicited from the surrounding churches. As many of the probationers had been soldiers in the war, this plan was the more readily adopted. An old boarding-house, with several small buildings surrounding it, was purchased and named Camp Blake. The money to pay for this property was secured, and an ample supply of provisions was also obtained. Nathan Green, the present chancellor, became superintendent of this novel encampment, and filled this position without any pay as long as this method of providing homes for our young men was continued. His services in that sphere were very valuable, for he not only managed the finances so as to keep the camp clear of debt, but also exercised the kindest fatherly oversight over the young preachers. Some of those who gathered there were very unpromising in appearance at first, but they improved afterward to a degree that placed them in the front ranks of the ministry of our church.

To many an old student the following paragraphs, clipped from one of Judge Green's published articles, will call up pleasant reminiscences:

Yielding to the suggestion of many older and wiser men, I have engaged the services of one of the most refined and elegant ladies of our church to supervise the cooking and grace the table at Camp Blake. The lady has her mother with her, who contributes much to the comfort of the cadets. It was thought indispensable that a lady should be among these young preachers to soften and refine their manners, as well as to protect them against the carelessness of servants. . . .

Already, though the next session will not begin for ten days, have the young preachers who intend to enter college next year begun to arrive. I am afraid to say how many will be here next session, for the old ones all remain. I am confident there will be fifty or more. What shall we do with them? They must all eat at once at the table, and they must all eat at the same table. The dining-room now used is too small for fifty men. We must have another, and take this for a dormitory. It has been determined, therefore, by the best advice, to erect a tabernacle.

From fifty to seventy young preachers were provided for every term. Some of these are now among the most successful pastors in the denomination. More young preachers went to college under this arrangement than any other our church ever had. When better times enabled the trustees to make better arrangements, the Camp Blake property, which was clear of debt, was rented out in the interest of the theological department, and is still so used.

One of the great difficulties the college encountered just after the war, was the utter lack of any regular preparatory schools in the South. In view of this, the trustees established detached preparatory schools in several Southern towns and cities. The number of pupils in these at one time reached seven hundred. The mission which these schools were designed to fill was temporary, and when their work was done they were abandoned.

Meantime the troubles about the purchase of the Caruthers buildings greatly increased. Only a small number of the building notes could be collected. About half the purchase money had been paid, and the remaining debt was pressing. Finally the property was condemned by the courts and its sale ordered. The theological school bought it, paying for it just half what it had cost the trustees.

This was one of the wisest steps the theological school ever took. This school had unimproved property in Chicago, which had been for years eating itself up with taxes and agent's fees. The trustees sold this Chicago property for twelve thousand dollars cash.

The theological school invested four thousand dollars of this money as endowment, and paid eight thousand for the Caruthers property, now called Divinity Hall. Thus buildings and land, which were valued at twice the money invested, were obtained, and the university was saved a sacrifice which would have placed both the theological school and the college of arts out of doors, with scarcely a hope of ever securing a shelter over their heads. Indeed this purchase saved the life both of the theological school and the college of arts. And yet a committee which knew nothing of the facts wanted the next General Assembly to censure the trustees for making it.

The darkest, saddest part of this struggle to build up the university was the bitter but unsuccessful conflict with the life insurance companies. Schemes for securing endowment by persuading men to take out insurance policies in favor of the university were pressed by five different companies. When these efforts were thwarted at Lebanon, the agents of the companies would visit churches and attend the meetings of presbyteries and synods to secure their influence in urging these plans upon the trustees. Some of our ablest ministers were induced thus to take an active part in pressing these schemes.

As the president had several times succeeded in defeating the efforts of these agents, they began to watch for opportunities to press their plans on the board in his absence. In 1871, while he was absent in Alabama, an agent of the St. Louis Mutual Life Insurance Company, who was also an elder in one of our strong churches, and a true friend of the university, prevailed on the trustees to adopt his scheme. Though this scheme was well meant, and looked plausible, and was indorsed by many friends of the institution, yet its adoption was a death blow to all the plans that had been formed by the president and those co-operating with him. The trustees claimed for the agents of the insurance companies a clear field, not permitting any other method of raising money for permanent endowment, or allowing the collection of cash contributions to supplement salaries. It being known that the author of this history, as president, had no confidence in the scheme, he was enjoined to keep silence. This he did except when conscience required him to speak. He did nothing to thwart the agents; but when the friends of other colleges wrote, making inquiries about the "grand scheme," they were warned to have nothing to do with it. The University of Virginia and other institutions were perhaps saved from burnt fingers by these warnings.

The insurance scheme amounted to a disaster. The insolvency of the company after the church had invested many thousands with it, and before the university had received any real benefit, came, sweeping away confidence and hope together. Under the anxiety growing out of this insurance business, and the suspense and final disaster it brought, the health of the president gave way, leaving him in a long struggle between life and death. He resigned in September, 1873, and the Hon. Nathan Green was placed at the head of the institution as chancellor.

Dr. Green receives pay as Law Professor, but his work as chancellor is done without salary. We can often judge of a man's clear-sightedness by looking backward. Dr. Green opposed the purchase of the Caruthers buildings for the law school. He opposed the schemes of endowment by life insurance. He opposed all the schemes for cheap scholarships, and all other clap-trap methods for securing endowment funds. The results now indicate the correctness of his judgment in all these matters.

The most important work of Dr. Green's administration has been that done for the theological school. When he was made chancellor that school had but one professor. It now has a faculty of three professors, and an indefatigable agent is making good progress toward its endowment. Two handsome buildings, large enough for two of the departments of the university, have also been secured since Dr. Green became chancellor.

The institution now has one building for each of its four departments. Its endowment is largely prospective—notes and lands being the main items.

A change of deep significance has taken place in regard to the endowment of the theological school. The General Assembly has awakened at last to the fact that this school belongs not to Cumberland University, but to the whole church. Not the trustees of the university, but the General Assembly planned and inaugurated this department. Cumberland University did not even ask the General Assembly to establish such a department. True, the friends of the university from all parts of the church are very earnest in their convictions that Lebanon is the proper place for such a school, and they urged those views on the General Assembly before the school was located.

At Bentonville, Arkansas, 1885, the General Assembly instructed its own Board of Education, located at Nashville, Tennessee, to appoint an agent to secure endowment for the theological school. So long as the trustees of Cumberland University appointed the agents to endow this department, that fact placed this school in a false light. It is not and never was a mere department of the university. It stands in relations to the university far different from those sustained by the law department. The latter was created by the trustees at Lebanon, and could be abandoned by them without asking the church or the General Assembly.

The church's theological school is a department of the university only so far as such relation is supposed to be serviceable to this school, but it is something more than a mere department. It has relations independent of the university. The propriety of having a separate board of trust for it has often been discussed, but its own interests are against such a separation.

The charter for this department differs greatly in its provisions from the charters of the other departments. One item included in the rules laid down by the Assembly when this school was established, and which was rigidly enforced for a few years, has unfortunately been allowed to pass into forgetfulness. It provides that a committee shall be appointed annually by the General Assembly to visit the institution and report concerning its prosperity and orthodoxy. At a time when so many theological schools are drifting away into heresies and something worse, our church should by no means relax its use of this fortunate provision. We have no right to assume that we are forever free from jeopardy, when some of our neighbors are even now in such trouble.

The fundamental laws of the institution, to which its charter was required to conform, were laid down by the General Assembly when the school was established. (See Assembly Minutes, 1852).

The last section of Article V. and three sections from Article VI. are here given:

ARTICLE V.

Sec. 7.—Each professor, before entering upon the duties of his office, shall solemnly adopt, in such form as the Assembly may prescribe, the Cumberland Presbyterian Confession of Faith and Form of Government.

ARTICLE VI.

Sec. 1.—That the theology taught in the school may be subject to the judgment of the Assembly, it shall be the duty of the Professor of Systematic Theology to write out his lectures to the classes, and when required, he shall submit them to the examination of the board, or to a committee of the Assembly.

Sec. 2.—Professors, as other ministers, will be amenable to the presbytery, and subject to be arraigned for immorality or heresy. But for their official character they shall be amenable to the Assembly, and upon a recommendation of the board or a committee of the Assembly, they shall be subject to removal for incompetency, gross neglect of official duty, or such irregularity in deportment or error in doctrine as shall render their continuance in office detrimental to the interests of the school.

Sec. 3.—As professors may be removed whenever the Assembly shall deem it expedient, appointments shall be made for an indefinite time, except in cases where the board may recommend an appointment for a definite period.

One of the strange questions of the times relates to the theological education of young ladies who are to go out as foreign missionaries. That there should be embarrassment and hesitation about receiving them into the classes of our theological seminary seems to some people very strange. To some of the staid old conservatives of Cumberland University, who have always objected to co-education, it is a matter of astonishment that such an innovation should be demanded. Now the question is to come before the General Assembly, and we shall see whether or not the world is moving. In this matter the Assembly has entire control.

The tables of statistics relating to the university, published in *The Theological Medium*, October, 1876, abound in mistakes. The dates, and the figures indicating the patronage, are unreliable. Omitting the temporary and detached schools, the following is a list of all those who have been members of the faculty of Cumberland University:

NAMES.	PROFESSORSHIP.	ELECTED.	CLOSED.
Rev. F. R. Cossitt, D.D	President	July 9, 1842,	Sept. 30, 1844.
Rev. T. C. Anderson, D.D	President	Sept. 30, 1844,	Aug. 24, 1866.
Rev. B. W. McDonnold, D.D., LL.D.	President	——, 1866,	——, 1873.
Hon. N. Green, LL.D	Chancellor	Aug. 30, 1873,	
Rev. C. G. McPherson	Mathematics	July 9, 1842,	Sept. 21, 1844.
Rev. T. C. Anderson	Languages	Aug. 3, 1842,	Sept. 21, 1844.
Mr. —— Price	Tutor for one session	Aug. 3, 1842,	——, 1842.
T. N. Jarman	Permanent Tutor	Sept. 9, 1842,	——, 1844.
B. S. Foster	Tutor	April 29, 1844,	——, 1846.
N. Lawrence Lindsley, LL.D.	Lin. Vetr	Sept. 21, 1844,	Oct. 13, 1849.
Gen. A. P. Stewart	Mathematics	Jan. 22, 1845,	Oct. 1, 1849.
Gen. A. P. Stewart	Mathematics	April 3, 1850,	Aug. 2, 1854.
Gen. A. P. Stewart	Mathematics	June 28, 1856,	Sept. 2, 1869.
Louis A. Lowry, A.B.	Mathematics (temporary)	Feb. 27, 1845,	——, 1845.
J. H. Sharp, M.D.	Chemistry	Feb. 27, 1845,	Sept. 4, 1847.
Hon. Ab. Caruthers	Int. and Const. Law and Political Economy	May 17, 1845,	May 1, 1847.
R. P. Decherd	Second Tutor	Jan. 3, 1846,	Feb. 20, 1847.
R. P. Decherd	Tutor	Feb. 22, 1849,	Feb. 16, 1850.
R. P. Decherd	Sup't. Prep. Dep't	Feb. 16, 1850,	Aug. 2, 1854.
Rev. Robert Donnell	Lecturer on Theology	July 10, 1846,	——, 1848.
Rev. Wiley M. Reed	Junior Tutor	Feb. 20, 1847,	——, 1848.
Robert Hatton	Tutor	June 26, 1847,	——, 1848.
Rev. N. J. Fox	Tutor	June 26, 1847,	——, 1848.
Wm. Mariner, A.M	Ass't Prof. Lin. Vetr	Dec. 31, 1847,	Oct. 1, 1849.
J. M. Safford, Ph.D.	Chem., Min., and Geo.	June 27, 1848,	——, 1873.
J. L. McDowell	Tutor	Sept. 11, 1848,	——, 1848.
Wm. Mariner, A.M.	Mathematics	Oct. 1, 1849,	July 12, 1850.
Wm. Mariner, A.M.	Lin. Vetr	July 12, 1850,	——, 1860.
Rev. J. C. Provine	Assistant Tutor	Feb. 16, 1850,	——, 1850.
Rev. T. C. Blake	Tutor	Sept. 20, 1850,	June 21, 1851.
Rev. T. C. Blake	Mathematics	Aug. 2, 1854,	June 28, 1856.
Rev. S. T. Anderson	Tutor	Jan. 18, 1851,	——, 1851.
Rev. W. W. Suddarth	Tutor for five months	June 27, 1851,	——, 1851.
Rev. E. B. Crisman	Tutor for one session	Oct. 10, 1851,	——, 1852.
Rev. A. H. Alsup	Tutor	April 2, 1852,	——, 1852.
Rev. R. Beard, D.D.	Systematic Theology	April 22, 1853,	——, 1881.
Hubert H. Merrill	Teacher Prep. Dep't	May 24, 1854,	July 3, 1856.
W. J. Craw	In Dr. Safford's absence	June 3, 1854,	
A. H. Buchanan	Eng. and Engineering Dep't	Aug. 2, 1854,	——, 1860.
A. H. Buchanan	Mathematics	Sept. 2, 1869,	
H. A. D. Brown	Teacher Prep. Dep't	Aug. 21, 1856,	——, 1858.
J. Blau	Modern Languages	July 11, 1866,	——, 1867.
E. G. Burney	Prin. Prep. Dep't	Nov. 17, 1866,	July 22, 1870.
Ben Decherd	Assistant Teacher Prep. Dep't	Aug. 24, 1869,	——, 1871.
T. C. Anderson, D.D.	Lecturer in Theology	June 30, 1870,	——, 1872.
W. D. McLaughlin	Adjunct Prof. Classics and Belles-Lettres	July 22, 1870,	Aug. 17, 1872.
W. D. McLaughlin	Prof. Lin. Vetr	Aug. 17, 1872,	
D. S. Bodenhamer	Teacher Prep. Dep't	June 6, 1871,	——, 1873.
H. T. Norman	Teacher Prep. Dep't	Oct. 18, 1871,	——, 1872.
John I. D. Hinds	Adj. Prof. Phys. Sci.	Aug. 30, 1873,	——, 1874.
W. J. Grannis	Prep. Dep't	——, 1852,	——, 1862.
W. J. Grannis	Prin. Prep. Dep't	Aug. 30, 1873,	
Samuel Y. Finley	Teacher Prep. Dep't	——, 1859,	——, 1860.
H. S. Kennedy	Prin. Eng. School	——, 1866,	——, 1871.
N. J. Finney	Teacher Prep. Dep't	——, 1866,	——, 1867.
Rev. T. M. Thurman	Tutor	——, 1866,	——, 1867.
Oliver Holben	Modern Languages	——, 1867,	——, 1870.
N. Green, Jr.	Tutor	——, 1844,	——, 1845.
T. H. Hardwick	Tutor	——, 1851,	——, 1852.
H. H. Merrill	Teacher	——, 1858,	——, 1859.
B. C. Jilson	Geology	——, 1854,	——, 1856.
E. H. Plumacher	Modern Languages	——, 1870,	——, 1871.
W. H. Darnall	Murdock Prof. Eccles. Hist.	——, 1873,	——, 1878.
H. W. Grannis	Teacher Prep. Dep't	——, 1875,	
Abram Caruthers	Law Professor	——, 1847,	——, 1862.
Nathan Green	" "	——, 1848,	——, 1866.
B. L. Ridley	" "	——, 1848,	——, 1852.
N. Green, Jr.	" "	——, 1856,	
John C. Carter	" "	——, 1859,	——, 1864.
Henry Cooper	" "	——, 1866,	——, 1868.
Robert L. Caruthers	" "	——, 1868,	——, 1882.
Andrew B. Martin	" "	——, 1878,	
S. G. Burney, D.D.	Prof. Bib. Lit.	——, 1877,	
R. V. Foster, A. M.	Prof. Belles-Lettres and Hebrew	——, 1877,	
John I. D. Hinds	Prof. Chem. and Nat. Science	——, 1874,	
J. D. Kirkpatrick, D.D.	Eccles. Hist.	——, 1880,	
E. E. Weir	Eng. Literature	Sept., 1880,	

From the first the law school has combined all the best methods of instruction with the services of the very ablest professors. The instruction does not consist of mere lectures by those who have turned aside for an hour from busy practice at the bar, but able lawyers give their whole time to the classes, teaching by recitations, lectures, and moot courts.

The first want of a student in his preparation for any profession is that mental discipline and development which a college of arts furnishes. To place a student in his professional studies before he learns how to think, is the road to professional failure. Cumberland University could furnish from its own long rolls, many an illustration of this fundamental truth. The department of arts demands larger facilities, and must have them if we would realize the best results.

Wiley A. Hatley, of Arkansas, in a tribute to the memory of his father, John Hatley, after describing many noble services which his father rendered to the church, closes the biographical sketch with these words: "No other part of the legacy he left to his children has been so precious in its influence on them as the money he contributed for the founding of Cumberland University, and for the support of other enterprises of the church. The large sums which he so freely gave to the church, and for the cause of Christian education, brought a greater blessing to those he left behind than the estate which they directly inherited."

Whenever the church resolves to have an endowed college, we shall have it. Not paper resolutions, but heart and pocket resolutions are meant. Small contributions from our entire membership can be secured, if the ministry will do their duty. This general action is the first great lever to prize up big donations. It was to Union College, long fostered by the gifts of a multitude of poor people, that Dr. Nott gave six hundred thousand dollars. "He that hath to him shall be given," is the law in college endowment. General action, even from the poor will make our colleges a success. The tax of one peck of corn on the poor colonists of Massachusetts saved Harvard College, and attracted large gifts even from England.

Let not our people foster the mistaken notion that we are

too poor to endow our colleges. Count over how much was lost by members of our church in your county by the war. They bore that loss and yet live. But they pleaded poverty before the war just as much as they do now. Suppose half as much as has been lost had been given to the church, could the donors not have supported their families and lived happily? Look around you and see what the members of the church are paying for railroads. Yes, and still the donors live.

Our men of large wealth have given us no examples of liberality proportionate to their ability. There is a wide field open for usefulness, for happiness, for honorable distinction—open to any wealthy man among us who will break the long spell of parsimony, and lead our rich men in deeds of munificence. Alumni of Cumberland Presbyterian colleges, the cause of learning in our church cries out to you for help.

CHAPTER XLV.

WAYNESBURG COLLEGE, LINCOLN UNIVERSITY, AND TRINITY UNIVERSITY.

> Delve we there for richer gems
> Than the stars of diadems.
> —*James Montgomery.*

BESIDES the university at Lebanon, Tennessee, whose work is described in the last chapter, Cumberland Presbyterians have three other principal educational centers. These are Waynesburg College, at Waynesburg, Pennsylvania, in the eastern part of the territory occupied by our people; Lincoln University, in the North-west, at Lincoln, Illinois; and Trinity University, in the extreme South-west, at Tehuacana, Texas. The object of this chapter is to sketch the history of these three institutions.

WAYNESBURG COLLEGE.

Some account of the first efforts of our people in Pennsylvania and Ohio to establish denominational schools is necessary as an introduction to the history of Waynesburg College. We have positive evidence that the missionaries who planted the first Cumberland Presbyterian churches in Pennsylvania recognized the importance of education, and the necessity for an institution of learning on that eastern border of our denominational field. The Rev. Le Roy Woods, who began his labors in that State in 1832, testifies[1] that: "To educate up to a high standard was a fixed purpose with Morgan and Bryan. Milton Bird occupied no equivocal position in reference to this question. Donnell, Burrow, Chapman, Aston, Shook—indeed all who took an active part in the

---

[1] Quoted from the *Religious Pantagraph* by Dr. A. B. Miller in his article on Waynesburg College in the *Theological Medium*, Vol. XIV. pp. 63-118, January, 1878. Dr. Miller gives a very full and satisfactory history of the institution over which he has so long and so ably presided, and many of the facts in this sketch are gleaned from his article.

commencement of our work in Pennsylvania—were outspoken friends of education—of collegiate education."

These pioneers showed their faith on this subject by their works. The Pennsylvania Synod at its first meeting, which was held at Uniontown, Pennsylvania, October, 1838, passed "a resolution encouraging the presbyteries to foster their educational interests." This synod at that time was made up of three presbyteries, Pennsylvania and Union in western Pennsylvania, and Athens, in Ohio. Each of these presbyteries "was making an effort to furnish the facilities necessary to the liberal education of the youth under its influence."[1]

Greene Academy, at Carmichaels, Greene county, Pennsylvania, in the bounds of Pennsylvania Presbytery, "was largely under Cumberland Presbyterian control, though it never sustained any ecclesiastical relation." The Rev. Joshua Loughran, a Cumberland Presbyterian minister, was its principal. "The congregation at Carmichaels was one of the first organized in western Pennsylvania, and under the blessing of God grew in numbers, strength, and usefulness." The influence of the Rev. Le Roy Woods and the Rev. S. E. Hudson, who were successively pastors of this church, did much to make Greene Academy an ally of Cumberland Presbyterians. Many candidates for the ministry were attracted to this school. Among our well-known and useful preachers who were in part educated here were A. J. Baird, Philip and Luther Axtell, Samuel McCollum, J. W. Cleaver, J. S. Gibson, and A. B. Miller. A. J. Baird for several terms did good service as assistant teacher in this institution.

In the bounds of Union Presbytery, at Uniontown, Pennsylvania, was Madison College. In 1838 this institution was under the controlling influence of Cumberland Presbyterians, though the nominal control was in the hands of a board of trustees, which, according to the statement of the Rev. J. P. Weethee,[2] "consisted of forty-five members, scattered through a dozen States." This school was probably established near the beginning of the century. Ac-

---

[1] Dr. A. B. Miller, in *Theological Medium*.

[2] See his "Review of Dr. Miller's Sketch," in *Theological Medium*, Vol. XIV. p. 345, July 1878.

Rev JOHN MORGAN.
The Only Existing Likeness.

cording to one statement, it was originally placed under the patronage of the Methodist Episcopal church; and another authority says that the Presbyterians at first exercised a dominant influence in its affairs, and that it afterward passed into the hands of the Methodists. By reason of a division in the Methodist church the work of the college dwindled, and was finally suspended; and about 1835 a young candidate for the ministry in the Presbyterian church was teaching a select school in the building.[1]

John Morgan was then pastor at Uniontown, and the Cumberland Presbyterian church had so grown in prominence and influence as to attract the attention of the guardians of Madison College; so they sought the alliance and patronage of this new church. J. P. Weethee, a young man twenty-two years old, a graduate of Ohio University, and a candidate for the ministry, was made president, and the college was opened for students. For the first three weeks there were but three pupils. The young man who had been teaching in the college building before Weethee took charge, opened a rival school in another part of the town. This school "was for many years under the supervision of a talented Presbyterian minister," and Mr. Weethee testifies that the sectarian opposition thus begun was continued throughout the eight years during which Madison College was under the patronage of our people.

The institution, however, prospered until it had one hundred and fifty students. John Morgan was for a time Professor of Moral Science, and, when failing health compelled him to resign, Milton Bird was chosen his successor. Among the graduates in the autumn of 1841 was Azel Freeman, so well known afterward throughout the church as an educator and writer. "Previous to his graduation," says Dr. Miller, "he rendered aid as tutor in the college, and immediately upon his graduation he was honored with the appointment to the Chair of Languages."

The Rev. Le Roy Woods gives the following incident, showing the deep interest which John Morgan felt in this school and in the cause of education. Describing his last visit to Mr. Morgan, Mr. Woods says:[2]

---

[1] Weethee's Article in *Theological Medium*. [2] Quoted from the *Religious Pantagraph* by Dr. Miller in the *Theological Medium*, January, 1878.

He was far on his way to the end of his race, and was so feeble that he could scarcely talk. After an interview of considerable length, during which we had in a very friendly manner reviewed the past and endeavored to forecast the future of our cause in Pennsylvania, when I announced to him that I would have to go, with much effort he arose from his couch, straightened himself to his full height, and looking me full in the face with an expression that I can never forget, he asked in an easy and familiar way, "Woods, how is Greene Academy getting along?" I gave him an appropriate answer. He then asked how many candidates were there. I gave him the number. I approached to bid him farewell. He took my hand in his, then hot with the fever that was consuming him, and said, with a tone of voice and with an earnestness of manner which showed clearly the deep interest he felt in the subject, and with a pressure of the hand more eloquent than words, "Don't give up your school—hang on to it." Then, referring to Bryan, in Pittsburg, and Bird, on Tenmile, both settled pastors but not connected with any school, he said, "they may have an easier time, and receive a better compensation than we, but our schools will be doing good after we are in our graves."

During Mr. Weethee's administration this question was brought before the board of trustees: "Are females, matriculated and pursuing a college course, students in the eye of the law?" This question was decided in the affirmative, and Mr. Weethee says this decision made Madison College "perhaps the first co-educational college in the Union."

In the spring of 1842 there was a serious rupture between the president and the board of trustees, and Weethee, Bird, and Freeman resigned; and the college passed for a time into the hands of the Presbyterians. Of his own labors in this school, and his final resignation, Mr. Weethee says:

My recitations began at sunrise, and continued through the day. I often heard twenty classes daily. To keep the college in motion, I at different times was called to fill every professorship. As the institution prospered and became an object of interest "worth having," the opposition increased, until finally by a general union of Presbyterian, Methodist, and Episcopal members of the board, . . . the opposition secured a majority of the votes. A change of administration being contemplated, and being well assured that the institution was lost to our church, I resigned.

Two years after Weethee's resignation the college was practically dead. The trustees heartily "repented of their folly in dispossessing Cumberland Presbyterians, and were quite ready to invoke their aid once more." In 1844 they were in correspondence with Pennsylvania Synod. That body at its meeting in the autumn of this year resolved "that the synod ought to take the necessary steps to secure the control" of Madison College. To carry out this resolution a committee was appointed "to offer proposals" to the trustees. In 1845 the synod adopted a report, "which sets forth that the trustees of Madison College had given it into the synod's control."

The Rev. A. Freeman was again elected as a professor, and an earnest effort was made to revive this college. Some students were gathered during the winter, and with the opening of the spring term an additional professor was appointed. But there was "only feeble, faint-hearted co-operation on the part of the synod," and the number of students was not encouraging. In the autumn of 1846 "the two professors resigned, and the synod relinquished all care and control." Thus ended the connection of our people with Madison College.

Within the bounds of Athens Presbytery, at Beverly, Ohio, in 1838, Benjamin Dana bequeathed certain coal lands to an academy to be built at that town. In 1842, John Dodge, of Beverly, deeded several lots to the Rev. Charles R. Barclay, in trust, "for the purpose and to the use of education at and within the Muskingum College (afterward called Beverly College) now erected or hereafter to be erected on said real estate, under and by the exclusive direction and control of the Pennsylvania Synod of the Cumberland Presbyterian church forever." A three-story brick building, which still stands, was erected on one of these lots for the intended college.

In 1840 the Pennsylvania Synod had discussed this question: Shall the Synod co-operate with the General Assembly in supporting Cumberland College, at Princeton, Kentucky, or undertake to establish a school of high order within its own bounds? A report was adopted by which the synod resolved "to act in its individual capacity," and to raise a fund of thirty thousand dollars for the endowment of a synodical college. A board of twelve trustees was elected, with authority:

1. To make proposals to any board of trustees within the bounds of the synod, or to any number of men who shall be incorporated within Pennsylvania, for the purpose of securing the erection of a college building.

2. To accept such terms as, in the clearest convictions of their judgments, afford the greatest advantages to the synod.

The Rev. J. P. Weethee, whose name stands first in the list of these twelve trustees, informs us that this board located the proposed synodical college at Beverly, Ohio, "induced to that action by the Dodge and Dana grants," and that this was the real origin of Beverly College. A liberal charter was granted to this institution by the legislature of Ohio, in 1843. Mr. Weethee was elected to the presidency. He says:

I removed to Beverly in the fall of 1842, and took charge of the students I could find. The location of the college was soon found to be not what we had anticipated. The town population was then inconsiderable, and the surrounding country was divided in its patronage by the Ohio University and Marietta College. Our denomination was weak, and could afford us but a few students. The college building was not sufficiently finished to be occupied. The winter that followed was very severe and protracted. We made our hotel room our recitation room. . . . The Dodge and Dana bequests did not then yield a dime, and we were left with scarcely enough to discharge our board bills.

How long Mr. Weethee continued his efforts in this school we are not informed, nor do we know who were his successors in the direct work of teaching. In 1848 the synod recommended "the tender of the Beverly property to the General Assembly for the use of a theological seminary." Reports were adopted in 1849 and 1850, deploring the condition of this college; and in 1851 a committee summed up the state of things in these words: "No school in operation at present, no agent in the field to solicit funds for the institution, no endowment fund on hand, no apparatus, no library, no professors or teachers." This institution never had a graduate, and it can scarcely be said that it "ever had an existence as a college." After the Ohio Synod was formed in 1853, the management of this school was handed over to that body, though, by some neglect or oversight, the charter was never so changed as to transfer the legal control and the ownership of the property from Pennsylvania Synod to Ohio Synod.

The efforts of Pennsylvania Synod to adopt and build up Madison College had failed; the hopes of those who had desired to make Beverly College the educational center of the synod had also been disappointed. Our people had no legal title to Greene Academy—no assurance that the control of its affairs might not at any time be taken out of their hands. Therefore, in April, 1849, Pennsylvania Presbytery declared that its educational interests imperiously demanded that an institution of learning should be established in its bounds, and appointed a committee of five "to receive proposals for the location and establishment of such an institution." When the presbytery met in the autumn following the committee reported proposals from Waynesburg and Carmichaels, both in Greene County, Pennsylvania. "Waynesburg offered a considerably larger sum than Carmichaels for the erection of a building, and was chosen as the location of what finally became the educational enterprise of the whole church in Pennsylvania." The same autumn "the Rev. Joshua Loughran left Greene Academy and went to Waynesburg, where he built up a high school simultaneously with the preliminary steps of the presbytery for the founding of a college, and which school was merged into the college."

The new building, "a three-story brick edifice, seventy by fifty feet," was erected by the citizens of Waynesburg at a cost of six thousand dollars. Work on it was begun in the spring of 1850, and it was fully completed in the fall of the following year. "On the first Tuesday in November, 1851, the college went into formal operation in this new building." The Rev. Joshua Loughran, A.M., had been chosen president, the Rev. R. M. Fish, A.B., Professor of Mathematics, and A. B. Miller and Frank Patterson, tutors. Miss Margaret K. Bell had been employed in the fall of 1850 to take charge of a school for young ladies, with the design of founding a female seminary in connection with the college. She became principal of what was afterward known as the Female Department. Three young ladies were graduated in this department in the autumn of 1852.

A year later, September 28, 1853, the first Commencement in the college proper was held. At this time, besides four young ladies who received diplomas from the Female Department, four young men, among them A. B. Miller, were graduated in the regular college course.

The charter, which was granted in March, 1850, placed the government of the college in the hands of a board of trustees, a majority of whom were to be elected by Pennsylvania Presbytery. In 1853 the college was transferred to the control of Pennsylvania Synod. Since then all the educational efforts of our church on its eastern border have been concentrated in this institution. Dr. Miller sums up the precise relations of the Cumberland Presbyterian church to Waynesburg College in these words:

1. The charter secures to the synod the perpetual use of the property, provided the synod sustains therein at least three professors. (The charter makes no requirement as to the *manner* in which the professors are to be supported.)

2. Of the twenty-one trustees, the charter grants to the synod the appointment of twelve. (The synod has, in fact, for twenty-four years, appointed the whole number of trustees.)

3. By mutual agreement it is a by-law that the trustees shall elect no person to a professorship until the synod has first nominated the person for the place.

4. The endowment fund of the college is held by another board, styled "The Board of Trust of the College Endowment Fund of Pennsylvania Synod," consisting of five members appointed by the synod, and acting under a charter securing to this board all needful powers and perpetual succession.

Prof. Fish having resigned, the Rev. A. B. Miller was elected to the chair of Mathematics, October, 1853, at a salary of three hundred dollars a year. The want of an adequate financial support was probably the chief cause of the resignation of President Loughran, which took place August, 1855. During his connection with the college Mr. Loughran also preached to the Waynesburg congregation. Dr. Miller testifies that he possessed "excellencies that made him a valuable man in the class-room;" that he was "a great reader, a good thinker, and could hold a class spellbound for an hour," and make a "recitation in his room a delight." But he was unable or unwilling to grapple with the financial difficulties which beset the college, and so yielded its management to other hands.

The synod nominated the Rev. J. P. Weethee as Mr. Loughran's successor, and he was elected president by the board of trustees. Though Mr. Weethee had ceased to be a Cumberland Presbyterian, and at that time "did not belong to any denomination,"[1] yet he professed unabated attachment to our church; and his doctrinal views, as explained by himself, were thought by the synod "to be no serious barrier to his nomination."[2]

Dr. Miller says: "Mr. Weethee entered upon his duties with a strong popular sentiment in his favor. . . . He brought into the college a spirit of improvement, and an earnest purpose to build up, and the first year of his labors was marked with decided progress." But difficulties afterward arose, growing in part out of dissatisfaction with the new president's peculiar religious views, and in part out of questions connected with the internal management of the institution. At the end of the third year of his presidency, in the autumn of 1858, on account of these difficulties, and because he "was not paid according to contract," Mr. Weethee resigned.

The friends of the college were much discouraged, and "feared that this educational effort would terminate in a repetition of the Madison College trouble." Some advocated the re-election of the Rev. Joshua Loughran to the presidency, and he was written to on the subject; "but having been once starved out, he made conditions which the synod pronounced impracticable."[3] The Hon. John C. Flenniken was made president *pro tem.* The Rev. S. H. Jeffery, A. M., pastor of the Waynesburg Presbyterian church, was called to the chair of Natural Science, and the Rev. A. J. McGlumphy, who had just graduated, was appointed Professor of Mathematics. The real work of managing the internal affairs of the institution fell on the Rev. A. B. Miller, who was vice-president by priority of appointment. Mrs. Miller (formerly Miss Margaret K. Bell) was still principal of the Female Department, and continued in this position until her death in 1874.

---

[1] Weethee's Review of Dr. Miller's Sketch, *Theological Medium*, July, 1878.
[2] Dr. Miller, Ibid., January, 1878. [3] Dr. Miller.

Dr. Miller was duly nominated and elected to the presidency in the fall of 1859. At the same time Milton E. Garrison, A.M., a graduate of Allegheny College, Meadville, Pennsylvania, was elected Professor of Greek and Latin. A year later W. G. Scott, A.M., became Professor of Mathematics.

Of the condition and prospects of the college when he was called to the presidency, and of his perplexing and responsible duties, Dr. Miller says:

A debt of over three thousand dollars hung upon the college. My salary was very inadequate; and, worse, there was no reasonable ground of hope that it would be paid if the other necessary professors were employed and paid. Dissension had turned a portion of the community against the college, and had begotten in the public mind a feeling of distrust in regard to the future. Accepting the position, and going to work under these unpromising circumstances, it seemed to me more like an effort to make a college than the honor of presiding over one— nor have I yet outgrown that feeling. My special aims were, first, to get the college out of debt, and to establish confidence in its value and permanence. To accomplish the former, and to keep the necessary teaching force in the college without incurring debt, has been the constant ever-perplexing problem through all these years. After looking in vain for other sources of reliable pecuniary dependence, I found it necessary to assume toward the college, in fact, the relation of president, financial agent, and board of trustees. Taught by bitter experience how great are these cares thus thrown on a college president, and admitting that ordinarily such a course could promise only financial ruin, I must record my profound conviction that in this case nothing but the unbounded liberty allowed me in the management of the college could have saved it from hopeless failure.

As tutor and professor and president, Dr. Miller has labored incessantly in this institution for nearly thirty-six years, and is still at his post faithful to his life-time work of building up a Cumberland Presbyterian college in Pennsylvania. In his article already quoted, he says:

I have been compelled to preach in order to live, sometimes supplying points twenty miles distant; I have been compelled to deny myself books greatly needed; to stay at home when I should have traveled; to walk many miles because I could not afford to pay hack fare; to be harassed with debts that have eaten up the mind as cancers eat the flesh; in short, to do a great many things, and to leave undone a great many things, which doing and not doing greatly hindered my usefulness as a public servant of the church. I once turned superintendent of schools, and walked all over Greene county in order to save a little money, and still the college went on, while the nation was fighting its battles. At another time I edited the *Cumberland Presbyterian*, did all the necessary correspondence of the office, and kept the books, at the same time teaching six hours a day in the college, exercising general oversight of its financial affairs, and often preaching twice on the Sabbath.

Through all the years until her death (1874), Mrs. Miller, as principal of the Female Department, was her husband's faithful co-worker. To the young ladies under her charge "she was at once a teacher, a counselor, a sympathizing friend." She labored almost without pecuniary return, her salary being "for a long time three hundred dollars a year, and never over four hundred dollars," and the full sum of even this pittance was not paid for any year. Through twenty-four years her time and strength were given with the utmost unselfishness and enthusiasm to this work. She really sacrificed her life to build up this institution. Without her brave self-denying work and influence, the enterprise would probably have failed. In addition to duties in her home, which was constantly open for the entertainment of the friends of the college, she usually taught six hours a day. "It can not be doubted that her early death was the result of exhaustion from overwork."

Since 1852 Waynesburg College has each year sent forth a class of educated men and women, many of whom have filled important places of trust and usefulness; and their influence and work have been no inconsiderable factor in promoting the progress of the Cumberland Presbyterian church. The largest class ever graduated by this institution was that of 1873, consisting of twenty members—eight young women and twelve young men. The same year the college had three hundred students, the largest number ever reported in attendance. The first five Cumberland Presbyterian missionaries sent to Japan were all graduates of this school.

Waynesburg College has not only sent forth preachers and missionaries, but it has furnished many successful teachers to other schools and colleges, and has trained up its own most valued and efficient teachers and professors. As has been seen, Dr. Miller was himself a member of the first graduating class. Prof. W. G. Scott, who has so long and with such ability filled the chair of Mathematics, was a member of the class of 1857. When Prof. M. E. Garrison died, April 7, 1870, after ten years of valuable service as Professor of Greek and Latin, the vacancy thus caused was filled temporarily by J. W. Freeland, A.B., who graduated in 1868. Afterward J. M. Garrison, A.B., a member of the class of 1870, was appointed to this chair. He was succeeded in 1872 by J. M. Crow, A.B., who had received his diploma from the college the year before. After teaching a year he spent two years in Germany and Switzerland prosecuting his studies. Returning in 1875, he resumed his work in the college, winning great popularity; but on account of the insufficiency of his salary he resigned his position. He was not the first nor the last valued instructor whom this institution has lost by reason of its meager financial resources. John F. White, B.S., who was graduated in the same class with Prof. Crow, was made Professor of Natural Science. Going to Harvard University to pursue his chemical studies, he was made assistant professor there, continuing several years in that position. Prof. Albert McGinnis, A.M., who graduated in 1878, and afterward studied in Leipsic, Germany, was elected to the chair of Greek and Latin, and proved a most thorough and successful teacher. He recently resigned this position to accept the chair of Belles-Lettres and the vice-presidency of Lincoln University, Illinois.

Among other graduates of Waynesburg College who served for a time as members of its faculty were James R. Rinehart, Lewis Sayers, John S. Hughes, H. D. Patton, J. C. Gwynn, and A. T. Silveus. Among the ladies who, after their graduation from this institution, proved efficient teachers in it, Dr. Miller mentions Miss Martha Bayard, now Mrs. J. M. Howard, of Nashville, Tennessee; Miss Minerva Lindsey, now Mrs. A. Freeman, of Colorado; Miss Juliet E. Barclay, now Mrs. Wilson, of Iowa; Miss M. C. Carter, afterward Mrs. W. L. Parkinson, and since deceased; Miss M. Lou Hager, now Mrs. M. L. Smith, of Illinois; Mrs. Estelle Biddle Clark, now of Nashville, Tennessee; and Miss Emma J. Downey, afterward Mrs. S. F. Hoge, now deceased.

As the Theological School, as well as all the other departments of Cumberland University, at Lebanon, Tennessee, was closed during the civil war, the necessity for some facilities for the theological training of our young men preparing for the ministry became pressing. From the Minutes of the General Assembly we learn that Pennsylvania Synod, in connection with the board of trustees of Waynesburg College, was, in 1863, "making efforts to establish a Chair of Theology." The Rev. S. T. Anderson, D.D., was elected to this professorship. He entered upon his duties in the autumn of 1864, and was also made vice-president of the college. In connection with his duties as pastor of the Waynesburg congregation, he did good service for several years as teacher of Hebrew and ethics. This theological professorship, being without endowment, was not made permanent. No successor to Dr. Anderson was elected.

In the autumn of 1873 "the purpose to erect a new building for the college was projected." A magnificent edifice, with splendid rooms for recitations, for libraries, apparatus, and all other requirements of a first-class college, was planned. In the erection of this building debts have been avoided, and the progress of the work has therefore been slow. Most of the rooms are now finished, and it is "the finest single college building in western Pennsylvania," and by far the most beautiful and imposing structure of the kind ever erected by Cumberland Presbyterians.

We have already seen that in 1840, when Pennsylvania Synod decided to act in its own individual capacity in establishing and sustaining a college, it resolved to raise thirty thousand dollars for endowment. Pennsylvania Presbytery, ten years later, when it accepted the control of Waynesburg College, determined to raise an endowment, and again the mark was set at thirty thousand dollars. When the institution was handed over to the Synod's control, the plan already adopted by the presbytery was continued. The congregations were canvassed by agents. In the General Assembly of 1853 the Committee on Education reported that the funds for the endowment of this school were in part already raised. A similar report next year says the endowment then secured was from three thousand to five thousand dollars. In 1855 fifteen thousand dollars was reported, and the next year the Minutes state that nearly thirty thousand dollars had been recently raised. The report of 1863 places the sum at twenty-five thousand dollars; that of 1865 at thirty-five thousand dollars. In succeeding years still larger sums were reported.

Up to 1881 all the endowment raised for this institution was by the sale of scholarships. A perpetual scholarship was sold for one hundred dollars, and a full course scholarship for thirty dollars. These scholarships were transferable, and could be used immediately. Ten or twenty thousand dollars raised in this way would create scholarships enough to crowd the college with students without yielding an income large enough to support one teacher. "It was," says Dr. Miller, "certainly an error to allow students to use these scholarships before a sufficient fund had been secured to support the required number of professors. As it was, the plan left no tuition fees, and but little in the stead." Purchasers were not required to pay actual cash for the scholarships, but only gave their notes, with the privilege of retaining the principal so long as they paid the annual interest. This interest often proved hard to collect, and many of the notes reported from time to time as endowment proved worthless. President Miller's sketch, written in 1878, says: "Any thing like an exact estimate of the amount of *reliable* endowment at this time can not be given, though the amount is certainly not less than at any previous period, recent additions fully making up for losses during the last three years of financial failures."

The year 1881 was observed by Pennsylvania Cumberland Presbyterians as a sort of denominational jubilee. Fifty years before, the missionaries sent by the General Assembly began their work in that field. The Pennsylvania Synod had recommended that an effort should be made to raise a sum sufficient to complete the endowment of three professorships as a fit offering to commemorate this semi-centennial year. Thirty thousand dollars was afterward fixed as the sum to be raised "as a semi-centennial offering." Mainly through the persistent efforts of the Rev. P. H. Crider, cash and notes reaching this amount were secured. Efforts further to increase the endowment are still continued, and the financial condition of the school is now more hopeful than ever before.

Up to the year 1878 over two thousand students had been enrolled in the several classes and departments of Waynesburg College. In the years which have followed hundreds of others have been added to the list. This school is not only a center of education and culture, but it has exercised a permanent and wide-spread religious influence. It has been the center of numerous revivals, in some of which nearly every student has been enlisted either as a worker or a convert. Speaking of the importance of the work and influence of Waynesburg College, President Miller says: "The money put into this institution, the prayers of the church in its behalf, and the labors and sacrifices of those who have been its faithful instructors, have been indeed as the 'handful of corn in the earth on the top of the mountain,' the fruit of which already shakes like Lebanon. Standing like a bulwark and a lighthouse on the eastern border of our denomination, it seems to me not only indispensable to the synod that controls it, but in some measure as involving in its future career the destiny of the Cumberland Presbyterian church."

LINCOLN UNIVERSITY.

Lincoln University was founded in the year 1864 by the Synods of Indiana, Sangamon, Central Illinois, Illinois, and Iowa. The civil war then raging had so divided the country that it was no longer practicable or indeed possible for the churches of the Northwest to patronize the schools in the South. These churches were compelled to establish schools for the education of their children.

Long before the war attempts were made in various parts of the country north of the Ohio to found schools of a high order. In the States of Ohio, Pennsylvania, Indiana, Illinois, and Iowa academies and colleges were started, and many of them accomplished much good in the cause of Christian education. At Virginia, Illinois, Union College did good service for a number of years. The same may be said of Cherry Grove Seminary and Mt. Zion Academy in Illinois, and Delany Academy, in Indiana.

When the States of the North-west established public schools, these academies for the want of sufficient endowment were forced to suspend operations. At the beginning of the war the free schools were in full blast, and they were at that time very popular. Private and denominational schools were almost entirely deserted. The churches of all denominations saw that if they would have the education of their children under their own care, they must build schools which could compete with and even surpass the schools of the State. Long years of struggle and anxiety passed away. Good men prayed and wrestled with the grave problem before them. At the meetings of presbyteries and synods, and in private gatherings, the subject of education was discussed.

In the darkest days of our civil strife the good men who stood by the church in the North-west did not abandon the cause of Christian education. It has often been charged against Cumberland Presbyterians that they oppose education. But no better evidence of their devotion to this cause can be given than the repeated and heroic struggles they put forth in the North-west in behalf of higher education. There was scarcely a presbytery in all that region that did not attempt to establish a school of high grade. All their efforts were not successful, nor were all of them wise and judicious, but the zeal of the people is to be commended if their judgment is not.

The war caused our people to feel more keenly and deeply than ever before the need of schools, and, at a time when thousands were faltering and ready to give up, the idea of founding Lincoln University was conceived. It is not known who was the first to suggest the idea. It is probable that the suggestion grew out of many anxious and prayerful conferences of brethren. There were at that time a number of educated and devoted ministers in the territory here mentioned. Among this number none stood higher than the Rev. Azel Freeman, D.D. He lived at Newburgh, Indiana, and was engaged in teaching in Delany Academy as its principal. He was a man of great and earnest piety, a most devout Christian scholar. He was always an ardent supporter of the cause of learning. The Rev. J. B. Logan, D.D., a man of great energy and activity, was editing a paper at Alton, Illinois, the *Western Cumberland Presbyterian*. He earnestly advocated the establishment of schools for the better education of the rising ministry. The columns of his paper were open for the discussion of this subject.

Dr. Freeman wrote many articles on the importance of a well-endowed school in the West.

It was in the Synod of Indiana, I think, that the suggestion of a school under the combined patronage of the five synods was first made. It is probable that the resolution passed by that synod was written by Dr. Freeman. At any rate he was one of its most enthusiastic advocates, and it was due to his sagacity and urgent appeals that the measure got before the Synods of Illinois and Iowa. When the proposition was once made, it became very popular. All over the three States the matter was discussed with great earnestness and approved with great unanimity.

Commissioners were appointed in the fall of 1864 to prosecute the work. They wrote and talked in the interest of the new movement. By order of the synods they advertised for bids for the location of the institution. Several places were put in nomination. Newburgh, Indiana, and Mt. Zion, Cherry Grove, Virginia, and Lincoln, Illinois, were the most prominent places in the contest. The commissioners visited each of the rival towns and heard the propositions of the people. Lincoln was finally chosen as the most eligible and suitable location for the new school. The citizens of that enterprising and flourishing young town made a very generous offer. They agreed to erect a building worth not less than thirty thousand dollars. The commissioners on their part pledged the church for fifty thousand dollars endowment. The agreement was that the school should not begin operations until the money was all raised.

A board of trustees was appointed and a charter was obtained. The institution was chartered as a university—a great mistake. Agents were sent into the field to secure endowment. The plan for endowing the institution was devised by the board of trustees. They had had but little experience in the work of building and endowing universities. They adopted the plan of selling scholarships, in order to secure the needed fund. Scholarships giving very great advantages were sold at very low figures. A two hundred dollar scholarship was made practically perpetual. It secured the tuition of one scholar at a time in the literary department. Five hundred dollars procured a scholarship admitting the pupil to all the departments of the proposed university. The liberal terms of the scholarships and the inflated condition of the currency made it very easy to sell them. Many bought them under the impression that they were making a good investment. The agents soon succeeded in raising in notes the sum agreed upon. Dr. Freeman did excellent service in this work of securing endowment. He raised about thirty thousand dollars of the fifty thousand. The Rev. James Ritchey, of Indiana, was also a very active and successful agent. Richard M. Beard, Esq., from first to last, was perhaps the most successful agent in the field. There was a great deal of enthusiasm in this work, and it was done in a very short time.

In the meantime the people of Lincoln began work on the building. In the year 1865 the corner-stone was laid. The governor of the State, Gen. Richard J. Oglesby, delivered the oration at the laying of the corner-stone. It was a grand day in the history of the church in the North-west. It is due to the people of Lincoln to say that they did far better than they agreed to do. Instead of a thirty thousand dollar house, such as they had agreed to build, they laid the foundation for a building, which when completed cost about sixty thousand dollars. By far the greater part of this sum was given by the people of the town.

It must be remembered that the currency was badly inflated at the time the work was undertaken. The money contributed to the endowment was not worth more than fifty cents on the dollar. Many who subscribed in flush times had to make their payments in hard times. This caused a great falling off in the collections. Many who had pledged contributions failed in business, and many others failed to pay. The trustees, however, did not stop at fifty thousand dollars. Agents were kept in the field nearly all the time for years. They more than made good the losses.

The school was opened in the year 1866, on the 16th day of November. The faculty consisted of the Rev. A. Freeman, D.D., President; the Rev. S. Richards, A.M., Professor of Ancient Languages; the Rev. A. J. McGlumphy, A.M., Professor of Mathematics; J. B. Latimer, A.B., Professor of Natural Sciences; Mrs. Mary E. Miller, Matron, and Teacher of English Literature. The school was co-educational from the first. The course of study laid down by the first faculty was full and complete. Young ladies were admitted to all the classes on terms exactly the same as those required of the young men.

The first year was typical in the history of the institution. During that time nearly all the main features of the school were outlined by its able and scholarly faculty, and particularly by its noble president. It is due to Dr. Freeman more than to any other man that the policy which has ever since guided the faculty in the management of the school was developed. The organization of classes, the formation of literary societies, the foundation of the library, the rules and the government of the institution were all developed by that most devout scholar and teacher and his assistants. He was at the head of the institution four years and during that time he showed a zeal and devotion to the school which has never been surpassed by any man in the church. He perhaps placed too many restrictions upon students. But the law of kindness was on his tongue, and he governed by love. He was driven from his great work by the unwise clamors of a few who were too zealous of orthodoxy. He held views not unlike those held by the professors of Andover Seminary in Massachusetts. These views he never sought to propagate. As a teacher of youth he never inflicted his theological opinions upon any one. If he had been at the head of a theological seminary there might have been some excuse for the war that was made upon him. After serving the institution most satisfactorily for four years, he retired without a word of remonstrance, and pursued a course worthy of all admiration.

He was succeeded by the Rev. J. C. Bowdon, D.D., who was pastor of the church at Evansville, Indiana. Dr. Bowdon was a man of great vivacity, most genial manners, and fine intellectual powers. He ruled by a method entirely different from that employed by his predecessor. He made but few rules, and yet he was universally loved and obeyed. He gave the institution a new impetus in the line of culture. Dr. Freeman was a man for thorough scholarship; Dr. Bowdon gave more thought to culture and social life. He made the faculty and the school the center of the social life of the community. He inspired young men with an ambition for the highest social as well as literary culture. He taught more by example than by precept. Never was there a more genial or more companionable man. He had a vast fund of humor and wit ever at ready command. He was a preacher of strong powers, and wherever he went he made a profound impression for the cause he represented. He had a great power over a popular audience. It was due to him largely that the school gained a wide popularity throughout the entire church. He was born and educated at the South, and he had hosts of friends and admirers in every part of the denomination. His brief career ended before he had time to develop his purposes. He died while in office in the year 1873 among his old friends in Mississippi, and there he was buried. He was loved as few men are ever loved.

The Rev. A. J. McGlumphy, D.D., LL.D., was elected to fill the vacancy caused by the death of Dr. Bowdon. He entered upon the duties of his office in the year 1873, and continued in that position until June, 1887. President McGlumphy was a good executive and an admirable teacher. During his administration an effort was made to start a law school and also a theological department. The Hon. R. C. Ewing, of Missouri, a son of Finis Ewing, was elected Professor of Law. He organized classes and had a number of pupils. About fourteen young men entered the school and studied through one year. The tuition was necessarily small and the attendance was not large. The want of funds compelled the trustees to suspend this school. About the same time the department of theology was opened, with the Rev. S. Richards, D.D., as Professor of Systematic Theology. There were but three or four pupils, and no money to support the teacher, and the undertaking had to be abandoned.

During this time the currency of the country had resumed a more healthy condition. Interest on money began to go down. No tuition was paid by students. The cheap scholarships that were sold to secure endowment were at the command of all who wished to use them. They drove tuition out, and it was impossible to increase the number of the faculty at a time when the number of the students was nearly double what it ought to have been. Nearly all the schools in the country where the patronage of the university came from had enlarged their faculties, and had put into their courses of study new departments. The competing schools had the advantage in wealth, and the people soon began to take advantage of the better opportunities that were offered them elsewhere. The trustees had no money to employ additional teachers, and none to procure libraries, apparatus, and museums. The result was a great falling off in attendance. Efforts were made time and again to increase the endowment. Most of the patrons had scholarships, and they did not see the necessity for more money. After years of struggle against odds and difficulties, President McGlumphy resigned.

The work of this institution, however, has by no means been a failure. It has more money now than any school in the church. There are nearly one hundred thousand dollars secured to the university, most of which is productive. There are many friends of the institution who are determined to stand by it. It has graduated some of the best scholars in the church. Its graduates take high rank in the ministry of the denomination. Several of them have been graduated in theology at Lebanon, Tennessee, Union Theological Seminary, New York, and elsewhere. A number of the graduates are prominent teachers in some of the best schools of the country. Hundreds of former students of this institution are useful members of the church. Two of them are missionaries in foreign lands, and two others have been accepted by the Board of Missions for the work in Japan, and are now preparing for their departure to that country.

The institution has always maintained a high standard of scholarship. No school in the church has more conscientiously adhered to the course of study laid down in its catalogue. No student can graduate who does not maintain a high grade of scholarship throughout the entire course.

Among the members of the faculty who have done valuable service in the institution should be mentioned Professor A. R. Taylor, A.M., Ph.D., who is now principal of the State Normal School of Kansas. For ten years he filled the chair of natural sciences with great ability. His enthusiasm in the class-room, his devotion to his pupils, and his accurate learning made him one of the most useful men in the church. As a disciplinarian and a

Christian educator he has had but few equals in the denomination. Under his instruction the natural science department became very popular, and his classes were always filled with the most eager and enthusiastic pupils. In 1882 he resigned to take charge of the important institution of which he is the successful president.

Another successful teacher in the university was Professor William Mariner, who for many years was a shining light in Cumberland University. He occupied the chair of Latin four years. His exact and painstaking scholarship and his rigid adherence to college methods did much to elevate the scholarship of this young and promising institution of the church. It was only the want of funds that compelled the board of trustees to accept his resignation. He was a man of great and varied general information, and he inspired young men and women to study that they might reach the high standard of learning to which their preceptor had attained. Since his resignation he has lived in Washington Territory, but in whatever sphere he lives and labors he carries with him the true scholarly spirit, and surrounds himself with an influence which brings him honor and respect. The Rev. B. F. McCord, A.M., Ph.D., filled the chair of Mathematics for fourteen years. He is a man of fine ability, correct literary taste, and excellent scholarship. He was graduated at the State University of Indiana, where he ranked at the head of the large class of which he was a member. In the school-room he was master of his subject. He taught with great enthusiasm and inspired his pupils with a love of study. In the summer of 1887 failing health caused him to seek relief from the work of the class-room in the less wearing duties of a business life.

Among the trustees there are several men whose self-sacrificing devotion to the institution deserves special mention. While the trustees have made mistakes, it will readily be granted by all who know the history of the school that they have been guided by the most unselfish motives in all their transactions. For nearly twenty years Col. Robert B. Latham was a member of the board—during the greater part of the time its president. He was always ready to make any sacrifice in his power to promote the good of the university. Being the best known citizen of the town and the county in which he lived, and still lives, he gave the school a good name throughout the State. His interest in the town and the community was always great, and every enterprise calculated to promote the welfare of his fellow-citizens secured his zealous support. He has always been a firm friend of the cause of education, and has given much wise counsel and years of earnest service to Lincoln University. He gave liberally of his means to secure the location of the school, and was ever ready to lead in any thing calculated to help the university. For years his beautiful and spacious house was thrown open with the most generous hospitality on Commencement occasions to receive the students, the faculty, and their friends. Not being a member of the Cumberland Presbyterian church, he deserves this honorable mention as a friend and generous benefactor to one of its most important enterprises.

The Hon. William B. Jones, for many years treasurer of the board of trustees, deserves respectful mention for the great interest which he has ever showed in the prosperity of the school. He labored hard for years to keep the finances in good condition. Much of his time was generously devoted to the interest of the college. He has frequently written for the church papers in behalf of the institution. Mr. George W. Edgar, an elder in the Lincoln congregation, has been a member of the board of trustees since the school was first organized. He has given freely of his money in the support of the college, and has been very liberal with his time in looking after the building and grounds. His home has always been open to the friends and patrons of Lincoln University. There are many other persons whose labors have contributed to the prosperity of the institution. It would require more space than can be given to the subject to record the deeds of all who are worthy of special mention. Such men as Samuel C. Parks, James A. Hudson, A. C. Boyd, the Rev. W. C. Bell, and the Rev. F. Bridgman have served as trustees with great fidelity and usefulness.

Among the endowing agents who have from first to last been engaged in working for the college must be mentioned the Rev. J. A. Chase, the Rev. Jesse S. Grider, and the Rev. J. C. Van Patten. They all did good work at various times. The Rev. J. S. Grider acted as agent but one year, but during that time he did a very valuable work. He secured in notes and bequests about thirty-five thousand dollars. One bequest of ten thousand dollars obtained by him has already been realized. It was made by Mr. Alfred Bryan, of Logan county, Illinois, who was for many years an active elder in the congregation known as Sugar Creek.

Lincoln University has been in existence but little over twenty years, but it may be safely said that no school in the church has done a better work in that time. It has graduated in the literary department alone just 186 pupils. These men and women are for the most part members in the Cumberland Presbyterian church, and in the General Assembly and our missionary boards, and in all the councils of the church, their influence is felt and acknowledged.

The foregoing sketch of Lincoln University is furnished for this volume by the Rev. D. M. Harris, D.D., Ph.D., who became Professor of Natural Science in that institution in the fall of 1868. He served in that position two years. In the fall of 1871 he was elected to the chair of Greek and Latin. He filled this important position with great ability until 1883. He did much to build up the interests of the institution and to promote thorough classical scholarship among the students. After nearly fifteen years of faithful and valuable service as a member of the faculty, he resigned and accepted his present position as editor of the *Cumberland Presbyterian* at Nashville, Tennessee.

In June, 1887, President McGlumphy and the entire faculty of this institution resigned. Subsequently A. E. Turner, A.M., Professor of Natural Sciences, was re-elected, and he has resumed the duties of that chair. Theodore F. Brantley was also re-elected to the chair of Greek and Latin, but did not accept it. Albert McGinnis, A.M., was elected Professor of Belles-Lettres, and vice-president, and he is at this time (October, 1887,) acting president. Albert T. Davis, A.B., of Hyde Park, Mass., was chosen Professor of Greek and Latin; I. W. P. Buchanan, A.B., Professor of Mathematics.

The full list of teachers in the Literary and Scientific department from the organization of this institution to the present time is as follows:

Presidents and Professors of Mental and Moral Philosophy.—Rev. A. Freeman, D.D., Rev. J. C. Bowdon, D.D., Rev. A. J. McGlumphy, D.D., LL.D.

Professors of Mathematics.—Rev. A. J. McGlumphy, A.M., Rev. B. F. McCord, A.M., Ph.D., I. W. P. Buchanan, A.B.

Professors of Ancient Languages.—Rev. S. Richards, D.D., Rev. D. M. Harris, D.D., Ph.D., William Mariner, A.M., Theodore Brantley, A.M., and Albert T. Davis, A.B.

Professors of Natural Sciences.—J. F. Latimer, A.M., Rev. D. M. Harris, A.M., A. R. Taylor, Ph.B., O. A. Keach, Ph.B., Rev. W. J. McDavid, A.M., Charles R. Krone, A.M., and A. E. Turner, A.M.

Professor of Belles-Lettres.—Albert McGinnis, A.M.

Professors of Elocution.—S. S. Hamil, A.M., Mrs. E. W. Felt, Rev. L. P. Marshall, A.B.

Matrons, and Teachers of English Literature.—Mrs. M. E. Miller, Miss Minerva Lindsey, Mrs. C. E. W. Miller, and Miss S. J. McCord.

Tutors.—J. R. Starkey, A.M., A. H. Mills, A.M., A. E. Turner, A.M., and M. A. Montgomery, A.M.

There are four literary societies connected with the university—the Neatrophean, the Amicitian, the Amasagacian, and Athenian. The first two are for ladies, and the others for gentlemen.

The property and assets of the university consist of:

A campus and buildings worth	$ 60,000
Furniture, library, and fixtures	5,000
Endowment fund invested and otherwise available	60,000
Endowment, good, but not yet available	40,000
Total property and assets	$165,000

TRINITY UNIVERSITY.[1]

Soon after the close of the civil war, there seems to have been a general sentiment among Cumberland Presbyterians in Texas

---

[1] This sketch of Trinity University is the work of a committee appointed by a voluntary meeting of ministers and members of the church in Texas, who were in attendance at the General Assembly, at Waco, in May, 1888. The committee consisted of J. A. Ward, D.D., H. F. Bone, D.D., E. B. Crisman, D.D., Rev. J. H. Wofford, and Rev. D. S. Crawford. It was prepared in June, 1888.

that the church ought to have in this State an institution of learning of high order, to supply facilities for the education of the children of the church in the State, and especially for the training of young men preparing for the ministry. Our people have manifested, in every State where they have established churches, their appreciation of thorough education. The pioneers of the church in Texas were not less appreciative and diligent in this respect than had been those of the older States. Before the civil war, three Cumberland Presbyterian colleges were in successful operation in the State, viz.: Chapel Hill, at Daingerfield; Larissa, at Larissa; and Ewing, at La Grange; besides other smaller schools.

It is here noted as a remarkable illustration of unselfish magnanimity that when the proposition was made to establish a central school of higher order, for general patronage, it had no warmer friends nor more ardent supporters than the men who had been managing the several colleges in the State. Brief sketches of the three pioneer colleges already named are here given.

Chapel Hill College was projected by the Marshall Presbytery, in the fall of 1849. A presbyterial committee located it at Daingerfield. At the fall meeting of the presbytery, 1850, a Board of Trustees was appointed, and a charter for a male school was that year obtained. A two-story wooden house was first built, and afterward a two-story house of brick. Prof. Fleming taught a primary school while the first house was in process of erection. The Rev. S. R. Chadick taught the first session in the new building, from February to June, 1852. He afterward had charge of the Preparatory Department, until 1856, when he resigned. The Rev. W. E. Beeson came to the school from Kentucky, March, 1852; and he and Mr. Chadick conducted the school for two years. The catalogue, during this period, shows the attendance of one hundred and seventy pupils, with patronage from Arkansas and Louisiana, as well as Texas. In the fall of 1853, Mr. Beeson was elected president, and held that position until he was elected President of Trinity University, in 1869. The Rev. S. T. Anderson, a graduate of Cumberland University, became Professor of Mathematics in 1855, and served until 1857, when he resigned. S. M. Ward, a graduate of the school, had charge of the Preparatory

Department from 1857 to 1860, and was Professor of Mathematics from 1860 to 1865. After 1869, the Rev. W. M. Allen was elected president, and conducted the school a year. Then the Rev. J. B. Renfro had charge until his death. Then the school was closed. From the beginning, the teachers of this school relied on tuition fees alone for their support, and taught free many young men preparing for the ministry, most of whom were also boarded without charge, either by teachers or citizens. Of the preachers educated there, the following are among the living: Benjamin Spencer, D.D., J. A. Ward, D.D., J. S. Patton, W. S. Glass, S. E. Black, and J. C. Blanton. Among the dead are W. Burgess Modrall, C. C. Givens, S. M. Johnston, T. W. Sego, Jerre Shetter, A. W. Johnston, and Y. H. Hamilton. Among the warmest and most efficient friends this school had, was the Rev. S. Awalt; and he has been equally earnest and active in helping forward other enterprises of the church in Texas.

Larissa College, located at Larissa, Texas, had its origin in the generosity of two noble elders, T. H. McKee and Nathaniel Killough, who each gave one thousand dollars to start the enterprise. The institution was chartered as a mixed school in 1855, and placed under the control of the Brazos Synod, with the Rev. F. L. Yoakum at its head. Larissa was a good location, and Mr. Yoakum and the Rev. J. B. Renfro, who was also connected with the school, were excellent educators. The prospects of the institution were flattering until the war. Its last catalogue numbered three hundred and thirty-seven pupils. Many who received training in its classes fill high positions of public trust. After the war, the trustees disposed of the property, and gave the proceeds to Trinity University. Mr. Yoakum had spent many years collecting a geological cabinet, which he donated to the University.

Ewing College, at La Grange, had its origin in the efforts and liberality of the Rev. A. H. Walker, the pastor, and the elders of the church at that place—Hiram Ferrell, W. B. McClellan, and I. B. McFarland. It was chartered by the legislature in 1852, as "The La Grange Collegiate Institute," to be under the care and control of the Colorado Presbytery. In 1854, the Colorado Synod was organized, and by amendment of the charter, the name of the school was changed to Ewing College, and its control transferred to the synod. In 1855, Prof. R. P. Decherd became president, and the school flourished under his management, and promised to become a permanent institution. Its work was stopped by the breaking out of the war. The close of the war found Prof. Decherd in charge of a school at Waco; Elder Ferrell was dead, and McClellan and McFarland had moved to Austin. Neither church nor school was ever revived at La Grange. Prof. Decherd afterward served with success as Professor of Mathematics in Trinity University. He died in 1887.

In the year 1866, each of the three synods of Texas, acting in concert, appointed a committee to consider jointly the propriety of establishing at that time such an institution of high order as the church in the State seemed to demand. The thought of such a school seems to have originated with the Rev. H. F. Bone and the Rev. A. J. Haynes at Corsicana. By them, with other brethren concurring, the proposition was made to the synods simultaneously.

The joint committee, thus appointed, met for consultation at Dallas, in December, 1867. The conclusion was reached that the immediate establishment of such an institution was not only desirable, but entirely practicable, and a report was submitted to the several synods, recommending its early location. It was stipulated that no point should be considered in selecting a location, unless twenty-five thousand dollars had first been raised as a bonus.

On the reception of this report, the synods appointed other committees of four each, to act jointly in selecting a location. In addition to making the location, the committees were instructed to take the steps necessary to put the institution in active operation.

Dallas, Round Rock, Tehuacana, and Waxahachie, each raised the required bonus. The joint committee met first at Tehuacana, November 14, 1868. After examining Tehuacana, the committee visited Dallas and Waxahachie, and most of the members visited Round Rock. They met for final action at Waco, April 20, 1869. After two days of deliberation, Tehuacana was chosen by unanimous vote, and Trinity University selected as the name.

The committee then arranged for opening the school by appointing a committee to procure a charter, naming the trustees, making temporary arrangements to pay teachers, and electing members of the faculty. T. B. Wilson, D.D., was chosen president, and the Rev. W. E. Beeson, the Rev. S. Doak Lowry, and the Rev. W. P. Gillespie, Professors. Agents were appointed to raise permanent endowment in the bounds of the synods, and were authorized to sell perpetual scholarships in the Literary Department for five hundred dollars, and five-year scholarships for one hundred and fifty dollars. The trustees were requested to organize as soon as practicable, and to take steps to put the school in operation by the first Monday in September, 1869. The committee finally adjourned, April 23, 1869, after a session of four days.

The point selected as a location had been previously known as Tehuacana Hills, sometimes Tehuacana Springs. It was not a business point, as it had only one very small trading house; and yet, such were its natural advantages as to water, health, and scenery, and its centrality as to population and territory in the State, that it had, twenty years before its selection by this committee, been in the race with Austin for the permanent seat of government, and was defeated by a very small majority. It is on an eminence or prolonged hill, in a prairie. There are many springs of water coming out on and around this elevation, besides water can be obtained in abundance by wells. The largest of these springs and many of the wells are rarely affected by droughts. Being free from temptations to vice, extravagance, and idleness, it is eminently fitted to be a seat of learning. In the particular of health, it is probably not surpassed in the State.

The bonus given by the friends of Tehuacana for the location, consisted entirely of real estate. Among the items, Maj. John Boyd had donated one hundred and thirty acres on the hill, on which the plot of the town of Tehuacana was afterward made, and on which the University building now stands, and a tract of fourteen hundred acres in the valley a half mile north-west. This last was subsequently sold in lots of twenty acres each, and the proceeds applied to erecting buildings, as were also the proceeds of the sale of lots in the town plot. Also, a company of friends of the enterprise, who had bought fourteen hundred and twenty acres of land, lying a half mile from the present building, donated to the school fifty acres of this tract, on which stood a large wooden residence, with eight rooms. In this house the school was opened in September, 1869, but the patronage soon outgrew the house, and another building became a necessity. The estimates put on the value of the lands donated to secure the location were high. Soon came the times of money stringency, and general shrinkage in values. The amount realized from sales was far short of the original estimates, and the buildings which were erected after the school opened have been paid for in large part by additional donations. In 1871, a new building of stone, with a large chapel and eleven other rooms, was projected, and the Rev. Alpha Young was appointed to manage its erection. In 1873, the school moved into this new building. It cost twenty-five thousand dollars. In 1886, extensive additions to this building were projected, to cost about twenty thousand dollars. On these additions, twelve thousand dollars has already been expended, and when they are completed, this school will have a most commodious building, substantial, and of great architectural beauty.

As the school began without a dollar of endowment, and projected its salaries for teachers at high rates—two thousand dollars for the president, and fifteen hundred dollars for professors—and as money depressions soon came, the trustees have had a long and hard struggle in keeping first-class teachers, erecting buildings, and securing endowment, and at the same time, avoiding debt. But in all these particulars they have succeeded, and the present status of the school is a monument to their caution and skill.

August 13, 1870, the legislature of Texas granted the school a charter, having the following as its most important provisions:

1. The corporate trustees were nine in number.
2. To the Board of Trustees was given the direct control and management of the institution.
3. The several synods of the Cumberland Presbyterian church of Texas were to have a general advisory supervision of the same.
4. The board once in each year was required to report to the synods the condition of the institution.
5. The school was to consist of both male and female departments, and was authorized to establish departments of law, medicine, theology, and other departments.

6. All property acquired by this institution was to be held by the board, in trust for the Cumberland Presbyterian church in Texas, with power to sell and manage the same for the benefit of the institution.

7. A majority of the board was to constitute a quorum for the transaction of all business except the election or removal of a member of the faculty, which requires the concurrence of at least two thirds of the members of the board. No meeting of the board was to be held elsewhere than at the institution, nor was any member of the board permitted to reside at a greater distance than twelve miles therefrom.

8. The successors of the corporate trustees were to be appointed by the three synods in Texas, three by each, and to hold office during the pleasure of the synod appointing them.

9. Any additional synod which might, after the granting of the charter, be organized in Texas, was to have the same rights and privileges, and thus the number of trustees would be increased.

10. The property owned and held by the institution, being set apart exclusively for educational purposes, was declared exempt from both State and county taxation.

An amendment to the charter in 1877 provided that the number of trustees should be increased to four from each synod, except the Brazos, which was to have five; that one more than half of the trustees should reside within twelve miles of the institution; and that an increase of two for every additional synod which might be organized in the State, should be necessary to constitute a quorum. Since 1877, one additional synod has been organized; hence, the board now consists of seventeen trustees, nine of whom reside within twelve miles of the institution. A quorum at regular meetings is seven, and at called meetings, nine.

Only one man, Judge D. M. Prendergast, of Mexia, has been a member of the Board of Trustees for the whole nineteen years of the history of the institution. He has served the board as president since 1885. It had previously two presidents. The first was J. S. Wills, M.D., who moved from Tennessee to Cotton Gin, Freestone County, Texas, in 1848, and was a ruling elder in the Cumberland Presbyterian church at that place until his death, which occurred at his home, August 6, 1877. He served as President of the Board of Trustees from its organization to his death.

Judge L. B. Prendergast, second president of the board, was born in what is now Giles County, Tennessee, November 25, 1808.

His mother was a sister of the Rev. Samuel King. He moved to Texas in 1839, and was a ruling elder in the Cotton Gin congregation for many years before and up to the time of his death. He served as president of the board from the death of Dr. Wills, in 1877, to his own death, March 23, 1885.

The following persons have served as teachers in this school:

W. E. Beeson, President, 1869-77.
R. W. Pitman, Acting President, 1877-78.
W. E. Beeson, President, 1878-82.
S. T. Anderson, Acting President, 1882-83.
B. G. McLeskey, President, 1883-85.
L. A. Johnson, Acting President, 1885-87.
L. A. Johnson, President, 1887-.
W. P. Gillespie, Latin and Greek, 1869-77.
S. Doak Lowry, Mathematics, 1869-71.
Mrs. Kate Gillespie, Music, 1869-78.
Mrs. M. E. Beeson, Music, 1869-.
D. A. Quaite, Belles-lettres, 1870-71.
D. A. Quaite, Natural Science, 1871-73.
Wm. Hudson, Commercial Department, 1870-83.
Wm. Hudson, Natural Science, 1883-.
R. P. Decherd, Mathematics, 1871-77.
V. W. Grubbs, Assistant Com., 1871-72.
Carl Danneberg, Music, 1871-81.
Mrs. Danneberg, Art and Music, 1871-81.
Mrs. M. F. Foster, Preparatory Dept., 1872-84.
Miss S. R. Young, Primary Dept., 1872-86.
D. M. Prendergast, Law, 1872-73.
I. S. Davenport, Natural Science, 1873-76.
R. C. Ewing, Law, 1874-78.
R. A. Shaver Assistant Teacher, 1875-77.
Mrs. E. B. Boyd, French, 1875-86.
T. M. Goodknight, Natural Science, 1876-77.
S. Richards, Latin and Greek, 1877-78.
R. W. Pitman, Belles-lettres, 1877-78.
R. W. Pitman, Natural Science, 1878-81.

S. T. Anderson, Mathematics, 1877-83.
Miss S. J. McCord, Natural Science, 1877-78.
W. E. Beeson, Theology, 1877-82.
Miss V. Henderson, Primary Dept., 1877-78.
J. H. Gillespie, Com. Dept., 1879-80.
Mrs. M. E. Pitman, Music, 1879-81.
Mrs. Mary Anderson, Music, 1880-83.
S. M. Templeton, Adjt. Mathematics, 1881-85.
P. M. Riley, Adjt. Languages, 1881-82.
Miss Georgie Lay, Music, 1881-82.
Miss Bettie Teague, Music, 1882-83.
Miss C. Wolverton, Music, 1883-84.
J. H. Miller, Assistant Teacher, 1883-84.
D. S. Bodendamer, Assistant Teacher, 1883-85.
D. S. Bodenhamer, Mathematics, 1885-.
S. T. Anderson, Mathematics, 1884-85.
J. H. Gillespie, Business College, 1884-88.
J. M. Riggs, Music, 1884-.
Mrs. M. L. Eads, Music, 1884-86.
Mrs. A. M. Riggs, Art, 1884-.
Mrs. D. Beaumont, Elocution, 1884-86.
V. S. Nelson, Penmanship, 1884-86.
W. P. Gillespie, Latin and Greek, 1882-.
E. B. Crisman, Aston Ch., 1886-.
Mrs. Bodenhamer, Art, 1885-.
Miss Lura Bell, English Literature, 1886-.
N. J. Clancy, High School, 1886-.
Miss L. Carothers, Primary Dept., 1886-88.
E. B. Kuntz, German, 1885-.
Miss Bessie Bell, Grammar School, 1887-.

T. B. Wilson, D.D., having declined the presidency, the Board of Trustees, at their first meeting, in 1869, elected Rev. W. E. Beeson president. Under him the school was opened, and he continued president, excepting one year, until his death, in 1882. W. E. Beeson, D.D., was born in Berkley County, Virginia, October 21, 1822. His parents moved to Logan County, Kentucky, when he was a child. There he grew up and became a candidate for the ministry in the Logan Presbytery. He was educated at Cumberland University, graduating in 1849. He was teaching a school near Bowling Green, Kentucky, when called to Chapel Hill College, Texas, in 1852. He was attacked with his last illness while from home, canvassing in the interest of the University, and died at the house of Dr. Craig, near Hillsboro, September 5, 1882.

B. G. McLeskey, D.D., was born near Dresden, Tennessee, July 24, 1834. He was educated at Bethel College, Tennessee. He served as pastor at Brownsville, Paris, and McKenzie, Tennessee, and Sherman, Texas. In 1883 he became President of Trinity University, and served two years. He died at Tehuacana, October 25, 1885. His administration was an eminently successful one.

The patronage increased very rapidly for the first few years, and then declined. This resulted, mainly, from the fact that there were but few schools in the State when this one opened, compared with the greater number which were speedily established as railroads were built and towns and cities grew up. The proportion of ministerial matriculations for the first eleven years was one to every thirty; for the last eight years it has been one to every eleven. This shows a great increase of interest in the thorough education of the ministry; and is probably in large part due to the influence of this school in the State, and to the advantageous arrangements in reduced expenses it is enabled to give students preparing for the ministry.

Almost immediately after the opening of this school, the trustees appointed soliciting agents, and at no period have they failed to have one or more in the field seeking donations in cash, land, and notes for endowment or building fund, supplementing teachers' salaries, selling scholarships, and raising money for various smaller wants of the enterprise.

The following persons have acted as agents: J. H. Wofford, D. W. Broughton, J. B. Renfro, A. J. Haynes, W. D. Wear, F. E. Foster, J. W. Riggins, S. E. Black, E. B. Crisman, and J. W. Pearson.

Very soon after the establishment of this institution, our country experienced the most remarkable shrinkage in values known in its history, causing unusual financial stringency. Thus, during almost the whole history of this institution, it has been compelled to contend with the difficulties resulting from this state of finances. No record is found of its financial condition until the Treasurer's annual report, of 1879, which is recorded with the minutes of the Board of Trustees. Similar records had been kept previously in a separate book, and were lost in a fire some years ago.

According to the report of 1880, the value of the endowment was then $21,501, of which only $2,146 was productive. The largest item included in this estimate was 4,360 acres of land, valued at $8,720. The college building and the lands surrounding it, with furniture, laboratory, and cabinet, were valued at $28,600. The total value of endowment and property, less debt, was $48,231, which represents the proceeds of the bonus given for the location, all the donations of every kind for eleven years, and the sale of about thirty-five scholarships. Most of these scholarships were for twenty-five years.

The financial condition July 1, 1888, is shown in the following exhibit:

ENDOWMENT:

Lands, 3,506 acres, worth, say	$ 6,740 80
Notes and Claims	10,940 00
Conditional Notes	2,800 00
Bequests, in shape	29,000 00
Productive Endowment	29,410 25
Total Endowment	$78,891 05

PROPERTY:

University Building and surroundings	$40,530 00
Furniture, Pianos, etc.	2,000 00
Laboratory, Cabinet, etc.	2,500 00
Divinity Hall and Furniture	1,841 07
Subscriptions for New Building	1,594 00
Total Property	$48,965 07
Total Endowment and Property	$127,356 12
Less outstanding claims	750 00
Balance	$126,606 12

In this exhibit, the items of notes and claims are of uncertain value.

The record of scholarships sold by this institution was destroyed in the fire heretofore mentioned, and hence the exact number can not be given. During the earlier years, probably more than a dozen perpetual scholarships were sold at the rate of five hundred dollars each, a very few for cash, which was partly consumed in agents' salaries, others for lands, which subsequently proved of little value. A few of these, by a mistake of the trustees, were allowed to be changed into twenty-five-year scholarships, two for one. Also, about twenty twenty-five-year scholarships were sold for cash or land, at three hundred dollars each; likewise, some half-dozen five-year scholarships at one hundred and fifty dollars each. The sale of limited scholarships, the sale of scholarships of any kind for other than endowment purposes, and the allowing the exchange of one perpetual for two limited scholarships, are all crippling mistakes, which the trustees, who began without experience in such things, soon discovered and stopped. During the past eight years, eight of the scholarships have been secured by the school, either by donation or by purchase at low rates; the five-year scholarships have expired, and the comparatively few others still in force are not likely to give any serious inconvenience.

Several of the financial benefactors of this school, who are now deceased, deserve special mention. First among these is John Boyd, who was born at Nashville, Tennessee, August 7, 1795. He moved to eastern Texas in 1835, and located the league of land at Tehuacana in 1836, to which he moved in 1845. He secured the bonus for the location of Trinity University, being himself the chief contributor. He died May 4, 1873.

Thompson Fletcher Fowler was born in Missouri, March 22, 1836, and while yet a lad moved to Texas with his father, an elder of the church, settling in Burnet County. He moved to California in 1861, but returned to Texas in 1873, and settled in Milam County. In 1883, he contributed eight thousand dollars, known as the Fowler Endowment. The interest of this fund is to be used in aiding young men studying for the ministry in Trinity University, in the items of boarding, clothing, and books. Mr. Fowler's idea was that the school would furnish free tuition to such pupils, and he wanted to help as many as possible in their expense account, thus increasing the number who would reap the benefits of the school. He died June 14, 1886.

James Aston was born in Wilson County, Tennessee, October 10, 1804. He was a merchant, doing business in Hardeman County, Tennessee, ten years; in Memphis, Tennessee, two years, and in Coffeeville, Mississippi, thirty-nine years. He moved to Farmersville, Texas, in 1883. In September, 1885, he donated nine thousand dollars in cash, and land and claims in Mississippi, to endow the Aston Chair in honor of his father. He died June 10, 1887. He was a man of strong logical mind and of few words, liberal to the poor and unfortunate, temperate, and physically well preserved to the age of eighty-three.

The Rev. G. N. Morrison was born in Bedford County, Tennessee, July 27, 1825. In 1850, he moved to Benton County, Arkansas, and from there to Texas, in 1864. In the fall of 1886, he and his wife deeded their farm, in McLennan County, Texas, to the endowment, to take effect at the death of the last survivor of the two. He died at home, May 28, 1887. He was a man of great power in the pulpit and in private life. Other deceased benefactors were J. C. McCuiston, of Corsicana, and Mrs. Ann Judson Farris, of Walker County.

Many of the the living benefactors of the University also deserve mention. Rev. R. O. Watkins and his sons donated, in 1883, two hundred and fifty dollars, as the first payment on the building and lot for Watkins Divinity Hall, for a boarding-house on the clubbing plan for theological students.

Mrs. M. M. Johnson, the widow of the Rev. James Johnson, who is mentioned on page 376 of this book, is now spending a pleasant old age at Corsicana, Texas. In 1884 she and her four sons contributed five thousand dollars to endow partially the Johnson Professorship of Mathematics.

Of the twelve thousand dollars recently spent in building, a number of persons have contributed as much as five hundred dollars each, and others smaller amounts. These names are all on record in a better and more enduring book than this.

CHAPTER XLVI.

OTHER SCHOOLS AND COLLEGES.

Whoever would effectually serve the interests of religion must befriend the cause of education.—*S. G. Burney, D.D.*

THE four leading institutions of learning whose history is sketched in the last two chapters are not the only schools that have grown up under the patronage of the Cumberland Presbyterian church. Though this church had its origin among the pioneer settlers of Kentucky and Tennessee, far from literary and commercial centers; though its first members were hardy and simple-hearted backwoodsmen, who gave more attention to the felling of forest trees and the opening of farms in the wilderness than to books; though the scholastic training of many of its first preachers did not meet the requirements of the rigid Presbyterian rule; yet its ministers and people have ever been the friends and promoters of liberal education.

We have seen how efforts to establish schools were joined to the evangelistic and pastoral labors of our first missionaries in Pennsylvania and Ohio. The same thing was true wherever Cumberland Presbyterian congregations grew up. In Indiana and Illinois, in Missouri and Arkansas, as well as in Kentucky, Tennessee, and Texas, our people were pioneers in the work of establishing schools. Cherry Grove Seminary, near Abingdon, Knox County, Illinois, a Cumberland Presbyterian institution, opened its doors to students in 1842, but a little while after the Congregationalists from New England laid the foundations of Knox College in the same county. Spring River Academy was doubtless the first high school ever opened in south-western Missouri. It was founded by Ozark Presbytery, and went into operation under the superintendence of the Rev. J. B. Logan, in November, 1844. Delany Academy flourished at Newburgh, in southern Indiana, before any other school of similar grade had been established in that part of the State. Such pioneer institutions sprang up wherever our people gained a foothold.

It is true that many of these pioneer schools had but an ephemeral career. The methods and policy adopted were not always the wisest. Many of our people did not have a very correct understanding of what was needed in the founding of an institution of learning. But the history of these efforts shows that the first Cumberland Presbyterians did not lack the spirit of education. The report prepared in 1855 by the Rev. S. G. Burney, chairman of the Committee on Education, and adopted by the General Assembly, declares that:

The founders and early friends of the Cumberland Presbyterian church were disinherited of their church patrimony, and deprived of the benefits of those literary institutions which they and their ancestry, by their money and prayers, had contributed to establish. These temples of knowledge were closed against them, and against their sons and successors in the ministry. It is not, therefore, strange that they were not profoundly learned in this world's wisdom. The wonder is, rather, that they were learned at all. What is now considered a demonstration of an increased educational interest, or "waking up," is only the development of a spirit which has always existed. . . . The fact is, and probably will not be questioned by any who have inquired into the subject, that the Cumberland Presbyterian church has not only taken the initiative, but has actually accomplished more for the cause of education in the great valley of the West than any other association whatever, in proportion to numbers and resources.

We have had schools which flourished for a while under the name of colleges, but which never had any endowment, and have long ago ceased to exist. Some of these were supplied with such meager facilities as to make their pretentious titles most inappropriate. But while we should protest against calling every little school a college, we are not to forget that even one or two earnest teachers in a log-cabin may do a valuable work. Every one of these schools, however meager its resources or brief its career, doubtless wrought out some good results. The report on education adopted by the General Assembly of 1871, and signed by Dr. Richard Beard, chairman of the committee, contains these words:

This church commenced, in its ecclesiastical capacity, the work of education in 1826. It has had reverses and disappointments; still much has been done. . . . The great want with us in this work has been to give a practical direction to our efforts. We have not had the experience of ages to guide us. We have not had foundations laid by predecessors upon which we could build. We have had to work out our own experience; we have been compelled to lay our own foundations. The wonder is that we have succeeded so well.

If the church could grasp the true theory of graded schools and thorough preparatory academies, and would build them wherever needed, and refrain from assuming for them the titles and prerogatives of colleges, and make each grade tributary to the next higher, all parts of the church would reap immense advantages from such a policy. But if every little town starts its academy, and every academy tries to teach college classes, then we shall never have either college or university. Neither shall we ever have any academies of high reputation. Show me the academy with mixed studies that can stand beside the Phillips Academy, or the Bingham, or the Philadelphia High-school.

The Minutes of the General Assembly show not only that our people have always been enlisted with great earnestness in the work of education, but also that, more than forty years ago, the importance of concentrating the efforts of the church on a few leading institutions, and of building up a graded system of preparatory schools, was recognized and insisted on by our most thoughtful men. Robert Donnell was chairman of the Committee on Education in 1845. The report which he presented to the General Assembly, and which was adopted, declares that it would "greatly enhance the prosperity of the higher institutions . . . under the auspices of the denomination to encourage inferior schools throughout the bounds of the church;" and recommends "to the presbyteries, ministers, and all members of the church," a school system which was to embrace: "First, schools in the bounds of every congregation; second, a presbyterial school in the bounds of every presbytery. These," continues the report, "crowned by the university at Lebanon, and the colleges at Princeton, Beverly, and Uniontown, would constitute a system of education worthy of the best efforts of the church." In the establishment of congregational schools our people were advised to co-operate with other Christians. It was recommended that "every congregation and every session should struggle to keep up a school in its bounds at all events; should strive to arouse others to co-operate, but maintain a school under any circumstances." It was suggested, also, that the presbyterial schools might in this way set up an advanced standard of education, "thus, better than by any other method, qualifying the students to enter the university and colleges."

The necessity of adopting this graded system of schools was for several years urged by the successive General Assemblies. From the Minutes we learn that, in 1846, "numerous congregational, presbyterial, and synodical schools" had been planted and were enjoying a high degree of prosperity.

In 1847 the most gratifying progress of the educational work under the auspices of the church was reported. In 1848 the report of the Committee on Education, of which Dr. F. R. Cossitt was chairman, contained these words:

> We are gratified to find the cause of education winning the favor and enlisting the efforts of your people almost throughout your bounds. Various and valuable improvements have been made in the institutions heretofore existing, and several new seminaries have been put in operation, and there is cheering evidence to believe that the time is not distant when the recommendation of a former General Assembly will be carried out, and every congregation will sustain its school, and every presbytery and synod its seminary. These preparatory schools, acting in their vocation of fitting students for college and university, will become so many tributary streams supplying the fountains. There can be but little doubt that the system of education heretofore so wisely recommended, and now being in many parts efficiently conducted, will greatly advance the interests of the church.

In 1849 the recommendation favoring congregational and presbyterial preparatory schools was approved and renewed by the General Assembly. The report, which was presented by Milton Bird, chairman of the Committee on Education, says:

> We must be faithful to this cause. . . . Its importance is such as requires us to be more determined, vigorous, and consecrated in our efforts than ever, in order that it may be increasingly advanced by the

upbuilding of our seminaries, the enlarged endowment of our colleges, and the constant augmentation of the number of our students.

But in spite of the wise recommendations of the General Assembly, new colleges, as well as new academies and high schools, soon began to announce themselves. In 1851 the names of three colleges not mentioned before appear in the General Assembly's Minutes; in 1853, three others, one of them a college for young ladies, were added to the list; in 1854, two others, one for young ladies exclusively; in 1855, two more colleges were announced; in 1856, one more; in 1858, one; in 1859, three; and in 1860, two. As early as 1851 the General Assembly began to protest against this tendency to multiply schools with collegiate pretensions. The report adopted that year says:

We suggest the necessity of much prudence and caution, lest in the eagerness to build up colleges the church squander its means, paralyze its energies, and ultimately fail of raising its institutions to the high standard desired. To build a college worthy of the name is the result of years of patient endurance and unremitting energy, requiring the concentration of means and of effort. . . . If such an enterprise, when fairly undertaken, fails to succeed, such failure, besides proving disastrous to those immediately concerned, involves the reputation of the church under whose auspices it was commenced.

In 1855 the General Assembly declared that "one college in each State, judiciously located and well endowed, with primary and preparatory schools so placed as to meet the local interests of the church," was fully commensurate with the needs of the denomination. In 1856 the report of the Committee on Education, adopted by the General Assembly, after commending the "zeal shown in the upbuilding of institutions of learning," adds these words:

Yet your committee would respectfully suggest that you commend again . . . sound discretion, lest by the multiplication of the places of learning the force of a general educational effort be distracted, and institutions already established be left to be impoverished and paralyzed, to pine and perish. Reason and sound policy seem most clearly to indicate that it would be the better plan to cluster around our older seats of learning, and cause them, by our patronage and money, fully to meet the wants of the church.

In 1859 the General Assembly again warned our people against the danger of attempting to build up too many schools, declaring that "it is better to encourage co-operative efforts on the part of our congregations, presbyteries, and synods to establish a few church institutions of the highest order, than to divide means and influence in efforts to establish a large number of small church schools."

We learn from the General Assembly's Minutes that there were, in 1849, "sixteen chartered institutions belonging to the church, together with a number of other male and female high schools under the patronage of, and partly belonging to, the Cumberland Presbyterian church." In 1856, the report on education, adopted by the Assembly, says: "There are now under the control of the Cumberland Presbyterian church, in whole or in part, and all fully subserving its educational interests, about thirty institutions of learning of high order. Invested in these we find a capital of some $331,725; employed in the same seventy-eight teachers, and under a course of training two thousand four hundred and fifty pupils." The next year "thirty-six or more institutions of learning of high order" were reported, in which there were "about six thousand pupils, taught by one hundred and twelve professors."

In 1860 the names of twenty-nine schools and colleges were reported to the General Assembly. The list included "one university, fifteen colleges, and thirteen academies, institutes, and seminaries," and the report says that there were "various other high schools, taught and patronized by members of our church, yet not controlled by any ecclesiastical body." The names of the colleges reported at that time, not including Cumberland University, were: Waynesburg College, Waynesburg, Pennsylvania; Beverly College, Beverly, Ohio; Ewing and Jefferson College, Blount County, Tennessee; Princeton College, Princeton, Kentucky; Bethel College, McLemoresville, Tennessee; Chapel Hill College, Daingerfield, Texas; Missouri Female College, Boonville, Missouri; Larissa College, Larissa, Texas; Cane Hill College, Washington County, Arkansas; McGee College, College Mound, Missouri; Columbia College, Eugene City, Oregon; Union College, Virginia, Illinois; Union Female College, Oxford, Mississippi; Cumberland Female College, McMinnville, Tennessee; Bacon College, Texas.

Chapel Hill College, Missouri, was for some reason omitted from this list. This school is mentioned in the Assembly's Minutes for 1849 as a chartered institution with several professors. In 1851 it reported one hundred and forty students and nine thousand dollars endowment. It was under the care of Missouri Synod, and the Rev. Robert D. Morrow was its president in 1853. In 1854 it reported two professors and forty students. In 1855 it had "good college buildings free from debt, four instructors, and one hundred students." It doubtless did a good work in its day, but the details of its history have not been obtained.

Of the fifteen institutions enumerated in the foregoing list, Waynesburg College was probably the only one which continued its work without interruption during the civil war; but four of the others still exist as Cumberland Presbyterian schools, viz.: Bethel College, Cane Hill College, Union Female College, and the Cumberland Female College. Efforts were made after the war to revive several of the others; and some of them in these latest struggles, before becoming finally inoperative, did valuable work. To give any thing like a full history of all of our dead schools and colleges would require a volume. Therefore a brief sketch of three of the number, one a co-educational college and two seminaries for young ladies, is all that is here attempted.

McGEE COLLEGE.

Among the Cumberland Presbyterian schools which accomplished an important work, and then, for lack of endowment, ceased to exist, McGee College, College Mound, Macon County, Missouri, was one of the most useful. It was first known as McGee Seminary, and was under the care of McGee Presbytery, but was afterward transferred to McAdow Synod. In the spring of 1853 it reported seventy students. James Blewett, A.B., was then principal. It was opened as a college in October, 1853, and the Rev. J. B. Mitchell became its president. For many long years he and his faithful co-workers toiled here under immense difficulties to train up consecrated workers for the church. In 1859 the faculty was composed of eight members, and the school had two hundred and three students, seventy of whom were females.

The work of this institution was suspended during the civil war. With the beginning of the year 1866 its doors were reopened for the reception of students. In 1867 a full faculty was elected, and Dr. Mitchell resumed his work as president. For seven years this college continued to do a valuable work. In 1869 it was reported as "enjoying a larger prosperity than at any former date." In 1872 it had two hundred and seventy-three students, twenty-nine of whom were preparing for the ministry.

The following list of prominent teachers in this institution is furnished by Dr. Mitchell:

NAMES.	PROFESSORSHIP.	DATE.
J. B. Mitchell, D.D.	President, Rhetoric, Logic and Ethics	1853 to 1874.
J. H. Blewett, A.B.	Ancient Languages and Mathematics	1853 to 1855.
Miss R. A. Hagan, M.A.	Natural Science and English Literature	1853 to 1856.
S. M. Weedin, A.M.	Ancient Languages and Chemistry	1854 to 1856.
G. S. Howard, A.B.	Mathematics	1856 to 1861.
A. B. Starke, A.M.	Ancient and Modern Languages	1857 to 1861.
Azel Freeman, A.M.	Natural Science	1858 to 1861.
J. M. Howard, A.B.	Ancient Languages and Mathematics	1866 to 1867.
J. N. Campbell	Natural Science and English Literature	1866 to 1867.
B. E. Guthrie, A.M.	Latin and Greek	1867 to 1874.
J. S. Howard, A.M.	Natural Sciences	1867 to 1874.
W. J. Patton, A.B.	Mathematics	1867 to 1874.
U. Vuielle, A.B.	Modern Languages and Hebrew	1868 to 1874.
F. T. Sheetz, A.M.	Assistant Latin and Greek	1871 to ——.
J. T. Mitchell, A.B.	Assistant Latin and Greek	1872 to 1874.
Miss S. J. McCord, B.S.	Assistant Natural Science	1873 to 1874.
Miss M. T. Henderson, B.A.	English Literature	1873 to 1874.

This institution had a revival of religion among its students almost every year. After the war it had a system of free boarding for candidates for the ministry, differing somewhat from the Camp Blake plan at Cumberland University. The details are thus given in the catalogue for 1869:

The trustees of the college furnish rooms and stoves therein to all known to be preparing for the ministry in the Cumberland Presbyterian church. Their meals are furnished by families at reasonable rates. The presbyteries sending probationers meet this expense, either by forwarding the money, or by furnishing supplies at cash rates. A committee here receive these funds or supplies, and appropriate them as directed, free of charge.

This institution gave instruction to thousands of pupils who have made valuable men and women, filling positions of honor and usefulness in church and State, and in the different callings and professions. Among those who, from first to last, attended its classes were more than one hundred and thirty young men preparing for the ministry in the different Christian denominations. Not less than fifty-three of these are still actively preaching the gospel, while several others have died in the service. Some of the best preachers in our own denomination received their literary training wholly or in part in this school. Among these are the Rev. J. S. Howard, of Hernando, Mississippi, for many years President of Union Female College, Oxford, Mississippi; the Rev. D. E. Bushnell, D.D., of Waynesburg, Pennsylvania; the Rev. W. O. H. Perry, President of Odessa College, Missouri; the Rev. H. R. Crockett, of Bethany, Illinois; the Rev. J. E. Sharp, of Marshall, Missouri; the Rev. W. B. Farr, D.D., Ph.D., of Westport, Missouri; the Rev. A. D. Hail, missionary to Japan; the Rev. S. H. McElvain, Fort Smith, Arkansas; the Rev. A. L. Barr, Alton, Illinois; the Rev. B. P. Fullerton, of Kansas City, Missouri; and many others. The work of McGee College as a Cumberland Presbyterian school finally ended in June, 1874.

GREENVILLE SEMINARY FOR YOUNG LADIES.

This school was located at Greenville, Kentucky, and was under the care of Green River Synod. It had property worth forty thousand dollars and in 1858 was in successful operation, with a full corps of teachers, and with good prospects of increasing usefulness. Under several able men its work was carried on for many years. The financial management and support of the school were connected with a joint stock company. Complications arose, and the school was transferred to an individual, and finally, in 1879, under circumstances which fully justified this course, it was transferred by him to a member of the Methodist church.

GREENWOOD SEMINARY.

This was a school for young ladies, and was founded by N. Lawrence Lindsley, LL.D., after he resigned his professorship in Cumberland University. He located his school in the midst of his fine estates near Lebanon, Tennessee, and conducted it from the first on a unique plan. The number of young ladies was limited to just sixteen, and no one was ever received without a thorough previous investigation. The pupils were as thoroughly cut off from outside associations as it was possible for them to be. Dr.

Lindsley and his assistants had the whole training of these pupils in their own hands. The largest private library in Tennessee was that of Dr. Lindsley. His correspondence with literary gentlemen both in America and Europe was also extensive. His death and that of his wife put an end to Greenwood Seminary.

Four colleges have already been named which, after suspending their work during the civil war, were revived and continue still in operation. A brief sketch of each of these will be in place here:

UNION FEMALE COLLEGE.

The incipient steps toward the founding of this institution were taken by Hernando Synod in 1851. The synods of Mississippi and Union, and afterward, in 1853, the synod of West Tennessee joined in this undertaking, and commissioners were appointed to decide upon a location for the new college. This combination was the result of a proposition from Bethel College that these four synods should enter into an agreement to co-operate in establishing two schools: Bethel College for young men, and a college for young ladies. A school known as Oxford Female Academy, controlled by a local board of trustees, had been chartered at Oxford, Mississippi, in 1838. The Rev. S. G. Burney, D.D., was elected principal of this school in 1852, and still held this position when the synodical commissioners met in 1853. The property belonging to this academy and other valuable donations by the citizens of Oxford were tendered to the new college on condition that it should be located at that town. The commissioners accepted this proposition, and the college was opened in the fall of 1853 with Dr. Burney as president. The institution received its new charter as Union Female College, February 4, 1854. In 1856, at a cost of twenty-five thousand dollars, a new brick building fifty by one hundred feet, and three stories high, was added to the old one, a two-story brick thirty feet square. With its enlarged field this institution became one of the educational powers of Mississippi, and, before the war, was making some progress in securing endowment. Dr. Burney resigned in 1859 or 1860, and was succeeded by the Rev. R. S. Thomas, D.D., who continued in charge of the institution until its work was suspended by the war.

The school was not re-opened until the autumn of 1865, when the Rev. C. H. Bell, D.D., was elected president. The institution rapidly regained its former prosperity, but owing to the prostration of Southern finances, no effort was made to renew the work of soliciting endowment. It is high time that this work was resumed and pushed to a happy completion. From the catalogue of 1870 we learn that "This institution is held by a board of trustees, under a charter from the State, for the benefit of the public, and is authorized to confer the highest educational honors. The property is supposed to be worth about thirty-five thousand dollars."

In 1873 Dr. Bell resigned the presidency, and was succeeded by R. J. Guthrie, A. M., who continued in charge of the school two years. His successor, the Rev. J. S. Howard, A.M., entered upon his duties as president in 1875, and served for twelve years, resigning June, 1887. W. I. Davis, A.M., succeeded him, and is still in charge. Two hundred and twenty-seven young ladies have graduated from this college, and more than one thousand others have here received their education. This institution has struggled with the usual difficulties incident to unendowed schools, and has at times been much involved in debt, but it is now entirely free from incumbrance, and in a better condition financially and otherwise than at any time in its past history. It is now owned and controlled by the synod of Mississippi.

CUMBERLAND FEMALE COLLEGE.

This institution was located at McMinnville, Tennessee, in 1850, and is now under control of Middle Tennessee Synod. Good buildings and handsome grounds, free from debt, were secured, and the first session opened in 1851. Apparatus and library were partially provided, but no endowment has ever been furnished. The location of this institution is one of the most healthful in the world. Romantic scenery adds to its attractions. A strong local support, that indispensable requisite, has always been enjoyed by this enterprise. No college ever succeeds without vigorous backing in the community where it is located. Our church at McMinnville, and our churches in the country around the place are strong enough to make the college feel their presence.

The institution has had five presidents: The Rev. A. M. Stone, 1851 to 1855; the Rev. J. M. Gill, 1855 to 1857; D. M. Donnell, A.M., 1857 to 1871; A. M. Burney, A.M., 1871 to 1880; N. J. Finney, A.M., 1880, to the present time (October, 1887). Its highest prosperity has been reached under the present administration. Additions to the handsome buildings have been recently made. The patronage has always been good, but at no time have its prospects been brighter than at present.

President Finney, is one of the very best graduates Cumberland University ever educated. He is an earnest Christian, a ripe scholar, an indefatigable worker.

BETHEL COLLEGE.

Bethel College was organized in 1851, and has done valuable work for the Church. Two interesting and precious facts connected with the inner life of this institution deserves special mention. The first is the intense religious interest which has been mingled with its educational work. Revivals of great power almost every year, bringing the pupils into the army of Christ, have been led and fostered by the faculty. As one of these seasons for protracted meetings approached, the young Christians in the college by mutual agreement each took an unconverted friend or comrade with him to secret prayer. Nearly all these comrades were led to Christ before the meetings closed.

The other special feature of the work of Bethel College is connected with the struggles of young men who had no money. The faculty and the surrounding community adopted their own peculiar method of encouraging this class of students. Their method was not to give the boys money, but to show them how to get along with little, and earn that little themselves. Poor students were encouraged to live in the "camps" or cabins which had been erected on the ground near the college building, where the camp-meetings were held. These students did their own cooking; work was given them so as to enable them to earn wages while going to college. The students who supported themselves in this way, not only stood as high in the respect of the community as the wealthiest, but often far higher.

The Rev. J. M. B. Roach roomed in one of these camps, preparing his own meals, and serving as college janitor. He was honored by the college and by the whole community above the very wealthiest students, and he deserved it. Though poor he was never a beneficiary; and his brief career after he graduated—alas, so brief!—was as heroic and as independent as was his life in Bethel College. He was not the only noble graduate of that institution. Its alumni in all parts of our denominational field are efficient and honored laborers for the Master. This school at first admitted only young men and boys to its classes, but is now a co-educational college.

There is a lesson from the experience of Bethel College about concentration. When some good brethren of West Tennessee Synod proposed to establish this institution, others opposed it on the ground that the church already had in Tennessee one college for the education of young men. These objectors were, however, outvoted, and the new enterprise was inaugurated. In a short time a small fragment of West Tennessee Synod, less than a presbytery, opened another school with a collegiate name, right in the field of Bethel College, using the very same arguments which had been used in favor of establishing that institution. Then the Bethel men became eloquent in their pleading for concentration, and sent special agents to Hernando and Mississippi Synods to try to dissuade them from a scheme which they were discussing looking toward the establishment of a college for young men. The agent sent to one of these synods succeeded in effecting an agreement by which the matter was compromised, and the founding of the rival college prevented. That compromise has continued until the present time, from 1853 to 1887.

Bethel College had one regular graduate at the end of its first collegiate year. There were six in its senior class the second year, and in the years following the classes continued to grow. Before the war this school had the best telescope to be found in any of our colleges. While the great conflict was raging, some soldiers carried this instrument off to the camps, believing that they had captured a brass cannon! When railroads drew the town, McLemoresville, away from the college, it pulled up stakes and moved to McKenzie, Tennessee, where it still continues its work.

It is said that the first president of this institution, the Rev. J. N. Roach, used to employ the switch as an instrument of discipline, not sparing even young men. He was regarded by the trustees as a master disciplinarian. But when he used the switch he often took the pupil with him into the woods, where he would pray with him awhile, and then whip awhile. After whipping and praying had alternated in one case for some time, he appealed to the student, asking, "What more can I do for you?" The answer was, "I think you would better pray again."

This president practiced the most rigid system of espionage on his pupils. Many a night he would be out nearly all night, watching to catch the boys in their mischief. He required the professors to take night and night about with him in these vigils. Whatever may be said against such a method of discipline, it was certainly popular in that community.

The succession of presidents in Bethel has been: the Rev. J. N. Roach, A.B., the Rev. C. J. Bradley, the Rev. Azel Freeman, D.D., the Rev. Felix Johnson, D.D., the Rev. B. W. McDonnold, D.D., the Rev. J. S. Howard, A.M., the Rev. W. W. Hendrix, D.D., W. B. Sherrill, A.M., the Rev. J. L. Dickens, A.M. This institution now has two hundred and thirty students enrolled; sixteen of these are preparing to enter the ministry.

CANE HILL COLLEGE.

As has been seen in a former chapter, efforts to establish an institution of learning on Cane Hill, Arkansas, were begun by our people as early as 1834. As there were then no State schools, all educational enterprises were carried on by personal effort. The influence of several private schools, conducted by teachers of good attainments, gave impetus to the educational spirit already among the people. They thought that they must have a college. Like many others, they supposed that a building a little better than the ordinary school-house, with two or three educated teachers, would constitute a college. Accordingly a brick house was built, and in 1852 a charter was secured from the legislature, and Cane Hill College was opened at Boonsboro, Washington County, Arkansas. This school was put under the care of the Arkansas Synod, and the Rev. Robert M. King, of Missouri, was elected president. He was assisted by Prof. S. Doak Lowry. After laboring efficiently for several years, Mr. King resigned, and moved back to Missouri. Professor Lowry was then in charge of the school, and was assisted by Prof. James H. Crawford and Prof. Pleasant W. Buchanan. An effort was made to raise endowment by scholarships, and the Rev. W. G. L. Quaite was appointed endowing agent. He secured in donation notes and scholarship pledges several thousand dollars, but the wreck and ruin wrought by the war, which soon followed, rendered all these utterly valueless.

Before the war a new building, worth about six thousand dollars, was erected. In March, 1859, the Rev. F. R. Earle, of Greenville, Kentucky, accepted the presidency, and was formally inaugurated in the following June. He found the college in good working order. At the close of the collegiate year, in June, 1859, two young men, S. H. Buchanan and J. T. Buchanan, were regularly graduated, receiving the first diplomas ever issued by the college. At that time, also, the first catalogue was issued. S. H. Buchanan was employed as tutor for the next session. In June, 1860, Prof. Lowry resigned. The Rev. W. P. Gillespie was afterward elected to fill the vacancy. The school prospered until 1861. Then came the war, by which its work was suspended. The college buildings, with a valuable little library, and some apparatus, were completely destroyed by fire in November, 1864.

One house belonging to the college, and formerly used as a boarding-house for young preachers, escaped the flames. After the war closed the president returned, and began to teach and preach in this building. In 1868 a new frame building, worth about five thousand dollars, was erected on the old foundation, and in September the president, assisted by Prof. James Mitchell, opened school in this new house. In September, 1869, Prof. J. P. Carnahan was added to the teaching force. In 1874 Prof. Mitchell retired, and accepted a more lucrative position in the State University. Prof. Harold Bourland was employed to fill the vacancy. He remained, however, for only one session.

In 1875 the trustees resolved to admit pupils of both sexes and the Rev. H. M. Welch was chosen as principal of the department for young ladies. In 1879 Prof. Welch retired. In the four years following, Mrs. Earle, Miss Welch, Miss Moore, and Mrs. Whittenberg were employed as teachers whenever the patronage demanded it.

In 1883 Prof. Carnahan retired, having taught fourteen years. The president then had entire control of the work until 1885, when he, too, resigned, and the Rev. J. P. Russell was called to take charge. He taught two terms and a half. In the second session of his administration the college building was burned. In this emergency the Methodists of the village generously tendered the use of their church, and this, with a small dwelling-house rented for the occasion, furnished room for the school, and the work went on.

After the resignation of Mr. Russell, Dr. Earle again undertook the labors and responsibilities of the work. In 1886 a new building on a new foundation was erected. This is better than either of the former buildings. In 1887, the president, assisted by two good teachers, opened school in the new building, with a good patronage and a fair promise of success. Excepting the two and a half sessions taught by Mr. Russell, and the vacation enforced by the civil war, President Earle has been in charge of the school from March, 1859, until the present time. In all that time he has been the only pastor of the congregation worshiping in the college chapel. Within this period thirty-four young men and young women have graduated. Of these all but three are living, and are doing good work, several of them as ministers. A large number of students who did not finish the college course have gone forth from this school to their life work. The institution still lives. It has property worth at least eight thousand dollars. It is situated, however, right under the shadow of a heavily-endowed State university, which furnishes practically free tuition, and therefore labors at a disadvantage.

The limits of this volume will not permit the introduction here of the history of all the schools founded by Cumberland Presbyterians since the close of the war, and now doing a good work. A brief notice of three or four of them is all that can be attempted.

WARD'S SEMINARY, NASHVILLE, TENNESSEE.

This school was founded by W. E. Ward, D.D., in 1865, who began the work when the country round him was still covered with the ruins the war had made. He had visited all the principal colleges for young ladies in America, thoroughly acquainting himself with modern methods. He made a brave beginning, and soon attained the highest rank as an educator. A long-tried son of the church, and giving the most liberal advantages to the daughters of its ministers, he commanded the hearty co-operation of our people in this private enterprise. From the first the school took high rank, and still maintains it. Over two hundred teachers have received their education at this institution. While laboring in this school, and securing its great success, Dr. Ward has been alive to the best interests of the church, taking an active part for over fifteen years as a member of our Board of Publication, as well as in the building up of our church in Nashville. The seminary is now in the prime of its career, and no doubt will go on to a greater success. It teaches one valuable lesson—that great enterprises must have time and patience, and a head to work out, through long years, the consummation they set out to make. The first year this school had one hundred and eight pupils. The patronage steadily increased, until in 1883 the number enrolled was three hundred and fifty-four. Its largest graduating class, that of 1884-1885, numbered fifty-six. The total number of graduates sent forth by this school up to 1887 was eight hundred and eighty.[1]

SPRING HILL INSTITUTE.

This school was founded by the Rev. J. L. Cooper, just after the war. It is located in Lauderdale County, Mississippi. Though private property it is regarded as one of our very useful institutions. Without any high pretensions, it goes steadily and earnestly on in its work of usefulness. The aim of Mr. Cooper was to establish an institution according to his own ideas, and place it out of the reach of contaminating influences. In carrying out his plan he

---

[1] Since this sketch was written, Dr. Ward has passed from his earthly toil to his reward. In the summer of 1887 he sought relief from severe illness, caused by overwork, in a voyage to Europe. After his arrival in England he grew worse and sailed for home, but died on shipboard in mid-ocean, July 20th, 1887. His death brought sorrow to the hearts of his pupils and his brethren throughout the church, and at Nashville was mourned as a public calamity. The school he founded continues its work with undimished success.

followed the example of N. Lawrence Lindsley, LL.D., of Greenwood Seminary, and placed his academy in the center of his own large area of land, so that he could control every lot and every settlement upon the premises. He has carried forward this enterprise successfully. His corps of teachers is always full, and the patronage of the school always about equal to the number it is able to accommodate. Of the results of co-education, after a pretty thorough test, Mr. Cooper speaks thus:

We have tried our plan of a male and female school for three years, and success has crowned our efforts thus far. Here brothers and sisters meet in the same chapel at roll-call and at prayers, after which the sister takes her seat in the study hall, and the brother retires to his boarding room. When the bell calls them to recitation, they again meet and recite to the same teachers; and, thus, all the stimulants to neatness of dress, purity of language, ease of manner and address, and high intellectual endeavor, growing out of contact with the other sex under wholesome restraints are secured. By having separate boarding-houses, and by holding the reins of government firmly, yet kindly, we find the school much more easily controlled than either a male or female school separate.

Several of our best living ministers were educated mainly at Spring Hill; some of them in the same classes with their wives, for married preachers are still thronging all our schools.

LOUDON HIGH SCHOOL.

Though it has only a modest name, this institution teaches a full college course. It was established by East Tennessee Synod, in 1869, at Loudon, Tennessee. It has had a very respectable faculty of real scholars. It has aimed to secure endowment, but its field is too circumscribed to give large hopes of success. Amid beautiful scenery, with historic surroundings, in ample buildings, the school presents a most fascinating exterior. Of its inner life the writer has no information.

EDUCATIONAL WORK IN MISSOURI.

The church in Missouri suffered a great loss by the closing of McGee College, in 1874. But our people did not become dispirited. It was decided to resume educational work and to profit by the disasters of the past. Several valuable schools had been lost by the want of permanent endowment, hence the synods of the State agreed to co-operate in raising one hundred thousand dollars as a permanent endowment fund, and not to open another college until that amount should be secured, this being considered a safe nucleus. The work of securing money has been going steadily forward for several years, and at this time it is believed that the one hundred thousand dollars has been fully provided for by the educational commission of the co-operating synods. The contemplated institution will, therefore, no doubt be founded in the near future.

Notwithstanding this action of the synods looking toward the founding of one central college for Missouri, several schools, controlled mainly or entirely by Cumberland Presbyterians, have been kept in operation in the State. Stewartsville Seminary, a private enterprise, under the charge of the Rev. W. O. H. Perry, had since 1863 been doing a good work. In 1879 it was chartered as Stewartsville College, and in the years following it sent forth about twenty graduates. On account of the loss of its buildings by fire, its work was, in 1887, brought to an end. Prof. Perry has recently taken charge of Odessa College, a school established by the citizens of Odessa, Missouri. Ozark College, at Greenfield, in the southwestern part of the State, belongs to Ozark Presbytery, and has grown into an institution of considerable importance. The Rev. A. J. McGlumphy, D.D., LL.D., formerly president of Lincoln University, Illinois, has recently taken charge of this school.

CHEAP SCHOLARSHIPS.

As so many of our colleges have committed themselves to cheap scholarships, and as circumstances in the past compelled the writer of this history to make an exhaustive investigation of all the questions connected with this plan for securing endowment, it may not be improper to give some of the general conclusions reached in that investigation.

The scholarship plan strikes a fatal blow at the only dependence any unendowed college has for support. Tuition fees may keep up a faculty for a little season, but for an unendowed college to adopt a scheme which reduces or destroys tuition fees is suicidal. The scheme of limited scholarships aims at endowing the college by defrauding three generations of teachers. "If we can only struggle through the limited period, then we will have a safe endowment." Yes, if—but O what a long and fraudulent if it is! "If we can only find professors to teach for us without adequate pay for a few years, then all the scholarships will have expired, and we shall have a safely invested endowment." As respectable and competent professors can not be secured without pay, the few years must be struggled through with such teachers as will work on less than one fourth an adequate salary. In some cases, long before the limited period expires the institution dies. In other cases the trustees save its life by a breach of trust—using the principal of these scholarships to retain the faculty. In still other cases the principal is so reduced by agent's fees, losses on investments, and other processes, that the institution finds itself bound to teach, without pay and without endowment, as many students as are likely ever to seek instruction within its walls. It then repudiates its scholarships, having no alternative left. By this process so many of the real friends of the institution are alienated that all prospects for real endowment are sadly diminished. Even the voluntary surrender of these scholarships, in view of obvious necessities, lessens the prospects of securing real endowment afterward.

In well-known cases a large number of scholarship claims have been bought up at low rates by *trustees* residing near the college. Though the original form of these scholarships did not allow them to be rented, yet these trustees, being the law makers of the institution, and having now a private interest to serve, have met together and enlarged the privileges of these claims so that they could be rented for a session at a time. Then these trustees, being on the ground, have underbid the faculty for the patronage of such students as would have paid the highest tuition!

The scholarship scheme appeals to wrong motives. It goes to men with offers and inducements of a financial character. They are asked to make an investment of money with an eye to future profits, not as a gift to the blessed Lord. All the high motives which influence earnest Christians to liberality and self-sacrifice— love for church and the ministry, love for the Master and the souls for whom he died—are sunk into the low, sordid hope of making a profitable investment of a few hundred dollars. No Abbot Lawrence will ever be developed among us by these sordid appeals. To the mistaken schemes for securing endowment by cheap scholarships is it chiefly due that no very large donations have ever been made by any one man to any of our colleges.

Let two agents start side by side, one to work for a college which never appeals to sordid motives, which asks only for unincumbered endowment, and the other for an institution which has adopted the plan of cheap scholarships; and, other things being equal, the former will secure far more money than the latter. The difference will grow immeasurably great if the former agent represents a college which is out-and-out and forever all for Jesus, and justly bases all its appeals for help on love to Christ's kingdom; while the other represents men, corporations, or towns, which have private axes to grind while pretending to ask assistance in the name of the sacred cause of religion.

The church educates its members by the methods it adopts. The agents whom it sends forth to solicit money are educators. Under those perverted methods employed in securing endowment funds through scholarships, and by kindred schemes for raising money for missions, or to sustain the work in our congregations, we have encouraged a species of giving which is in many cases a sham and a cheat. There are those who think themselves the most devoted Christians on earth, who have not learned the first lesson in consecration and self-denial.

The scholarship evil is but one of the many substitutes which men are prone to adopt instead of the divine plan of raising money for the Master's kingdom. Some of these substitutes might be innocent enough in themselves if they were not used to crowd out God's own appointed method of training a church to give systematically and from principle.

Is there no supreme love to Christ? Is there no heart so full of devotion to him that its utmost possible gift would be gladly bestowed, and which weeps bitter tears because it has no more to offer? Once an agent of one of our colleges was accosted by the wife of a wealthy man. Her husband was not a Christian, and though he controlled vast estates, he dealt out money to his wife with a sparing hand. When she was alone with the agent she said to him: "My heart is nearly breaking because I can not do something for my Savior through your institution. I believe that work is sacred to my Redeemer, but I have only one thing in the world which I am at liberty to give you without asking my husband: that is my diamonds. I have a full set that cost a large sum. I want the Savior to accept the poor little offering, and use it in training men to preach the gospel." That was giving to Jesus. "*O si sic omnes.*"

CHAPTER XLVII.

PUBLICATION, NEWSPAPERS, REVISION, AND TEMPERANCE.

> For the cause that lacks assistance,
> For the wrongs which need resistance,
> For the future in the distance.
> —*Dr. Guthrie.*

FOUR subjects which belong to more than one period of this history have been reserved for this special chapter. They are Publication, Newspapers, Revision, and Temperance.

PUBLICATION.[1]

Cumberland Presbyterians manifested very early their appreciation of the printing-press. The founders of this church, before the organization of its first presbytery, sent forth to the world, "The Remonstrance of the Council," an "Address to the Christian Reader," and probably other short publications. The first official document issued by our people was probably the "Circular Letter," published in 1810, by which the church announced and vindicated its own existence. Old Cumberland Synod at its first meeting, held in October, 1813, at Beech meeting-house, Sumner County, Tennessee, appointed a committee to prepare a complete account of the rise, history, and doctrines of Cumberland Presbytery, to be published in Woodward's third edition of Buck's Theological Dictionary. This account was accordingly prepared and published.

When the synod of 1814 adopted the Confession of Faith, Catechism, and Discipline, Finis Ewing and Hugh Kirkpatrick agreed with the synod to print the book at eighty-seven and one half cents per copy, "upon good writing paper, neatly bound and lettered." It is not certain that this contract was ever carried out. The Confession was probably not printed until seven years later,

---

[1] This sketch of the publishing work of the church was prepared by J. M. Gaut, Esq., President of the Board of Publication.

The oldest copy now known to be extant was printed at Russellville, Kentucky, in 1821, by Charles Rhea. This was the first book ever issued by Cumberland Presbyterians.

For the first ten or fifteen years of the church's existence, its preachers were too intent on bringing sinners to Christ to think of ecclesiastical machinery; but in course of time they began to think more of the equipments of the church. The first step looking toward a publishing department was taken by the synod in 1825. In adopting the plan of old Cumberland College, the synod provided that the commissioners should be authorized to connect with it, if they thought expedient, a printing office, to publish a "periodical paper," books, tracts, etc. This was not deemed expedient however.

The aspirations of the young church seem to have been kindled in a number of directions about this time. The synod at its meeting in 1823 required each presbytery to report its history to the synod. All of the twelve presbyteries, except two, complied; and these documents were filed with the clerk of the synod, and the presbyteries were ordered to continue their reports. In 1824 the synod appointed a committee to collect materials for a church history. In 1825 it made arrangements for publishing the lectures which Finis Ewing had delivered in his school in Missouri. A committee was appointed to secure from the records of the Presbyterian church the history of the Cumberland Presbyterian preachers who had been connected with that church. It also appointed a committee, consisting of Samuel King, Robert Donnell, and James B. Porter, to compile a hymn book. This committee made the compilation and by authority published the book, and sold six thousand copies; ultimately, in 1848, the plates of this hymn book, with the committee's debts, were transferred to the Board of Publication.

The Assembly of 1845, carrying out the spirit of resolutions adopted in 1843, provided for the committing of its business transactions to the care of boards. A Board of Publication was created, called a "Publishing Association." A constitution was adopted, prescribing its powers and duties, and making it a sort of stock company. The members of the board were Richard Beard, Milton

Bird, H. A. Hunter, Le Roy Woods, J. F. Wilkins, Wm. Miller, James M. Rogers, and Alonzo Livermore. It seems to have been a cumbersome piece of machinery; and was never called together even for organization until about two years after its creation, and the very day before the Assembly abolished it. The Assembly of 1847 appointed a simple Committee of Publication, consisting of five members, the Rev. Milton Bird, the Rev. Laban Jones, and Ruling Elders T. E. McLean, A. M. Phelps, and James L. Stratton, and instructed them to procure a charter of incorporation. This board located its work at Louisville, Kentucky, where Milton Bird lived, and who sooner or later was president, corresponding secretary, publishing agent, book editor, and salesman.

The business of the board was carried on at Louisville, from 1847 to 1858. A general statement of its history during this period has been given on pages 313–316 of this volume. Only a few details will be added. During the years 1848 and 1849, about $2,900 was donated to it, and the sales amounted to about $1,400. In 1850 Dr. Bird resigned as publishing agent, and the Rev. Le Roy Woods was appointed in his stead. After this the donations dropped down to a few hundred dollars per year, and the main dependence was upon sales. Up to 1853 the total donations were reported at $3,129.76, and the assets then amounted to $3,725.62, showing an increase of $595.86. The agent was paid $500 for five sixths of his time. The printing was done by contract. Difficulty was experienced in getting frequent meetings of the board, a quorum not living in Louisville. Complaints were made by several General Assemblies because the board failed to report fully or in due time, and, on one occasion, because it did not report at all. A memorial from the Pennsylvania Synod was presented to the Assembly of 1850, praying a removal of the "Book Concern" to a place farther eastward. The prayer was refused. It is quite remarkable that two reports of the board, doubtless written by Dr. Bird, announce business principles whose soundness it has required years of sad experience to enable our own and other churches to appreciate. He condemned the extending of credit and the contracting of debts. He opposed the fixing of too low prices on the books, the clamor to the contrary notwithstanding. He protested against the keeping up of depositories at the risk and expense of the board, and favored, instead, agencies conducted by the presbyteries or individuals. He opposed changes in the location of the board, and recognized the need of a book editor, and the necessity of paying for manuscripts. The books then most needed were, in his opinion, a treatise on our theology, a church history, biographical sketches of our ministers, children's books, and doctrinal and practical tracts.

But all of this good preaching against the credit system was followed by some very bad practice on the part of somebody. By 1854 the board had become largely indebted to its printers, Morton & Griswold, Louisville, Kentucky. This debt, according to the board's statement, was more than $2,000. There was due on sales of books for 1853, $856, and for 1854, $1,042—about one third of the entire amount of the sales. The board became alarmed and reduced the salary of the agent, and he resigned. The Rev. Jesse Anderson was appointed in his stead.

The Assembly of 1854 gave some very pointed orders about reporting, and abstaining from the credit system. As measures of relief, it recommended the employment of soliciting agents and colporteurs, and an increase in the price of the books. It recommended further that none but an experienced book-keeper should be appointed agent. The board's report for that year is not clear, but the Assembly's committee reported the assets at about $4,500, and the debts about $2,500. A committee of three was appointed to audit the books of the board. Resignations became frequent about this time. The number of the members of the board was increased to seven. There was no improvement, however, in the financial results, and the Assembly of 1857 passed a resolution to wind the business up. Thus ends the first period of the board's history. Its assets at this time, as reported to the Assembly of 1858, amounted to $4,913.88. In this estimate, however, were included notes and accounts due the board, amounting to $2,795.22, worth not more than fifty cents on the dollar. The remainder of the assets consisted of plates, books, and a small amount of cash. The liabilities amounted to $1,189,44. The actual net assets were therefore supposed to be about $1,310.00. During that period there had been published about thirty thousand volumes, consisting largely of hymn books and Confessions of Faith. The sales had amounted to about $11,000. The books of the church consisted of the Hymn Book, Social Harp, Confession of Faith, the Manual, Ewing's Lectures, Donnell's Thoughts, Guide to Infant Baptism, Infant Philosophy, and A Commentary on the Sixth Chapter of Hebrews.

The General Assembly of 1858, which convened at Huntsville, Alabama, appointed a special committee on publication, including some of its best men. They were Richard Beard, chairman, R. Burrow, M. B. Feemster, H. B. Warren, R. L. Caruthers, A. J. Baird, Milton Bird, and Isaac Shook. In accordance with the recommendations of this committee, a complete re-organization of the publishing work of the church took place. A permanent "Committee of Publication" was provided for, to consist of three practical business men, known to be devoted to the interests of the church, and "located contiguous to each other." This committee was to appoint a general agent, and require him to give bond. It was instructed "to adopt all necessary means" to raise money, "by subscription or otherwise," to carry forward the work of publication. The agent was to be paid a sufficient salary to justify him in giving as much time as was necessary for the vigorous prosecution of the work. The committee was not to involve itself in debt or extend its business beyond the means under its control. The members were to be subject to removal by the General Assembly. The committee was to have power to fill vacancies in its membership, occurring between the meetings of the Assembly, subject to the confirmation of the next Assembly. It was instructed to secure a charter of incorporation. Its location was to be determined by a committee of seven, who were to receive propositions from various places with the view of establishing a general book depository and store, and ultimately, if the prospects should justify, "a house of publication." The men appointed to constitute this permanent committee were Elder Andrew Allison, the Rev. W. E. Ward, and the Rev. Wiley M. Reed.

The committee was located at Nashville, Tennessee, and the Rev. Wiley M. Reed was chosen its chairman. The Rev. W. S.

Langdon was appointed general agent. He went to Louisville and took charge of the assets. All the stereotype plates, except those of the catechism were lost in the manner stated on page 315 of this history. The assets removed to Nashville consisted of the plates of the catechism, books valued at $641, and notes and accounts, which, after paying the debts, yielded about $900. In 1860 the board was chartered by an act of the legislature of Tennessee. One thousand dollars was borrowed to publish the hymn book, which had been revised by a committee consisting of the Rev. A. J. Baird, the Rev. J. C. Provine, and Elder N. Green, Jr., appointed by the Assembly of 1858. The lenders of this money were the Hon. Robert L. Caruthers, Judge N. Green, Sr., the Hon. Horace H. Harrison, the Rev. Carson P. Reed, John Frizzell, Esq., and others whose names can not now be ascertained. Most of the money thus loaned was subsequently donated to the board. E. Waterhouse, Sr., donated the money with which the Confession of Faith was stereotyped.

The publishing work of the church was suspended by the war till 1863, when it was transferred to Pittsburg, Pennsylvania. Of the publishing committee appointed at that place, Joseph Pennock was made chairman, and the Rev. S. T. Stewart, the publishing agent. The assets, when removed from Nashville, amounted to $5,892.25, less debts amounting to $2,254.69. A new committee was appointed in 1865, consisting of the Rev. I. N. Cary, the Rev. S. T. Stewart, and Alexander Postley. The business was for a time under the management of Mr. Stewart. The printing and selling were afterward done on commission by Davis, Clark & Co., of Pittsburg. This arrangement was continued until the work was again transferred to Nashville. This was done by order of the Assembly which met at Memphis, in 1867. The Rev. A. J. Baird, the Rev. L. C. Ransom, and Ruling Elder D. C. Love, were then appointed the members of the board.

The Assembly had recommended that a book editor and publishing agent should be employed, who should be *ex officio* a member of the board. It also appropriated to the publishing work $2,460 from the interest on the Finley Bequest. This, added to the assets received from Pittsburg, made the total resources

$5,217.74. The Rev. J. C. Provine, D.D., was chosen book editor and publishing agent. The receipts from sales during ten months were $6,971.24. Although the General Assembly had passed a resolution calling the attention of the presbyteries to the necessities of the board, and requesting them to have collections taken up in the congregations for the cause of publication, yet the donations for the entire year amounted to only twenty dollars. The expenditures for the ten months were just equal to the donations and the receipts from sales. The next Assembly re-adopted the "quarterly system" of collections. During the following year only thirty-five out of twelve hundred congregations took up collections for the cause of publication—ten of them in Missouri, and nine in Tennessee, and not exceeding three in any other State. The total donations were $391.75. This, with the receipts from sales, amounted to $9,807.13. Thus the net profit for the year was a little more than $380.

The report of the board to the Assembly of 1869 set forth in appealing terms the need of more books for the church, and the need of more money with which to produce them. Attention was called to the board's condition of absolute dependence on other publishing houses for its printing. The Assembly resolved to raise fifty thousand dollars to place the enterprise on a firmer and broader basis. It also increased the number of members composing the board to five. In 1869, Dr. Provine resigned his position, and W. E. Dunaway was elected publishing agent. The report to the Assembly of 1870 showed a marked increase in donations, sales, profits, and assets. The appointment of an agent to raise the fifty thousand dollars was recommended. A store was opened January 1, 1871, for the purchase and sale of religious and literary books, in connection with the sale of the church's own publications. Rev. T. C. Blake, D.D., was employed in 1871 as financial agent to raise the fifty thousand dollars. Exclusive of his compensation and expenses, he secured $7,107.47. By permission of the Assembly of 1873, this money, with accrued interest, was used for the purposes of publication, with the understanding that a certain portion, supposed to have been contributed expressly to build or buy a publishing house, should be appropriated, with interest, to that purpose, whenever a sufficient sum was secured. The treasurer still holds the agent's notes for the same.

In August, 1872, the Rev. M. B. De Witt, D.D., was made soliciting agent and book editor, and became editor of the Sunday-school periodicals, and of the *Theological Medium*. He continued his editorial work in these several departments until the fall of 1879, when he resigned, and other arrangements were made.

During the year 1872 the board purchased of Dr. T. C. Blake the *Sunday-school Gem* and the *Theological Medium* for $2,500, the board filling out the unexpired subscriptions of each. As early as 1851 a memorial from Mackinaw Presbytery had called the attention of the General Assembly to the necessity for a Sunday-school paper, and of a missionary paper. The committee on publication to whom the memorial was referred, reported favorably, but the whole subject was referred to the next Assembly. When the next Assembly met, no action was taken in regard to this matter. The *Gem* had when purchased 15,000 subscribers, and the *Medium* 1,180. The number of subscribers to the latter diminished during the succeeding year to 525, and in 1879 it had ceased to be self-sustaining. Then the board, by order of the Assembly, filled out its unexpired subscriptions and donated this quarterly to the theological faculty of Cumberland University. The subscriptions to the *Gem* increased during the year 1873 to 24,000. Its patronage has since been divided with *Our Lambs*, the publication of which was commenced by the board in 1877, and both together have now (1887) a circulation of about 35,000.

Prior to 1874 the church never owned a newspaper. Once, on condition of being allowed to appoint the editors, it made a private newspaper its organ, but left the ownership still in private hands. After a very unsatisfactory experience in pursuing this plan, the whole newspaper business was again left to private enterprise. Several evils, however, seemed to be inseparable from this system of independent church journalism. At some periods newspapers multiplied beyond the prospect of support, and their quality often deteriorated in proportion to the increase of their number. There were frequent controversies and rivalries among them, and at times some of them were arrayed against leading enterprises of the church. Owing to lack of financial support, however, many of these publications were short-lived, and it happened not infrequently that two or more of them were forced to consolidate.

In the Assembly of 1852, the Rev. J. N. Roach read a paper on the subject of a religious journal under the control of the Assembly.

The Assembly of 1858 adopted a resolution favoring a consolidation of all the church papers owned and published by individuals. In 1868 a memorial from Princeton Presbytery was presented to the Assembly, asking that the Board of Publication should be directed to begin the publication of a religious journal for the church. The report of the Committee on Publication, adopted by the Assembly, approved the proposed step, but did not recommend immediate action because of the board's lack of money. Another memorial on this subject was presented to the Assembly of 1873 by Bell Presbytery, and, in its report to that Assembly, the board expressed the opinion that an effort should be made to bring about a consolidation of the existing newspapers. The report of the Committee on Publication, adopted by the Assembly, favored the measure, setting forth the reasons therefor at considerable length. Expressing a desire that the church should not enter into competition with the owners of the existing papers, it recommended that the board should be "instructed to negotiate with them, and, if possible, procure their interests in their respective publications at reasonable rates."

To the Assembly of 1874 the board reported that it had been found impracticable at that time to purchase the papers then in existence. That Assembly adopted a report, which said: "It is the sense of this General Assembly that fair terms should be offered to the proprietors of the present weekly church papers, not to be less than the estimate fixed by disinterested parties mutually chosen, and should the terms thus offered be not accepted, the board will report to the next General Assembly its views on the propriety of establishing a weekly newspaper for the church." The owners of the *Banner of Peace* and *Cumberland Presbyterian* declined to submit their property to the valuation of disinterested parties, stating that the property was not for sale. By private negotiation, however, in the fall of 1874, "the good-will" of the *Banner of*

Peace was purchased by the board from the Rev. S. P. Chesnut, D.D., for ten thousand dollars. Soon afterward, the board purchased of Brown & Perrin the good-will of the *Cumberland Presbyterian*, together with a printing-press and other machinery, for thirteen thousand dollars. The machinery was supposed to be worth about three thousand dollars. The good-will of the *Texas Cumberland Presbyterian* was purchased of the Rev. J. H. Wofford for twenty-five hundred dollars.

All the papers were consolidated at Nashville, Tennessee, at the total cost of $25,500, the Board of Publication agreeing to fill out the unexpired subscriptions of the three papers. The consolidated paper was first called the *Banner-Presbyterian*, but the name proved unsatisfactory, and was changed to the *Cumberland Presbyterian*. Rev. J. R. Brown, D.D., was chosen sole editor, and continued in that position till July 1st, 1883, when Rev. D. M. Harris, D.D., was made joint editor. Dr. Brown's connection with the paper ceased April 1st, 1885, when Dr. Harris was made editor in chief. The Rev. J. M. Howard, D.D., at this time became associate editor of the *Cumberland Presbyterian* and book editor.

After the purchase of the three weekly papers, the former owner of one of them, and one of the joint owners of another, became interested in the publication at the same places of papers similar in character to those sold. It was contended that such action not only involved disloyalty to the church, but also impaired the "good-will" purchased by the board, and was in violation of the contract. These questions gave rise to extended discussion in the church, and to deliverances by four General Assemblies. What principles, if any, are settled by these deliverances, it would perhaps be unprofitable now to discuss.

The subscriptions to the papers, when consolidated, amounted to about seven thousand five hundred. The consolidated paper now has a circulation of about fifteen thousand. The price of the consolidated paper is two dollars. It furnishes about twice as much reading matter as any one of its predecessors. It has grown steadily in influence and usefulness. Thus the church has one large weekly to which all our people can justly look with satisfaction—strong, able, and under the church's own control.

In 1874 the board began the publication of a monthly journal, *Sunday Morning*, for the use of Sunday-school teachers, officers, and advanced pupils. It attained a circulation of about twenty-eight hundred, but from considerations of economy was discontinued in 1879. It was followed in the same year by *The Comments*, a Sunday-school quarterly, and in 1885 a quarterly of lower grade was commenced, called *The Rays of Light*. These two publications have now a combined circulation of about thirty-five thousand.

Since 1879 Rev. R. V. Foster, D.D., has been the editor, except during a short interval, of the *Comments*, *Rays of Light*, and *Lesson Leaf*. He was also the editor of the *Gem* and *Our Lambs* until July, 1883, when they were committed to the editorial management of Mrs. Caroline M. Harris.

Mr. W. E. Dunaway was business manager of the board from 1870 to the latter part of 1874, when he resigned and was succeeded by Rev. T. C. Blake, D.D., who filled this position until failing health compelled his resignation in October, 1878. November 1, 1878, John M. Gaut was made corresponding secretary, and, at the request of the board, took temporary charge of the business, exercising a supervisory control over it. He continued in this position till December 1, 1880, when T. M. Hurst was appointed agent and business manager. Mr. Hurst's resignation took place May, 1886, at which time John D. Wilson was elected agent.

The assets of the board gradually increased from $5,217, in July, 1867, to $81,879.05, May 1, 1887. Their valuation approached this latter sum during some of the previous years, but, as was afterward ascertained, they were largely overvalued. The liabilities also increased from nothing in 1867, to $12,390.53 in 1887, having at times during the intervening years been larger than that. The indebtedness in 1879 was so great and the receipts so small that the board was very seriously embarrassed. Without the individual credit of several members of the board freely extended for several years, it would have been difficult, if not impossible, to have averted a suspension of business. An extension of time had to be asked of its creditors, a general retrenchment of expenses was made, and its income largely increased by an increase in the subscribers to the periodicals. In this way the house was greatly relieved. A large burden of debt continued upon it, however, till 1884, when the church by donations in sums of ten dollars, in response to what was known as "the Uncle Josh Proposition," generously contributed upward of ten thousand dollars to pay off the indebtedness. The originator of this proposition was Mr. Joshua D. Spain, of Nashville.

Since 1867 the books published by the board have increased about threefold, and a large number of valuable pamphlets have been issued.

It is curious to note how long the church has been in realizing its desire for certain publications. A committee was appointed in 1824 to collect materials for a history of the Cumberland Presbyterian Church. In 1847 the General Assembly resolved to have such a history written, and a committee was appointed to do this work. In 1848 this committee reported progress. The necessity for such a history was urged in the report of the Board of Publication in 1850. The Rev. H. S. Porter, D.D., of Memphis, Tennessee, began the writing of the church's history, but died before the work was finished. In 1856 his widow tendered to the General Assembly his incomplete manuscript and the papers which he had collected. The donation was accepted and a committee appointed to engage a competent person to complete the work. Then the enterprise seems to have slumbered. In 1884—sixty years after the initial effort—the board took the step of which this volume is the result.

The Assembly of 1852 appointed Rev. Milton Bird to prepare for publication "a copious abstract" of the Minutes of the Council, of Old Cumberland Presbytery, of New Cumberland Presbytery, of Cumberland Synod, and of the several General Assemblies from the first to that date; and the Board of Publication was authorized to publish the same. This abstract was prepared and is still in existence. Why it was not published is not known. In 1858 the stated clerk was requested to publish an abstract or digest of these records; and the next Assembly by resolution inquired what he had done toward complying with this request. In 1869 a resolution was adopted, recommending that the Board of Publication should have a digest of the Assembly's deliverances prepared and published as soon as practicable. A subsequent Assembly appointed the board and the stated clerk to do this work. The stated clerk, Hon. John Frizzell, prepared such a digest, and the Assembly of 1878 appointed a committee to review it, and ordered its publication if it was approved. The Assembly of 1885 appointed another committee to take this matter in hand. This committee reported in 1886, when the whole subject was referred to the next Assembly. That Assembly appointed the Hon. John Frizzell to complete the work, and it will doubtless be ready for the press early in 1888.

The preparation of a hymn and tune book was recommended by the Assembly of 1869. The manuscript of such a work was presented to the Assembly of 1870 and referred to the Board of Publication. The board, fearing that the selections were not adapted to the wants of the church deferred publishing the book. In 1873 the Assembly again expressed itself in favor of such a publication. In that year the Rev. A. J. Baird, D.D., of Nashville, proposed to undertake the compilation of such a work, asking as his only compensation that the board should furnish his church with a supply of the books. The proposition was accepted, and after many months of painstaking labor, his manuscript was ready to be presented to the General Assembly of 1874. By this General Assembly it was referred to a committee for examination. It was slightly amended by this committee, and abridged by the author. Then the revised manuscript was approved by the Assembly of 1875, and the first edition of the work was published by the board in 1876.

The long, faithful, and arduous labors of one of the late honored presidents of the board, the Rev. W. E. Ward, D.D., deserve special mention. From 1858 to 1879, excepting the years when the Pittsburg committee was in charge, he taxed an already overburdened heart and brain with the additional cares and responsibilities of this struggling institution.

The following list contains the names of all who have ever served as members of the board or the Committee of Publication, and shows, with approximate accuracy, the time of each member's service. Except in a few instances, it has been found impossible

to ascertain exact dates. Most of the dates here indicated show when the several elections, resignations, or deaths are first mentioned in the board's annual reports.

Rev. Milton Bird	From 1847 to 1855	President and Cor. Sec.
Rev. Laban Jones	" 1847 to ——	
F. E. McLean	" 1847 to 1854	
A. M. Phelps	" 1847 to 1852	
James L. Stratton	" 1847 to ——	
Rev. S. M. Aston	" —— to 1851 or 1852	
Rev. S. B. Howard	" 1851 or 1852 to 1856	
E. C. Trimble	" 1852 to 1857	
Charles Miller	" 1854 to 1858	
Rev. B. Hall	" 1855 to 1856	
Rev. F. G. Black	" 1856 to 1858	
Rev. Le Roy Woods	" 1856 to 1858	
A. F. Cox	" 1856 to 1857	
Rev. Caleb Weedin	" 1856 to 1858	
F. P. Detheridge	" 1857 to 1858	
P. N. Frederick	" 1857 to 1858	
Andrew Allison	" 1858 to 1862	
Rev. W. E. Ward	" 1858 to 1862	President.
Rev. W. E. Ward	" 1867 to 1879	
Rev. Wiley M. Reed	" 1858 to 1862	President.
Joseph Pennock	" 1862 to 1865	Chairman.
Rev. S. T. Stewart	" 1862 to 1867	
Samuel Morrow	" 1862 to 1865	
Alexander Postley	" 1862 to 1867	
T. C. Leazear	" 1862 to 1865	
Rev. I. N. Cary	" 1865 to 1867	Chairman.
Edward De Barrenne	" 1867	President.
Rev. A. J. Baird	" 1867 to 1870	President.
Rev. L. C. Ransom	" 1867 to 1867	
David C. Love	" 1867 to 1874	
John Frizzell	" 1869 to 1881	Vice-president and President.
Terry H. Cahal	" 1870 to 1872	
John M. Gaut	" 1870—now a member	President, Treas., Cor. Sec.
W. C. Smith	" 1872 to 1880	Secretary.
Wm. Porter	" 1874 to 1876	
P. H. Manlove	" 1876—now a member	Secretary.
R. L. Caruthers, Jr.	" 1879 to 1881	Secretary.
Travis Winham	" 1879 to 1883	
W. F. Nisbet	" 1881 to 1886	
Thos. W. Campbell	" 1881 to 1887	
E. Waterhouse	" 1881 to 1885	
Rev. R. M. Tinnon	" 1882 to 1884	Secretary.
Isaac T. Rhea	" 1883 to 1887	
Rev. J. P. Sprowls	" 1884 to 1886	Secretary.
John H. Reynolds	" 1886—now a member	
Rev. W. J. Darby	" 1887— " "	
Rev. J. C. Provine	" 1887— " "	
H. Parks, Jr	" 1887— " "	Secretary.
W. T. Baird	" 1887— " "	

NEWSPAPERS.

The church's first paper, as has been seen, was the *Religious and Literary Intelligencer*. Its publication was begun by Cossitt & Lowry, at Princeton, Ky., early in 1830. It was moved to Nashville in 1832, and its name changed to the *Revivalist*. In 1834 its name was changed to the *Cumberland Presbyterian*. In 1839 its publication, after a brief suspension, was resumed at Springfield, Tennessee, where it expired in May, 1840. Its editors from first to last were F. R. Cossitt, David Lowry, and James Smith; assistants, T. C. Anderson and John W. Ogden.

THE BANNER OF PEACE—1840 TO 1874.

In March 1840, Dr. Cossitt, at Princeton, Kentucky, began the issue of a monthly pamphlet with this title. It was removed to Lebanon, Tennessee, January, 1843. Soon after this it was changed to a weekly. In 1850 the Rev. W. D. Chadick, D.D., bought this paper and continued its publication at Lebanon, at the same time purchasing and consolidating with it *The Ark*, a monthly, hitherto published at Athens, Tennessee, by Rev. Robert Frazier. Then he took Rev. David Lowry into partnership, both as proprietor and editor. He and Lowry sold the *Banner of Peace* to the Rev. Isaac Shook and the Rev. J. C. Provine. The paper was then moved to Nashville, where it remained till it was absorbed by the consolidated paper in 1874. Its succession of editors, after its removal to Nashville, was as follows: J. C. Provine, W. S. Langdon, W. E. Ward, J. C. Provine, J. M. Halsell, T. C. Blake, S. P. Chesnut. Some of the articles which appeared in the *Banner of Peace* were afterward collected and published in book form. Mahlon's Letters, by Dr. A. J. Baird, is one example. Others might well have been preserved in a similar manner.

CHURCH PAPERS IN PENNSYLVANIA.

A Cumberland Presbyterian newspaper was started in Pennsylvania before John Morgan began the publication of the *Union and Evangelist*, but no record of its name or its work has been found. It is alluded to sarcastically by Smith in his editorials. It ran a very brief course. In 1840 the *Union and Evangelist* began its career at Uniontown, Pennsylvania. After some time the Rev. J. P. Weethee became assistant editor. The next year Morgan died, and Milton Bird continued the publication for a short time at Uniontown. He then moved his paper to Pittsburg, Pennsylvania, and changed its name to the *Evangelist and Observer*. In 1846 we find the paper back at Uniontown, and its name changed to *The Cumberland Presbyterian*. Afterward the Rev. A. B. Brice became associate editor along with Bird. In 1847 Brice bought out Bird's interest, and continued to publish the paper at Uniontown till 1850. Then he removed to Brownsville and associated the Rev. J. T. A. Henderson with himself in the editorial work.

In 1857 the Rev. William Campbell was editor, and in 1860 the paper was issued from Waynesburg. In 1863 we find the name of the Rev. A. B. Miller, D.D., as editor, and after a while the name of Azel Freeman, associated with Dr. Miller's.

In November, 1868, Dr. Miller sold out his subscription list to Dr. J. B. Logan, of Illinois, and Pennsylvania for more than eight years had no Cumberland Presbyterian paper. In May, 1877, at Pittsburg, Pennsylvania, the Rev. Philip Axtell began the publication of *The Religious Pantagraph*, a large weekly. It was continued until November, 1878, when its subscription list, which had reached eleven hundred, was transferred to the *St. Louis Observer*. During a part of the year 1881, a small monthly, the *Semi-Centennial*, was issued at Pittsburg by Mr. Axtell, but its publication was suspended before the year closed.

THE CUMBERLAND PRESBYTERIAN PULPIT.

This was a monthly devoted to the publication of sermons. The first number was issued at Nashville, Tennessee, in January, 1833, by the Rev. James Smith. The first volume contains three sermons from Finis Ewing: one on the atonement, one against slavery, and one on Christian union; two sermons each from David Lowry, Robert Donnell, and Abner McDowell; and one each from Hiram A. Hunter, James Guthrie, George Donnell, William Ralston, Laban Jones, David Foster, Isaac Shook, David Morrow, John W. Ogden, James Smith, Richard Beard, A. G. Gibson, Robert Sloane, J. L. Dillard, David M. Kirkpatrick, Alexander Anderson, and C. P. Reed. One of the sermons furnished by Robert Donnell was preached at the Rev. William McGee's funeral, and the one contributed by John W. Ogden, was preached at the funeral of the Rev. William Barnett. Richard Beard's contribution was a sermon on The Church. It abounds in poetical quotations.

These sermons show what was the character of the preaching in Cumberland Presbyterian pulpits during the first two decades of the church's history. In all of them there is the utmost plainness and directness of manner. Reading them reminds us of Moody and his stirring appeals to sinners. In Donnell's sermon, preached at the funeral of William McGee, we are told that there were conversions under almost every sermon that McGee ever preached. That statement calls up a remark which the writer, when only a child, heard Robert Donnell make to the Rev. Samuel McSpeddin. He used something like these words: "Brother McSpeddin, there is something wrong. I have now preached two sermons in succession without witnessing one single conversion." How many sermons in succession do our preachers now deliver without witnessing a conversion? How many preach without either expecting or praying for conversions? Some have set times in the future, and look forward to the protracted meeting season, when they expect and pray for conversions; and they grind their ecclesiastical organs to entertain and hold their congregations together the rest of the year.

THE ARK—1841 TO 1850.

In September, 1841, the Rev. Robert Frazier began the publication of *The Ark*, at Athens, Tennessee. This was a monthly. It at first had three special departments: 1. Doctrinal, 2. Ecclesiastical, 3. Moral. An historical department was afterward added. One thing might have been safely predicted in advance of all Frazier's editorials. He would run in no ruts. He called no man master. There was a boldness and vigor about his writings which constituted their chief charm. Oftener wrong, perhaps, than right in the positions he took, it is manifest at least that he was honest and thoroughly in earnest in all these positions. He was fearless, too, attacking every thing in the church which he believed to be wrong. His paper earnestly advocated the divorce of the church courts from all secular enterprises.

THE TEXAS PRESBYTERIAN.

In November, 1846, the Rev. A. J. McGown issued the first number of this paper at Victoria, Texas. It was a large four-page weekly. Its location was several times changed. After publishing this paper nine years as a private enterprise, he tried to induce his synod to take charge of it. In this, however, he was not successful, and so he continued to plead for the interests of the Texas churches in its columns. Not only was the paper valuable to the local interests, but some of the best materials for a history of the progress of the church in other fields have been gathered from articles published in it. It is asserted by some that this was the first

Protestant newspaper ever published on Texas soil. McGown and his paper received strong commendations from members of other churches, from old soldiers of San Jacinto, and from authors of stately volumes.

TEXAS CUMBERLAND PRESBYTERIAN—TEXAS OBSERVER.

The *Texas Cumberland Presbyterian* was not the same paper McGown edited, but a new enterprise, undertaken after his death. Its publication was begun by Rev. J. B. Renfro and Rev. J. H. Wofford, at Tehuacana, April, 1873, and it was continued until the Assembly's consolidation scheme absorbed all the private newspapers of the church. The sale of this paper to the church was accomplished in December, 1874. Wofford had previously bought out Renfro's interest. In 1879 Mr. Wofford began the publication of a new paper, the *Texas Observer*, at Tehuacana. This paper has changed owners and editors several times, and the place of publication has also been frequently changed. It is now issued as the organ of Trinity University by a stock company. Under this arrangement Dr. E. B. Crisman and the Rev. J. S. Groves were until recently the editors. The Rev. W. B. Preston has lately become editor. Its name has been changed to the *Texas Cumberland Presbyterian*.

THE WATCHMAN AND EVANGELIST—1850 TO 1859.

Milton Bird, after he sold the *Cumberland Presbyterian*, at Uniontown, Pennsylvania, to the Rev. A. B. Brice, moved to Louisville, Kentucky, and, in 1850, started the *Watchman and Evangelist* there. After several changes of editors, this paper was, in 1859, consolidated with the *Missouri Cumberland Presbyterian*, and moved to St. Louis.

PAPERS IN MISSOURI AND ILLINOIS.

St. Louis, Missouri, and Alton, Illinois, have for a long time jointly constituted an important newspaper center for our people. In May, 1852, at the earnest solicitation of a number of Missouri ministers and leading laymen, the Rev. J. B. Logan began the publication of the *Missouri Cumberland Presbyterian* at Lexington, Missouri. He had the promise of five hundred subscribers to begin with, and the list was to be increased to one thousand by the close of the year; but he began with three hundred. In a year he moved the paper to St. Louis. In 1858 or 1859 the *Watchman and Evangelist*, published at Louisville by A. F. Cox, and edited by the Rev. Milton Bird, D.D., was united with the *Missouri Cumberland Presbyterian*, and the consolidated paper was called the *St. Louis Observer*. Dr. Bird was for a time its editor. Mr. Cox afterward bought this paper. About the beginning of the war the list was sold to the *Cumberland Presbyterian*, then published at Waynesburg, Pennsylvania.

About 1861 the Rev. J. B. Logan began the publication of the *Western Cumberland Presbyterian*, at Alton, Illinois. It was continued under this name until November, 1868, when it became the *Cumberland Presbyterian*, its proprietor having purchased from Dr. A. B. Miller, of Waynesburg, Pennsylvania, the paper bearing this latter title. The Rev. J. R. Brown became joint editor and also joint proprietor of this consolidated paper. In 1874 it was sold to the Board of Publication by Brown and Perrin, and removed to Nashville, Tennessee.

In September, 1875, the publication of *Our Faith* was begun at Alton. This was a monthly, and the Rev. J. B. Logan, D.D., was its editor. It was continued about a year and a half, when it was merged into the *St. Louis Observer*. The latter was a weekly paper, and the Rev. W. B. Farr, D.D., was made its editor. The Rev. W. C. Logan afterward became associate editor. Mr. Logan and the Rev. J. R. Brown, D.D., are its present editors.

The Ladies' Pearl—1852 to 1884.

This was a monthly magazine for women. Its publication was commenced at Nashville, Tennessee, by W. S. Langdon and J. C. Provine, in 1852. It was the testimony of Dr. Herschel S. Porter that this magazine did more to develop the talents of the women of the Cumberland Presbyterian Church than all other agencies put together. Hosts of sprightly writers were called out who knew nothing of their own powers till the *Pearl* developed them. J. B. Logan, J. R. Brown, John Shirley Ward, J. M. Halsell, and S. P. Chesnut were all at one time or another editors of this magazine. Dr. Chesnut finally sold it, and Cumberland Presbyterians ceased to have any periodical specially for ladies.

THE PACIFIC OBSERVER.

In 1860, at Alamo, California, the Rev. T. M. Johnston started the first Cumberland Presbyterian paper on the Pacific coast. It was first called *The Presbyter*, afterward *The Pacific Observer*. At first it was issued monthly, but was soon changed to a weekly. It was removed to Stockton, and was of good size and well printed. The subscription price was four dollars a year. The isolated condition of our feeble churches in California gave a poor prospect for sufficient patronage to sustain such a paper; but Johnston persevered, though at a heavy pecuniary loss. He felt that the paper was a necessity to the church in that country; and he spared neither toil nor money in the struggle to meet the pressing demand. In 1871 this paper was bought by Dr. D. E. Bushnell, and moved from Stockton to San Francisco, where it ran a short course and then ceased to exist. Its fruits, however, still live.

CENTRAL CUMBERLAND PRESBYTERIAN.

The publication of this paper was begun at Owensboro, Kentucky, January, 1865, with the Rev. Jesse Anderson as editor. Near the close of that year the Rev. J. M. Halsell became editor and proprietor. Its largest circulation was in Kentucky, Indiana, Illinois, and Missouri. Its influence helped to prepare the way for the conservative action of the General Assembly in 1866. It was consolidated with the *Banner of Peace* at Nashville, June, 1866.

THE THEOLOGICAL MEDIUM—1845 TO 1884.

In 1845, at Uniontown, Pennsylvania, the Rev. Milton Bird issued the first number of the *Theological Medium*. It was at first a monthly, devoted to theological discussions. Its first article was a discussion of the subject of election, by the Rev. Albert Gibson. It frequently published sermons. Its location was several times changed. Finally it was changed into a quarterly. It passed through various hands. Dr. T. C. Blake owned and edited it a while. Then it was bought by the Board of Publication, and the Rev. M. B. DeWitt was its editor. After this the theological professors in Cumberland University were its proprietors and editors. Then W. C. Logan, of St. Louis, Missouri, in whose hands it died, was its owner and editor. Its name had, in the meantime, undergone some transformations. Its last name was the *Cumberland Presbyterian Quarterly.*

The doctrines and policy of the church were ably discussed in this quarterly. So, also, were many questions of general interest. Nearly all our best scholars and writers were at one time or another contributors to its pages. Its files furnish a striking record of the views and the progress of our people, and indicate a gratifying unity of doctrine and harmony of feeling. No arguments against the inspiration of the Bible, no clerical infidelity, no "scientific apostasy from the faith" is to be found in any of these productions of our writers. Solid, old-time views on all the great leading doctrines greet us everywhere as we peruse these pages. The doctrine of the plenary inspiration of the whole Bible, of the eternal punishment of the finally impenitent, of the vicarious atonement of Christ, of the spiritually dead state of the unconverted, and, therefore, of the absolute necessity of regeneration and of justification by faith, together with all the other standard doctrines of our Confession of Faith, are ably enforced. Some little differences in minor matters there are, of course, but there is a general unity in sound and orthodox teaching. We find, too, in these files many able articles from recognized leaders on the necessity of holy living. Prominent among those pleading for holiness of life were Samuel McAdow and Dr. Beard.

Cumberland Presbyterians have had in all over fifty periodicals, and over one hundred editors. There have been six newspaper centers in the Cumberland Presbyterian church: one in Kentucky, one in Tennessee, one in Pennsylvania, one in Texas, one at Alton or St. Louis, and one on the Pacific coast. The Rev. F. Lack's paper in the German language, and some occasional publications in the Japanese tongue, are the only periodicals ever published by our people not in the English language. There have been transient issues of some sort in the Choctaw language and, perhaps, in the Cherokee, but no regular periodicals. The church has an important work to do in furnishing a periodical literature for our children and young people. Our Sunday-school publications are doing great good, and have a most inviting field of usefulness to cultivate.

REVISION OF THE CONFESSION OF FAITH—1854 AND 1883.

From the first there was dissatisfaction with the arrangement of the chapters of our Confession of Faith. Besides this, there were in the book scraps of the Westminster Confession that belonged naturally to the rejected system of fatality, and were hard to fit into the system held and preached with great unanimity by our ministers. This fault of our first Confession was freely admitted by the men who compiled the book. Strong statements to this effect, from Ewing in particular, exist now in manuscript, to be filed in the library of Cumberland University. In spite of these admissions, not only the original compilers of the book but a great number of younger men feared to open the door of revision, lest too great innovations should be made. What greatly strengthened these fears was the fact that one or two strong men in the church who rejected vital points in our system of doctrines were acknowledged leaders among revisionists.

In 1852 the following paper was submitted to the Assembly by the Rev. Samuel Dennis:

WHEREAS, It is believed by many, whose opinions deserve respectful consideration, that in order to a more clear, definite, and literal rendering of the distinctive tenets of Cumberland Presbyterianism, a revision of the Confession of Faith and Form of Government is necessary; and, whereas, it is believed that such revision can be safely undertaken by this General Assembly; therefore,

Resolved, 1. That a committee of nine be appointed by this General Assembly, whose duty it shall be to take under consideration every part of the Confession of Faith and the Form of Government, and report the result of their labors to the next General Assembly.

2. That said committee shall have no power to diminish any chapter or section, or add thereto, only in so far as they may esteem it necessary to present the doctrines and government of the church in as literal, clear, and unambiguous manner as possible; and they are hereby forbidden to introduce a new chapter or section, unless they shall esteem an additional section to the sixteenth chapter of the Form of Government necessary to carry out the provisions of said chapter; nor shall they be permitted to add foot-notes.

After considerable discussion, this was negatived. The yeas and nays being called stood, yeas, 14; nays, 69.

But the revisionists were not to be put down, even by so decided a vote. The very next year they came with a synodical memorial, asking for revision. The Assembly of 1853 yielded so far as to appoint a committee to prepare a revised Confession. As soon as this was done, the *Banner of Peace* closed its columns against the discussion of the question. Its editor was a revisionist, but Milton Bird, who was opposed to revision, kept the columns of his paper open to this discussion. The committee prepared a new creed, and printed it and the creed of 1814 in parallel columns. This was a very fair and satisfactory mode of presenting the case. This amended Confession was reported by the committee to the Assembly of 1854. It contained no new doctrines, but presented a rearrangement of the order of the chapters. A few objectionable phrases were struck out, and words more in keeping with the general method of presenting our doctrines in the pulpit substituted. The first, second, fourth, seventh, twelfth, sixteenth, seventeenth, eighteenth, nineteenth, twentieth, twenty-first, twenty-second, twenty-third, twenty-fourth, twenty-fifth, twenty-sixth, twenty-seventh, and twenty-ninth chapters of the Confesssion were presented unchanged.

On the question of accepting this report and of submitting the proposed amendments to the presbyteries, speeches were made by Dr. S. G. Burney and the Rev. Reuben Burrow in favor of the revision; and by Dr. Richard Beard and Judge R. L. Caruthers against it. Very deep interest was felt in the discussion. Robert Donnell, who helped to prepare our first Confession, was present and took sides with the opposers of revision. There was not time during the sitting of one Assembly thoroughly to examine and discuss the proposed amendments. Men feared evils which these changes did not involve. When the vote was reached there was a very large majority against the new book.

One of the strangest things in all the history of the church took place after that. A synod went so far as to pass a vote of censure upon the Assembly for refusing to refer that revised Confession to the presbyteries, and published its action in the *Banner of Peace*.

An effort to revise our Form of Government has already been

alluded to. It engaged the attention of every General Assembly from 1867 to 1874. A committee consisting of Richard Beard, S. G. Burney, J. H. Coulter, R. L. Caruthers, and John Frizzell was appointed in the year first named, and reported to the Assembly of 1868 a revised Form of Government and Discipline, which was approved and submitted to the presbyteries. Fifty-eight of the one hundred presbyteries reported action on it, and but eight of these approved the revision as a whole; twenty accepted parts of it, while twenty-eight rejected the whole. A new committee, consisting of F. G. Black, H. D. Onyett, A. Templeton, C. H. Bell, and Nathan Green was however appointed to perfect this work of revision. By the order of the Assembly of 1870, fifteen hundred copies of this new committee's report were printed and the whole matter referred to the next Assembly. Much of the time of the Assemblies of 1871 and 1872 was spent in discussing and amending this proposed revision. Twenty-one chapters, composing a new Form of Government, were approved by the Assembly in 1872, and submitted to the presbyteries. Thirty-seven presbyteries voted in favor of these chapters, and forty-two against them, while twenty-five presbyteries were not heard from. By the Assembly of 1873 the same matter was referred back to the presbyteries to enable them to review their action. But in 1874 but forty-three presbyteries reported in favor of this revision, while forty-six voted against it. The matter was then indefinitely postponed.

In 1881 a memorial was presented to the General Assembly, again asking for a revision of the Confession of Faith. That Assembly appointed two committees, one to revise the book, and another to revise this revision. The first committee consisted of S. G. Burney, A. Templeton, and John Frizzell; the second, of C. H. Bell, J. W. Poindexter, A. B. Miller, W. J. Darby, and R. L. Caruthers. These committees early in 1882 published the result of their work in the *Cumberland Presbyterian*, presenting a "Revised Confession of Faith, and Government." This report was also printed in pamphlet form, and mailed to all the ministers of the church. It was introduced by a statement, signed by all the members of the committee who participated in the work, setting forth in a very forcible manner the reasons why the revision was thought desirable. This introduction gave the following account of the work of the committees:

The first committee met at Lebanon, Tennessee, November 18, 1881, all the members being present, and continued its labors until the evening of the 24th, holding three sessions daily, Sunday excepted. The second committee convened November 25, 1881, at the same place, Ministers C. H. Bell and W. J. Darby, and Ruling Elder R. L. Caruthers being present; and continued its labors one week, holding three sessions daily, Sunday excepted. By request the first committee was present with the second at its meetings, and participated in its deliberations. The discussions were full and free, evincing a wonderful harmony of opinion. Some preferences as to verbal form had, of course, to be surrendered. This, however, was always done in the true spirit of compromise, and in no instance was there a negative vote. Mindful of the fact that the committees were appointed not to make a new Confession, but to revise the old one, we have studied not to transcend our authority; and we have no hesitation in saying that we have not changed a single doctrine fundamental to your scheme of theology, or any of its logical correlates.

It was announced that the object of publishing this report before the meeting of the Assembly was "to secure to the committees the benefit of the suggestions and criticisms or objections" that any person might wish to make before the revised book should be finally presented to the Assembly. The secretaries of the two committees published the following statement:

The committees feel that they have discharged the trust assigned them by the General Assembly with a conscientious regard to its importance, but they will meet again for a final revision previous to the meeting of the Assembly. Any suggestion forwarded to them in the meantime will be carefully considered before the matter is submitted to the Assembly.

The discussion of this report and of questions connected with it was excluded from the church paper until after the meeting of the Assembly of 1882, the editor assigning the following reasons:

The report being yet in the hands of the committee, and incomplete, it of course is not yet presented for adoption, and is not legitimately before the church for discussion. . . . To enter upon a general discussion of the report while it is in this incomplete state would not be justice to the committee nor profitable to the church, as it would be necessary to go over the whole ground again. . . . We want the report considered and the issue met on its merits, which can not be done now. . . . The work is incomplete and in the hands of a committee, and has not been considered by the General Assembly. Therefore the time for a discussion in the paper has not come.

It probably would have been well, in order to remove all possible grounds of dissatisfaction or complaint, to have allowed those not in favor of revision to state their objections in the church paper, even before the report was submitted to the Assembly. There would have been no injustice to the committees in this. They would have been helped rather than hindered by the suggestions which such a discussion would have called forth. There was really no danger of any angry or distracting controversy. A full and impartial discussion at that time, while it could not have changed the final result, would have satisfied the few who were opposed to the new book. But these few really had no serious ground of complaint. The committees called for suggestions from the whole church, giving every man in the denomination a chance to file his objection or record his protest; and in the Assembly, and afterward in the papers and before the presbyteries, the fullest possible opportunity for discussion was afforded. The Assembly of 1882 made considerable changes in the proposed book, and then referred it to the presbyteries, requiring them to accept or reject the new Confession as a whole.

There were some who thought final action should have been deferred another year, to give time for further suggestions and amendments, but the majority thought otherwise. A large portion of the new book is the work of the Assembly of 1882. As a system it differs from the old in nothing but its omissions. It contains no new doctrines. No original Cumberland Presbyterian could reject the new Confession.

Improvements, which an anti-revisionist is obliged to admit, are found in very many places. For example the order of subjects in our first Confession is Justification, Adoption, Sanctification, Saving Faith, Repentance; while the order in the revised book is Repentance, Faith, Justification, Regeneration, Adoption, Sanctification. Every old-time Cumberland Presbyterian recognizes the landmarks of our theological system in the second arrangement, but not in the first. Throughout the new book, harmony with our pulpit theology is clearly discernible.

The only just grounds for complaint against the new book are in its omissions, and in its loose and hastily written portions. After all, Confessions of Faith are smaller, far smaller matters now than they were in the preceding century. The Bible, studied as a book, without reference to creeds, is very different from the Bible studied in the light of a particular creed. The Bible as a book is what our International Sabbath-school System puts us all to studying. The Bible as a book will, it is hoped, one day be studied in all our theological schools. It is the utter abuse of creeds to use them as candles for studying the Scripture. They have their appropriate place, but that place is a very subordinate one.

The report of the committees contained no list of proof-texts, and there is no record of such a list ever coming before the Assembly. These proof-texts were not, therefore, submitted to the presbyteries, and are left by the committees just where they ought to be left, as mere suggestions and nothing more. They are helpful, and there their mission ends. So too the preface is properly left in the same loose connection with the creed. It is not and should not be a part of our doctrines. It was very properly never referred to the presbyteries, and contains historic statements which may be questioned without incurring the charge of heresy. Whether we think it good or bad, true or false, is a matter of no importance.

One thing that did go down to the presbyteries and meet their approval, and now stands as a law of the church, was improperly or by oversight omitted from the stereotyped book, though it was in the earlier and cheaper edition. It is this:

It being hereby distinctly understood and declared that those who have heretofore received and adopted the Confession of Faith approved by the General Assembly in 1829, and who prefer to adhere to the doctrinal statements contained therein, are at liberty to do so. [First (printed) edition of new Confession, page 137. See also Assembly's Minutes, 1882, page 36.]

This is the edition on which the presbyteries acted. This item went far toward satisfying the anti-revisionists.

The presbyteries voted almost unanimously in favor of the adoption of this new creed. There has been nothing like this unanimity in all ecclesiastical history. It amazed and silenced those who were opposed to revision. Most of these determined at once to acquiesce. A few may still be unhappy about it, but even they are bound to admit that the new creed is by no means what they apprehended that it would prove to be.

After Paul came as an appendix to the apostleship, God sent Peter (one of the fathers) to write a few words, in his old age, to let the churches know that he indorsed what this fiery apostle to the Gentiles had taught in his epistles. So, in 1883, God in his goodness allowed John L. Dillard, who was a full-grown man before our church was organized, in 1810, and who was a companion in the gospel with all the first Cumberland Presbyterian ministers, to speak in terms of approval of the doctrinal teachings and the spirit of the church in this generation. He not only saw and read the new creed, but expressed himself as well pleased with it. It is not likely that such an old watch-dog of our orthodoxy could be deceived.

TEMPERANCE.

Among the items taken down by the author of this history from the lips of the Rev. Thomas Calhoun, in 1845, was the following: "Samuel King was the first man I ever heard come out publicly against even the moderate use of whisky. He refused to ask a blessing at a public dinner because the table had whisky on it." In the Minutes of Elk Presbytery for April, 1816, page 21, Vol. I., are resolutions pledging all the members to total abstinence, and binding them to enforce this rule to the utmost among their people, and wherever else their authority or influence extended.

Our church papers have all been agreed in their opposition to intemperance and the whisky traffic. Whatever else they may have differed about, they all have spoken with one voice on this subject. It would be hard to determine which of our one hundred editors has been the most outspoken against whisky and in favor of temperance. Those now in the editorial work are all earnest advocates of total abstinence and prohibition, but they are not more earnest or outspoken on this subject than was David Lowry, who belonged to the first editorial corps of our first church newspaper.

The Rev. Le Roy Woods gave in the *Cumberland Presbyterian* the following reasons for going to the legislature of Indiana, in 1855:

The facts in the case are these. I had given up my place as publishing agent, and had taken a very active part in the temperance cause, which has agitated our State from one end to the other. I was a member of the State convention, which resolved to ignore all party questions and make the passage of a prohibitory law the issue at the polls. I had advocated the same in a convention in our own county, and strongly advocated the nomination of a temperance ticket for the county in the event of the politicians refusing to do so. They did refuse, and we had no alternative left us but to have our county represented by men opposed to our whole temperance scheme, or nominate a ticket of our own. This we determined to do. When we came to look over the ground and see the difficulty, we had some trouble in finding men who would assume the responsibility of pleading the claims of our cause before the public. In this dilemma the convention, without a single dissenting voice, demanded of me that I should accept the nomination and make the canvass. No one but myself knows the struggle which it cost me to obtain my own consent. Nothing but my deep solicitude for the cause of temperance, and a sense of duty to our common country, could have induced me to accept this expression of confidence on the part of so many of my fellow-citizens. On the day of my nomination, and throughout the whole canvass, I publicly refused to be a politician. I made the race exclusively on the question of "Search and Seizure," no other question was discussed.

He was elected on this prohibition ticket, called the "Search and Seizure" ticket.

When our church had but three presbyteries, and drinking whisky was as common as drinking coffee is now, each of these presbyteries declared it to be an offense worthy of discipline to make, sell, give away, or drink intoxicating liquors. Our church courts have kept up these utterances, only making them stronger and stronger as the years have passed away. All of our recent Assemblies have declared it to be the duty of Cumberland Presbyterians to co-operate in all lawful efforts to secure the prohibition of the manufacture and sale of intoxicating drinks. The Assembly of 1851 passed the following resolution:

Resolved, That it is the sense of this General Assembly that to make, buy, sell, or use as a beverage any spirituous or intoxicating liquors is an immorality; that it is not only unauthorized, but forbidden by the word of God. We do, therefore, recommend to the several churches under our care, to abstain wholly from their use.

The Assembly of 1853 adopted a report which, after setting forth the evils of intemperance, asks:

What is the duty of the church relative to this important question? We believe there is but one answer. It is the duty of the Christian to use every reasonable effort within his power to advance the glorious cause of temperance. If he fails in this he fails in one material branch of his duty, and will be held accountable for the failure. We regard the efforts now being made in the temperance cause as requiring the co-operation of the church, . . . as one of the means of reforming and finally converting the world; and the failure of church members thus to co-operate amounts to a sin against light and knowledge. So far as our information extends, this branch of Zion is discharging her duty in this great work with commendable zeal.

The efforts which Christians should use for the furtherance of this work consist not alone in abstaining from the use of ardent spirits, and being Washingtonians or Sons of Temperance. The true and devoted advocate of temperance will labor for the enactment of such laws as will prohibit the making, vending, or use of intoxicating liquors.

To this preamble the following resolutions were added:

1. It is incompatible with the character of a Christian, and particularly the Christian character of a Cumberland Presbyterian, to use or in any way to encourage the use of ardent spirits as a beverage.

2. If he fails to use reasonable efforts to bring about, by legal enactments or otherwise, an entire prohibition of the liquor traffic, he acts beneath his duty as a professor of religion.

3. Christians not only have duties to discharge to the church and the world as Christians, but also to their government and society as citizens.

4. In discharging the latter duty they should be governed by the broad principles of Christian philanthropy, advocating the extermination of alcoholic drinks . . . by the enactment of prohibitory laws for that purpose, with such penalties as will cause those laws to be respected and enforced.

With some slight verbal changes, this preamble, accompanied by the same resolutions, was adopted by the Assembly of 1854.

Time after time the Assembly and subordinate judicatures have called on all our ministers and churches to pray for the overthrow of the whisky traffic. Sunday-schools have been again and again urged to teach the doctrine of total abstinence and prohibition. Men who sell intoxicating spirits have repeatedly been declared unfit for church membership.

In 1876 the managers of the Philadelphia Centennial Exhibition made provisions to allow whisky to be sold on their grounds. Our General Assembly that year, by a unanimous rising vote, protested against this action as "a flagrant violation of the moral and Christian sense of the American people," and appealed to the Centennial Board of Finance to revoke this license, adopting the following resolution:

Resolved, That we do hereby earnestly recommend that all the members of the Cumberland Presbyterian church refrain from patronizing the Centennial Exhibition until the ruling of the Board of Managers be changed on this subject.

The Assembly of 1884 appointed "a day of special prayer for divine guidance in the selection of discreet and godly men by the great political parties" in the national conventions then approaching. It urged that greater prominence should be given to the subject of temperance in Sunday-schools, and that temperance meetings for children should be held. It indorsed the various societies organized to promote the temperance reform, enumerating "the several State Temperance Alliances, the Woman's Christian Temperance Union, the Order of Good Templars, the Young Men's Christian Association, and the Band of Hope."

In 1885 the Assembly declared "the manufacture or sale of ardent spirits as a beverage inconsistent with Christian character and the high relation of church membership;" and in 1886 the cause of prohibition was indorsed in this strong language:

Recognizing the manufacture and sale of intoxicating liquors as the source of very great evils, we re-affirm our unflinching devotion to the cause of absolute constitutional prohibition, and we are glad to note that other ecclesiastical bodies are taking high ground on this subject.

The Assembly of 1887 declared "that the failure or refusal of any professed follower of our divine Master to use his profession in favor of, to pray for, labor for, and vote for such legislation as will free the country and God's church from this drink curse, is inconsistent with the teachings of holy Scripture and the example of our Savior."

David Lowry, in an article published not long before his death, adduces an array of testimonies to prove that the use of fermented wines was forbidden at the Jewish passovers,[1] presenting Jewish instructions about the time and the manner in which the passover wine should be prepared, and denying that Christ made fermented wine or wine that would intoxicate. He showed that all the direct utterances of the Bible on this subject condemn strong drink in the most unmistakable terms. Incidental mention of harlots and of thieves there are, in which the sacred writer does not stop to express condemnation, but in every direct declaration concerning their character and their deeds they are condemned. Of the same nature are all the Bible utterances about strong drink. Many incidental mentions of it we find, but in every case where its character is directly pronounced upon, it is either condemned or prohibited, or both. All persons are forbidden even to look upon the wine when it is red.[2] We are forbidden to induct into the ministry any man who is given to wine-drinking.[3] Such is the tone generally of the direct declarations of God's word.

By the grace of God the sober people of the land are determined to give the matter no rest until the manufacture and sale of intoxicating drinks are as thoroughly prohibited by law as are theft and murder.

The following anecdote concerning the Rev. J. M. Berry, which appeared in one of our church papers, is given as a fitting close for this chapter:

Abraham Lincoln was once the partner in a little store with William Berry, the Rev. J. M. Berry's son—his prodigal son. After Lincoln had retired from the "store," and had gained considerable

---

[1] It was an offense punishable by death to be found with leaven in the house. Leavened or fermented wine would have incurred that penalty.—Ex. xii. 19.
[2] Prov. xxiii. 31, 32. [3] 1 Tim. iii. 3; Titus i. 7, 8.

notoriety as a lawyer, some women banded together and broke up a grog-shop which had become an intolerable nuisance to the neighborhood. They knocked in the heads of the barrels and kegs, and smashed the bottles. When the dram seller threatened them with the law or violence, one of the women said to him: "Be quiet, for we are determined to knock in the head of every thing that has liquor in it; and your own head is in danger." Lincoln volunteered to plead the cause of the women. The case was tried in the town where the Rev. J. M. Berry lived. A large crowd had collected to hear the pleading. The evils of intemperance were so eloquently presented as to touch most of those present, and many were bathed in tears. "There," said the speaker, pointing his long bony finger toward Mr. Berry, "is the man who years ago was instrumental in convincing me of the evils of trafficking in and using ardent spirits." Tears ran in streams down the aged preacher's cheeks. His thoughts at that time were probably something like this: "O my ruined boy! I lost you, but saved your partner. Thank God my labors were not in vain in the Lord."

CHAPTER XLVIII.

NEW FIELDS, EVANGELISTS, PROGRESS, REFLECTIONS.

> Springs of life in desert places
> Shall thy God unseal for thee;
> Quickening and reviving graces,
> Dew-like, healing, sweet and free.
> —*F. R. H.*

PIONEER missionaries of the Cumberland Presbyterian church have penetrated to almost all the Territories of the West. The lack of an adequate home mission fund has crippled the efforts of our people to establish congregations, but in spite of the lack of strong support from the churches in the older States, a good work has been done in many towns and country places in these new fields.

COLORADO.

As soon as the Territory of Colorado was open to white settlers, Cumberland Presbyterian preachers and private members joined the tide of emigration that flowed thither. The Rev. B. F. Moore was perhaps the first of our preachers to make his home in this Territory. He was there and at work when the Rev. J. Cal. Littrell and the Rev. S. D. Givens arrived in the fall of 1870. The Board of Missions rendered some little assistance to Littrell and Givens, whose work in that Territory was crowned with great success.

In November, 1870, these three ministers, Moore, Littrell, and Givens, organized the Rocky Mountain Presbytery.[1] This presbytery had at first but one congregation under its care. The missionaries traveled from house to house, laboring among the families of the emigrants, and holding meetings wherever they could gather the people together. In 1872 there were six congregations, one hundred and nine members, and one hundred and forty-eight

---

[1] Sketch furnished by stated clerk, the Rev. W. W. M. Barber.

pupils in the Sunday-schools. The church property in the presbyterial bounds was valued at five thousand dollars. In the year ending May, 1874, Littrell traveled over five thousand miles, and preached one hundred and eighty-seven times. There were four congregations in his field of labor.

The Rev. T. H. Henderson was laboring as missionary at Colorado Springs in 1874. In 1875 the board reported that this mission had been taken under its care. The congregation then had a "good church edifice finished and paid for, and a small organization of energetic and liberal members." The Rev. P. A. Rice, who succeeded the Rev. T. H. Henderson as missionary, had also resigned. Afterward the Rev. J. H. Steele, the Rev. J. Cal. Littrell, and the Rev. W. A. Hyde successively served as missionaries here. To the Assembly of 1881 the board announced that this mission had been declared self-sustaining.

The city of Pueblo was a point of interest to Cumberland Presbyterian pioneers, and a good beginning in denominational work was made there mainly by private enterprise. Then the congregation was adopted by our board as a mission. A comfortable church was built and paid for. When the Board of Missions made its report in 1886, this congregation had a membership of twenty, and church property valued at $3,500.

NEW MEXICO.

In 1875 that zealous pioneer, the Rev. J. Cal. Littrell, published the following account of an exploring trip made by him in New Mexico:

Through the kindness of my congregations and friends at home, I was granted time to visit Colfax County, New Mexico. I had been for over a year receiving earnest requests from the people there, urging me to visit them and preach to them. This I have done during the past twenty-five days. I found large communities gospel hungry. They have no preaching, no Sunday-schools, no assembling together on the Sabbath day. I preached where the gospel had never been proclaimed before. Some had not heard a sermon for more than ten years. We were blessed with gracious outpourings of the Holy Spirit. Christians were made happy in a Savior's love afresh, and some for the first time learned the joy of believing. Men of the world wept and trembled. There was much earnest pleading for help. Many said: "Won't you come and preach to us, or send some one? We are poor, but we will do all we can." I thank God that I went, although it was a hard trip, and I received less than my expenses. I have the assurance that I did them some good. I met several Cumberland Presbyterians. O that the missionary spirit would fire some faithful and efficient man to go into that field! It is extensive, and white unto harvest. I traveled four hundred and fifteen miles, and received one dollar and fifteen cents.

No attempt has been made to plant Cumberland Presbyterian churches in New Mexico.

NEBRASKA.

Before Nebraska was a home for white settlers it was part of the great highway to the Pacific. Fur traders, soldiers, daring adventurers, and miners had their regular routes of travel across its wide plains, and their posts for supplies along its water-courses. Along with these travelers were some of our own people, as well as along with the very first permanent settlers on this soil. Like most pioneers, however, they published no history of their labors. It is by no means to be presumed that their lives were destitute of adventures. Indian difficulties and Indian massacres we know there were, and questions growing out of some of these came up for discussion and decision before the national authorities ten years after Nebraska became an organized Territory of the United States.

When all became peaceful, it did not follow that Indians were no longer Indians. It is said that when the kind-hearted Quakers of Philadelphia heard that the Nebraska squaws wore no bonnets, they immediately sent an ample supply. On the reception of these, the Indian braves held a council and decided to use the bonnets for "crow cushions," bound upon the persons not of the squaws, but the warriors!

The men who organized and managed the celebrated express company for overland passengers and freight from the "States" to California before the war, were members of the Cumberland Presbyterian church. The history of this enterprise with the biographies of the men who planned it and carried it out, would, if published, form a volume of thrilling interest. Large-hearted, brave, adventurous men they were, and all the West teems with stories of their wonderful energy and liberality. This company had one of its important stations in what is now Nebraska City.

The following account of the introduction of the Cumberland Presbyterian church in the Territory of Nebraska was written in 1868 by the Rev. R. S. Reed, then pastor at Nebraska City, and published in the *Banner of Peace:*

I am not positive, but believe that the first sermon by a Cumberland Presbyterian minister in Nebraska was preached in the spring of 1858 or 1859, by the Rev. Robert Renick, of Missouri. It occurred in this way: Alexander Majors, Esq., formerly of Independence, Missouri, and for many years a ruling elder in our church at that place, had settled in Nebraska City, and was extensively engaged in the freighting business. The rules by which he governed his teamsters—usually a rough class of men—were peculiar to himself, but of very extensive notoriety in this Western country. Among other wholesome requirements, drunkenness and profanity were positively prohibited under penalty of immediate dismission from service without pay. These rules were strictly enforced; and, in addition, it was Mr. Majors' custom to rest on the Sabbath, and hold prayer-meetings with his men. These meetings he usually conducted himself, often delivering extempore exhortations, in which he was not a little gifted. Sometimes a minister in the company preached, and in this way it is possible that some Cumberland Presbyterian minister preached in this Territory before Father Renick.

A wave of moral influence was started through the untiring efforts of Mr. Majors, whose effects will be seen and felt in eternity. But few men, if any, have such moral power in this country as that which he exercised. Would to God we had many more such elders. About the time to which reference has been made, he induced Father Renick to come to Nebraska City, paying him a good salary out of his own pocket to preach to his men while in camp. Father Renick came and preached for some months in a beautiful grove adjoining the city and known as the "Outfitting Grounds." Mr. Majors expected to secure the organization of a Cumberland Presbyterian church, but Father Renick returned to Missouri, and the purpose was abandoned for the time. About this time one or two camp-meetings were held near this city by Mr. Majors, and perhaps some other Cumberland Presbyterians, in connection with brethren of the Methodist Episcopal church. Gracious revivals were enjoyed at these meetings, and many sinners were converted.

The first Cumberland Presbyterian church organized in the Territory of Nebraska was at Nebraska City. The great civil war, and especially the troubles in Missouri consequent upon this war, had brought quite a large emigration to this city. Among these emigrants were quite a number of Cumberland Presbyterians and Southern Methodists, who were as sheep without a shepherd. Business had called Mr. Majors and a few others here prior to this. The most of these united, temporarily, with the Methodist Episcopal church; but such were the political influences brought to bear in this church and from the pulpit during the exciting times of war, that it was impossible for them to live in peace here. They accordingly quietly withdrew. It was then proposed to find a home in the Presbyterian church (O. S.). The Rev. J. G. Dalton, a worthy brother and member of the Lexington Presbytery of our church, being here at the time, did, by invitation, occupy the pulpit of that church for a few months. But such was the discourtesy with which the proposition to unite with that church was treated, that our brethren felt they could not find a congenial home with that people.

It was, perhaps, about this time that the Rev. O. D. Allen, from Missouri, gathered up a few Cumberland Presbyterians in the neighborhood of Rock Bluff, about eighteen miles above Nebraska City, and preached for them for a time. About the same time, perhaps a little later, the Rev. Mr. Starnes, of Missouri, commenced operations near Brownsville, some thirty miles below Nebraska City. His labors have since resulted in the organization of a respectable congregation of Cumberland Presbyterians.

Our people at Nebraska City, driven from the Methodist Episcopal church, and denied sympathy and encouragement when they sought to unite with the Presbyterian church, were shut up to the necessity, as were our fathers, of an independent organization. Then the question came up, What kind of church should be organized—Cumberland Presbyterian, or Methodist Episcopal, South? The number of members was nearly equally divided between the two. The Rev. George W. Love, a minister in the latter church, very generously proposed that all should unite in the organization of a Cumberland Presbyterian church. The Rev. C. B. Hodges, a Cumberland Presbyterian minister, was sent for, and, on the 16th day of July, 1865, the organization was effected, and the names of fifty-four members were enrolled. Five elders were elected, and Mr. Love was selected pastor temporarily. He and Mr. Hodges alternately and conjointly occupied the pulpit until the fall of 1866, during which time two extensive revivals of religion were enjoyed, in which many souls were converted and added to the church. A large and flourishing Sabbath-school has been in successful operation ever since the organization of the church.

On the 28th of October, 1866, I took charge of the church, devoting all my time to its interests. On the 15th of December, 1867, a new and beautiful brick edifice, built entirely by the liberality of our own church and some friends in the city, was dedicated. But many of our members from Missouri were here only temporarily, so that by the time we entered the new church, although about one hundred had been added since the organization, we were reduced to about fifty. Soon after entering the new church we were blessed with a powerful work of grace, and quite a number were added to the membership.

A sketch written in 1886 by another faithful worker in this field gives some of the same facts, but in different connections:

During the late civil war, many persons from Missouri and other border States came to Nebraska. Among these were some Cumberland Presbyterians. Russell, Majors & Co., the noted overland freighters, had established their headquarters in Nebraska City. Mr. Majors, being a Cumberland Presbyterian, and well acquainted in Missouri, had induced some ministers of that denomination to locate here. Among these were Robert Renick, C. B. Hodges, James G. Dalton, and Martin Hughes. A large, two-story frame building had been erected by Mr. Majors for a store-room. This building was used also as a place of worship by the few scattered members of our church in the city.

Here a series of meetings was held, resulting in a revival. Some time afterward it was decided to organize a church. On the 16th day of July, 1865, the first Cumberland Presbyterian church was organized by Rev. C. B. Hodges. The Rev. G. W. Love became pastor, but was soon followed by the Rev. C. B. Hodges, who was very efficient in building up the church during his six months' pastorate.

In the spring of 1866, Rev. R. S. Reed, of Salem, Illinois, accepted a call from this church, and entered upon his work on the 28th of October the same year. Under his management the church prospered greatly, both in its spiritual and financial interests. A beautiful house of worship was erected on the corner of Tenth and Laramie streets, and dedicated December, 1867. The work on this building was begun the first year of Mr. Reed's pastorate. In October, 1869, after three years of faithful service, he resigned.

In November, 1869, the Rev. J. B. Green, of Kentucky, took charge of this church. During his pastorate, the work so well begun by his predecessor has gone steadily on. There has been no change of pastor since 1869. For a number of years this congregation has been on a sound financial basis, and out of debt. The Sunday-school was organized in July, 1865, and has prospered from the first, doing a good work.

Some time after the organization of the Nebraska City church, a congregation was organized near Brownsville, Nemaha County. After a few years it built a good brick house of worship. This church has had several pastors, and is now under the care of the Rev. B. J. Johnson. Eight or ten years ago, a congregation, known as the Weeping Water church, was established in Cass County. Some of its members had been connected with the Nebraska City church. This congregation has recently been merged into a new one, and is now known as the Factoryville church. A few years ago this church erected a neat frame meeting-house, and now holds services twice each Sabbath. The Rev. R. F. Powell is the pastor.

Later a congregation, first known as Harmony, was formed six miles west of Nebraska City. This organization was finally moved to the village of Dunbar, and it is now known as the Dunbar church. Its members have built a substantial frame house, and services are held each Sabbath. The Rev. R. A. Williams is now its pastor. Two or three other smaller congregations have been organized more recently.

All Nebraska was formerly included in the Leavenworth Presbytery, and in the Missouri Synod. In 1873 Leavenworth Presbytery was divided and the Nebraska Presbytery formed. The first meeting of this new presbytery was held at Harmony church on the 6th day of March, 1873. Rev. J. B. Green was the first moderator. The following ministers composed the presbytery: B. J. Johnson, J. B. Green, I. Wayne Snowden, J. C. Hamilton, and Amasa Rippetoe. Four congregations were represented at this meeting.

The missionary operations in this State have been mainly supported by home contributions. But little help has ever been received. The Board of Missions has never had a missionary or a mission in this State. Rev. R. F. Powell, under appointment from the board, labored for a few months, but his work was mostly confined to Kansas. The denomination has lost much in not giving more attention to this important territory. The Nebraska City congregation was never a mission church, but has been self-sustaining from its organization.

At the Assembly of 1886, the Nebraska Presbytery reported six ordained ministers, thirteen churches, four hundred and seventy-eight members, and four hundred and eighty-eight pupils in the Sunday-schools.

WASHINGTON TERRITORY.

In 1872, the Rev. H. W. Eagan went to the new Territory of Washington. Without assistance from the Board of Missions he began his labors at the town of Walla Walla. With no house of worship, no organized congregation, and no private estate to rely on, he determined to cast himself upon the Lord for support, and give himself to the ministry among the pioneers. He preached faithfully, and God put it into the hearts of the people to furnish him a temporal support. A working congregation was gathered, and a good church house built and paid for. When this faithful pioneer was no longer able to meet the growing demands of the work, an appeal was made to the Board of Missions for assistance. In answer to this call, the Rev. W. W. Beck was, in 1886, commissioned and sent to Walla Walla as missionary. To the General Assembly that year, this church reported sixty resident and sixty-six non-resident members, and church property valued at five thousand dollars.

The Rev. A. W. Sweeny has spent most of his life in the far West. In one of his letters, written in 1874, and published in the church paper, we get a glimpse of his work in Washington Territory. Describing one of his meetings, he says:

The Rev. H. W. Eagan, of Walla Walla, came on Monday. That night a large number of the anxious came forward. Some were converted every night during the week. The second Sabbath came. At night fifty-five came to the altar. We could not close the meeting. We were there the next Sabbath. At night forty-five were at the altar, and there were eleven professions. So we spent two weeks at that meeting. Certainly there had never been before, in this part of the country, such a deep religious interest felt.

The same letter shows how these pioneer missionaries went forth, trusting God for a support. Mr. Sweeny says:

The Rev. E. P. Henderson and myself visited Waitsburg and held a meeting, two years ago last September and October. He remained until spring with the little congregation which we organized here. I then took charge of it. I was alone, bishop, circuit rider, preacher, and exhorter. In the fall Brother Eagan came. God sent him. I gave him part of my field. Forty dollars a year was all the salary that he or I positively knew of. God has supported him. He has not lacked for any thing. The Rev. R. H. Wills came recently. I turned over to his support all but three of my contributing members of Waitsburg congregation. The way looks dark. What are we to do? A question often asked, and easily answered. Go forward, trust in God, and he will open the way. The additions at our camp-meeting will make up my loss by dividing with Brother Wills. I am slowly learning to "have faith in God." At Brother Eagan's basket meeting with his country congregation there were nine additions. So you see we have encouragement in this new country. God be praised!

We now (1887) have in Washington Territory one presbytery, the Walla Walla, with twelve ordained preachers, four candidates for the ministry, eleven congregations, six hundred members, and five hundred pupils in the Sabbath-schools.

There are some ministers and members of the Cumberland Presbyterian church in Montana Territory, but no presbytery has been formed.

EVANGELISTS.

In the last twenty years, not only in the Cumberland Presbyterian church, but throughout all Christendom, the work of evangelists, both lay and clerical, has been among the wonderful things connected with religious activity and development. We have had our full share of those remarkable preachers. There seems to be a special movement in this direction, brought about by the Spirit of the living God. While there have no doubt been abuses, yet the great harvest of souls among those who were ready to perish is far too precious to permit us to doubt that God is in this work. One thing of special value is the use which these evangelists make of the Scripture. This is true pre-eminently in the work of our own evangelists, the Rev. R. G. Pearson and Dixon C. Williams.

One of our aged ministers once traveled some distance to attend the meetings of the Rev. R. J. Sims, another Cumberland Presbyterian evangelist. There was an immense congregation. The evangelist made a very simple, earnest address with no loud tones, violent gestures, or exciting appeals. The talk was conversational, and in subdued accents. Then the speaker asked those occupying the four pews in front of the pulpit to vacate them, to accommodate the penitents. To the aged preacher, who sat behind the evangelist, this seemed a foolish proceeding. "Four seats indeed!" thought he. "If one mourner comes forward it is more than I expect." The evangelist said: "Let all who want to be saved here to-day come quietly to these seats." In a few moments all the four seats were filled; then four more were called for and filled; then two more. The visiting preacher was amazed—almost frightened. He continued with that evangelist a week, and watched him closely, to find out how all this was accomplished. The first day and night he found that the evangelist spent about six hours alone in prayer, and that he gathered two or three chosen ones to join him in short, special prayers. This was the daily programme. The secret of his success was that God was with him.

It is true that this evangelistic work puts into the hands of the pastors greatly increased labors in organizing and training converts. But this is not a valid objection. It would be inconsistent in parents to object to their children being converted in early life, because the duty of training the little believers rests upon fathers and mothers, and involves much prayer and patient labor; hardly less inconsistent is it for pastors to object to the sudden conversion of large numbers in their congregations. Would it be better to risk the eternal loss of all these souls than to have the pastor's labors and embarrassments multiplied?

In the Cumberland Presbyterian church this modern method of evangelistic work began in 1873. For several years our people had just one evangelist at large. He visited nearly all the States in which the church had a membership, spending twelve years in this work. His was purely a life of faith, so far as the support of his family was concerned. He had no assurance of compensation, no contract with man, and no private means of his own; but neither he nor his family suffered for any of the necessaries of life. Such a life of trust brings a laborer into closer relations with God than any other life. It by no means includes the neglect of teaching the people their duty about money. In 1880 the church had twelve of these evangelists at large—men who "reported only to God." This does not include ministers sent out by synods or presbyteries.

Lay evangelists were a part of the original machinery of the Cumberland Presbyterian church. At first these were selected and commissioned by the presbytery, choice being made of men who had shown some fitness for the work. Of late years this custom had fallen into desuetude. One little experiment on the old plan, which was made a few years ago by Bethel Presbytery, in the Choctaw country, was thus described at the time by the Rev. W. S. Langdon in the *Banner of Peace:*

Some time since the Rev. I. Folsom furnished an account of the proceedings of Bethel Presbytery. The business was conducted in the

Choctaw language. It seems to have been a very spiritual meeting, and resulted in much immediate good. One item that I did not notice when I first read it, now strikes me more forcibly than any thing else in the record. This is probably because the subject is one that has occupied my thoughts a great deal recently. Here is the item: "During the meeting of the presbytery, loud Macedonian cries came up from different parts of the Nation. At first we were utterly at a loss to know what to do, as we had more fields already than we were able to supply, and as some of us were advanced in years, and were becoming infirm. For some time we remained silent, in deep, prayerful reflections. So, on the following day, after asking counsel of God, the presbytery determined to send forth the elders and deacons, and appoint exhorters to go and read the holy Scriptures to the people, sing and pray with them, and exhort in their meetings, until ministers could go round and baptize converts and organize them into churches according to the apostolic usage."

Here, I think, we have a perfect copy of the "Apostolic usage." Our Indian brethren have taken a step in the right direction, and have set their white brethren an example that it would be well for them to consider. Has not the Christian church departed from the plan of ministerial labor and church extension devised by the great Head of the church?

For three hundred years the disciples and their successors operated upon a plan similar to that set forth in this extract from the proceedings of this Choctaw Presbytery. They went forth and preached, organizing churches, administering sacraments, and ordaining elders. Then they proceeded to some other place, leaving the new church members to conduct their own services. These services were very different from those held in the churches in this day. Then they met to study the Scriptures and learn what their duties were, and inquire what was the will of God concerning them. Their meetings were religious sociables. It was the privilege of every member to take part, under the rules prescribed by the apostles. Once in a while some of the ministers came round, and corrected any errors into which the converts had fallen, preaching to them and strengthening them by words of counsel. The people were thus aided and encouraged in their religious work, and they helped the preacher in his.

The error of the ministry for fifteen hundred years has been that it has taken the work of Bible-readings, religious discussion, and personal exhortation too much out of the hands of the people, and substituted sermons instead.

Lay preaching, but without presbyterial appointments, has been a prominent part of the evangelistic work of recent years. Among our own lay preachers are Dixon C. Williams and General A. P. Stewart. General Stewart has never abandoned his secular business to go out as evangelist, but has preached a great deal. While he was chancellor of the University of Mississippi, he spent most of his vacations holding meetings, and these meetings were owned of Heaven, resulting in the conversion of many souls. Mr. Williams, familiarly known as "Dixie" Williams, gave up his business and his pleasant home, leaving his young wife and little children behind him, in order to devote his whole strength to preaching.

One of our old preachers, who knew Williams from childhood, speaks thus of him and his work:

When Dixie first became a church member, his life was a disappointment. He is of the stock to which Thomas Calhoun belonged, and I hoped he would become a preacher. I was troubled to find his life not what I hoped for. Then Hammond came along, and Dixie got worked over, and went to holding meetings in the by-ways and hedges. I went to hear him. I had been all the time thinking of my former disappointment. He rose, and, with deep feeling, made confession about past failures, and declared his fixed determination, by God's grace to be what he professed—out and out the Lord's. He is doing just that, and the Lord is using him. It is a curious fact that both in the early and the recent history of Cumberland Presbyterians, our most successful preachers have been Christians worked over.

Many of our evangelists prefer the plan of "reporting only to God," and never publish any accounts of their meetings. It is, therefore, not easy to obtain details of their work.

OUR DENOMINATIONAL PROGRESS.

In 1810 there were three Cumberland Presbyterian preachers; no churches. In 1812 we had eight preachers and thirty-three congregations. In 1829 there were eighteen presbyteries, and a General Assembly was organized. The number of ministers and churches at that time is unknown. In 1842 there were fifty-three presbyteries; other statistics unknown. In 1860 the church had ninety-seven presbyteries, and not less than fifteen chartered colleges. The total membership was estimated at one hundred thousand, twenty thousand of whom were colored people. In 1887, notwithstanding the loss of all its colored members and ministers, the church had one hundred and nineteen presbyteries, fifteen hundred and sixty-three ministers, two thousand five hundred and forty congregations, and over a hundred and forty-five thousand members.

The small number of candidates for the ministry and licentiates —less than one third the number of ordained ministers—is a discouraging feature in our recent denominational statistics. The old-time plan of going to God with fasting and prayer, and asking him to call more men to the work of the ministry should be revived. There was a time when parents solemnly asked the Lord to lead their own sons into this sacred calling. It would be well if such personal prayers were still daily offered by parents. In nearly every thing else our progress is most hopeful. In giving money systematically to missions and other church work there is steady and encouraging growth. In a few years more, at the present rate of advancement, our people will not be ashamed of financial comparisons. There is a heresy of the pocket and the life which is worse than heresy in the creed. The Moravians, it is said, are the freest of all people from this practical heresy—this financial disloyalty to Jesus. It would be well if a good large Moravian element could enter into our membership.

A most hopeful sign of progress is the increasing number of regular pastors. A far larger proportion of our congregations now have permanently settled ministers, giving their whole time to the work, than at any former period. Another most potent auxiliary to church progress is the very large circulation of the church paper. Never before was so large a number of our members reached through our own weekly organ. If its subscription extended to every family in the church, all our congregations and all our enterprises would be quickened into new life.

Another auxiliary to this progress is the improved condition of our theological school. The encouraging success of the endowing agent gives promise that this school will soon be furnished with a full faculty, and equipped with all needed facilities for its work. When this is done, will not Dr. Beard bend over the battlements of heaven and weep tears of rapture over the realization of his hopes and the answer to his prayers?

Some comfort in our deficiencies and hope for our future growth may be derived from comparisons. The Presbyterian church in America in 1819 was about one hundred and fourteen years old— that is, about thirty-seven years older than ours is to-day. At that date it had, in all America, eleven synods and fifty-three presbyteries. It had no Board of Publication and no Board of Foreign Missions. Its Board of Domestic Missions was only two years old. It is true that this slow progress may have been caused in part by the revolutionary war, and adverse influences in colonial times; but there were difficulties and hindrances in the early days of the Cumberland Presbyterian church scarcely less embarrassing.

In a letter written by Rev. John L. Dillard, in 1883, when he was over ninety years old, he says. "I think the outlook of the Cumberland Presbyterian church is very bright. I think increasing attention is paid to experimental and spiritual religion. So far as I can learn the facts, God is greatly blessing the work of our ministry." On the subject of doctrines, also, this veteran gives utterance to the belief that our people are maintaining the original purity and soundness of the faith.

We have a far larger number of real scholars now than ever before; but our spirituality will not stand comparison with that which once made all our pulpits a blaze of fire. A young preacher, talking recently to one of our old men, used something like these words: "Doctor, how is it that so few of our preachers ever have any earnest, spiritual conversations with each other. You and Dr. M. are about the only ministers I think of now who ever seem to desire such conversation." All this was vastly different once. John Barnett used to say that he made it an invariable rule to speak at least a few words for Jesus in every conversation he held with his fellow-men. Something for Jesus, some little word for eternity in every conversation, every letter, every visit, would make a vast difference in the aggregate influence of a life-time.

GENERAL REFLECTIONS.

In preparing such a history as this, an author necessarily studies many subjects which he can not discuss in his book. The impression on his own mind is far broader and deeper than that which he can convey to his readers. Some few thoughts growing out of these unrecorded impressions are now to be presented. Our people will perhaps be startled by the declaration that Ewing, King, and McAdow were not the first Cumberland Presbyterians. Yet in a very important sense this declaration is true. Every sacred principle, for which the men of 1800 struggled and suffered, had been struggled for and suffered for in the Presbyterian church of Scotland before any white man's cabin stood on the soil of Tennessee.

The study of Hetherington is like reading over again the history of McGready's difficulties. It was the injected element, thrust by the State into the true Presbyterian church, which opposed revivals, which objected to laymen leading in prayer, which trampled down the rights of presbyteries, as Lyle's synodical commission did. It was the same old struggle, when field meetings in Kentucky took on the form they bore so long ago in the land of our forefathers. The same old struggle between a hide-bound fatality and a liberalized Calvinism had sprung up in almost every revival the Presbyterians of past generations ever had. The same struggle to reach the perishing masses, without being held back by conditional red tape, had involved revival Presbyterians in controversies long before the Cumberland Presbyterian church was born.

Our church was raised up to be the conservator of evangelical, liberal Presbyterianism.

The first Cumberland Presbyterian preachers all belonged to the Scotch-Irish race. They were soldiers' sons, ecclesiastically, and they felt bound to walk erect, but none the less were they genuine Presbyterians. Their true kinsmen, ecclesiastically, must ever be sought in the liberal party of the Presbyterian church. There have always been two schools or shades of doctrine among Calvinists. Of later years there are many minor shades, but even in the Westminster Assembly there were two shades of doctrine. Our doctrines are no new element in Presbyterianism. There has been a scarlet thread of the same sort running through the whole woof from the first. The doctrine of grace, a belief in the divine influence of the Holy Spirit extending to all hearts, and the divine longing for the salvation of all lost sinners, has in every age been found in the church. When liberal Calvinists work in revivals, they become practically Cumberland Presbyterians. We have not even added any new measures, except it be camp-meetings. Itinerant evangelism, and even lay evangelism were among the earliest measures adopted by the revival party in the Scotch Presbyterian church.

Our church is a conservator of the best and holiest elements of revival Presbyterianism. The mother church is our debtor in these things. We are her debtor, too, in many things. From the liberal element in her doctrines our theology is derived—the Bible system, which makes salvation the gift of God, while it makes death the wages of sin. We are indebted to her for our whole system of church government, and for that revival policy which rests on God's truth and God's Holy Spirit given in answer to prayer, and not on any human device. We are also indebted to her for the system of settled pastorates. Though it was impossible for our preachers and congregations to adopt this system at first, we have ever clung to it in theory, and are now struggling to establish it throughout the denomination.

We owe the mother church a large debt also in the matter of ministerial education. Even the abuse and misrepresentations of our methods and policy by some of her writers did us great service. That some of our presbyteries had drifted into laxness can not be called in question, but the worthy example of the Presbyterian church through her whole history has all the while been calling us to higher things. Her schools and her literature have been trumpet voices in our hearing. Above all else her theological schools have been precious examples to our people. Cumberland Presbyterians, in their efforts to make their seminary all that it should be, find great help in the history of similar institutions built by Presbyterians. When our young men have sought better facilities than our own school could furnish, they have nearly always gone to the schools of liberal Calvinists—seldom or never to those of the Methodists. The number of such young men has been very large.

Our natural and historic affinities are with the Reformed churches. We have taken our place in the Presbyterian Alliance; now, let us maintain it. If there are driftings in another direction they promise no good to our cause. Let us hold to our anchorage. Let us cling to the system of doctrine which has been so blessed of Heaven in our denominational career. Let us have done with the battles about decrees. Fatality is nowhere preached now. There is no use in forever fighting it. Organization, drill, work, missions, progress, souls immortal, are the prizes now to be struggled for; and in most of this work the Presbyterian church will furnish models for our imitation.

CHAPTER XLIX.

ANECDOTES.

*Be noble! and the nobleness that lies
In other men, sleeping, but never dead,
Will rise in majesty to meet thine own.*
—*Lowell.*

THE sources from which these anecdotes are derived are the church papers, and manuscript accounts written by eye-witnesses. The incidents described in the manuscripts are so numerous that it is impossible to put them all in this short chapter. Selections have been made of such only as give the greatest promise of usefulness. These anecdotes belong to all periods of the church's history. We begin the list with those dating farthest back, but are not careful to preserve any exact chronological order afterward.

ANECDOTE OF MRS. SAMUEL KING.

The wife of Rev. Samuel King was a daughter of Joseph Dixon, of the Presbyterian church. Her son, the Rev. R. D. King, published the following anecdote of his mother. The scene of this incident was Mrs. King's girlhood's home, in the wilds of Tennessee. The people were exposed to attacks from hostile savages, and every settlement had its fort:

On one occasion, early in the morning, something attracted Mr. Dixon's attention in the direction of the fort to which he belonged. He immediately took his rifle in his hand, and cautiously proceeded about one hundred or one hundred and fifty yards from the door of his cabin. His manner was so unusual as to attract little Anna's attention. She stood in the door watching her father with a throbbing heart, though she knew not why. Suddenly a band of savage warriors sprang from where they had been concealed, and, in a moment, Joseph Dixon lay a corpse.

The savages, with hideous yells, rushed for the house. Anna's only safety now lay in flight. She determined to reach the fort, which was six miles distant. With a sagacity and determination that far surpassed her years, she commenced her flight. Soon she heard the band of savages yelling behind her; but she evaded them, and after a while all but one of the Indians ceased their pursuit. The race between the two at last became a silent race for life, in which a child in her twelfth year fled from a young athletic warrior. Often the blood-thirsty pursuer would hurl his tomahawk with all his power, at his intended victim; yet each time it fell harmless, not at her feet, but far beyond her.

As they approached the fort, the man who was on guard saw the race and threw open the gate. Just as the little girl sprang in, the cruel and determined savage poised himself steadily, and as the last fearful act of his life, hurled his tomahawk at her as she lay fainting from exhaustion. But, as before, the weapon missed its aim, and fell far beyond her. At the report of the sentinel's rifle, the pursuer fell dead twenty or twenty-five steps from the gate of the fort.

A TIMELY ARRIVAL.

The Rev. Le Roy Woods published the following incident connected with the history of the church in Pennsylvania:

Morgan's health, never very robust, had, by travel and incessant labor, become very much impaired, and he had arranged to leave Pennsylvania for the South at the close of the Waynesburg meeting. Aston remained in Washington County. This would leave Bryan alone. December had come, the cold was becoming intense, and Morgan had to leave. The hearts of these two men, Morgan and Bryan, had become knit together as the hearts of Jonathan and David. The idea of being separated, especially at this time, was very painful. It had been arranged that they should spend the night together at the house of a Mr. Jennings, one mile out of Waynesburg, and that one of them should preach in this private residence. The religious interest was still very deep, and at an early hour the house was filled. Every room was crowded; the hall and the stairway were packed with people, anxious to hear. Morgan was too ill to sit up, and was compelled to leave the room, and lie on a bed up-stairs. Bryan was expected to preach.

Just before service began a stranger came to the gate. His clothing and appearance indicated that he was a traveler on a long journey. His apparel was rather plain and somewhat worn. He was evidently suffering from the severe cold, and the fatigue of the day's travel. He inquired for the Rev. A. M. Bryan. Who was this stranger? What was he, and what did he want with the minister? These thoughts passed through the minds of all, and all were anxious for an explanation.

Bryan came to the door. One glance at the stranger, and in an instant he was at the gate, grasping the hand of the new-comer, and bidding him to alight and come in. He then introduced him as his dear friend and fellow-laborer from Kentucky, the Rev. Milton Bird. Bryan was relieved; Bird would preach. Bryan ran up stairs to tell Morgan that Bird had come just at a time when help was indispensable. They both wept for joy, thanking God and taking courage. Bryan would not now be left alone.

Morgan was too ill to come down to take part in the service. He was intensely anxious to hear the man who was to take his place when he was gone. He said: "I listened closely, but I heard but little of the prayer; I was disappointed, I felt discouraged, I tried to pray God to help the new preacher. The first part of the sermon I lost entirely. I grew more despondent. But as the discourse progressed, and the speaker began to warm with his subject, I could hear an occasional sentence. I was favorably impressed. As he proceeded, and I began to hear more distinctly, I became more deeply interested. I found myself sitting on the side of the bed. In that position I could hear every sentence, and my feelings became more deeply enlisted. I went to the head of the stairway; I was delighted. There was thought, there was reason, there was the Bible, there was logic in every sentence. His words were falling like burning coals on the hearts and consciences of his hearers. The close was a most happy one. I went back to my bed, weeping tears of joy, and feeling that our cause was safe in the hands of such men as Bryan and Bird."

A QUARREL SETTLED BY A SONG.

The following was also published by the Rev. Le Roy Woods:

On a certain occasion, when a large congregation was assembled to hear Mr. Bryan preach, a dispute arose between the Presbyterians and our people, in reference to which were entitled to the use of the house at a certain hour. Many present forgot the proprieties of the time and place, and the controversy became very hot and unchristian in spirit. In the midst of their wrangling and contention, Mr. Bryan rose up in the pulpit and began to sing, in a clear, solemn voice the hymn,

> Amazing grace! how sweet the sound,
> That saved a wretch like me.

The effect was wonderful. Before the first stanza was completed, the storm of passion was stilled, and all were silent. Before "the sweet singer" had completed the closing lines,

> And God who called me here below
> Shall be forever mine,

tears in many eyes proclaimed the deep emotion of the audience. At the close of the hymn, the difficulty was amicably and lovingly adjusted, and the two denominations continued to occupy the house with uninterrupted good feeling and harmony.

CONQUERED BY KINDNESS.

This camp-meeting anecdote was published in one of the church papers:

Once at a camp-meeting, before the first service commenced, a huckster wagon drove up. The man had given great trouble at a meeting held by members of another denomination a few weeks before, and had been fined heavily for disturbing religious worship. The Rev. J. M. Berry proposed that all the preachers and people present should visit the huckster in a body. This plan was adopted, and Mr. Berry began a friendly conversation with the huckster. The man stated that he did not wish to create any disturbance, and that he did not sell intoxicating liquor. Mr. Berry said "Our intention is to worship God." He pointed out the good effects of religion. "Now," said he to the huckster, "if you intend to do no harm, but wish to do good, will you not promise us that you will attend preaching when we do, and, when the services are not going on, supply those who wish to purchase any thing you have for sale?" "Yes," said he, "if you will agree that I may take my position near the camps, so that I may be in sight, should any one be disposed to disturb my wagon." This also was agreed to. "But," said Mr. Berry, "the Sabbath is not our time, and none of us have the right to buy or sell on that holy day. You will also agree not to wound the feelings of the good people, and sin against God, by keeping open on the Sabbath." The man agreed to this also. He kept his word in every particular, and wept like a child under preaching. On Sabbath he carried his cakes around in armfuls, and distributed them gratuitously among the camp-holders and their children. On Monday morning he left us. He reported that Cumberland Presbyterians were all gentlemen.

THROUGH HEAD AND HEART.

When Samuel M. Aston was preaching in Pennsylvania he visited one of our churches in which a learned Universalist had proved too powerful in argument for the session and the pastor. When told of the case, Aston replied: "I will shoot him through the head Sunday morning, and through the heart Sunday night." At the service Sabbath morning Aston's sermon swept away all the arguments of the Universalist, till he writhed and groaned in his seat. At night, Aston's presentation of Christ's dying love to lost sinners melted the poor man to tears, and won him to a personal trust in Christ alone for salvation.

TARDINESS CURED.

The Rev. Samuel M. Aston begun his labors with a Pennsylvania congregation whose people were rather noted for their tardiness in attending the services. When he had preached once or twice, and had discovered how slow the people were, he announced that there would be services the next Sabbath at 10:30 o'clock *precisely*. The people did not notice, particularly, the emphasis he placed on the last word. The next Sabbath, punctual to the minute, Mr. Aston arose and began the services, though not more than a dozen members of his usually large congregation were in attendance. His discourse was a little shorter than usual, and his congregation was dismissed and the people on their way home by 11:30 o'clock. It was amusing to see the tardy worshipers coming in. Some arrived just as the preacher was closing his discourse, some during the last hymn, and some just in time for the benediction; while the latest stragglers met the returning congregation, and turned homeward without reaching the church. On the next Sabbath, at 10:30 o'clock precisely, the people were all in their seats, waiting for the services to begin.

"THE ROOT OF THE MATTER."

Here is a little picture of Dr. Beard's as a school-boy, drawn by himself in an article in the *Banner of Peace*. It shows that if a student has "the root of the matter" in him, he will somehow find the road to noble attainments.

I made up my mind to preach. It was a great trial, but I had, in a great measure, to "let the dead bury their dead." In the course of the winter I had the opportunity of spending a few weeks at what seemed a good school. A young man, who was preparing for the Methodist ministry, was teaching in one of our congregations, and I bought Murray's English Grammar and turned in with him. His stock of knowledge, however, was soon exhausted, and I had not learned much about the grammar. But in the following spring a good old patriarchal elder of the church heard of my case. He lived within four miles of one of the best schools in the country. He proposed to board me a few months gratuitously, if I could stand the walk to that school. I thought of nothing but being able to stand it. A neighboring congregation made me up seven dollars and a half for the purchase of necessary books. I bought Cumming's Geography and Atlas, Ferguson's Astronomy Abridged, Watts' Logic, and the whole set of Murray's Practical Exercises, Key, etc., and set myself earnestly to work for the summer. My reader will perhaps smile, but I can not help it; this was my literary outfit. I think I had the root of the matter in me. I walked the four miles in the morning, and back in the evening, over a hilly road, day in and day out. I literally committed to memory large portions of Watts' Logic. I studied every thing with a mind to it; I had crossed the Rubicon; my heart was upon the ministry. I did a good work that summer. My testimonials from that school are still in my possession—fifty-three years old. They were read at the following meeting of the presbytery by one of the old men, and pronounced *very good*.

ANECDOTE OF THE REV. R. D. MORROW.

One of the church papers many years ago published the following anecdote:

About the year 1820 the legislature of Missouri was in session at the town of St. Charles. The Hon. John Miller, a Cumberland Presbyterian, was the representative from Howard County. The Rev. Mr. R., who was then regarded as the giant of the Baptist church in Missouri, visited St. Charles, and preached to the legislature on this text: "For I say unto you, That except your righteousness shall exceed the righteousness of the scribes and Pharisees, ye shall in no case enter into the kingdom of heaven." The next day the Hon. Henry S. Guyer, of St. Louis, also a member of the legislature, approached Mr. Miller, and criticised the sermon, remarking that Mr. R.'s views of law were unsound, and that, before a competent jury, his reasoning could easily be torn into fragments. Mr. Miller replied: "We have a little circuit rider up in our country who can preach law which you can not tear to pieces." A few weeks afterward, on returning to his room, Mr. Miller found that his "little circuit rider"—the Rev. R. D. Morrow—had called to see him. It was arranged for Morrow to preach in the Senate chamber. Mr. Miller took special pains to notify Mr. Guyer to attend. The hour arrived, and a promiscuous crowd of law-makers and law violaters had assembled. When the preacher entered the door, and walked down the long aisle of the chamber, dressed in plain homespun jeans, with his saddle-bags on his arm, all eyes were turned to get a view of Mr. Miller's circuit rider. Mr. Morrow's unprepossessing appearance caused many eyes, among them Mr. Guyer's, to be turned upon Mr. Miller, with an inquiring glance, as much as to say, "Is that your law preacher?" The services proceeded. Strange as it may seem, Mr. Morrow, without any knowledge of what had passed on the former occasion, announced the same subject upon which Mr. R. had preached. In a few minutes the audience was spell-bound, and for one hour many hearts were made to burn within them, while the preacher opened up God's glorious plan of justification and redemption. Even Mr. Guyer could not refrain from emotion; and as they walked out of the chamber he said to Mr. Miller, "That law will do; I can't pick any flaws in that man's views of law."

THE RULING PASSION STRONG IN DEATH.

When the Rev. R. D. King lay dying the members of his congregation resolved to visit him in a body. King was notified of their coming; and, when his beloved flock were gathered around him, he had them bring him his Bible and prop him up in bed. Taking a text, he then proceeded to preach them a sermon. The voice was feeble; the body was sinking into the grave; but his soul was filled with God's Spirit; and an unconverted woman that day, in that chamber of the dying saint, found Jesus and salvation. He had been in the ministry sixty-two years, and winning souls had been his ruling passion through all these years. For that work he had patiently borne the most wonderful hardships, and he rejoiced on his death-bed that he had been counted worthy of suffering such hardships for Christ's sake. So, greatly to his delight, God used him even in death in bringing one more soul into everlasting light. O happy servant he whom his Master finds thus watching! King's death was at his Texas home, in 1883. He was then past his three-score and ten, and glad to meet his summons home to heaven.

COMFORT THROUGH FAITHFULNESS.[1]

In Mississippi, forty years ago, there was a young lady who, in her childhood, had professed conversion, but had afterward fallen into doubt. Her doubts grew upon her, and at the annual camp-meeting she sought counsel of the preachers and other Christians, and struggled alone in prayer to God for light and comfort. But she found no relief; the darkness was not dispelled, but grew

---

[1] This and the following incident are furnished by the Rev J. G. Boydstun, of Mississippi.

thicker. Finally she settled it in her heart that she had committed the unpardonable sin, and was hopelessly lost. Along with this conclusion came also the determination to spend all the rest of her life in laboring to keep others from falling into the same lamentable condition. When the usual call for mourners came at the next service, she began to act on her resolution. Going to a seat filled with unconverted young ladies, she told them that she was herself hopelessly lost, but she wanted her young friends to escape so bitter a destiny. One of them rose and went to the mourner's bench, saying she felt as if a lost spirit had been sent from the dead to warn her. Others followed her example. The despairing messenger still went with her warnings among the young people, and at last a large number of her associates were among the happy converts. Then all her doubts forever vanished, and from that day she has lived in the sweet assurance of her own salvation.

ANECDOTE OF THE REV. F. M. FINCHER.

Many years ago the Methodists were holding a camp-meeting in the neighborhood where the Rev. F. M. Fincher, of the Cumberland Presbyterian church, lived. The meeting dragged through its allotted time without any conversions. The campers advised the presiding elder to close the meeting. The congregation was at that time gathered in front of "the stand." The elder asked Mr. Fincher to say a few words, intending then to close the meeting. Fincher rose and stood for some moments in front of the stand, silently weeping. Then he quoted Jeremiah ix. 1: "O that my head were waters, and mine eyes a fountain of tears," and proceeded to make an earnest exhortation. The Holy Spirit was poured out; mourners were called; conversions followed. The meeting was protracted, and was given over almost entirely into Fincher's hands. There was a great spiritual victory whose fruits still abide.

Mr. Fincher and the Rev. John Nicholson, of the same presbytery, were comrades in toil, and their labors were often blessed with gracious results similar to those just described. To this day the people of Mississippi remember a sermon preached by Nicholson, when he was so worn down with toil that he could scarcely stand on his feet. Every sentence from his lips went like an arrow to the people's hearts. At the close of that wonderful sermon a little boy led the prayer, and people said it was an angel's voice pleading for sinners. This boy afterward became a minister of the gospel.

A MISSOURI CAMP-MEETING.

The year 1854 was one of great drouth in some parts of Missouri, the severest ever known to the people of that State. It continued from June 1854 to May 1855. Trees died, stock perished, people were in extreme suffering for lack of water. The "Salt Fork" Cumberland Presbyterian church had a pretty large membership. About one third of these members wanted to hold their annual camp-meeting, drouth or no drouth. The other two thirds earnestly objected, and positively refused to co-operate. Only three families were willing to move to the encampment. Still the minority resolved to hold the meeting. They secured the services of the Rev. J. B. Morrow, and the Rev. P. G. Rea. They got permission to use a dry well near the camp-ground. From a big spring, three miles distant, they hauled water in barrels and filled the well. By keeping a wagon constantly running all through the meeting, they kept a supply of water in this reservoir. At first only a few people were present. Part of the few were rowdies who attended for the purpose of making disturbance, and for several days resorted to various methods of interrupting the services. At last some of them went so far as to pretend to be seeking religion. The instructions which these pretended mourners received were such as to make their ears tingle. Finally they became so frightened at the solemnity of the meeting, that they ran away. Then their leader began to feel real conviction, and sought his Savior in good earnest. In spite of drouth, opposing members, and lawless rowdies, God blessed his faithful servants with a gracious revival. About seventy conversions were counted among the results of the meeting.

THE BARN MEETING.

In 1851 there was in Saline County, Missouri, a neighborhood which had no church of any denomination. The Rev. P. G. Rea made arrangements to hold an out-door meeting in a grove near a large barn in that neighborhood. Rain setting in, the services were held in the barn. There was good interest, and the meetings were continued two weeks. One of the mourners was a bright little girl whose father was an unconverted man. This father feigned to be sick, and kept away from the meetings more than a week, but his wife was praying for him. At last, on Sabbath, he ventured to attend. That day his daughter was still a mourner, but before the services ended she was converted. Then she went to her father and asked him to seek his Savior. He promptly agreed to do so, and went with her to the mourner's bench, where he also found peace in believing. Though now old, he still maintains a consistent Christian life. This meeting in the barn was the origin of the Mt. Horeb church.

A TRIAL AND A TRIUMPH.

In Logan County, Kentucky, in the great revival of 1800, a youthful daughter of George McLean became a Christian. Her father was at that time a gambler, distiller, and man of the world generally. The daughter, Elizabeth, was a disturbing element in the godless revels of the family. The father tried through several of her associates to win her back to a worldly life. Then, as now, the dance was relied upon as the entering wedge to divide asunder the Christian and the Savior. But all efforts to entangle Elizabeth in this snare of Satan utterly failed. Then her father changed his tactics. As she would not go to balls, he resolved to have one at his own house. When the guests were assembled, and all inducements had failed to make her dance, he said to her: "You profess to go by your Bible. The Bible commands you to obey your parents. I now order you positively to dance the next set with me, your father." She obeyed, but spent the time while she was dancing in solemn prayer to God for the conversion of her father. Her face was pale, her countenance sad, her eyes were filled with tears. All present felt impressed by her conduct. Her father broke down, publicly asked her pardon, and began to pray for salvation. He never rested until he became a rejoicing Christian. Other members of the family were brought into the fold. Year after year McLean was found in his tent at old Mt. Moriah camp-ground, ready to co-operate with Chapman and Harris in their annual camp-meetings. The family all became Christians, and have all of them made their record among the best workers of our church. When it became necessary for him to move to another neighborhood, where there was no camp-ground, Mr. McLean established one. He built five camps, and agreed to furnish all the provisions if his neighbors would occupy his camps and feed the people. Elder A. J. McLean was his son, and the Rev. George D. McLean, of precious memory, was his grandson.

ANOTHER DANCING INCIDENT.

In 1867 in a Tennessee town lived a beautiful and wealthy lady who was fond of dancing. There was a revival in the town, and the only daughter of this fashionable lady was among the converts. She wanted to join the church, but her parents opposed. The pastor visited them, and discussed the question very earnestly with them. They said: "No; she shall not join. You would not let her dance, and we intend her to be a society woman." They carried their point. A society woman she became. She is still a society woman, but the scene of her sad career has changed. She now leads a life of shame in the great city, and the mother lives with her daughter. The tree is known by its fruits.

A WAR INCIDENT.

At the battle of Murfreesboro, Rev. W. P. McBryde, who was afterward chaplain, went along with his regiment. After the great battle was over, he found a bullet hole in his shoe, another in his haversack, and another through the back of his coat. A ball had torn off the front part of his vest pocket. Another had passed between his sleeve and breast, cutting the coat. Taking out his Bible from his side pocket for his regular scripture reading that night, he found a bullet hole through the Bible. And yet McBryde himself had received no wound. Some will say all such things are the result of chance, or of nature's laws; and some of us prefer seeing the protecting hand of a loving Father shielding a life for which he still had other uses.

A CASE OF FASTING AND PRAYER.

The Rev. R. J. Sims was holding a meeting in Arkansas. Two sisters were attending, one a Christian, the other not. The

Christian sister asked Sims what he thought about fasting. He is an earnest believer in its efficacy. He gave the young lady incidents pointing to the divine blessing on fasting as a means of grace. She resolved to observe a protracted season of fasting and prayer for her sister's conversion. At the closing hour of her appointed fast she was seated beside that sister in the church. Up to this time no indications of any answer to her prayer had been given. The unconverted sister had made no public demonstration of interest or concern; but now she rose to her feet, and, extending her hand, said very quietly: "Your prayers are answered; I am saved." Going through the congregation in the same quiet way, she communicated the same intelligence to her friends and acquaintances. Her life since that day gives evidence of genuine conversion.

A GAINSAYER CONVERTED.

At one of Mr. Sims' meetings, a woman who ridiculed experimental religion, carried her Bible to church and made a vigorous canvass among the mourners, trying to prove that the minister's teachings about repentance, and faith, and the love of God in the heart were unscriptural and false. She was noisy, insolent, and persistent. Sims inquired about her, and learned that her parents were good Methodists. Taking an elder with him to the grove, the two joined in prayer to God for the fulfillment of the promise made in Psalms lxxiv. 10-12. The meetings went on, and the mocker pursued her opposition. Then her daughter was among the rejoicing converts. The mother railed on her, argued with her, but the daughter, after hearing respectfully all that her mother had to say, replied calmly: "I can not but testify to what I know and feel in my own soul. I know I am happy in Jesus." At this the mother fell prostrate and began praying for salvation. She continued to seek, until she was enabled to testify before the whole congregation that she now knew for herself the reality of that spiritual experience which she had ridiculed. Members of her church then interfered, and took her home. They said she was crazy. Her husband was absent, driving stock to market. They wrote to him that his wife had lost her reason. He sacrificed his stock, and hurried home, expecting to find his wife a hopeless wreck. To his delight he found her in her right mind more than she had ever been before. After a few days' observation he went to the church of which he and his wife had both been members, and asked them to take his name off their rolls.

A BAND OF ROWDIES CONQUERED.

At one of the meetings which Mr. Sims held in Arkansas, a band of unconverted men determined to break up the meeting. Sims went to God in fasting and prayer. The wife and daughter of the ringleader of the band became deeply concerned about their souls, and went to the mourner's bench. This enraged the wicked man. At the next service he took his stick and went with his family to church, declaring it to be his purpose to beat the preacher with his stick. Sims, who had just ended one of his seasons of fasting and prayer, made his usually solemn though simple talk, and then started through the congregation to the spot where the man with his stick was seated. There was a power in the preacher's presence which made this boastful opposer of religion tremble. Along with this power, given in answer to prayer, the minister showed that fearlessness which the conscious assurance of divine protection always imparts. As Sims approached, the ruffian retreated, leaving the church and going to his home. The wife and daughter were converted that day, and when they entered their house they found the wicked man prostrate in prayer. He was at last converted and went to work for other lost souls. He held prayers in his family, and gave of his money freely to the cause of Christ. Other violent opposers were also reached by the Holy Spirit, and became part of the praying band.

THE KEYSTONE OF THE ARCH.

When the Rev. W. H. Crawford was young in the ministry, he and another minister held a series of meetings not far from his home in East Tennessee. The congressman for that district was present. While this man was very popular, he was not a Christian, and his presence was a terror to the young preachers. During the sermon, however, the preacher forgot the fear of man, and proclaimed with power the plain truth of God. The congressman was in tears. Seeing this, Mr. Crawford went to him when the sermon closed, and said: "Mr. C., you need no argument from me to convince you that you ought to be a Christian." He answered: "I do not." The preacher said: "There is one thing more that you ought to know, if you do not already know it. You are standing in the way of others."

The congressman rose to his feet, and speaking aloud, said: "I want it distinctly understood that I will stand in the way of nobody. If you want to be Christians, come along with me to the mourner's bench." Grasping a prominent friend in each hand, he led the way to the place of prayer. There were sixty conversions there that day, including nearly all the adult sinners of the neighborhood. A church was organized, a house built, and Crawford was called to be pastor of the new flock. In this relation he remained for many years. The congregation still lives.

A PRESBYTERIAN ELDER CONVINCED.

At this meeting just described, there was a Presbyterian elder who had been bitterly prejudiced against "the Cumberlands." When, however, he saw the conversion of the congressman, and after that the conversion of his own children, his prejudices were all swept away, and he became as demonstrative in his religious raptures as any one else at the meeting. This elder, like thousands of others in that day, had been taught to believe that "Cumberlands" and "New Lights" were one and the same, and that our church had no written creed, but was opposed to Confessions of Faith.

A CHRISTMAS PARTY.

The unconverted young men of an East Tennessee neighborhood met to decide how to enjoy the approaching Christmas. After some conversation it was proposed to send for the Rev. W. H. Crawford, have a meeting, all of them agreeing to seek their souls' salvation. The proposition was adopted, and a petition was drawn up stating that they desired Mr. Crawford to come and hold a meeting with a view to their conversion. They all signed the petition. Mr. Crawford complied with their request. At the first service he read the petition to the congregation. One dear old Methodist shouted when he heard the paper read. The meetings were wonderfully successful. About one hundred conversions were reported. Among these were all but one of the young men who had signed the petition. One declared it to be a mere joke. He mocked at the meeting, and opposed it. A few days afterward, in the same church at a public meeting, he was attacked with a sudden illness, and fell dead from his pew.

TWO CASES CONTRASTED.

On the last day of one of our great camp-meetings in the olden time, a preacher was going silently about among the people, talking with the unconverted. One of the persons whom he approached was a young man named Joe. After some preliminaries Joe said: "I have deliberately made up my mind to wait till the Providence camp-meeting, two weeks from now, and then to seek religion." Afterward the preacher had a conversation with a young lady who was also unconverted. She said, "I don't intend to leave this camp-ground till I find my Savior." She kept her word. When the last service was over and the congregation was dismissed, she refused to go away. Some friends remained with her, and at two o'clock that night she found peace in believing. The next week she and Joe both died. Joe said, with his last breath, "Lost, forever lost!" The young lady, with her last breath, proclaimed the joys of salvation. Her face was radiant with heavenly light even until the pulses ceased to beat.

A DEFEAT CHANGED TO VICTORY.

Bethel and Shiloh were the names of two camp-grounds in West Tennessee where the beloved Robert Baker used to win many a triumph as God's own chosen minister. After Christ called Baker home, there was one camp-meeting at Bethel which, though attended by even larger congregations than usual, seemed to be an utter failure. The last day of the meeting came. The campers loaded their wagons to return to their homes. They were disappointed and sad. Never before had Bethel camp-meeting closed without any conversions. Parents were there who had been looking fondly to that meeting as the time when their unconverted children would be brought to the Lord. There were many bowed heads and heavy hearts. Although the wagons were all loaded and every thing ready for going home, still all seemed reluctant to leave the encampment. Men were seated silently about the camps; women were weeping. Mrs. Lou. Bigham was one of the best Christians in that neighborhood. She sat with her head bowed upon a table, not weeping, but praying. After a while her prayers grew articulate. Then they became audible. Others seated about also began to pray. In a few moments there was a girdle of prayer around the encampment. It was not social prayer, but each one prayed apart. Some lay prostrate, some were on their knees, and some were seated. After a few moments more Mrs. Bigham's voice rang with the accents of victory. God had given her assurance that her prayer was accepted. The power of the Spirit touched the unconverted, and soon in every tent there was some poor sinner seeking salvation. Outside, scattered here and there, were little groups of praying ones bowed together with some anxious inquirers after salvation. No dinner was eaten. At night the wagons were unloaded, and public services were held. Before that meeting closed the names of more than two hundred converts had been enrolled. Among these converts were several young men who afterward became ministers of the gospel.

A MOTHER'S PRAYERS.

About forty-eight years ago the grandmother of the Rev. J. N. McDonald was living with her son, Alexander McDonald, in Vermillion County, Illinois. She was a devoted member of the Presbyterian church, but her son was not a Christian. She, however, kept up regular family worship with her son's household. By and by her prayers became very personal. She pleaded for the conversion of her son. He did not like this, and expostulated with her. She told him that she would agree to refrain from such direct prayers on condition that he would go at once for the Rev. Mr. Ross (a Cumberland Presbyterian minister), and have him come and hold a meeting there in their own house. There was no meeting-house in the neighborhood. The ground was then covered with snow, but with some reluctance and misgivings the condition was accepted. Ross came and held the meeting. A gracious revival was the result. Many persons were converted, and a Cumberland

Presbyterian church was organized with forty members. The first name on its roll was Mrs. McDonald's. That church still exists. Nearly all the members of that branch of the McDonald family, wherever they are now scattered, are Cumberland Presbyterians.

A JEW CONVERTED.

Many years ago Mr. D., a thriving Hebrew merchant, lived in a Tennessee town. The services of the Rev. C. A. Davis, D.D., were secured to hold a series of meetings in the Cumberland Presbyterian church. This Jewish citizen attended the meetings and became an ardent admirer of the preacher. One day Dr. Davis discussed the prophecies which point to Christ as the Messiah of the Old Testament. D. was present, and gave close attention. As the proofs were brought nearer and nearer to a demonstration, the sweat rolled from D.'s face. At last the preacher closed up the last link in the chain of his argument. The Jew saw it all like a flash of lightning. In an instant, right in the midst of the sermon, he cried out at the top of his voice, "O thou son of David, have mercy upon me." He became an earnest Christian, and his whole family followed him into the Cumberland Presbyterian church, where he maintained a consistent membership until the day of his death.

L. C. RANSOM'S DISCIPLINE.

While L. C. Ransom was pastor at Memphis, Tennessee, a lady who had been an active and faithful member in his congregation attended the theater. Afterward she began to have some anxiety about what her pastor would say on the subject. Finally she made up her mind to put on a bold face. She would resent any attempts to lecture her as an interference with her private rights, and assert her ability to judge for herself what was proper conduct for a church member. Her first meeting with the pastor was in his study alone. He met her kindly, took her cordially by the hand, and, bursting into tears, turned away and hid his face from her sight. She then and there resolved never again to attend the theater.

PRESENTIMENT OF DEATH.

In 1871 the Rev. A. J. McGown was attending the meeting of Trinity Presbytery. He preached Friday. Saturday he was again appointed to preach. When he rose in the pulpit those who had long known him say that they never before saw on his face such an expression of solemnity. He commenced by saying: "Brethren, I feel impressed that this is to be my last sermon, and I want to take this text, 'Go ye into all the world, and preach the gospel to every creature.'" The sermon was one of great power. He returned after services to the house of Mr. Murchison, where he took his bed, from which he rose no more.

INDEX.

A.

ADAIR, REV. WAYMAN, enters the ministry, 162; in Mississippi, 259.

ALABAMA, planting churches in, 155; an incident, 161; beset with trials, 162, 163.

ALABAMA PRESBYTERY, manner of organization, 158; a hard field, 159; its candidates, 161; condemning the convention, 236.

ALLEGHENY PRESBYTERY, when organized, 291.

ALLEN, JOSEPH W., an incident of, 455.

ALLEN, REV. O. D., 622.

ALTON (Ill.), Board of Missions, 382, 441.

ANECDOTES, 635-652.

ANDERSON, REV. ALEXANDER, written discourse of, 48; licensed, 49; gifts of, 54; prayer answered, 55.

ANDERSON, REV. JESSE, publishing agent, 588; 604.

ANDERSON, REV. DR. S. T., missionary to Trinidad, 479-481; return of, 482; professor in Waynesburg College, 539.

ANDERSON, REV. DR. T. C., biographical sketch of Rev. George Donnell, 145, 146; assistant editor, 231; in Ohio, 298; an incident, 305; professor in Cumberland University, 509, 510; president, 511; resignation, 516.

ANTI-REVIVAL PARTY, 61.

ARK, THE, 601.

ARKANSAS, planting of church in, 188-200.

ARKANSAS PRESBYTERY, when and where constituted, 195; no quorum, 196; extension, 196; meetings, 197.

ARMSTRONG, REV. J. C., missionary to Turkey, 335; commissioned to go to the North-west, 338; an incident, 338; organizes churches, 339; glimpses of his work, 339, 340, 443-447.

ASHMORE, REV. H. H., extract from manuscript of, 172; incidents of, 424, 425.

(653)

ASTON, REV. S. M., sent to East Tennessee, 145; in Pennsylvania, 284; in Ohio, 299; anecdotes of, 638, 639.

AUSTIN (Texas), 458.

AXTELL, REV. PHILIP, editor *The Religious Pantagraph* and *Semi-Centennial*, 600.

B.

BACON, REV. SUMNER, rejected as a candidate, 263; first Protestant to preach in Texas, 264; adventures of, 263-266; licensed and ordained the same day, 266; at a meeting of Mississippi Synod, 268.

BAIRD, REV. DR. A. J., compiler of hymn book, 597; corresponding delegate, 449, 450; instructor in Greene Academy, 528; author of Mahlon's Letters, 599; death, 467.

BAKER, REV. MR., 429.

BAKER, REV. ROBERT, sent to East Tennessee, 145; to West Tennessee, 149; 649.

BAKER, REV. ROBERT W., missionary to the Indians, 330; principal of Armstrong Academy, 330.

BALCH, REV. MR., opposition of, 39, 80.

BALDRIDGE, REV. W. H., testimony of, 32.

BANNER OF PEACE, 238, 389, 599.

BARNETT, REV. JOHN, first sermon in Illinois, 168; lease of, 216.

BARNETT PRESBYTERY, when organized, 185; its original members, 185.

BARNETT, REV. WILLIAM, biographical sketch of, 92; won to missions, 136; in West Tennessee, 150.

BAXTER, REV. DR., testimony of, 23, 24; jerks, 47.

BEARD, REV. DR. R., testimony of, 36; sketch of Rev. W. Harris, 95; sketch of Rev. Robert Bell, 141; sent to Forked Deer circuit, 149; 222; elected president of Cumberland College, 224, 227; his assistants there, 227; closed his work at, 228; in charge of Sharon Academy, 259; a corresponding delegate, 317, 318; anti-slavery record, 412, 413; 450; page in Assembly's Minutes set apart to, 458; professor in theological department Cumberland University, 514, 515. report on education, 564; anecdote of, 639, 640.

BECK, REV. W. W., 625.

BEECH CHURCH, 15; historic interest, 121.

BEESON, REV. DR. W. E., president of Chapel Hill College, Texas, 552; president of Trinity University, 558.

BELL, REV. DR. C. H., address of, 475; in St. Louis, 471; lectures in Theological School, 506; president of Union Female College, 573; president Board of Missions, 476.

BELL, REV. ROBERT, at school, 6; testimony of, 17; biographical sketch, 91; prepares constitution for first missionary society, 129; sent as an evangelist, 130; school opened, 133; convictions as to education, 134; government aid secured, 134; could not be driven away, 135; his correspondence, 136–140; mission closed, 140, biographical sketch by Rev. Dr. Beard, 141; sent to Hunt's Spring, 156.

BELL, REV. R. S., missionary to the Indians, 330; 441.

BERRY, REV. J. M., anecdotes of, 306, 616, 617, 638.

BETHEL COLLEGE (Tenn.), 574–576; origin of, 574; struggles of young men, 574, 575; a lesson on concentration, 575; its succession of presidents, 576.

BETHEL PRESBYTERY (Indian), when organized, 389; 476, 477.

BEST, REV. JAMES, in Logansport (Ind.), 474.

BEVERLY COLLEGE (Ohio), origin of, 531, 532.

BIDDLE, REV. J. G., professor in Cumberland College, 227; at Winchester, Tenn., 228.

BIG SPRING CHURCH, origin, 121; Rev. Thomas Calhoun first pastor, 122.

BIRD, REV. DR. MILTON, reply to the *Presbyterian*, 46; paper of, 239, 240; arrival in Pennsylvania, 283, 636; editor of the *Union and Evangelist*, 291; opening sermons, 311, 391; chairman Committee of Publication, 314; chairman of Committee on Fraternal Correspondence, 318; clerk of General Assembly, 320; opposed to concentration, 362; opposed to abolition of synods, 389; editor, 603, 604; professor in Madison College, 529; publishing agent, 587; sermon of, 391; report of, 566; death of, 449; 637.

BLACK, REV. F. G., at Lebanon, Ohio, 298; in Cincinnati, 323, 377.

BLACK, REV. W. H., in St. Louis, 472; not admitted to Pan-Presbyterian Council, 462; report of, 463.

BLACKBURN, REV. DR., "tokens," 19; revivals, 24; a revival meeting, 43; "jerks," 47; a leader in East Tennessee, 143; mission to the Indians, 128.

BLACKWELL, WILLIAM, a specimen elder, 188.

BLAKE, REV. DR. T. C., secretary Board of Missions, 313; established the *S. S. Gem*, 389; agent Cumberland University, 513, 515; editor *Banner of Peace*, 599; editor of the *Theological Medium*, 604; publishing agent, 595; financial agent Board of Publication, 591; stated clerk General Assembly, 459.

BONE, REV. DR. M. H., began his work, 152; an incident, 154; as agent visits Ohio and Pennsylvania, 273; president Board of Education, 316; organized church at Lebanon, Ohio, 298; two incidents, 373, 377.

BOOKS, of fourth period, 367; names and character of, 367–369; new, 461.

BOONE, DANIEL, 5.

BOWDON, REV. DR. J. C., 435; president of Lincoln University, 545.

BOWLING GREEN (Ky.), a great revival, 301; an incident, 377; school (col.), 437, 455.

BOYDSTUN, REV. J. G., 641.

BRADLEY, REV. C. J., president Bethel College, 576.

BRALY, REV. FRANK M., an incident, 183, 184.

BRALY, REV. J. E., in Oregon, 343; incidents by the way, 343, 344; arrival in California, 349, 350; 353.

BRICE, REV. A. B., editor *Cumberland Presbyterian* (Uniontown), 599, 602.

BROWN, COL. JOE, 3, 109.

BROWN, REV. DR. J. R., editor, 460, 603; author of "Lights on the Way," 489; editor *Cumberland Presbyterian*, 594; editor *St. Louis Observer*, 603; editor *The Ladies' Pearl*, 603;

BROWNSVILLE (Neb.), 623.

BRYAN, REV. DR. A. M., appointed to visit Pennsylvania, 274; first to work in Pittsburg, 283; at Meadville (Pa.), 289; his work in Pittsburg, 290; anecdotes of, 290, 636, 637.

BUCHANAN, REV. ANDREW, as a preacher, 196; a fearless hero, 199.

BUCHANAN, REV. JOHN, his work and influence, 305.

INDEX.

BUCHANAN, REV. DR. S. H., 472; tutor in Cane Hill College, 577.

BUIE, REV. DANIEL, first to settle in Missouri, 175; last days of, 375.

BUNYAN, REV. JOHN, quotation from, 67.

BURNEY, A. M., president Cumberland Female College, 574.

BURNEY, REV. DR. S. G., on abolition of synods, 370, 389; president Union Female College, 572; report on education, 564.

BURNEY, REV. W. S., abundant in labors, 259.

BURROW, REV. A. G., chaplain, 430.

BURROW, REV. DR. REUBEN, sent to Missouri, 179; an incident, 180; small salary, 182; physical power, 193; an incident, 194; visit to Pennsylvania, 274; camp-meeting, 281; an incident, 282; on sanctification, 370; infant justification, 370; rights of presbyteries, 370.

BUSHNELL, REV. DR. D. E., quotation from, 354; 440; editor *Pacific Observer*, 604.

C.

CALHOUN, REV. THOMAS, an incident, 30; prayer of, 31; an incident, 33; answer to prayer, 35; camp-meeting, 89; biographical sketch of, 91; life work, 123; first evangelistic tour, 128; in East Tennessee, 143; glimpse of pioneer life, 147; through West Tennessee, 149; at Hunt's Spring, 156; public confession, 246; first president Board of Missions, 312; testimony of, 612.

CALHOUN, REV. T. P., secretary Board of Missions, 313.

CALIFORNIA, planting of churches in, 348-356; first Protestant preaching in, 350; fascinations of, 355; difficulties, 355, 356; advantages of, 356.

CALIFORNIA PRESBYTERY, when and where organized, 352; original members, 352.

CAMPBELL, REV. DR. W., editor *Cumberland Presbyterian* (Pa.), 600.

CAMPBELL, REV. DR. W. S., 436.

CAMP-MEETINGS, first in Christendom, 13; description of, 14; order of the day, 15; held in churchless communities, 117; an example, 117; first held in East Tennessee, 147; "old Shiloh," in Carroll County, 149; first held in Illinois, 171; in Missouri, 184; in Texas, 265; in Pennsylvania, 279, 282; in Arkansas, 192; in Ohio, 293; in Iowa, 337; "died a lingering death," 370; colored people at, 433, 434.

CANE HILL CHURCH (Ark.), 198, 199.

CANE HILL COLLEGE, "a school for Jesus," 199; its first board of trust, 304; our oldest school, 305; building destroyed by fire, 577, 578; charter procured, 576; both sexes admitted, 577.

CANE RIDGE (Ky.), meetings at, 44.

CANE RIDGE (Tenn.), 17.

CARMICHAELS (Pa.), church at, 287; Greene Academy, 528.

CARNAHAN, REV. JOHN, labors in Alabama, 156; in Arkansas, 189; first Protestant sermon, 189; a solitary standard-bearer, 190

CAROLINAS, Synod of the, 10.

CARUTHERS, JUDGE ABRAM, professor in law department Cumberland University, 512.

CARUTHERS, HON. R. L., president trustees Cumberland University, 509, 512.

CATECHISM, examination in, 116.

CAVE SPRING, camp-meeting at, 31.

CHADICK, REV. W. D., missionary in Chattanooga, 474; agent Cumberland University, 514; editor *Banner of Peace*, 599.

CHAPEL HILL COLLEGE, 569.

CHAPMAN, REV. ALEXANDER, an incident, 33; special prayer, 35; answer to prayer, 36; first exhortation, 56; biographical sketch of, 92; in Indiana, 164; a camp-meeting, 168; a missionary tour, 171; visits Pennsylvania, 274.

CHAPMAN PRESBYTERY, ordination by, 31.

CHASE, REV. J. A., agent Lincoln University, 549.

CHATTANOOGA (Tenn.), mission in, 474; convention at, 383.

CHAUTAUQUA, assembly at, 31.

CHEAP SCHOLARSHIPS, 581-584.

CHEROKEES, mission to, 476; first church organized, 477; first presbytery, 477; schools, 478.

CHEROKEE PRESBYTERY, organized, 477; items of interest, 478, 479.

CHERRY GROVE SEMINARY, 563.

CHESNUT, REV. DR. S. P., editor *Banner of Peace*, 599; editor *The Ladies' Pearl*, 603.

CHICKASAWS, mission to the, 476.

CHICO, JUDGE, 476.

INDEX.

CHOCTAWS, mission to the, 476.

CHOCTAW PRESBYTERY, proceedings of a, 627, 628.

CHURCH, THE, change of name, 320.

CHURCH ERECTION, the Board of, its organization, 316.

CHURCH PAPERS, THE, difficulties connected with our first paper, 229–239; *Religious and Literary Intelligencer*, 229; moved to Nashville—*The Revivalist*, 230; changed to *Cumberland Presbyterian*, 231; assistant editor, 231; plans of Assembly's committee, 232; Smith's conditions accepted, 233; paper suspended, 234; proposed consolidation, 365; a sample argument used, 365, 366; proposition failed, 367; debates, 371; papers in Pennsylvania, 599.

CHURCH TRIALS, an unusually large number, 371.

CIRCUITS, extent of, 54.

COLBERT, LEVI, a Chickasaw chief, 131, 132, 140; a letter of, 137.

COLESBURG PRESBYTERY, when organized, its extent, 340.

COLLEGE, CUMBERLAND, convention of delegates, 61; necessity of establishing a, 201; theory of manual labor, 201, 214; a printing establishment with, 202; commissioners to locate, 214; "on credit," 214; doubters as to location, 215.

COLORADO, 618.

COLORADO SPRINGS, self-sustaining, 619.

CONCORD CHURCH (Pa.), 282.

CONCORD CHURCH (W. Tenn.), 302, 303.

CONFESSION OF FAITH, necessity for, 98; outline statement of doctrine, 98–100; adherence to the word, 100; synod's committee, 100; Robert Donnell's memoranda, 100, 101; Dr. C. H. Bell's exhibit, 101–103; much in the Westminster Confession left unchanged, 104; additions, 104; guards against abuse, 104, 105; medium theology taught, 106; diagram of representative creeds, 107; committee appointed to revise, 458; consideration of revision, 459; transmitted to presbyteries, 459; declared adopted, 459.

CONTROVERSIES, on doctrinal questions, 369, 370; on rights of presbyteries, 370; abolition of synods, 370; tone greatly improved, 370; revision of Confession of Faith, 370; in the newspapers, 371; Dr. Cossitt and the Presbyterians, 372.

CONVENTION, THE, 233–236; the defense of, 235; resolution to publish a paper at Lebanon, Tenn., 234.

INDEX.

COOPER, REV. J. L., general missionary, 428; work of, 438; principal of Spring Hill Institute, 579, 580.

CORNWALL, REV. J. A., first Cumberland Presbyterian minister in Oregon, 343; difficulties of, 345, 346; first Oregon church organized by, 346.

COSSITT, REV. DR. F. R., president of Cumberland College, 202, 225; his assistants, 225; editor *Banner of Peace*, 238; 274, 275; president of Board of Missions, 312; in favor of Japan, 335; in favor of concentration, 362; president of Cumberland University, 509; report on education, 566.

COULTER, REV. J. H., 418; in St. Louis, 470.

COUNCIL, THE, sent commissioners to Kentucky Synod, 68; organization and agreement, 82; struggle for reconciliation, 82–84.

CRAIGHEAD, REV. THOMAS B., 7; testimony of, 8; opposition of, 15; opposition to revivals, 39.

CRAWFORD, REV. C. H., 440.

CRAWFORD, REV. JOHN, pioneer in Illinois, 168; autobiography of, 169; an incident, 170.

CRAWFORD, REV. N. J., missionary to the Indians, 477.

CRAWFORD, REV. W. H., three anecdotes of, 647, 648.

CRIDER, REV. P. H., 441; agent Waynesburg College, 540.

CRISMAN, REV. DR. E. B., agent Trinity University, 559; editor *Texas Observer*, 602; secretary Board of Missions, 476; sketch of Trinity University, 551.

CUMBERLAND, country of, 1, 9; first school in, 5.

CUMBERLAND CHURCH (Ohio), when organized, 298.

CUMBERLAND PRESBYTERIAN, THE, name changed to, 231; committee to form stock company for, 234, 235; location of, 460; in Pennsylvania. 389, 599.

CUMBERLAND PRESBYTERY, opposition to heresy, 44; created, 56; extent of, 56; two parties in, 77; refusal of majority to submit, 78; right to originate process, 79; failed to appeal, 82; dissolved by order of Kentucky Synod, 82; re-organized, 84; no charges brought against its members, 84; Dr. Ely's testimony, 85; opposition, 85; first meetings, 86; last effort at reconciliation, 86; purchase of a library, 86, 115; adjustment of "union" difficulties, 87; dealing with probationers, 87; regard for the Sabbath,

87, 88; ordained missionaries, 90; its school of science and divinity, 90; heroism required, 90; biographical sketches of ministers, 90–92; names of licentiates, 92; names of candidates, 92; union desired, 93; epithet "Cumberland Presbyterian," 1, 114.

CUMBERLAND PRESBYTERY (Nashville), its members, 94; its boundaries, 94, 111; manner of representation, 110; fast days, 111; plan of work, 112, 113; in favor of a school, 116; established circuits in West Tennessee, 148.

CUMBERLAND PRESBYTERIAN CHURCH, name of, 1, 114; origin of, 10; spiritual power, 28; its high calling, 74–76; a separate church not aimed at, 93; origin of the name, 1, 114; difference in growth in two States, 173; great transition period, 207; extent of in 1829, 207; two parties in, 362; mushroom colleges, 362; attitude on the slavery question, 410–419; conservative spirit of, 419.

CUMBERLAND PRESBYTERIAN CHURCH (colored), 432–439; claims of, 437, 438; representative from Greenville Presbytery, 436; ecclesiastical separation, 434, 435; growth of, 437, 468; prosperity of, 436, 437; school at Bowling Green (Ky.), 437; committee to cooperate with, 435, 459.

CUMBERLAND COLLEGE, opened, 215; agents and debts, 215; proposition to lease, 216; joint stock company formed, 217; transfer threatened, 217; board of trust appointed, 217, 218; report of committee on education, 218; commission meets, 218; accepted the offer from Lebanon, Tenn., 218; report of the commission, 219–221; the Assembly's decision, 221, 222; protest, 223; plan presented by the minority of the committee on education, 222; friends resolve to keep it alive, 223; its useful career, 224; ceased to be a Cumberland Presbyterian institution, 224; glimpses of its inner history, 224–228.

CUMBERLAND COLLEGE (California), 353.

CUMBERLAND FEMALE COLLEGE, 573, 574.

CUMBERLAND PRESBYTERIAN PULPIT, 600.

CUMBERLAND UNIVERSITY, 509–526; a new charter, 510; re-opening after the war, 515, 516; Camp Blake, 518; changes, 511; faculty, 509, 510, 524; great prosperity, 513, 514; Finley bequest, 517; Murdock library, 518; pro-rata salaries, 510; purchase of Caruthers building, 516, 519; law department, 512, 513, 515, 525; theological department, 514, 521; law concerning, 522, 523; trustees of, 509; war closed the departments, 515; struggles with life insurance companies, 520; table of statistics, 523, 524.

CUMMINGS, REV. CHARLES, first preacher in Tennessee, 6.

CUNNINGHAM, REV. W. N., missionary and educator, 354.

D.

DALTON, REV. J. G., 622, 623.

DANCING, Assembly's deliverance, 460.

DARBY, REV. DR. W. J., his pamphlet history, 165, 167; 457, 460, 488.

DARNALL, REV. DR. W. H., missionary in Chattanooga, 474.

DAVIDSON, REV. DR., 7, 40, 83.

DAVIESS, JOE, 2.

DAVIS, REV. DR. C. A., 651.

DAVIS, W. I., president Union Female College, 573.

DELANY ACADEMY (Ind.), 542, 563.

DELANY, REV. H. F., sermon of, 31; an incident, 153.

DENNIS, REV. DR. SAMUEL, a paper by, 606.

DE WITT, REV. DR. M. B., chaplain, 430; 435; soliciting agent Board of Publication, and editor of various periodicals, 592, 604; superintendent of Sunday-schools, 456.

DICKENS, REV. J. L., president Bethel College, 576.

DICKERSON, REV. J. H., missionary, 477.

DICKEY, REV. DR. C. A., 450.

DILLARD, REV. DR. JOHN L., first itinerant, to West Tennessee, 148; approval of revision, 612.

DOCTRINES, 73; committee to prepare synopsis of, 98; comparison of creeds, 106, 107; test at the sacrament of the Lord's Supper, 108.

DONNELL, D. M., president Union Female College, 574.

DONNELL, REV. GEORGE, sent to East Tennessee, 145; not paid, 147.

DONNELL, REV. ROBERT, an incident of, 29; his covenant, 34; an agent, 60; camp-meeting in Alabama, 89; biographical sketch, 92; in Nashville, 127; president Board of Missions, 132; first evangelist in East Tennessee, 143, 144; sent to Hunt's Spring, 156; doubts as to location of Cumberland College, 215; defends the convention, 236; visits Pennsylvania, 274; last letter, 320; organized church in Memphis, 373; a prayer and a vow, 412; 565.

INDEX. 663

DONNELSON, COL., 2.

DOOLEY, REV. LINVILLE, a faithful minister, 351; 440.

DOOLEY, REV. O. D., 440.

DRENNAN, MRS. A. M., arrival in Japan, 494; school opened, 495; classes for young men, 495.

DUFFIELD, MISS BETTIE A., arrives in Japan, 500; work with Miss Orr, 500.

DUNAWAY, W. E., publishing agent, 591.

DUNBAR (Neb.), 624.

DURANT, ELDER, facts from the life of, 376.

DUVALL, REV. C. P., 472.

E.

EAGAN, REV. H. W., pioneer, 624, 625.

EARLE, REV. DR. F. R., president Cane Hill College, 577, 578.

EDGAR, GEO. W., trustee Lincoln University, 549.

EDUCATION, without books, 5.

EDUCATION, THE BOARD OF, its organization, 316; instruction to appoint agent for theological school, 522.

EDUCATION, MINISTERIAL, 48–65; questions of that day still debated, 57; errors concerning, 57; slander refuted, 58; held in esteem, proof, 58–61; a curious inconsistency, 61; a change, 62; licensing catechists, 64; woman's sphere, 64; the necessity of, recognized, 201.

ELK PRESBYTERY, organized, 93, 94; original members, 94; manner of representation, 110; its extent, 111; plan of work, 112, 113; first to move in Indian missions, 129; mission work in southern Alabama, 157; favored a Board of Missions for the whole church, 132.

ESTILL, REV. MILTON, organized first church in Texas, 269.

ESTILL, CAPT. WALLACE, account of Gasper meeting, 12.

EVANGELISTS, 626, 629; work began, 627; lay evangelists, 627–629; error of the ministry, 627, 628.

EVANGELICAL LUTHERAN CHURCH, correspondence with, 458.

EVANSVILLE (Ind.), 167; Assembly at, 448, 456.

EWING, REV. FINIS, at school, 6, 7; testimony of, 27; an anecdote of, 28; before Transylvania Presbytery, 48; licensed, 49; testimony in favor of an educated ministry, 59; biographical sketch of, 91; testimony concerning sanctification, 104; settled in Missouri, 178; opened school of the prophets, 178; sermon on slavery, 411; emancipated his slaves, 410.

EWING, HON. R. C., professor in law department in Lincoln University, 546.

F.

FACTORYVILLE (Neb.), 624.

FARR, REV. DR. W. B., editor *St. Louis Observer*, 603.

FAST DAYS, appointed, 319.

"FENCING" THE TABLE, 110.

FERGUSON, REV. DR. FERGUS, visit of, 18; 452, 453.

FINCHER, REV. F. M., anecdote of, 642.

FINNEY, N. J., president Cumberland Female College, 574.

FIRST PREACHERS, privations of, 3; unconverted, 7; testimony in favor of an educated ministry, 59, 60; preferred the wilderness, 187; thorough preaching, 118, 119.

FOLSOM, REV. ISRAEL, 329; devotion to his people, 330, 331.

FOSTER, REV. DAVID, biographical sketch of, 92; extract from letter, 139; ordered to East Tennessee, 145.

FOSTER, REV. DR. R. V., editor Sunday-school periodicals, 595.

FRATERNAL CORRESPONDENCE, a committee on, 317; correspondence with the General Assembly of the Presbyterian (New School) church, 317–319; with General Assembly (Old School), 319.

FRAZIER, REV. R., editor *The Ark*, 601.

FRAZIER, REV. SAMUEL W., a missionary to Texas, 269.

FREEMAN, REV. DR. AZEL, professor in Cumberland College, 227, 228; professor in Madison College, 529, 531; principal Delany Academy (Ind.), 542; president Lincoln University, 544, 545; president Bethel College, 576.

FRIZZELL, JOHN, stated clerk, 449, 456; resigned, 459; moderator General Assembly, 459; appointed to prepare a digest, 597.

FULLERTON, REV. B. P., in Kansas City, 472.

FUQUA, A. J., 435.

G.

GALLAGHER, REV. JAMES, narrative of, 15; testimony of, 25; discussion by, 37.

GASPER RIVER, meeting at, 13; medical treatment of "the jerks,", 47; commission met at, 80; of historic interest, 121.

GAUT, J. M., corresponding secretary Board of Publication, 595.

GENERAL ASSEMBLY of the Cumberland Presbyterian church, first meeting, 207, 208; college, paper and the "book concern" sources of anxiety, 208; home missionary work a bright feature, 209; resolved to co-operate with the American Board, 209; benevolent enterprises receive indorsement, 209; opposition to statistics, 209; fast days declared, 210; few appeals, 210; few exciting debates, 210; declaration against making, selling, or giving away ardent spirits, 211; theological department postponed, 211; biennial instead of annual meetings, 212, 311; growth of synods and presbyteries, 212; passing away of the fathers, 213; the credit system, 213; large bodies not competent to manage financial enterprises, 213; its organ, 230; struggle and controversy, 232; plans of committees, 232; committee of investigation church paper, 239; opening sermon of 1843, 311; great speech of 1845, 312; missionary work of the church, 312; a Committee on Publication, 313; report of the board unsatisfactory, 314; new committee, 314; Board of Education organized, 316; Board of Church Erection organized, 316; Committee on Fraternal Correspondence, 317-319; a complete history of the church, 319; day of meeting changed, 320; ratified the formation of California Presbytery, 352; from 1861 to 1870, 380; smallness of that of 1861, 380; temporary committees appointed, 381; committees re-organized in 1863, 382; meetings in Lebanon, Ohio, and Evansville, Ind., 382; distressing condition of affairs, 382, 383; convention at Chattanooga, 383; convention at Selma, Ala., 383, 384; convention at Memphis, Tenn., 384; Assembly at Owensboro, Ky., 384; mission boards at Lebanon, Tenn., and Alton, Ill., re-organized, 384; Pacific coast committee taken under care of, 384; Assembly at Memphis, 385; a Committee on Organic Union, 385; Board of Publication re-organized at Nashville, 385; Assembly at Murfreesboro, Tenn., 387; Boards of Missions consolidated and located at St. Louis, 388; a sharp discussion, 388; a compromise,

389; new presbyteries, 389; consolidation of synods, 389; action in regard to slavery, 417, 418; at Nashville, 448, 459; at Evansville, 448; at Huntsville, 449, 458; Austin, Texas, 458; Jefferson, Texas, 455; Lebanon, 455; Lincoln, 455; McKeesport, Pa., 459; Memphis, 456; semi-centennial, 456; action concerning the Pan-Presbyterian Council, 464; on co-operation in foreign missions, 504; on dancing, 460.

GENERAL ASSEMBLY of the Presbyterian church, testimony of, 128; apology of Kentucky Synod, 67; deliverance of, 68, inquiries to, 68; disapproved the action of Kentucky synod, 80.

GENERAL SYNOD, its management of Cumberland College, 201; minor matters, 202, 203; expediency of organizing a General Assembly; 203; strong feeling in favor of a delegated synod, 204; minor rules and transaction, 204, 205; resolved into four synods, 205; necessary changes in Form of Government, 205; synodical period, 205; final adjournment, 206; Minutes lost, 310.

GENERAL REFLECTIONS, 631–634.

GEORGIA, planting of the church in, 357; extent of the work in, 358.

GILL, REV. DR. J. M., 459; president Cumberland Female College, 574.

GILLESPIE, REV. E. J., 440; in St. Louis, 471.

GILLESPIE, REV. JACOB, manuscript of, 347; a pioneer in Oregon, 348.

GILLIAM, REV. F. M., in St. Louis, 470.

GIVENS, REV. S. D., 618.

GOODPASTURE, REV. A. H., 417.

GORDON, REV. DR. M. L., missionary to Japan, 480, 482–484.

GOSHEN, 121; an incident, 126.

GREENE ACADEMY, work of, 528.

GREEN, REV. DR. J. B., sent to Kansas, 361; 441; 623.

GREEN, NATHAN, reminiscences of, 518, 519; work of, 521.

GREEN, HON. NATHAN, SR., professor in law department Cumberland University, 512.

GREENVILLE SEMINARY, 571.

GREENWOOD SEMINARY, 571.

GRIDER, REV. J. S., agent Lincoln University, 549.

GROVES, REV. J. S., editor *Texas Observer*, 602.

INDEX. 667

GUTHRIE, ROBERT, 7.

GUTHRIE, REV. J. S., extract from letter, 139; sent to Hiwassee circuit, 145; sent to West Tennessee, 149; in Alabama, 161.

GUTHRIE, R. J., president Union Female College, 573.

GUTHRIE PRESBYTERY, when organized, 389.

H.

HAIL, REV. A. D., accepted as a candidate, 482, 484, 485; ordained to mission work, 485; sailed, 485; general mission work, 486; letter from, 488; translations by, 489; author of principles governing mission work, 493; in America, 502.

HAIL, REV. J. B., accepted as a candidate, 482, 484, 485; sailed for Japan, 485; first baptism, 487;. translation by, 489.

HALL, REV. BENJ., 441.

HALL, REV. DR. THOMAS, an incident, 55.

HALSELL, REV. J. M., editor *Banner of Peace*, 599; editor *The Ladies' Pearl*, 603; editor *Central Cumberland Presbyterian*, 604.

HARRIS, MRS. C. M., editor *The Gem* and *Our Lambs*, 595.

HARRIS, REV. DR. D. M., professor Lincoln University, 550; editor *Cumberland Presbyterian*, 550, 594.

HARRIS, REV. WILLIAM, prayer of, 35; biographical sketch of, 92; dedication of his grandson, 95; pen pictures, 96; first in Indiana, 164; in Pennsylvania, 284.

HAWKINS, REV. A. W., in Logansport (Ind.), 473.

HAYS, REV. DR. J. S., address of, 453-455.

HENDERSON, REV. E. P., 625.

HENDERSON, REV. J. T. A., a pioneer, 176; an incident, 287; pastor of Hopewell (Pa.) church, 289; in Sedalia (Mo.), 473.

HENDERSON, REV. DR. ROBERT, an orderly meeting, 43.

HENDERSON, REV. T. H., 619.

HENDRIX, REV. DR. W. W., president Bethel College, 576.

HENSON, J. C., 418.

HESS, MRS. MARGARET, memoir of, 3.

HESS, REV. N. J., an incident, 148.

HILL, REV. HUGH B., in Ohio, 299; pastor Oak Grove (Tenn.) church, 303; an incident, 373.

HILL, REV. H. H., in Alabama and Mississippi, 259.

HODGE, REV. DR. CHARLES, on Old Side views, 8; on "the jerks," 47.

HODGE, REV. WILLIAM, pastor at Shiloh, Tenn., 13; testimony of, 47.

HODGES, REV. C. B., 622, 623.

HOGAN, REV. DAVID, incident of, 477.

HOPEWELL CHURCH (Enfield, Ill.), first organized, 171.

HOPEWELL CHURCH (Iowa), organized by Rev. J. C. Armstrong, 339.

HOPEWELL CHURCH (Pa.), its origin, 288.

HOPEWELL PRESBYTERY, when and where organized; its original members, 150.

HOUGHTON, REV. A. H., sent to northern Iowa and southern Minnesota, 340; 441.

HOWARD, REV. JOSEPH, second church in Iowa organized in his house by Rev. Cyrus Haynes, 336.

HOWARD, REV. DR. J. M., editor *Cumberland Presbyterian*, 594.

HOWARD, REV. J. S., president Union Female College, 573; president Bethel College, 576.

HUDSON, REV. G. G., arrival in Japan, 502; report of, 487.

HUDSON, REV. S. E., 418; influence of, 528.

HUGHES, REV. MARTIN, 623.

HUMPHREY, REV. J. F., appeal of, 439.

HUNTER, REV. DR. H. A., testimony of, 28; professed religion, 133; an incident, 153; touching accounts, 166; 417, 425.

HUNTSVILLE (Ala.), Assembly at, 449.

HUNTSVILLE PRESBYTERY, when organized, 389.

HURST, T. M., publishing agent, 595.

HUTCHINSON, ELDER, 7.

HUTCHINSON, JAMES, statement of, 52, 53.

HYDE, REV. W. A., 619.

HYMN BOOK, THE, its history, 315, 316.

I.

ILLINOIS, planting of churches, 168; first sermon, 168; first church, 171; hardships, 172; first presbytery, 173; papers in, 602.

ILLINOIS PRESBYTERY, when organized; its original members, 173.

INDIANA, planting churches, 164; date of first churches, 165; hardships, 166; early camp-meetings, 167.

INDIANS, mission to the, 128; societies formed for special work among the, 129; a constitution for a ladies' missionary society, 129; an organization in Russellville, Ky., 129; arrangements for a school among the, 130; the Chickasaw Nation never at war with our people, 130; traditions of Tombigbee River, 131; establishment of a school, treaty signed, 132; government aid for, 134; Rev. William Barnett won, 136; hardships, 139; programme of duties, 140; mission closed, 141; Lowry's mission to the Winnebagoes, 324.

IOWA, origin of the church in, 336; first church in, 336; ruffianism, 337; sufferings of pioneer preachers, 340.

IOWA PRESBYTERY, when organized, 337; original members, 337.

ISH, REV. T. A., a letter from, 350, 351.

J.

JACKSON'S PURCHASE, the work in, 150, 151.

JARMAN, T. N., tutor Cumberland University, 510.

JEFFERSON (Texas), 455; an incident, 445.

JENKINS, REV. J. E., allusion to pamphlet by, 165.

JERKS, THE, 46, 47.

JOHNSON, REV. B. J., 624.

JOHNSON, REV. DR. FELIX, 431; president Bethel College, 576.

JOHNSON, REV. JAMES, autobiography of, 376.

JOHNSON, L. A., president Trinity University, 558.

JOHNSON, REV. NEIL, in Iowa, 337; in Oregon, 345; his journey, 346.

JOHNSON, REV. ROBERT, statement of, 436.

JOHNSTON, REV. T. M., editor *Pacific Observer*, 604; 354, 355.

JONES, HON. W. B., trustee Lincoln University, 549.

K.

KANSAS, beginning of work in, 358; opened to white settlers, 359; a descriptive letter, 359; first church organized, 360.

KANSAS CITY, self-sustaining, 472.

KANSAS PRESBYTERY, when and where organized, 360; original members, 360; prohibition, 360; strength of, 361.

KENTUCKY SYNOD, commission of investigation, 77; commission met, 77; no right to *originate* process, 79; Dr. Davidson's concession, 79; General Assembly of 1807 disapproves, 80; place of meeting unfortunate, 80; revised its actions, 83; extent of, 44; charges brought by, 67; terms laid down by, 68; exciting controversies, 1.

KENTUCKY SYNOD (Cumberland Presbyterian), date of formation, 320; disappears from rolls, 390.

KING PRESBYTERY, when organized, 389.

KING, RICHARD, conversion of, 7, 13.

KING, REV. R. D., autobiography of, 157; an incident, 159; sent to Missouri, 179, 180; closed his life in Texas, 181, 194; ordained, 191; hardships in Arkansas, 193; in Louisiana, 261; anecdote of his mother, 635; ruling passion strong in death, 641.

KING, REV. R. M., president Cane Hill College, 577.

KING, MRS. SAMUEL, anecdote of, 635, 636.

KING, REV. SAMUEL, at school, 6; evangelistic tour, 34; before Transylvania Presbytery, 49; first against whisky, 54; an agent, 60; biographical sketch, 91; 94, 124, 126; sent to the Indians, 129; moved to Missouri, 180; sketch of, 185; visitation by order of Assembly, 211; in Louisiana, 261; attitude on temperance, 612.

KIRKPATRICK, REV. HUGH, biographical sketch of, 92; heroic endurance, 148.

KNOXVILLE PRESBYTERY, when organized, 147; its original members, 147.

L.

LADIES' PEARL, THE, 389; 603.

LANGDON, REV. W. S., financial agent Committee of Publication, 315; rule for newspaper discussions, 370; in St. Louis, 471; publishing agent, 590; editor *Banner of Peace*, 599; editor *Ladies' Pearl*, 603; description of lay evangelism, 627.

LANSDEN, REV. ABNER W., sent to East Tennessee, 145.

LATHAM, COL. R. B., trustee Lincoln University, 548, 549.

LATTA, REV. E. C., description of meeting, 352; 440.

LOUGHRAN, REV. CORNELIUS, a Presbyterian minister, 273; changed relation, 283.

LOUGHRAN, REV. J., president Waynesburg College, 533; resigned, 534.

LAWYER, REV. F. P., ordained missionary to Mexico, 506.

LAY EXHORTERS, 53, 54; activity needed, 64.

LEAVENWORTH PRESBYTERY, organization of, 360, 389; strength of, 361.

LEAVITT, MISS JULIA, arrived in Japan, 490; work at Osaka, 500, 501; at Shingu and Tanabe, 501.

LEBANON BOARD OF MISSIONS, 441, 442, 447.

LEBANON CHURCH (Ohio), organization, 298; Rev. Dr. M. H. Bone its first pastor, 298; work of Rev. F. G. Black, 298; church bell, 298, 299; an incident, 377, 378.

LEBANON PRESBYTERY, crossed the mountains to hold its meeting, 147.

LEBANON (Tenn.), 455.

LINCOLN (Ill.), 455.

LINCOLN UNIVERSITY, origin of, 541–544; a charter, 543; endowment, 543, 544; co-educational, 544; efforts to establish law and theological departments, 546; decline in attendance, 546, 547; work of, 547; trustees, 548; faculty resigned, 550; list of teachers, 551.

LINDLEY, REV. JACOB, a Presbyterian minister, 273; report of first camp-meeting, 280; autobiography of, 285; at the meeting of his presbytery, 286; becomes a Cumberland Presbyterian, 286; his work in Ohio, 292, 293; at Beverly, 296; incidents, 294, 295.

LINDSLEY, REV. DR. J. BERRIEN, services rendered by, 86.

LINDSLEY, DR. N. LAWRENCE, professor in Cumberland University, 510, founder of Greenwood Seminary, 571.

LITTLE ROCK (Ark.), self-supporting, 472.

LITTRELL, REV. J. CAL., 618, 619.

LOGAN, REV. DR. J. B., secretary Board of Missions, 475; editor, 542, 602, 603; in charge of Spring River Academy, 555; editor *The Ladies' Pearl*, 603.

LOGAN, REV. W. C., editor *St. Louis Observer*, 603; editor *Theological Medium*, 604.

LOGAN PRESBYTERY, organized, 94; original members, 94; its extent, 111; plan of work, 112, 113; ladies' missionary society, 132; missionaries sent to other States, 132; districts and missionaries, 164; fast days, 165; condemning the Nashville convention, 236.

LOGANSPORT (Ind.), 473.

LOUDON HIGH SCHOOL, 580.

LOUISIANA, planting the church in, 261; first church organized, 261.

LOUISIANA PRESBYTERY, when organized, 261; original members, 261; dissolved and again revived, 262; Sumner Bacon licensed and ordained by, 266.

LOVE, REV. G. W., 623.

LOWRY, REV. DAVID, professor in Cumberland College, 225, 226; editor, 230; missionary to the Winnebago Indians, 324–327; appeals for missions, 328; organized first Protestant church in Iowa, 336; in favor of concentration in the North-west, 337; reply to Dr. Wilson, 62; testimony on temperance, 616.

LOWRY, S. DOAK, in charge of Cane Hill College, 577.

LYLE, REV. JOHN, bearer and defender of Minutes of Kentucky Synod, 83.

M.

MACCRAE, REV. DR., quotation from, 71.

MADISON COLLEGE, work of, 528, 529, 531.

MAJORS, ALEXANDER, pioneer in Nebraska, 621.

MARINER, WILLIAM, professor in Cumberland University, 513; professor in Lincoln University, 548.

MARSHALL, MRS. MARY, a pioneer worker, 199, 200.

MATTOX, REV. G. N., work of, 423, 424.

McADOW, REV. SAMUEL, two sermons, 36; night spent in prayer, 84; biographical sketch, 90; sermons, 105; settled in Illinois, 174.

McBRYDE, REV. W. P., an incident, 645.

McCALLAN, REV. J. B., an incident, 302.

McCORD, REV. B. F., professor in Lincoln University, 548.

INDEX. 673

McCorkle, Rev. Archibald, a Missouri pioneer, 182.

McCrosky, Rev. E. J., in Chattanooga, 474.

McCutcheon, Rev. J. F., 429; an incident, 429, 430.

McDaniel, Rev. Hiram, in Arkansas, 195.

McDonald, Alexander, a mother's prayers, 650, 651.

McDonnold, Rev. Dr. B. W., president Cumberland University, 516; Life Insurance Companies, 520, 521; president Bethel College, 576.

McDonnold, Rev. James, first itinerant in West Tennessee, 148; "a circuit rider" in Texas, 270.

McDonnold, Rev. Philip, wonderful career, 96.

McGee College, 569; list of teachers, 570; importance of, 570, 571; names of men educated at, 571.

McGee, Rev. John, 12, 16, 17.

McGee Presbytery, when organized, 173, 178; "intermediate meeting," 191.

McGee, Rev. William, biographical sketch of, 91.

McGhee, Rev. Z. M., first to settle in Georgia, 358.

McGhirk, Dr. N. H., 479; missionary, 480.

McGinnis, Albert, professor in Waynesburg College, 538; professor and acting president Lincoln University, 550.

McGlumphy, Rev. Dr. A. J., professor in Waynesburg College, 535; professor in Lincoln University, 544; president of Lincoln University, 546; president Ozark College, 581.

McGown, Rev. A. J., heroism and integrity of, 267; an incident, 268; at Mississippi Synod, 268; returns to the United States, 271; a presentiment of death, 651, 652.

McGready, Rev. James, statement of, 8; friends of, 9; covenant of, 10; work began, 11; singing hymns an offense, 41.

McKeesport (Pa.), 459.

McLean, Rev. Ephraim, a true hero, 55, 56; ordained, 84; biographical sketch, 91; perplexed on the slavery question, 412.

McLean, George, a trial and a triumph, 644, 645.

McLean, J. S., 417.

McLeskey, Rev. Dr. B. G., president Trinity University, 559.

McLin, Rev. D. W., biographical sketch, 92; in Illinois, 171.

McMurray, Mrs. Elizabeth, narrative furnished by, 13.

McMurray, Rev. J. M., agent Cumberland University, 511, 512.

McPherson, Rev. C. G., professor in Cumberland University, 509, 510.

McSpeddin, Rev. Samuel, at school, 6, 7; testimony about, 8; about the origin of the revival, 17; his character, 95.

Meek, Rev. J. J., 418.

Memphis, 456.

Methodists, no opposition from, 26.

Mexico, work in, 504–506.

Miller, Rev. Dr. A. B., 450; tutor in Waynesburg College, 533; professor in, 534; president of, 536; his life work, 536, 537; editor *Cumberland Presbyterian* (Pa.), 600, 603.

Miller, Rev. Barnett, 435.

Miller, Mrs. M. K. B., work of, 533, 537.

Miller, Rev. Dr. Samuel, letter of, 30; his ninth letter and its answer, 43; correction of, 45.

Milligan, Rev. Mr., resolutions of, 426.

Ministerial Relief, Board of, organized, 458, 460.

Ministry, preaching on a call to the, 115.

Missions, work of synods and presbyteries, 322; city missions, 322, 469–475; Winnebago Indians, 324–327; two young ladies sent out under the A. B. C. F. M., 328; appeal of Rev. David Lowry, 328; his report, 328, 329; work among the Indians pressed, 330–332; a growing feeling for our own board, 332; first foreign missionary, 333; from 1860 to 1870, 440–447; home mission work, 440, 441, 475; foreign, 441; progress of, 469; work of city missions, 469–475; a list of growing mission churches, 475; missions among the Indians, 476–479; mission to Trinidad, 479–481; work in Japan, 482; first convert baptized, 487; first official report, 487; extended preaching tour, 488; need of denominational literature, 489; book and tract store opened, 490; arrival of Miss Orr and Miss Leavitt, 490; the annual report, 491; first elders, 492; principles governing mission policy, 493; liberality of, 494; great fruitfulness, 495–498; Corea, 496; names of missionaries, 502; great gain to the home churches, 503; co-operation with other churches, 504; the *Missionary Record*, 506; systematic giving, 506, 507; home churches can not live without, 507, 508.

INDEX. 675

MISSIONS, BOARD OF, organized 312; not chartered until 1845, 133, 209; no paid officers at first, 312; first president, 312; secretary with salary, 312; appeal for Liberia, 334; in favor of China, 335; Rev. J. C. Armstrong appointed to Turkey, 335; sends Rev. P. H. Crider to Iowa, 339; resolved to establish a mission at St. Cloud, Minn., 340; Bell's mission closed, 141; board located in St. Louis, 388; discussion over the plans of, 388.

MISSIONARY RECORD, THE, 506.

MISSISSIPPI, planting the Church in, 253; a slander denounced, 254; vacating the Choctaw and Chickasaw country, 254; speculation rife, 255.

MISSISSIPPI PRESBYTERY, when and where organized, 256; original members, 256; an incident, 258.

MISSISSIPPI SYNOD, when organized, extent, 258; organizes Louisiana Presbytery, 258; Texas Presbytery, 258, 268; new presbyteries created and dissolved, 258; Oxford and New Hope organized, 258.

MISSOURI, origin of the church in, 175; first sermon, 175; home supply of ministers, 181; noble women, 181; camp-meetings, 184, 643; a pioneer scene sketched, 188; educational work in, 580, 581; papers in, 602.

MITCHELL, REV. DR. J. B., 450; president McGee College, 569.

MIYOSHI SAN, at Cumberland University, 502.

MODRALL, REV. N. P., 418.

MONTANA, 626.

MOODY, D. L., an illustration from, 28; record of, 63.

MOORE, REV. A. A., sent to Kansas, 361.

MOORE, REV. B. F., first in Colorado, 618.

MOORE, REV. WILLIAM, sent to the Indians, 129; interesting incident, 136; sermon by, 161; his grave, 162.

MOORMAN, REV. R. A. A., an incident, 378.

MORGAN, REV. JOHN, becomes a preacher, 156; visits Pennsylvania, 274; account of work, 275; camp-meetings, 281, 293; an incident, 281; began the publication of the *Union and Evangelist*, 291; visits Ohio, 292, 293; a distillery closed, 293; professor in Madison College, 529; incident of, 530; death, 291.

MORRIS, REV. DR. E. D., corresponding delegate, 456, 467.

MORRISON, REV. DR. JAMES, 452.

MORROW, REV. J. B., 643.

MORROW, REV. R. D., sent to Missouri, 175; punctuality, 176; report, 177; opened School of the Prophets, 178; anecdote of, 640, 641.

MOTHERAL, REV. N. W., in Chattanooga, 474.

MOURNER'S BENCH, its use and abuse, 42.

MOUNTAIN VIEW CHURCH, 353.

MT. MORIAH, first congregation organized as a Cumberland Presbyterian church, 125; historic sketch, 125, 126.

MT. ZION, first church organized in Indiana, 166.

MUDDY RIVER, meeting at, 11.

MURRAY, REV. GIBSON W., account of, 160.

N.

NASHVILLE, jail of, 7; Robert Donnell began preaching in, 127; much opposition, 127; Assembly at, 448.

NEBRASKA, early settlers, 620; not supported by the Board of Missions, 624.

NEBRASKA CITY, first Cumberland Presbyterian church organized, 621–623.

NEBRASKA PRESBYTERY, when and where organized, 624.

NELSON, REV. DAVID, testimony of, 24.

NELSON, REV. DR. H. A., 450.

NEWBURG CHURCH (Ind.), 167.

NEW FIELDS, 618.

NEW HOPE CHURCH, an historic place, 123, 124.

NEW HOPE PRESBYTERY, when organized, 258; efficiency and energy of, 259; united with Columbus Presbytery, 259.

NEW LEBANON CHURCH (Mo.), 178; when organized, 187.

NEW LEBANON PRESBYTERY, facts from Rea's history, 375; resolutions in favor of the Maine law, 375.

NEWMAN, REV. A. M., death of, 131.

NEW MEXICO, 619, 620.

NEWSPAPERS, 598-605.
NICHOLSON, REV. JOHN, a sermon by, 642.
NORTH CAROLINA, missionary work in, 357.

O.

OAK GROVE CHURCH, its annual camp-meetings, 303.

OGDEN, REV. BENJAMIN, 7.

OGDEN, REV. JOHN W., agent Cumberland College, 215; corresponding editor, 236; in Louisiana, 261; as agent visits Ohio and Pennsylvania, 273.

OHIO, origin of the church in, 292; John Morgan visits Athens, 292, 293; his preaching closes a distillery, 293; first camp-meeting in, 293; first church in, 294; first camp-meeting, 294; itinerants appointed from Pennsylvania Presbytery, 296; work at Senecaville, 297; not strong in numbers, 300.

OHIO PRESBYTERY, prayer for a revival, 10.

OREGON, origin of church in, 342, 343; Whitman's massacre, 344; facts concerning emigration, 344, 345; first church in, 346; manuscript sketch by Rev. Jacob Gillespie, 347.

OREGON PRESBYTERY, when organized, original members, 347; resolved to have a college, 347.

ORGANIC UNION, a committee appointed to confer with a committee from the Presbyterian church, South, 385; Presbyterian deliverance on the subject, 386; meeting of committee in Nashville, 449-451; plan of, 450; response of Presbyterian committee, 451; agreement that negotiations should continue, 451; action of the Cumberland Presbyterian Assembly, 451; two ideas to be considered, 451.

ORR, MISS ALICE M., arrived in Japan, 490; work in the out stations, 500, 501.

OSAKA, JAPAN, first sermon preached in, 486; first converts, 487; second church organized, 502.

OSBORN, REV. A. G., a chaplain, 424.

OUR DENOMINATIONAL PROGRESS, 629-631; a discouraging feature, 630; hopeful signs, 630; comparison, 631.

OUR LAMBS, 592.

OXFORD PRESBYTERY, when organized, 258.

OZARK COLLEGE, 581.

OZARK SYNOD, 390.

P.

PACIFIC PRESBYTERY, when and where organized, 353.

PARKS, REV. R. C., a native Cherokee, 477.

PASTORS, none in the first and second periods, 89; transition from missionary evangelists to, 242; opposition to, 242; a growing sentiment in favor of, 243; the difference between pastors and evangelists, 244; their difficult calling, 245; mistakes and false views concerning, 246; their duty and their compensation, 249; robbed by the churches, 249–252.

PATTON, REV. DANIEL, sent to South Alabama, 158; in Missouri, 185; glimpse of his work, 186; an account of last meeting of General Synod, 203.

PEARSON, REV. R. G., evangelist, 626.

PENNSYLVANIA, origin of church in, 273; visited by Bone and Ogden, 273; invitation and visit of our missionaries, 273–277; first Presbyterian ministers to open their churches, 277; first Cumberland Presbyterian church, 278; first camp-meeting, 279; reports in church papers, 283; formation of a presbytery, 283; examples of our noblest congregations, 287–290.

PENNSYLVANIA PRESBYTERY, when and where organized, 284; original members, 284; its rapid growth, 290; appointed itinerants for Ohio, 296.

PENNSYLVANIA SYNOD, when and where organized, 291; its prosperous condition, 291; action of, 417, 528; resolutions, 531; Waynesburg College under control of, 534; semi-centennial, 540; memorial from, 480; pledges of, 483, 485.

PERRY, REV. W. O. H., president of Stewartsville College, 581. president Odessa College, 581.

PHELPS, REV. DR. AUSTIN, quotations from, 71, 73.

PIERSON, REV. DR. B. H., 151, 304.

PINER, REV. F. D., superintendent of Burney Academy, 330.

PINEY, 121.

PITTSBURG (Pa.), temporary location of Committee of Publication, 382; committee discontinued at, 385.

PITTSBURG CHURCH, when organized, 290.

PLANTING OF CHURCHES, 142.

PORTER, REV. JAMES B., power in preaching, 32; his education and conversion, 56; biographical sketch, 91.

POWELL, REV. R. F., 624.

PRAIRIE GROVE, first church organized among the Cherokee Indians, 477.

PRESBYTERIAN, THE, its charges against Cumberland Presbyterians, 45; its statement corrected, 46.

PRESBYTERIES, organization of new, 468.

PRESBYTERIAN ALLIANCE, constitution of, approved, 458; delegates elected to, 458; relation of the Cumberland Presbyterian church to, 461, 462; delegates refused admittance, 462, 463; wide-spread interest in, 463; delegates appointed to, 464; result of the application, 464-466; report to the General Assembly, 466.

PRESBYTERIAN CHURCH, divisions in, 39, 40; propositions for union with, 385-387, 449, 452; our debts to, 633.

PRESBYTERIAN CHURCH (South), considering a change in standard of education, 63; negotiations for union with, 385-387.

PRESBYTERIANS, Scotch Irish, church erected by, 6.

PRESTON, REV. W. B., editor *Texas Observer*, 602.

PRIME, REV. DR. S. IRENÆUS, recommendation of, 479.

PROVINE, REV. DR. J. C., secretary and treasurer of Board of Education, 316; author of deliverance of Assembly, 1866, 405; book editor and publishing agent, 591; editor *Banner of Peace*, 599; editor *The Ladies' Pearl*, 603.

PUBLICATION, 585; first book published, 586; first step toward a publishing department, 586; arrangements made for publication of books, 586; hymn book, 586; Board of Publication created, 586.

PUBLICATION, BOARD OF, committee appointed, 313; programme changed, 314; management often changed, 314; new committee located at Nashville, 314; inheritance from the Louisville Board, 315; charter secured, 315; missing stereotype plates, 315; re-organized, 385, 387; debt paid, 461; periodicals purchased by, 460; its origin, 586; its first members, 587; a Committee of Publication,

587; book editor chosen, 591; assets and liabilities, 595; located at Louisville, 587; difficulties, 587, 588; chartered, 590; moneys donated to, 590; permanent committee chosen, 589; transferred to Pittsburg, Pa., 590; re-organized at Nashville, 590; publication of newspapers, 592, 593; papers purchased, 593, 594; books published, 596, 597; names of members of, 598.

PUEBLO, 619.

PYATT, JACOB, an incident, 190.

Q.

QUAITE, REV. W. G. L., agent Cumberland College, 224; agent Cane Hill College, 577.

R.

RANSOM, REV. L. C., editor *Southern Observer*, 384; a sermon by, 385; in St. Louis, 469; discipline, 651.

REA, REV. J. W., sent to West Tennessee, 149.

REA, REV. P. G., interesting facts from, 375; correction of Hon. R. C. Ewing's dates, 375; a barn meeting, 643, 644.

RED RIVER, meeting at, 12; of historic interest, 120.

REED, REV. R. S., Secretary of Board of Missions, 475; in Nebraska, 621, 623.

REED, REV. WILEY M., chairman Committee of Publication, 315; speech of, 404.

RENICK, REV. ROBERT, a pioneer, 621, 623.

REPUBLICAN VALLEY PRESBYTERY, strength of, 361.

REVISION OF CONFESSION OF FAITH, 606-612; a demand for, 606; a committee appointed, 607; its report, 607; a synod's vote of censure, 607; appointment of committees and their work rejected by the presbyteries, 608; the two committees of 1881, 608; work of the committees, 609; changes made by the Assembly of 1882, 610; grounds of complaint, 611; proof texts, 611; preface, 611; an omission, 611; its adoption by the presbyteries, 612; record of the vote on, 459.

REVIVALS, prayer for, 10; revival of 1800 a genuine work, 20; extent of, 26; opposition to, 39; a cause of division, 40; churches closed against, 40; personal violence, 40; hyper-Calvinism logically opposed, 41; objections to measures used, 42; defended, 42, 43.

REZNER, MISS RENA, arrived in Japan December, 1886, 502.

RICE, REV. DAVID, his removal to Kentucky, 6; testimony of, 7; a sermon by, 20, 21; opposed to revival "measures," 42; visit to McGready's field, 48; a favorble report, 49; a letter on education and answer, 49.

RICE, REV. GREEN P., an incident, 170, 171; first sermon in Missouri, 175.

RICE, REV. P. A., 619.

RICHARDS, REV. DR. S., a chaplain, 426; professor in Lincoln University, 544, 546.

RIDLEY, HON. BROMFIELD L., professor in law department Cumberland University, 512.

RILEY, PROF. PHILIP, an incident, 227.

ROACH, REV. J. M. B., struggles of, 575.

ROACH, REV. J. N., president Bethel College, 576; 593.

ROARK, REV. AMOS, first delegate to the General Assembly from Texas, 269; return to the United States, 271.

ROBINSON, REV. CALVIN, 476.

ROCHESTER, REV. DR., diagram of progress, 26.

ROCKY MOUNTAIN PRESBYTERY, its organization, 618.

ROSS, REV. R. L., a liberal helper in church work, 259; an incident, 260, 261.

ROUND PRAIRIE CHURCH, first in Kansas, 360.

RUSH, JOHN R., delegate to Presbyterian Alliance, 462.

S.

SACRAMENTO PRESBYTERY, strength of, 356.

SACRAMENTO SYNOD, name changed, 390.

SCHAFF, REV. DR. PHILIP, Westminster Confession, 72, 73.

SCHOOLS AND COLLEGES, 555, 564; importance of a lower grade of, 565; multiplication of colleges, 567; warnings of the Assemblies, 567, 568; names reported, 568.

SCOTT, REV. DR. W. A., left the church, 240; in Louisiana, 261.

SEDALIA (Mo.), 473.

SELMA (Ala.), temporary Committee on Missions for the South at, 384, convention at, 383, 384.

SHAKERS, attitude of the first Cumberland Presbyterian ministers toward the, 25.

SHARP, REV. J. E., in Kansas City, 472.

SHARP, JAMES H., professor in Cumberland University, 511.

SHELBY, REV. AARON, his lease of Cumberland College, 216.

SHERRILL, W. B., president Bethel College, 576.

SHILOH CHURCH, 13; meeting at, 14; identical with De Sha's, 18.

SHOOK, REV. ISAAC, secretary of Board of Missions, 312; his missionary magazine, 312; his resignation, 313; agent of Board of Publication, 315; visit to Mississippi, 255; an incident, 257; pastor at Columbus, Miss., 258; in Ohio, 298; story of the "stars falling," 304.

SHOUTING, origin of, 18; opposition to, 41.

SIMS, REV. R. J., an evangelist, 626; a case of fasting and prayer, 645; a gainsayer converted, 646; a band of rowdies conquered, 647.

SIMMONS, A. M. C., 435.

SLOAN, REV. ROBERT, a circuit rider, 181; died in Missouri, 196.

SLAVERY, relation of Cumberland Presbyterians to, 410; relation of first ministers to, 410; a sermon by Ewing, 411; McAdow opposed to, 411; some preachers perplexed, 412; men forced to become slave owners, 413; attitude of *The Revivalist*, 413-416; attitude of the *Cumberland Presbyterian*, 416; report of the Assemblies of 1848 and 1851 on the subject, 416-418.

SMALL, REV. J. M., work of, 353.

SMITH, REV. HUGH R., services of, 182.

SMITH, REV. JAMES, editor, pastor, and stated clerk, 230; resignation, 232; continued as editor, 233; call for convention, 233; in the convention, 234; re-appearance of paper, 235; attitude on the college question, 237; ubiquitous, 238; his inconsistent course, 239; history by, 16.

SMITH, REV. JOHN C., appointed missionary, 134.

SMITH, REV. J. J., missionary, 477.

SMITH, REV. DR. J. T., 450.

SMYRNA, 121, 122.

SOLDIERS, preaching to, 420; chaplains in Confederate armies, 420, 421, 426; in the Union armies, 423-426; programme of services, 428.

SONOMA ACADEMY, 353, 354.

SPAIN, J. D., 596.

SPARKS, REV. S. M., goes to Pennsylvania, 284.

SPEER, REV. DR., narrative of, 15, 26, 46.

SPRINGFIELD (Mo.), Assembly at, 451-453.

SPRINGER, REV. DR. F., chairman Committee on Correspondence, 458.

SPRING HILL ACADEMY, the first school in Cumberland, 5, 6.

SPRING HILL INSTITUTE, aim and origin of, 579.

SPRING RIVER ACADEMY, 555.

SPROWLS, REV. DR. J. P., chairman of Committee on Correspondence, 458.

STATISTICS, prejudice against, 116; Dr. Burrow opposed, 117; 468.

STEELE, REV. A. J., work in Alabama, 156.

STEELE, REV. J. H., 619.

STEPHENS, REV. A. H., in Sedalia, 473.

ST. LOUIS, mission work in, 469-472.

STEWART, GEN. A. P., professor in Cumberland University, 511; offered the presidency of University, 516; evangelist, 629.

STEWART, REV. S. T., publishing agent, 590.

STEWARTSVILLE COLLEGE, 581.

STONE, REV. A. M., president Cumberland Female College, 574.

STONE, REV. BARTON W., 44.

SUNDAY MORNING, 595.

SUNDAY SCHOOL COMMENTS, 595.

SUNDAY-SCHOOL GEM, THE, 389; 592.

SWEENY, REV. A. W., 625.

SYNODS, consolidation of, 467.

SYNOD, FIRST, when and where organized, 94; a sketch of its members, 94; report of committee to prepare statement of doctrine, 98, 99; old customs, 109-119; manner of representation, 110; effort to organize a presbytery in South Alabama, 157; plan for a school adopted, 201.

T.

TATE, REV. ROBERT, his work and death, 269.

TAYLOR, A. R., professor in Lincoln University, 547; principal Kansas State Normal School, 547.

TEHUACANA, site of Trinity University, 552.

TEMPERANCE, 612; early attitude of the church on, 612; church papers a unit, 612, 613; utterance of the church courts, 613–615.

TEMPLETON, REV. DR. A., in Chattanooga, 474; anecdote of, 358.

TENNESSEE PRESBYTERY, when organized, 159; an intermediate session of, 159; resolved to establish and endow a college, 362.

TEXAS, planting the church in, 263; first Protestant sermon in, 264; first camp-meeting, 265, 269; the revolt of, 267; first church organized, 269; first Protestant minister ordained, 271; rapid growth, 272; table of dates, 272.

TEXAS CUMBERLAND PRESBYTERIAN—TEXAS OBSERVER, 602.

TEXAS PRESBYTERY, when organized, 268; original members, 268; decided measures adopted, 269; elders sent to help to organize churches, 270; incidents, 270; a period of darkness, 271.

TEXAS PRESBYTERIAN, THE, 601.

TEXAS SYNOD, when organized, 271; its presbyteries, 271.

THE THEOLOGICAL MEDIUM, 389, 592, 604, 605.

THEOLOGICAL SCHOOL, efforts to establish a, 363; location at Lebanon, Tenn., 363; action of Bethel College, 363; action of General Assembly, 364; new missionary life awakened in, 506; more than a department of the University, 521, 522; laws binding on professors in, 522; co-education, 523; first, 178, 179; no theological department in Cumberland College, 211, 212.

THE PACIFIC OBSERVER, 354, 604.

THE WATCHMAN AND EVANGELIST, 602.

THOMAS, REV. DR. R. S., principal Union Female College, 572.

THOMAS, REV. S. Y., sent to East Tennessee, 146; pioneer in West Tennessee, 150; his labors in Concord church, 302.

TOKENS, their use dropped, 109.

TOMBIGBEE PRESBYTERY, when organized, 158.

TOPP, COL. JOHN S., an anecdote of, 254.

INDEX. 685

TRANSYLVANIA PRESBYTERY, 48, 49; division of, 1, 56.

TRINITY UNIVERSITY, origin of, 552, 554; endowment, 555, 559, 560; list of teachers, 558; its work, 559.

THE RAYS OF LIGHT, 595.

TULARE PRESBYTERY, strength of, 356; when organized, 389.

U.

UNION FEMALE COLLEGE, founding of, 572.

UNION PRESBYTERY (Presbyterian), 4.

UNION PRESBYTERY (Pa.), when and where organized, 291.

UNION SYNOD, name changed, 390.

UNIONTOWN CHURCH (Pa.), one of the first in Pennsylvania, 287.

V.

VAN PATTEN, REV. J. C., agent Lincoln University, 549.

VENEZUELA, as a mission field, 480, 481.

W.

WALLA WALLA (W. T.), 624, 625.

WALLA WALLA PRESBYTERY, 626.

WARD, JOHN SHIRLEY, editor *The Ladies' Pearl*, 603.

WARD, REV. DR. W. E., appointed a delegate to Presbyterian Alliance, 462; agent Cumberland University, 514; an incident, 515; founder Ward's Seminary, 578, 579; president Board of Publication, 597; editor *Banner of Peace*, 599.

WARD'S SEMINARY, 578, 579.

WAR RECORD, 391; sermon by Rev. Dr. Milton Bird, 391-395; resolutions in 1861, 395; report in 1862, 396, 397; in 1863, 398, 399; the deliverance of 1864, 399, 400; protest, 401-403; resolution of 1865, 403; action of Southern conventions, 404; secession of Oxford Presbytery, 404; Chattanooga convention, 404; determination to avoid schism, 405; deliverance of 1866, 405; resolutions of Pennsylvania Synod, 406; deliverance of 1867, 407; report of 1868, 408-410.

WARREN, REV. J. H., superintendent Sunday-schools, 456.

WASHINGTON (Tenn.), work of first evangelists at, 143.

WASHINGTON TERRITORY, 624–626.

WATKINS, REV. R. O., first candidate for the ministry in Texas, 268; driven from his work, 270; first Protestant minister ordained in Texas, 271.

WATSON, REV. BENJAMIN, reflections of, 374; his history, 374, 375.

WAUKON CHURCH (Iowa), organized, 339.

WAYNESBURG CHURCH (Pa.), organized, 283.

WAYNESBURG COLLEGE, 527–541; founded, 533; charter granted, 534; passed under control of Pennsylvania Synod, 534; its relation to the Cumberland Presbyterian church, 534; labors of Dr. Miller in, 536, 537; of Mrs. Miller, 537; work of, 537, 538, 541; professors and teachers, 533, 535, 538; theological department, 538, 539; endowment, 539, 540.

WEEKLY PAPERS, consolidation of, 460, 593, 594.

WEETHEE, REV. J. P., 528, president of Madison College, 529; president Beverly College, 532; president Waynesburg College, 535.

WEIR, REV. EDMOND, missionary to Liberia, 333; commissioned to raise funds, 333; work in Liberia, 334, 335; 441–443.

WEIR, REV. J. C., a pioneer in Alabama, 162.

WEIR, REV. MOSES T., seeks separate organization for colored people, 435; at Warrensburg Assembly, 436.

WESTMINSTER CONFESSION, reservations in adopting, 66; meaning of the word "fatality," 66: doctrinal difficulty, 67; ecclesiastical deliverances in 1811, 68; proposed substitute for, 69; doctrines not accepted as of old, 70; difficulties of liberal defenders, 71; utterance of Rev. Dr. MacCrae, 71; protests coming from Calvinists, 71–73; the third chapter rejected, 73.

WEST TENNESSEE, 148–160; an incident, 377.

WEST VIRGINIA, a small beginning, 357.

WHATLEY, REV. A. H., missionary to Mexico, 504, 505; work commenced, 505, 506.

WHITE, REV. A. W., his work under Christian Commission, 423.

WHITE, REV. J. G., evangelist in Iowa, 337; missionary at St. Louis, 469.

WICHITA PRESBYTERY, strength of, 361.

WILLIAMS, DIXON C., evangelist, 626, 629.

WILLIAMS, REV. R. A., 624.

WILLS, REV. R. H., 625.

WILSON, REV. A. M., 441.

WILSON, JOHN D., publishing agent, 595.

WILSON, REV. DR. J. L., statement of, 62; one of the commission, 81.

WINCHESTER, REV. G. L., his work as chaplain, 427, 431.

WOMAN'S BOARD OF MISSIONS, organization, 457, 487, 488; its success, 457; first Board of Missions a Woman's Board, 457; arrival of Miss Orr and Miss Leavitt in Japan, 490; arrival of Mrs. Drennan, 494; the girls' school opened, 495; Mrs. Drennan's classes for young men, 495; arrival of Miss Duffield, 500; arrival of Miss Rezner, 502; names of missionaries, 502.

WOODS, REV. J. W., work as chaplain, 426.

WOODS, REV. LEROY, his journey to Pennsylvania, 284; his marriage, 285; publishing agent, 587; testimony concerning first Presbyterian preachers, 527, 528; reasons for going to the legislature, 613; incidents furnished by, 529, 636, 637.

Y.

YAGER, REV. C., in California, 351, 440.

YOUNG, REV. A. A., a pioneer, 185.

YOUNG, REV. T. E., 435.

www.ingramcontent.com/pod-product-compliance
Lightning Source LLC
Chambersburg PA
CBHW031423160426
43195CB00010BB/598